Peoples of Color in the American West

Peoples of Color in the American West

SUCHENG CHAN
University of California, Santa Barbara

DOUGLAS HENRY DANIELS
University of California, Santa Barbara

MARIO T. GARCÍA
University of California, Santa Barbara

TERRY P. WILSON
University of California, Berkeley

D. C. HEATH AND COMPANY
Lexington, Massachusetts   Toronto

Address editorial correspondence to

D. C. Heath and Company
125 Spring Street
Lexington, MA 02173

ACQUISITIONS EDITOR: James Miller
DEVELOPMENTAL EDITOR: Sylvia L. Mallory
PRODUCTION EDITORS: Sarah Doyle, Heather Garrison
DESIGNER: Cornelia Boynton
PHOTO RESEARCHER: Mary Lang
PRODUCTION COORDINATOR: Richard Tonachel
PERMISSIONS EDITOR: Margaret Roll
COVER DESIGN: Tama Hochbaum
COVER PHOTOGRAPHS: *(top)* Hispanic women Southern Pacific railroad workers, World War II, Tucson. Arizona Historical Society Library. *(right)* Arthur Walker, black cowboy. Schomburg Collection, New York Public Library (SC-CN-87-0136). *(left)* Young Nez Percé woman, probably Peo-na-nikt, c.1900. Photo by Dr. Edward Latham, U. S. Indian Agency physician. Special Collections Division, University of Washington Libraries (NA996). *(bottom)* Don Chun Wo and family. Arizona Historical Society Library. *(Background)* Map exhibiting the routes to Pike's Peak, by D. McGowan, 1859. Geography and Maps Division, Library of Congress.

PREFACE

This anthology, by bringing together readings on Native Americans, Mexican Americans, African Americans, and Asian Americans—here collectively called peoples of color—in the American West, represents a new stage in the writing of western American history. While the early works on the American West either ignored peoples of color or treated Native Americans and Mexican Americans mainly as obstacles impeding the westward march of European Americans across the continent, more recent studies that do discuss peoples of color have tended to depict them mostly as victims of successive waves of conquest.

The readings in this book, in contrast, attempt to transcend the perspectives of both the "old" and the "new" western American history. The selections sketch the lives of nonwhite peoples who have worked hard to survive economically, to establish families and communities, to retain elements of their cultures as they interact with other groups, to cope with myriad forms of prejudice and discrimination, to organize themselves politically, and to participate in the larger, complex world of the American West. This focus on the everyday lives of peoples of color helps to underline the fact that they have been, and remain, *subjects* of history, and not simply the objects of other people's actions. For that reason, we have included a number of autobiographical and biographical accounts that convey the thoughts and sentiments of individuals. Students can "hear" the "voices" of these persons as they recall and reflect upon their experiences.

This book provides new perspectives—different ways in which to look at western American history. However, we have not tried to fashion a master narrative—a single, seamless story line—or a definitive conceptual framework by which to interpret the stories told in the readings. Given the many remaining gaps in our knowledge of the numerous ethnic groups that have peopled the American West, it is premature to attempt such a synthesis. Rather, we intend the readings to serve as intellectual building blocks that offer glimpses of hitherto hidden dimensions of western American history and that suggest innovative ways of interpreting that history. Any future synthesis must be based on careful empirical studies of the multifaceted experiences of the diverse racial and ethnic groups that call the region home. While waiting for the appearance of a sufficiently large number of good monographs to make such a synthesis possible, we have compiled an anthology for this transitional period—one that is opening itself up to multiple points of view and that values equally the struggles and contributions of men and women of many different origins and positions in life.

Certain consequences follow from our effort to present peoples of color as agents in the making of their own history, as well as of western American history. We have extended the geographic boundary of the American West outward to include Alaska and Hawaii, where many different groups of Native Americans and Asian Americans live. We have also employed a time frame longer than that used in other books on the American West: the story begins in the days before people of European ancestry entered the region. Further, we have stretched the definition of what counts as historical documents by including several Native American myths and legends that reveal how Indians saw themselves in the interconnected worlds of nature and of human beings. Finally, in an effort to counter the heroic, male-centered approaches used in the older writings, we have featured many readings by or about women. In light of our multiple goals, we have inevitably omitted certain topics or readings that other editors might have chosen, but we have tried our best to balance many conflicting demands and to publish a book of manageable length.

This interdisciplinary anthology can be used in a variety of history, social science, and ethnic studies courses as either a main text or a supplementary reader. Drawn from the best scholarly writings—books and journal articles—as well as from more personal life stories published in the last two decades, the readings should prove interesting, challenging, and comprehensible to lower-and upper-division students alike. Headnotes briefly contextualize each selection and pose questions to alert readers to important issues. A bibliography at the end of each chapter serves as a guide to further study.

For their helpful suggestions and constructive criticisms, we thank all of those who reviewed the various drafts of the table of contents. They are Sue Fawn Chung, University of Nevada, Las Vegas; Margaret Connell Szasz, University of New Mexico; Richard Griswold del Castillo, San Diego State University; Ramón A. Gutiérrez, University of California, San Diego; Lisbeth Haas, University of California, Santa Cruz; Donald Hata, California State University, Dominguez Hills; Dale T. Knobel, Texas A&M University; Guillermo Lux, New Mexico Highlands University; Franklin Ng, California State University, Fresno; Wendy Ng, San Jose State University; Peggy Pascoe, University of Utah; Roberto Mario Salmón, University of Texas, Pan American; William S. Simmons, University of California, Berkeley; Quintard Taylor, University of Oregon; Michael Welsh, University of Northern Colorado; and Richard White, University of Washington. We also appreciate the professional contributions made by D. C. Heath's staff—history editor James Miller, developmental editor Sylvia Mallory, production editors Sarah Doyle and Heather Garrison, permissions editor Margaret Roll, editorial assistant Daphne Zervoglos, designer Cornelia Boynton, and photo researcher Mary Lang—that made our collaboration with them such a pleasure.

S. C., D. H. D., M. T. G., T. P. W.

ABOUT THE EDITORS

 SUCHENG CHAN is professor and chair of Asian American Studies at the University of California, Santa Barbara. She received her Ph.D. in political science from the University of California, Berkeley, in 1973. She is the author of *This Bittersweet Soil: The Chinese in California Agriculture, 1860–1910* (Berkeley and Los Angeles: University of California Press, 1986), *Asian Americans: An Interpretive History* (Boston: Twayne, 1991), and *Asian Californians* (San Franciso: Boyd and Fraser, 1991), and the editor of five other books. She edits the *Asian American History and Culture* series, published by Temple University Press.

DOUGLAS HENRY DANIELS is professor of black studies and former chair of the Black Studies Department at the University of California, Santa Barbara. He received his Ph.D. in history from the University of California, Berkeley, in 1975. He is the author of *Pioneer Urbanites: A Social and Cultural History of Black San Francisco* (1980; repr. Berkeley and Los Angeles: University of California Press, 1990) and *Lester Leaps In: The Life and Times of "Prez" Young* (New York: W. W. Norton & Co., 1993).

 MARIO T. GARCÍA is professor of history and Chicano studies at the University of California, Santa Barbara. He received his Ph.D. in history from the University of California, San Diego, in 1975. He is the author of *Desert Immigrants: The Mexicans of El Paso, 1880–1920* (New Haven: Yale University Press, 1981), *Mexican Americans: Leadership, Ideology, and Identity, 1930–1960* (New Haven: Yale University Press, 1990), and *Memories of Chicano History: The Life and Narrative of Bert Corona* (Berkeley and Los Angeles: University of California Press, 1993), and the editor of one other book. He edits the *Latinos in American Society and Culture* series, published by the University of California Press.

TERRY P. WILSON is professor of Native American studies in the Department of Ethnic Studies at the University of California, Berkeley. He received his Ph.D. in history from Oklahoma State University in 1974. He is the author of *The Cart that Changed the World: The Career of Sylvan N. Goldman* (Norman, Okla.: University of Oklahoma Press, 1978), *The Underground Reservation: Osage Oil* (Lincoln, Neb. and London: University of Nebraska Press, 1985), *A Bibliography of the Osage* (Metuchen, N.J.: Scarecrow Press, 1985), and *The Osage*, vol. 11 in *The History of Indians in North America* series (New York: Chelsea Pub., 1988). He has served as coeditor of the *American Indian Quarterly* since 1985.

Contents

CHAPTER 15 DIVERSITY   550

Western American Historiography and Peoples of Color

W e have compiled this anthology because we believe that it is time to make available a reader on the American West that presents peoples of color as more than conquered and oppressed victims. Although many books have been published in recent years depicting peoples of color as active agents in the making of western American history, all focus on only one group at a time. This book is the first to adopt a comparative approach, placing the four major "umbrella" groups of minorities alongside one another. By putting the experiences of these diverse peoples in the foreground, we are deliberately deemphasizing approaches that treat the entry of Euro-Americans into the American West as the beginning of that region's history. To show how this book fits into the intellectual traditions of western American historiography, we will briefly review some of the major organizing themes and core narrative structures that have informed historical writing on the American West in the last one hundred years.

Frederick Jackson Turner (1861–1932), Walter Prescott Webb (1888–1963), and Herbert Eugene Bolton (1870–1953), three widely acknowledged founding fathers of western American historiography, each introduced a captivating set of ideas for thinking about the American West. In his 1893 essay "The Significance of the Frontier in American History," read before the American Historical Association, Turner argued that the American national character did not derive from European roots but had been forged, rather, in the crucible of the frontier, which he described as a moving zone in which "civilization" encountered "savagery."

According to Turner, two conditions on the frontier played a crucial role in shaping Americans into the exceptional people that they became. First, the relative abundance of "free land"—free not in the sense of being devoid of inhabitants, but free from rents paid to landlords—made the distribution of wealth and opportunity relatively egalitarian. The vast majority of the population thus could become yeoman farmers, each owning his or her own plot, rather than living out their days as an oppressed peasantry. And economic equality gave rise to political independence. Second, in the rough living conditions of the frontier, Euro-

American settlers were forced to "regress" to an earlier stage of social evolution, thereby getting a chance to develop a set of uniquely American traits. In Turner's eyes, it was the rigors of the frontier experience that made the settlers the energetic, rugged lovers of democracy and freedom that they became, possessing minds at once idealistic and pragmatic.

Turner's thesis captivated both the scholarly and the popular imagination, for it gave Americans, especially ordinary men and women, a flattering way to perceive of themselves. The essay was basically pessimistic, however, because it noted that the 1890 census had shown that the frontier—defined as land with a population density of two or fewer persons per square mile—had disappeared, a development that in Turner's view signaled the end of the formative period of U.S. history. Henceforth Americans would be preoccupied with the problems of industrial strife that accompanied a maturing capitalist economy characterized by mergers and monopolies, and with the assimilation of the millions of immigrants flooding into the nation's filthy, overcrowded cities. Because his analysis simultaneously massaged the egos of ordinary Americans during their country's expansionist, nationalist phase and offered them an explanation for the glaring problems born of industrialization and immigration, Turner enjoyed an influence far out of proportion to his limited publications.

Turner never produced the historical works, based on careful, systematic study, that he intended to write, and so the task of putting empirical flesh on his conceptual skeletons fell to his two most influential disciples, Frederic Logan Paxson and Ray Allen Billington, each of whom wrote several books on the American frontier. Paxson's major work, *History of the American Frontier, 1763–1893*, appeared in 1924 and won a Pulitzer Prize. In it, he emphasized the settlers' battles with Native Americans, the importance of railroads and other transportation routes, the absorption of new territories, the admission of new states, the cattle industry, and a host of other topics. Billington published *Westward Expansion: A History of the American Frontier* in 1949, *The Far Western Frontier, 1830–1860* in 1956, and *America's Frontier Heritage* in 1966. As Turner's most ardent defender, he worked hard to modify and fine-tune his mentor's arguments, seeking to shore up the master's legacy. In response to the criticism that Turner's thesis was too vague, Billington defined the frontier more precisely as a "series of contiguous westward-migrating zones, each representing a different stage in the development of society." He specified six such zones, each dominated by a different group: fur traders, cattlemen, miners, pioneer farmers, farmers with machinery, and urban dwellers.

Paxson's and Billington's works, however, did not address certain substantive criticisms against the Turner thesis raised by historians who argued that other factors were more crucial than the frontier in shaping the American national character. Economic historian Charles A. Beard thought that the conflict between capitalists and workers had a stronger influence on

American historical development than did the frontier. Social historian Arthur M. Schlesinger, Sr., believed that immigration was a more central theme in American history. Writer Lewis Mumford demonstrated that European cultural roots continued to exert a strong influence on Americans and that the latter's experience on the frontier did not constitute a decisive break from the European legacy.

The contribution of the Turnerian school to western American historiography is, overall, a paradoxical one. By claiming that frontier history was quintessentially American history, Turner and the neo-Turnerians established it as a field whose importance transcended that of a mere regional history. At the same time, however, by putting so much emphasis on the pre-1890 frontier, they made western American history virtually synonymous with frontier history. It took other scholars many decades to break out of this conceptual straitjacket. Until they did, few wrote about those aspects of western America not directly associated with the frontier.

Unlike Turner's difficult-to-pin-down moving frontier, Walter Prescott Webb's American West had definite geographic boundaries. Webb introduced three particularly significant ideas about western history: the transforming power of an arid landscape, the "colonial" status of the West, and the peopling of the American West as but part of a larger process—a "four hundred year boom" that had begun in Europe and eventually spread to other continents.

To Webb, aridity (or, more accurately, semiaridity) was the defining feature of the West. Following the surveys of geologist John Wesley Powell, Webb understood the West to comprise the lands lying west of the 98th meridian, where the annual rainfall measured less than twenty inches and where few trees grew. In *The Great Plains* (1931), Webb demonstrated how settlers had to adapt the crops they grew, the tools they used, the houses and fences they built—indeed, their very behavior—to survive in such a forbidding environment. In short, the environment largely determined the kind of community or society that developed in the region. In Webb's writings, western American history was more the history of a region than the history of a process.

Webb's second important intellectual contribution was spelled out in his *Divided We Stand* (1937), in which he echoed an argument first made by Bernard DeVoto in a 1934 essay in *Harper's* magazine. DeVoto had called the American West a "plundered province"—one whose natural resources had been exploited for the profit of eastern and foreign capitalists, not for the benefit of the region's inhabitants. Although Webb's book focused on the South, it spoke eloquently to westerners, who, like almost everyone else in the country during the Great Depression, were suffering great privation. Conceiving of their region as an exploited "colony" gave westerners someone, something, or someplace else to blame for their troubles.

Webb made his third major contribution in his *Great Frontier* (1952). The conquest and settlement of the West, argued Webb, culminated a long boom that had originated in Europe. During four centuries of European expansion, millions of people had moved across the face of the earth—either of their own free will as explorers, traders, or immigrants, or under coercion as slaves and indentured servants—to open new lands to cultivation and to mine precious metals and minerals. The rate of economic growth that the United States, particularly its western region, experienced during the tail end of this process was unprecedented in world history. But by the mid-twentieth century, the movement was just about completed, and Americans, like people elsewhere, would have to adapt to the economic, social, and political constraints that would emerge in the ensuing era of resource scarcity.

Such a prognosis was not well received by an audience basking in the postwar prosperity of the 1950s, an era of abundance that seemed to contradict Webb's gloomy predictions. Although many of the arguments in *The Great Frontier* seem simplistic today, Webb performed an important function by placing western American history in a global context—an endeavor only recently resumed by a small number of historians of the American West.

Historian Herbert Eugene Bolton saw the American West from yet another perspective, that of Western Hemispheric history. Concentrating on what he called the Spanish borderlands, he depicted a frontier that moved not from east to west but from south to north. By meticulously plumbing voluminous archives in Mexico, Bolton became aware of the enormous scope of Spain's colonization efforts—efforts that transformed what eventually became the American Southwest long before English-speaking colonizers entered the region.

In book after book and in M.A. theses and Ph.D. dissertations he directed, but particularly in *The Spanish Borderlands: A Chronicle of Florida and the Southwest* (1921), Bolton demonstrated that western American history cannot be fully understood without studying the history of Spanish colonization in the Americas. To use current vocabulary, it was he who first emphasized the multiethnic, multicultural nature of western American history.

Influential as they were, these founding fathers had their critics, among whom Henry Nash Smith, Earl Pomeroy, and Gerald D. Nash offered the most substantial critiques. In *Virgin Land: The American West as Symbol and Myth* (1950), Smith introduced a whole new dimension to the study of the American West. Through a close reading of both highbrow texts and works of popular culture, he theorized about how meaning is created out of words and images. Americans who knew little about the "virgin" land they were attempting to conquer and settle, Smith argued, projected their own desires and fantasies upon it.

Smith traced how the image of the supposedly empty continent had slowly changed. Initially considered a barrier to a western passage to India, the New World eventually became an agricultural utopia in the eyes of

Americans, one that, according to the ideology of manifest destiny, was theirs to take. Thus, according to Smith, Turner's thesis was but one of the many myths that helped to form an American identity.

Pomeroy's critique, which he most clearly expressed in two essays, "Toward a Reorientation of Western History: Continuity and Environment" (1955) and "The Changing West" (1962), was of a different order. He believed that instead of creating a new civilization, the westering pioneers had in fact acted quite conservatively: more often than not, they had perpetuated old patterns brought from Europe or the eastern seaboard rather than develop new ways. "The Westerner has been fundamentally imitator rather than innovator," declared Pomeroy.

In other studies, Pomeroy examined how territorial governments functioned, and he concluded that they had served well as vehicles for the replication of national institutions. He also charged that by focusing so much on the agrarian sections of the American West in the pre-1890 period, the Turnerians had neglected the urban West and twentieth-century western American history—topics that he himself explored in *The Pacific Slope: A History of California, Oregon, Washington, Idaho, Utah, and Nevada* (1965).

In various articles and books, Gerald D. Nash also has probed the twentieth-century West. In *The American West Transformed: The Impact of the Second World War* (1985) and *World War II and the West: Reshaping the Economy* (1990), Nash argued that modern western American history can best be divided into a colonial era preceding World War II and a postwar period during which the region became a pacesetter for the nation. The West's economic and consequent social and political transformation was made possible mainly by federal-government investments, particularly in massive irrigation and water-control projects that provided cheap (because subsidized) water to large-scale farmers and manufacturers, and in defense industries, which created well-paying jobs for hundreds of thousands of workers and handsome profits for those who owned the plants and received the government contracts.

Whereas Turner's early critics chipped away at his thesis rather gently, some of his later critics have attempted to overturn it completely and to cast the entire field of western American history adrift from its former heroic, male-centered, individualistic, and romanticized moorings. Patricia Nelson Limerick, in *The Legacy of Conquest: The Unbroken Past of the American West* (1987), has mounted the most sustained challenge. The year 1890 was no watershed, Limerick asserts. Rather, the American West can best be understood as a place that has experienced wave after wave of conquest. As the meeting ground of diverse peoples, most of whom have been hitherto left out of the picture, the American West and its history constitute part of the "global story of Europe's expansion." The heart of this story has to do with how the conquered peoples were dispossessed of their land. It is "this intersection of ethnic diversity with property allocation [that] unifies Western history," Limerick proclaims. She then demonstrates by selected examples how the region's natural and human resources have been wastefully used for the benefit of the few and to the misery of the many.

Unlike another recent work of synthesis, *The American West: A Twentieth-Century History* (1989), by Michael P. Malone and Richard W. Etulain, which confined most of its discussion of peoples of color to a chapter entitled "Social Patterns in the Modern West," Limerick's book devotes three out of ten chapters to peoples of color—one to Native Americans, a second to Mexican Americans, and a third that groups Asian Americans, African Americans, and Mormons. Much of her discussion of these peoples, however, concerns how Euro-Americans have perceived, depicted, and treated them. Readers do not learn a great deal about the internal life of the communities these diverse groups established.

The same themes of exploitation and oppression are found in Richard White's *"It's Your Misfortunes and None of My Own": A New History of the American West* (1991). White has synthesized a stunning amount of information and integrated the story of the various nonwhite groups into various topical chapters. Race and ethnicity form the central themes in White's narrative, because the three most distinctive factors about the American West, in his view, are its "peculiar pattern of race relations," by which he means "a segmented labor structure based partially on race"; its economy, dominated by extractive and service industries; and its dependence on the federal government. In the book, he is careful to emphasize, as he put it in his article "Race Relations in the American West" (1986), that "race in the West has always been not so much a biological fact as a cultural and historical creation." Despite the importance he accords to race and ethnicity, however, White's account largely depicts peoples of color as victims, as objects of other people's actions, rather than as subjects or as agents of historical change.

Whereas Limerick and White primarily scrutinize the exploitation of people, William C. Robbins worries about the West as an exploited region. In the articles "The 'Plundered Province' Thesis and the Recent Historiography of the American West" (1986) and "Western History: A Dialectic on the Western Condition" (1989), Robbins revives and modifies the "plundered province" thesis and proposes that we can best understand the region's history by examining its location in the world capitalist system. According to Robbins, the impressive post–World War II transformation of the American West notwithstanding, those areas within the region where the local economies are still based primarily on extractive industries remain "colonial" in their status. Now, however, the metropolitan centers on which they depend for capital and to which profits flow are found in the financial centers not only of the eastern United States but also of California. Robbins then notes a trend that is becoming increasingly clear: a third financial metropole may also be emerging in the rapidly industrializing Asian countries along the Pacific Rim. "Indeed, if there is continuity to western history," Robbins states, "it rests not in the realm of its exceptional qualities and successes, but in the perpetually unstable nature of its material and economic base and relations with the rest of the world."

Yet another kind of exploitation—of the land itself—has been analyzed by environmental historian Donald Worster. In his article "New West, True West: Interpreting the Region's History" (1987), Worster identifies two very different "Wests"—one pastoral, based on cattle raising and a cowboy subculture; the other hydraulic, resting on an irrigated agriculture made possible by the technological wonders wrought by reclamation engineers and, it might be added, by armies of migrant farmworkers, the vast majority of them (with the exception of the Okies and Arkies in the 1930s) peoples of color. "This water empire," according to Worster, "is a purely western invention," whose salient features he has described at length in *Rivers of Empire: Water, Aridity, and the Growth of the American West* (1985). Manmade wonder though the modern hydraulic society may be, its days are numbered as the water table falls, salinity increases, and the soil subsides.

Despite all of these efforts to expose the dark underside of western American history, Turner's ghost has not yet been laid to rest. As William Cronon put it in his essay "Revisiting the Vanishing Frontier: The Legacy of Frederick Jackson Turner" (1987), "However much we understand [Turner's] *analytical* shortcomings, we still turn to him for our *rhetorical* structure" [emphasis added]. For Cronon, the "most useful elements of Turner's frontier are its focus on the history of how human beings have interacted with the American landscape; its ability to relate local and regional history to the wider history of the nation; its interdisciplinary focus; and, not least, its commitment to putting ordinary people at the center of the story." In other words, wrong though Turner may have been with regard to details, emphasis, and interpretation, his *intentions* are nevertheless worth emulating.

Perhaps to give western American historiography a new "sound," Cronon has proposed some ear-catching vocabulary. In a coauthored essay, "Becoming West: Toward a New Meaning for Western History," published in *Under an Open Sky: Rethinking America's Western Past* (1992), he calls upon his colleagues to examine six processes involved in the westward movement: species shifting (introducing alien plants and animals into new ecosystems), market making, land taking, boundary setting, state forming, and self-shaping. Looking at this list, however, one cannot help but ask, are these processes unique to the American West, or are they aspects of human settlement in any part of the world?

The above historiographical review shows that, despite fine efforts to include groups until recently left out of the master narrative, the treatment of peoples of color even in the newest works still falls short. For that reason, although many gaps exist in the literature, we have put together this book of readings specifically to place peoples of color at center stage. Our effort to reconceptualize western American history parallels what feminist (male and female) historians have tried to do in works such as *Frontier Women: The Trans-Mississippi West, 1840–1880* (1979), by Julie Roy Jeffrey; *Women and Men on the Overland Trail* (1979), by John Mack Faragher; *Westering Women and the Frontier Experience, 1800–1915* (1982), by Sandra L. Myres; *No Step Backward: Women and Family on the Rocky Mountain Mining Frontier, Helena, Montana, 1865–1900* (1987), by Paula Petrik; and *The Female Frontier: A Comparative View of Women on the Prairie and the Plains* (1988), by Glenda Riley, as well as such anthologies as *The Women's West* (1987), edited by Susan Armitage and Elizabeth Jameson, and *Western Women: Their Land, Their Lives* (1988), edited by Lillian Schlissel, Vicki L. Ruiz, and Janice Monk.

Changing the vantage point from which western American history is written requires us to change the time frame of that history, its geographical boundaries, and what constitutes "legitimate" sources. Our decision to open this book with several Native American legends illustrates the kind of re-visioning that we hope will eventually take place. We realize that these are myths, not documents. But such materials offer valuable glimpses of how the indigenous peoples themselves recollect the coming of strange-looking Euro-Americans and the significance of that encounter in their historical consciousness. Including myths is a way of redressing some of the omissions, distortions, and biases that have infused western American historiography as far as peoples of color are concerned.

Legends have occupied a central place in the lives of Native Americans. Children learned of life by dwelling in close contact with their extended families and by observing the interactions among individuals and between people and their surroundings. Their closest experience with formal instruction traditionally has come in the form of stories told by elders to the young. Although labeled as mere "folklore" by non-Indian scholars, these stories have offered lessons in what we would today call philosophy, history, politics, diplomacy, psychology, sociology, agricultural science, military science, astronomy, and so forth—all combining to form distinctive worldviews. The storytellers have accomplished their task in seemingly effortless fashion because the plots were exciting and memorable, brimming with drama and humor. Carriers of an oral tradition—a finely honed art in the absence of written languages—the storytellers were masterful teachers.

By opening this book with several of these stories, we give recognition to a history that began before Europeans colonized, conquered, and settled the Americas. We thus simultaneously lengthen the time frame of western American historiography, redefine its subjects or protagonists, change the direction of their "gaze," and enlarge our sources of knowledge.

In terms of geographic boundaries, we extend the definition of the American West to cover the forty-ninth and fiftieth states. Alaska and Hawaii have seldom been included in western American historical writings. In their textbook on the twentieth-century West, *The American West* (1989), Michael P. Malone and Richard W. Etulain explain that they purposely have left out Alaska and Hawaii because they are "not arid, nor do they exhibit another key factor of western regionalism: a commonly shared history." And what constitutes this "shared history"? In "Beyond the Last Frontier: Toward a New Approach to Western American History" (1989), Malone singles out four "fundamental bonds of regional identity: the abiding aridity of the West, its exceptional reliance upon the federal government, the recency and residual aura of its frontier experience, and its still heavy dependency upon extractive industries." He and Etulain claim that the two noncontiguous states lack all these characteristics.

Not so, responds John Whitehead, the author of "Hawai'i: The First and Last Far West?" (1992). Whitefield points out how, despite the fact that the world's wettest spot (with over 450 inches of rain per year) is located in one of the Hawaiian islands, other areas in the state receive less than six inches of rain. Sugar plantation owners have gone to great expense on the island of Maui to build miles of irrigation ditches to bring water to the cane fields, and on the island of Oahu, artesian wells have been dug with technology imported from California. Thus semitropical Hawaii is not devoid of aridity. In any case, aridity does not characterize the entire American West—the Pacific Northwest and northern California are quite wet.

As in the "classic" American West, the federal presence in both Hawaii and Alaska in also obvious. A very large proportion of Alaskan land remains in the federal public domain, and Hawaii is one of the most heavily militarized states in the nation. As for the aura of the frontier, if cowboys are its quintessential symbol, there is a thriving cattle industry in Hawaii. It is home to the Parker Ranch, now the largest in the nation, an enterprise worked by real cowboys. Finally, in terms of extractive industries, there are oil, timber, and fishing in Alaska and sugar, pineapple, and coffee cultivation in Hawaii. Although agriculture is not "extractive," it does depend on the use of the land.

From our point of view, however, more important than any of the above is the fact that the indigenous peoples of Hawaii and Alaska share a common history of conquest, colonization, and exploitation with peoples of color on the mainland. Native Hawaiians lost their land and were impressed into hard plantation labor. Their numbers were greatly reduced by diseases brought by Euro-Americans—diseases to which the New World inhabitants had no immunity. In Alaska, large corporations drilling for oil, cutting down timber, and mining for metals and minerals have impinged upon the livelihoods of the Eskimos and other Native Americans. In short, whether one thinks that common experiences exist between the indigenous peoples of the two noncontiguous states and those in the forty-eight "mainland" states depends on the reference group one uses.

Pointing out some of the commonalities among all peoples of color in the American West does not imply that the histories of the individual groups have been completely similar. By juxtaposing selections that at first glance might seem wildly disparate in some of the chapters, we encourage readers to search for characteristics shared by several groups as well as for the differences among them. By organizing the chapters topically, in some instances including readings that span several centuries, we also encourage readers to look for patterns that persist from one period to the next.

A number of underlying concerns have guided our choice of materials. First, we believe that race and ethnicity have circumscribed the lives not only of all peoples of color but also of Euro-Americans. Race and ethnicity have been used as fundamental dividing lines to separate people with pale skins from those of darker hues in terms of economic rewards, social prestige, cultural dominance, political control, and the attendant privileges flowing therefrom. Given the profound impact of race and ethnicity, we need to understand how they function in everyday life.

Second, virtually all studies of minorities in the United States have focused on the relationship between them and Euro-Americans. We believe that studies of interactions among different peoples of color are also needed. Interracial marriages, master-servant relationships, cooperation and competition in the labor market, the exploitation of one people of color by another people of color, and myriad forms of social commingling, as well as the problems that arise from such mixing, are historical phenomena that urgently require documentation and analysis. The three selections in Chapter 8 suggest some of the intellectual possibilities in researching this set of topics.

Third, because work has been the major arena in which peoples of color have encountered Euro-Americans, it is sometimes tempting to treat *all* peoples of color far too simplistically as a single working class or "proletariat," and all Euro-American employers as "capitalists." But life is considerably more complicated than is suggested by the concepts that social scientists invent to make sense of the world. We think that it is important to examine the internal stratification within each racial/ethnic community and the conflicts that have arisen from intracommunity class divisions. Furthermore, because so many jobs available in the American West have been in agriculture, fishing, lumbering, and mining—outdoor extractive industries, many of them requiring a migratory labor force that is extremely difficult to organize—the classical Marxist concept of class, based on the factory experiences of European and Euro-American workers, may not be all that pertinent for the labor history of peoples of color in the American West. Any class analysis, therefore, must pay careful attention to the specific contexts and actors involved.

Fourth, gender relations among peoples of color may have been and continue to be quite different from those found among Euro-Americans. Because such a large proportion of women of color have worked, whether as unpaid family labor or as wage earners, the neat demarcation between the private and public spheres suggested by Euro-American feminist scholars may not always hold among peoples of color. More studies are needed of the work performed by women of color in the American West, as well as of the impact of such labor on women's social status, economic worth, self-esteem, life satisfaction, family dynamics, political power, and role in the mediation, transformation, and transmission of culture. When more is known, we will better understand how and why the politics of liberation among women of color may differ from that of middle-class Euro-American women. In this book, we do not relegate readings on women and gender-related issues to discrete chapters of their own. Instead, there is at least one reading on women in most chapters. In short, we have integrated gender with more general topics.

Fifth, although we have compiled this anthology partly in response to the call for a more diverse, multicultural curriculum, our perspective differs from the liberal stance that suggests that interracial and interethnic conflicts stem from ignorance of the "contributions" made by peoples of color, and by women, to American life. Proponents of multiculturalism tend to overlook the fact that tensions have just as often arisen from *knowledge*—from the recognition that groups compete for scarce resources. Indeed, at any point in time in most societies, one group has taken most of the rewards of its society for its own members through its control over that society's forces of coercion, be they physical, political, economic, cultural, social, or psychological. Until we can cognitively untangle the roots of conflict, we will not discover viable bases for cooperation in the real world.

Sixth, as historians interested in depicting peoples of color as historical agents, we disagree with postmodernist writers who call into question the very idea of subjects. Instead, we consider it important to assert that new (because hitherto neglected) subjects, like those presented in this book, are constantly emerging as our historical consciousness broadens. For this reason, about one-sixth of the selections in this volume are autobiographical or biographical; we have included them in order to convey some sense of the consciousness—the thoughts, feelings, attitudes, and perceptions—of men and women of color.

Finally, we must say a word about the terminology we use in the book, particularly in the introductions to each chapter and selection. We prefer the term *peoples of color* to *minorities* because at one time some of the groups we discuss were majorities. If current demographic trends continue, nonwhites will outnumber whites within a few decades in certain western states. We say *peoples*, rather than *people*, in order to emphasize the diversity among and within the groups. We use *African Americans* and *blacks* interchangeably, but in some of the readings published in earlier years, the terms *Negroes* and *Afro-Americans* can also be found. *Asian Americans* is preferred over *Orientals* because *Oriental*, meaning "Eastern," harks back to a colonialist era that took Europe as its point of reference. We also use *Chicanos* and *Mexican Americans* interchangeably; *Latinos* refers to people from Mexico as well as from Latin American countries other than Mexico. *Native Americans* appears alongside *American Indians* or simply *Indians*. Americans of European ancestry are called *Euro-Americans*, *Anglos*, *whites*, or *Caucasians*. The term *Euro-Americans*, or more properly *European Americans*, was coined to create a parallel term to *African Americans*, *Asian Americans*, and so forth. It is relatively new but is being adopted by more and more scholars and journalists. When we take the experiences of all these groups into account, it becomes clearer than ever that the history of the American West is richly textured and full of exciting possibilities.

— Sucheng Chan

FURTHER READING

Susan Armitage, "Women and Men in Western History: A Stereoptical Vision," *Western Historical Quarterly* 16 (1985): 381–395.

Susan Armitage and Elizabeth Jameson, *The Women's West* (Norman and London: University of Oklahoma Press, 1987).

Allan G. Bogue, "The Significance of the History of the American West: Postscripts and Prospects," *Western Historical Quarterly* 24 (1993): 45–68.

Antonia I. Castañeda, "Women of Color and the Rewriting of Western History: The Discourse, Politics, and Decolonization of History," *Pacific Historical Review* 61 (1992): 501–533.

William Cronon, "Revisiting the Vanishing Frontier: The Legacy of Frederick Jackson Turner," *Western Historical Quarterly* 18 (1987): 158–176.

William Cronon, Howard R. Lamar, Katherine G. Morrissey, and Jay Gitlin, "Women and the West: Rethinking the Western History Survey Course," *Western Historical Quarterly* 17 (1986): 269–290.

William Cronon, George Miles, and Jay Gitlin, eds., *Under an Open Sky: Rethinking America's Western Past* (New York: W. W. Norton & Co., 1992).

Brian Dippie, "The Winning of the West Reconsidered," *Wilson Quarterly* 14 (1990): 70–85.

Richard W. Etulain, ed., *Writing Western History: Essays on Major Western Historians* (Albuquerque: University of New Mexico Press, 1991).

John Mack Faragher, *Women and Men on the Overland Trail* (New Haven: Yale University Press, 1979).

Christiane Fischer, ed., *Let Them Speak for Themselves: Women in the American West, 1849–1900* (Hamden, Conn.: Archon Books, 1977).

Gene M. Gressley, "The West: Past, Present, Future," *Western Historical Quarterly* 17 (1986): 5–23.

Elizabeth Jameson, "Toward a Multicultural History of Women in the Western United States," *Signs: Journal of Women in Culture and Society* 13 (1988): 761–791.

Julie Roy Jeffrey, *Frontier Women: The Trans-Mississippi West, 1840–1880* (New York: Hill and Wang, 1979).

Joan M. Jensen and Darlis A. Miller, "The Gentle Tamers Revisited: New Approaches to the History of Women in the American West," *Pacific Historical Review* 49 (1980): 173–213.

Richard Jensen, "On Modernizing Frederick Jackson Turner: The Historiography of Regionalism," *Western Historical Quarterly* 11 (1980): 307–322.

Patricia Nelson Limerick, *The Legacy of Conquest: The Unbroken Past of the American West* (New York: W. W. Norton & Co., 1987).

Patricia Nelson Limerick, Clyde A. Milner II, and Charles E. Rankin, eds., *Trails: Toward a New Western History* (Lawrence: University Press of Kansas, 1991).

Michael P. Malone, "Beyond the Last Frontier: Toward a New Approach to Western American History," *Western Historical Quarterly* 20 (1989): 409–427.

Michael P. Malone, ed., *Historians and the American West* (Lincoln and London: University of Nebraska Press, 1983).

Michael P. Malone and Richard W. Etulain, *The American West: A Twentieth-Century History* (Lincoln and London: University of Nebraska Press, 1989).

Clyde A. Milner II, *Major Problems in the History of the American West* (Lexington, Mass.: D. C. Heath and Co., 1989).

Ruth B. Moynihan, Susan Armitage, and Christine Fischer Dichamp, eds., *So Much to Be Done: Women Settlers on the Mining and Ranching Frontier* (Lincoln and London: University of Nebraska Press, 1990).

Sandra L. Myres, *Westering Women and the Frontier Experience, 1800–1915* (Albuquerque: University of New Mexico Press, 1982).

Gerald D. Nash, *Creating the West: Historical Interpretations, 1890–1990* (Albuquerque: University of New Mexico Press, 1991).

Gerald D. Nash and Richard Etulain, eds., *The Twentieth Century West: Historical Interpretations* (Albuquerque: University of New Mexico Press, 1989).

Roger L. Nichols, ed., *American Frontier and Western Issues: A Historiographical Review* (Westport, Conn.: Greenwood Press, 1986).

Spencer C. Olin, Jr., "Toward a Synthesis of the Political and Social History of the American West," *Pacific Historical Review* 55 (1986): 599–611.

Rodman W. Paul and Michael P. Malone, "Tradition and Challenge in Western Historiography," *Western Historical Review* 16 (1985): 27–53.

Paula Petrik, *No Step Backward: Women and Family on the Rocky Mountain Mining Frontier, Helena, Montana, 1865–1900* (Helena: Montana Historical Society Press, 1987).

Vicki Piekarski, *Westward the Women: An Anthology of Western Stories by Women* (Albuquerque: University of New Mexico Press, 1984).

Earl Pomeroy, "The Changing West," in *The Reconstruction of American History*, ed. John Higham (London: Hutchinson and Co., 1962), 64–81.

Earl Pomeroy, "Toward a Reorientation of Western History: Continuity and Environment," *Mississippi Valley Historical Review* 41 (1955): 579–600.

Gerald E. Poyo and Gilberto M. Hinojosa, "Spanish Texas and Borderlands Historiography in Transition: Implications for United States History," *Journal of American History* 75 (1988): 393–416.

Martin Ridge, "The American West: From Frontier to Region," *New Mexico Historical Review* 64 (1989): 125–142.

Glenda Riley, *The Female Frontier: A Comparative View of Women on the Prairie and the Plains* (Lawrence: University Press of Kansas, 1988).

William G. Robbins, "The 'Plundered Province' Thesis and the Recent Historiography of the American West," *Pacific Historical Review* 55 (1986): 577–597.

William G. Robbins, "Western History: A Dialectic on the Modern Condition," *Western Historical Quarterly* 20 (1989): 429–449.

Virginia Scharff, " 'Else Surely We Shall All Hang Separately': The Politics of Western Women's History," *Pacific Historical Review* 61 (1992): 535–555.

Lillian Schlissel, *Women's Diaries of the Westward Journey* (New York: Schocken Books, 1982).

Lillian Schlissel, Byrd Gibbens, and Elizabeth Hampsten, *Far from Home: Families of the Westward Journey* (New York: Schocken Books, 1989).

Lillian Schlissel, Vicki L. Ruiz, and Janice Monk, eds., *Western Women: Their Land, Their Lives* (Albuquerque: University of New Mexico Press, 1988).

Michael C. Steiner, "The Significance of Turner's Sectional Thesis," *Western Historical Review* 10 (1979): 437–466.

David Weber, "Turner, the Boltonians, and the Borderlands," *American Historical Review* 91 (1986): 66–81.

Richard White, "Race Relations in the American West," *American Quarterly* 38 (1986): 396–419.

Richard White, *"It's Your Misfortune and None of My Own": A New History of the American West* (Norman and London: University of Oklahoma Press, 1991).

John Whitehead, "Hawai'i: The First and Last Far West?" *Western Historical Quarterly* 23 (1992): 153–177.

Donald Worster, "New West, True West: Interpreting the Region's History," *Western Historical Quarterly* 18 (1987): 141–156.

Donald Worster, *Rivers of Empire: Water, Aridity, and the Growth of the American West* (New York: Pantheon Books, 1985).

Donald Worster, *Under Western Skies: Nature and History in the American West* (New York: Oxford University Press, 1992).

Mary Young, "The West and American Cultural Identity: Old Themes and New Variations," *Western Historical Quarterly* 1 (1970): 137–160.

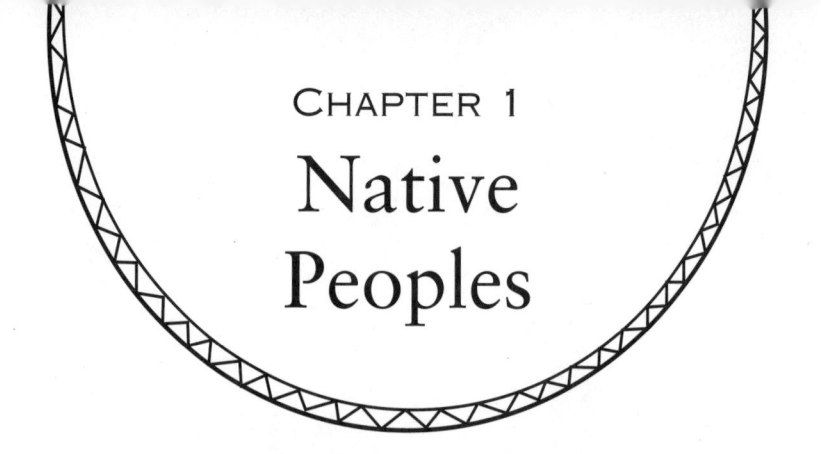

CHAPTER 1

Native Peoples

Generations of schoolchildren have learned that American history began with the voyage of Columbus in 1492. Until recently, history textbooks invariably started their chronicle of the United States with a chapter on the European age of discovery and colonization. The course of subsequent events was couched within the framework of the frontier—that ever-westward-shifting boundary where "civilization" met, and inevitably replaced, "savagery." And until the past decade or so, history textbooks scarcely mentioned the native peoples' presence in America before their contact with Europeans. Students seldom learned that a thriving and diverse indigenous, or native, population had occupied the land long before it was invaded by outsiders.

In one sense, all "American" history textbooks and anthologies, including this one, are woefully unbalanced. By emphasizing the most recent five hundred years of cultural interactions and conflicts, historians, consciously or unconsciously, relegate the thousands of years of pre-Columbian or "prehistorical" Native American life to lesser importance. The disregard or severe abbreviation of precontact aboriginal history not only distorts the true picture but also serves as a rationalization for subsequent events. Positing the past of Native Americans as "prehistory" dehumanizes the cultures that were subjugated by the European invasion, and places them on the same level as the deserts, mountains, forests, and wild animals that writers have long depicted as "obstacles" in the path of civilization or progress.

Descriptive and explanatory studies about the nature of Native Americans before the uninvited incursions of Europeans and Euro-Americans are needed. But the Americas' geographic vastness and diversity of peoples makes it nearly impossible to provide any systematic representation of the indigenous cultures. The readings in this chapter can only give glimpses of some of these cultures.

Richard Erdoes and Alfonso Ortiz edited the oral traditions of several Indian tribes, and these stories, excerpted in the first selection, are the closest that modern readers can get to aboriginal thought patterns. Ramón A. Gutiérrez describes the southwestern Pueblo world in the sec-

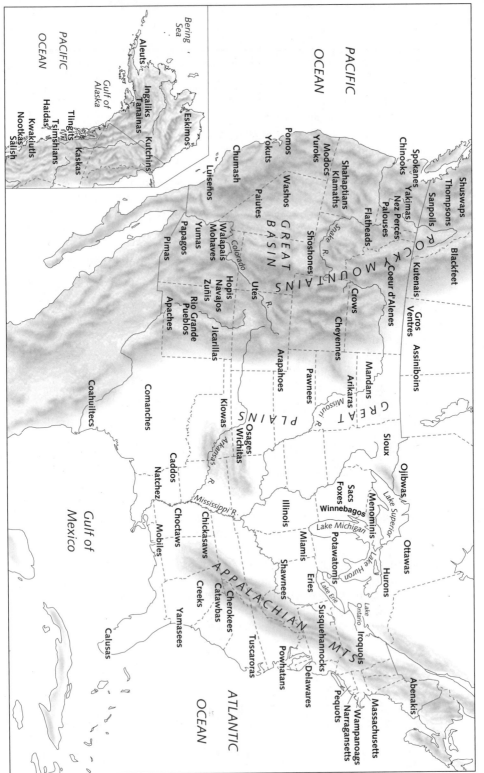

Location of selected Indian Tribes, A.D. 1500

ond selection, followed by John Fahey's account of the Flatheads in Montana. Finally, shifting the focus far beyond the North American continental landmass, Edward D. Beechert offers insights into how native Hawaiians lived. It is important to remember that, together with many other indigenous peoples, these groups constituted the *majority* culture of the American West until the Euro-American conquest.

FOR ANALYSIS AND DISCUSSION

1. How do the Native Americans' accounts of their origins compare with the biblical version of the creation of the earth and its peopling? Why are the former classified as "myth" and the latter as "religion"?

2. How did the climate and geography of the regions where the various indigenous peoples lived affect their patterns of life and ways of thinking? Cite examples from each reading.

3. Compare and contrast the lifestyles of the Pueblos, the Flatheads, and the Hawaiians.

4. How do the ways in which the indigenous peoples viewed themselves and their surroundings, as described in this chapter's readings, differ from the ways that we Americans today see ourselves and our relationship to the environment?

5. How did Native Americans deal with gender-related issues of marriage, family, work, and spiritual life?

6. How was knowledge about various aspects of life passed on from one generation to the next among each of the native peoples discussed in this chapter?

7. Did the readings in this chapter change the perceptions you had about tribal peoples? If so, in what ways?

American Indians' Ideas About Themselves

RICHARD ERDOES AND ALFONSO ORTIZ

Discerning historians and social scientists have learned to respect and value American Indian myths and legends. Along with the bodily remains and extant man-made structures and objects, these oral traditions are all that survive to shed light on thousands of years of Native American life. Handed down from generation to generation, these stories, though their details might be changed and their form and content altered after exposure to European thought and translation into non-Indian languages, nonetheless retain a power and significance that cannot be dismissed.

Storytellers through the ages have told their tales not simply to amuse or divert, although their entertainment value is readily perceived by those of other cultures. The myths and legends contain no reliable keys to specific events and dates. They do, however, reveal the ethos of the ancient native peoples, who told them as truths to be believed in. Varied as the multiplicity of geography, language, and culture they represent, the myths and legends nevertheless share common themes and rhythms. Native Americans' sense of oneness with their natural surroundings, based on their faith in a spiritual presence that connects all things, provides a commonality to the stories. The ordered universe of pre-Columbian life is explained in the early tales, while later stories attempted to rationalize the changes and confusion that followed the arrival of Europeans.

The following selections come from the Yuma Indians, who still reside near the junction of the Gila and Colorado rivers in southern Arizona; the Jicarilla Apaches, whose reservation is located in northwestern New Mexico; and the Modocs, who live on a reservation in southern Oregon. All of the stories contemplate the genesis of the earth and humans' place within it. These creation accounts collected by Richard Erdoes and Alfonso Ortiz reveal how three groups of American Indians explained the natural features of the world around them and the foibles and fancies of the tribespeoples who populated the land.

STUDY QUESTIONS

1. What are the similarities in the myths and legends of the three groups of Native Americans represented in this reading?

2. What can you deduce about Indians' sense of humor from these stories?

3. How do these Native American stories compare with European and Euro-American explanations for natural phenomena?

THE GOOD TWIN AND THE EVIL TWIN (YUMA)

This is how it all began. There was only water—there was no sky, there was no land, only nothingness. Then out of the waters rose a mist, and it became the sky. Still there were no sun, no moon, no stars—just darkness. But deep down in the waters lived Kokomaht, the Creator. He was bodiless, nameless, breathless, motionless, and he was two beings—twins.

Then the waters stirred and rushed and thundered, and out of the spray and foam rose the first twin, the good twin. With closed eyes he cleaved the waves and came to the surface. He stood upon the waters, opened his eyes, and saw. There he named himself Kokomaht—All-Father.

And from beneath the waters a second voice called out to Kokomaht: "Brother, how did you rise? With eyes open or with eyes closed?"

Bakotahl was the evil twin, and Kokomaht wanted to make it more difficult for him to do harm. So Kokomaht lied to him, saying: "I opened my eyes while I was under water." The second twin opened his eyes as he rose, and when he reached the surface he was blind. Kokomaht said: "I name you Bakotahl—the Blind One."

Then Kokomaht said: "Now I shall make the four directions." He pointed with his finger and took four steps, walking on the water. Then he stood still for a while and said, "Ho, this is north." Then he went back to his starting place, and in the same manner made the west, the south, and the east—always taking four steps in each direction and always returning to the center.

"Now," Kokomaht said, "I shall make the earth."

Blind Bakotahl answered: "I don't think you have the power to do this."

"Certainly I have," said Kokomaht.

"Let my try to make the earth first," asked Bakotahl.

"Certainly not," said Kokomaht.

Kokomaht stirred the waters into a foaming whirlpool with his hand. They frothed and swelled and bubbled, and when they subsided there was land. And Kokomaht sat down upon it.

Bakotahl was angry because he would have liked to create the earth, but he said nothing and settled down by Kokomaht's side. The Blind Evil One said to himself: "I shall make something with a head, with arms and legs. I can make it out of the earth." Bakotahl formed something resembling a human being, but it was imperfect. Instead of hands and feet there were lumps; it had neither fingers nor toes. Bakotahl hid it from Kokomaht.

Then Kokomaht said: "I feel like making something." Out of mud he shaped a being that was perfect. It had hands and feet, fingers and toes, even fingernails and toenails. Kokomaht waved this being four times toward the north and then stood it on its feet. It moved, it walked, it was alive: it was a man. Kokomaht made another being in the same way, and it was alive: it was a woman.

Bakotahl went on trying to make humans, piecing together seven beings out of earth. All were imperfect. "What are you making?" Kokomaht asked.

"People," answered Bakotahl.

"Here," said Kokomaht, "feel these people I've made. Yours have no hands or feet. Here; feel; mine have fingers, thumbs, to work, to fashion things, to draw bows, to pick fruit." Kokomaht examined the beings Bakotahl had formed. "These are no good," he said, and stamped them to pieces. Bakotahl was so enraged that he dove down deep beneath the waters amid rumblings and thunderings. From the depths he sent up the whirlwind, bringer of all evil. Kokomaht stepped on the whirlwind and killed it—except for a little whiff that slipped out from under his foot. In it were contained all the sicknesses which plague people to this day.

So Kokomaht was by himself except for the two beings he had made. These were the Yumas, and in the same way that he had created them, Kokomaht now made the Cocopahs, the Dieguieños, and the Mojaves. In pairs he created them. Then he rested. Four tribes he had created. After having rested, he made four more tribes: the Apaches, the Maricopas, the Pimas, and the Coahuilas. In all, he made twenty-four kinds of people. The white people he left for last.

The one he had made first, the Yuma man, said to Kokomaht: "Teach us how to live."

"You must learn how to increase," said Kokomaht. In order to teach them, he begat a son. Out of nothing, without help from a woman, he sired him and named him Komashtam'ho. He told men and women not to live apart, but to join together and rear children.

Still something was missing. "It is too dark," said Kokomaht. "There should be some light." So he made the moon, the morning star, and all the other stars. Then he said, "My work is done. Whatever I have not finished, my son Komashtam'ho will finish."

Now, among the beings Kokomaht had made was Hanyi, the Frog. She was powerful; fire could not destroy her. She envied Kokomaht his power and thought to destroy him. Kokomaht knew this because he knew the thoughts of all the beings he had made, but he said to himself: "I taught the people how to live. Now I must teach them how to die, for without death there will soon be too many people on the earth. So I will permit Frog to kill me."

Hanyi burrowed down underneath the spot where Kokomaht was standing and sucked the breath out of his body through a hole in the earth. Then Kokomaht sickened and lay down to die. He called all the people to come to him, and all came except the white man, who stayed by himself in the west.

The white man was crying because his hair was faded and curly and his skin pale and washed out. The white man was always pouting and selfish. Whatever he saw, he had to have at once. He had been created childish and greedy. Komashtam'ho, tired of hearing the white man crying, went over to him and tied two sticks together in the form of a cross. "Here, stop crying," he said. "Here's something for you to ride on." The white man straddled these sticks and they turned into a horse, so the greedy one was satisfied— for a while.

For the last time now Kokomaht taught the people. "Learn how to die," he told them, and expired.

"I have to make what my father could not finish." said Komashtam'ho. He spat into his hand and from his spittle made a disk. He took it and threw it up into the sky toward the east. It began to shine. "This is the sun," Komashtam'ho told the people. "Watch it move; watch it lighting up the world."

Then Komashtam'ho prepared to burn the body of his father, but since there were no trees yet, he had no wood. Komashtam'ho called out: "Wood, come in being! Wood, come alive! Wood, come here to where I stand." Wood came from everywhere and formed itself into a great funeral pyre.

Navajo children learning from the stories of a tribal elder

Before he died, Kokomaht had told Coyote: "Friend, take my heart. Be faithful. Do what I tell you." Coyote misunderstood Kokomaht and thought that he was supposed to eat the heart. Komashtam'ho knew this because he could see into Coyote's mind. So he told Coyote: "Go get a spark from the sun to light a fire."

As soon as Coyote was gone, Komashtam'ho took a sharpened stick and twirled it in some soft wood until he sparked a flame. "Look, my people," he said, "this is the way to make fire. Quick now, before Coyote comes back." With these words he lit the funeral pyre. The people did not lament for Kokomaht because they did not yet understand what death was. But before the flames had consumed the body, Coyote returned and leapt up quick as a flash to seize Kokomaht's heart. He ran off with it, and though all the other animals and the people too chased after him, he was too fast for them.

Komashtam'ho called after Coyote: "You have done something bad. You will never amount to anything. You will be a wild man without a house to live in. You will live by stealing, and for your thefts the people will kill you."

After Kokomaht's body had been burned, the people asked Komashtam'ho: "When will Kokomaht come back."

"He will never come back," he told them. "He is dead. He let himself be killed because if he had gone on living, then all you people would also live forever, and soon there would be no room left on the earth. So from now on, everybody will die sometime."

Then all the people began to lament. They wept for Kokomaht and for themselves. They did not want to believe that he would never come back. As they sat grieving, they saw a little whirlwind like a dust devil rising from the spot where Kokomaht had been burned. "What is it? What can it be?" they cried.

Komashtam'ho told them: "It is the spirit of Kokomaht. His body died, but his soul is alive. He will go someplace—north or south, east or west—somewhere his spirit will dwell. He will never tire, he will never be hungry or thirsty, and though we weep because he has died, Kokomaht's spirit will be happy always."

And Komashtam'ho instructed the people in the nature of death. "When you die, you will be again with those you love who have gone before you. Again you will be young and strong, though you might have been old and feeble on the day you died. In the spirit land the corn will grow and all will be happy, whether they were good or bad when they were alive. So death is not something to be afraid of." And when they heard this, the people stopped weeping and smiled again.

Then Komashtam'ho chose one man, Marhokuvek, to help him put the world in order. The first thing that Marhokuvek did was to say, "Ho, you people, as a sign that you mourn the death of your father Kokomaht, you should cut your hair short." Then all the people, animals, and birds did as they had been told. The animals at this time were people also: they looked like humans. But when he saw them Komashtam'ho said: "These animals and birds don't look well with their hair cut," and changed them into coyotes and deer, into wild turkeys and roadrunners—into the animals and birds we have now.

After some time, Komashtam'ho let fall a great rain, the kind that never stops. There was a flood in which many of the animals were drowned. Marhokuvek was alarmed. "Komashtam'ho, what are you doing?" he cried.

"Some of these animals are too wild. Some have big teeth and claws and are dangerous. Also, there are simply too many of them. So I am killing them off with this flood."

"No, Komashtam'ho, stop the flood," pleaded Marhokuvek. "The people need many of these animals for food. They like to hear the songs of the birds. Rain and flood make the world too cold, and the people can't stand it."

So Komashtam'ho made a big fire to cause the waters to evaporate. The fire was so hot and fierce that even Komashtam'ho himself was slightly burned. Ever since that time, the deserts around here have been hot, and the people are used to the warmth.

After that, he called the people together and told them: "Over there is your father Kokomaht's house. We must pull it down, because when a man dies, the spirits of his house and of all his belongings follow him to the spirit land. So people must destroy all the things he owned in this life so that their spirits can serve him in the other world. Also, after a man has died, it is not good to look upon the things that he used to own. One sees his house, but he who dwelt in it is gone. One sees his water olla, but he who owned it is no longer here to lift it to his lips. It makes people sad, and they sicken with grief and longing. Therefore you Yuma people must always burn the house and possessions of those who die, and you must move to another dwelling where nothing reminds you of the dead. Also, never again mention the name of him who is gone. He belongs to another life, while you must start on a new one." And from that time on, the Yuma have followed these rules.

Komashtam'ho took a huge pole, smashed the house of Kokomaht, and rooted up the ground on which it had stood. Water welling up from the rut made by the pole became the Colorado River. And in it swam the beings that Bakotahl—the Blind Evil One—had formed, the creatures without hands or feet, toes or fingers. These were the fish and other water animals.

Now Kahk, the Crow, was a good planter and reaper. He brought corn and all kinds of useful seeds from the four corners of the world. He flew south to the great water, stopping four times on the way and crying: "Kahk, kahk!" Each time he did this, a big mountain arose. After the overflow of the river which Komashtam'ho had made, Crow brought many seeds from the south for the people to plant.

The tribes had been scattered over all the world, but Komashtam'ho kept the Yuma near him because they were the special people he loved. "Listen closely," he said to them. "I cannot stay with you forever. I am now only one, but soon I will become four. My name will no longer be Komashtam'ho. I will turn myself into four eagles—the black eagle of the west, the brown eagle of the south, the white eagle of the east and the fourth eagle, whose name is 'unseen,' because no man has ever caught a glimpse of him."

When Komashtam'ho had turned himself into the four eagles, he dwelt no longer among the Yuma in the shape of a man. He kept watch over them, however, and in their dreams he gave them power from Kokomaht. Thus Kokomaht advises the people through Komashtam'ho and tells them while they sleep: "Think about me, think of what I taught you. Sick people especially should follow my teachings."

Now Bakotahl, the Evil Blind One, is under the earth and does bad things. Usually he lies down there quietly, but sometimes he turns over. Then there is a great noise of thunder, the earth trembles and splits open, and mountainsides crack, while flames and smoke shoot out of their summits. Then the people are afraid and say: "The Blind Evil One is stirring down below."

Everything that is good comes from Kokomaht, and everything evil comes from Bakotahl. This is the tale—how it was, and how it is, and how it will be.

> — Retold from several sources, among them Natalie Curtis's report in 1909

THE JICARILLA GENESIS (JICARILLA APACHE)

In the beginning the earth was covered with water, and all living things were below in the underworld. Then people could talk, the animals could talk, the trees could talk, and the rocks could talk.

It was dark in the underworld, and eagle plumes were used for torches. The people and the animals that go about by day wanted more light, but the night animals—the bear, the panther, and the owl—wanted darkness. After a long argument they agreed to play the thimble-and-button game, and if the day animals won there would be light, but if the night animals won it would always be dark.

The game began. The magpie and the quail, who love the lights and have sharp eyes, watched until they could see the button through the thin wood of the hollow stick that served as a thimble. This told the people where the button was, and in the first round, the people won. The morning star came out and the black bear ran and hid in the darkness. They played again, and the

---

Ibid., pp. 82–86.

people won. It grew bright in the east and the brown bear ran and hid in a dark place. They played a third time, and the people won. It grew brighter in the east and the mountain lion slunk away into the darkness. They played a fourth time, and again the people won. The sun came up in the east, and it was day, and the owl flew away and hid.

Even though it was light now, the people still didn't see much because they were underground. But the sun was high enough to look through a hole and discover that there was another world—this earth. He told the people, and they all wanted to go up there. They built four mounds to help them reach the upper world. In the east they mounded the soil and planted it with all kinds of fruits and berries that were colored black. In the south they heaped up another mound and planted all kinds of fruits that were blue. In the west they built a mound that they planted with yellow fruits. In the north they planted the mound with fruits of variegated colors.

The mounds grew into mountains and the bushes blossomed, fruited, and produced ripened berries. One day two girls climbed up to pick berries and gather flowers to tie in their hair. Suddenly the mountains stopped growing. The people wondered, and they sent Tornado to learn the cause. Tornado went everywhere and searched into every corner, and at last he found the two girls and brought them back to their people. But the mountains did not grow any more, and this is why a boy stops growing when he goes with a woman for the first time. If he never did, he would continue to grow taller.

The mountains had stopped growing while their tops were still a long way from the upper world. So the people tried layering feathers crosswise to make a ladder, but the feathers broke under weight. The people made a second ladder of larger feathers, but again they were too weak. They made a third ladder of eagle feathers, but even these would not bear much weight. Then a buffalo came and offered his right horn, and three others also contributed their right horns. The horns were strong and straight, and with them the people were able to climb up through the hole to the surface of the earth. But the weight of all those humans bent the buffalo horns, which have been curved ever since.

Now the people fastened the sun and moon with spider threads so that they could not get away, and sent them up into the sky to give light. And since water covered the whole earth, four storms went to roll the waters away. The black storm blew to the east and rolled up the waters into the eastern ocean. The blue storm blew to the south and rolled up the waters in that direction. The yellow storm rolled up the waters in the west, and the varicolored storm went to the north and rolled up the waters there. So the tempests formed the four oceans in the east, the south, the west, and the north. Having rolled up the waters, the storms returned to where the people were waiting, grouped around the mouth of the hole.

The Polecat first went out, when the ground was still soft, and his legs sank in the black mud and have been black ever since. They sent the Tornado to bring him back, because it wasn't time. The badger went out, but he too sank in the mud and got black legs, and Tornado called him back. Then the beaver went out, walking through the mud and swimming through the water, and at once began to build a dam to save the water still remaining in pools. When he did not return, Tornado found him and asked why he had not come back.

"Because I wanted to save the water for the people to drink," said the beaver.

"Good," said Tornado, and they went back together. Again the people waited, until at last they sent out the gray crow to see if the time had come. The crow found the earth dry, and many dead frogs, fish, and reptiles lying on the ground. He began picking out their eyes and did not return until Tornado was sent after him. The people were angry when they found he had been eating carrion, and they changed his color to black.

But now the earth was all dry, except for the four oceans and the lake in the center, where the beaver had dammed up the waters. All the people came up. They traveled east until they arrived at the ocean; then they turned south until they came again to the ocean; then they went west to the ocean, and then they turned north. And as they went, each tribe stopped where it wanted to. But the Jicarillas continued to circle around the hole where they had come up from the underworld. Three times they went around it, when the Ruler became displeased and asked them where they wished to stop. They said, "In the middle of the earth." So he led them to a place very near Taos and left them, and there near the Taos Indians, the Jicarillas made their home.

— Based on a tale reported by James Mooney in the 1890s

WHEN GRIZZLIES WALKED UPRIGHT (MODOC)

Before there were people on the earth, the Chief of the Sky Spirits grew tired of his home in the Above World, because the air was always brittle with an icy cold. So he carved a hole in the sky with a stone and pushed all the snow and ice down below until he made a great mound that reached from the earth almost to the sky. Today it is known as Mount Shasta.

Then the Sky Spirit took his walking stick, stepped from a cloud to the peak, and walked down to the mountain. When he was about halfway to the valley below, he began to put his finger to the ground here and there, here and there. Wherever his finger touched, a tree grew. The snow melted in his footsteps, and the water ran down in rivers.

The Sky Spirit broke off the small end of his giant stick and threw the pieces into the rivers. The longer pieces turned into beaver and otter; the smaller pieces became fish. When the leaves dropped from the trees, he picked them up, blew upon them, and so made the birds. Then he took the big end of his giant stick and made all the animals that walked on the earth, the biggest of which were the grizzly bears.

Now when they were first made, the bears were covered with hair and had sharp claws, just as they do today, but they walked on two feet and could talk like people. They looked so fierce that the Sky Spirit sent them away from him to live in the forest at the base of the mountain.

Pleased with what he'd done, the Chief of the Sky Spirits decided to bring his family down and live on the earth himself. The mountains of snow and ice became their lodge. He made a big fire in the center of the mountain and a hole in the top so that the smoke and sparks could fly out. When he put a big log on the fire, sparks would fly up and the earth would tremble.

Late one spring while the Sky Spirit and his family were sitting round the fire, the Wind Spirit sent a great storm that shook the top of the mountain. It blew and blew and roared and roared. Smoke blown back into the lodge hurt their eyes, and finally the Sky Spirit said to his youngest daughter, "Climb up to the smoke hole and ask the Wind Spirit to blow more gently. Tell him I'm afraid he will blow the mountain over."

As his daughter started up, her father said, "But be careful not to stick your head out at the top. If you do, the wind may catch you by the hair and blow you away.

The girl hurried to the top of the mountain and stayed well inside the smoke hole as she spoke to the Wind Spirit. As she was about to climb back down, she remembered that her father had once said you could see the ocean from the top of their lodge. His daughter wondered what the ocean looked like, and her curiosity got the better of her. She poked her head out of the hole and turned toward the west, but before she could see anything, the Wind Spirit caught her long hair, pulled her out of the mountain, and blew her down over the snow and ice. She landed among the scrubby fir trees at the edge of the timber and snow line, her long red hair trailing over the snow.

There a grizzly bear found the little girl when he was out hunting food for his family. He carried her home with him, and his wife brought her up with their family of cubs. The little red-haired girl and the cubs ate together, played together, and grew up together.

When she became a young woman, she and the eldest son of the grizzly bears were married. In the years that followed they had many children, who were not as hairy as the grizzlies, yet did not look exactly like their spirit mother, either.

All the grizzly bears throughout the forests were so proud of these new creatures that they made a lodge for the red-haired mother and her children.

They placed the lodge near Mount Shasta—it is called Little Mount Shasta today.

After many years had passed, the mother grizzly bear knew that she would soon die. Fearing that she should ask the Chief of the Sky Spirits to forgive her for keeping his daughter, she gathered all the grizzlies at the lodge they had built. Then she sent her oldest grandson in a cloud to the top of Mount Shasta, to tell the Spirit Chief where he could find his long-lost daughter.

When the father got this news he was so glad that he came down the mountainside in giant strides, melting the snow and tearing up the land under his feet. Even today his tracks can be seen in the rocky path on the south side of Mount Shasta.

As he neared the lodge, he called out, "Is this where my little daughter lives?"

He expected his child to look exactly as she had when he saw her last. When he found a grown woman instead, and learned that the strange creatures she was taking care of were his grandchildren, he became very angry. A new race had been created that was not of his making! He frowned on the old grandmother so sternly that she promptly fell dead. Then he cursed all the grizzlies:

"Get down on your hands and knees. You have wronged me, and from this moment all of you will walk on four feet and never talk again."

He drove his grandchildren out of the lodge, put his daughter over his shoulder, and climbed back up the mountain. Never again did he come to the forest. Some say that he put out the fire in the center of his lodge and took his daughter back up to the sky to live.

Those strange creatures, his grandchildren, scattered and wandered over the earth. They were the first Indians, the ancestors of all the Indian tribes.

That's why the Indians living around Mount Shasta would never kill a grizzly bear. Whenever a grizzly killed an Indian, his body was burned on the spot. And for many years all who passed that way cast a stone there until a great pile of stones marked the place of his death.

— Reported by Ella Clark in 1953

The Pueblo Indian World in the Sixteenth Century

RAMÓN A. GUTIÉRREZ

One of the biggest challenges confronting scholars who seek to describe and analyze American Indian cultures and societies is the relative paucity of native sources. An additional problem is determining how best to understand the meaning and significance of the information found in the various kinds of sources available. Europeans and Euro-Americans looking at native customs have frequently misunderstood what they beheld: coming as they did from alien backgrounds, they have often failed to perceive the broader cultural context for their observations.

Pueblo is a generic term for several groups of Indians living in permanent villages or towns in what is present-day New Mexico and Arizona. Among the best known are the Hopi, Zuni, Acoma, Laguna, and Tewa tribes. In the following selection, Ramón A. Gutiérrez offers a remarkable ethnohistorical glimpse of Pueblo Indians at the time of their contact with the Spanish. (Ethnohistory, a method of studying the past by combining a knowledge of anthropology and history, rests on the idea that an understanding of a group's culture allows us to appreciate the people's motivations and actions.) Gutierrez begins with a creation account and goes on to elaborate on the ideology of the Pueblos as revealed in their cosmology.

The author, a historian with a deep appreciation of the Pueblo worldview, discusses familial relationships, the tribe's harmony with the universe, individual obligations within community life, sexuality, hunting, and warfare. The composite picture that emerges gives readers an idea of how stable and sophisticated Pueblo life was and how the Pueblos managed to cope with the aggression of surrounding raider tribes, among them the Navajos and Apaches. Unfortunately, the Pueblos' delicately balanced universe could not withstand the encroachment of the Spanish conquistadors and priests, who were undeterred by the circles of sacred cornmeal that the Pueblo shamans drew around their towns to ward off invasion.

STUDY QUESTIONS

1. Does this account of Pueblo life differ from or conform with the notions you have of the daily lives of Native Americans? Explain in detail.

2. After reading about the Pueblos, what strikes you as the most significant aspect of their spiritual life?

3. What place did women occupy in Pueblo society?

In the beginning two females were born underneath the earth at a place called Shipapu. In total darkness Tsichtinako (Thought Woman) nursed the sisters, taught them language and gave them each a basket that their father Uchtsiti had sent them containing the seeds and fetishes of all the plants and animals that were to exist in the world. Tsichtinako told the sisters to plant the four pine tree seeds they had in their basket and then to use the trees to ascend to the light. One grew so tall that it pushed a hole through the earth. Before the sisters climbed up the tree from the underworld, Thought Woman taught them how to praise the Sun with prayer and song. Every morning as the Sun rose, they would thank him for bringing them to the light by offering with outstretched hands sacred cornmeal and pollen. To the tones of the creation song, they would blow the offering to the sky, asking for long life, happiness, and success in all their endeavors.

When the sisters reached the earth's surface it was soft, spongy, and not yet ripe. So they waited for the Sun to appear. When it rose, the six directions of the cosmos were revealed to them: the four cardinal points, the earth below, and the four skies above. The sisters prayed to the Sun, and as they did, Thought Woman named one of the girls Iatiku and made her Mother of the Corn clan; the other she named Nautsiti, Mother of the Sun clan.

"Why were we created?" they asked. Thought Woman answered, "Your father Uchtsiti made the world by throwing a clot of his blood into space, which by his power grew into the earth. He planted you within it so that you would bring to life all the things in your baskets in order that the world be complete for you to rule over it."

When the first day ended, the girls slept. They awoke before dawn to greet the Sun with a prayer on their lips and an offering of cornmeal and pollen. When Sun rose and gave them warmth, the sisters were very happy. Tsichtinako then took several seeds from their baskets and showed the sisters how to plant corn. With a dig stick she poked holes into Mother Earth and deposited seeds in her womb. The corn germinated and grew. When its ears were ripe and plump, Thought Woman showed them how to pick it, how to collect its pollen, and how to mill its kernels into the meal they would offer their father daily.

That night a flash of brilliant red light fell from the sky and when it touched the earth, it exploded into fire. "Your father Sun gives you fire to cook your food and to keep you warm," explained Thought Woman. "The fire's tongues will stay alive if fed branches from the pine tree that gave you passage from the underworld." From that day forward, Iatiku and Nautsiti had fire with which to cook corn. They flavored the corn with the salt they found in their baskets and ate to their hearts' content.

Next, Thought Woman taught the sisters how to give life to the animal fetishes in their baskets so that the animals would give them life in return. Mice, rats, moles, and prairie dogs were created and were given grasses on which to forage and multiply. The sisters cast pebbles in various directions and from these emerged mountains, plains, mesas, and canyons. From the seeds they next strewed about, pine, cedar, oak, and walnut trees grew and underneath them beans and squash sprouted and yielded their fruit. Rabbits, antelope, bison, and deer were dispatched to the open plains. To the mountains went the elk with their predators the lions, wolves, wildcats, and bears. Eagle, hawk, and turkey were cast into the sky, but turkey fell back to earth and never learned to fly. In the earth's waters fish, water snakes, and turtles were placed, and there they flourished and multiplied. Now Thought Woman told the sisters to kill an animal. "Roast meat and corn together and flavor it with salt," she instructed. "Before you eat, always pray and offer morsels of these to your father Uchtsiti who created the world and lives in the fourth sky above."

Tsichtinako cautioned Iatiku and Nautsiti to handle their baskets carefully. At first they did. But as they were giving life to the snakes one fetish fell out of a basket unnoticed and came to life of its own power as the serpent Pishuni. Pishuni bred selfishness and competitiveness between the sisters. Soon Nautsiti became sullen and refused to associate with Iatiku. When this occurred, Pishuni asked Nautsiti: "Why are you lonely and unhappy? If you want what will make you happy, I can tell you what to do. If you bore someone like yourself, you would no longer be lonely. Tsichtinako wants to hold back this happiness from you," he said. Nautsiti believed Pishuni and agreed to meet him near a rainbow. On a rock near the specified rainbow, Nautsiti lay on her back, and as she did drops of rain entered her body. From this rain she conceived and bore twin sons. Father Sun had strictly forbidden the sisters to bear children, and when he learned that Nautsiti had, he took Thought Woman away.

When Nautsiti's sons grew up, the sisters separated. Nautsiti departed East with her favorite child; Iatiku remained with Tiamuni, the son Nautsiti disliked. Iatiku and Tiamuni eventually married and had many daughters to whom they gave clan names representing all the things that their father had given them at emergence: Sky, Water, Fire, and Corn.

After Thought Woman departed, Iatiku took earth from her basket and made the season spirits: Shakako, the ferocious spirit of winter, Morityema, the surly spirit of spring, Maiyochina, the warm spirit of summer, and Shruisthia, the grumpy spirit of fall. Iatiku told the people that if they prayed properly to these spirits they would bring moisture, warmth, ripening, and frost, respectively.

Next Iatiku, their Corn Mother, took dirt from her basket and created the katsina, the Cloud-Spirits or ancestor dead who were to live beneath a lake in the West at Wenimats. Tsitsanits (Big Teeth) was brought to life first as ruler of the katsina; then many other katsina were brought to life. Some looked like birds with long beaks and bulging eyes, others had large animal snouts, and still others were moon creatures with horns sticking out of their heads like lunar crescents. "Your people and my people will be combined," Iatiku told the katsina. "You will give us food from your world and we will give you food from our world. Your people are to represent clouds; you are to bring rain." Iatiku then took cornmeal and opened a road four lengths long so that the katsina could travel to Wenimats and along which they would return when called.

"Now we are going to make houses," said Corn Mother. Suddenly a house made of dirt and trees grew out of the earth resembling in shape the mesa and mountain homes of the season deities. Each of Iatiku's daughters constructed a house for their children and when they were all ready, Iatiku laid them out into a town. "All is well but . . . we have no sacred place, we have no *kaach* [kiva]," Iatiku said. She taught the oldest man of the Oak clan how to build religious houses underneath the earth's surface to resemble Shipapu, the place of emergence.

The people did not have a father of the game animals, so Iatiku appointed a Shaiyaik (Hunt Chief), taught him the songs and prayers of the hunt, gave him an altar, and showed him how to make stone fetishes and prayer sticks to secure the power of the prey animals. Hunt Chief eventually became overburdened with work and so Corn Mother made Tsatia hochani (War Chief or Outside Chief) to rule over everything outside the pueblo. Iatiku gave him a broken prayer stick with four tails marked on four sides to extend from the earth to the sky. "When you hold [the prayer stick] clasped in your hands," Iatiku told Tsatia hochani, "you are drawing all the people together so they will not be scattered. With this you will have great power over all the rest of the people." Iatiku gave the War Chief twin sons, Masewi (Wren Youth) and Oyoyewi (Mocking Bird Youth), to assist him. The boys were the Twin War Gods, sons of Father Sun.

The people had never known sickness until the serpent Pishuni returned as a plague. The people tried to cure themselves, but could not. To break Pishuni's spell Iatiku created the *chaianyi*, the Medicine Man. The oldest man of the Oak clan was made Fire Medicine Man because fire was the strongest thing that Sun had given them and oak burned hottest. Corn Mother told Oak Man to go to North Mountain and there in a pine tree that had been struck by lightning he would find an obsidian arrowhead that would be his heart and his protection. She taught him how to make black prayer sticks as symbols of the night in which he would work, and then made him an altar. Iatiku taught the Medicine Man how to mix medicines and how to secure the power of bears to destroy disease-causing witches. "Now I will make you *honani* [corn fetish] so that you will remember me," Iatiku said to the chaianyi, "it will have my power." Into a corn cob she blew her breath along with a few drops of honey to symbolize all plant food.

The cob was wrapped in four husks and dressed with the tail feather of a roadrunner and of a magpie to make it useful in prayers, Iatiku also placed turquoise on the corn fetish so that it would always have the power to make one attractive and loved.

Everything was ready for a cure so Iatiku said to Fire Medicine Man, "Let us try it out." For four days the medicine man did not touch women, salt, or meat, and only sang and prayed. On the fourth night he performed a cure. The people quickly recovered. When Iatiku saw this, she also created the Flint, Spider, and Giant Medicine Societies.

Eventually it came to pass that the young people no longer respected Iatiku. So she returned to Shipapu. After she departed, Outside Chief led the people in search of their home at Haako (Acoma), "the place where the echo returned clearest." They settled at White House for a while but the katsina refused to visit because the young had insulted Iatiku. Rain clouds would not form and famine came. Flint Medicine Man and an ordinary man worked very hard, prayed, and fasted, and finally got the katsina to visit, bearing rain and gifts.

Iatiku's people were happy for a long time until sickness again befell them. The War Twins believed that this was a sign from Iatiku that they should move to Haako, and so they did, gathering everything in four days and traveling until they reached Washpashuka. They settled there until the people began to quarrel. When this occurred, Outside Chief told the people that it was time to move again. They walked south for many moons until they reached Tule Lake. The people settled at Tule Lake for a while too. But after they suffered a severe famine there, they decided to continue their search for Haako.

They traveled south until they reached Dyaptsiam, a place of many turkeys and antelope. There they built a town. The people lived very happily until Outside Chief reminded the Medicine Men and the War Twins that they still had not reached Haako. The chiefs searched in the south and came upon a large rock. Outside Chief yelled out, "Haako!" and listened. Four more times he yelled and each time the echo came back clearly. After four days of preparation the people moved to Haako and were happy knowing that their journey had ended.

PUEBLO IDEOLOGY

The origin myth of the Acoma Indians just presented likened human life to plant life. Seeds held the potential to generate life. When planted deep within Mother Earth and fertilized by the sky's vivifying rain, seeds germinated, grew into plants, and eventually bore seeds that repeated the cycle of life. Like a sprouting maize shoot rooted in the earth or a child coming forth from its mother's womb, so the Pueblo Indians described their emergence from the underworld.

All of the Pueblos have origin myths that dramatically depict the ideological structure of their world. Myths express the values and ideals that organize and make people's lives meaningful. They explain how the universe was created, its various components, and the tensions and balances that kept it intact. Whether through the deeds of gods, the feats of heroes, or the abominations of monsters, the Pueblo origin myths expressed life's generic prospects: birth, marriage, sex, quarreling, illness, migrations, and death. The Pueblo Indians conceived their history as instances of these generic forms. When pestilence struck, when famine engulfed the land, or when invading warriors demanded submission, it was through comparison with patterns in remote mythological events that the particular was understood.

The Western mind's linear concept of time imposes chronology on all events and struggles to comprehend the causes and consequences of moments that have irrevocably altered history. Such a concept of time was alien to the Pueblo Indians until quite recently. Time to them was not linear but cyclic; . . . the particular was simply comprehended through those experiences of mythic progenitors. . . . The structural principles of Pueblo culture were not a static set of symbolic oppositions but a dynamic process that unfolded and constantly created and recreated the basic cultural categories and relationships. . . .

PUEBLO RITES

From birth until death every phase of a Pueblo Indian's life was marked by rites of transition and incorporation. Before children of either sex could be considered adults they needed a host of essentials. Girls needed religious fetishes, esoteric knowledge in curing, pottery production, household construction, basket making, and a husband. Boys likewise needed sacred fetishes, knowledge in hunting, warfare, curing, rain-conjuring, and a wife. Boys and girls, however, were incapable of obtaining these goods for themselves. Seniors had to secure them for their children and did so by offering gifts to those seniors who could provide the required goods. . . .

Thus when girls and boys began life they were already indebted to their parents for the payment of gifts to the medicine man on their behalf. As a result of this debt and the many others they would incur to reach adulthood, juniors had to reciprocate with obedience and respect toward their parents. Concretely, respect meant that girls had to work for their mothers grinding corn, cooking, and tanning hides; boys had to tend to the corn crops, hunt, and weave cloth. Seniors, by appropriating the products of their children's labor, obtained gift stuff to offer seniors of other households so that their children could receive those blessings, knowledge, and gifts they needed to become adults.

Gift exchange in Pueblo society created dyadic status relationships between givers and receivers. A gift properly reciprocated with a countergift established the exchanging parties as equals, there being no further claim one could make of the other. If a gift giver initiated an exchange with a highly respected or knowledgeable person to obtain blessings, religious endowments, or ritual knowledge, such as when a parent offered a medicine man gifts so that he would present their child to the rising sun, the obligation created was fulfilled through a proper countergift. But if only one side gave and the other side could not reciprocate, the receiver out of gratitude had to give the presenter unending obedience and respect. . . .

The debts children incurred by obtaining unreciprocated gifts from or through their parents created bonds of obligation they had to fulfill. As the Acoma myth notes, before the Corn Mothers even knew that they needed baskets, seeds, and fetishes to create life, their father had already fulfilled his duty to provide them with these things. So with children, before they became conscious that they needed gifts, parents had already overfulfilled their duty to provide them. Children had never reciprocated these gifts and were thus indebted to their parents, owing them respect and labor. The fact that juniors did not own the products of their labor and possessed nothing the seniors needed meant that if juniors were to continue to accumulate the things that conferred adult status they had to do as seniors commanded. Children exhibited respect for their elders when they did as they were told. Seniors would only endow respectful juniors, and no elder would ever listen to or speak up for a disrespectful junior.

The Acoma origin myth also describes what could happen if the rules of reciprocity that governed gifting and structured generational obligation faltered. These themes surface in reference to the katsina, the beneficent rain spirits that represented the ancestral dead. In Pueblo thought, with increasing age one approached the godliness of katsina. The myth explains that the katsina first fought with the people, abandoned them, refused to shower them with rain and happiness, and ultimately severed the ties that bound them with the people because the young no longer respected the katsina and instead mimicked their gestures, burlesqued their dances, and refused to call them properly with gifts. Seniors scolded juniors for their disrespect, but the juniors continued to misbehave. When the katsina discovered this, they became very angry and refused to accept the peoples' prayer sticks. When the katsina finally visited they killed many people. . . . To teach the young the respect they had to show the katsina, that is, the reciprocity which regulated generational relations and labor exchange between juniors and seniors, every adolescent had to be initiated into the katsina cult and learn what death and destruction awaited those juniors who did not observe these rules.

Marriage, the mark of transition from junior to senior status, was similarly enmeshed in gift exchanges. Girls married when they were about seventeen years old, . . . boys when they were about nineteen. This occurred in the standard boy-meets-girl way. The young man would then inform his parents that he wanted to marry. If the parents and kin agreed to the match, the senior members of his household gathered the necessary marriage-validating gifts on the boy's behalf. The willingness of elders to gather these gifts testified that the boy had been respectful of his elders, had toiled for them tirelessly, and had been obedient. Had he not, they could withhold the gifts he needed to present to his prospective in-laws, reminding him of his past failures and of their anger at him. . . .

When the boy's elders had gathered their marriage-validating gifts, they took them to the girl's household. If the girl's kin agreed to the marriage and accepted the gifts, each person that accepted a gift had to give one in return. The gifts the bride's kin collected for her in-laws were usually taken to them on the fourth day after the initial gifts were received. Jane Collier characterizes this marital system as one of "equal bridewealth" because "equal" amounts of wealth are exchanged between the boy's and girl's households to validate the marriage. When these exchanges were complete a marital rite followed. . . .

Marriage was not conceptualized as a monogamous life-long tie. The Indians "make agreements among themselves and live together as long as they want to, and when the woman takes a notion, she looks for another husband and the man for another wife," asserted Joseph Brondate in 1601. Serial monogamy was the norm except among successful seniors who were always described as polygamous. Shortly we will see why.

Marriage and procreation marked one as an adult. Children triggered a new cycle of indebtedness. But if because of few or sickly children a couple was unable to produce those socially desired goods exchanged as gifts, then these unsuccessful seniors would have to indebt themselves to successful seniors in order to provide their own children with the prerequisites for adulthood. Unsuccessful seniors who obtained gifts they could not reciprocate for their child from successful seniors were indebted to them and could be expected to render labor, respect, and obedience. Heads of successful households, by having numerous juniors as well as unsuccessful seniors whose labor they could appropriate to accumulate gift-stuff, were thus in a position to support large extended households consisting of secondary wives, widows, orphans, and strays.

These "papas," as the sixteenth-century Spanish explorers called the heads of successful households, were often polygamous. "The men have as many wives as they can support," wrote Gaspar Pérez de Villagrá in 1610. "I saw Indians who had five or six wives," attested Marcelo de Espinosa. Brondate concurred and added that the marital system was sexually asymmetrical: men could have several wives but "women have only one husband." . . .

Pueblo seniors who became successful by virtue of their superlative skills and knowledge as hunters, warriors, rain-conjurers, or medicine men received many gifts from seniors who wanted their knowledge or their blessings for themselves or for their children. Successful seniors were the individuals best capable of community leadership because of the available wealth they stood prepared to offer the gods and unsuccessful seniors as gifts. This, then, was how gifting structured inequality both between juniors and seniors and between successful and unsuccessful households.

Relationships of superordination and subordination among the Puebloans were based on age and personal characteristics. Such societies are often called egalitarian because theoretically all men and women had equal access to those things a person of either sex needed in life, be it ritual blessings, esoteric knowledge, tools, land, or seeds. . . . Age grading was one source of inequality in the Pueblos, but as one advanced through life and married, became a parent, a household head, and finally an elder, one's power and prestige also grew. Senior men, successful or unsuccessful, controlled social well-being. Senior women likewise commanded great respect and authority through ownership of the household, of its sacred fetishes, and of its seeds, whatever the household's size or productivity. . . .

. . . When a chief died or became so senile that he was no longer able to accumulate the gift-stuff to stage ceremonials and to indebt others, his following dissolved. The chief's children might be advantaged in obtaining ritual knowledge, blessings, and gifts, but every person who aspired to leadership had to obtain his own ritual knowledge, his own bride, and his own following. Leadership was not hereditarily based in one household or matrilineage until the eighteenth century, thus minimizing inherited inequalities. Additionally, the Pueblos prized generosity and equated conspicuous wealth with witchcraft. Chiefs were above all successful seniors who generously gifted those who sought their help and selflessly provided all the goods necessary to stage religious ceremonials through which the gods' blessings were obtained.

The Pueblo Indians viewed the relations between the sexes as relatively balanced. Women and men each had their own forms of wealth and power, which created independent but mutually interdependent spheres of action. The corn fetish every child was given at birth and the flint arrowhead with which boys were endowed symbolized these relations and expressed the basic preoccupations of a people living in a semi-arid environment. Corn and flint were food and water, but they were also the cosmic principles of femininity and masculinity. Female and male combined as corn seeds and rain combined to perpetuate life. Corn plants without rain would shrivel and die; water without corn was no life at all. The ear of corn infants received represented the Corn Mothers that had given life to all humans, plants, and animals. At Acoma Pueblo this corn fetish is still called Iatiku, because it contains her heart and breath. For this reason too the Hopi called this corn fetish "mother." "Corn is my heart, it will be to [you] . . . as milk from my breasts," Zia's Corn Mother told her people. Individuals kept this corn fetish throughout their entire lives, for if crops failed its perfect seeds held the promise of a new crop cycle.

If the corn ear represented the feminine generative powers latent in seeds, the earth, and women, the flint arrowhead represented the masculine germinative forces of the sky. Father Sun gave men flint arrowheads to bring forth rain, to harness heat, and to use as a weapon in the hunt. The noise emitted by striking together two pieces of flint resembled the thunder and lightning that accompanied rain. Rain fertilized seeds as men fertilized their women. Without rain or semen life could not continue. The flint arrowhead was the sign of the hunter and warrior. Sun gave his sons, the Twin War Gods, arrowheads with which to give and take away life. From flint too came fire. When men struck flint and created that gift Sun gave them at the beginning of time, they transformed that which was raw into that which was cooked. To the Pueblo Indians flint, rain, semen, and hunting were to male as corn, earth, and childbearing were to female. . . .

The natal home was the primary unit of affiliation in Pueblo society. Everyone belonged to a home. Humans, animals, deities, and even the natural forces were believed to each have a home within which they lived. In the sixteenth century the Pueblos were matrilineal, anchoring maternity to matrilocal households. "The houses belong to the women, they being the ones who build them," observed Espinosa in 1601.

The household was preeminently a female domain of love and ritual. Women joined together to fashion houses out of the entrails of Mother Earth, setting her stones in charcoal ash and dirt mortar, assiduously building those multistoried edifices they still call home. Though houses were clustered together in hive-like compounds, each had its own entrance, a hearth for heat and cooking, sleeping rooms, and a room for the storage of seeds, sacred fetishes, and religious objects. The interior walls of a house were whitewashed and decorated with the clan's eponym. Reed mats for sleeping, pottery utensils for cooking and storage, and a mill stone for grinding corn were basic furnishings. When a household outgrew its space, usually when daughters married, adjacent rooms were added as vertical or horizontal extensions to the hearth.

Towns were an aggregation of households. Each town contained anywhere from 50 to 500 houses grouped around a central plaza in which several kivas stood. Houses rarely had ground floor entrances; they were usually entered by ascending moveable ladders that connected the various terrace levels of a housing compound. This was supremely a defensive architectural design. If enemies attacked, town residents climbed up to the highest terrace, removed the ladders to the lower ones, and from these heights, pelted outsiders with arrows and stones. From these heights, too, women protected their homes, rallying assistance with smoke signals or by "lifting their hands to their mouths and letting out a loud cry which could be heard far away."

The role men played in the construction of homes was rather limited. "The women mix the plaster and erect the walls; the men bring the [roof and support] timbers and set them in place," observed Pedro de Castañeda in 1540. Timber came from distant mountains outside of the town—the province of men and gods. Women owned the domestic hearth, exercised authority over those that lived within it, and at death passed on the edifice to their daughters. The female household head was custodian of its rights and possessions; the agricultural plots their husbands and sons worked, all food and seed reserves, and the sacred fetishes and ritual objects of the clan. The implication of these facts for domestic politics was clear to Fray Alonso de Benavides in 1634: "[The woman] always commands and is the mistress of the house, and not the husband."

The typical household unit consisted of a grandmother and her husband, her sisters and their husbands, her daughters and their husbands, various young children, and perhaps an orphan, slave, or stray. Women were attached to their natal dwelling throughout their lives, said Hernán Gallegos in 1582, and did "not leave except when permitted by their mothers." Men moved from house to house according to their stage of life. During childhood boys lived with their mothers, and at adolescence they moved into a kiva to learn male magical lore. When they had mastered these skills, and were deemed worthy of marriage by their kin, they took up residence in their wife's home. A man nonetheless remained tied to his maternal home throughout his life. For important ceremonial events, men returned to their maternal households. When this occurred the household became a matrilineage. Matrilineages that acknowledged descent from a common ancestor, usually through ownership of a similar animal or spirt fetish, formed larger, primarily religious aggregations known as clans.

When a child was born, the umbilical cord was buried—inside the household underneath the grinding stone if it belonged to a girl, outside in a cornfield if it belonged to a boy. This natal practice nicely delineated the sexual division of space and labor. The house and compound were female space invested with descendent earth-bound symbols. In the household women gave men their love and their bodies. They bore children, reared them, and engaged in that ritual activity that was at the core of kinship—feeding. Women fed their children, their mothers and grandmothers, their brothers and maternal uncles, and their husbands. Kinship was reckoned through genealogical principles—born of blood and substance. But just as importantly, kinship was created through feeding, what the Puebloans call "adoption." Any life or spirit form was transformed into kin through feeding. . . .

Large portions of a woman's day were spent preparing meals for her household. Corn, beans, and squash were the main staples of the diet. Corn was the most important and symbolic of these. It was boiled whole, toasted on the cob, or dried and ground into a fine powder easily cooked as bread or gruel. Every day a woman and her daughters knelt before metates, grinding corn to feed their gods, their fetishes, and their kin. The women worked joyful at this task, observed Castañeda in 1540. "One crushes the maize, the next grinds it, and the third grinds it finer. While they are grinding, a man sits at the door playing a flageolet, and the women move their stones, keeping time with the music, and all three sing together."

> Oh, for a heart as pure as pollen on corn blossoms,
> And for a life as sweet as honey gathered from the flowers,
> May I do good, as Corn has done good for my people
> Through all the days that were.
> Until my task is done and evening falls,
> Oh, Mighty Spirit, hear my grinding song.

Within the household an age hierarchy existed, for as Hernán Gallegos observed in 1582, "women, if they have daughters, make them do the grinding." The production of pottery (e.g., storage jars, cooking utensils, ritual medicine bowls), moccasins, ceremonial apparel, and turkey-down blankets was also women's household work. Men appropriated and circulated some of these goods throughout the Southwest. Pottery was widely coveted and brought a handsome barter in hides, feathers, and meat.

After feeding, the activity of greatest cultural import to Pueblo women was sexual intercourse. Women were empowered through their sexuality. Through sex women bore the children who would offer them labor and respect in old age. Through sex women incorporated husbands into their maternal households and expected labor and respect from them. Through sex women domesticated the wild malevolent spirits of nature and transformed them into beneficent household gods. Accordingly, then, sexuality was deemed essential for the peaceful continuation of life.

Female sexuality was theirs to give and withhold. In marriage a woman gave her husband her love and her body because of the labor he gave her mother, and because of all the marriage-validating gifts that had been given on her behalf to her in-laws. When women gave the gift of their body to men with whom no obligational ties existed, they expected something in return, such as blankets, meat, salt, and hides. For a man to enjoy a woman's body without giving her a gift in return was for him to become indebted to her in a bond of obligation.

Erotic behavior in its myriad forms (heterosexuality, homosexuality, bisexuality) knew no boundaries of sex or age. Many of the great gods—the Zuñi Awonawilona, the Navajo First Man/First Woman, the Hopi Kawasaitaka katsina—were bisexual, combining the potentialities of male and female into one—a combination equally revered among humans. If the Indians sang of sex, copulated openly, staged orgiastic rituals, and named landmarks "Clitoris Spring," "Girl's Breasts Point," "Buttocks-Vagina," and "Shove Penis," it was because the natural world around them was full of sexuality.

Sexuality was equated with fertility, regeneration, and the holy by the Pueblo Indians, a pattern Mircea Eliade has found to be common to many societies. Humanity was dependent on sexuality for its continuation. . . .

Modesty and shame were not sentiments the Pueblo Indians knew in relationship to their bodies. Before European contact they wore little clothing and were "entirely naked except for the covering of their privy parts."

Women wore what resembled "table napkins, with fringes and a tassel at each corner, tying them around the hips." Most men left their genitals totally exposed; some tied their penis "near the prepuce with a maguey fiber" to protect it from evil spirits.

Sexual intercourse was the symbol of cosmic harmony for the Pueblo Indians because it united in balance all the masculine forces of the sky with all the feminine forces of the earth. . . . Society was made whole through libidinous female sexuality. Through intercourse, outsiders (men from other towns or clans) became insiders (household and community members). . . .

Warfare was a male activity among the Pueblos that was outside and beyond the moral order of society. In the continuum of reciprocities that regulated a pueblo, the taking of human life through violence was at the negative end; gifting was at the positive end, signifying the avoidance of war. Through the gifting of food and the offering of hospitality in the form of intercourse women assured communal peace. Violence was domesticated and tamed through such female ritual. And through the issue of women's bodies—children—foreigners and natives became one and were incorporated into households.

These ideas were expressed poignantly during the scalp dance performed by Pueblo women when their men returned from war. Women would jubilantly greet returning war parties outside the pueblo, reported Fray Atanasio Domínguez in 1776, and together with their men would carry the scalps of the enemy dead, "singing on the way about the events of the battle . . . [with] howls, leaps, shouts, skirmishes, courses back and forth, salvos, and other demonstrations of rejoicing." When the scalps entered the pueblo, said Domínguez, "the women scornfully touch their private parts with the scalp." Another observer said that the women "bared their buttocks to it [the scalp]. They said it was their second and third husband and lay down on it as if having sexual intercourse. All of this was to take power away from the enemy." After the scalps had been robbed of their power in this way, they were attached to a large wooden pole and a dance was performed for them, which included much singing about the feats of battle and the prowess of Pueblo warriors.

The Pueblos believed that an enemy's head and scalp were invested with the person's spirit: if not properly adopted, they would wreak havoc. To forestall this possibility, after the scalps were robbed of their power through intercourse, they were entrusted to women who fed them cornmeal and thereby incorporated into a household. Beneficent fetishes now, the scalps were considered potent rain makers. "We are going to have a little rain," the Keres say, "the scalps are crying.". . .

The power women enjoyed by virtue of their control over the household, feeding, and sexuality was rivaled by the power men enjoyed as a result of their control over the community's relationships with its gods, which made hunting, warfare, rain making, and trade possible. . . .

"A man's place is outside of the house," Hopi women assert. As we saw, out in the fields they would bury a baby boy's umbilical cord, signifying that that was the place for males. But this was the female's point of view. Men had a much more expansive notion of their space, which encompassed everything that was at the core and center of society, as well as everything that was outside and beyond it.

Men's spatial location in village life correlated closely with their roles in the sexual division of labor. Three distinct but overlapping spaces were defined as masculine. The first zone was created through kinship and marriage obligations to women. Sons had to work their mothers' corn plots, brothers those of their sisters, husbands those of their mothers-in-law. "The men attend to the work in the cornfields," observed Gallegos in 1582. "The day hardly breaks before they go about with hoes in their hands." He continued: "The men bear burdens, but not the women." When wood was needed for the construction of a house or to stoke the cooking fires, the household's matriarch dispatched the men to "bring the firewood . . . and stack it up," noted Castañeda in 1540.

The space outside and beyond the pueblo was authentically the province of men and gained meaning in opposition to the space men controlled at the symbolic center of the town. The male conceptualization of space outlined here comes from Pueblo origin myths. . . . By outlining the organization of society in mythic times, detailing who helped whom emerge when and where, men asserted their spatial claims, their rights, and their precedence in their relationships both with women and with the members of other households and clans.

The men of every pueblo considered their town to be the center of the universe and placed their main kiva at the vortex of a spatial scheme that extended outward to the four cardinal points, upward to the four skies above, and downward to the underworld. Kivas were usually round (sometimes square) subterranean structures that conjoined space and time to reproduce the sacred time of emergence. Located at the center of the kiva's floor was the *shipapu*, the earth's naval, through which the people emerged from the underworld and through which they would return.

The kiva was circular to resemble the sky. A hole in the center of the roof, the only entrance and source of light, symbolized the opening through which the Corn Mothers climbed onto the earth's surface. The profane space outside and the sacred space within the kiva were connected by a ladder called "rainbow" made of the same pine tree the sisters had used to emerge. The kiva floor had a fire altar that commemorated the gift of fire, and a hollow, dug-out place that represented the door to the house of the Sun, the Moon, and the mountains of the four cardinal points. The walls had altars on which were placed stone fetishes representing all the animals and deities of the world. Around the entire base of the kiva was an elevated ledge covered with bear and lion skins known as "fog seats." When the spirits that lived outside the pueblo were invoked and came to participate in ceremonials, they sat on these. Men's claims to precedence over women lay precisely in this capacity to bring what was outside the village into its core during religious rituals, to communicate with the gods, and thereby to order and control an otherwise chaotic and hostile natural world.

Radiating outward horizontally from the kiva toward the four cardinal points were a series of tetrads that demarcated the sacral topography. The outermost tetrad was formed by the horizontal mountain peaks in which the seasonal spirits lived. In between the horizon and the pueblo were the shrines of the outlying hills and mesas. Shrines were "heaps of small stones which nature [had] formed," reported Hernán Gallegos in 1582, or holes in the earth's surface that resembled navels. People "worshiped and offered sacrifices" at these places, said Diego Pérez de Luxán, when they were "weary from their journey or troubled with any other burdens." Within the town the tetrad was repeated as directional points that all ceremonial dance circuits touched. At the center of the pueblo, the kiva united the cosmic six directions. Men owned the kivas and the sacred fetishes, altars, masks, and ritual paraphernalia contained therein.

The kiva, as the naval that tied the people with their gods, was the physical symbol of political society. Each pueblo was a theocracy. At the center of political life stood the cacique, the town chief or Inside Chief, who exercised broad authority over all matters. Around him stood men of superlative knowledge in hunting, warfare, medicine magic, and rain-conjuring who by virtue of their abilities had accumulated large followings as well as large amounts of gift-stuff with which they could stage communal rites and offer gifts to others on behalf of unsuccessful villagers. Next were the unsuccessful seniors, their veneration increasing with age. Young male aspirants to the religious knowledge that would translate into political power came next. And finally, at the margins, as men saw it, were women, children, slaves, and strays. . . .

Presiding over the town's main kiva, the quasi-divine Inside Chief was simultaneously a lawgiver and a peacemaker, a war lord and a high priest. He symbolized cosmic harmony and the embodiment of those forces of attraction that constituted society. He conjoined the human and the divine, the cosmological and the political, the mythic and the historic, and organized those three functions on which Pueblo religio-political life depended: administration of the sacred, exercise of physical force, and control over well-being and fecundity.

The Inside Chief controlled the sacred in Pueblo society. He was the town's chief priest, a direct descendant of the Sun, "the holder of all roads of men," and the person who brought order to an otherwise chaotic cosmos. . . .

The religious system the Inside Chief administered was fundamentally monistic. Humans, animals, natural forces, and supernatural spirits were all intricately related in balanced ties of reciprocity. The cosmic harmony every person desired was subject to human mechanistic control. So long as people performed religious rites joyfully and precisely, careful that every prayer was word-perfect and full of verve, and that the ritual paraphernalia was exact to the last detail, the forces of nature would reciprocate with their own uninterrupted flow. The sun would rise and set properly, the seasons of the year would come and go, bringing rainfall and verdant crops in summer, and in the winter, game and snow.

The cacique's central imperative was to keep the cosmos properly balanced so that humanity did not swerve from life's road. So long as the forces of evil that threatened to disrupt society were rendered impotent through ritual, peace and prosperity reigned. The Inside Chief accomplished this by calling together the men in the town's households and clans for ritual purposes and by acting as arbiter of law and order. As high priest, the cacique was the keeper of sacred time. From the heights of the town's dwellings he watched the course of the sun and moon and with amazing accuracy announced the summer and winter solstices, the vernal and autumnal equinoxes, and all the dates for planting, harvest, initiations, and rain and curing rites. At appropriate points in the lunar year, the cacique entered the town's main kiva, and by ritually recreating the primordial time of emergence when humans and gods were one, and when all a town's clans, kivas, and esoteric societies were in harmony, he temporarily obliterated local enmities and tensions.

Through these ceremonials (which women could watch but not participate in) the Inside Chief integrated the town into one communal whole. The fragmenting pull of clan, lineage, and household affiliations was suspended as each clan, village-wide kiva, and esoteric society (for example, hunt, war, rain, and medicine societies) contributed its special role to a ceremony or performed a certain dance in a dance complex. . . .

The cacique's frequent promotion of communal peace through ritual was necessary because fragmentation constantly threatened to tear society asunder. . . . Factionalism was the normal state of affairs, and ceremonial harmony was the ideal men tried to create. Each pueblo was an aggregation of matrilineages, each with its own rituals, fetishes, and patron deities. Marital exogamy and cross-cutting lineage affiliations in kiva and esoteric societies fostered village integration. But in times of stress, whether caused by political, social, or environmental factors, communities splintered along lineage and household lines, leading to those town abandonments and population dispersals which were so rife in the Pueblo world between 1250 and 1600.

If the Inside Chief's administration of the sacred was a harmonizing power, the antithesis—violence, human domination, and the negation of the community's moral order, what we will call physical force—was in the hands of the Outside Chiefs, war chiefs who protected the village from external, natural, and supernatural enemies.

Protecting the village from enemies was perhaps the Outside Chiefs' most important duty. A decade rarely went by without war over women, land, water, salt, turquoise, or hunting grounds. A village with an abundant supply of any of these resources was always at risk of losing them. The threat was met in part by constructing impenetrable fortress-like towns. From the heights of the towns the war chiefs could easily spot intruders and marshal their defenses. The war chiefs also participated in hunts, salt expeditions, wood-gathering trips, and visits to sacred springs for waters. When a foreign bride entered a pueblo, it was the war chiefs who escorted her. . . .

How was the Outside Chiefs' violence domesticated for community life? The problem is an important one because the war chiefs lived among their people and performed vital functions within their towns. . . . As we saw, during the scalp dance females transformed the malevolent spirits of the enemy dead into beneficent community members through intercourse and feeding.

Warfare was the most generalized masculine task in Pueblo society. Before boys could become men, they had to establish themselves as competent warriors. To do this, young men sought out a "warrior father" (usually the war chief or Outside Chief) of great bravery and skill to teach them the prayers, songs, dances, and esoteric lore that would give them power over enemies. Through offering the warrior father numerous gifts, aspiring warriors were gradually taught how to harness the power of the prey animals for success in battle. . . .

Besides the town's main kiva, male ritual associations devoted to war, curing, hunting, and rain-making each had its own kiva that doubled as a lodge house. Warrior novices lived in the warrior society kiva and there their warrior father taught them bravery, endurance, and agility. Before the arrival of European horses in the Southwest, all warfare was conducted on foot, so running fast was also a cultivated skill.

When men practiced war magic they had to have pure minds and hearts. For the four days before and after war, they refrained from sexual intercourse and purified themselves with sweat baths and emetic drinks. Offering smokes to the war gods and singing war songs, they prayed for success. To obtain the ferocity and strength of bears, the cunning of lions, and the sharp vision of eagles, the warriors took their war fetishes shaped in the likeness of animals, bathed them in human blood and fed them pieces of human hearts that had been torn from the breasts of enemies in previous victories. When all the ritual preparations for warfare were complete, the warriors marched into battle.

Once a young man had proven himself by killing an enemy he was inducted into the warrior society through an ordeal. The Zuñi Bow War Society required its initiates to sit naked atop a large ant hill for a day and submit stolidly to the insects' bites. Members of the Hopi, Zuñi, and Tewa Cactus War societies whipped themselves with cacti. Such a benumbing ordeal also marked the installation of a war chief.

The opposing forces harmonized by the town chieftaincy—Inside Chief versus Outside Chiefs, center versus margin, old versus young, native versus foreign, law versus force—were dependent on the existence of fecundity and well-being. This third essential component of religious life was controlled competitively by three chieftaincies: the rain chiefs, the hunt chiefs, and the medicine men.

The chiefs who directed the hunt, rain, and medicine societies knew well the godly transmitted mysteries of life and death. Women might know the life-giving secrets of Mother Earth, seeds, and child-bearing, but through ritual men controlled the key to the positive and negative reciprocities in their world, which at any moment could be turned to life or death. The heart (which contained the breath and spirit of humans, animals, and deities) and blood were the symbols of the rituals staged by men to assure communal peace and fertility. Just as feeding was a central part of female ritual, so too men regularly gave life to their fetishes, bathing them in nourishing blood and symbolically feeding them bits of heart. Men also fed the earth with their own blood, whipping themselves crimson when they sought those blessings that assured fertility.

Rain was the Pueblo Indians' central preoccupation and the essential ingredient for fecundity. Men recognized that Mother Earth and women had immense capacities to bring forth life, but to realize this potential the sky had to fructify the earth with rain and men their wives with semen. Thus what the people worshipped most, said Hernando de Alarcón in 1540, was "the sun and water." Why did they worship water? According to Coronado it was "because it makes the maize grow and sustains their life, and that the only other reason they know is that their ancestors did so."

The rain chief was one of the most powerful men in every village because he knew how to conjure rain both by calling Horned Water Snake and the katsina. The Pueblo equated serpentine deities with rain. The Horned Water Serpent of the Pueblos united the vertical levels of the cosmos. He lived both upon the earth and below it and so combined the masculine germinative forces of the sky (rain) with the feminine generative power of the earth (seeds). The phallic representations of Horned Water Snake were cloaked in feathers as a god of lightning and rain. The earliest Pueblo rock drawings depict him as a zigzag line with a horned triangular head and as a lightning snake attached to a cloud burst.

Horned Water Serpent was also feminine and lunar. "Sun is male, Moon is female," maintain the Acoma Indians. The serpent's ability to shed its skin and to be born anew undoubtedly resembled the moon's birth and death every 28 days. In decorative motifs the measured zigzags of the lightning snake and the coiled spiral of the rattlesnake evoked those rhythms governed by the moon: the rains, the agricultural calendar, and a woman's menstrual flow. Water Serpent's horns, too, were lunar. Each horn represented the moon's crescent; with two, the lunar cycle was complete.

Horned Water Serpent, then, provided the Pueblo Indians with fecundity and abundance by joining together the levels of the cosmos (sky/earth, earth/underworld) and social existence (male/female, life/death). . . .

After warfare, hunting was the broadest male task in Pueblo society. Thus, after katsina initiation young men entered a hunt society. Men contributed meat to the maize diet at every pueblo, but it was at those villages dependent exclusively on rainfall for crop irrigation that hunting magic was most important. Boys learned hunting techniques by observing renowned hunters and by listening to their animal stories. When a boy killed his first rabbit, he was initiated into a hunt society and apprenticed to a hunt father who gradually taught him the prayers, songs, and magical ways of the hunt in return for gifts of corn and meat. The novice became a full member of the society when he captured a large game animal (deer, antelope, or mountain sheep). If by chance he killed a prey animal (bear, lion, or eagle), he automatically became a member of the warrior society, because hunting and warfare were considered very similar activities. . . .

A pueblo's prosperity was fundamentally dependent on the physical and psychological well-being of its members. Thus every village had several *chaianyi*, medicine men who cured illnesses and exorcised disease-causing witches who robbed human hearts of their breath and spirit. As knowledgeable herbalists, the *chaianyi* cured minor ailments; but if a disease seemed unique, longlasting, or particularly debilitating, witchcraft was its cause. Witches wrought calamities and illnesses by shooting objects into the body of their victim or by stealing their heart. Using tactics similar to those of hunters, witches sapped people of their strength by attacking their heart. Since witches plied their craft disguised as animals, medicine men had to fight them as animals. That is why *chaianyi* were known as bears (the fiercest animal humans knew) and their magic as "bear medicine." In such form medicine men could help people regain their health, winning back their heart and sucking out the objects shot into them by the witch.

When an individual or a community was afflicted by disease, a cure by the medicine man known to have power over that illness was requested through gifts. For four days the medicine man prepared himself, smoking, making prayer-sticks, reciting the necessary prayers and songs, and abstaining from meat, salt, and sex. He made offerings at appropriate shrines, obtained water for medicines from sacred springs, erected an altar, and arranged on it fetishes, medicine bowls, and curing paraphernalia. When all was ready, the sick individual was placed on the floor before the altar. Near the patient, the medicine man made a circular sand painting representing all the powerful forces in the cosmos. Then, to obtain the power to cure from the "real" medicine men, the animals, he prayed to the bear fetish for the power of all the animals on earth, to the eagle fetish for the power of the animals in the air, and to the weasel fetish for the power of the animals in the ground. Each of these fetishes was fed and bathed in blood from the heart of the animal they represented. Wearing a bear claw necklace with four claws, and holding eagle plumes in each hand, the medicine man "whipped away" the disease with cutting motions. If a quartz crystal with which the person's body was examined revealed foreign objects, the medicine man sucked them out. If the patient's heart had been stolen, the *chaianyi* fought with the witches to retrieve it. When the ceremony ended, the patient drank medicines and returned home cured. If for some reason the patient died, the presumption was that the ceremony had not been properly conducted or that the *chaianyi*'s heart was impure.

In sum, entering male ceremonialism from the edges and moving toward the center, we first find the chiefs who controlled well-being and fertility (rain, hunt, and medicine chiefs), then the Outside Chiefs who organized physical force, and finally at the core the Inside Chief who represented the sacred powers of attraction that constituted political society. Through apprenticeship in a town's various societies, junior men gradually learned the religious knowledge they needed to assure prosperity and guarantee their personal advance to senior status. Religious knowledge allowed men to harness and control those natural forces outside the pueblo, which the gods ruled, and to bring them peacefully into the core; it gave them the power to kill, and by so doing assured life. By carefully executing prescribed ritual formulas, they preserved the relationship of reciprocity that existed between men and the spirit world and kept the fragile structure of the cosmos intact.

Men envisioned a cosmos in which masculinity and femininity were relatively balanced. But the social world really was not so. In a largely horticultural society women asserted and could prove that they had enormous control and power over seed production, child-rearing, household construction, and the earth's fertility. Men admitted this. But they made a counterclaim that men's ability to communicate with the gods and to control life and death protected the precarious balance in the universe by forestalling village factionalism and dissent. The tendency of women to overproduce had to be properly controlled through the religious activities of men. Women's voraciousness for semen and the earth's infinite capacity to soak up rain sapped masculinity of its potence. This was indeed the case, explains Jane Collier, regarding gender concepts in "equal bridewealth" societies. On a daily basis women appropriated men's vital energies: the crops they planted, the children they engendered, and the meat from their hunts. Men thus frequently renewed their energies by segregating themselves from women and staging ceremonials to assure successful hunts, war, curing, and rain-making. Because potent femininity polluted and rendered male magic impotent, men abstained from sex with women for a prescribed period before and after their rituals. It is easy to understand the roots of these gender concepts in the social division of labor. The ecological constraints of the habitat in which men pursued their productive activities made their world precarious. Who could predict defeat in battle, disease, factionalism, drought, or poor hunting? . . .

Pre-menopausal women polluted male ritual and were thus excluded from active participation in all kiva-centered ceremonials. According to Gallegos, when men gathered to renew the universe or to recreate primordial time "only the men take part, the women never." The participants in these rituals "wore the masks and dress of both men and women even though they were all men," attested Don Esteban Clemente in 1660, even to the point of smearing the insides of their legs with rabbit blood to resemble menstrual discharge. . . .

These, then, were the contours of Pueblo Indian society in the sixteenth century. Each pueblo was an aggregation of sedentary horticulturists living in extended matrilineal households, supplementing their existence through hunting and warfare. Elders controlled the organization of production and, through the distribution of its fruits as gifts and ritual blessings, perpetuated the main inequalities of life; the inequality between juniors and seniors and between successful and unsuccessful seniors. The household and all the activities symbolically related to it belonged to women; the kivas and the pueblo's relationships with its gods was the province of men.

Flathead Life
Before the Horse

JOHN FAHEY

The Flathead tribe of western Montana did not encounter white people until more than two centuries after the Spanish had penetrated Pueblo territory far to the south. Writing twenty years before Ramón A. Gutierrez, John Fahey was clearly less comfortable about exploring the psyche of a culture not his own. Moreover, he was handicapped by an almost complete lack of Indian sources—a problem made all the more difficult in the light of the Flatheads' tendency to adapt their accounts to white people's perceptions rather than to rely on their own memories. Fahey therefore had to deduce his observations from a "mirror history" based on Euro-American documents that reflected outsiders' notions about the Flathead tribespeople.

Using language and analysis less Freudian than Gutierrez's, Fahey nonetheless sketches an arresting picture of the Flatheads. Classified anthropologically as Plateau Indians, the Flatheads were Salish-speaking buffalo hunters. Today they belong to the Confederated Salish and Kutenai tribes, along with the Kutenai and Pend Oreille Indians. Fahey believes that their culture is that of a society in transition—one susceptible to the blandishments of Euro-American civilization.

Among the salient points raised in this selection is the way in which the Flatheads are almost indistinguishable from other related groups. Indians and non-Indians alike have a tendency to assume that discrete twentieth-century tribal configurations have always existed that way. However, as Fahey shows, there is a widespread borrowing of traditions, social mores, and living spaces, as well as the formation of political affiliations. The reading ends by describing the astonishing changes that occurred as a result of the Flatheads' acquisition of the horse.

STUDY QUESTIONS

1. Compare the Flatheads' traditional account of their origins with the story that they told white people.

2. How did Flathead healers deal with health and sickness?

3. What was the impact of guns and horses on Flathead life?

In the beginning the Sun created the heavens and the earth. And the earth was void and empty. And the Sun created every living and moving creature. And he gave them power according to their kind, commanding: Increase and multiply, fill the waters, and the earth, and the air. But the Sun perceived that many creatures were evil. And he created Coyote, saying to him: Behold, the earth is a dwelling place for monsters. And he sent Coyote to change earth into a place of cool mountains, forests with game, and streams with fish. And Coyote caught the wild gale and tamed it, and he cooled the hot and warmed the cold winds. And as he traveled over the earth, his wives bore him children who begat Indian tribes.

As time passed, Coyote roamed the land. Where he found wayward Indians, he transformed them into animal, wood, or stone. Their shapes remain in trees and rocks. Monsters he turned into mountains and valleys. The Coriacan Defile (O'Keefe Canyon) north of Missoula, Montana, was a monster that swallowed unsuspecting travelers until Coyote killed it. Although he played many tricks, Coyote also gave the Indians useful gifts such as fire and taught them to make weapons and utensils. Many times Coyote died at the hands of enemies, but Fox revived him by jumping over him.

The Flathead Indians of Montana descended from Coyote. Although common in the folktales of many peoples, Coyote remained the Flatheads' particular friend; he howled to warn of enemies nearby; he yipped three times to signal approaching strangers. By origin, the Flatheads are *skéligu*,

From *The Flathead Indians* by John Fahey, pp. 3–17. Copyright © 1974 by the University of Oklahoma Press.

their own word for angels and Indians that is loosely translated as "human beings."

Coyote is central in the mythical heritage of the Flatheads, a tradition passed from old to young around winter campfires where venerable men told stories. The old women talked among themselves and recited tales for young children. Formal storytelling was taboo in summer. Generally members of the tribe agreed on an approved version of the stories known best. A number of the Flatheads' tales occur in a time before *skéligu;* they portray animals acting with human motives, talking, sometimes wearing clothing, and possessing magical powers. When Coyote stories were intended to be comic, the narrator might use a high-pitched tone, while his listeners laughed uproariously. When the speaker was serious and faithful to an accepted version, listeners interjected approving remarks.

Traditional tales, often spun in contests to determine the best storytellers, suited the Flatheads to explain natural phenomena and to illustrate moral principles for children. All but the youngest knew the fabulous elements were only good stories. The narratives served well enough to explain his world to the Flathead, to amuse him, and to illumine his relationship to unseen forces—the spirit world around him.

As depicted in tales, and as the Flatheads knew from experience, animals exercised supernatural powers. Disturbed robins could cause rainfall; ants could stop it; eggs found by chance were an omen of rain. Certain spirits—those of eagle, grizzly, and elk—were most powerful. Animal relics representing these powers served the Flatheads as talismans to influence forces that decided human fates.

Certain trees and rocks, as well as animals, possessed strong powers. On the plain of the Bitterroot River stood a pine more than three hundred years old with a ram's horn imbedded in it seven feet from the ground. Wishes spoken to this tree were fulfilled, and the Flathead who hung a wisp of his hair on it was assured long life. An isolated tree, or one deformed by wind or lightning, also frequently possessed powers that the Indians discovered by experience.

Thus the Flatheads' affinity for the land and its creatures was spiritual. Indians did not conquer earth or bring it under their sway; they regarded earth as a mother, nurturing and sustaining them. The Flatheads thought of their homeland as a broad area they could never use for farming. In early times they did not think of farming the land at all. The unfortunate estimate that each Indian required eighty square miles of wild country to sustain his natural mode of living eventually convinced white men of the impracticality of the Indians' concept of land.

As earth was eternal, time was the present. Until the advent of white men among them, the Flatheads recognized no historical continuity, although they kept short chronological records by memory, tying knots in cords, or notching sticks to mark events and passage of time. The Flathead past, except as expressed in their folk tales, ended with the recollections of the oldest men and women. Virtually all stories about the past concerned events the teller saw himself or heard from a participant. . . .

When the white man demanded to know the history of the Flatheads, however, the Indians obliged him. In the earliest times they could recall, the Flatheads migrated from an older home to the Bitterroot Valley of western Montana, finding it already occupied by fabulous bands of giants, dwarves, and a small tribe of dirty, stupid Indians regarded as the Foolish people—very useful for moralistic stories.

An outline of the Flatheads' real past may emerge some day from archeological research and further studies of Salish dialects. Salish is the Indian language family that the Flatheads share with such peoples of the interior Pacific Northwest as Shuswaps, Thompsons, Wenatchis, Columbias, Okanogans, Sanpoils, Nespelims, Colvilles, Lakes, Lower Pend Oreilles (Kalispels), Upper Pend Oreilles, Spokanes, and Coeur d'Alenes, and with more than twenty tribes on the coasts of Washington and British Columbia. Salish is also the name by which the Flatheads prefer to be known. It means simply, "The people who speak Salish."

Despite the presence of the Foolish people, who disappeared in a way unknown, the Flatheads settled in the enveloping Bitterroot where high mountains and narrow passes partially protected them from pestilence carried up the Missouri and Columbia rivers and from Blackfoot raiders skulking from the buffalo plains of the Upper Missouri and the Saskatchewan. How long ago this may have been, none of the Flatheads seemed to know. . . .

Linguistic evidence indicates the various Salish speakers lived together in the interior of British Columbia several thousand years ago before separating into bands that preserved the language and some of the folk tales. Some bands remained inland; others migrated to the ocean shores. Probably their separation was friendly, for interior bartered with coastal Salish for slaves, seashell ornaments, small utensils such as bone needles, and other goods, trading a few of these in turn to other peoples east of them. Approximately four thousand years before Christ, by European reckoning, the Pacific Northwest interior turned drier, requiring its inhabitants to borrow tools and methods of the desert people to their south, probably by progressive trading along the western slopes of the continental divide, a route that grew in importance as sections of the interior plateau turned to desert and as, centuries later, horses became the prime item of barter.

By two thousands years before Christ, Athabascan-speaking peoples north of the Salish began to edge southward in migrations of varying intensity. Some Athabascans stalled after penetrating Salish areas, but others continued to move, generation after generation, for perhaps six hundred years. Under the pressure of this migration, a number of Salish were jostled from position.

Some Salish consequently drifted through the Okanogan Valley onto the Columbia Plateau, but possibly others, including the Flatheads, crossed the Rockies eastward before turning south. Confined by unfamiliar plains to a narrow corridor of mountain parklands and river systems, these Salish withstood the rip current of Athabascan migration flowing into the American southwest about 1000 A.D., but felt its vigor, traded with its people, and bobbed in its periphery until they encountered Sahaptin speakers who slowed the Flatheads' drift southward and bent their course into the Bozeman River valley. Perhaps the Flatheads stayed close to their mountain valleys, venturing onto the plains in comparatively recent times.

The Flatheads adopted social forms as well as manufacturing techniques and weapons from peoples they encountered in these early times. Other borrowings seem relatively recent. A pure Flathead tradition, if one existed, was progressively diluted by cultural borrowings, intermarriages, and adoptions, so that the Flatheads as a society combined features of the original Plateau and adopted Plains cultures. So lively was the cultural infusion, in fact, that older Blackfeet consider the Flatheads a Plains people.

Due to movement and adaptation, the Flatheads underwent continual change in habitat and social organization in the half millennium preceding European settlement in their homelands. In that five hundred years, change accelerated for the Flatheads, first with their own migration, then with acquisition of horses, and finally at its most rapid pace when they encountered white civilization. Modifications that once took centuries soon occurred in one generation. Aware of the process, and of the peril of extinction if they did not adapt, the Flatheads accommodated or fled each new circumstance thrust on them. . . .

By perhaps 1700 A.D. the Flatheads' gateway position between the Plains tribes and those of the plateau enhanced use of Salish as a common tongue. The first literate white men among the Flatheads observed that with Salish alone "one can converse from the United States to the Willamette . . . without the necessity of an interpreter. . . . [Also] he will find many among the Blackfeet, the Crows, and the Crees who speak the Flathead language.". . .

Utilization of the Flathead dialect as a universal tongue indicates widespread trading and also suggests considerable shifting of position among Salish-speaking bands over an area which, from archeological evidence, stretched from Canyon Ferry, twenty-five miles east of modern Helena, westward to the present Grand Coulee Reservoir in north central Washington, and from The Dalles on the south to the Fraser on the north, during the several hundred years immediately before white men reached western Montana. The pattern of Indian settlement in this region lay in river valleys where bands located as string communities along waterways.

The movement of Salish and neighboring peoples reflects not only pressures of migration but their roving searches for food and raw materials. Despite abundant game, there was not enough in one area to feed the Flathead population. They moved to find more. Indians of the intermontane region relied on Mother Earth to replenish roots and berries which they gathered seasonally, but, wherever game existed in small quantities, the Flatheads soon depleted the supply. No faunal balance between supply and demand allowed the Flatheads to remain in one place; they sought meat beyond their immediate residence as long as they depended on wild foods.

For these reasons the Flatheads established an annual cycle of gathering and hunting that followed the seasons. From the time of their arrival in modern western Montana until approximately 1840, the Flatheads hunted buffalo west of the Rocky Mountains. . . . While hunting methods were primitive, the western bison survived, but as the Indians' destructive capability grew with acquisition of horses and guns, buffalo rapidly disappeared. Until these western bison were virtually exterminated, the Flatheads ventured onto the plains to hunt mainly in spring. . . .

Before they had horses and guns, the Flatheads hunted by surrounding a few buffalo or stampeding animals over cliffs to be dashed to death. A man with powerful spiritual assistance lured buffalo to places where they could be killed. Occasionally in winter a lone buffalo could be driven into a snowdrift and, mired, dispatched with spears and arrows. The Flatheads on occasion used cliffs ("buffalo kills") near Thompson Falls and the present Martinsdale forest ranger station. Near such sites, discarded arrow and lance heads, shards, and other debris indicate considerable economic activity. The time spent to skin and butcher animals and to conduct thanksgiving rites made buffalo kills important locations for intertribal trading.

Despite dwindling herds west of the Rockies, the Flatheads considered the buffalo inexhaustible; when the herds eventually thinned, they regarded the cause as supernatural and complained that "buffalo are not close or plenty as they were before the white man came among us."

With buffalo products among their trade goods, the Flatheads bartered manufactured items and seasonal surpluses. This trading differed from the exchange of reciprocal gifts, which was customarily limited to friends and relatives. The trade covered a broad area. Incised dentalium and abalone earrings from southern Oregon (and perhaps from California, brought north to coastal tribes by Spanish seamen) reached northward to the Fraser and eastward to Plains tribes. Watertight bags and baskets made by the Nez Percés, flat wallets, bows, and similar goods passed through Salish hands to the plains in return for pipestone, manufactured pipes, and molded Blackfoot pottery.

Goods occasionally moved surprising distances. For example, in 1789 a Siouan battle-ax reached Indians of the lower Columbia. Flatheads also traded for obsidian points (arrow heads) with the Shoshonis and Thompsons, who used them in burial ceremonies. From the Thompsons, the Flatheads received dressed moose skins, painted hide bags, and fish products.

By the eighteenth century blue glass beads appeared among the Shoshonis and Klamaths, who passed them to Flatheads. Soon afterward a trickle of iron knives, white trade beads, and assorted European items reached western Montana from the east. (Common butcher knives came without handles because the Indians preferred to fashion their own from bone or wood.) Only horses and guns at first were commodities the Flatheads did not possess in some form. . . . Trading occurred at established meeting places or where Indians gathered to dig, fish, or hunt. Although much of the Flatheads' trading stock came from buffalo, among Spokanes and Coeur d'Alenes whitened deerskin clothing made by Flatheads was popular.

Despite intertribal warfare, periods of peace allowed hunting and trading with enemies. Blackfeet and Flatheads, characterized as unrelenting foes, concluded truces for barter. . . . As the easternmost of the Plateau tribes, the Flatheads bore the first fury of Blackfoot retaliation for offenses, . . . while the Flathead land served as the collecting place for western tribes bound for buffalo plains.

Not all Flatheads hunted buffalo. Customarily the youngest children, some women, and the elderly remained in camp in the Bitterroot Valley while the hunters and able members of families went to the buffalo grounds, and certain small bands are said to have eschewed the bison hunt. Hunter or not, the Flathead economy included useful tasks for each person, according to age and sex, from making and repairing equipment to teaching skills and tradition, this last the contribution of the aged. The instruction by the elders in food gathering, weaponry, and ritual was a foundation of Flathead survival in a world where the wisdom of an experienced warrior or fetish of a shaman might prove the tribe's most important resource.

The mode of life that the Flatheads evolved in the Bitterroot Valley was the last phase in their swiftly changing aboriginal culture. Their tribal ceremonies relating to conflict and food were simple, consisting mainly of dances and prayers to sun and earth for success and abundance. Flatheads occasionally offered bits of their flesh to the sun. A culture of longer duration would have developed more complex rites and, perhaps, select orders for its men. But men and women participated together in rites. . . .

Despite their brief tenure in the Bitterroot Valley, the Flatheads appeared to dominate their intermontane territory when white men arrived. The geographer-explorer David Thompson in 1787 confidently asserted the Salish claim to past dominion over a larger area, reporting that a region east of the Rockies also had been "in full possession" of the Flatheads, Pend Oreilles, Kutenais, and Shoshonis at one time. The Pend Oreille chief, Alexander, would make the same assertion sixty-two years later at a treaty council, and Victor, chief of the Flatheads, would advise his son, Charlot, to retreat toward that eastern ground if he were driven from the Bitterroot Valley.

Flathead community life was mobile due to its seasonal migrations to hunt, gather, dig, and fish. White trappers and traders reported this life as they saw it, but Indian lives through the eyes of an alien culture often seem to lack motivation beyond food or war, and the traits of one or several individuals easily become generalized as those of a band or a nation. We can be sure, however, that the Flatheads were a geographic grouping of highly individualistic persons, many born into other tribes and adopted by the Flatheads, who drew together for security and society.

Except in winter, the Flatheads rarely camped more than ten or fifteen days in one location. The women prepared and preserved foods, made clothing, and maintained the households, which included moving the lodges of poles and skins. The men procured meat and hides, guarded the camp, and made weapons.

In spring the Flatheads hunted buffalo. The hunters returned in time to accompany the camp to camas, bitterroot, and onion fields, judging the season by a "bitterroot moon," where women dug with paddle-shaped sticks or elk-horn diggers while the root was tender before flowering. Bitterroot, which grows abundantly on gravel terraces flooded in spring, pushes shoots above ground under the snow, and in late June blooms with pink petals. It occurred in the Bitterroot Valley, at places along the Clark's Fork, in Grass Valley, in the Big Hole, and near Philipsburg. Dried by baking three days in pits or steamed in skin bags, stored in parfleches (skin bags), and pounded into flour for small cakes or boiled with berries, bitterroot was a Flathead staple.

Camas, also cooked in pits, served as a sweetener prized by many tribes. With light blue flowers so thick that fields of camas sometimes resembled lakes, it grew near Potomac, Darby, Lake Como, and Rock Creek, where Nez Percés and Pend Oreilles joined Flatheads to dig; on occasion, even Plains bands participated under tenuous compacts supposed to guarantee the Flatheads safe passage on the plains. A favorite meeting place to council was a spirit tree twelve miles south of Darby. Visiting tribes scrupulously observed the customs of the host tribe as they dug. In turn the Flatheads respected the practices of a host tribe when some of them fished for salmon with the Nez Percés, Colvilles, or Spokanes. In later times, when Indians owned horses, a short summer hunt was held by agreement among bands that joined for camas digging.

As occasion offered, Flatheads also dug sunflower roots; stripped the bark of pine, larch, and fir for sap and the edible cambium layer; gathered black moss from pine trees to be washed and baked into cakes; pulled wild carrots and parsnips; fished the local streams; and snared or shot fowl and small game. Raw meats and roots usually were boiled in woven or skin bags containing water heated by dropping hot stones into it. Cakes were baked over open fires. In winter, foods were cooked inside the tipis in stone-lined pits or by boiling in bags sunk into the ground. For seasoning and supplemental foods, Flathead women gathered choke, service, and huckleberries in bark baskets.

To be sure they would find enough wild foods, Flatheads observed rituals marking the passage of seasons. Both in tribal and individual prayers, the number of supernatural beings was indefinite. The Flatheads agreed on no hierarchy of spirits, and the male sun approached most nearly their notion of a supreme being. Individual prayers to the sun were occasional; tribal prayers to the sun were seasonal. . . .

The Flatheads' individual communication with the supernatural centered on visions and special powers conferred by spirit helpers. For access to spirits, Flatheads relied on practices and charms which the white men called "medicine." Medicine involved the intervention of personal helpers. Charms might be talismans, potions, powders, or private songs used to promote supernatural help in achieving success in warfare, hunting, courting, seduction, or gambling. Charms also offered protection against someone else's power.

Power was demonstrated by luck and wealth. The poor were believed to have ineffectual powers. An individual Flathead carried a small leather pouch, usually hung by a thong around his neck, containing relics of a highly personal nature connected with his *sumesh,* his power. Special songs summoned his spirit ally—songs usually learned in adolescence by a youngster sent alone into the forests or mountains to fast and await a vision of a spirit guardian from whom he obtained influence. Boys nearly always went on such spirit quests; girls often did, but were guarded. Spirit helpers might also come in unsought visions and dreams. Formal quests were preceded by fasting, sweating, and ritual bathing. The pragmatic Flatheads, even if impressed by the questor's report of his spirit vision, waited to see a demonstration of power before believing in it.

Certain men and women who showed unusual powers as seers, prophets, and physicians came to be regarded as shamans. . . . These special people were respected but did not act as full-time medicine men. Shamans forewarned of raids, located and summoned bison, cured illnesses, and were forever being asked to find lost articles. While Flathead shamans apparently did not engage in public contests of power, feuds between strong ones were not unknown. . . .

Doctoring included natural plant remedies for minor ailments as well as ritual. Shamans and herb doctors borrowed techniques from each other, although most herb doctors were women, some of whom specialized in a single illness. Flatheads learned herb medicine in dreams or exchanged remedies with other tribes. Sweating, the universal tonic and curative, was both therapeutic and ceremonial purifier. Flatheads built hollow mounds of sticks covered with grass mats or turf as sweat lodges, heated by hot rocks dashed with water.

Among common remedies the Flatheads employed carrot roots to relieve headaches, a yellow-flowered herb (probably agrimony) of the rose family to stop diarrhea or cure a sore throat, and a woodpecker's beak or rattlesnake fang thrust into caries to allay toothache. They made teas of Oregon grape to assist delivery of the placenta, prevent conception, or treat venereal disease; yarrow tea to aid colds; wormwood, applied lukewarm from boiling, to reduce swelling. They used the dried leaves of the common evergreen plant, kinnikinnick, to promote rapid healing of burns; inhaled powdered false hellebore roots to induce sneezing or relieve nasal congestion; and covered open sores with herb, dung, mud, or pitch poultices. The doctors also splinted broken arms or legs, and occasionally amputated. They pried out infected teeth. If the patient cried out or moaned, he was jeered.

Ritual physicians blew upon affected parts of the body, uttering incantations, shaking rattles, dancing, and wearing costumes for the purpose because Flatheads realized that major illness or injury resulted from the stronger power of a rival or invasion of the body by an unfriendly spirit which must be driven out. The successful shaman expected payment; one who failed might be killed by survivors of the patient. When dogs barked all night, the Flatheads understood sickness was coming and burned juniper to purify their lodge interiors with smoke.

Flatheads used herbs and plants for purposes other than medicinal. Oregon grape root and pine moss colored quills yellow; berries supplied red dyes; clay, requiring a hard trip east, also was used for red coloring; and black came from beds of natural asphalt. The Flatheads made perfumes and insect repellants from grasses and shrubs, employing yarrow as an aromatic body deodorant and strands of sweetgrass, folded into clothing, as a garment deodorant. Meadow-rue seeds, chewed and rubbed over the body, served as perfume. A shampoo of orange honeysuckle grew longer hair, and the sap of western larch held it in place. Fir needles could be ground for baby powder. Paint was also part of the Indian's toilet. "Paint is like anything else of an Indian's dress or fancy; and feathers likewise. . . . Paint is part of his dress," observed a white who lived among the Flatheads.

Far from libertine, the Flathead lived within bounds imposed by his spiritual world, tangible and unpredictable. Yet no somber mood prevailed. He enjoyed jokes and laughter. Inconsequential activities of each day required no supernatural assistance, but the Flathead prudently summoned his guardian's aid for important ventures, including play.

Favorite games among the Flatheads were common to many tribes. They included the hand game, or stick game, in which opposing teams, facing each other, concealed bones—one decorated—which they passed from one player to another by hand, using feints and distractions, singing lucky songs. Players and bystanders wagered, and colored sticks were used to tally the score when the decorated bone was located by an opponent. Another popular game required contestants to throw arrows or small spears at rolling hoops with colored spokes, attempting to hit a chosen color, and again betting against each other and with spectators. The games not only supplied recreation but functioned as practical exercises in hand and eye skills, although no Flathead thought of them in this way.

Spiritual influences affected a Flathead from birth. In order to protect her child from namelessness, a Flathead mother named him for the first object she saw after his birth. He might be Dry Wood or Old Moccasin until he earned a name by deeds or received one from his father or an uncle. The gift of a name from a relative was not uncommon, and the name often recalled an incident of the hunt or war. To make him placid in later life, a child's mother would rub heart of a fool-hen, mashed with white clay, over his chest. Ants mixed with white clay as a poultice made him energetic, and heart of eagle or hawk conferred courage. The heart of mouse assured him stealth to steal horses.

Many facets of Flathead life changed when the Indians acquired horses. The horse extended the tribe's range and recast its values. Caravans with horses to carry their loads might travel thirty miles in one day; mounted warriors could ride one hundred if necessary. The manner and date of acquiring horses, according to Flathead timekeeping and recollection, was from the Shoshonis by theft about 1600. Probably they actually obtained horses by peaceful exchange with the Shoshonis sometime between 1700 and 1730.

The plausible source lay in the established trade route to the Flatheads' south along which Spanish goods trickled for a century or more. The Spanish forebade selling guns to Indians or allowing them even to ride horses, but stories of both came northward, and by 1659 the Spanish reported Apache raids for horses. About the same time, the Apaches traded slaves for horses from the Pueblos. By 1692 the Utes were mounted, and then the Comanches. When the Utes and Comanches acquired horses, they turned into bison-hunting nomads, foreshadowing the Flatheads' conversion to Plains bison hunters.

The Comanches, Utes, and Kiowas—all of Shoshoni linguistic stock— formed a chain of commerce from New Mexico to Montana by way of the Colorado, Grand, Green, and Snake river courses. Not only had these tribes provided a pathway for native and European bartered wares, but the Salish, when mounted, would consider them allies against the Blackfeet. By 1705 Kiowas appeared in Comanche raiding parties of Spanish ranches near Amarillo, and a few years later occasional Flatheads joined them. The chain thus passed horses northward from one tribe to the next, west of the continental divide, until they reached the Shoshonis, the funnel for horses into the interior Pacific Northwest. The exchange of horses for guns owned by northern tribes doubtless speeded the spread of horse bands.

As a result of this route, the Flatheads adopted the Spanish saddle, bridle, and handling, modified to suit Indian life. As they adapted, the Flatheads fashioned rawhide bridles (the Nez Percés preferred braided hair) and devised a pad saddle, a soft pillow of animal skin stuffed with hair or grass, without stirrups. For a time, Plains and mountain tribes armored their horses in the Spanish manner with several thicknesses of leather. In 1806 Meriwether Lewis would watch Flatheads castrate a stallion with Spanish technique and declare their way better than those of Americans or British.

Ancient Hawaii: An Agrarian Society

EDWARD D. BEECHERT

The people who today are called native Hawaiians were not indigenous to the Hawaiian Islands. Rather, scholars generally believe that the first settlers in Hawaii came from the Marquesas Islands and that later arrivals originated from the Society group of islands, most likely Tahiti.

In the following reading, Edward Beechert has reconstructed a picture of ancient Hawaii, a society organized around extended families, called *'ohana,* and divided into three status levels—the *ali'i* or high chiefs, the *konohiki* or headmen, and the *maka'āinana* or common people. The people did not own the land but had the right of usufruct, that is, the right of using and enjoying the produce of the land as long as they did not alter or damage it. Each piece of land assigned to an *'ohana* provided the family members with a variety of food. Taro (a starchy root) and sweet potatoes were the principal staples, and fish supplied the main dietary protein. Because taro requires moist soil, ensuring a steady flow of water was an important task. The Hawaiians consequently became experts in building ditches and ponds.

In ancient Hawaiian society, a close relationship prevailed between production and political authority. The *ali'i* not only controlled production but also distributed the products of human labor. Generosity was an important basis of an *ali'ihi*'s power. However, the nature of Hawaiian society began to change as one of the *ali'i,* who came to be called Kamehameha I (ruled 1795–1819), conquered and unified the island chain by using weapons he bartered from Europeans, who had begun visiting the islands toward the end of the eighteenth century. The introduction of commodities that were not locally produced affected not only food production but also the pattern of land tenure, thereby fundamentally disrupting the agrarian way of life.

STUDY QUESTIONS

1. Compare and contrast the social structure and economic organization of ancient Hawaii with those found in the Pueblo world and among the Flathead Indians.

2. Who held power in each of these societies—Hawaiian, Pueblo, and Flathead—and on what basis?

3. In what major ways do the three societies described in this chapter differ from modern American society?

Hawaii before the arrival of the European was a complex communal society, one with standards of material well-being markedly different from
those of the western world. Although the evidence is scanty, the first settlers
arrived in Hawaii in approximately A.D. 124, with successive waves coming
until approximately the thirteenth or fourteenth centuries. Although authorities disagree, the first Hawaiians probably arrived from the Marquesas
Islands. Later arrivals came from the Society group, notably Tahiti. The
influence of Tahiti was certainly strong in the language, and some postulate
that the Hawaiian society which greeted Captain Cook in [1778] was a dual
society: a class of commoners ruled by an elite derived from the Tahitian
experience.

The first people brought only a few plants and small animals with them.
They settled at the ocean's edge. Taro and sweet potatoes, supplemented by
fish and complemented with such items as sugarcane and coconuts, made up
the basic diet of the Hawaiian. Pigs, chickens, and dogs were supplementary
and often ceremonial foods rather than items of regular consumption.

Hawaiian society was organized around a single extended family unit,
the 'ohana. These units formed the basis of the land divisions of Hawaii. The
land was divided into segments which gave each kinship group access to
resources from the sea to the upland forests. Ideally these *ahupua'a* extended
from the mountain tops to the offshore reefs. The title to the area was held
by the chief of the group. Basically *ahupua'a* followed the watershed where
there were streams or were arbitrarily drawn from mountain to sea, forming
a district for levying taxes on produce.

The major task of the 'ohana was agricultural. One of the Hawaiian
accounts of life before the arrival of the European described the basic condition of agriculture.

From *Working in Hawaii: A Labor History* by Edward D. Beechert, pp. 1–11. Copyright
© 1985. Reprinted by permission of The University of Hawaii Press.

Sources drawn on in the original work are Gavan Daws, *A Shoal of Time* (1968); Timothy K.
Earle, *Economic and Social Organization of a Complex Chiefdom: The Halelea District, Kaua'i,
Hawaii* (1978); Kenneth Emory "Origins of the Hawaiians," *Journal of the Polynesian Society*
68 (1959): 29–35; Abraham Fornander, *Collection of Hawaiian Antiquities and Folklore*, series
1–3, vol. 6 (1916); Irving Goldman, *Ancient Polynesian Society* (1970); E. S. C. Handy and
Elizabeth Green Handy, *Native Planters in Old Hawaii: Their Life, Lore, and Environment*
(1972); E. S. C. Handy and Mary Pukui, *The Polynesian Family System in Kau* (1972); Melville
Herkovits, *Economic Anthropology* (1952); Stella Jones, "Economic Adjustment of the Hawai-
ians to European Culture," *Pacific Affairs* 4 (Nov. 1931): 957–974; Samuel Kamakau, *Na Hana
a ka Pa'e Kahiko* (1976); Ralph S. Kuykendall, *The Hawaiian Kingdom*, vol. 1, *1778–1854:
Foundation and Transformation* (1938); David Malo, *Moolelo Hawaii* (1951); Nakuina,
"Ancient Hawaiian Water Rights, in *Thrum's Hawaiian Almanac and Annual* (1894); Marshall
D. Sahlins, *Social Stratification in Polynesia* (1958); and Elizabeth Wittermans, *Interethnic
Relations in a Plural Society* (1964).

[The farmers] were not well supplied with proper tools; they had no iron digging implements, no cattle, no horses. Their tools were their hands and their backs—these were their cattle. Their hands were their lifting implements and their shoulders their carts for hauling rocks, great logs, and all the heavy things. . . . Fire was a man's plow and his clearing implement. With his hands he softened the earth, weeded, raked, and spaded, with only the help of a wooden digging stick.

With this limited technological development, a reasonably systematic agriculture was essential for maintaining an adequate flow of food.

Furthermore, given that food storage techniques were rudimentary, a smoothly functioning system of work allocation was a basic requirement for survival. Tasks were apportioned according to spiritual tradition. Taro planting, for example, was essentially a male task. Women, tabooed from participating in this activity, cultivated and harvested the sweet potato, gathered shellfish and seaweed, and collected fibers. Fishing was another major activity. Deep sea fishing was the work of the specialist, while shallow, inshore fishing was conducted by the family. The result of organizing crop rotation, the harvesting of fish, and the gathering of a variety of plants and fibers through an integrated system of communal activity was the gradual

Hawaiians tending a taro field

development of a complex system of agriculture balanced with fishing and other marine resources that made up the basic Hawaiian economy.

TARO PLANTING

Depending on the location of the plot, taro could be grown on either "dry land" or "wet lands." Both systems in fact required a considerable flow of water. Wet taro, in a land characterized by a limited distribution of water, meant the construction and maintenance of irrigation dams, ditches, and terraces. Where rainfall was abundant, dry taro was planted in burned-over fields that had been mulched with grass.

Taro planting was a stylized activity carried out only by men. On the day of planting, the men went to fish in the morning, feasting on the catch. Women made leis (headbands) to be worn by the men while planting. Marking out the field with fishing lines for straight rows, the men lined up with their digging sticks and made holes for the taro slips. Traditionally the stick was held in the right hand and the taro in the left. . . . Once the taro took root, the field was burned again and then mulched. The taro grew rapidly. Where conditions were not so favorable, a much more difficult process had to be followed. Underbrush had to be cut away before burning the field and planting. In some cases, the taro grew slowly, taking more than a year to mature. It was customary to offer ripe taro, fish, or even pigs to those who assisted in this extra work.

Frequently taro was grown in large terraces or ponds; typically, these plots were the property of the chiefs. Building the terraces, large or small, was a heavy task. Large groups of men were required for a project that could take months or even years to complete, depending on the size and shape of the land. From one hundred to a thousand workers were assembled to perform this work. First water was allowed to flow over the land selected. Again, the men would feast beforehand; then they lined up at the lower edge of the field where they began to heap up the soil with their hands. This process continued until the terrace was level. After the sides had been packed by tramping, sugarcane tops, coconut fronds, and grass were tamped into the sides, which were then covered with flat stones, fine soil, and grass to prevent drying out. When the terrace was completed, the next step was to make a floor. At this point the women and children joined in. Water was flooded over the floor and the people packed the mud with their feet. This task frequently took on the air of a festival. Finally, the men planted the taro and lined the banks with sugarcane and banana plants.

SWEET POTATOES AND YAMS

Sweet potatoes and yams were the most important supplement to the taro plant. Not so dependent on water, they were often a more reliable food source than taro. Not only did sweet potatoes grow in a variety of soil conditions but some varieties could be stored for long periods. Moreover, the sweet potato was not surrounded by the religious restrictions of taro: women could plant, tend, and harvest the sweet potato.

As with taro, the conditions for planting sweet potatoes varied with the climate and type of land available. Lowland fields were burned over and then softened by digging with an *o'o* (digging stick). Stubble and brush were removed in order to bring the level of moisture to the surface. After a month, slips were prepared. Since both men and women participated, planting was a festive occasion. New *malos* (loincloths) were donned; leis and flowers were worn. Slips were planted in mounds about twelve feet apart. Men made the planting hole with their digging stick and women inserted the potato vines, two to each hole. On good land, about five acres could be planted in one day. Different techniques were used on slopes and dry land—small patches were the rule here, scattered wherever the opportunity presented itself.

WATER SYSTEMS AND LAND

Closely related to the planters were the irrigators or controllers of water. Irrigation projects were generally simple and apparently completed in stages so that the labor requirement was not excessive. The early Hawaiian regarded water as inseparable from the land. In perhaps no other area did western ideas have a more devastating effect than on the possession of water and the right to its use. The importance of a consistent flow of water is reflected in the careful arrangements for access. Wet taro requires a steady flow of moisture to maintain a narrow range of temperature. The use of land and water depended upon the contribution of the user and his family. So long as a family lived on the land and contributed their share of the work required to maintain the water supply, they were considered to have a right to a portion of the water. . . . "Water, then, like sunlight, as a source of life to land and man, was the possession of no man, even *ali'i nui* [chiefs] or the *mo'i* [ruler]."

Because of the poor distribution of water, the cycle of wet and dry seasons, and the contour of the land, the need for an efficient water system was a matter of continuing urgency. In a prolonged drought, "sometimes famine, bitter famine, came over the land. . . ."

Deforestation and soil erosion were serious problems brought on by the slash and burn techniques. Overcutting of timber in some areas seems to have produced a desiccation of the land. Many of the fish ponds were filled with silt from soil erosion. Because of the uneven quality of the land, people tended to congregate in the coastal areas and wherever there were favorable soil and water conditions. As the expanding population pushed people from the ocean's edge onto less desirable land, by the time of European contact a wide diversity of land was being cultivated. . . .

FISHING

Fish provided the primary source of protein in Hawaii's basically agricultural economy. Two types of fishing were characteristic: offshore fishing from canoes and inshore fishing with nets, spears, traps, and hands. . . .

Deep sea fishing involved the use of long fishing lines especially braided for this purpose. Hooks were made of a variety of materials, including human bone. The fishermen obtained their lines from farmers who raised the *olonā* plant with its long, supple fibers that were also used to make ropes. Boggy interior valleys and upland areas were favored for the planting. The preparation of the bark for cord was a skilled task performed by women: "The work of twisting was laborious. The palm of the hand was used to rub the fibers over the thigh, to make a firm, tight cord of two or three strands, even throughout." The cord so laboriously made was then fashioned into nets. The largest nets, if filled with fish, required "from ten to twenty" canoes to hold them all. According to the size of the catch, the fisherman first filled a container with choice fish for his wife, for "over her chafed thighs the cords for the nets had been twisted." . . . The location of the deepwater fishing sites was the well-guarded secret of each fisherman. Elaborate precautions were taken to conceal the location of these places. . . .

Shallow inshore fishing, requiring less skill and being less intensive, was a family activity: "These were not expert ways of fishing; they were just for the taking of fish to make life more pleasurable." To offset the unpredictable nature of deep sea fishing, the Hawaiians also cultivated fish. The farming of fish ranged from individual efforts in small taro patches to seawater ponds of massive construction, of which many survive today. One of these sea ponds had a sea wall extending some five thousand feet. Since the labor to construct such ambitious dikes had to be communally organized, ponds of this size were in the nature of public works. . . . Although the stonework was crude and largely undressed, considerable engineering was needed to move and place the stones. Sluice gates and weirs were constructed to take advantage of the tides to trap the fish.

Another type of pond widely used was the freshwater pond. Where circumstances permitted, taro patches were used to raise mullet. Others used a brackish pond varying in size according to the resources of the farmer. A community resource was the "fish trap"—a low wall with openings that were flooded at high tide. Nets were placed across the openings on both the flood and ebb tide to snare the fish. This type of trap was usually community property, the use of which was assigned in rotation.

CANOE MAKING

Although the basic activity of the Hawaiian system was a subsistence agriculture, the economy did support a number of specialized craftsmen. Canoe making was held in a special high status in pre-European Hawaii. An apprenticeship was required before the craftsman was permitted to engage in the work. . . . The process was surrounded by an elaborate ritual involving a special priest who conducted the appropriate ceremonies in selecting a log to be felled. After the felling, the canoe was hollowed and shaped. Some forty-eight feet long, in the case of the larger canoes, the roughly finished vessel was ready to be dragged down the mountain. For these large canoes, both men and women joined in the effort: "Many pigs were provided for them. The dragging of a canoe was a great occasion." At the shore, the specialist assembled his varied tools, the chisel, the broad tanged adze, the narrow adze, the axe, the finishing adze, and scrapers. The comprehension of the canoe was monitored by the priest to ensure integrity of construction and thus the safety of the vessel.

POLITICAL STRUCTURE

KINSHIP SYSTEM

To understand the labor system upon which Hawaiian society was based, it is necessary to consider the kinship-political structure which governed the society. There were basically three status levels. At the top, the high chief or *ali'i* ruled with his family. The units of this family were generally the chiefs of the districts of the island. A second level of authority was that of the *konohiki*, the stewards or headmen of the *ahupua'a*, persons of intermediate rank who administered the divisions of the domain. These men were generally distant relatives of the high chief. Below the varying gradations of chiefs were the bulk of the people, the *maka'āinana* (literally "people living on the land"). The *maka'āinana* were divided roughly into three groups: the largest group was farmers; the smaller and more specialized group included fishermen and canoe builders; there was also a very small, ambiguous group of social outcasts, the *kauwa* (untouchables). Generally the *maka'āinana* were planters—the base of society—who made up the *'ohana* or family group. . . .

. . . Only at the level of high chiefs were genealogical titles of great importance, and marriage within these families was frequently practiced in order to maintain the blood lines. Family was more loosely defined in commoner society where neither political power nor property rights depended upon genealogical ties. The large populations involved and the movement toward the consolidation of political authority further blurred the closeness of kinship ties. After 1450, attempts to consolidate political authority led to increasing warfare. In effect, a conquest hierarchy was imposed over the genealogical hierarchies and the focus of power was determined by warfare as much as by marriage. With conquest came a reallocation of stewardship and a redistribution of land that erased kinship lines in the *ali'i* class. The defeated *ali'i* slipped easily out of the class and into the status of commoner. The *maka'āinana*, moved about by the ebb and flow of warfare, increasingly operated through the extended family and loosely defined relationships.

In summary, then, these definitions describe two different economic systems. In one, the extended family, there is implied specialized economic activity organized into self-sufficient units. In the other, there is a greater degree of independence of the household units. Given the diversity of conditions in Hawaii and the fact that much of the evidence dates from 1800 or later, it is likely that both types of organization were maintained. . . .

Under the *ali'i* system, the chiefs indeed controlled production to provide the resources they required to maintain their position. That revenue, however, carried with it the obligation to meet and discharge the related duties of land tenure. It was at this juncture of land tenure that the *ali'i* class met the commoner class. The chiefs could not separate their revenue from the productions of the families on the land without destroying the basis of the system. Since the chiefs did not recirculate their revenue as investments designed to augment their wealth through increased production, the Hawaiian system did not lead to the accumulation of wealth in the sense of the accumulation of capital. Chiefly power resided "not [in] the possession of goods, . . . but [in] their disposition; hence generosity is the sine qua non of chieftainship. . . . [In] the evolution of culture as a whole, productivity, the tribal economy, and political power proceed together."

CONCEPTS OF WEALTH

The notion of wealth must be carefully defined in relation to the Hawaiian system. Goods were not accumulated for wealth; there were no established market systems for such exchange. . . . [T]here was no common medium of exchange. The up-country people traded their tapa, fibers, sweet potatoes, and stone adzes for fish and poi. In some cases, they traded koa logs to be made into canoes. Few areas were self-sufficient. Not all of the trading could be arranged within the group of the *'ohana*. . . . For those goods produced by outside sources, periodic fairs were held to facilitate the exchange of needed items. . . .

The trappings of the *ali'i* status—feather capes, garlands, pendants, helmets, and emblems of rank—constituted a form of wealth, but not in the sense of exchange wealth. That is, these goods could not be acquired by persons not entitled to them by status. . . . [T]he status of chiefs in Hawaii was measured more in terms of political power and jurisdiction than in the amount of produce to be gained by conquest. There was a close link between authority and production. The successful collection and distribution of goods guaranteed the prestige and stability of the chief.

RIGHTS AND RESPONSIBILITIES

. . . Under the *ali'i* system, the *ahupua'a* functioned as a tax unit. The head of the *ahupua'a*, the *konohiki*, had the duty of ensuring that the people of the unit met the levy specified by the administrative officer. . . . The Hawaiian tenant held the land apportioned to him to maintain his family. He owed a portion of his produce to the *ali'i* above him. Commoners were bound neither to the *ali'i* nor to the land or the district. In fact, the commoner had the right to abandon his district and move to another if he regarded his treatment as abusive or unfair. Three principles ruled: Water, like land, was governed by use considerations rather than by possession; neither land nor water could be transferred or owned in the sense of excluding others from their use; and those who did not utilize their share, and who did not contribute, lost both the land and the water.

The role of labor expended in the production of goods and services in ancient Hawaii should be seen, then, as part of the social system—a role in society rather than as a commodity. Hawaiian society was predominantly agricultural—an agrarian community:

> The Hawaiians, more than any of the other Polynesians, were a people whose means of livelihood, whose work and interests, were centered in the cultivation of the soil. . . . It was the practice of systematic agriculture more than anything else that produced qualities of character in the Hawaiian common people that differed markedly from those typical of other Polynesians.

. . . Work was a matter of maintaining the 'ohana and the political community at large. It was the success in meeting these two objectives which constituted the reward for labor expended. Both geographic and political considerations dictated the boundaries of the ahupua'a. In effect, Hawaiian society encompassed two contradictory notions of wealth. On the one hand, high consumption and adornment were symbols of high status; on the other, there was a marked generosity in giving and sharing. . . .

WAR AND THE POLITICAL ECONOMY

Warfare of the type which characterized the consolidation of the eighteenth century involved drastic changes in land tenure. The displacement of chiefs, both high and low, frequently resulted in changes of tenancy as well. . . .

Kamehameha I radically altered the practice of Hawaiian warfare and, therefore, the traditional economic and political structure. He changed the conduct of war by employing European weapons—firearms and ships—to carry out his strategies. These commodities, however, unlike all previous commodities required to carry out warfare, were not produced by the commoner class. Their purchase was accomplished by drafts of labor and goods which were taken out of the local political economy.

The traditional system of accumulating the necessary weapons and canoes for war spread the gathering of supplies over a long period of time and lessened the burden on the commoner. Given the level of technology, canoe making alone required a considerable investment of time and energy. The production of foodstuffs to feed the army was also a time-consuming process. Given these conditions, armies could not be mobilized for long periods of time or called up frequently. When Kamehameha I completed his conquest of Oahu, for example, he set about building large taro ponds in preparation for the attempted invasion of Kauai, using upward of one thousand men drafted for the task. . . .

The implication of Kamehameha's change in warfare as an exercise in political power was that the basic activity of the Hawaiian people, agriculture, was severely disrupted. The rhythms of a low-technology agriculture require careful timing and attention to sequence. Although Hawaii was the most productive of the Polynesian societies and generally produced an adequate food supply, in the absence of drought and severe weather, the margin of surplus was small. Under normal conditions, the people could have produced easily for their own subsistence and for that required by the political structure. The requirements added by the *ali'i* to support their increasingly concentrated and complex political system, however, added an intolerable burden to the commoner's need to produce.

The intensive cultivation, with increasing population, also produced considerable changes in the terrain. The removal of forest land and the cultivation of valleys, all well before the arrival of the European, created a series of far-reaching changes. Erosion poured silt into ocean fish ponds, reducing the yield; upland cultivation of taro and sweet potato made the crops more vulnerable to changes in the weather pattern. One can fairly conclude that these ecological changes, in addition to the damage wrought by the wars of consolidation, put undue pressure on the system of food production.

FURTHER READING

Louis A. Brennan, *American Dawn: A New Model of American Prehistory* (New York: Macmillan, 1970).

Peter Farb, *Man's Rise to Civilization as Shown by the Indians of North America from Primeval Times to the Coming of the Industrial State* (New York: E. P. Dutton and Co., 1968; London: Seeker and Warburg, 1969; New York: Avon Books, 1971).

Robert J. Hommon, "Social Evolution in Ancient Hawaii," in *Island Societies: Archaeological Approaches to Evolution and Transformation*, ed. Patrick V. Kirch (Cambridge: Cambridge University Press, 1986).

Wilbur R. Jacobs, "The Tip of the Iceburg: Pre-Columbian Indian Demography and Some Implications for Revisionism," *William and Mary Quarterly*, 3d ser., 31 (1974): 123–132.

Alice Beck Kehoe, *North American Indians: A Comprehensive Account* (Englewood Cliffs, N.J.: Prentice-Hall, 1981; 2d ed., 1992).

Patrick V. Kirch, *Feathered Gods and Fishhooks: An Introduction to Hawaiian Archaeology and Prehistory* (Honolulu: University of Hawaii Press, 1985).

Malcolm Margolin, *The Ohlone Way: Indian Life in the San Francisco–Monterey Bay Area* (Berkeley: Heyday Books, 1978).

T. Stell Newman, "Man in the Prehistoric Hawaiian Ecosystem," in *A Natural History of the Hawaiian Islands*, ed. E. Allison Kay (Honolulu: University of Hawaii Press, 1972).

Valerio Valeri, *Kingship and Sacrifice: Ritual and Society in Ancient Hawaii* (Chicago: University of Chicago Press, 1985).

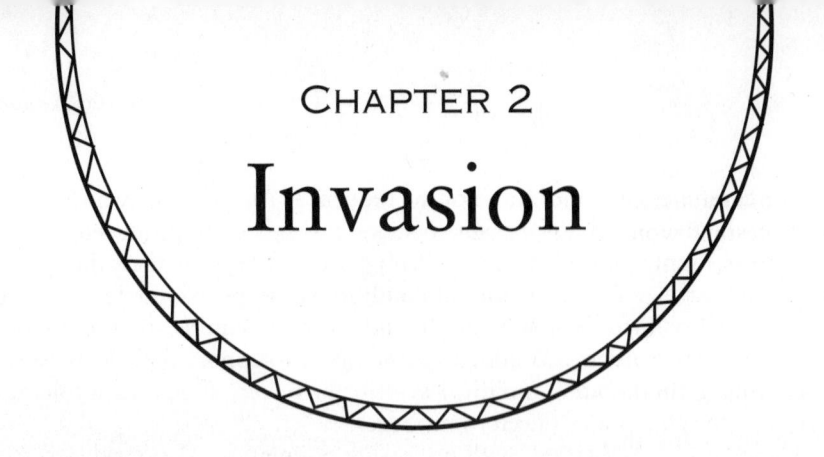

CHAPTER 2

Invasion

A harsh reality of human conflict permeates the history of the American West. Native Americans, the aboriginal inhabitants of long standing, endured successive waves of conquest, beginning with the Spanish conquistadors' ventures from central Mexico into what is now the American Southwest. Later, Anglo-Americans penetrated the same region, irretrievably altering the lives of the surviving Indian tribes, as well as those of people of Mexican descent. Not until the last decade of the nineteenth century did the military phase end, although it has been forever mythologized in Hollywood movies about the Indian wars.

Indians and Chicanos continue to be subjected to economic, political, cultural, and psychological domination. Obviously, the permutations on this theme are many, although we can give only a few examples here. In the opening piece, Carey McWilliams explains why we need to see beyond the "fantasy" culture presented in a great deal of the popular literature about the Spanish-Mexican heritage to examine the more "prosaic" aspects of the Spanish conquest. Quintard Taylor points out in the second selection that blacks were among the earliest settlers in the Oregon Territory and that they therefore, ironically, formed part of the Euro-American penetration into the region—even as they themselves struggled to maintain their rights in the face of efforts to perpetuate slavery in what became a free state. In the third reading, Robert Utley reminds us that the West was won by military campaigns that many Native American groups fiercely resisted. Finally, Sarah Deutsch highlights the role that women missionaries played in a form of cultural invasion. These readings show that the ancestors of today's minority groups were not always minorities; rather, they were reduced, in various way, to their current subordinate status.

FOR ANALYSIS AND DISCUSSION

1. Many old Hollywood movies depict Indians as aggressors who attacked Euro-Americans moving westward across the continent. Have the readings in this chapter changed your understanding of this history of the westward movement? If so, how?

2. Compare and contrast the methods used by settlers, the U.S. Army, and Protestant women missionaries in their efforts to subjugate peoples of color in the American West.

3. What did each of these methods accomplish?

4. What ideological justification did Euro-Americans use to assert their dominance in the American West?

5. Do you think that similar methods of conquest and domination are still at work today, though perhaps in more subtle ways? Explain your answer.

North from Mexico

CAREY MCWILLIAMS

People of Mexican descent (Chicanos) officially became residents of the United States following the U.S. conquest of northern Mexico in 1848, but they possess a much longer history in the area that today is the American Southwest. Chicano history can trace its origins to the contact between pre-Columbian native peoples and the conquering Spanish in what is now Mexico and the Southwest. The resulting racial and cultural mixing between Indians and Spaniards produced what in Mexico is referred to as the *mestizo*. Most Chicanos are *mestizos*.

Carey McWilliams, who wrote the first history of Chicanos, *North from Mexico* (1949), from which the following selection is taken, notes that the deep roots of the Mexican-American experience as exemplified by the Spanish conquest and Spanish settlements in the Southwest. Rather than valorizing this experience, McWilliams emphasizes the prosaic nature of these settlements and their contributions to an evolving Mexican-American culture.

STUDY QUESTIONS

1. What were some of the prosaic material items that the Spanish introduced to the region that is now the Southwest?

2. How did these contributions promote the region's development?

3. What does the author mean when he states, "While the form or model was often Spanish, the ultimate adaptation showed unmistakable Mexican and Indian influences"?

Despite the insurmountable obstacles which they encountered, the Spanish left an imprint on the borderlands which, as Bolton once said, "is still deep and clear." The names of three states in the region are Spanish in origin: California, Nevada, and Colorado. "Scores of rivers and mountains and hundreds of towns and cities," to quote Bolton again, "still bear the names of saints dear to the Spanish pioneers." From Los Angeles to San

Antonio, the Spanish language is spoken today by upwards of two million people. Thousands of Indians living in the region speak Spanish in preference to English and profess the Catholic faith. The imprint of Spain is to be found in the land systems of the region; in the law of waters, of minerals, and of community property; and in many institutions now firmly planted in the Southwest. "It is to them and their followers and descendants," writes Dr. Frank C. Lockwood, "few though they were, and opposed as they were by harsh nature and hostile savages, that our Anglo-Saxon pioneers owed from the first a degree of exemption from such extremes of ignorance and crudity as most American pioneer settlers have experienced."

A major factor in the prosaic success of the Spanish in the Southwest consisted in the similarity of the climate and environment to that of Spain. Spain is the only European country with an arid or semi-arid environment. Over a period of thirty generations, the Spanish had acquired a profound knowledge of the nature and limitations of such an environment. The Spaniards knew and understood irrigated farming, for irrigation is necessary throughout the whole of the Spanish peninsula as it is throughout the Southwest. They had solved the problem of building without timber by the use of adobe, brick, and stone, a practice which proved of great value in the Southwest. In almost every respect, their institutions and culture were adapted to the environment which they found in the borderlands. "The scale was higher," writes Dr. Walter Prescott Webb, "but the difference was more of degree than of character or quality."

Everything that the Spanish brought to the Southwest was either driven or carried in saddlebags or *carretas*. But what they did bring was of enormous importance. . . . They brought the first cattle, horses, goats, pigs, cats, and barnyard fowls to the Southwest. At great effort they brought from Europe the first hoes, spades, grinding stones, clamps, plows, files, and pliers used in the region. The first wheels that turned on American soil were Spanish in origin. "There was no product contributed to the agriculture of America by the English," writes Harvey Bernstein, "which the Spanish had not planted earlier."

The list is a long one, indeed, including peaches, figs, oranges, apples, grapes, apricots, limes, pomegranates, pears, olives, and lemons. Over 260,000 orange trees were planted in the older mission groves of California by 1880. The vineyards that developed so rapidly in California after 1848 were planted in or near the original vineyards which the Spanish had laid out. Up to 1860, there was only one grape grown in California,—the Mission grape; but in that year the state's thirty million vines were producing upwards of seven million gallons of wine. The Spanish introduced raisin culture to California. The first wheat seeds brought to California came from Spain and were, on their arrival in 1770, already well-adapted to climatic and soil conditions not unlike those which existed in the state. The first wheat planted in Colorado was Spanish in origin and was known as "Sonora wheat." The grandfather of Don Amado Chaves brought the first alfalfa seed to New Mexico tied in a *manta*. The Spanish brought the important seed of the alfilaria or filaree to California as well as the first flax seeds. In 1806 the Spaniards introduced a cotton seed from Mexico that produced exceptionally large, wide, open bolls. Introduced by way of New Orleans, this seed spread rapidly throughout the Deep South.

While the area farmed by the Franciscans in California was not large—perhaps not more than 10,000 acres—the mission "gardens" provided a preview of the state's agriculture. "The fruits and nuts known to have been grown by the padres," writes Dr. Frank Adams, "included almost all those now produced in California, and some that have not succeeded commercially. There were pears, peaches, apples, almonds, plums, quinces, pomegranates, oranges, lemons, citrons, limes, dates, cherries, plantains, walnuts, grapes, olives, figs, strawberries and raspberries." Not only did the Franciscans demonstrate that all these crops could be produced in California, but some of the fruits now grown in the state have come directly from the mission gardens, notably the Mission grape, Mission fig, and Mission olive.

From the Spaniards, the Indians of the Southwest learned to hammer silver and copper; to work iron; and to use plows and hoes. From the Spanish the Navajo took over much of their present-day pastoral culture, including a knowledge of how to card and to weave wool. To this day, the Indians use Spanish terms to designate the colors used in their blankets: *morada subido, rosa baja, oro, amarillo, tostado, grano*. The Spanish introduced sugar cane to Louisiana and built the first sugar refinery in New Orleans in 1791. Spanish gardeners, farm laborers, blacksmiths, millwrights, and artisans brought a variety of skills to the Southwest. In fact it would take pages merely to list the things which the Spanish brought to the region that have long since been incorporated in its culture. Savants have written learned papers on what the introduction of the cat meant to the people of the New World.

What the Spaniards contributed to the Southwest, in addition to their language, religion, law, and institutions, were the seeds of things which were later of enormous importance. They were the trail blazers and seed planters. In most cases, the key to the success with which these seeds were transplanted is to be found in the similarity of the Southwest environment to that of Spain. The horses, sheep, cattle, and goats that the Spanish brought to the region, as well as the plants that they imported, were alike well adapted to the environment; and so were many of their cultural practices and institutions. That many of these seeds failed to reach full development and maturity under Spanish rule is due to a variety of factors: the intractable character of the plains and desert Indians; the dead weight of tradition; the highly centralized character of Spanish administration; the senseless restrictions imposed on initiative and innovation; the cheapness of Indian labor; and the feudal, caste-like social system which the Spanish also brought to the Southwest. That the Spanish failed to make the most of their opportunities, however, cannot detract from the importance of their prosaic accomplishments.

Still another key to the amazing success with which Spanish cultural influences were planted in the Southwest is to be found in the isolation of the borderlands. Isolated in time and space, the settlers were compelled to plant things firmly in the soil. What survived may later have appeared to be scrawny, crude, and misshapen; but it was unquestionably tough, well-adapted, and indigenous. While the form or model was often Spanish, the ultimate adaptation showed unmistakable Mexican and Indian influences. If the Spanish were the carriers of seeds and plows, Mexicans and Indians were the planters and plow hands. Beyond all doubt the culture of the Southwest, in 1848, was a trinity: a whole consisting of three intricately interwoven, interpenetrated, thoroughly fused elements. To attempts to unravel any single strand from this pattern and label it "Spanish" is, therefore, to do a serious injustice to the Mexicans and Indians through whom, and only through whom, Spanish cultural influences survived in the region. "I do not agree with all this talk about Coronado," Pablo Abeyta, the governor of the Isleta Pueblo, has said; "I don't know what they mean by Spanish culture. . . . The Spaniards got lost on the ocean and accidentally ran across the country." Whether by accident or otherwise, however, the prologue to the settlement of the borderlands is indubitably Spanish in origin.

Freedmen and Slaves in Oregon Territory, 1840–1860

QUINTARD TAYLOR

Slavery played a significant role in the European and American domination of the American West, as in the South and in Mexico. Black freedmen as well as slaves had accompanied Spanish conquistadors during their first centuries of conquest. In the eighteenth century, slaves had often preceded Euro-Americans in forays into Louisiana and Texas. On the Pacific Coast during the mid-nineteenth century, territorial politics was shaped by the question of whether territories that wished eventually to join the Union should become free or slave states. Such was the case in both Oregon and California, and so a reading on how blacks were viewed and treated in the Oregon Territory is most appropriate in this chapter on the Euro-American conquest of the American West.

The following selection by Quintard Taylor analyzes the concerns of African-American pioneers living in Oregon in the antebellum years, a time when antislavery and abolitionist forces were capturing the nation's attention. Euro-American migrants to the Pacific Northwest often came from those areas of the country most affected by slavery and antiblack attitudes, and they sought to place similar restrictions on black settlers with regard to the latters' right to vote, to own property, or even to remain in the region. Taylor describes how African Americans actively fought discrimination and did not passively accept attempts to prohibit them from exercising their rights. His study nevertheless reveals how slavery—the "peculiar institution"—persisted in the Oregon Country, which became a "free" state in 1859. Furthermore, one of the incidents that Taylor discusses provides evidence of the deep complexity characterizing social relations among blacks, Native Americans, and Euro-Americans in the Oregon Territory. This is a theme that we will explore further in other chapters.

STUDY QUESTIONS

1. How did European immigrants and Americans in Oregon discriminate against blacks?

2. In what ways did the black freedmen who had made their way to Oregon fight against such discrimination?

During the 20-year period between 1840 and 1860 the Afro-American population of the Pacific Northwest (Oregon and Washington territories) never exceeded one per cent of the total population. Yet the status of slavery, slaves, and free blacks greatly occupied, and in many instances dominated, the political debates of the region during this period. To be sure, the slavery question loomed ominously over the national political scene during these years and culminated in a bloody civil war. But the Pacific Northwest was at least 2,000 miles from either Northern or Southern states which had a vested interest in slavery's destruction or preservation.

Yet the West in general and the Pacific Northwest had always been part of the struggle, with this region being viewed by both sides as one of the major prizes. Some proslavery advocates saw the acquisition of the Oregon Country as an opportunity to establish a slave state or at least a proslavery free state in the Far West. Two antislavery groups sought influence in Oregon as well. "Popular sovereignty" advocates felt the new region fell into their sphere of influence, an area which could be settled without slavery or free blacks, while abolitionists wanted to see the region open to both blacks and whites and become a strong western bulwark against slavery. Neither the proslavery nor abolitionist interests dominated the Pacific Northwest.

From "Slaves and Free Men: Blacks in the Oregon Country, 1840–1860" by Quintard Taylor, *Oregon Historical Quarterly* 83 (1982), pp. 153–158 and 159–169.

Antislavery and antiblack popular sovereignty Democrats held sway in the region for the entire period until the Civil War brought about a major political realignment.

Most of the adult white residents in the Pacific Northwest during this period had migrated last either from four states of the "Old Northwest" (Iowa, Illinois, Indiana, and Ohio) or the border states of Kentucky, Tennessee, and Missouri, with the latter providing nearly 25% of the total non-Indian residents of Oregon Territory in 1850. These seven states had much in common including a recently experienced frontier period. . . . Migrants . . . brought their racial attitudes to the Pacific Northwest, transforming them into a series of black exclusion laws. . . .

The first code contained no prohibition against free blacks residing in the region. However, Oregon's population was growing rapidly; 900 settlers arrived by the fall of 1843, a far cry from the "63 Americans and 400 British

George Washington, an emancipated slave who migrated to Oregon Territory in 1850 and later became a wealthy farmer

subjects" that were residents. . . . When new elections were held in 1844 only two of the original nine members of the legislative committee were reelected. One of the new members, Peter H. Burnett, . . . felt a black exclusion bill necessary to "keep clear of that most troublesome class of population. We are in a new world, under most favorable circumstances, and we wish to avoid most of the evils that have so much afflicted the United States and other Countries." On June 25, 1844, he introduced a bill to prevent slavery in Oregon [that] . . . provided that persons who brought slaves to Oregon were required to remove those slaves within three years. If the owners refused, the slaves would be freed. The sixth section stated that any free black person over 18 who did not leave the territory in two years if male, and three years, if female, would be subject to trial and if found guilty would "receive upon his or her bare back not less than twenty nor more than thirty-nine stripes, to be inflicted by the constable of the proper county." Should the individual still refuse to leave, the punishment would be repeated every six months until he or she did. The next day the bill passed by a vote of six to two. The following December the "whipping" section was repealed and the law was amended to include a provision for hiring out violators at public auction, with the employer being responsible for removing the black person when his service was ended.

A major factor in the passage of the 1844 exclusion act was the Cockstock incident, a dispute between James Saules, a black settler, and Cockstock, a Wasco Indian, over ownership of a horse. The dispute precipitated the first major confrontation between Native Americans and Oregon's growing non-Indian population and resulted in the deaths of Cockstock and George LeBreton, clerk and recorder of the Oregon Provision Government. Saules had little legal claim to the disputed horse and exploited local prejudice against Native Americans by accusing Cockstock of making threats against the lives of settlers in the area. His inflammatory remarks angered Cockstock, who along with several Indians, came to Willamette Falls. In a confrontation shots and arrows were exchanged, and Cockstock was killed by Winslow Anderson, another black resident. However, LeBreton and another settler, Sterling Rogers, died of wounds received in the melee.

Local whites blamed Saules and Anderson for the incident and threatened Saules' life. Saules, who had married an Indian woman three years earlier, issued a counterthreat, claiming ability to bring the wrath of the Indians on the settlers. Local authorities charged him with threatening to incite the Indians and both Saules and Anderson were "encouraged" to leave the area. They moved to Clatsop County in northwestern Oregon.

The Cockstock affair had a number of implications for future black-white relations. White settlers were angry at the blacks for creating an incident that could have precipitated an Indian war but they were more apprehensive about a potential black-incited Indian uprising against them led by Saules or some other Afro-American. . . . [T]his fear must have played a part in the first black exclusion legislation. . . .

. . . As a result of the Treaty of 1846, Oregon was a firmly established possession of the United States and on March 2, 1849, its first territorial governor, Joseph Lane, arrived at Oregon City. During the remainder of that year a territorial legislature was organized and a delegate was sent to Congress. In September 1849 the legislature met and passed a bill to prohibit blacks and mulattoes from settling in the Territory. . . .

This law varied from the original exclusion bill of 1844 in that it was to take immediate effect and that Afro-Americans had 40 days to leave the Territory. However, blacks already residing in the Territory and their offspring were exempted. The territorial exclusion law remained in effect until supplanted by provisions of the 1859 Oregon constitution which continued the ban of black migration into the state and specifically denied black voting rights. . . .

The early Afro-American population in the Pacific Northwest was small, 58 in 1850 and 154 in 1860, but they were in a variety of occupations. That population included farmers, merchants, skilled laborers and artisans, sailors and personal servants. The largest numbers were farmers and farm laborers (17), perhaps reflecting the agricultural nature of the region's early economy and the fact that most blacks in the region were from rural areas of border states like Missouri. The second and largest groups, cooks (15) and barbers (12), resided in major towns such as Portland and Oregon City.

Two of the region's more noted early black residents, George Bush and George Washington, eventually became wealthy farmers after settling in western Washington. In 1845 George Bush was among the first party of American settlers that entered Washington Territory. Six years later George Washington settled on land in Lewis County and in 1872 founded the city of Centralia on that claim. Both men came from Missouri, and each gave as a reason for migrating to the Pacific Northwest a desire to live in an area with fewer restrictions on the free black population. Yet due to incipient racial prejudice each had difficulty in securing a claim.

George Bush brought his Caucasian wife and his family to western Washington in 1844–45. . . . Bush was a free mulatto in the slave state of Missouri in the 1830s, a period when the state legislature was encouraging emigration of "people of color." Although relatively prosperous and living in a northwestern county not dominated by slaveholders, Bush was cautious about his status and the future status of his five sons. . . . Bush saw the Oregon Country as a new land but not necessarily one that would be totally under American control, and he may not have shared what many Americans then or at a later date saw as a grand design to bring Oregon under U.S. jurisdiction. . . .

Twenty miles south of Bush Prairie another Afro-American, George Washington, settled in Lewis County in 1852. Washington was born a slave on August 15, 1817, in Frederick County, Virginia. He was emancipated and reared by a white couple, James and Anna Cochran, who in 1826 migrated to Missouri. Although Washington was granted Missouri citizenship in 1838, his difficulty as a "free man of color" forced him in 1850 to leave Missouri for the Oregon Country.

Like George Bush earlier, George Washington turned his attention toward the area north of the Columbia. . . . By moving north of the Columbia to a distant part of the Territory, Washington hoped to remain in the region until the Oregon territorial legislature either repealed the black exclusion act (as the Provisional Government had done in 1845), or passed an exemption petition, as the Missouri legislature had done for him in 1837. The Oregon territorial legislature took the latter course and passed the exemption allowing him to remain in the region on December 20, 1852.

Other black residents in Oregon found themselves subject to the territorial legal obstacles. . . . [T]hese individuals, like Bush and Washington, challenged the law. In 1851, two years after the passage of the black exclusion law by the territorial legislature, the first and only successful attempt to enforce the law was made against a black sailor, Jacob Vanderpool. Vanderpool, a West Indian, had come to Oregon in 1850 on the bark *Louisiana* and in 1851 was living at Oregon City. In August, 1851, Theophilus Magruder, a white resident of Oregon City, swore out a complaint against the sailor before Justice Thomas Nelson of the territorial court. Vanderpool was arrested and brought to trial on August 25. Although his lawyer argued that the exclusion law violated the federal Constitution and the articles of the Northwest Ordinance, and that the complaint was technically invalid since it did not specify Vanderpool was black, the judge ordered the defendant out of Oregon in 30 days. . . .

In spite of the individuals previously discussed, not all of the early Pacific Northwest blacks were either prosperous or free. . . . [T]here is ample evidence that a number of blacks brought to the Pacific Northwest between 1840 and 1860 were slaves in fact if not in name. . . . The census records for 1850 and 1860 show numerous instances of blacks living with white families; although all were listed as "servants" because of the territorial prohibition on slavery, no doubt many, if not most, were slaves regardless of the classification they were given by the census enumerators or the families with whom they lived. . . . Of the 135 blacks and mulattoes listed . . . as residing in Oregon between 1850 and 1860 at least 14 were clearly slaves. During a debate over the ban on slavery in the territorial legislature in 1858, William Allen, a representative from Yamhill County, declared that there were already slaves in Benton, Lane, Polk and Yamhill counties. Thus, in spite of laws supposedly prohibiting it, slavery existed in Oregon because the provisional and territorial governments chose not to enforce strictly the ban against it.

Blacks resisted slavery in Oregon either through the legal process or by flight. Their actions, among other reasons, kept the institution from becoming entrenched in the Pacific Northwest. Probably the most celebrated legal case was that of Robin Holmes *vs.* Nathaniel Ford. In 1844 Ford, a Missouri farmer, brought a slave couple, Robin and Polly Holmes, to Oregon. Before leaving Missouri, Ford promised freedom to the Holmes family upon their arrival in Oregon. Ford settled in the Willamette Valley and built a small cabin for the Holmeses. Although allowing them limited travel and the right to sell some of their agricultural produce, he still denied the family its promised freedom.

Finally in 1849 Ford manumitted Robin and Polly and their newborn son but refused to free the other four children, three of whom were born in Oregon Territory between 1844 and 1858. In the interim, Robin and Polly moved to Salem and opened a nursery. Harriet, one of the children still held by Ford, died on a visit to her parents in 1851. Realizing that Ford would not voluntarily free the surviving children and blaming him for the death of Harriet, Holmes brought suit in Polk County District Court the following year to gain custody of his children.

The case languished in various courts for 11 months. Finally in July, 1853, Judge George A. Williams, recently arrived Chief Justice of the Territorial Supreme Court, placed it at the head of his docket. Williams, a "Free Soil" Democrat from Iowa, decided against Ford, declaring that slavery could not exist in Oregon without specific legislation to protect it. He said: "in as much as these colored children are in Oregon, where slavery does not legally exist, they are free." Williams' decision marked the last attempt by Oregon's proslavery settlers to maintain slavery through the judicial process.

A second case involving slaves who used the legal process to establish their rights came in 1854, when a black woman, Luteshia Carson, sued the estate of her former owner. She hoped to "recover the value of her services" after working for him from 1845 until his death in 1852. The case, heard by Judge Williams, was tried before a jury which could not reach a verdict. . . . Although slavery existed in both Oregon and Washington territories, these incidents indicate that the "institution" was in a far more precarious condition than in the South.

Custer's Last Stand, 1876

ROBERT M. UTLEY

No other person's name more readily summons an image of Indian-white confrontation in western American history than that of George Armstrong Custer. Cinematic, pictorial, literary, and historical portrayals of his "last stand" at the Little Bighorn River in 1876 abound, yet each generation produces more such interpretations as this quintessential westerner and his Seventh Cavalry, juxtaposed against Sitting Bull's Sioux and other Indian allies, still elude a wholly satisfactory analysis. In the next reading, frontier and military historian Robert M. Utley provides a straightforward and thoughtful narrative of this famous battle that affords useful insights about the Native American actors who have been all too frequently slighted or misunderstood by early investigators. (The original work from which the selection was excerpted closely examines all aspects of the battle.)

The news of Custer's defeat shocked a nation hitherto confident that the war against the "wild Indians" of the western plains and mountains was nearing an inevitable victory. Dismay and surprise underlie much of the fascination that the reports from the Little Bighorn held for Custer's countrymen: how could this commander and his presumably peerless regiment blunder into military debacle? Utley notes that the continuing strenuous efforts to explain Custer's fall in terms of military failures in tactics, strategy, and leadership have overlooked the simple fact that the cavalry lost primarily because the Indians defeated them. The allied tribes were strongly motivated, well armed, and ably led. That many Americans still perceive the battle as a seemingly inexplicable aberration in the conquest of Indian America, rather than as a symbol of Native American resistance to aggression, attests to the power of the enduring myth of the frontier as Anglo-American progress in "taming" a "savage" wilderness and its aboriginal inhabitants.

STUDY QUESTIONS

1. How does the description of the Battle of the Little Bighorn fit with your own image of the nature of battles between Euro-Americans and Native Americans on the plains?

2. For what reasons were the Indians who defeated Custer fighting?

On May 14, 1876, the Seventh Cavalry, all twelve companies brought together for the first time, shivered in a tent city laid out with military precision on the Missouri River flats two miles below Fort Lincoln. Cold rains soaked the valley into a quagmire, immobilizing the heavily loaded supply wagons and casting uncertainty over the departure set for next day. On this wet morning Mark Kellogg, reporter for the *Bismarck Tribune* and also representative of the *New York Herald*, wrote in his dispatch of the day of a newly reenergized Indian fighter:

> Gen. George A. Custer, dressed in a dashing suit of buckskin, is prominent everywhere. Here, there, flitting to and fro, in his quick eager way, taking in everything connected with his command, as well as generally, with the keen, incisive manner for which he is so well known. The General is full of perfect readiness for a fray with the hostile red devils, and woe to the body of scalp-lifters that comes within reach of himself and brave companions in arms.

Kellogg caught the spirit of the Seventh and its leader, dampened only by the rains that delayed the departure of the Dakota Column. Three days later, although still threatening, the weather freed the expedition to head for the Sioux country. . . .

As Sitting Bull's following made its way slowly up the Rosebud through early June, a scattering of people arrived from the agencies. Others left, however, on hunting forays, to scout the enemy's movements, and even to trade for arms and ammunition at distant points on the Missouri River. The size of the village, therefore, remained about four hundred tipis. . . .

On the back trail from the Rosebud down Reno Creek, and down the Little Bighorn itself, the agency Indians converged on their destination. They came in small groups and large, trailing on the ground behind them, in a chaos of size, direction, and age, the marks of their progress. It was this jumble of Indian sign, abruptly intruding on and muddling the easily read trail of the Sitting Bull bands up the Rosebud, that perplexed Custer and his officers on the afternoon of June 24.

Over a span of only six days Sitting Bull's village more than doubled, from 400 to 1,000 lodges, from 3,000 to 7,000 people, from 800 to 2,000 warriors. In 6 separate tribal circles they crowded the narrow valley of the Little Bighorn. Hunkpapas, Oglalas, Miniconjous, Sans Arcs, Blackfeet, Two Kettles, Brules, and a scattering of Yanktonnais and Santees (Sioux, but not Tetons) made up the 5 Sioux circles, while 120 Cheyenne lodges rounded out the array. Even a handful of Arapahoes cast their lot with their friends.

From *Cavalier in Buckskin: George Armstrong Custer and the Western Military Frontier*, by Robert M. Utley, pp. 165, 178–180, and 187–193. Copyright © 1988 by the University of Oklahoma Press.

The tribal leaders had planned to move even farther up the river, toward the Bighorn Mountains (exactly where General Terry had expected to find them). Scouts, however, brought word of antelope herds to the north and west, downstream. On June 24, therefore, as Custer puzzled over the scarred valley on the other side of the Rosebud divide, they moved the village northward, back down the Little Bighorn in the direction from which they had come.

The new location afforded an appealing setting. The upper end of the camp, anchored by the Hunkpapa circle, lay about two miles below the mouth of Reno Creek. The rest of the tipis sprawled along the west bank of the river for nearly three miles downstream. On the west the valley ended in low grassy hills and benches where the huge pony herd grazed. On the eastern edge of the valley, the river, cold and brimming with the spring runoff from the Bighorn Mountains, meandered among thickets of shady cottonwood trees. A series of ragged bluffs rose steeply from the east bank of the river to a height of some three hundred feet.

There in the valley of the pretty stream the Sioux called the Greasy Grass lay a village of unusual size. Such numbers consumed immense quantities of game, forage, and firewood and so could not remain long in one place, or even together in one village. It had come together in this strength only in the few days preceding, and it could stay together for more than a few days or a week only through luck, frequent moves, and constant labor. White apologists, seeking to explain the disaster this coalition of tribes wrought, would later endow it with an immensity it never approached. Still, it was big by all standards of the time, and it was more than twice as big as any of the army officers looking for it had anticipated.

Equally significant, the village contained a people basking proudly in the fullness of tribal power. Contrary to the assumptions and the mindset of the [military], the Indians felt little inclination to avoid conflict. Their grievances united them in a determination to fight against those who would seize the Black Hills and send soldiers to force them out of the unceded territory, where even the white people's paper conceded their right to roam.

The coincidence of timing that brought the Seventh Cavalry to the vicinity of this village during the few days of its peak strength was only the beginning of a run of ill fortune that ended in the utter collapse of "Custer's Luck."

> "Passed several large camps," recorded Custer's itinerist, Lieutenant George D. Wallace, as the Seventh Cavalry made its way up the Rosebud on the afternoon of June 24. "The trail was now fresh, and the whole valley scratched up by the trailing lodge poles." The Crows pushed far in advance, seeking more information for the expectant Custer.

Shortly, after nightfall the Crows rode into the Seventh's bivouac on the Rosebud. They related exactly what Custer needed to know. Ahead the Indian trail veered to the west and followed a tributary of the Rosebud over a low mountain pass toward the Little Bighorn. Fading daylight had prevented the scouts from learning more. . . .

The Crows had presented Custer with critical intelligence. It placed the Indians on the Little Bighorn, as assumed. But the freshness of the trail meant that they could not be on the *upper* Little Bighorn. They, or a large part of them, had to be on the *lower* Little Bighorn, hardly a day's ride to the west. . . .

. . . The Crow scouts, released by Custer from the coming fight, watched part of it from a slope overlooking Medicine Tail Coulee from the south, but their recollections were badly garbled. The Indians who fought Custer left equally confused stories. Even so, the Indian accounts are vital pieces of the puzzle. When added to other pieces—the placement of the bodies on the battlefield, the testimony of Reno's survivors, and archaeological evidence plotted on topographical maps—they provide a basis for informed speculation. Indeed, one problem is not too little evidence but too much. Following is what may have happened.

Shortly after sending Trumpeter Martin back for Benteen and the packs, Custer divided his command. He sent Yates's two-company battalion galloping down Medicine Tail Coulee toward the Little Bighorn, and he posted Captain Keogh's three-company battalion on a ridge separating Medicine Tail from the next drainage to the north, Deep Coulee. Keogh's troopers took up dismounted positions overlooking Medicine Tail and the mouth of the ravine they had just descended from the bluff tops.

These dispositions probably reflected news Custer received shortly after reaching Medicine Tail. Boston Custer, who had been with the packtrain, had hurried to join his brothers as soon as it became apparent that a battle was about to take place. Trumpeter Martin met him on the ride back to Benteen. Boston would have informed Custer that Benteen had ended his scout to the left, returned to the main trail, and now, followed by the packtrain, was riding toward the scene of action.

A plausible theory is that Custer intended Yates to hold the ford and threaten the Indians, thus relieving the pressure on Reno, until Benteen could come up and join in a powerful thrust into the village itself. Keogh's mission was to cover Benteen's approach route and then accompany him to the attack position. Whether Custer went with Yates or remained with Keogh is unknown.

Whatever Custer's plans, two crucial developments elsewhere doomed them.

First, Benteen dawdled on the back trail, falling farther and farther behind the rest of the regiment. Sergeant Kanipe, en route to McDougall, told Benteen about the battle taking shape ahead, but that news failed to stir the battalion's pace from a leisurely walk. When Trumpeter Martin dashed up with Cooke's urgent summons, Benteen ordered a trot. Only a gallop would have been responsive to Custer's expectation, and even that pace might not have brought Benteen to Medicine Tail in time.

Second, Reno did not hold his position at the upper end of the village. Flanked on the skirmish line, after fifteen minutes he withdrew into the timber along the river. Then, pressed by Sioux for half an hour or more, he ordered a retreat. It turned into a demoralized rout back across the river to the bluff tops from which Custer had first looked over the valley. The "charge," as Reno termed it, cost forty dead and thirteen wounded. . . .

The actions of his two subordinates left Custer to fend for himself. Reno's retreat freed all the Indians to concentrate on Custer. Benteen's languor brought him to Reno's hilltop position and thus under Reno's command. The demoralization of Reno's shattered battalion, combined with the indecision of the two ranking officers, kept seven companies and the pack-train, which also reached the bluff tops, out of action at the most critical moment for the other five.

Yates's two companies reached the Little Bighorn at the mouth of Medicine Tail Coulee, roughly opposite the center of the Indian camp. A hot fire greeted them from warriors posted in the brush on the other side. The bullets flew so thickly, recalled a Sioux participant, "that the head of his command reeled back toward the bluffs after losing several men who tumbled into the water." Sitting Bull later described the action succinctly: "Our young men rained lead across the river and drove the white braves back."

At first only a handful of warriors, perhaps thirty, held the ford against Yates. But they quickly received help as men returned from the pony herd with their mounts, and others, freed by Reno's withdrawal, reached the new scene of action. The Hunkpapa Gall rallied the forces and led them across the river.

Back from the river Yates's two companies retreated, returning a ragged defensive fire as they rode, dismounting skirmishers to hold back the Indian advance. The soldiers "held their horses' reins on one arm while they were shooting," remembered Low Dog, "but the horses were so frightened that they pulled the men all around, and a great many of their shots went up in the air and did us no harm." The line of this fighting retreat lay up the northern slope of Deep Coulee toward a high ridge that offered the prospect of a better position.

Gall's warriors also hit Keogh, posted on the heights between Medicine Tail and Deep Coulee. From dismounted skirmish lines the troopers laid down a heavy fire, including some volley firing, that kept the Indians at bay. Although not seriously threatened, Keogh probably realized that Yates was in trouble and that the Indians gathering in Deep Coulee, to his rear, might isolate the two battalions from each other. After half an hour or more Keogh began to withdraw northward toward a union with Yates.

Gall's warriors pressed closely. On the slope north of Deep Coulee, Keogh dismounted and formed a line. The Indians fired into the horsehold-ers and dropped enough men to stampede the horses and put much of the battalion on foot. With the horses went the extra carbine ammunition.

Rain in the Face, a Sioux warrior who fought at the battle of Little Bighorn

"After this," related Gall, "the soldiers threw aside their guns [carbines] and fought with little guns [pistols]." Dismounted, Keogh's men moved up the slope to join with Yates.

The union occurred on a flat hill, tilted toward the river and overlooking Deep Coulee, that is now named Calhoun Hill. . . . Calhoun Hill formed the southern nose of a high ridge extending half a mile northward. This elevation came to be known as Battle Ridge, commanding a sweeping vista of the river valley and the Bighorn Mountains beyond, Battle Ridge fell abruptly, amid tumbles of steep hills and deep ravines, to the valley below. On the east a narrow ravine heading on Calhoun Hill bordered Battle Ridge and widened and deepened as it ran northward. On Calhoun Hill, Battle Ridge, and the slopes on the east and the west, the final scenes of Custer's Last Stand unfolded.

What role Custer himself played can never be known. Almost certainly no Indian recognized "Long Hair" in the smoke, dust, grime, and excitement of battle, or indeed even knew they were fighting his soldiers. As hinted in some Indian accounts, he may even have fallen, dead or wounded, in the first fire at the mouth of Medicine Tail Coulee and been carried to the spot where his body was found. If he remained in the saddle on Calhoun Hill, he must by now have recognized how desperate, indeed hopeless, his plight. Faced with overpowering numbers of well-armed warriors, caught in rough terrain unsuited to cavalry, partly dismounted, and with no trace of Benteen or the packs on the hills to the south, even Custer's robust self-confidence must have wavered. . . .

The warriors made few if any grand mounted charges. Rather, they kept up a long-range fire, mostly from dismounted positions. They took advantage of hillocks, sagebrush clumps, tall grass, and folds and troughs of the terrain. From these hiding places they struck down the cavalrymen with bullets and arrows. Many had rifles, some Winchester and Henry repeaters, others carbines and pistols taken from Reno's dead in the valley, and still others old trade muskets. Arrows took heavy toll. Loosed in high arcs, they fell with deadly effect on clusters of exposed troopers.

The soldiers fought back with a bravery that earned high tribute from Sitting Bull himself. They were veterans, not readily stampeded if they had able leadership. Confusion, scattered pockets of panic, and even a few suicides probably occurred. But the stories of mass suicide and mass hysteria that spared the foe serious casualties flowed from a few self-serving Indian accounts or simply from faulty interpreters. Other Indian testimony, combined with burials discovered in the vicinity of the battlefield and along the Indians' route of retreat, indicate that at least one hundred Indians, and possibly many more, were killed or died later of their wounds.

The fatal blow hit from the north. Crazy Horse had led a large force of warriors down the Little Bighorn valley to a crossing below the village, forded the river, and swept in a wide arc to climb Battle Ridge from the north. They struck the units with Custer and Yates and thrust up the ravine on the east leading to Calhoun Hill. There they crushed Keogh's men against Gall's warriors beyond.

Although each of the companies made its "last stand," the last stand of history and legend occurred at the northern end of Battle Ridge, now known as Custer Hill. There most of Company F, part of E, and remnants of the other companies gathered with the headquarters group. Whether in panic or deliberate counterattack, a large contingent broke toward the head of the deep ravine in the direction of the river. "We finished up this party right there in the ravine," said Red Horse. . . .

The hot June sun hung low over the Bighorn Mountains when the last man fell, possibly two hours after Yates had opened the battle at the mouth of Medicine Tail Coulee. Exultant warriors raced their ponies around the battlefield, dispatching wounded men, firing their rifles in triumph, and raising great clouds of dust. Women and children made their way up the slopes from the village to rob, strip, and mutilate the bodies.

Four miles to the south, a trace of blue appeared atop a peaked hill beyond Medicine Tail Coulee. Hearing firing from the north and irate over Reno's indecision, Tom Weir had simply mounted his company, D, and moved to the sound of the guns. The rest of the command had followed hesitantly. Reaching the high hill later named Weir Point, the troops scanned the rugged terrain beyond. It rose to distant hills and ridges obscured by rolling dust. Indistinctly amid the dust, recalled Lieutenant Winfield Scott Edgerly, "We saw a good many Indians galloping up and down and firing at objects on the ground." Then, as Lieutenant Edward S. Godfrey recalled, "clouds of dust arose from all parts of the field, and the horsemen converged toward our position."

Falling back to their original hilltop position, the seven companies fought desperately until darkness brought relief. During the night they entrenched, and next day they held out as the emboldened Sioux and Cheyennes tried to carry their defenses. Reno displayed weak leadership. Benteen, fearlessly stalking the lines as Indian sharpshooters tried to drop him, inspired the troopers to valiant efforts. By midafternoon the firing had tapered off.

In the valley the Indians fired the dry prairie grass. A wall of thick smoke screened the village. About 7:00 P.M. an immense procession of horsemen, women and children on foot, travois, ponies, and dogs emerged from behind the smoke. Slowly it wound up the slope on the west side of the valley and made its way across the benchland to the southwest, toward the Bighorn Mountains.

Next morning, June 27, a blue column approaching up the valley explained the hasty withdrawal of the Indians. Some on Reno Hill believed it was Custer at last. Others thought Terry. A few even guessed Crook. Two officers rode down to investigate. A short gallop brought them to the leading ranks of the Second Cavalry, General Terry in the van. Both general and lieutenants burst out with the same question: Where is Custer?

Lieutenant Bradley and his Crow scouts brought the answer, and on the morning of June 28 Reno and his men rode down the river to see for themselves. "A scene of sickening ghastly horror," Lieutenant Godfrey remembered. The bodies, many of them stripped, scalped, and mutilated, all grotesquely bloated from the burning sun, lay scattered about the battlefield where they had dropped.

Undiscovered until next day was the body of Mark Kellogg, the correspondent who was to report Custer's great victory over "the hostile red devils." In unintended irony the "scalp lifters" he had ridiculed on the eve of the campaign had repaid the compliment. Except for cutting off an ear, they had not mutilated him. They had only lifted his scalp.

On Custer Hill the knot of fallen men graphically portrayed the drama of the last stand. Although Cooke and Tom Custer had been badly butchered, most in this group escaped severe mutilation. "The bodies were as recognizable as if they were in life," Benteen wrote to his wife.

Although naked, "The General was not mutilated at all," Lieutenant Godfrey later wrote. "He laid on his back, his upper arms on the ground, the hands folded or so placed as to cross the body above the stomach: his position was natural and one that we had seen hundreds of times while [he was] taking cat naps during halts on the march. One hit was in the front of the left temple, and one in the left breast at or near the heart."

A third wound may have been invisible to Godfrey and the others who looked down on their former chief. The Cheyenne woman Kate Big Head related that two Southern Cheyenne women recognized Custer from his campaign in the Indian Territory in 1868–69. At that time he had been much admired by the women taken captive at the Washita, who had envied Monahsetah her good fortune in gaining the affection of the long-haired white chief. Thinking of Monahsetah, the two women prevented some Sioux men from mutilating the body by explaining that he was their relative. Continued Kate Big Head:

> The women then pushed the point of a sewing awl into each of his ears into his head. This was done to improve his hearing, as it seemed he had not heard what our chiefs in the South said when he smoked the pipe with them. They told him then that if ever afterward he should break that peace promise and should fight the Cheyennes the Everywhere Spirit surely would cause him to be killed.

 # Women Missionaries and Cultural Conquest, 1900–1914

SARAH DEUTSCH

When we think of conquests and invasions, whether they be military, political, or economic in nature, we usually picture male protagonists. Although we are aware that women teachers, nurses, or missionaries often entered other societies to serve and transform them, we seldom think of women as the main agents of social change.

In the following excerpts, however, Sarah Deutsch points out that in certain parts of what became the American Southwest, Euro-American women missionaries "often found themselves not just the only Anglo women, but the only Anglos at all in their Hispanic villages. They were not merely the vanguard; they were the whole army." It was these women who first tried to impose Protestant Christianity and American culture on the people already living in the Southwest. Deutsch's study not only uncovers the key role played by "Anglo" women in the Euro-American conquest and settlement of the region but also reveals how Spanish-speaking and Native American women coped with this cultural invasion.

Beyond bringing women into the picture, Deutsch introduces a framework that views the "frontier" not as a place where one culture subjugated another but as one where two or more cultures interacted, each mutually influencing the other. In her view, there was not just an Anglo frontier but a Hispanic frontier as well: as Hispanic villagers found work in the developing capitalist economy, they spread out geographically. Members of many families migrated to work seasonally in other areas and in the growing urban centers. In the process, they created a "community bound by ties of kinship as well as economy"—a community based on "mutual dependency" between "migrants and villagers." Deutsch's work is important because the pattern that she has identified and described has distinguished other communities of color as well.

STUDY QUESTIONS

1. What does the author mean in saying that Anglo women missionaries saw their work as a "moral imperative"?

2. Why did the women missionaries concentrate on changing Hispanic women rather than men?

3. Deutsch states, "According to popular stereotypes of the time, all but the most elite Hispanic women were voluptuous, poor, dirty, and morally lax." Do you think that such stereotypes still exist? If so, give examples. If not, how has the situation changed?

"Had I been set down upon some other planet," Harriet Benham marveled in 1900, "the country, the people and their customs would, probably, not have been stranger to me than those of New Mexico." Foreign in language and dress, Catholic in heritage and fact, Hispanic New Mexico seemed to many Americans not harmlessly peculiar, but a threat to national unity and virtue. Such a threat created its own imperatives, demanded a second conquest. It was the Protestant churches who claimed the privilege.

By 1900, churches in the United States had come to think of mission fields as frontiers of Christian civilization and missionaries as a vanguard. Anglo Protestants spoke in one breath of Americanizing and of "Christianizing" New Mexico, of conquering this frontier. Presbyterian minister George McAfee exulted biblically in 1903, "The whole land is before us. Shall we go up and possess it?" Through church and school, the Protestants hoped for a more effective conquest, one that would bring the recalcitrant former Mexicans firmly into the English-speaking Protestant nation spiritually and culturally as well as geographically.

. . . [B]y and large it was women who went up and did the possessing. In New Mexico in 1900 nineteen of twenty-one mission schools were run by women. Over two hundred mission women came to New Mexico and southern Colorado between 1900 and 1914 alone. These women, as Rev. Robert Craig explained in 1903, were "compelled in the prosecution of their work to invade a foreign speaking community and to overcome time honored prejudices." The mission women were not always comfortable with their new role as invaders, but they recognized a moral imperative. Congregationalist Honora deBusk, after describing a "picturesque and quaint" New Mexico village scene with children's "happy voices ringing out in the clear cold air," continued, "if we did not know the awful sinfulness and the real soul hunger of the people . . . it would seem too bad for us to invade such an Arcadia." Since these women felt they did "know so well the depravity of their [Hispanic] lives," the apparent idyllic nature of village life proved an inadequate defense for Hispanics on this women's frontier. . . .

Representatives of this invading force often found themselves not just the only Anglo women, but the only Anglos at all in their Hispanic villages. There they were not merely the vanguard; they were the whole army. In the Hispanic heartland and the women's world of the northern New Mexico villages, the most direct intercultural contact was thus female. Examining the missionaries themselves as well as the contact reveals the significance of the female nature of this frontier, for the character of the assailants intimately affected the ways in which villagers were able to protect the village from the cultural threat within as they protected it in the larger context by the regional community and its migratory networks. While other Anglos determined the nature of cultural interaction elsewhere in the regional community, in the villages it was the missionaries whose backgrounds, attitudes, aims, and actions, in conjunction with those of the villagers, formed the pattern of relations.

The missionaries proclaimed a multiple purpose for their schools in New Mexico:

> to convince of a full and free salvation through the savior of the Cross; to make true American citizens, intelligent and enthusiastic supporters of our institutions, and to give a moral and technical education that will enable them to cope with the social temptations and problems of the twentieth century.

Such a mission, frequently consolidated under the rubric of teaching Hispanics "what real living is," obviously went beyond the purely religious. To these missionaries, the task of creating "in a generation or two . . . good American citizens and loyal servants of Christ" required that they "change in every respect the homes and habits of these Mexicans.". . . [T]he women who came to New Mexico drew no distinction between the religious and the secular facets of their message. . . .

And yet for all their enthusiastic evangelical patriotism, the missionaries recognized that many back east did not see their schools as true mission work. It seemed to these doubters that at least part of this multidimensional mission in New Mexico should have been performed by the public sector. . . . [But] in 1912, the year of statehood, seven school districts in mountainous Rio Arriba County had no schools, and nine-tenths of the schools with teachers met for three months or less. The county had no public high school until 1917. Unable to collect the requisite tax levy, cash-poor Rio Arriba lost matching state aid for education. Other Hispanic counties of northern New Mexico enjoyed a similar dearth of facilities.

The attitude of teachers, too, was not uniformly constructive. Anglo teachers tended to regard "teaching Spanish American children . . . as a last resort," an educator revealed in 1915. Some of these reluctant "missionaries" considered Hispanic children sadly lacking "the spirit of liberty and that love of education . . . the ambition . . . courage and determination," in short "the aspirations of the Pilgrims" that presumably came to Anglo children as their "birthright." Such teachers, according to another educator in 1912, led Spanish-American children "to believe that they can not do as well as others."

On the other hand, the resulting lack of qualified teachers did not imbue villagers with great respect of public education. Children were kept home from school by parents who relied on them for various agricultural and domestic chores such as herding goats, planting and harvesting, and doing the laundry. One villager remembered with devastating candor, "very few people would go to the public schools. They just didn't learn, the teachers did not know how to teach, they were not educated. . . . [Thus] the way lay open for the women missionaries.

By 1902, 1500 New Mexican children attended mission schools. That year, twelve requests for schools from unserved villages reached the Presbyterian Women's Board of Home Missions, by far the most active in the field. But the impact of the schools reached beyond the sites and certainly beyond the approximately 1400 Hispanic converts. Matilda Allison's Presbyterian school for Hispanic girls in Santa Fe had seventy-seven pupils from twenty-eight plazas and towns; only slightly over a third were Presbyterian. Since many had the resources to attend for only a year, former pupils scattered over the landscape. In plaza day schools, students were largely Catholic, but mission teachers who stayed in one village, as Sue Zuver did for nineteen years, found they had taught nearly the entire village. In addition, graduates of Presbyterian schools, particularly the high schools, were in great demand. In 1909, mission teachers in Chimayo found that five of the public schools near them had former mission pupils as teachers, and of fifty-five teachers at the annual teachers' institute for Taos County three years later, fifty-one had attended Protestant mission schools. The Anglo women missionaries represented a cultural contact at once diffuse and intense, one that penetrated deeply into the Hispanic hinterland and found few Anglo competitors for influence.

The mission schools, in their teaching force and organization, stood in direct contrast to the villages' school system. Hispanic schools were locally controlled and often staffed, through political patronage, with sons, daughters, wives, or widows of long-established families. While Hispanic women occasionally served on county school boards after receiving school suffrage in 1912, and the feminization of the Hispanic teaching force proceeded with relative rapidity between 1912 and 1916, even in the latter year only 34 percent of Rio Arriba County's public school teachers were women. The Presbyterian schools, in contrast, were controlled by the women of the Women's Board of Home Missions in distant New York. Approximately 80 percent of the teachers were single Anglo women in their twenties, most of whom came from the Midwest or Pennsylvania and spoke no Spanish on arrival in the villages. The missionaries at once feminized and Anglicized the teaching force and education in general in northern New Mexico.

The feminine nature of the mission force was no accident. "The teachers," declared the Presbyterians in 1905, "—faithful, gentle, persevering, brave, unfaltering . . . are the power used to drive the wedge." This was to be an invasion propelled by the "pedagogy of love," the "nurturant approach," which had gained favor with American educators elsewhere in the mid-nineteenth century accompanying the shift in emphasis from role learning to moral inculcation. Only the American woman, as "the natural and appropriate guardian of the young . . . who has those tender sympathies . . . who has that conscientiousness and religious devotion," as reformer Catharine Beecher had put it, could inspire in the children the virtue "indispensable to the safety of a democratic government like ours." This tradition of moralism and more personal pedagogy was clearly what the Presbyterians called forth when, recognizing that Hispanics were more eager for Anglo knowledge than Anglo religion, they insisted "that where the preacher can not go the teacher may, and with *her* loving service and ready sympathy win the love and confidence of the people."

Teaching itself was already regarded as a highly respectable calling for women among Anglos, and missionaries cut a heroic figure on speaking tours throughout the United States. For girls imbued with both the optimistic, adventurous activism of the 1890s and a spirituality derived from missionary or ministerial relatives, or simply from the centrality of the church in the small-town social life of the midwest, the opportunity to become a missionary seemed a shimmering promise. . . .

Mission women found themselves living in adobe houses and "trying to cook on an open fireplace" in villages where infant mortality ranked among the highest in the nation, and typhoid, diphtheria, and malaria swept with depressing regularity. The teachers' home in Truchas did not have running water or electricity until 1922, and the house in Holman lacked indoor plumbing until the late 1930s. Yet the women seemed to glory in overcoming these difficulties, to glory in a strength that was not only spiritual. . . .

These devout and independent invaders were also proud of their professionalism, for mission teaching was a "calling" in this sense as well. Most of these women had taught in public or in mission schools before coming to New Mexico, or had trained in normal schools. Even those women who had not trained as academic teachers, but as musicians or matrons, insisted their professional training be used and refused mission work outside it. . . .

Their spirituality drove the missionaries to New Mexico, but other attributes equally influenced their impact there. Not just their independence and professionalism, but their pride in those characteristics shaped them as models of Anglo womanhood in the village. Whatever other contrary images they attempted to convey would suffer by comparison with their own vivid example.

When these professionals arrived on the field, they at first experienced certain difficulties in finding acceptance in the villages. Some problems were due to lack of preparation. In her first year at San Juan, Colorado, Mollie Clements was "thankful that I could smile . . . for not knowing the language, to smile was about all I could do!" Other difficulties had their basis in moral and cultural concerns. In 1900 Anna McNair reported, "[W]hen our mission teachers visit the homes in some of the plazas they feel the stigma put upon them by the priests, through the frown that greets them, and the fingers held firmly in the form of the cross until they leave the house." Slotted into the category of "witch," the missionaries found the villagers at new sites less than open. Eventually, however, villagers chose other slots for women missionaries to fill, and by the 1920s, if not before, the "witches" had become, in the words of the villagers. "Protestant nuns." . . .

In their anxiety to prove themselves as valid, courageous, and heroic as those missionaries in more remote stations, these women at times magnified their adventures for the audience back east. Some of these fantasies found an outlet in short pieces of fiction created for mission magazines, often by women with little actual experience on the field. In such stories, for example, women missionaries who lived alone in New Mexico faced stoning and death from the hostile villagers, although actually only two women missionaries were known to have had anything like such dangerous encounters in the eighty years these women served in New Mexico, and in both of these cases the perpetrators were outsiders to the village. Other stories depicted an oppressive and barren life for Hispanics and an exaggeratedly humble gratitude for the mission presence. The stories brought out the fundamental racism of the period, in which many of the women missionaries participated, enhanced by the mission need to emphasize the "otherness" or foreignness of their subjects at the same time they struggled to eliminate it.

Some of the missionaries had faith that Anglo settlement would in itself sufficiently improve the "natives." Josephine Orton wrote from Tierra Amarilla of a "general awakening on the part of the native population toward a bettering of their condition," apparently stimulated largely by the fact that "with the opening up of large tracts of land for settlement in this vicinity, there is a healthy influx of Americans and foreigners, a good working class, who have come here hoping to build up homes." . . .

This conviction of their own superiority often led to a self-imposed isolation and loneliness that not only impeded but precluded their cultural mission. Like other frontier women, separated by living styles so different that missionaries were convinced "no American could live as they do," these Anglo women resisted integration and found their most "trying ordeal was being shut off from associates of like interests." "I confess to you," one missionary wrote the Board, "It is a dreadfully lonesome place."

Anglo women, however, were more likely than men to overcome the popular images of Hispanics planted in their minds and to retain at least an ambivalence toward Hispanics and Hispanic culture marked by a like ambivalence toward their own. Firmly rooted in America's Victorian ideology of domesticity, the women missionaries' vision was of a world more nurturing and less competitive than that outside the walls of middle-class homes. They had less of a stake than Anglo men in defining civilization and progress as cutthroat competition for commercial ends. While the men, including the men of the church, were more likely to note waste of New Mexico's "latent resources" and see in them a "Mexican" who lacked "a vista, an ambition," some of the women found their preconceptions modified by the universal "efforts at homemaking," the "clean white walls," and "carefully tended plants." In direct contrast to the men, at least one of these Anglo women missionaries concluded, "I believe the majority of the people have high aspirations." The communal sharing of wages and other resources so criticized by the industrialist seemed to many women to be virtues. "They give their best to their guests, they treat strangers kindly, and to the poor they give freely," praised Harriet Benham. Some of these Anglo women were less than enchanted with "our exceedingly hygienic methods of living," with "Americans who have located in New Mexico with a view only of money-making," with, in short, "the merciless white man." They could more easily than Anglo men admire an industriousness that did not hinge on industrialism or large-scale commercial agriculture. Ambivalent toward both their own and the Hispanic culture, they did not merely seek to perpetuate the civilization from which they had come, nor did they wish to leave unchanged what they found.

The women missionaries, in fact, determined to take over the direction of the entire village and to reshape it, in a brand of miniature empire building. If male empire builders evinced paternalism, then this was maternalism. "'She is the mother of us all,' is heard constantly on the lips of the people," Alice Blake revealed, "till one comes to feel one's self so much a necessity that it is hard to go away even for the needed vacation." These women, often trapped by their sense of necessity and their divinely appointed mission, tried to deliver a female version of the imperial message. The female nature of this cross-cultural contact influenced both the particular targets chosen and the nature of the culture conveyed.

Mission boards recruited women by urging each "to respond to the plea of her sister who, 'suffering as a slave or beast, knows not the meaning of womanhood.'" The New Mexico missionaries' perceptions of Hispanic women's lot lay firmly within the more general secular tendency to credit Christianity with "the elevated status of Western women" and to deplore "the depraved condition of women in heathen lands." Hostility to education for women, the loveless marriage, cruel, non-Protestant husbands, and tyrannical parents or parents-in-law became stock elements in missionary literature of such diverse fields as China, Africa, and New Mexico.

According to popular stereotypes of the time, all but the most elite Hispanic women were voluptuous, poor, dirty, and morally lax. Hispanic men were lazy, filthy, stupid, cowardly, and conniving. To mission women in New Mexico who had grown unaccustomed to women working outside the home, it did seem that Hispanic women were forced to do the men's work, while the men were not men enough to make sufficient provision for them to stay within doors. Missionaries complained, too, that the tyranny of the mother-in-law, if not the other members of the family, made marriage "little more than slavery." . . .

Mission women determined to wrest control of child-rearing, in part, at least, so that they could remedy the perceived abuses of womanhood along with the other flaws in Hispanic culture. Some complained of brutal parents, others of Hispanics "disposed to be too lenient with their children." It did not really matter. If the Hispanic child were to grow up to be "American," if the missionaries were to succeed in their mission, the children had to be trained by representatives of that culture, that is, by the Anglo women, and not by their own parents.

The obvious answer was the boarding school. It may have seemed to the Anglo women a natural choice and an easy adjustment, given the system of fostering which they at first perceived as resulting from parents "nearly devoid of a feeling of responsibility for their families, if only they can shift it onto someone else." They soon found, however, that parents were reluctant to leave their children at the schools. . . .

. . . [C]ultural disputes over child-rearing methods placed the Anglo missionaries and the Hispanic mothers in direct conflict as teachers and, more particularly, as women. Parents were naturally loathe not only to part with their children, but to leave them for the day or overnight in the hands of those whose teaching in both spiritual and secular matters would counter their own, and who would, if they could, usurp authority and control. Only the tremendous value placed on education and the opportunities it afforded both boys and girls kept the Presbyterian boarding schools full to overflowing and the Presbyterian day schools packed. By the constant instruction in religion and manner—aggression rather than reserve for both girls and boys—as the parents feared, and missionary Alice Hyson reported, "the child's mind in many cases is divided, because they must decide who is right, the mother or the teacher." Hispanic parents and missionaries were simply fulfilling their socially assigned roles as cultural bearers and conveyors, but the cultures were in competition.

Women missionaries made special efforts to bring Hispanic girls into the day schools as well. They believed, at least in part, in the maxim, "Educate a man and you educate an individual; educate a woman and you educate a family." In the 1880s, the Anglo women had found Hispanics reluctant to send their girls to school. The villagers had viewed education as unnecessary for the village-centered functions of the women and gazed askance at coeducational school rooms. By the turn of the century, however, parents had changed their minds. Missionaries had argued the need for female literacy to enable women to take their places in the modern world and to teach and provide nurses for the villages, and by 1900 the men and women villagers agreed. One Hispanic woman moved into town with her daughters, telling, not asking, her husband. "I don't want them to be raised like tontitas [dummies]," she insisted. Another woman, who had at times been responsible for her own livelihood, wanted her girls educated in order to be independent. By 1900 the villagers realized that the maintenance of the relatively egalitarian relations between the sexes demanded that both sexes "benefit from the more modern training."

Although the missionaries emphasized the need for literacy and the training of independent women, the strongest message they broadcast, perhaps even stronger than the strictly spiritual message, was quite different. "The native girls need Christian help no less than the boys," wrote Judge William Pope in *Home Mission Monthly,* "that they may make homes for coming generations." The Allison School gave a regular academic course, but the Home Mission Board's male superintendent, Mr. Allaben, insisted that the Allison School's "emphasis should be on home economics and general training for homemaking," which included the use of an adobe oven, that the girls might "be expert in native cooking if they are to prove equal to home demands." And when the Anglo women set out to educate Hispanic girls, what they, too, had in mind was education for domesticity. The future roles they allocated to Hispanic women were quite clear: "better housekeepers, more devoted mothers, and more intelligent and economical wives."

Housekeeping, mothering, and wifehood encompassed a far more limited round of activities than the Hispanic women and certainly than the Anglo missionaries habitually enjoyed. But the Anglos blamed Hispanic poverty, at least in part, on the idleness and mismanagement of these village women and the laziness of their husbands. In their schools, as they trained the girls in homemaking, the missionaries trained the boys to manage the traditional female fields of gardens and poultry. They spoke in this context of ". . . training the young men, and . . . developing the young women among the Spanish Americans in Colorado and New Mexico for the manifold responsibilities of a Christian-American citizenship." The key message of the missionaries, then, involved the Americanization of Hispanic gender roles, the replication in the plazas of Anglo gender patterns—women in the home, men outside it—in short, the cult of domesticity. This was the elevated status of women for which they held Christianity responsible.

While their reports were replete with the mention of the training, establishment, and impact of Hispanic girls as homemakers, it was quite clearly not the traditional Hispanic home they had in mind. The women missionaries demanded "the right sort" of homes, which alone would produce "the right sort of men and women." Despite the fact that most observers regarded

Hispanic women as house-proud, as "excellent housekeepers," many Anglo women missionaries saw their adobe houses as "cheerless homes" which produced "sad-eyed and spiritless," "idle, cigarette-smoking women." Not content to meddle with or "Americanize" home life through the school, mission women attacked the home within. In some sense, they entered these homes only to change them. From homes so distressingly unlike their own, they concluded that "decency and true refinement are not found among the Mexican people." Agreeing with the China missionary who declared, "civilization is shown so clearly in the way one eats," the missionaries were appalled to see families who not only slept on the floor, but ate there from a common dish with tortillas for spoons. "We hope," wrote Alice Blake, "to be able to establish better habits in these matters."

The missionaries were particularly concerned with the twin themes of respectability and refinement. They taught women to sew "respectable" dresses, and rejoiced when, through the influence of their schools, a "filthy, uncombed, unkempt, sad-eyed" Hispanic became "a frank, bright, clear-eyed, neatly-clothed and combed lady-like girl." Much ink was spent here as elsewhere by these middle-class women with different notions of privacy, deploring, however neat the home, the customary "crowding of large families into one living and sleeping room" as "necessarily productive of much evil" and as "not at all favorable to the development of the true moral nature."

The missionaries tended to count their moral victories by tables "set with American dishes," tablecloths, "cooking utensils and furniture." When filled with these new items, the homes at last would display "a general air of refinement." "The evolution of the Mexican home," concluded Alice Blake triumphantly, "is now making toward Americanism." Americanization was thus defined in terms of spreading material culture; "America" meant bedsteads and board floors, closed stoves and sewing machines. As did other interested Anglos, these women tended to confuse enthusiasm for cultural artifacts with enthusiasm for the entire cultural complex. They seemed to believe deeply in the power of material culture to recreate the entire culture which produced it.

They also firmly believed in the power of this reformed home to effect "the salvation of the Mexicans," and, inseparably, believed that flowers, curtains, the multitude of "things" and rooms of which the Hispanics "cannot seem to understand" the need were essential to that salvation. Middle-class morality, taste, and gender patterns, Americanism, and Protestantism were all tightly bound together in mission teaching. As the missionaries pursued their efforts in the areas of child-rearing, refinement, respectability, and the elevation of Hispanic women, as well as in homemaking, which encompassed all four, consciously or unconsciously they were not simply trying to turn Hispanics into Americans, but into Americans of a particular class. In so doing, they threatened the variety and relative autonomy of Hispanic women's activities and the survival patterns dependent on them.

Not just in the home but in the wider village, the mission woman threatened the integrity of village society. Simply her presence, as a representative of an alternative religion, disrupted patterns of hierarchy. Catholic priests, resident on less than half of the Protestant church sites in New Mexico and on an even smaller proportion of mission school sites, felt vulnerable. The Presbyterians, while charging a minimal tuition fee payable in kind, provided free services for baptism, marriage, and burial, whereas the priests often demanded cash payments for each of these rites. And although the ratio of Presbyterian ministers, Anglo or Hispanic, to Presbyterian Hispanic churches and schools was even lower than that of the Catholic clerics, the mission teachers carried the pastoral work between visits much the way the Catholic village women did for the priests. By her presence, her education, and her prominent role in local church affairs, the woman missionary provided a rival authority to the nearest Catholic priest.

The women missionaries not only threatened the power of the priests, they threatened the status of Hispanic women in religion. They condemned the "worship" of Mary and its related rituals. Ironically, the Protestants praised women as uniquely religious creatures through whom mankind could be brought to salvation, but were horrified at the attention paid to Mary in village churches. . . .

Converts . . . posed perhaps the most tangible threat to a village unity which depended at least in part on all inhabitants attending the same church, school, fiestas, and bailes. Missionary Alice Hyson "was disturbed by the rather riotous Sundays honoring the patron saint of Taos and Taos Pueblo." Such fiestas involved dancing, drinking, racing, and gambling, all anathema to the missionaries. But according to anthropologist Wesley Hurt, the fiesta was "more than a religious ceremony. . . . It also tend[ed] to strengthen the community bond between the various inhabitants of the town.". . .

Even resettlement could not erase all the problems of a conversion so loaded with cultural meaning. Hispanic religious conversion was tantamount to a confession that Hispanic religion, at least, and the concomitant facets of Hispanic culture were not only inferior, but wrong. Polita Padilla, a young Hispanic missionary in 1905, confessed a feeling of distance from and rejection of her own Hispanic culture as a result of mission school training: "I am a Mexican, born and brought up in New Mexico, but much of my life was spent in the Allison School where we had a different training, so that the Mexican way of living now seems strange to me." Her ambition was "to aid my people . . . as by God's grace I have been helped," that is, helped away from Hispanic culture.

For some girls, conversion meant at least temporarily "a disastrous breach in her closest family ties." More common was a feeling of isolation on the part of the converts similar to that of the Anglo mission women. Anglo women missionaries made an effort to provide for some of these young Hispanic women a network of their own. This informal system of protégées was an intense form of maternalism on the part of Anglo women who found the adults, once they had trained them, as acceptable as they found the "lovely adorable Spanish children." Yet there were limits to the ability of mission patronesses to help establish their protégés, male or female, in a new community. They could not, for example, overcome the segregation of the wider society. Not fully acceptable as equals to most Anglos, including most Anglo Presbyterians, labeled "extinguished lights" by their Catholic neighbors, and prohibited from participating in most village activities by their Protestant mentors, the Hispanic converts often found themselves caught in a perpetual marginality to both worlds, and neither Mary nor the women missionaries could provide for them an effective mediator.

Having requested the mission presence for its educational benefits, however, the villagers did their best to prevent it from disrupting their society. . . . They particularly resisted the spiritual message and avoided, as one frustrated missionary noted, "conversation that will touch their special beliefs." "The great majority," reported Jeanette Smith, "are willing to accept social good times, medical aid, education, everything that the mission has to give, except its religion." With equal determination Catholic and Protestant alike attended the same dances, participated in each others' services, and attended the same school. There were tensions. . . . To the missionaries, disruption of the social fabric seemed unfortunate but necessary before it could be rewoven, and the efforts of the villagers to minimize the conflict only frustrated these women. But villagers had found few alternatives which so met their needs as their integrated village community. Even converts made compromises to remain part of their village, marrying Catholics in Catholic ceremonies, for example, and they usually discovered that "natural parental affection overcame religious opposition" within six months to three years.

Hispanic definitions of village membership could, in fact, mitigate friction arising from the missionary presence. . . . Slightly over half of the missionaries spent only three years or less on a single site in the Hispanic field. Both their itineracy and their ideas and aims could keep them . . . at the village margin. Anglos who wished to "change in every respect the homes and habits of these Mexicans" and who rejected the society around them without trying to understand, roused resentment on the part of the villagers and found themselves shut out from the villagers' life and from influence on the cultural direction it would take.

New Mexico novelist Orlando Romero, however, has noted that the chain of social relations securing house to house in a plaza and thus encircling it could be broken by the settlement of an outsider in one of those houses. Given the delicate nature of such a system, it was in the interest of the villagers, particularly when confronted with a more enduring and intrusive mission presence—many mission teachers stayed not three years, but five, ten, and even twenty—to find some way besides exclusion to defuse the threat mission teaching represented. At the same time, such missionaries, in the interest of the mission, made every effort to penetrate that dense social network.

As part of their mission to "get into the hearts of the families," missionaries made a point of visiting the homes. Village fathers tended to visit the school, in keeping with their role of handling external relations. Mothers, however, could be reached most effectively at home. Politeness, and village mores of not offending witches, ensured a universal reception. This acquaintance helped to lower barriers raised by priests and other rival authorities, and led to a pattern of rapidly rising enrollments, with an increase of 700 percent not uncommon.

Alice Hyson found visits to the homes "in times of affliction" particularly "effective." According to Miss Hyson, "they realize that you have no other motive than that of love when you try to relieve them." The mission women adopted visiting as their strategy, and participation in critical life stages as a crucial part of their "pedagogy of love." They did not realize that village women also used visiting as a strategy, but as a strategy of integration rather than as one of cultural tutelage. Inadvertently, by participating in the normal functions of village women, the women missionaries had begun their own integration into the village on terms they neither fully understood nor controlled.

In much the same way, mission women participated in the customary pattern of mutual exchange of goods and services, with a few variations. Plaza teachers received an annual salary of approximately $350. By the standard of the national public school average, $485, it was small, but it easily outstripped that of local New Mexico teachers. This relative wealth often proved insufficient for vacations, retirement, and luxuries, especially if the missionaries helped support other members of their families. But coupled with the fact that theirs was often the only cash income earned in the village, it gave the missionaries some patronage to dispense. They employed selected villagers, usually the elderly or children, on odd jobs, and sent children to school and even to boarding school at their own expense. Missionaries who had independent sources of income gave playground equipment or school buildings to the villagers.

The largesse of the missionaries could have created a permanent sense of inequality and could have distanced them from the villagers. Once the lopsidedness of the exchange became equal, however, once the missionaries, too, became recipients, their status as elite outsiders diminished. Missionaries found that those hired to do odd jobs were in return "always doing little things for us that we couldn't pay for." One villager put his "conveyance" at the disposal of the missionaries; other villagers built new kitchens, cleaned house, and helped erect new teachers' houses by furnishing adobe bricks and hauling fence posts, all without charge. Sometimes the villagers even reversed the teacher-student roles, as when a dozen Chimayo women taught Jennie Clark to spin. "How it did please them," wrote her sister, "to find that there was something that her fingers could not do as well as theirs! . . . and how proud they were of her success."

Most important, given the villagers' own valuation of it, was the donation of food by the villagers to the missionaries. "Many times," reported Victoria MacArthur from Truchas, "have we been invited to stay for supper, and been given a little bucket of beans, peas, potatoes or apples to bring home with us when we left." Louise Conklin at Chacon realized such gifts represented a great sacrifice, but found the villagers "so eager to do something to prove their gratitude that I cannot refuse." The missionaries interpreted the gifts as signs of affection, gratitude, and devotion, but to the villagers the gifts also initiated a set of actions designed to incorporate the mission women into the group as peers.

Perhaps the single most effective mission role giving these teachers access to village families was that of healer. The entry of Anglo women "medicas" could have led to competition and tension with Hispanic female practitioners. But the mores of the Hispanic healers placed as their first responsibility healing the patient and learning all they could, and demanded they accept any help that might aid in that end. Because of the exalted place of parteras [midwives] and curanderas [healers] within the community of women and the village in general, and the distrust, cost, and scarcity of Anglo male doctors, the female missionaries' establishment of themselves as technologically superior resident medical advisers paved the way for their acceptance by the villagers beyond the confines of the classroom. Leva Granger described how initial suspicion turned to trust because of the effectiveness of her medicine. Granger bent over a sick woman, trying to force medicine between the patient's teeth, when:

> the door opened suddenly, a woman, much excited, hurried in and pushed us aside so rudely that the cup was dashed to the floor. . . . For some time she refused to allow us to approach the sick woman, but, fortunately, the medicine began to act favorably, the friend at last realizing that we really wished to help and not harm, stood aside, and before we left even tried to assist.

Granger fully recognized the cause for the woman's initial terror—"for were we not strangers and, above all else, Protestants?" But actions and results carried more weight with the bulk of the Hispanic population than the strictures of the priests, and once a healer had established herself, she had little further trouble. Unlike other mission territories where no model, in particular no female model, existed that allowed the natives to assimilate their would-be ministers, Hispanic Colorado and New Mexico had their curanderas and parteras, their maestras [teachers], and their female heads of households, as well, of course, as their nuns at convent boarding schools and their witches. These pre-existing female models eased the way for the integration of women missionaries who desired a deeper involvement with the village. In a sense, they found their place awaiting them.

At the same time, mission women created new roles for themselves and new social forces within the villages. They tried to channel the integrative rituals of the community into forms not only acceptable to themselves, but which replicated their own society. After all, integration into village society without changing it did little to further mission aims. Reasoning that "our Protestant Mexicans are not yet far removed from their Romanist training, and love to have special days and special doings," missionaries held social gatherings in their schools. They brought the Anglo import, Santa Claus, to the plazas and organized literary and Christian Endeavor societies, and, of course, women's missionary societies. It was as though the villagers had suddenly acquired a social director. And the mission teachers were tempted to associate the high degree of attendance with success of their aims. Most, however, remained properly skeptical. One missionary acknowledged that church programs were always "packed" simply because "the mission school was the only place aside from the saloon for any recreation." More mission functions complemented than competed with traditional gatherings; they coexisted, uneasily on the part of the missionaries, with saints' days and other fiestas.

In their varied roles as maestras, curanderas, and informal social directors, mission women had indeed assembled a formidable arsenal and achieved a strategic position for changing the Hispanic village into an American small town, or so it seemed. Mission workers pointed with pride to developments whose origins they attributed to themselves rather than to larger social and economic imperatives. They commented on increased male industry, migration for work, more fruit trees and vegetables, and an unspecified "decided improvement" among the young. These mission women partook of the reform impulse of the progressive era in their desire to create a new world, and, unlike some missionaries elsewhere, they had access to both sexes to do it. And the mission women did indeed fulfill vital roles in the Hispanic villages. But their desire to use those roles to change the villages was matched by the villagers' desire to incorporate the missionaries on village terms. The enthusiastic village-wide welcome mission women received after an extended absence epitomized the conjunction of acculturative strategies. Like the exchange of food, it met the cultural needs of both missionaries and villagers. It legitimized the place of the missionaries as part of the village society in the same way the fiesta held each fall reincorporated the migratory male laborers. At the same time its rituals reinforced the mission women's own sense of how essential they were to the village. Intercultural relations in the village took this confusing route of common experience diversely interpreted, though occasionally distilled through common values, as each group sought to channel the activities of the other into safe and constructive passages. . . .

Their mission gave these women missionaries the opportunity to try to shape a society. They had been sent by home mission boards to turn Hispanics into "Americans." Away from direct male supervision, or direct supervision at all, they had trouble fulfilling this function in the way anticipated by the mission boards. It was difficult if not impossible for a woman alone to convey an entire culture, particularly when women in the late nineteenth and early twentieth century seemed to have their own culture. Not bound to the image of the Anglo world from which they came, they aimed for an improved version of that society, a more feminized version, with its emphasis on the power of the "Christian" female-created home to transform society.

Just as the role of social control and cultural bearer was allotted to the women missionaries, that of social integrator and cultural and community maintainer was the role adopted by the women villagers. Intercultural relations in the village thus took the form of a struggle, largely female, to integrate two peoples, each of whom tried to control and dominate the union, to bring it closer to their own culture. But the women missionaries had come so far, so alone, to reach the villages, that they had little chance. Those who did not retreat at the first opportunity founded an empire more personal than national. Those whose sense of racial and cultural superiority walled them off from the village community found the barrier worked both ways. Without some integration into the village to breach the defenses, the mission message remained, like these missionaries, isolated, unanchored, and ephemeral.

Even missionaries who partially abandoned the industrial definition of "American" could not always implement their own cultural program as intended. As female bearers of Anglo culture, they had sought most to replicate the women's world that they knew, with its language, family values, tablecloths, and tea services. The life these women promoted for the Hispanic women, however, bore little resemblance to the life the missionaries themselves led in the villages. Anglo women as cultural messengers could not help but convey a message ambiguous at best, as the very act of conveying it required transgressing the roles it relayed. Not only had they themselves ventured far from the domain of home and hearth, unmarried, but they disrupted Hispanic family life and community at their core, as rival authorities in child-rearing, education, and religion.

In turn, the recipients of this mixed message proved selective in the lessons they learned from the Americanizers in their midst, the "Protestant nuns." Language and technology they accepted, but separated these aspects from their over-arching culture as they had separated sewing machines and other Anglo material goods they acquired. They selected those elements of an evolving Anglo culture best suited to their own evolving culture, and refused, for the most part, to receive the message in exactly the spirit it was given. Just as they slotted Anglo mission women into traditional Hispanic roles (curandera, maestra, nun), they interpreted their message and actions through the prism of their own female world of visiting, exchange, and labor.

4Further Reading 107

FURTHER READING

John F. Bannon, *The Spanish Borderlands Frontier, 1513–1821* (Albuquerque: University of New Mexico Press, 1974).

Dee Brown, *Bury My Heart at Wounded Knee: An Indian History of the American West* (New York: Holt, Rinehart, and Winston, 1971; New York: Bantam Books, 1972; New York: Pocket Books, 1981; New York: Washington Square Press, 1981).

Albert Camarillo, *Chicanos in a Changing Society: From Mexican Pueblos to American Barrios in Santa Barbara and Southern California, 1848–1920* (Cambridge, Mass.: Harvard University Press, 1979).

Angie Debo, *Geronimo: The Man, His Times, and His Place* (Norman, Okla.: University of Oklahoma Press, 1976).

Peter Gerhard, *The Northern Frontier of New Spain* (Princeton, N.J.: Princeton University Press, 1982).

Ramón A. Gutiérrez, *When Jesus Came, the Corn Mothers Went Away: Marriage, Sexuality, and Power in New Mexico, 1500–1846* (Stanford: Stanford University Press, 1991).

Neal Harlow, *California Conquered: War and Peace on the Pacific, 1846–1850* (Berkeley and Los Angeles: University of California Press, 1982).

Robert W. Johannsen, *To the Halls of the Montezumas: The Mexican War in the American Imagination* (New York: Oxford University Press, 1985).

Alvin W. Josephy, Jr., *The Nez Percé Indians and the Opening of the Northwest* (New Haven: Yale University Press, 1965; abridged ed., 1971; Lincoln: University of Nebraska Press, abridged ed., 1979).

Douglas Monroy, *Thrown Among Strangers: The Making of Mexican Culture in Frontier California* (Berkeley and Los Angeles: University of California Press, 1990).

Robert J. Rosenbaum, *Mexicano Resistance in the Southwest: "The Sacred Right of Self-Preservation"* (Austin: University of Texas Press, 1981).

Edward H. Spicer, *Cycles of Conquest: The Impact of Spain, Mexico, and the United States on the Indians of the Southwest, 1533–1960* (Tucson: University of Arizona Press, 1962; 1967).

Russell Thornton, *American Indian Holocaust and Survival: A Population History Since 1492* (Norman, Okla.: University of Oklahoma Press, 1987; 1990).

David J. Weber, *The Mexican Frontier, 1821–1846: The American Southwest Under Mexico* (Albuquerque: University of New Mexico Press, 1982).

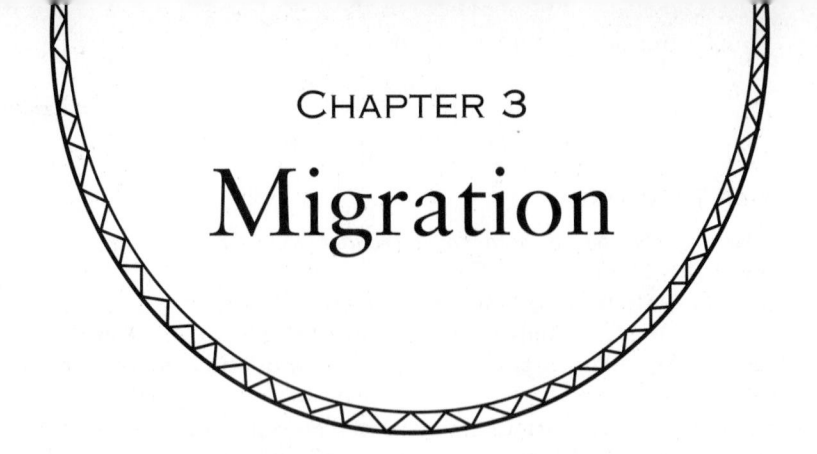

CHAPTER 3

Migration

Scholars traditionally have discussed the American West as a region characterized by people in motion. The westward movement of explorers, settlers, merchants, soldiers, and others of European ancestry has often taken center stage. When race and ethnicity are factored into this process, however, the migration of peoples to the West becomes more complicated. By the time Euro-Americans arrived, the so-called West was already populated by Native Americans and Spanish Mexicans.

Moreover, the demographic movement associated with the settlement of the American West has not just occurred from east to west; for Asian Americans and Mexican Americans, it has taken quite different trajectories. As Shih-shan H. Tsai and Manuel Gamio remind us in two of this chapter's readings, the West is not always "west." Chinese immigrants crossed the Pacific Ocean, traveling eastward to reach California, the "Gold Mountain." Mexican immigrants, as had earlier Spanish Mexicans, journeyed to *El Norte*—the north—in search of jobs and escape from political revolution.

The selections on internal migration call for yet another major reconsideration of western American history: not only did European, Asian, and Mexican immigrants come to the American West, but, as Douglas Henry Daniels and Charles Roberts note in the two other readings in this chapter, so did African Americans and Native Americans from other parts of the United States. Together, these immigrants and migrants of color added to the diversity of the western experience; by their labor, skills, and tenacity, they helped to construct a multicultural and multiethnic society in the region.

FOR ANALYSIS AND DISCUSSION

1. How did the migrations of peoples of color to the West differ from the immigration and internal migrations of peoples of European ancestry?

2. How were the migrations of various peoples of color similar to and different from each other?

3. What conditions "pushed" people out of their homelands or places of birth, and what factors "pulled" them to the American West?

4. What difficulties did each group discussed in this chapter encounter, and how did they overcome them?

5. What differences existed between the journeys of the Chinese and the African Americans who arrived in the West in the nineteenth century and the trips of the Mexicans and the Native Americans who migrated during the twentieth century?

 # Chinese Immigration, 1848–1882

SHIH-SHAN HENRY TSAI

Almost 1 million persons from five Asian countries—some 300,000 Chinese, 400,000 Japanese, 7,000 Koreans, 8,000 Indians, and 180,000 Filipinos— came to the continental United States and to Hawaii between the late 1840s and the mid-1930s. Each group managed to land without restriction for only a relatively short period before the U.S. Congress, responding to strong anti-Asian sentiment, enacted laws severely limiting their entry.

The Chinese, the first sizable group of Asians to migrate to the New World, had a long tradition of going overseas. Traders and emigrants from China's southeastern provinces of Guangdong (Kwangtung) and Fujian (Fukien) had established settlements all over Southeast Asia by the time the California Gold Rush drew Chinese people across the Pacific Ocean in the early 1850s.

California contained a majority of the Chinese in the United States until the end of the nineteenth century. They eventually fanned out to other states and territories in the American West, especially locations where gold had been found. Many Chinese also went to Hawaii, but their numbers in the islands remained small until the 1870s, even though a handful of Chinese skilled in sugar making had found their way to Hawaii in the early years of the nineteenth century.

The peak period of Chinese migration to the Pacific coast (1852–1882) roughly coincided with the infamous Chinese coolie trade (under which Chinese were kidnaped or tricked into indentured servitude) to Cuba, Peru, and other places in Latin America. For that reason, anti-Chinese forces claimed that Chinese immigration was a new form of slavery. Shih-shan Henry Tsai, who has studied Chinese immigration to the United States as well as the coolie trade to Latin America, argues, however, that the Chinese who ventured to California were free immigrants in search of economic opportunities.

STUDY QUESTIONS

1. Why does the author contend that Chinese immigrants to California were free immigrants similar to European newcomers?

2. How did Chinese workers contribute to the economic development of the American West?

Various motives and inducements brought Chinese to the Pacific Coast of the United States. In addition to the influences of overcrowding, poverty, war, and other catastrophes in China, there were effective external influences. Chinese Marxist scholars have emphasized exploitive elements among these factors. Ch'ing Ju-chi, a prominent Chinese historian, has remarked, "In the forties of the nineteenth century a big Mexican territory was annexed into the United States. . . . In order to cultivate and exploit this newly obtained Western land and resources, to develop a modernized industry, to build a trans-continental railway, to pioneer a channel for American commerce with China, the United States needed labor badly. Naturally, she looked to the large numbers of hard-working, resourceful, and good-quality Chinese people for help." Chinese Marxist historians generally have contended that America's need for labor was the most important external inducement to immigration. Chu Shih-chia, a Columbia University Ph.D., stated, "American capitalists, in order to exploit Chinese laborers, whipped them to dig gold mines, to build railroads, to plant. The answer to the question of why industry and agriculture developed so fast in Western America was to be found in the Chinese laborers' sweat and blood exploited by American capitalists." Writing at the height of the Korean War, Chang Jen-yu asserted that the United States suggested the principle of free immigration in the 1868 Burlingame Treaty because "the United States needed the Chinese laborers and American businessmen wanted to trade with the Chinese." Liu Ta-nien, a member of the Chinese Science Academy, made the same point: "American capitalists were aware of the fact that Chinese labor was cheap. Therefore, they used all kinds of fraud and propaganda to bring Chinese laborers to the United States."

American scholars generally agree that the demand in California and other western territories for labor was the most important motivation for Chinese immigration. The Chinese were needed for cooking, laundering, grain farming, fruit growing, tide-land draining, mining, and other labor demanded in frontier communities. Several American scholars have added other factors. Mary R. Coolidge, for example, wrote in 1909 that the discovery of gold in California drew Chinese peasants to the West Coast. She noted that the news of the discovery of gold in the Sacramento Valley in January 1848 reached Hong Kong in the spring and created much excitement there. "Masters of foreign vessels afforded every facility to emigration, distributing placards, maps, and pamphlets with colored accounts of the Golden Hills." Elmer C. Sandmeyer saw the transportation companies as a powerful promotional influence. By carrying Chinese laborers between Hong Kong and San Francisco and by charging them high passenger rates, American

Reprinted by permission of the University of Arkansas Press from *China and the Overseas Chinese in the United States 1868–1911* by Shih-shan H. Tsai, copyright 1983.

shipowners could make good money. Sandmeyer wrote, "In 1866 the Pacific Mail Steamship Company entered the China trade, under government subsidy, and a little later the Occidental and Oriental Steamship Company was organized as a competitor." Gunther Barth provided a statistical account to support this assertion. "The fare," Barth stated, "at the lowest estimate, amounted to forty dollars for transportation to San Francisco and twenty dollars for the return trip. . . . During the year 1852 alone, thirty thousand Chinese who embarked at Hong Kong for San Francisco paid $1,300,000 for the voyage. At the beginning of 1856, William Speer calculated that all Chinese in California had paid a total of $2,329,580 for the trip."

The facts support the thesis of opportunity rather than of exploitation. Almost all of the Chinese who emigrated to the United States in the nineteenth century were natives of Kwangtung, a southern Chinese province of about eighty thousand square miles, approximately the area of the state of Oregon. In this hilly province only 16 percent of the land was cultivated as late as 1955, and, in the eighteenth and nineteenth centuries, much of this cultivated land was used to grow such commercial crops as fruit, sugarcane, indigo, and tobacco instead of rice, the staple food of the Chinese. Consequently, the common folk suffered from the ever-rising price of rice. This situation was further aggravated by the increase in population throughout the eighteenth and nineteenth centuries. After the suppression of the Three Feudatories Revolt in 1681, Kwangtung enjoyed a long period of peace and stability. As a result, its population grew rapidly. In 1787 the population of Kwangtung numbered 16 million; by 1850 it had increased to 28 million. But during the 1850s and 1860s Kwangtung was devastated by the Taipings and the Triad-led rebels. Fighting also broke out between Punti (Cantonese speaking) and Hakka (Guest Settlers) people in the region southwest of the Pearl River Delta. These conflicts resulted in political disorder, social chaos, and economic dislocations. The *Hsin-ning hsien-chih* (Gazetteer of the Hsinning district) graphically described the situation. "The fields in the four directions were choked with weeds. Small families found it difficult to make a living and often drowned their girl babies because of the impossibility of looking after them." Emigration was very much in evidence.

The largest portion of the Chinese in America came from Kwangtung's most populous prefecture, Kwangchou, which contains the city of Canton, and from the colony of Macao. The Cantonese were more venturesome than most Chinese because of their early contact with foreigners, and because British Hong Kong served as a steppingstone for their adventures. Emigrant ships that carried Chinese to California seldom sailed directly from any other port in China. More than nine-tenths of the Chinese emigrants embarked for San Francisco at Hong Kong. The emigrants traveled in junks, lorchas, or rafts over the waterways of the Pearl River Delta from their native villages to Hong Kong. The officials at Canton normally did not interfere with their countrymen going to Hong Kong, nor did the British authorities try to detain them. Chinese emigrants obtained the money to pay their passage in various ways. Some had saved money, others sold their property, including land or hogs, to secure passage. Some borrowed money from friends or relatives. Some pledged their families as security for the loan. They came at their own option, and when they arrived in California they were free to go where they pleased and to engage in any occupation they liked.

Those Chinese who arrived in California without means were credit contract laborers. That is, the foreign shippers paid their passage fees and, in most cases, advanced them three or four months' wages for their family needs. This sum would be deducted from their wages in America. In chapter 23 of *K'u she-hui* (The Bitter Society), the author describes how the credit labor system worked. "The foreman Hsieh gave each person three hundred dollars and said that each month thirty dollars would be deducted from their wages, so that within ten months all their debts would have been deducted. The three men were extremely glad. They each kept a hundred dollars and remitted two hundred back to their families. At the end of the month, foreman Hsieh sent someone to tell them that they had to go on board the next evening." An agreement signed in 1849 between an English company called the Tseang Sing Hong in Shanghai and a group of Chinese laborers exemplified the operation:

> The Tseang Sing Hong having now hired the American ship called the Ah-mah-san [Amazon] for voyaging purposes, the mechanics and laborers of their own free will, will put to sea, the ship to proceed to Ka-la-fo-ne-a [California], and port of Fwh-lan-sze-ko [San Francisco], in search of employment for the said mechanics and laborers. From the time of leaving Shanghai, the expenses of provisions and vessel are all to be defrayed by the head of the Tseang Sing Hong. On arrival, it is expected that the foreign merchant will search out and recommend employment for the said laborers, and the money he advances on their account, shall be returned when the employment becomes settled. The one hundred and twenty-five dollars passage money, as agreed by us, are to be paid to the said head of the said Hong, who will make arrangements with the employers of the coolies, that a moiety of their wages shall be deducted monthly until the debt is absorbed: after which, they will receive their wages in full every month.

It is obvious that whether they came with their own money or under credit contract, the Chinese were free agents, as were the European immigrants. Two Chinese ministers in charge of migration affairs characterized these people as "dwellers upon the sea-coast" who "have flown thither as the wild geese fly." In their opinion, the Chinese did not go to the United States as a result of deceit or by being kidnapped but because they regarded America as a land of abundance and great opportunities.

The Chinese who journeyed to the United States in the nineteenth century were mainly male peasants and workers. Of these immigrants, at least one-half were married and expected not merely to make their personal fortune but also to support a family back home. They went to California after hearing of gold and higher wages there. The facts do not indicate that they were homeless drones or criminals or slaves. They were mostly poor, ignorant, and uneducated, but they were free. They were accommodating and they could be easily governed, and they came to the United States voluntarily to get a good price for their labor.

The merchant class constituted only a small portion of the total Chinese population in the United States. Some Chinese came to California with a business background, and a few turned to business after a long period of industrious and frugal living as laborers. Mr. Lee Chew, one of the heroes in Hamilton Holt's *Undistinguished Americans,* was a good example. Lee was born in a farming village of the Kwangchou prefecture. Lee told Holt, "My father gave me $100, and I went to Hong Kong with five other boys from our place and we got steerage passage on a steamer, paying $50 each." After Lee arrived in California, he worked as a house servant for an American family for two years and saved $410. He then opened a laundry in a mining town, and after three years he increased his capital to $2,500. He finally settled down in New York City and ran a grocery store. It is interesting that the merchants, who ranked near the bottom of the Chinese social scale, were leaders among the Cantonese in America. If after accumulating an adequate amount of money they did not retire to their native towns in Kwangtung, the Cantonese immigrants usually entered business in the Chinatown community.

Before 1880 only a few Chinese women came to the United States. It was a Chinese tradition that a respectable woman should not leave home even with her husband. Most of those who did leave, at a time when Chinese society decreed foot-binding, were large-footed and of the working class or prostitutes. In 1875, the prostitute traffic between Hong Kong and San Francisco was so serious that the U.S. Congress passed the Page Law to stop women of "disreputable character" from coming to the United States. But after 1880 public sentiment in China changed, and many small-footed Chinese women emigrated with their husbands to the United States. Still, as the Chinese loved to say, "there were more monks than rice porridge." According to the U.S. Census of 1900, there was only one Chinese female for each twenty-six males in this country.

A few Chinese had come to America even before California's admission to the Union in 1850. According to pioneer historian Hubert H. Bancroft and contemporary observer Daniel Cleveland, the first Chinese immigrants were two men and a woman who arrived in San Francisco aboard the *Eagle* in 1848. Several sources, however, vary with regard to the number of the Chinese immigrants during the nineteenth century. Elmer C. Sandmeyer, for example, compares figures from the Immigration Commission, the Bureau of Immigration, and the San Francisco Customs House to show a considerable discrepancy among the estimates of the three governmental agencies. These discrepancies may be explained by the fact that every year hundreds of Chinese returned to their native land because of the seasonal character of their occupations. Or they may be the result of official exaggeration or poor census practices. The first decennial census in California was in 1850; others followed in 1860, 1870, and 1880. Although each census gives the country of birth of all nonnatives enumerated, the color categories in the censuses of 1850 and 1860 were limited to white, black, and mulatto. Not until the census of 1870 were the codes for Chinese, Japanese, and Indians added. Unfortunately, 99 percent of the records of the 1890 census, including California, were destroyed by a fire in the Department of Commerce in 1921.

Authorities also differ as to exactly when the Chinese came in large numbers into California. Some claim that major Chinese immigration began in 1854, while others believe that it began in 1852. Daniel Cleveland reported to Minister Ross Browne, "Eighteen thousand four hundred and thirty-four arrived during the year 1852, nearly three times as many as in any subsequent year, except 1854, and almost equal to the number for the past four years." Bancroft recorded that in 1851, 4,018 men and 7 women arrived in

Chinese in San Francisco's Chinatown

the United States; in January 1852, the figure was 7,512 men ad 8 women; by May, the number had increased to 11,787; and it soared in August to more than 18,040.

After they arrived in this country, the Chinese immigrants were engaged in many different occupations. A statistical report prepared for Minister Ross Browne and Secretary William Seward in 1868 gives some idea of the Chinese occupations in California:

Merchants and traders	2,000
Engaged in manufacturing for themselves	2,00
In other occupations	1,000
Washhouses	1,800
Laborers in factories and in other capacities in cities and towns	3,500
Mechanics	1,000
House servants	3,000
Laborers on the Pacific railroad	10,000
Miners	13,084
Farm laborers	2,000
Fishermen	200
Total of male Chinese in California	39,584

These statistics show that about two-thirds of the Chinese immigrants were either working for the railroad or digging in the mines. Approximately one-eighth of the Chinese were engaged in independent commerce and industry.

Many Chinese chose to return to their native Kwangtung villages as soon as they obtained enough money. Some of them traveled between the Pearl River Delta and San Francisco Bay like migrating birds because of the seasonal character of their occupations. An interesting census recorded by the San Francisco Customs House indicates that in some years more Chinese returned to China than arrived in the United States. It should also be pointed out that, although California absorbed most of the Chinese immigrants, there were Chinese working in almost every state of the Union in 1880.

In the 1870s and 1880s, the Chinese not only raised hops and fruit, reclaimed marshy lands, fished, and worked in the manufacturing industries of California, they also dug mines, canned salmon, laid railroad tracks, and washed clothing in Oregon, Nevada, Idaho, Washington, and Montana. Even the South was experiencing the presence of the Chinese, whose "cheapness" and industriousness were attractive to southern planters and railway magnates. In 1882, when the U.S. Congress passed the anti-Chinese Exclusion Act, the Chinese immigration was not just a California issue but a national concern.

Travelcraft and Black Pioneer Urbanites, 1850s–1870s

DOUGLAS HENRY DANIELS

Blacks inhabited San Francisco, the first big city on the Pacific coast, in sizable numbers beginning in the 1850s, and they constituted the largest body of African-American city dwellers in the region until 1900, when black Los Angelenos surpassed them in population. Numbering more than a thousand in the nineteenth century, black San Franciscans were assertive, highly mobile, versatile, and skilled city folk. These qualities stand in stark contrast to the stereotypical image of blacks as people mired in poverty and helplessness.

In this reading, Douglas Henry Daniels focuses on these people's unusual combination of skills, attitudes, and outlook, which he calls travelcraft. Travelcraft permitted African Americans to reach the West Coast and to inhabit San Francisco at a time when most Euro-Americans, as well as black Americans, were rural dwellers. It allowed them to range along the Pacific coast and into the interior, searching for mineral ore, adapting their talents to specific occupations as needed, and founding black communities and social and cultural organizations wherever they settled. The black migrants naturally relied on the modes of travel available at the time. They crossed the continent on ocean and river steamers or on foot (until the completion of the transcontinental railroad), often working on these conveyances along the way as sailors, porters, chambermaids, cooks, and waiters.

The variety of means that blacks used to communicate information on travel, to describe opportunities in new settlements, and to document racial problems reflected their urbanism, as well as their versatility. Black newspapers published their private letters and their travel tips; through word of mouth, too, these experienced city dwellers communicated vital information very quickly over thousands of miles. By the twentieth century, more reliable means of travel and communication, along with formal labor recruiting, served to draw African Americans to the San Francisco Bay Area, Los Angeles, Chicago, and New York in large numbers, and the term *great migration* was fittingly coined to describe the phenomenon.

STUDY QUESTIONS

1. What does the author mean by the term travelcraft?

2. How did community newspapers become important to black migrants to California?

Many Black pioneers migrated to, then temporarily left, San Francisco, to wander in search of fortune. Their movement resulted from the specific urban setting and from the obstacles facing all Afro-Americans: initially caused by political weakness, the propensity to travel became a source of strength. . . . I will focus on the pioneers' travel abilities—what made them capable of acquiring and sorting out information, selecting the best option, and journeying distances that were remarkable in the nineteenth century, especially for a group which had recently been enslaved. Their ability to travel to San Francisco, to cross and recross the continent, and to roam the Pacific slope highlights their determination and pluck, their resourcefulness, and their adventurousness, all traits rarely attributed to Blacks.

I use the term *travelcraft* to designate the outlook and complex of skills that facilitated both long-distance travel and residency in the Bay Area. Travelcraft distinguished Pacific slope Black urbanites from the mass of Negroes tied to the land in the south, and set them apart from Black city folk in the east who chose to stay close to the Atlantic shore. Before analyzing travelcraft, we must delineate the habits which underlay it and the frequency with which Black pioneers undertook lengthy trips.

Letters in San Francisco's Black newspapers of the 1860s and 1870s indicated that Afro-Americans valued information on the geography of distant places, on travel routes, on the likelihood of economic advancement after migration, on the presence of race discrimination, and on the successes of other Negroes. To help collect and disseminate such information, pioneers sent foreign and domestic newspapers to the offices of the San Francisco *Pacific Appeal* and the San Francisco *Elevator* for interested citizens to read. William H. Hall was thanked by the *Pacific Appeal* in 1863 for furnishing issues of a Panamanian and several Jamaican newspapers. . . . Seamen delivered copies of San Francisco's Black papers to Afro-Americans in distant lands.

Before leaving San Francisco, travelers were asked to give information based on their personal experiences and observations; others supplied intelligence because of a felt need for such information. Correspondents prefaced their letters with such statements as, "I promised you, when leaving the Bay City, to write you a few lines on reaching my destination.". . . Daniel Seales, a prosperous businessman, sought to "drop . . . a few lines of information which may be of interest to the traveling community.". . .

Black pioneers' letters indicate a coordinated effort to aid one another by sharing information and insights derived from actual experiences. Their letters and newspaper columns trace the movements of Negro westerners and suggest the extent to which some continued to travel after migrating west.

Pioneers' obituaries also indicate that nineteenth-century Pacific slope Negroes moved distances with a frequency that jars our notion that Black folk were demoralized and dehumanized first by slavery, and then by industrialization and urbanization. . . .

. . . Afro-American travelers included businessmen who, in the eyes of their contemporaries, were self-made men and successful entrepreneurs. Henry M. Collins came west shortly after the Gold Rush, returned to the Atlantic coast to collect his wife and family, then moved to San Francisco, from where he made frequent trips to the mining country. . . .

Some pioneers were lifelong travelers. Inclination, habit, and job opportunities at sea or on the road made long-distance journeys an integral part of their life and work. . . . Mifflin W. Gibbs, an Arkansas judge during Reconstruction and U.S. consul to Madagascar in the 1890s, lived in California in the 1850s and made lengthy trips all his life. As a young man he sailed from the Atlantic states to San Francisco shortly after the Gold Rush. In 1858 he migrated to British Columbia with a number of other Black Californians. The next year he returned to the east coast to marry and to visit friends in Rochester, New York, and Philadelphia before undertaking the 4,000 mile trip by steamship to Victoria, Vancouver Island, with his bride. . . . For Gibbs, as for a number of pioneers, travel remained a lifetime habit.

Heads of Black institutions also ranged over the Pacific slope. Reverend T. M. D. Ward probably traveled more than any other Black San Franciscan in 1868, covering 14,000 miles in seven months. After going from San Francisco to the east coast on church business, he returned to the city by the bay. A week later he headed for Virginia City, Nevada. The next month he steamed to Portland, Oregon, and British Columbia to attend to church matters before returning east. . . .

. . . The frequent long-distance movement, and the travelcraft on which it was based, is striking in the historical context of a homeless people searching for a place to develop its potential and achieve wealth and status without the injustices of American racism.

Afro-Americans differed from other Americans because of the circumstances surrounding their migration, settlement, and status in the New World. Black slaves were unwilling migrants and unwilling workers. As freedmen they did not enjoy the same political privileges and economic and social opportunities as whites. . . .

. . . Black pioneers expected to prosper from mining and from the high wages unique to pioneer California. But when the legislature passed laws severely limiting the rights of Afro-Americans, many reluctantly concluded that California was not the place they sought. Articles and letters in the newspapers reveal that in the 1860s, particularly before Emancipation, Black San Franciscans still searched for a place where they could realize their ambitions. The debate concerning prospects and conditions of life overseas sheds light on travelcraft and, specifically, on the manner in which the Black pioneers collected evidence, disseminated it through their journals, and used it to make decisions.

In the early 1860s the *Pacific Appeal* featured specific articles and letters reflecting Afro-Americans' interest in finding a suitable place to live. In late 1862 a westerner could peruse "The Future of the Colored Race in America." "Thoughts on Colonization," and "On Colonizing"—all of which ran for at least two issues. "The Liberian Republic" was reprinted from an eastern source along with "Eight Reasons for Objecting to the Haytian Scheme." In April 1863, the *Pacific Appeal* published the "Forty-Sixth Annual Report of the American Colonization Society" for interested readers. . . .

Advocates of overseas migration remained a minority among Afro-Americans, including San Franciscans, and interest in remaining in the United States increased after the Civil War. The Reconstruction amendments seemed a guarantee that the United States was serious about equal rights and opportunities for Blacks. . . . Interest in new settlements and a better life persisted, and so scouts sought news of new places. Before and after these national developments, Black San Franciscans ranged over the entire Pacific slope in search of opportunity and wealth. . . . Their letters in the *Pacific Appeal* and the *Elevator* informed readers of the conditions of life and travel in these places.

In the mid-nineteenth century, Reverend John J. Moore went to the mining country and encountered "many personal friends and acquaintances" from California among the one hundred Afro-Americans in Cariboo, Canada. He believed they had "fine prospects ahead," referring to this particular mining bonanza as "the Ophir of modern times" and "a blessing to many of our colored Californians." As for race prejudice, it was reported, initially at least, that the situation was "of course more encouraging than in California, for the reason that the laws know no distinction.". . .

Black scouts visited and commented on the mountain communities in the Sierras and settlements in the valleys and along the coast. A pioneer in Wadsworth, along the Central Pacific railroad above Sacramento, claimed that wages were magnificent. . . . Nor was this the only favorable report on the mountain towns. . . .

Travelers noted the material progress of the colored families in towns a few miles from the bay, south along the coast, and in the inland cities of Sacramento and Stockton. Napa City, north of the bay, received praise; one correspondent emphasized the successes of wheat growers in the region. Others reported on the few Black pioneers in San Jose, Petaluma, Vallejo, and Benicia. . . . Sacramento earned favorable reports, and in Stockton, the colored inhabitants "appear[ed] to be in very comfortable circumstances.". . .

Despite its reputation as a place of opportunity, the American west withheld some benefits from Black citizens while it extended others. Years of experience with discrimination in the west taught Blacks to view the rest of the nation differently after the end of slavery. Travelers in eastern cities reported favorable conditions for Afro-Americans, causing some westerners to return. The author of a "Letter from Chicago" compared the midwestern city to New York, Sacramento, and San Francisco. He found little prejudice, as "all the churches . . . receive colored persons kindly and respectfully.". . .

Black San Franciscans constituted the largest urban Negro contingent in the far west until 1900, but with new mining discoveries and improved conditions in the south and east, they wondered how long this would last. In 1863 the *Pacific Appeal* expressed concern about the exodus from the Pacific coast metropolis. "We are certainly getting jealous of Victoria and British Columbia, for attracting so many of our most valuable men to their domain." About the same time, the *Elevator* noted: "Several of our warm personal friends have lately left this State to return east as under the new

African-American and Euro-American gold miners in California

conditions of affairs the southern and western states offer a better field for enterprising colored men than California.". . .

. . . Partly because of racial loyalties, San Francisco's (and California's) Black population remained at a few thousand until the growth of Negro Los Angeles around 1900. Nevertheless, the remaining pioneers believed the Bay Area was the best place for Negroes even if they could not convince many others, and even though they themselves left the city from time to time.

Train or steamer fare often presented a greater obstacle to Blacks than to whites. In the 1870s, sea passage from New York cost about $50, and a rail-road ticket cost from $65 to $140. These prices must have been prohibitive for most country dwellers, and were quite a sum of money for workers in eastern cities. . . .

The rigors of sea travel also discouraged many prospective Black migrants. Unless they wished to make the difficult journey overland, the pio-neers traveled by sea until the completion of the transcontinental railroad in 1869. They sailed either around the Horn or to Central America, where they crossed the isthmus. . . .

In addition to the usual hardships. Black travelers faced special difficul-ties. Aboard the *Pocahontas* in 1852, Negro passengers with tickets for cabin passage were denied admission to the cabin and forced to occupy the sailors' berths while the crew took their places in the cabins. More humilia-tions followed. Black travelers were prevented from eating until both white passengers and crew had dined. When the ship stopped in Puerto Rico, one distinguished Black passenger was evicted from the "first table" of a restau-rant on shore. Similar problems were encountered in California. . . .

If these obstacles did not discourage Black travelers, there were other dif-ficulties unique to their ethnic group. . . . For Black pioneers, the large for-eign-born presence in San Francisco indicated they received aid more readily than native Afro-Americans, even though the foreign-born had to cross an ocean to reach the New World. In 1880, more than 100,000 San Franciscans (44 percent) originated overseas. Most came from Europe, but the figure also included 21,213 Chinese. . . . Despite the demand for domestic workers and westerners' reported preference for Black servants over Chinese or white, no one promoted large-scale Afro-American migration. In fact, Californians preferred Asian and foreign white laborers over native Black citizens. Fur-thermore, whites were often aided by "Immigration Societies whose agencies are spread over the Eastern States and in Europe," while Blacks did "not possess like facilities." The fares of Chinese migrants were paid by capitalists who needed cheap labor, because merchants and businessmen profited from Chinese migration as they had from the migration of other foreigners.

The unique situation of American Blacks was highlighted by the fact that whites asked compatriots in their native land to join them in the New World. Chinese told their brethren of the opportunities awaiting them in California. Black Americans, on the other hand, were more likely to scour the African continent for opportunities rather than recruit African workers for the New World. Afro-Americans traveled entirely on their own, or depended upon personal ties as servants, or migrated as a result of their work on ships and trains.

. . . [T]ravelcraft served Afro-Americans just as immigration societies, capitalists, and Chinese companies aided foreign-born and brought them to San Francisco. It involved a particular outlook in which the determination to succeed, reflectiveness and rationality, and racial consciousness assumed important roles.

Because the best jobs were closed to them, Negroes had to be especially alert for opportunities, actively pursuing chances for money instead of waiting for them to arrive, and traveling to dismal, forlorn places. In a letter to his wife, Jeremiah B. Sanderson explained why he left Sacramento for Shasta county, hundreds of miles to the north. . . . When offered the chance to earn $2.50 a day in winter and more in the spring, he left for the distant mountainous region in northern California. The isolation he endured was typical of that suffered by many Black pioneers.

Hardships were compounded by separation from relations. As noted, some left families in the east, while others housed them in San Francisco before heading for the interior. Sanderson described the travails of the Blacks, and the reasons they endured prolonged separations and hardships. "My thoughts are continually of home, of you and the children—at times I have felt anxiously and wretchedly enough to get up and start at once for home poor as I am—Heaven help me to be patient for a few months longer. I am now making one more effort to get together a few dollars, at least enough to come home to my family.". . .

Discrimination in employment and travel produced a racial dimension to travelcraft. To avoid embarrassment and inconvenience, Negroes traditionally looked after their own, using an "intricate and involved system of reciprocal entertaining" to "soften the impact of prejudice on the Negro traveler." By lodging and entertaining visitors and then enjoying similar privileges while on the road, Black folk found "a method of avoiding insults in restaurants, refusals in hotels, and discrimination in places of public entertainment." Debate in ethnic associations, conventions, and newspapers heightened the racial consciousness caused by oppression and developed racial awareness and pride by knitting Afro-Americans together and providing intelligence. . . .

. . . The methods of Black pioneers were predicated on their rationality and their racial outlook. Race-conscious correspondents and agents for the newspapers collected subscriptions and obtained information. The newspaper offices were clearing houses, and the editors were intelligence officers who solicited information, then decided what to publish, and perhaps even suggested what correspondents should note and communicate.

The names of a newspaper's agents and correspondents were frequently printed on the front. The October 4, 1862, *Pacific Appeal* listed thirty-three intelligence officers, including a "traveling agent," Reverend T. M. D. Ward. . . . [A]gents reported from such nearby cities as San Jose, Stockton, and Sacramento, from the interior towns of Marysville, Grass Valley, and Placerville, and from Nevada, Los Angeles, Portland, Oregon, and Canada. One agent was to be found as far away as Panama, and Peter K. Cole sent information from Japan. . . . Thanks to the agents, Black pioneers could stay abreast of business and personal affairs in distant cities and states.

Pioneers also sought the wisdom of prominent Blacks on the lecture circuit. The Bay Area churches frequently featured well-known and well-traveled Afro-Americans who spoke on a variety of topics of the day, including conditions in foreign lands or in the eastern states. Peter K. Cole addressed Black city dwellers on the economic possibilities resulting from trade with Asia. Reverend E. T. Anderson, "who spent four years in Great Britain, visited Rome and many other continental cities," lectured at the A. M. E. Church in 1890. . . . Another visitor was Ida B. Wells, a leading Afro-American at the turn of the century. After lecturing in the United States and Europe, this courageous journalist visited the west coast and addressed San Francisco's citizens in 1895. Other speakers were the Reverend Adam Clayton Powell, Sr., father of the late congressman; James Weldon Johnson, the lawyer, scholar, and songwriter; and Booker T. Washington, head of Tuskegee Institute. Through both speaking engagements and less formal occasions, well-traveled Black citizens increased residents' understanding of their larger situation and the opportunities it held.

Other important disseminators of travel information have been neglected by scholars. Workers on trains and ships aided Negro travelers, providing information, amenities, and some protection from prejudice. Because many Black San Franciscans worked on ships and trains, it is necessary to consider their importance for travelers.

"Clio," a correspondent for the *Elevator*, wrote of the important roles played by porters on the Central Pacific Railroad. While it is not clear that all porters were Black, some were, including such leading pioneers as James R. Phillips. . . . Afro-Americans listened to these respected workers "because they knowd [sic] the porters [have] been everywhere" and were "able to let people know what was happening." Whenever the pioneer urbanites landed in a strange place, without friends or knowledge of the city, the service workers, who also suffered from prejudice, were invaluable. . . .

By the late nineteenth century, travel to the Bay Area was easier and information was more readily obtained. Cheaper fares, new railroad lines to southern California, and the dissemination of travel intelligence by Black newspapers, societies, and Pullman porters brought drastic changes. These factors, combined with increased hostility and oppression in the south, prompted mass migration. When they emerged at the end of the nineteenth century, Black migration societies might have provided settlers to enlarge San Francisco's Afro-American population. But most migrants settled in northern or eastern cities, and as early as 1886 migrants to the west chose southern California over the Bay Area. . . .

In 1910 Los Angeles contained 7,599 Blacks, and the number continued to grow while the Bay Area's contingent remained comparatively small. Elsewhere along the Pacific slope, new Black communities grew in such booming cities as Seattle, whose Black population increased from a handful in the nineteenth century to 2,296 by 1910, when it surpassed San Francisco's. By 1920 these increasing populations indicated that the new cities offered more chances for success than the old metropolis, which could not match their growth.

The difficulties that the nineteenth-century pioneers overcame made them unique. They viewed adversity as a challenge, and valued courage and self-reliance. They were individualists who journeyed by themselves, or with family and a few friends, but never in large organized groups. When Afro-Americans finally traveled en masse with the help of colonization societies or recruiters, it was another era and they settled in another place. . . .

Other characteristics acquired in their travels aided the pioneers. They developed the habit of befriending influential whites and the traveling public to obtain the things that whites won by right or because of union, family, or business associations. Black urbanites cultivated their knowledge of human character because their fortunes rose and fell according to the whims of white Americans. Especially among San Francisco's Negroes, years of traveling, working as porters or servants, and meeting with different people constituted a valuable education. . . .

Their jobs and the travel experience constituted an education which could never be obtained from formal institutions of learning. A Pullman worker, Nat Love, explained what he eventually learned on the job about the public. He maintained that "porters must necessarily be good judges of human nature to be able to please the majority of people who travel under our care." Mary Ellen "Mammy" Pleasant, who rose to power, wealth, and influence to become a legend in her own time, explained that she needed no "book education," for she succeeded by studying people. "You will find such knowledge much more advantageous than all the book-learning you ever knew." After all, those "that have studied books till they knew nearly all the books in the library" become "lost out in the world" when they meet people because their knowledge remains "locked in the library." The Bay Area Afro-Americans' knowledge of humanity was a singular characteristic that underlined their acute sensitivity to human needs and problems. Ironically, this characteristic was rarely recognized in Blacks in the nineteenth century, and is not attributed to them today.

Black travelers enriched the Afro-American world in the city by the bay. In 1870 Peter K. Cole noted that critics might wonder whether Negroes overseas were only returning to reap the rewards of freedom, and question why they were not around during the lean years. The Japan-based correspondent answered: "In being where we have been and being where we are in this wide world, we can bring to you a knowledge of how mankind is ruled in other spheres, from this knowledge, we will help you to deduce facts for important legislation—facts to be gathered from our demonstrations of the great peculiarities of the Eastern world." The intelligence that underlay such a statement filled the newspaper columns and provided a sorely-needed perspective. It allowed readers to see their problems in a way not ordinarily permitted the descendants of slaves.

Travelcraft highlighted devotion to race, because Afro-Americans needed one another to find a place to realize their potential, to assess the degree of prejudice in various lands, and to soften the effects of racism. Jeremiah Sanderson's devotion as a provider, father, schoolteacher, and minister exemplified this love of Black folk who, according to some modern sources, are filled with self-hatred. The sentiments and actions of John G. Wilson, wandering along the Pacific coast, are an example of the race consciousness of a people often separated from family and from the mass of Afro-Americans. About to undertake an overland trip and resigned to a short life expectancy, he told *Pacific Appeal* readers, "If I fall by the way, remember, I depart with an ardent love for the rising progress of the great Afro-American people, the only love I know, next to my God, and that of my brother. . . . who I hold as dear to me as my own existence."

Besides reminding us of their devotion to their cause, travelcraft was significant as an essential element in the life of the Black citizens of the Bay Area. It accounted for their presence and continued residency, for new arrivals could succeed in the urban center if they watched for the right opportunity, consulted informed citizens, and cultivated their relationships with the influential. Collecting and sifting data on routes and places was a skill that could be used in real estate or mining schemes, or in figuring where a Black person could quickly find a job. This talent was also useful for keeping an old job or acquiring a new one, so that the Pacific slope residents survived the onslaughts of white labor unions, competition with the foreign-born, and the increasingly large-scale, specialized nature of industry and commerce.

A Mexican Immigrant, 1910s–1920s

Manuel Gamio

By the late nineteenth century, the territory conquered by the United States from Mexico—the present-day Southwest—had become integrated into the national industrial economy. Indeed, needing new sources of raw materials and foodstuffs for the industrial armies of the East and Midwest, American captains of industry turned increasingly to outlying regions such as the Southwest and California for these extractive resources. Accelerating the process, the railroads had penetrated the Southwest by the 1880s and opened it up for new mining, smelting, ranching, and farming enterprises.

Unable to persuade sufficient numbers of European immigrants to settle in a distant region lacking the more coveted industrial jobs, and having abandoned the importation of Asian labor, owing to the alleged "Yellow Peril," U.S. corporate interests began actively recruiting Mexican laborers from across the border. The result was the first massive migration of Mexican immigrants to the United States. Between 1900 and 1930, well over 1 million Mexicans entered the country, mainly seeking work, although many also fled the violence of the Mexican Revolution of 1910.

In one of the first major studies of Mexican immigrants, Mexican anthropologist Manuel Gamio interviewed southwestern immigrants of varied backgrounds during 1926–1927. In the following excerpt, immigrant Pablo Mares tells Gamio of his experiences in the United States. Although Mares's story is generally positive, it has to be seen in the context of the different working and living conditions of immigrant life.

STUDY QUESTIONS

1. Why did Pablo Mares leave Mexico for the United States?

2. In Mares's case, and perhaps that of other Mexican immigrants to the United States, can we differentiate among political, economic, and social factors to explain why they left their homeland? Explain.

[Pablo Mares] is a miner, a native of a little village near Guadalajara, Jalisco, *mestizo.*

"In my youth I worked as a house servant, but as I grew older I wanted to be independent. I was able through great efforts to start a little store in my town. But I had to come to the United States, because it was impossible to live down there with so many revolutions. Once even I was at the point of being killed by some revolutionists. A group of revolutionists had just taken the town and a corporal or one of those who was in command of the soldiers went with a bunch of these to my place and began to ask me for whiskey and other liquors which I had there. But, although I had them, I told them that I didn't sell liquor, but only things to eat and a few other things, but nothing to drink. They didn't let me close the store but stayed there until about midnight. The one in command of the group then went to another little store and there got a couple of bottles of wine. When he had drunk this it went to his head and he came back to my store to bother me by asking for whiskey, and saying that he knew that I had some. He bothered me so much that we came to words. Then he menaced me with a rifle. He just missed killing me and that was because another soldier hit his arm and the bullet lodged in the roof of the house. Then some others came and took the fellow away and let me close the store. On the next day, and as soon as I could, I sold everything that I had, keeping only the little house—I don't know in what condition it is today. The Villistas [followers of Pancho Villa, a leading figure in the Mexican Revolution] pressed me into the service then, and took me with them as a soldier. But I didn't like that, because I never liked to go about fighting, especially about things that don't make any difference to one. So when we got to Torreon I ran away just as soon as I could. That was about 1915.

"I went from there to Ciudad Juarez and from there to El Paso. There I put myself under contract to go to work on the tracks. I stayed in that work in various camps until I reached California. I was for a while in Los Angeles working in cement work, which is very hard. From there I went to Kansas, and I was also in Oklahoma and in Texas, always working on the railroads. But the climate in those states didn't agree with me, so I beat it for Arizona. Some friends told me that I could find a good job here in Miami. I have worked in the mines here, in the King, the Superior and the Globe. In all of them it is more or less alike for the Mexicans. Here in the Miami mine I learned to work the drills and all the mining machinery and I know how to do everything. The work is very heavy, but what is good is that one lives in peace. There is no trouble with revolutions nor difficulties of any kind. Here one is treated according to the way in which one behaves himself and one

From *The Mexican Immigrant: His Life-Story* by Manuel Gamio, pp. 1–4. Copyright 1931, reprinted by permission of Ayer Company Publishers.

Mexican gas company workers in Los Angeles

earns more than in Mexico. I have gone back to Mexico twice. Once I went as far as Chihuahua and another time to Torreon, but I have come back, for in addition to the fact that work is very scarce there, the wages are too low. One can hardly earn enough to eat. It is true that here it is almost the same, but there are more comforts of life here. One can buy many things cheaper and in payments. I think that as long as we have so many wars, killing each other, we will not progress and we shall always be poor. That is what these *bolillos** want. It is here that the revolutions are made. It is over there that the fools kill each other. It is better for the *bolillos* that we do that, for they want to wipe us out in order to make themselves masters of all that we possess. It is a shame that we live the way we do and if we go we shall never do anything. I don't care about political matters. It is the same to me to have Calles as Obregón in the government. In the end neither one of them does anything for me. I live from my work and nothing else. If I don't work I know that I won't eat and if I work I am sure at least that I will eat. So that why should we poor people get mixed up in politics. It doesn't do us any good. Let those who have offices, who get something out of it, get into it. But he who has to work hard, let him live from his work alone. It is not, as I

---

* Nickname given to the Americans by the Mexicans.

have already told you, that I like it more here. No one is better off here than in his own country. But to those of us who work, it is better to live here until the revolutions end. When everything is peaceful and one can work as one likes, then it will be better to go back there to see if one can do anything. There are no profits in small businesses. Only the large businesses make money. They sell to the little stores and these just manage to get by. Here in Miami one can live as one wishes without being bothered. I am a Catholic because my parents taught me that faith. But to tell you the truth since I left Mexico I haven't gone to a single church, nor do I pray except when I think of it, and when I am not very tired when I leave my work. But I know that since I harm no one nothing is going to be done to me either. Let each one believe that which seems to him best. Whether a man is Catholic or Protestant makes no difference to me if he does no evil, but if anyone does me a wrong regardless of what faith he may be, if I can hurt him, I will hurt him, or at least defend myself. I hardly ever read the papers for I know that they tell nothing but lies. They exaggerate everything, and besides, I hardly know how to read, for my parents didn't have the means with which to send me to school. I, by myself, with some friends, have learned to read a little and to write my name. I had to do this when I went back to Mexico. If I hadn't, they wouldn't have let me come back in."

A Choctaw Odyssey, 1900s–1950s

CHARLES ROBERTS

After suffering a drastic reduction between the 1760s and 1860s, the Native American population of California has risen from a nadir of 30,000 to well over 200,000 in 1990. Several observations about the nature of that growth are required to give an appreciation of its realities. While California can boast the largest Indian population of any state in the Union, the vast majority of Native Americans living there migrated from other states or are the descendants of such migrants. In direct contrast to the Indians of the late nineteenth century, who lived in largely rural, reservation, and ranchería settings, today's California Indian residents dwell predominantly in urban areas. More often than not, native people in these West Coast cities go unrecognized as being Indian. Frequently they are assumed to be part of more publicized immigrant groups such as Asian American–Pacific Islander and Mexican-Latino. Moreover, Indians sometimes resemble members of other racial groups, including Caucasian, as the majority are of mixed racial descent. Despite composing a significant percentage of the national Indian population, California Native Americans receive relatively scant attention compared with peoples of color who make up noticeably larger groups.

A major factor in the urbanization of Indians was the relocation program conducted by the Bureau of Indian Affairs during the 1950s. With government assistance, tribal families left rural and reservation areas for new lives in cities—Los Angeles–Long Beach proved one of the chief centers of relocation. Others moved earlier or later, independently seeking economic opportunities unavailable at home. Scholars have devoted considerable attention to relocation policy and the general effects of interstate migration, especially to urban areas from rural and reservation communities. In this reading, mixed-blood Choctaw historian Charles Roberts offers a needed, highly personalized account of one Indian's move to California—his grandmother's.

STUDY QUESTIONS

1. Compare and contrast the account of this Indian family's migration to California with the descriptions of the immigration of other ethnic groups featured in this chapter.

2. How does twentieth-century Indian life differ from Indian life in earlier centuries, as described by Gutierrez and Fahey in Chapter 1?

3. Do you think that the author's relationship to Lesa Phillip Roberts is a plus or a minus in his ability to tell her story? Explain.

Early last month my grandmother, Lesa Phillip Roberts, who lives in Chowchilla, California, became ninety-eight years old. Since Lesa doesn't know exactly when in February her date of birth is, she has arbitrarily selected the first as a day of celebration. My wife and I, and our two children, ages nine and five, drove down from Sacramento to share in this celebration. I have a need to be near my grandmother in these last years of her life and want my boys to know her in ways that Highway 99 does not permit.

Lesa lives in a duplex with her youngest son, William, in a neighborhood that we have lived in since 1950, moving about from one rental house to another. My aunt Juanita and my cousin Judy, with their families, live across the street, and I have other relatives whose homes are only a few blocks distant. Lesa rarely leaves her home, taking only a monthly trip to the local Bank of America to deposit the check she receives from the Veterans Admin-

From Charles Roberts. "A Choctaw Odyssey: The Life of Lesa Phillip Roberts," *American Indian Quarterly* 13 (1989), pp. 259–273. Reprinted by permission of *American Indian Quarterly*.

istration. My aunt and cousin take care of the shopping, do most of the cooking and cleaning, and help my grandmother in numerous ways. . . . She suffers from arthritis, and her eyesight is weakened by cataracts. Lesa moves about now only with the help of a walker, but in my mind she is still a powerful woman, who ministered to my needs and nourished my growth. She has always been the core to which my family had adhered. It may be that, except for us, her life has been insignificant, yet within its course may be felt currents of wider meaning.

Sometime in February, 1890, Lesa was born in a cabin secluded in the backwaters of rural Mississippi. Her home was in Cushtusa, a small Choctaw community some twenty miles southeast of Philadelphia in Neshoba County. Her parents, Buckhorn and Lucie Phillip, were descended from Choctaw who had remained in Mississippi after the tribe had signed a treaty in 1830 that required them to move west to the new Choctaw Nation in Indian Territory. These Mississippi Choctaw, having chosen to remain in their ancestral lands, had struggled for decades to maintain their identity in a society that defined itself in polarities of white and black, the racial categories demanded by slavery and maintained after the Civil War by segregation.

Prior to the 1880s, the Choctaw had little contact with their white and black neighbors. Their villages were built in the areas marginal to swamps, and they eked out a living by hunting and trapping and by raising garden crops. But in that decade, and in the backwash of powerful forces unleashed by the abolition of slavery, they began to lose their isolation and to enter the local economy. By the 1880s railroads had been constructed through central Mississippi, timber companies had begun to clear-cut the yellow pine and broadleaf forests, and more land was opened for cultivation. As the freedmen departed in large numbers for the richer soil of the Yazoo delta, the Choctaw were recruited as laborers. Most became sharecroppers, working long, hard years for local white farmers, raising only enough corn and cotton to make the barest margin of existence. Others cut and hauled timber for a living or helped in the manufacture of turpentine. Only a few continued to hunt and trap for their livelihoods. The women and young girls wove cane mats and baskets and sewed patchwork quilts and bartered them locally to storekeepers and to the wives of white farmers. . . .

At some time early in the 1890s Buckhorn Phillip moved his family to Tucker. Lesa attended the Catholic mission school there for less than a year. When she was nearly seven years of age, her father cut his foot severely in a lumbering accident and bled to death. He was buried at the Holy Rosary Mission cemetery, in a service that was probably conducted by Father Bekkers. The low voices and the candles flickering above his coffin are indelibly fixed in Lesa's memory. After her father's death, Lesa returned to Cushtusa along with her mother and older sister, Fannie.

In 1898 Congress sent representatives of the Special Commission to the Five Civilized Tribes, more commonly known as the Dawes Commission, to identify Mississippi Choctaw and advise them of their eligibility for land in the Indian Territory. The Choctaw Nation was to be dissolved, and its land divided among its members, prior to absorption into the new state of Oklahoma. Over the next three years the Dawes Commission worked to establish a roll of eligible Mississippi Choctaw. On May 3, 1901, Lucie Phillip, on behalf of herself and her two daughters, signed an application enrolling them as Mississippi Choctaw.

Late in July, 1903, H. Van V. Smith, a special agent of the Dawes Commission, circulated among the Mississippi Choctaw, offering to take them to the western Choctaw Nation. By terms of the Indian Appropriation Act of March 3, 1903 (32 Stat. 982), Congress had allocated $20,000 for the removal of all Mississippi Choctaw identified as eligible under the 14th article of the 1830 Treaty of Dancing Rabbit Creek, but too impoverished to pay their own removal expenses. On July 21, one of Smith's enrolling agents, J. V. Harris, reached Cushtusa. Lesa's mother applied for removal on behalf of her family. Fannie, who had recently married Putwood Billey, applied separately. Seventeen other Choctaw from Cushtusa also decided to emigrate. Shortly thereafter, as Lesa recalls, her mother sold most of their belongings to a neighbor for $12. On August 10, Harris took them to Meridian, Mississippi, to be interviewed by Special Agent Smith.

After Smith confirmed their eligibility as "identified and indigent" Choctaw, he sent them to the county fairgrounds, where they joined other Choctaw who had accepted the offer of land in the Indian Territory. Smith had scheduled a special train to depart from Meridian on August 12. As they waited, Lesa overheard other Choctaw express their fears and apprehensions. Some were disturbed about having to leave relatives behind, while others worried about debts owed to the farmers whose lands they worked. Local merchants who would lose the Choctaw as customers hovered about the campground, urging them to stay. Land agents and speculators from the Indian Territory pestered them as well, "offering whiskey and money as inducements to sign contracts, alleging that the Government would allot them only low grade lands in the Choctaw and Chickasaw Nations." On the morning of August 12, a speculator from Ardmore, Indian Territory, attempted to organize a stickball game. Apparently he wanted to delay the departure and use the ensuing confusion to induce the Choctaw to doubt Smith's authority. Smith rushed to the fairgrounds, threatened to arrest the speculators, and suspended the game. His actions convinced most of the Choctaw of the government's good faith and persuaded them to pack for departure.

At 5:00 P.M., two hours behind schedule, a special train of the Queen and Crescent Railway pulled out of the station at Meridian. As Lesa boarded the train she realized that her journey would take her hundreds of miles from the sacred soil of Mississippi and from Nanih Waiya, the mound that marked the center of the Choctaw universe. She knew that her ancestors had once taken this route, coming out of the west and carrying the bones of all those who had died on the migration. They had emerged out of the vastness of the continent and settled in Mississippi, charged with the veneration of their dead. For Lesa the movement of the train was a palpable reminder of what the departing Choctaw were losing. On board were 259 full-blood Choctaw whose journeys had begun several days earlier in Leake, Jasper, Newton, Kemper, and Neshoba counties, Mississippi. From Meridian the train made its way to Vicksburg and then crossed the Mississippi River, carrying with the Choctaw their personal belongings and their memories of the past.

At 11:00 P.M. the train halted in Monroe, Louisiana, to pick up five more Choctaw. The next morning it passed through Shreveport and arrived in Texas that afternoon. At Dallas the passengers were transferred to the Missouri, Kansas and Texas line. Their route turned north to Denison, across the Red River, and into the heart of the western Choctaw country. Precisely at midnight, August 13, they arrived at Atoka, where the Choctaw Land Office was located. The Choctaw remained on the train overnight, but Lesa and some of the other youngsters stepped off into the streets of the town, still wet from an early evening shower. The morning air was heavy with their excitement. . . .

Each of the newly arrived Choctaw was required to file a proof of settlement with the Choctaw Land Office. On August 15, the day after their arrival, Lesa and her mother reported to William H. Angell, the Commissioner of the Land Office, and indicated their intention to take allotments. From Atoka their applications would be forwarded to the Dawes Commission in Muskogee and then to the Secretary of the Interior in Washington, D.C. For nearly two months, Lesa remained at the camp near Atoka. The Atoka firm of Reynolds and Sample furnished rations to each family on Thursdays, consisting of flour, beef, bacon, cornmeal, dried fruits, coffee, sugar, soda, baking powder, salt, potatoes, and fresh vegetables. Lesa and her mother cooked their own meals, using pots and pans provided by the Commission. When the weather permitted, some of the Mississippi Choctaw hired themselves out to local farmers to pick cotton and to perform other chores. As her mother and sister worked in the fields, Lesa remained in camp to take care of the younger children. On other days she walked in the woods, picked blackberries and wild grapes, and gathered firewood. On one glorious afternoon, as Lesa remembers, she attended a performance of the Sells Brothers Circus in Atoka. . . .

On September 15 the Choctaw Land Office finally acted, sending sixty-six of the Mississippi Choctaw to Bennington in Blue County, where another temporary camp had been erected. Lesa and her mother were not included among this initial group. The Land Office intended to assign the newcomers to an area bounded by the Red River to the south, the line of the Arkansas and Choctaw Railway to the north, the Missouri, Kansas and Texas Railroad to the west, and the St. Louis and San Francisco Railroad to the east.

Although this area had been used primarily for pasture and some of it was heavily wooded, Commissioner Angell described it as "a strip of country well adapted for agricultural purposes. . . ." The Land Office expected to place the Mississippi Choctaw on their allotments before the onset of cold weather, and it provided each family with a set of tools: one hammer, one axe, one hatchet, and one plow at a cost of $3 a family. With these tools they were expected to build log cabins and to prepare the land for cultivation in the spring. Angell ordered Thomas Bayless, who was in charge of the camp at Bennington, "to impress upon them the necessity of immediately building log houses and advise them that it will be necessary to build a house within a week or ten days in order that you may secure the tent to loan to other Indians." . . .

On September 29 the Choctaw Land Office awarded allotments to Lesa and her mother. They had to wait another week, however, before the Dawes Commission approved these selections. On October 6 Lesa, her mother, and fifty-five other Choctaw were taken to the camp at Bennington. By this time the Commission realized that not all of the Mississippi Choctaw could be accommodated in the area near Bennington, so it opened another camp at the Honey Springs Church near Soper. Within fifteen days, the remaining Choctaw were taken to Soper, and the camp at Atoka was abandoned.

Because of the lateness of the season, Lesa remained at the Bennington camp until the following March, when she and her mother were settled upon her mother's homestead. She helped build a cabin, clear the land, and put in a garden. With these labors Lesa began to adjust to the country that would be her home for the next forty-one years. In the next two years she was often hired by local farmers to help with their harvests. She did not attend any of the Choctaw schools, which were now under federal receivership. The sum of her formal education remained the few months of attendance at the Holy Rosary Mission school at Tucker. Her social life was confined mostly to other Mississippi Choctaw and was restricted to the Bennington area. . . .

In 1907, at the age of seventeen, Lesa was married to Daniel Williams, an Oklahoma Choctaw who worked for a cattle ranch near Bokchito. Daniel's enrollment card shows that he was twenty-four years old at the time of his marriage and was three-fourths Choctaw by blood. Lesa has always been reluctant to discuss her marriages, wishing to keep her memories private. In the few offhand moments that she has talked about her husbands, her feelings were released only with hesitation and tentativeness. In her memory Daniel remains a skillful horseman and possessor of an exuberant personality, yet their marriage was marked by tragedy. A first child lived just for a few weeks after birth. A second son, Morris, was born with a lame foot; he lived to the age of ten, when he died of influenza. Daniel died three years after their marriage, succumbing to pneumonia.

After Daniel's death, Lesa returned to her mother's home. After she observed the appropriate period of mourning, she was married in 1911 to

Charles Billey, a Mississippi Choctaw who had emigrated to Oklahoma on the same special train that brought Lesa in 1903. Charles, the son of Rena Billey, was originally from Toles, Mississippi. In 1915, Lesa gave birth to a daughter, Nellie. Her life continued to be shadowed by tragedy. In 1916 she again became a widow when Charles died of tuberculosis. Her mother, Lucie, died in the same year and was buried at the cemetery at Good Springs. Her grief, Lesa recalled, was nearly inconsolable.

In 1916 Lesa was married for a third time. Her marriage to Dawson Billey, Charles's younger brother, also proved short-lived. Two years later Dawson was called to active military duty. Several hundred Choctaw were eventually sent to France, and some were highly decorated, but Dawson Billey never made it to the Western Front. He contracted influenza during the epidemic of 1918, and his life ended at Camp Logan, a training base near Houston, Texas. The most tangible legacy of their marriage was a son, Carl, born July 4, 1917.

On July 14, 1919, Lesa was married to Jesse Roberts, an Oklahoma Choctaw who had recently been discharged from the United States Army. Jesse was born in Blue County, Choctaw Nation, on June 23, 1886. His father was Benjamin Roberts, who was a successful farmer, and his mother was Mulsie Belvin. Jesse's military career was less than glorious. He had enlisted as a Private in Company B, 21st Battalion, United States Guards, on May 20, 1918, and was released from active duty seven months later. During this brief period he served at training bases in Texas and Louisiana. From May 31 to June 2 he was treated in the infirmary at Camp Nicholls, Louisiana, for vaccinia. He was also diagnosed as having a case of chronic gonorrheal urethritis.

After so many tragic times Lesa now found in this marriage a measure of security and happiness. Jesse had three brothers and a sister, thus providing Lesa with an extended family. These family ties also introduced her to the Presbyterian church, Chish Oktok, located about six miles southeast of Bennington. Jesse built a three-room frame house on forty acres of land that he and Lesa purchased shortly after their marriage, which became known as the "old Yellow House" after its first coat of paint. Later Jesse added an additional room. This house had neither electricity nor indoor plumbing, and it was lit by kerosene lamps. It was located three miles west of Chish Oktok on RFD #2, and access to it was over a dirt road.

During the first eight years of the marriage Lesa gave birth to four children: Pearl, born in 1920; William, in 1922; Juanita, in 1924; and Gladys, in 1926. Lesa's life settled into a pattern that flowed from the needs of her children and from the cycle of a farming season. She rose early in the mornings to light a wood stove and to prepare breakfasts of bacon, sausage, fried eggs, biscuits and gravy, all washed down with thick coffee. She prepared suppers of fried chicken, pork steak, sweet potatoes, pinto beans, black-eyed peas, corn-on-the-cob, hominy, okra, and peach cobbler. She hauled water from the spring behind the house and gathered firewood. She washed clothes in a large tub, blackened from the fire used to heat the water. She used the same tub to bathe her children. She gathered black walnuts, pecans, and hickory nuts in the woods. She did most of the gardening, raised chickens and guinea fowl, slopped the hogs, and lavished affection on the dogs that gathered beneath the front porch and in the space underneath the house. She told stories to her children, especially in the cold of winter nights, nursed them when they were ill, disciplined them when they misbehaved, and sent them off to school.

Neither Lesa not Jesse could read or write. Since they lived in one of the poorest counties in Oklahoma, they did not see any compelling reason to require their children to attend school on a regular basis. With the exception of Carl, who spent several years at Jones Academy, the tribal boarding school at Hartshorne, none of their children became proficient in reading. In 1930 an educational survey prepared by C. L. Crutcher for the Bureau of Indian Affairs revealed that five of Lesa's children were of school age. They were expected to attend Manning School, located one-and-a-half miles from the old Yellow House. Nellie, mistakenly identified as age 17, was enrolled in the sixth grade. Carl, listed as age 15, was enrolled in grade four. Pearl, age 10, and William, age 8, were both in the first grade. Juanita, who had just turned 6, was not yet enrolled. . . .

It is not surprising that Lesa's children failed to progress beyond the ninth grade nor that public education left them with only a rudimentary knowledge of reading, writing, and computation. Yet it helped them to become bilingual and to acquire an understanding of the world outside Bryan County. Their intelligence was shaped primarily by other forces: the experience of working on and with the land, the culture of a rural community, and the spiritual life that centered on Chish Oktok. . . .

To a great extent the life of the family centered on Chish Oktok, the Presbyterian church where Jesse's father had once been minister. The congregation was mostly Choctaw, and services were conducted in the Choctaw language. Lesa enjoyed listening to hymns sung in both Choctaw and English. Her children also shared this joy. . . .

With the onset of the Great Depression, Jesse found working the farm increasingly difficult. He borrowed money on five occasions from the First National Bank of St. Paul, Minnesota, to buy seed and meet expenses. He spent a year in the state prison at McAlester for stabbing a man during an argument over a debt Jesse was trying to collect. When his health began to fail in late 1932, he sought a disability payment from the Veterans Administration. In March, 1933, Jesse was given a thorough physical examination at the V.A. hospital in Dallas, Texas. He was suffering from chronic arthritis and glycosuria, but his claim was dismissed because his illnesses were not related to his military service. The next year his health rapidly deteriorated, despite medical attention from Dr. S. M. Toney of Bennington. At 5:00 P.M., March 7, 1934, Jesse died of "tuberculosis of the lungs.". . .

Throughout the Depression Lesa had a hard time managing the farm. As the family's income fell she sought relief from the regional office of the Bureau of Indian Affairs. On two occasions in 1933 the Bureau issued vouchers to Lesa to pay for groceries, the first for $10 and the second for $9.95. . . .

These hard times eroded the family's confidence, forcing them to think about an alternative to farming. As early as 1936 Homer's sister, Effie, and his brother-in-law, Daniel Collum, had emigrated to California and settled in the San Joaquin Valley. A number of Pauline's relatives also moved to California and found work in the Santa Clara Valley. One of her uncles, Ed Pearson, established a home in Berkeley. Their letters back to Bryan County had a disquieting effect on Carl. When reports about the plethora of jobs created by the war industries in California reached him, Carl decided to act. In July, 1943, he took his family to Durant and boarded the Greyhound bus for California. For a time they stayed with Pauline's uncle in Berkeley. Eventually Carl found work as a welder in one of the four Kaiser shipyards in Richmond and moved his family into a labor camp on Dam Road, located in the hills behind the city. Later that year Nellie and her family also emigrated to California. Homer worked briefly in the Richmond shipyards but, disliking the work and the pressures of living in a large city, soon took his family to the San Joaquin Valley. He found a job with a dairy a few miles outside the town of Madera.

Lesa was perturbed by the splitting of her family, and she decided to join Carl and Nellie in California. Carl began sending her money for transportation. To generate more income Lesa took her family to work in the cotton fields near Bonham, Texas. During the fall of 1943 they picked cotton in fields next to German prisoners of war. Finally, in early June, 1944, Lesa had enough money to travel to California. She bade farewell to her sister, Fannie, and to other relatives and friends. She left most of their belongings and the old Yellow House in the keeping of an uncle, Ed Billey. Thus her family began a journey that would have momentous consequences. . . .

Late in the afternoon of June 4, 1944, they arrived at the station in Richmond. They were greeted by Carl and taken to his apartment at 4301 Cutting Boulevard. Shortly before their arrival, Carl and his family had moved into an apartment complex recently constructed by the federal government and for which they paid a monthly rental of $40. Until the summer of 1945 at least ten persons occupied its four rooms, sharing the two beds and sleeping on the floor. This number was frequently enlarged by friends and relatives from Oklahoma, who also came to Richmond to find work. Other refugees from Bryan County lived in this complex. . . .

The shipyards at Richmond offered jobs to all who came during these war years, and the city itself was in a frenzy of growth and demographic change. Before the war Richmond was a relatively placid industrial city sprawling along a low-lying point on the northeastern shore of San Francisco

Bay. Its population of 24,000 was supported mainly by a Standard Oil refinery, a Ford assembly plant, and a dozen smaller industries located on the waterfront. After the United States entered the war, four Kaiser shipyards were constructed in Richmond, and its population mushroomed to over 100,00 persons. The thousands of emigrants who poured into the city created enormous problems in housing and municipal services. The federal government erected huge barracks-style, public-housing projects in the mud flats between the harbor and the town. Schools were so overcrowded that for a time they were run in four shifts. By 1944 they had settled into two shifts. The older residents of Richmond, who were mostly whites, were torn by pride in their city's accomplishments and by resentment of the newcomers, especially the 14,000 Blacks and the group they disparagingly identified as Okies.

After their arrival Lesa's children obtained jobs at Kaiser. Pearl was hired as a welder on a segregated night shift, composed exclusively of Indians. William became a trucker's helper, and Juanita worked on a cleanup crew. Gladys, the younger of Lesa's daughters, stayed at the apartment and helped with housework and the grandchildren. Lesa seldom left the apartment, except to buy fruit at Bruno's and to shop at the local Lucky's Market. She could not speak English, and she was always apprehensive around strangers. Her rich interior life could only be released in the soft words of the Choctaw language, in the conversations she had with her children, in the stories she told her grandchildren, and in the songs she sang to them. Often, into the deep of the night, Lesa listened patiently as her children came to her, bringing their discoveries, joys, hopes, and fears.

Coming from the rural isolation of southeastern Oklahoma, Lesa's family did not have the knowledge necessary to accommodate the powerful forces of the urban world. They were overwhelmed by the frenetic pace of the Bay Area, alternately perturbed and exhilarated by the crowded streets of Richmond and its rich mix of nationalities. Nor could they comprehend the money they received each payday. The average worker at Kaiser made $61 a week. Such sums were intoxicating to a family that only a few months before was picking cotton for measly wages in Texas. In moments of respite from work, they took the ferry across the Bay, shopped in San Francisco, had their pictures taken at Fisherman's Wharf, ate at restaurants in North Beach and Chinatown, watched as ships sailed through the Golden Gate into the maelstrom of the war. They became immersed in movies. Several times a week they went to the cinemas in Richmond to be drawn into a world of fantasy and dreams. They went to the USO that was located a few blocks from the apartment, and in the evenings they went to Wade Ray's country and western place where they danced to the music of the Maddox Brothers & Rose and other groups. This music, rooted in the Southwest and adapted to California conditions, appealed strongly to their memories and emotions.

Lesa gave cautious advice to her children, but she could do little to counteract the Bay Area's allurements. Her children began to drink socially at the bars, and for some alcohol would remain a problem for many years after the war. The girls were courted by sailors and soldiers, finding pleasure in transient relationships. For a time Pearl was attracted to Nick Novak, who worked for the Southern Pacific in Oakland. He often accompanied Pearl, her son, and Carl's children to a playground near the apartment and bought them candy and soft drinks. Gladys became pregnant and, in June, 1945, gave birth in Richmond to a son, Richard. Carl and Pauline also had a third child, Linda, born in Oakland a few hours after Gladys's delivery.

As the war came to an end Lesa had a difficult choice to make. She could return to Oklahoma and to the hard times they remembered too clearly, or she [could] stay in California and pursue its promise of abundance. Lesa never forced the issue, allowing her children to make the decision. In the summer of 1945 they worked in the orchards near Santa Paula and for Libby's Cannery in Sunnyvale. Then, in September, they packed their belongings into William's 1938 Ford sedan and made their way over the winding course of the Pacheco Pass and onto the expanse of the San Joaquin Valley. They drove to Madera County where a number of Bryan County refugees had settled during the Depression and where Nellie's husband was already employed. They moved into two tar-paper shacks on the north bank of the Berenda Slough, about eight miles west of the small town of Chowchilla. . . .

Since 1945 Lesa has resided in Madera County. For five years after the war her family followed a migratory lifestyle, but always within the county. They found agricultural jobs: cropping and picking cotton, harvesting grapes, knocking almonds and walnuts. Thus they drifted into a pattern that gave them little security. Winters were especially difficult, for jobs were scarce then. William occasionally found work digging out hardpan or tending smudge pots. . . .

A degree of stability was achieved when Lesa's family moved to Chowchilla in December, 1950, even though they continued to work as farm laborers. Lesa has returned to Oklahoma twice for brief visits, once in the summer of 1948 and again in 1952. But over the years her ties with Oklahoma have been mostly broken. Lesa's sister, Fannie, had died, and she has outlived nearly all the friends and neighbors who shared her activities at Chish Oktok. She has sold all of the property that she inherited from her husbands, and she has sold most of her own allotment with the exception of her inalienable homestead. . . .

Lesa is now linked to California by powerful bonds of kinship. Her oldest daughter, Nellie, died in 1972, and Nellie's husband, Homer Neal, died a few years later. Their daughter, Anna Mae, committed suicide in the spring of 1971 in Salt Lake City. Pearl's son, Randall, was fatally involved in an automobile accident on the night of November 16, 1963, when the car in which he was a passenger rammed into a concrete standpipe. Most recently, in February, 1985, Pauline Billey died of a heart attack. With the exception of Anna Mae, all were buried in the Chowchilla Cemetery. Lesa now has fourteen grandchildren, nine of whom were born in California, thirty-two great-grandchildren, and nine great-great-grandchildren. This extensive family is scattered over the country from Florida to Alaska, but the greater number of them lives in or near Chowchilla.

When Lesa celebrated her most recent birthday, many of her extended family were present. The four rooms of the duplex resonated with their voices. Clearly this woman, born nearly a century ago in Mississippi, has created a substantial legacy, and in her person there is a strength that I would like my sons to understand. As we left for Sacramento at the end of our visit, I was pleased when my older boy, Christopher, went directly to Granny and gave her a kiss on her cheek and talked about his pet frogs. My younger son, Matthew, more hesitant, merely put his hand over hers. Then he smiled and headed for the door.

FURTHER READING

Lawrence A. Cardoso, *Mexican Emigration to the United States, 1897–1931* (Tucson: University of Arizona Press, 1980).

Hilary F. Conroy, *The Japanese Frontier in Hawaii, 1868–1898* (Berkeley and Los Angeles: University of California Press, 1953).

Norman L. Crockett, *The All Black Towns* (Lawrence: Regents Press of Kansas, 1979).

Douglas Henry Daniels, *Pioneer Urbanites: A Social and Cultural History of Black San Francisco* (Philadelphia: Temple University Press, 1980; Berkeley and Los Angeles: University of California Press, 1990).

Mary Dorita, *Filipino Immigration to Hawaii* (San Francisco: R&E Research Associates, 1975).

Donald L. Fixico, *Termination and Relocation: Federal Indian Policy, 1945–1960* (Albuquerque: University of New Mexico Press, 1986).

Ernesto Galarza, *Barrio Boy* (Notre Dame: University of Notre Dame Press, 1971).

Juan Ramón García, *Operation Wetback: The Mass Deportation of Mexican Undocumented Workers in 1954* (Westport, Conn.: Greenwood Press, 1980).

Mario T. García, *Desert Immigrants: The Mexicans of El Paso, 1880–1920* (New Haven: Yale University Press, 1981).

Kenneth B. Goode, *California's Black Pioneers: A Brief Historical Survey* (Santa Barbara: McNally and Loftin, 1974).

Joan Jensen, *Passage from India: Asian Indian Immigrants in North America* (New Haven: Yale University Press, 1988).

Rudolph Lapp, *Blacks in Gold Rush California* (New Haven: Yale University Press, 1977).

Bruno Lasker, *Filipino Immigration to Continental United States and to Hawaii* (Chicago: University of Chicago Press, 1931; New York: New York Times and Arno Press, 1969).

Alan Takeo Moriyama, *Imingaisha: Japanese Emigration Companies and Hawaii, 1894–1908* (Honolulu: University of Hawaii Press, 1985).

Nell Irvin Painter, *The Exodusters: Black Migration to Kansas After Reconstruction* (New York: Alfred A. Knopf, 1977; Lawrence: University Press of Kansas, 1986).

Wayne K. Patterson, *The Korean Frontier in America: Immigration to Hawaii, 1896–1910* (Honolulu: University of Hawaii Press, 1988).

Kenneth R. Philp, "Stride Toward Freedom: The Relocation of Indians to Cities, 1952–1960," *Western Historical Quarterly* 16 (1985): 175–190.

Mark Reisler, *By the Sweat of Their Brow: Mexican Immigrant Labor in the United States* (Westport, Conn.: Greenwood Press, 1976).

Ivan Van Sertima, *They Came Before Columbus* (New York: Random House, 1976).

C. Matthew Snipp, *American Indians: The First of This Land* (New York: Russell Sage Foundation, 1989).

Russell Thornton, Gary D. Sandefur, and Harold G. Grasmick, *The Urbanization of American Indians: A Critical Bibliography* (Bloomington: Indiana University Press, 1982).

Shih-shan Henry Tsai, *China and the Overseas Chinese in the United States, 1868–1911* (Fayetteville: University of Arkansas Press, 1983).

Jack O. Waddell and O. Michael Watson, eds., *The American Indian in Urban Society* (Boston: Little, Brown, 1971; Lanham, Md.: University Press of America, 1984).

Zo Kil Young, *Chinese Emigration into the United States, 1850–1880* (New York: New York Times and Arno Press, 1979).

CHAPTER 4

Work

The greatest contributions of peoples of color have come in the blood, sweat, and tears they put into the building (literally) of the West. In certain areas, a particular racial minority, sometimes in tandem with other peoples of color, has been prized for its labor. Employed in agriculture, railroads, mining, smelting, ranching, local industries, and services, racial minority workers have taken part in the economic development of the West for many centuries.

While at times providing the crucial muscle and genius for such growth, peoples of color unfortunately have not fully shared in the fruits of their labor. Subjected to both race and class discrimination, these workers often performed segregated labor in the most undesirable jobs, received the lowest wages, and lived in impoverished conditions. Though heavily exploited in the particular hierarchies of race, class, and gender established in the American West, racial minority workers have nevertheless acted as anything but helpless victims. As shown in this chapter's readings by Albert Hurtado, Clarence Glick, Kenneth Porter, Michael Smith, and Mario García, men and women of color have made history through their economic contributions and their struggles to achieve equality and justice.

FOR ANALYSIS AND DISCUSSION

1. How did the jobs in which most peoples of color were employed differ from the jobs held by many Euro-Americans?

2. How did racism affect the working conditions of the groups discussed in this chapter?

3. What work did women of color typically do? What were the similarities and the differences in the kind of jobs they found and those that their men were hired to perform?

4. How did the poor pay and harsh working conditions of minority workers affect their overall lifestyles?

5. After reading this chapter, have your ideas about the contributions made by different ethnic and racial groups to the building of the American West changed? If so, in what ways?

Indian Labor in California in the 1850s

ALBERT L. HURTADO

Albert L. Hurtado's study of Indian survival on the California frontier won the Ray Allen Billington Prize for the best book in American frontier history in 1989. It focuses on the mid-nineteenth-century experiences of Native Americans in coping with the beginnings of Anglo-American dominance in the northern interior counties of California from the early Gold Rush to 1860s. While analyzing the effects of governmental policy on Indian life, it emphasizes the active participation of California tribes in the development of a capitalist economy that, although providing a means of survival for some, contributed drastically to overall demographic losses and to the restructuring of native institutions, particularly the family.

Any study of California Native Americans is driven by the depressing reality of population reduction. When the Spanish frontier advanced to the state's present boundaries in 1769, approximately 300,000 Indians resided in that region. At the time of the Mexican Revolution in 1821, this number had fallen by a third. By 1848 it was down to about 150,000. During the 1850s, the period examined in the following selection, an 80 percent decline resulted in a native population of just 30,000, while the numbers of non-Indians made that total a minority.

California constitutes a special case in the history of Indian-white relations in the Far West. California Indians' resistance to U.S. encroachments did not feature dramatic large-scale military confrontations as California native groups were small and as they often fought outsiders individually or as small communities. Further, the long interaction of California tribes with the Spanish and Mexicans had conditioned them to a pattern of often violent resistance coupled with near-servile adaptation. Hurtado offers examples of the several subtle strategies California Native Americans employed in their "quest for survival."

STUDY QUESTIONS

1. How did the Gold Rush affect California's Indians?

2. How did California's Indians adapt to a minority status?

3. What can you deduce from this reading about how non-Indians historically have viewed Native Americans?

When opponents of the 1851 treaties [agreements that provided California tribes with reservations and federal agents] declared that Indians were already in "the best school of civilization," they assumed that employment in the white economy had intrinsic value beyond the pecuniary benefits that it provided. Indians who worked for whites were surely on their way up the ladder of civilization, or at least on the bottom rung, far above native people who remained in a "savage" condition. That whites benefited from Indian labor was well understood and nobody questioned the right of an employer to profit from the work of his employees, regardless of their race. The civilizing effects of an honest day's labor were highly regarded on the temporary reservations as well as on private farms. It was a happy coincidence that native labor would make the reservations self-sustaining. At first, the reserve system seemed to promise the best of all possible worlds: while permitting Indian workers to remain on white farms, it would remove troublesome natives to places where hard work would redeem them with little or no expense to the taxpayers.

To bureaucrats, humanitarians, ranchers, and perhaps even the Indians themselves, labor on and off the reservation seemed to be the only certain way for native people to survive in the 1850s. Surely, Indians who adapted so readily to the changes of previous decades would prove flexible enough to meet the new requirements of California Indian life. In looking back on those turbulent years, it is tempting to view peaceful labor as preferable to the pervasive violence that was a growing cause of Indian population decline. Warfare killed untold numbers of Indians and drove thousands into marginally productive environments where malnutrition, starvation, and disease took a further toll. In view of this grim reality, reservations and ranchos seem to have been relatively benign institutions which, if properly managed, could have helped Indians to survive in the 1850s. As it turned out, they were peculiarly ill suited for this purpose, regardless of what whites said at the time.

Contemporary observers seemed unable to understand why reservations failed to live up to the extravagant claims of [Edward F.] Beale [California Superintendent of Indian Affairs] and his supporters. Failures were almost always portrayed as the result of corruption rather than any fundamental unsoundness of design. Typically, the 1858 reports of special agent J. Ross Browne showed corruption and mismanagement at all levels in the California superintendency, as indeed there were. He claimed, however, that the reservation system should not be pronounced a failure since it had not been given a fair trial. Properly managed by honest men, Browne believed, the temporary reserves could work.

From Albert L. Hurtado, *Indian Survival on the California Frontier*, 1988, pp. 149–154, 159–161, 163–168, reprinted by permission of Yale University Press.

The Office of Indian Affairs was shocked at Browne's reports. To get a second opinion, its administrators sent special agent G. Bailey to California. Bailey confirmed Browne's charges, but decided that there was something wrong with the theory behind the institution. Referring to Nome Lackee [one of the temporary reserves], he wrote: "The Government provides a magnificent farm of 25,000 acres in one of the finest grain countries in the world, and stocks it at lavish expense: $17,160 are annually expended in salaries of overseers; $32,427 87/100 more are applied to the purchase of clothing, provisions and supplies of every description: an unlimited supply of Indian labor is furnished, and finally a net result is attaining of 11,950 bushels of grain." The system, wrote Bailey, did not "look beyond the mere feeding and clothing of Indians." Consequently, "there was no gain in the way of civilization to go to the credit side of the account," as Beale's plan had originally envisioned. Instead of self-supporting government farms operated by Indians who gained civilized habits, Bailey explained, the reservations were "simply Government Almshouses where an inconsiderable number of Indians are insufficiently fed and scantily clothed, at an expense wholly disproportionate to the benefits conferred." An average of only forty men were actually employed in farming, a tiny fraction of the total Nome Lackee population, which was estimated at twenty-five hundred. Since the produce of the farm could not feed all of them, almost two thousand were off "gathering berries, grass seed." About a half dozen Nevada County Nisenan girls were employed making straw hats, "but the great mass of the Indians appeared to have no occupation whatever." . . .

Reservation administrators soon learned that agricultural production alone would not support the Indians. In the summer of 1856 [California] Superintendent [of Indian Affairs] Henley faced a small congressional appropriation and food shortages caused by the drought of the previous year. Consequently he ordered the agents at Klamath, Tejon, Nome Lackee, and the Fresno River Farm to send out the Indians to gather wild food. Old men and women should be kept "constantly in the fields and woods, collecting such articles of food as can be procured," thus reducing "the issues from the products of the farm." The agents' reports commonly included estimates of the amount of natural food on hand. Grass seed, acorns, and salmon continued to be a substantial part of the Indian diet, and they were often procured off the reserves. Yokuts at the Fresno River Farm hunted wild horses to supplement their diet. At the same time, reservation Indians mined gold and worked for white ranchers. . . .

Nonreservation Indians sometimes went to reserves to work. Tulare Lake Yokuts gleaned the Tejon fields; Yokuts and Tubatulabals from the San Joaquin, Kern, and Kings rivers helped with the harvests at the Fresno and Kings River farms. Indians from Tuolumne and Mariposa counties lived part of the year on reservations and spent the rest of their time in their homelands. In the winter of 1857, the Monache Indians came down from the mountains to ask the Fresno subagent for blankets and clothing. Although he sent them away disappointed, their arrival shows that they were aware of the agency as a potential source of provisions.

While many Indians were willing to work at reservations on a seasonal basis, most wanted to live in their traditional territory. Even if they had wanted to go to reservations, there would not have been enough food to support them. . . .

By the late 1850s the relationship of the Indians to the reservations had been turned on its head. To feed the Indian inmates, the agents had to rely on hunting and gathering. Independent natives used the reserves as part of their seasonal round, a situation hardly describable as the school of civilization that bureaucrats and politicians had envisioned. Instead of receiving security, food, and modern means of subsistence, the Indians subsidized the reservations with traditional food gathering. . . . Most Indians lived off the reservations, preferring to survive in the midst of a white society. . . . [T]heir experiences varied considerably: some entered the school of civilization by way of the indenture system; others were free laborers. . . .

Before the gold rush most working Indians were employed in agriculture, yet the 1852 census enumerated comparatively few Indians in the interior agricultural counties. Sutter County, with more than five hundred, had the largest Indian population in the Sacramento Valley, but less than a fifth were definitely located adjacent to white farms. The rest were at the west end of Yuba City, at the mouth and along the banks of the Feather River, and across the Sacramento River opposite Colusa. Not surprisingly, sixty-five Indian people lived on John Sutter's Hock Farm and thirty-one resided on the ranch of Nicholaus Allgeier, a former Hudson's Bay man who had worked for Sutter in the 1840s. Regardless of their location, many of these Indians no doubt worked for white farmers part of the year, using Sutter and other ranchers as part of their seasonal round. The male and female populations were nearly equal, but since ages were not recorded it is impossible from these statistics to speculate on the Indians' reproductive potential.

Continued agricultural work did not necessarily enhance Indian opportunities for survival. In 1856 John Sutter explained the deteriorating condition of Sutter County's Indians in a letter to Superintendent Henley. At Nicholaus there were only 15 Ollash Nisenans, down from 52 in 1846. In 1856 the Yukulme Nisenans, three miles down the Feather River from Sutter's Hock Farm, were "nearly extinct" and combined with the Hock Nisenans to form a community of 35, compared to 101 a decade earlier. About three miles up the Feather River from Hock Farm the diminishing Sisums had united with the Yubu Nisenans, rowdy Indians who Sutter thought were leading the other tribes astray. They would drink and gamble all night, then go into the towns to amuse themselves during the day. Drinking in their rancherías led to frequent fights over women. Because "not all of them have Women," Sutter explained, competition for females was intense and sometimes ended in murder, as in the 1854 case of a Yukulme man who wanted to marry the widow of an Ollash chief. When she refused him, he shot and stabbed her to death, then eluded Sutter's attempt to capture him. Assaults on Nisenan women were common, according to Sutter, when the Indians were drinking.

Another aggravating problem that concerned Sutter was that Indians refused to work for less than one dollar a day. Consequently, he preferred to hire white men who received slightly higher wages but ate less than Indians and were more reliable. Indians would work for a week, then rest for another, Sutter explained, taking their wages to Marysville to buy "bad Rhum and Whiskey and get Drunk and disorderly." Formerly Sutter had paid the Indians with "clothing and provisions," but in 1856 "nothing as the Dollars bring them to work."

In towns, Sutter continued, the Indians did a little domestic work, fetching water and chopping wood. Nisenan men, some of whom had firearms, still hunted and fished when they could, but sold their game to whites for money and whiskey. Likewise, they sold their bows and arrows and other "curiosities" to buy bad liquor. Nisenans may have decided that bow hunting was archaic after they had acquired guns. Besides, not all traditional food gathering techniques were still permitted. Sutter complained that some settlers would not let Nisenan women gather acorns or grass seed, which were formerly staples of the Indian diet. With only men's work to supply the Indians, and with much of the men's earnings going for liquor, Sutter feared that the Nisenans would steal from his fields, orchards, and vineyards. Exasperated, Sutter asked Henley to remove the Indians, "or if you would give me the control *only of the* Hock & Yukulme Indians, I would make them work and pay them a reasonable Compensation, in food and Clothing." . . .

. . . Tulare County had a unique population structure among California's enumerated interior tribes in 1852: it was the only region where large communities remained the basis of Indian social life. Regrettably, the data are incomplete, for the census enumerator merely estimated the aggregates of men and women in fourteen rancherías, which were listed separately from the white population. Despite its shortcomings, the census shows that, as usual, men outnumbered women by more than two to one, although some rancherías had more women than others. Like so many other native people, the Tulare County Indians survived by combining hunting, gathering, mining, and working for whites; but with nearly fifty Indians for every white in the county, the Yokuts' main advantage was in numbers that gave them a measure of security from wanton white attacks. Living in large communities permitted the Yokuts to control their own social lives more than Indians who were forced into smaller and smaller native settlements as a result of demographic losses and white pressure on local resources. Moreover, in 1852 the sparseness of white settlement left large areas open to Indian exploitation.

During the 1850s the school of civilization in California had a limited enrollment and many truants. On federal reserves, agricultural labor did not sweep away traditional subsistence patterns, but rather complemented them. As self-sufficient enterprises, the reservations became dependent not merely on Indian labor, but on traditional native provender as well. Furthermore, no reservation provided enough work to absorb the total Indian labor pool; unemployment and underemployment were the lots of most reservation Indians.

Outside the reserves, Indians found comparatively few employment opportunities. Even as early as 1852, at the height of the gold rush demand for food, surprisingly few Indians worked in seasonal agricultural occupations. Why were Indians, who had been the principal source of agricultural labor until the gold rush, so quickly displaced in the interior farming counties?

Part of the answer is found in the nature of the new white population that employed Indians. Bound by racist ideas and unfamiliar with Indian labor, whites were reluctant to rely on native workers. And, as Sutter pointed out, Indian labor was no longer all that was available; white workers were more efficient, especially when Indians insisted on cash for their services. Sutter's statement of Indian wages may have been a little high, since others reported that Indians received seventy-five cents per day. Low Indian wages could have been offset by the increased efficiency of more-expensive white laborers who, according to Indian Office employees, did twice as much work. Furthermore, some farmers who relied on Indian labor set aside fields to help support rancherías year around, a practice provided for in the Indian indenture law. Most farmers were unwilling to exchange productive land for Indian labor, which is one reason why the 1852 census shows comparatively few Indians living among farmers.

There were few incentives to hire Indians in the 1850s, and the best-informed sources advised white farmers to reduce their reliance on manual labor. In 1854 the *California Farmer and Journal of Useful Sciences* urged farmers to substitute machines for people. The reason was simple: when a machine could "at a smaller cost . . . do the work which you are now doing with human hands, buy the machine if you can; and if you have not the means get them as soon as possible." Farmers heeded the suggestion. Two years later Eliza Farnham described the proliferation of farm machinery. Where in 1852 there had been undeveloped land, she saw "continuous grain fields, of six or eight miles in length, with, perhaps, a dozen reapers, of the best patent, marching up and down, leveling the tall thick harvest." Some of the reapers were manufactured locally, but by the mid-fifties Cyrus McCormack and other eastern manufacturers were exporting their wares to the West Coast. Reapers, seed drills, mowers, and threshers mechanized California agriculture. On the large farms horse-powered treadmills ran threshers, and by 1860 portable steam engines had made their appearance. According to a twentieth-century estimate, the horse-drawn reaper alone cut the labor requirement to about half that of hand harvesting. If, as Indian Office employees claimed, native harvesters using sickles were only half as efficient as whites, then a mechanical reaper could reduce the need for Indian labor by three quarters. Moreover, farm laborers were plentiful in California. In 1860 the federal census showed California with the highest ratio of farm laborers to farmers in the United States. Two farmers in the Golden State shared one farm worker, while in Illinois the ratio was three to one, and in Indiana, four to one. While Indian population declined precipitously in the 1850s, native labor became a marginal rather than a critical resource. There were too many hands for too few jobs and Indian labor had become a surplus commodity on the California market. Just as the California economy could not absorb numerous Indian workers, the stopgap temporary reservations were incapable of supporting the native inmates who were already enrolled, much less care for the thousands of dispossessed native migrants who needed assistance.

Thus, the public and private institutions that were supposed to save the Indians from extermination managed to provide salvation for only a small minority, at a cost of fragmenting Indian society and exacerbating population decline. For insofar as jobs were available for Indians, whites usually hired young men for heavy seasonal work. Consequently, women and children were ordinarily left behind to shift for themselves, a perilous situation in the 1850s. By no means were women irrelevant to the Indian economy, for wherever possible they continued to gather wild food against the lean winter months. The chronic shortage of women virtually everywhere in the interior in 1852 was a serious problem that threatened Indian survival, just as the shrinking Indian resource base did. Although there were not enough jobs for native men in the California economy, there were too many tasks for women as fewer of them became responsible for providing food to native communities. In addition, the lack of women presented a long-term demographic problem. Imbalanced sex ratios, coupled with shrinking populations in community after community, reduced chances for family formation.

Chinese Sugar Plantation Workers in Hawaii, 1860s–1900s

CLARENCE E. GLICK

According to the U.S. census of population in 1870, 25 percent of the gainfully employed persons in California were Chinese. Though less numerous elsewhere in the American West, Chinese played a significant role in the region's economic development, helping to build not only the western portion of the first transcontinental railroad but also some of the earliest public works. They mined for gold, drained swamps, dug irrigation ditches, built levees, grew and harvested a great variety of corps, cleaned houses, washed clothes, served as cooks not only in private homes and on large ranches but also in restaurants, hospitals, and prisons, and sold groceries and Chinese merchandise.

In Hawaii, however, the work available to the Chinese was more limited: most worked on sugar plantations, having been brought to the islands under contract. If they violated the terms of these contracts, they could be arrested, fined, or even imprisoned. Clarence Glick, who did research on the Chinese in Hawaii in the 1930s for his Ph.D. dissertation, revised and published the work after he retired in the 1970s. Having carried out his research at a time when many of the early Chinese immigrants were still living, Glick uses numerous quotations from the individuals whom he interviewed, offering glimpses of why the Chinese came and what their life was like on the plantations.

After restrictions on Chinese immigration to Hawaii were imposed in 1886, Japanese and eventually Filipinos became the largest work forces on the sugar plantations. In Hawaii, Asian immigrants and their children attained social mobility only when they managed to leave the plantations to enter other kinds of employment.

STUDY QUESTIONS

1. What conditions in China prompted people to emigrate to Hawaii?

2. What problems did Chinese workers encounter on Hawaii's sugar plantations?

3. To offset the monotony of work, what kinds of recreation were made available to the Chinese plantation workers?

O f the estimated 46,000 Chinese migrants who came to Hawaii before Annexation [1898], probably two-thirds to three-fourths began as laborers on sugar or rice plantations, with the larger number working initially on sugar plantations. Hawaiian sugar plantations during this period, though having some unusual features, shared the basic characteristics of the plantation system as it was developing in many parts of the nonindustrialized world.

In the premechanized era, sugar plantations needed not only a large supply of laborers willing to work at wages low enough to return a profit to investors, but also a stable force of workers remaining on the plantation long enough to pay for the costs of recruiting and importing them and to carry through from one crop to the next. To keep imported laborers on the plantation for at least a minimum period, sugar planters in Hawaii during the latter half of the nineteenth century availed themselves of two legal measures that were generally integral parts of the plantation system: first, a form of indenture or contract binding the laborer to the plantation for a stated period under stipulated conditions; second, legal sanctions with judicial machinery to enforce the contract. The indenture system lessened the risks incurred by entrepreneurs who undertook plantation agriculture on economic peripheries by assuring them labor over a given period. The legal basis for this arrangement in Hawaii was the Masters and Servants Act which had been enacted two years before the first Chinese laborers were imported to Hawaii in 1852. It applied not only to plantation labor but also to other types of employment. . . .

From a purely utilitarian point of view the Chinese imported workers had characteristics which made them one of the most satisfactory labor groups in the early phases of plantation development. Their industriousness, perseverance, and adaptability became proverbial. The willingness of Chinese workers to endure hardships, undergo the physical risks of penetrating and opening up undeveloped areas, and put up with the minimum essentials of living accommodations became well known. Employing them was profitable not only because they were willing to work for low wages but also

------

From *Sojourners and Settlers: Chinese Migrants in Hawaii*, by Clarence E. Glick, pp. 23–29, 31–34, 36–39. Copyright © 1980. Reprinted by permission of The University of Hawaii Press.

Sources drawn on for the original work are "An Act for the Government of Masters and Servants," Penal Code of the Hawaiian Islands (1850); Board of Immigration, *Report* (1899); Department of Foreign Relations, Chinese Bureau, records; *Honolulu Advertiser*, 14 August 1932; Interior Department, "Miscellaneous: Immigration—Chinese" (1864–1865); interview with George N. Wilcox, Honolulu (1930); information from a student paper submitted in one of the author's classes, University of Hawaii; and the author's notes from the records of a social welfare agency in Hawaii, 1937.

because the cost of their maintenance was minimal since they rarely brought families with them. . . .

While it is generally true that poverty at home and the hope of economic betterment abroad were basic in bringing thousands of Chinese to the plantations, many different circumstances and motivations led individual Chinese to migrate. The following cases show how the context varied:

> Mr. Lum, born in 1869, was the only son and oldest child in a family of seven children. His early life was one of poverty and hardship. His father used the larger, middle room of their three room house for a store, selling foodstuffs and a few necessities. The people in the village, however, were poor and bought the goods "on account." Often these bills remained unpaid. Money became scarce, and debts were incurred. Suddenly the father died, leaving debts and the support of the family to his wife and thirteen year old son. An uncle who returned to the village about this time from the Hawaiian Islands, where he was a partner in a sugar plantation, finally persuaded the widowed mother to let her young son go with him to Hawaii. The boy made a contract with his uncle whereby he was to work on his uncle's sugar plantation on the island of Hawaii for ten years at ten dollars a month. His passage was to be paid by the uncle, but upon reaching the Islands an amount of his monthly pay was to be taken until the passage expenses were refunded. With his [clothing] in a small bamboo valise, he left his native land, in 1882, for Hawaii.

> Wong Wai was born in 1871 in a village in Duck Doo, Chung Shan district. He comes from a family of four children, being the second son and child. His parents were rice farmers and were of the poorest class of laborers. Although it is customary for a boy to marry early, he could not afford this because of extreme poverty. He did not go to school. . . . Wong heard stories of the better conditions [in Hawaii], told by returning laborers. Seizing the opportunity in 1894, he signed up with the Hawaiian Sugar Planters' Association as an immigrant laborer to work on the sugar plantations and was brought to Honolulu, to be immediately assigned to the _____ Sugar Company on Maui. . . .

A weak government and local instability in South China during the latter half of the nineteenth century added to the conditions which led some Chinese to sign contracts for plantation work in Hawaii:

> We came as contract laborers through lack of steamer fare. . . . You see, although we belonged to a family of wealth we were impoverished by feud. Our family owned 40 to 50 *mou* . . . and dozens of workmen were hired during the harvesting season. We had two steady watchers of the fields the year-around. . . . In a bloody feud between the Chang family and Oo Shak village we lost our two steady workmen. Eighteen villagers were hired by Oo Shak to fight against the huge Chang family, and in the battle two men lost their lives protecting our pine forests. Our village,

Wong Jook Long, had a few resident Changs. After the bloodshed, we were called for our men's lives, and the greedy, impoverished villagers grabbed fields, forest, food and everything, including newborn pigs, for payment. We were left with nothing, and in disillusion we went to Hong Kong to sell ourselves as contract laborers. We were very young then. I was 22, and my brother was four years younger.

Most of the Chinese migrants came from villages in delta regions south and east of Canton or from the central coastal districts of Kwangtung province. In order to reach the ports from which the emigrant ships sailed— chiefly Canton, Whampoa, Hong Kong, and Macao—the men usually started out in groups, walked to the inland ports, and traveled by small vessels, along canals or rivers, through districts which were unfamiliar and sometimes unsafe. Chinese migration to Hawaii was not characterized by the atrocious and harrowing experiences of kidnapping and shanghaiing, imprisonment behind barracoons in the port cities of South China, maltreatment on shipboard, or inhuman dealing in "coolie flesh" which have blackened accounts of the "coolie trade" to many other areas. . . . Each man who embarked was to be given a free passage to the Hawaiian Islands, a present of eight dollars, two suits of clothing, a winter jacket, a pair of shoes, a bamboo hat, a mat, a pillow, and bed covering. The vessels were prepared for a 56-day passage and fitted out with berths, water, firewood, cooking utensils, Chinese provisions, medicines, and a "hospital" on deck; an interpreter and a Chinese doctor were to be provided on each vessel; twenty of the passengers were to act as cooks for the five hundred immigrants, six as overseers and two as stewards, each to receive payment in advance for such services. And a rail partition was to be erected on the vessels to separate the "male and female passengers on board.". . .

Even with such provisions, the passage, some four thousand miles by the most direct route, was long, tedious, and often trying. Before 1880 most of the migrants came on sailing vessels which sometimes took as long as seventy days for the trip. Conditions on the ships were crowded and uncomfortable; there was much uneasiness, even near panic when contagions broke out. . . .

Precautions by immigrations authorities to minimize the danger of introducing contagious diseases proved as obnoxious to the Chinese as such efforts have been to steerage immigrants elsewhere. After several epidemics in the early 1880s had caused many deaths, chiefly among the already diminishing Hawaiian people, quarantine facilities were set up on an island near the mouth of Honolulu harbor, where Chinese immigrants were landed and kept under the observation of physicians for a few days. Chinese residents and others protested this procedure. . . .

Even though the government tried to avoid the worst abuses of laborer recruitment, some migrants were disillusioned after reaching Hawaii. Men who had agreed to ship to the plantations often came to feel that they had been exploited and deceived by government officials or by Chinese who assisted the plantations in securing contract laborers. . . .

Caring for and handling Chinese contract laborers, once they arrived on the plantations, posed several problems which were complicated by the differences in race and culture between planters and workers. One of the first problems had to do with food. In the early decades of Chinese importation the contracts required the planters to furnish food for the laborers. At that time most workers already on the plantations were Hawaiians whose diet consisted primarily of such locally available foods as poi (made from taro), fish, and sweet potatoes—a diet quite different from that of the South Chinese for whom the staple food was rice. Until locally produced rice became plentiful and cheap, stinting on the amount of rice provided Chinese workers was a source of complaint. . . .

The housing furnished by the plantations, though simple, seems to have caused few problems. Men were usually housed in long, unpainted, frame buildings. The Chinese were accustomed to sleeping on a mat thrown over a wooden platform, and plantation houses usually had wooden ledges, two or three feet from the ground and about three feet wide, where the men could place their mats and, if they wanted to, hang mosquitos nets. From six to forty men would be assigned to a single room.

Since the Chinese were brought to the plantations primarily for unskilled manual work in the fields and around the mills, no complicated or extensive communication between them and their employers was expected. . . . Chinese workers who became familiar with Hawaiian or pidgin English commonly acted as interpreters. . . .

On a large plantation the contract laborer actually had little direct contact with the Caucasian owner or manager. On the job he was supervised by, and at the orders of, a luna (overseer) who was generally of a different ethnic group—in the early days a Hawaiian or part-Hawaiian, later on perhaps a Portuguese, Norwegian, or German imported migrant—someone who did not know his language, his cultural background, or even the extent of his agricultural knowledge and skills. Probably the greatest single source of trouble on plantations was friction between field workers and lunas, certainly not unusual in worker-supervisor situations but exacerbated here by cultural differences.

Apart from field work under the direct supervision of a non-Chinese luna, two other systems of sugar cane production developed that gave Chinese workers more discretion and independence: the *ukupau* (Hawaiian for "job done") and the "contract." Under the *ukupau* system a certain quantity of work was set by the plantation as a day's job. The laborer could work as rapidly or as slowly as he pleased and could quit when the stipulated work was completed. [One] planter . . . said that in his long experience the *ukupau* system had proved to be the best to use with Chinese labor. Under the contract arrangement a group of Chinese laborers worked under a Chinese who

contracted with the plantation to carry out a given undertaking at a stipulated sum per acre, per ton, or per job. At one time more than three hundred
Chinese laborers were under the control of two Chinese contractors on one
of the larger plantations on Maui. It was expected that Chinese laborers
would be more content to work under this system than under the more
impersonal control of non-Chinese lunas; they could work under arrangements which took account of the demands and values of their cultural background. Sometimes the contractor, with plantation approval, recruited his
laborers from among his own clansmen or fellow villagers in the expectation
that they would compose a more stable group because of their traditional
ties and would work harder because of their personal obligations to the contractor. The system also lent itself to cooperative arrangements by which the
laborers could share in the profits with the contractor.

Another type of cooperative scheme worked out among the laborers
themselves was described by the same planter:

> The Chinese usually made one of their gang the cook. He would fix their
> breakfast, and then cook their dinner and bring it hot to the field. They
> had to have hot dinner and hot tea to drink. The man who was made the
> cook usually shared just the same as the rest of the men. They would
> divide up what they made, so that all got the same. . . . Another thing
> was the dope. Y —— Fat was the one I learned this from: He told me
> that when he went to the field to work, and the cook brought his meals
> to him, he found that in the top of the bucket was a little paper or enve-
> lope with the dope in it. All the men, he said, took their dope that way
> with their dinner. The cook would have to see about getting the stuff and
> fixing it up the same as the rest of the meal.

On some Hawaiian plantations the daily life of the workers was closely
regimented in the interest of maintaining an efficient work force. The nature
of this regimentation was implicit in the rules that plantations usually drew
up and posted. . . . Workers felt, with some cause, that the laws were more
readily enforced for the employers than for themselves. There is some evidence to support complaints about collusion between the planters and the
legal authorities to the disadvantage of the laborers. . . .

Most contracts in the nineteenth century stipulated twenty-six working
days of ten hours [per month]. Work started early, and even though men
worked overtime during busy seasons there was a good deal of free time in
the late afternoons and evenings and on Sundays and holidays. Until about
1910 most of these men were young—of 6,894 Chinese entering contracts in
1895–1897 almost half were under twenty-five years old, three-fourths
under thirty, and nine-tenths under thirty-five. . . . [T]he plantations provided little for these men to do when they were not working. Most plantations, during the years most Chinese were employed on them, were quite
isolated and the laborers under contract seldom got into town. Since there
were few Chinese women and families, and on some plantations none, there

was little semblance of the stabilizing family and clan life these young men had left behind. There were no clan or village elders to exert control. Usually the plantation did house Chinese workers separately from those of other ethnic groups in what was generally called "the Chinese camp," with an older Chinese, who had several years' experience on the plantation, as "headman" or manager. Sometimes he was responsible for order in the camp, collected rents from the day laborers living in the camp, assisted in paying wages, and served as interpreter, labor contractor, labor recruiter. Commonly the headman operated a store selling the men Chinese and other goods. This store was a common meeting place for workers with nothing else to do. Sometimes the headman had his wife and family with him; if so, they helped tend the store and often made and mended clothes for the bachelor laborers.

One spare-time activity was gardening. Most of the workers had been farmers at home, and on the plantation they cultivated plots where they grew the vegetables favored in Chinese cooking. Growing bananas and raising pigs, ducks, and chickens were other ways laborers could supply themselves with the kinds of food they liked to eat and at the same time reduce their food costs. This arrangement became more prevalent when contracts no longer required planters to supply food to the laborers and also when Chinese remained on the plantations as day laborers.

Nevertheless, the young men who lived in the camps were often bored with the monotonous plantation life. It is little wonder that vices spread as they usually do in frontier communities with an abnormal preponderance of males. Opium smoking was widespread. . . . Gambling flourished on the plantations. . . .

During most of the decades that Chinese migrants entered Hawaii as contract laborers, the plantation work force also included a large number of Hawaiians, both men and women. . . . [Some] Caucasians encouraged liaisons between Chinese men and Hawaiian women as a way of "rebuilding the native race"; others concluded that such relations were "demoralizing the natives." In any case, numerous migrants did associate freely with Hawaiian women, some casually, others establishing permanent family ties. The migrants' relations with Hawaiian women were a factor in some of the anti-Chinese feelings among Hawaiian men.

Although several hundred Chinese workers brought to the plantations as contract laborers remained on them throughout their working life in Hawaii (as day laborers after they were no longer on contracts), by far the greater number left the plantations when their contracts expired. In spite of the arrival of over 14,000 Chinese during the six years prior to 1882, only 5,007 of the plantations' 10,253 workers in 1882 were Chinese. During periods when importation of Chinese contract laborers was restricted—roughly from

1886 to 1895 and from 1898 on—the number of Chinese plantation employees diminished rapidly. Less than half as many were on the plantations in 1892 as in 1888, and of the 8,114 Chinese working on sugar plantations on 31 December 1897 over half had left by 1902.

 # African Americans in the Cattle Industry, 1860s–1880s

KENNETH W. PORTER

Kenneth W. Porter was one of the first historians to explore ethnic and racial themes in the American West, including studies of black Seminoles and black cowboys. The following excerpt on African-American workers in the cattle country contradicts the more common portrait of a biracial West consisting of white cowboys and Native Americans. Not only did blacks work as cowboys, but they also were often highly skilled wranglers, riders, and ropers, who, along with Mexicans and Mexican Americans, made up as much as 25 percent and 12 percent, respectively, of the multiracial enterprises that have been almost invariably portrayed as all-white in western films. Porter provides the complex racial portrait that we need to understand that the region (and the United States at large) has multiracial historical origins; he also offers evidence of a spirit of cooperation, as well as competition, among these different groups.

Besides examining their skills, working conditions, wages, and social life, Porter discusses the presence of racial discrimination in the lives of black cowboys. In contrast to the South, in the western cattle industry, relations between African-Americans and Euro-Americans were comparatively equal, although blacks could not rise through the ranks to top ranch positions. Significantly, and underlining the close ties between racism and sexism, Porter indicates that the relative equality found on the range and in gambling houses diminished considerably when white women were present in ranch houses and restaurants. Despite the racial discrimination, Porter contends that conditions for black cowboys in the American West allowed them to lead better and safer lives than in the Deep South.

STUDY QUESTIONS

1. What jobs did black ranch hands perform?

2. What were race relations like in the western cattle industry?

The range-cattle industry . . . was rendered possible by such factors as vast expanses of grazing land, projected railroad lines across the Missouri and onto the Great Plains, the rise of heavy industry and the consequent demand for beef of less-than-high quality by the meat-hungry industrial population. But like the steel, mining, packing, and other industries, it also needed a labor force—workers with special abilities and qualities—for although the cowhand or cowboy possibly was no more than a "hired man on horseback," he was a hired man with skills in riding, roping, and branding which could not be easily acquired. Most of his working hours were spent in such routine tasks as riding the range and turning back drifting steers; rounding up, branding, and castrating calves; selecting beeves for the market; and, even on the "long drive," jogging along and daily "eating dirt" on the flanks or in the rear of a few thousand "cow critters." But he also needed the inborn courage and quick thinking to use these skills effectively while confronting an enraged bull, swimming a milling herd across a flooded river, or trying to turn a stampede of fear-crazed steers.

But the general public, under the influence of decades of "Western" movies and, more recently, television shows has come to regard the cowboy's workaday activities as altogether secondary to fighting off hostile Indians, pursuing rustlers and holding "necktie parties" for them, saving the rancher's daughter from Mexican raiders, and engaging in quick-draw gunfights in dusty streets. From similar sources this same public has also learned that cowboys, with the exception of an occasional low-browed villain or exotic and comic-accented *vaquero*, were all of the purest and noblest Anglo-Saxon type, as in Owen Wister's *The Virginian*.

In reality, as George W. Saunders of the Texas Trail Drivers Association has authoritatively estimated, of the fully 35,000 men who went up the trail from Texas with herds during the heroic age of the cattle industry, 1866–1895, "about one-third were Negroes and Mexicans." This estimate is closely confirmed by extant lists of trail-herd outfits which identify their members racially. These lists also demonstrate that Negroes out-numbered Mexicans by more than two to one—slightly more than 63 percent whites, 25 percent Negroes, and slightly under 12 percent Mexicans.

The racial breakdown of individual outfits, of course, varied widely. Some were nearly all of one race, such as the 1874 outfit which was all-Negro, except for a white boss, or the 1872 outfit which consisted of a white trail-boss, eight Mexicans, and a Negro; but more typical were the two 1877 outfits composed, respectively, of seven whites and two Negro cowboys, and a Negro cook; and seven whites, two Negroes, and a Mexican hostler. Many

From Kenneth W. Porter, "Negro Labor in the Western Cattle Industry, 1866–1900," *Labor History* 10 (1969), pp. 346–364, 366–368, 370–374. Used by permission of *Labor History*.

outfits had no Mexicans at all, but it was an exceptional outfit that did not have at least one Negro and enough outfits were nearly all Negro, or a third or more Negro, to bring the number up to the estimated twenty-five percent of the total. . . .

The racial make-up of ranch outfits, with their seasonal and day-by-day fluctuations, was not so well recorded as that of the trail-herd outfits, but available information indicates that ranch hands, in Texas at least, were white, Negro, and Mexican in proportions varying according to locality and to ranchowner tastes; probably the overall proportions differed little from those of trail outfits. . . .

Negro trail drivers swarmed west and north with herds from the Texas "hive" and, though most returned, a few remained as ranch hands as far north as Wyoming, the Dakotas, and even Canada and as far west as New Mexico, Arizona, and even California and Oregon.

Negroes occupied all the positions among cattle-industry employees, from the usually lowly wrangler through ordinary hand to top hand and lofty cook. But they were almost never, except in the highly infrequent case of an all-Negro outfit, to be found as ranch or trail boss.

Negroes and also Mexicans were frequently wranglers, or *remuderos*—in charge of the saddle horses not immediately in use—usually regarded as the lowliest job in the cattle industry, except for the boy who sometimes served as wrangler's assistant. There were exceptions, however, including some Negro wranglers who became "second in authority to the foreman" in a few camps. Such wranglers were "horse men" in the highest sense: capable of detecting and treating illness and injury, selecting the proper horse for each job, and taking the ginger out of unruly animals. . . .

The majority of Negroes on the ranch or "long drive" were neither wranglers nor yet authoritative cooks. . . . They were top hands or ordinary hands who, on the long drive, rode the point, the swing, the flank, or the drag, according to their experience and ability. The point—the position of honor—was at the front of the herd where the steers were strongest, most restless, and most likely to try to break away. There the most experienced top hands rode. Farther back, the cattle were somewhat less troublesome, while in the rear, where the tired beasts were comparatively easy to manage, could be found the fledgling cowboys of the drag, "eating the dust" of the entire herd. Negroes rode in all these positions. . . .

Old, experienced Negro cowhands frequently served as unofficial, one-man apprentice systems to white greenhorns. This was particularly true, of course, when the fledgling was the employer's son or relative. Will Rogers, for example, got his first lessons in riding and roping from a Cherokee Negro employee of his father. Almost any young would-be cowboy who showed the proper spirit, however, might have the good fortune to be "adopted" and "showed the ropes" by one of these black veterans, who would sometimes take on the inexperienced boy as partner when white cowboys were unwilling to do so. . . .

Negro cowhands confronted all the dangers and met all the tests of the long trail. . . . Crossing the wide, deep, frequently flooded rivers was even more dangerous than stampedes. According to a white ex-cowboy, "it was the Negro hand who usually tried out the swimming water when a trailing herd came to a swollen stream"—either because of his superior ability or because he was regarded as expendable. . . .

Although every top hand had to be a skillful rider and roper, some were so outstanding as to be considered "bronco busters" and/or ropers *par excellence* rather than as merely uncommonly able cowboys. Numerous references suggest that Negroes and Mexicans were widely regarded as particularly expert in both these capacities—the Mexicans especially noted for their prowess with the *reata* (or lasso). . . .

A white ex-cowpuncher-writer states that Negroes were hired largely for their ability to cope with bad horses which the white cowhands did not want to tackle. "The Negro cow hands of the middle 1880s . . . were usually called on to do the hardest work around an outfit. . . . This most often took the form of 'topping' or taking the first pitch out of the rough horses of the outfit. . . . It was not unusual for one young Negro to 'top' a half dozen hard-pitching horses before breakfast.". . .

The list of Negro bronc riders—the comparatively few whose names have survived—is still a long one. [Among a] few of the better known, partly because they attracted the attention of published writers, [was] Isam, Isom, or Isham Dart of Brown's Hole, "where Colorado, Wyoming, and Utah cornered," who, although now remembered principally as a reputed rustler, was also "numbered among the top bronc stompers of the Old West.". . .

While most of the famous riders were bronco busters only as one aspect of their work as cowhands, some, including a number of Negroes, were officially recognized as ranch horsebreakers, and a few were full-time or nearly full-time professionals. . . . Other Negro cowhands were particularly renowned as ropers, such as Ab Blocker's Frank, who was, according to a white cowboy, "the best hand with a rope I ever saw," and whose roping skill once saved his employer from an angry steer. . . .

Naturally enough, many of the famous Negro riders, such as Isom Dart and Jim Perry, were almost or quite as renowned as ropers. One of the most spectacular at both riding and roping was "Nigger Add," "one of the best hands on the Pecos," who would as a matter of course "top off" several bad horses of a morning. . . . Indeed, the prowess of such Negro riders, horse-breakers, and horse-trainers was so outstanding as to contribute to the commonly held belief of the time that there was some natural affinity between Negroes and horses. . . .

High in the hierarchy of cow-country employees was the ranch or trail cook, who ranked next to the foreman or trail boss and, in camp, ruled supreme over an area of sixty feet around the chuckwagon. . . . He could do more than anyone else to make life pleasant and many a cowboy selected an outfit because of the reputation of its cook. In compensation for duties which few men could satisfactorily perform, the cook normally was paid from $5 per month more than the ordinary cowhand up to even twice as much. . . .

African-American cowboy Jess Stahl

. . . [T]he cow-camp menus on record seem to have been disproportionately the work of Negro cooks. Good cooks occasionally supplemented the
filling but somewhat monotonous diet of biscuits, "sowbelly," beef,
molasses, and coffee by carrying a gun in the wagon and, between dishwashing and starting the next meal, hunted deer, turkey, and other game. . . .

The Negro cook often possessed other skills beyond the culinary. So
many Negro cooks, in fact, were noted riders and ropers that something of a
pattern emerges. The wild-game cook extraordinary, Black Sam, was such a
good rider that "frequently one of the boys would get him to 'top' a bad
horse.". . . When an associate of one of the famous Blockers expressed some
doubt about his roping ability, Blocker told his Negro cook, "Goat," to wipe
the dough off his hands and get a rope and a horse. Blocker swung a regular
"Blocker loop" on the first cow, which picked up her front feet, and the cow
pony did the rest. "Goat" similarly roped and threw the next cow, Blocker
the third, and so on, until they had roped about twenty, never missing. . . .

All cowboys . . . were expected to be able to "sing" in order to soothe the
restless cattle. Just as they were expert riders and ropers, Negro cooks were
frequently singers, musicians, and even composers. Although hard-worked,
they were about the only men in an outfit with the opportunity to carry and
play a musical instrument. "The Zebra Dun," a song about a supposed
greenhorn who surprised everyone by riding an outlaw horse, is said to have
been composed by Jake, who worked for a Pecos River ranch. One chuckwagon cook who supplemented his menu with deer and turkey which he
shot himself, also sang and played the guitar. . . .

That the Negro cow-country cook frequently possessed unusual abilities
was due in part to limitations imposed because of racial discrimination. He
was much more likely than the average white man to have been brought up
about the kitchen and stables of a plantation or ranch and there, at an early
age, to have become acquainted with cooking and horses. He was less likely
to regard kitchen chores as somehow beneath him. The unusually able and
ambitious white cowboy could look forward to possible promotion to foreman or trail boss; the Negro of equal ability knew he had little chance of
attaining such a position. To become a ranch or roundup cook was about as
much as could be expected. Age, inexperience, or physical handicap might
preclude a white man from any ranch job outside of the kitchen; but for the
superior Negro cowboy to preside over a chuckwagon or ranch kitchen
meant an increase in pay and prestige.

The Negro cowhand, however able, could . . . rarely rise to a position
higher than chuckwagon or ranch-house cook. The principal obstacle to his
becoming a ranch foreman or trail boss was a general belief that a Negro
simply did not possess the qualities necessary for such a position. But even if
a ranch owner or group of cattlemen were confident that a Negro had the
necessary intelligence, initiative, and general capacity, there was always the
practical consideration that such a man, even if in charge of an all-Negro

outfit, would on occasion have to deal with white foremen and trail bosses who might refuse to recognize his authority, and that expensive trouble might ensue. A Negro, however great his ability, thus had difficulty in attaining greater authority than could be exercised over a chuckwagon or kitchen. The phenomenal success of Ora Haley, who for three decades was the dominant figure in the range-cattle business of Northwestern Colorado, is said to have been partly due to his Negro top hand Thornton Biggs, who although he "taught a whole generation of future range managers, wagon bosses, and all-round cowpunchers the finer points of the range-cattle business," himself "never became a range manager or even a foreman." The fairer-minded recognized the handicaps under which their Negro cowhands labored. Jim Perry, redoubtable cook, rider, and fiddler of the XIT ranch, once wryly remarked: "If it weren't for my damned old black face I'd have been boss of one of these divisions long ago." "And no doubt he would have," a white employee commented. . . .

Paradoxically, the race prejudice which prevented more than a very few Negro cowhands from rising to the status of foreman or trail boss may have spurred able and ambitious Negroes into taking up land, acquiring cattle, and setting up as independent small ranchers, whereas, lacking the incentive such an obstacle provided, they might have remained satisfied with a position as ranch foreman. . . .

Some especially able and trustworthy cow-country Negroes fulfilled roles for which there was no equivalent among white cowhands; as confidential assistants, factotums and, when it was necessary to transport large sums of money, bodyguards and "bankers."

Colonel Charles Goodnight wrote of Bose Ikard, his right hand man: "I have trusted him farther than any living man. He was my detective, banker, and everything else." Bose would sometimes have on his person proceeds from his employer's cattle sales amounting to as much as $20,000, since it was reasoned that a thief would be unlikely to search a Negro's belongings. . . .

In view of the racial situation which then prevailed throughout the United States, particularly in the South and West, it can be assumed that Negro cowmen encountered discrimination and segregation. The question therefore is not: Did discrimination and segregation exist? But rather: What was their extent and character? And how uniform were they? For although racism was general, it did vary from region to region, from state to state, and even from community to community. It also varied from period to period, probably increasing rather than diminishing during the years in question. . . .

Discrimination was probably least evident on the job. As to wages, cowpunching was, of course, by no means a highly paid occupation, regardless of race. Wages of various categories of cowhands varied widely not only from year to year and from region to region, but even within the same year and region and sometimes within the same outfit as well. Wages were generally low, but increased somewhat from the 1860s into the 1890s and were higher on the Northern Range than in Texas and Kansas. . . .

Strange though it may seem, there is no clear-cut evidence that Negro cowhands were generally or seriously discriminated against in the matter of wages, though this was obviously so with Mexicans, who sometimes received one half to one third that of white cowboys earning $20–25. . . . Wages were so much under the control of the individual employer that no doubt Negroes were sometimes discriminated against; but such discrimination seems not to have been characteristic and, when it occurred, was never nearly as serious as that to which Mexicans were subjected. . . .

Negroes were not discriminated against in the work permitted them— below the rank of foreman and trail boss. An experienced Negro would not be told to help the wrangler or to "eat dust" on the drag while a white greenhorn rode at point. On the other hand, Negroes may have been worked harder and longer than whites. John M. Hendrix, a white former cowpuncher and rancher, writing in the middle 1930s, approvingly presented the most extreme picture of discrimination. Negroes, he says, "were usually called on to do the hardest work around an outfit," such as "taking the first pitch out of the rough horses," while the whites were eating breakfast. "It was the Negro hand who usually tried out the swimming water when a trailing herd came to a swollen stream, or if a fighting bull or steer was to be handled, he knew without being told that it was his job." On cold rainy nights, moreover, Negroes would stand "a double guard rather than call the white folks" and would even launder everyone's clothes when the opportunity offered. "These Negroes knew their place, and were careful to stay in it."

The Negro, to be sure, was occasionally given unpleasant chores, but due to individual unfairness rather than to accepted custom. They might be given jobs which no one else would do—such as killing the calves dropped during the night on a cattle drive. They were sometimes tricked or bullied into doing more than their share of work. But there is no evidence that Negroes were normally expected to do double night-herding duty or guard the cattle while the whites went on a spree—merely that some cowboys were cheats or bullies who were ready to take advantage of Negroes, or, for that matter, of inexperienced white cowhands.

Discrimination and segregation off the job, whether on the ranch or the cattle trail, would have been difficult. . . . [F]irsthand accounts of ranch and cattle-trail life indicate about as much segregation as prevailed on Huckleberry Finn's and the "Nigger Jim's" raft before the appearance of "The King" and "The Duke." The sleeping arrangements were usually such as to defy any idea of racial segregation. Ranchowner, trail boss, Negro and white cowhands—particularly in bad weather—frequently not only slept in the same shack or tent but also shared the same blankets. . . . But when white women began to appear, those extreme manifestations of racial "integration" belonging to the womanless world of the cattle trail and the wintering camp yielded to a more formal and conventional pattern of conduct. When a highly respected Negro cowboy, in the midst of a blizzard, was permitted to sleep on the kitchen floor of a shack in which a camp manager was living with his wife it was regarded by the Negro as an example of extreme condescension or of humanity or both. . . .

The Negro cowboy engaged in the same amusements as the white—on a basis ranging from apparently complete integration to rigid separation. The extent of this segregation depended upon how well the parties knew one another and, more important, upon whether or not the whites included women.

To understand the character and degree of this segregation, and the way in which it was regarded by both whites and blacks, one must remember that the white men and women of the cow country were largely Southerners, or Westerners with a Southern exposure, while the Negroes, if not former slaves, were usually the children of ex-slaves. Both whites and Negroes were thus acquainted, by personal experience or recent tradition, with racial *discrimination* far more severe than anything practiced in the post-bellum cow country, even though racial *segregation* under slavery was less rigid than it became during the late nineteenth century.

When ranch work was slack, particularly in the winter, the hands sometimes held a dance, either a "bunkhouse 'shindig'" in which the participants were all males or a "regular dance" with girls from neighboring ranches or from town if one was close enough. On these occasions the Negro hands had the opportunity to shine, as musicians or dancers or both. Although serving as musicians at either type of dance, they were more conspicuous as dancers in the womanless bunkhouse affairs. Indeed, they might not appear on the dance floor with white women, though, singly or in groups, they might present dancing exhibitions as part of the entertainment.

Segregation in a cattle town, where the Negro cowhand was more of a stranger and white women were present, was much more clearcut than on the familiar ranch. But even here the restrictions were not always as rigid as one might perhaps expect. On the town's streets and among members of the same outfit, segregation might be non-existent. . . .

Even in Texas, however, segregation in the saloons was apparently informal. Whites, it seems, were served at one end of the bar, Negroes at the other. But should a white man and a Negro choose to drink and converse together in the "neutral zone" between the two sections probably no objection would be raised. . . .

If the Negro, however, moved from the saloon to a restaurant, he would encounter a completely segregated situation, partly because of the symbolic value attached to sitting down and eating together—as opposed to standing up at the same bar—but principally because women might be guests in the dining room or cafe. In a town without a colored restaurant, the Negro might have food handed to him at the back door of a cafe—perhaps he might even be permitted to eat in the kitchen—but more probably would, like many white cowboys, prefer to purchase groceries and eat sitting on a hitching rail.

Negroes, of course, were not lodged in "white" hotels—unless they were in attendance on prominent white cattlemen—but cowboys, black and white, usually felt that they had better use for their money than to spend it on hotel rooms. They preferred to spread their "hot rolls" in a livery stable or some other sheltered spot.

The most rigorously segregated cow-town establishments, at least so far as Negro cowhands were concerned, were brothels staffed with white prostitutes. . . . The cow-town gambling-house, on the other hand, was apparently entirely unsegregated. A gambler who intended to separate a Negro trail hand from his wages through the more than expert use of cards and dice could hardly do so without sitting down with him at the same card or crap table.

The Negro cowhand was accustomed to a degree of segregation and apparently did not resent it—at least not to the extent of risking his life in defiance of the practice. Clashes between Negro cowhands and whites were exceedingly rare. When racial encounters occurred in cattle towns, the Negroes involved were almost always colored soldiers.

Without the services of the eight or nine thousand Negros—a quarter of the total number of trail drivers—who during the generation after the Civil War helped to move herds up the cattle trails to shipping points, Indian reservations, and fattening grounds and who, between drives, worked on the ranches of Texas and the Indian Territory, the cattle industry would have been seriously handicapped. For apart from their considerable numbers, many of them were especially well-qualified top hands, riders, ropers, and cooks. Of the comparatively few Negroes on the Northern Range, a good many were also men of conspicuous abilities who notably contributed to the industry in that region. These cowhands, in their turn, benefitted from their participation in the industry, even if not to the extent that they deserved. That a degree of discrimination and segregation existed in the cattle country should not obscure the fact that, during the halcyon days of the cattle range, Negroes there frequently enjoyed greater opportunities for a dignified life than anywhere else in the United States. They worked, ate, slept, played, and on occasion fought, side by side with their white comrades, and their ability and courage won respect, even admiration. They were often paid the same wages as white cowboys and, in the case of certain horsebreakers, ropers, and cooks, occupied positions of considerable prestige. In a region and period characterized by violence, their lives were probably safer than they would have been in the Southern cotton regions where between 1,500 and 1,600 Negroes were lynched in the two decades after 1882. The skilled and handy Negro probably had a more enjoyable, if a rougher, existence as a cowhand then he would have had as a sharecropper or laborer.

Mexican Labor in Oklahoma, 1900–1945

Michael M. Smith

The economic development of many areas of the Southwest in the early twentieth century depended on the availability of Mexican immigrant labor. Throughout the region, Mexican immigrants worked in railroad maintenance, agriculture, mining, construction, and domestic service. Not only men but also women and children found employment. Married women augmented their families' income by taking in boarders or doing various forms of work in the home. Single women labored as domestics, laundrywomen, and factory workers in urban areas. Child labor was widespread in most southwestern industries. Mexicans received little in return and often were paid less than other workers for comparable work.

Such were the characteristics of Mexican immigrant labor, as Michael M. Smith notes in the following study of Oklahoma. Though not often perceived as a state where Mexicans worked, Oklahoma in fact depended on Mexican labor in its major industries: railroads, mining, and agriculture. In the excerpts reprinted here, Smith examines the role of Mexican railroad workers. Despite their employment by the thousands to maintain railroad tracks throughout the United States, Mexican railroad workers have not yet been the focus of any significant study. Although Smith's information is limited, he conveys a flavor of the particular experiences of these workers.

STUDY QUESTIONS

1. How was discrimination against Mexican railroad workers exhibited?

2. What kinds of housing were available to Mexican railroad workers?

Between 1900 and the depression [of the 1930s], Mexican immigrants played an increasingly vital, yet largely ignored role in the economic development of Oklahoma. They perhaps comprised a majority of the railroad maintenance crews and constituted a significant segment of the labor force in coal mines. Thousands of Mexican migrants annually worked the cotton harvests. Throughout the state they held numerous unskilled positions in industries, packinghouses, municipal services, and domestic employment.

From *The Mexicans in Oklahoma*, by Michael M. Smith, pp. 37–41. Copyright © 1980 by the University of Oklahoma Press.

No immigrant group in American history has been so intimately tied to the railroads as the Mexican. Railways provided the major arteries of migration from Mexico, and railroad companies were the principal employers of Mexican nationals in the United States. The railroads brought thousands of Mexicans to Oklahoma, and their routes often determined the patterns of settlement of Mexicans in the state. Between 1910 and the depression, Mexicans lived in nearly every city and important town along Oklahoma railroad lines. The companies often furnished their workers housing in tents, boxcars, or section houses along the right of way or encouraged them to live nearby, thus establishing the Mexican *colonia* "across the tracks." The large turnover rate in railroad gangs forced these corporations to draw a constant stream of workers into the country in order to maintain their crews at full strength.

Although the major portion of Oklahoma's railroad network was completed before 1907 and therefore prior to the heaviest migration of Mexicans to the state, they worked on construction crews in the 1880s and 1890s. Most of these "Mexicans" were probably *tejanos* [Mexican Texans] who had entered the state as *vaqueros* [cowboys] on the cattle drives and remained or returned for more lucrative employment in railroad construction. They evidently worked a short time and then found other jobs or returned to Texas.

After statehood, most railroads in Oklahoma were consolidated under the control of four major companies—the Atchinson, Topeka, and Santa Fe (Sante Fe), the Chicago, Rock Island, and Pacific (Rock Island), the St. Louis and San Francisco (Frisco), and the Missouri, Kansas, and Texas (Katy). All of these companies had direct or indirect connections to El Paso or Laredo and drew heavily upon the Mexican labor force there. While most of the railroads had employed European immigrants, blacks, and white Americans on the construction gangs, after 1907 they increasingly relied upon Mexicans for track maintenance. The most important recruiting center for Mexican track labor was El Paso, which had a seemingly endless supply of Mexican workers. During an eight-month period between 1907 and 1908, six El Paso companies supplied almost 16,500 Mexicans to various railroad corporations. The railroads needed track labor from February to October, and most Mexican immigrants, perhaps 95 percent, came to the United States intending to work only a short time. They signed contracts for three, six, or nine months, and, if they fulfilled their agreement, received free or reduced-rate transportation back to the border. One railway official stated that his company sent an agent to the Río Grande every spring to get men for the summer. He declared that the company had to keep its agreements with the men or it could not get any help the next year. Many Mexicans returned annually to work for the same railroad, often in the same geographical region.

Mexicans initially filled positions on extra gangs. Their principal jobs were ballasting, laying ties, and ordinary pick and shovel work. Most were *solos*, bachelors or married men who had left their families behind. Some workers on extra crews did bring their families. Life on the extra gang was extremely nomadic. Laborers constantly moved to locations where emergency or temporary work was required. They repaired washed-out embankments, moved track to higher ground, laid new rails, or installed double tracks. They lived in dilapidated boxcars converted into crude living quarters and parked along sidings. These bare shelters contained few facilities, except perhaps a small cookstove. The company furnished water and fuel; the commissary provided food. The workers slept on straw or, if they were fortunate, rough bunks. Although men usually traveled alone on extra gangs, when there were women and children along, boxcars housing families would be parked at a distance from the rest to allow greater privacy.

The nature of extra-gang work caused many to break their contracts, and they drifted into other kinds of unskilled jobs. Farmers and ranchers frequently lured them away from the tracks by offering more money. In an attempt to keep their employees, railroad companies in Oklahoma paid wages that were higher than those generally available in Texas or other southwestern states. During the summer of 1907, Mexicans received $1.50 a day, but many still deserted to the grain and cotton fields when they had a chance. The turnover rate in track workers was consistently high until the depression. The Santa Fe, which in 1928 employed a total of 14,300 Mexicans nationally, had a turnover rate of 300 percent. No doubt the principal reasons for leaving railroad work were the unsteady nature of employment, the constant moving about, and the desire of many men to be near their families.

Extra-gang employment frequently led to work on a section crew, a maintenance group assigned to a specific portion of the track line. Crews of six to thirty or more men lived in a particular community and traveled back and forth to their job on handcars. Mexicans also found employment in the railroad shops and roundhouses. Although these jobs were only semipermanent at best, they did lead to the establishment of some of the first Mexican communities in Oklahoma.

In the early years the assessment of the quality of Mexicans' work on the railroads was often unfavorable. In 1908 some railroad officials complained that Mexicans lacked ambition, were irregular in shop attendance, and drank hard after paydays, thereby losing part of their working time. Other sources, however, reported the Mexicans compared favorably with other nationalities in most respects and surpassed them in performance. Later evaluations of Mexican labor were more favorable. A Rock Island engineer listed several disadvantages of Mexican workers, including their inability to speak English, their status as temporary immigrants, and their difficulty in acclimating to harsh winters. But their refusal to be clannish, excellence as gang laborers, ability to do a full day's work in a hot climate, and faithfulness made them perhaps the best of all foreign workers. A Santa Fe official agreed that the Mexican laborers as a whole were about as steady as could be obtained for the price. He also noted that when they first arrived in this country many Mexicans were weak and malnourished. After they had been here for a month or so, however, they regained their strength and made commendable workers.

Mexican railroad laborers in Oklahoma did not experience the wage discrimination or physical abuse that their countrymen often suffered in the southwestern or Pacific states. In 1911 Mexicans were the lowest paid of any ethnic group of maintenance workers in the Pacific and Rocky Mountain regions. Over 90 percent of the Mexican workers received less than $1.50 a day. Beyond that area, however, Mexicans earned a wage comparable to that of any ethnic group. Mexican laborers earned at least $1.50 a day in Oklahoma in 1907; in the 1920s they received an average of $2.50 to $2.80 for an eight-hour day. Many Mexicans did complain of mistreatment. The Southern Pacific and the Union Pacific railroads received much criticism for their abusive handling of Mexican laborers. The Santa Fe, which probably employed the largest number of Mexicans in Oklahoma, enjoyed a generally good reputation because of its greater consideration for Mexican employees and also because it paid well. A Santa Fe engineer in the 1920s intimated that anyone who knew how to manage Mexicans could get more work out of them than any other class. A general foreman writing an article on "How to Handle Mexican Labor" stated that when properly managed, they were willing to do a great deal for their boss even if they received ridiculously low wages. In one respect, the Mexican worker in Oklahoma suffered a great disadvantage. He seldom advanced beyond the status of an extra- or section-gang member. Companies rarely hired Mexicans as foremen or assigned them the better jobs in roundhouses or repair shops. The usual reason given was that the Mexicans did not speak English well enough or did not possess the requisite skills.

By 1913 the Mexicans' predominance on railroad gangs forced Santa Fe officials to make an effort to overcome the language difference between Anglo foremen and Mexican track workers. Noting that almost all the section work on its line was done by *hombres*, the Santa Fe issued foremen Spanish-English dictionaries to assist them in giving orders to their Mexican crews. Although a few Americans of Mexican descent served as foremen and most Anglo bosses spoke some Spanish, the dictionary would aid those of the latter group who had not mastered the "tongue twisters."

By the outbreak of the Mexican Revolution, railroad companies such as the Santa Fe were already endeavoring to retain Mexican workers on a more permanent basis as a result of both the scarcity of track workers in general and the positive performance of Mexicans in western divisions. To attract a better and steadier class of workers, the company began to build housing for its employees so that those with families could locate on each railroad section. Santa Fe officials noted that the seminomadic life of the homeless workers encouraged the development of a vagrant class much like the American hobo. The company also noted that while many Mexicans in the western area built dugouts or tie houses with mud roofs, the earth beyond the arid region did not endure like adobe. After a heavy rain washed away the roofs of their crude shacks, many workers abandoned both the dwelling and their job.

In 1912 the Santa Fe began to erect houses on railroad property and rented them to employees for a minimal charge of one or two dollars a month. These houses were generally constructed of scrap pieces and cheap, secondhand material. Builders utilized sawed or hewn railroad ties for walls, old rails for rafters, and sheet metal for roofs. Mud or concrete filled the cracks and interstices. The dwellings did not contain furniture, plumbing, or electrical facilities. The company did provide coal, water, and stoves for heating in winter.

Not all railroads supplied even these bare shelters. The first Mexicans who worked on the Frisco line in Tulsa lived in tents pitched along the right of way. The firemen on the locomotives often cast them their quota of coal as the train passed. The companies encouraged workers who did not live along the right of way to settle nearby. They preferred that the labor force reside in a compact settlement so that the entire crew of a particular section could be summoned immediately in an emergency such as a washout or derailment at night.

Until the depression and even after, the needs of the railroads dictated the distribution of many Mexicans in Oklahoma. These settlements varied considerably in size and location. They included small groups of Mexicans at such places as Blackwell, Edmond, Purcell, Pauls Valley, and Ardmore along the Santa Fe, or Medford, Enid, El Reno, Chickasha, Duncan, and Waurika beside the Rock Island. Many more worked on a large section crew or in a roundhouse in Oklahoma City, Sapulpa, or Tulsa.

A position on a section gang did not provide year-round or permanent employment. Many Mexicans in Oklahoma accepted the offer of free passage to the border and returned to Mexico after fulfilling their contract. Others saw little advantage in going home and sought alternate jobs until the railroads needed them again. A large number of railroad employees worked the cotton harvest, which began almost coincidentally with the termination of their contract period. Some found work in coal mines and industries, on farms and ranches, or as municipal employees. Numerous Mexicans had to join the great migrant agricultural pool. Families packed their few belongings and followed the sugar beet, tomato, strawberry, wheat, peach, or cranberry harvests to Kansas, Nebraska, Colorado, Iowa, Illinois, Michigan, and elsewhere.

The depression dramatically affected the employment of Mexicans on the railroads. Pressured by federal officials, labor unions, and unemployed citizens, corporations drastically reduced the number of Mexican track laborers or eliminated them entirely. The experience of the Mexican *colonia* in Sand Springs revealed the impact of the economic crisis on Mexican railroad workers. In 1917 about sixty Mexicans and their families moved to Sand Springs to construct the Sand Springs Railway. A large proportion of the men came from the coal mines in southeastern Oklahoma. The company provided "shotgun houses" near the roundhouse for the men and their families. After the railroad was completed, many remained as maintenance laborers while others found employment as section hands or in the shops or roundhouses of the Santa Fe or Frisco in Tulsa or Sapulpa. When the depression struck, they were given the option of staying in the houses which had been built for them or accepting a free pass to the border or anywhere in the United States they wished to go. Those who chose to remain would receive free rent and utilities and a few days' work a month on the railroad. Only the Fabela, Rodríguez, and Ramírez families accepted the offer and stayed.

Mexican Women Workers in Texas, 1880–1920

MARIO T. GARCÍA

Although present in smaller numbers than men, Mexican immigrant women formed part of the "great migration" from Mexico to the United States during the early twentieth century. Married and single women, along with female children, all took part in the Mexican diaspora north of the border. Most married immigrant women remained in the home to take care of their families' needs or earned small sums looking after boarders. However, as time passed, increasing numbers of single women and female heads of households were forced to seek paid employment in the U.S. job market. Women thus are a significant part of the history of Mexican immigrant workers.

In his study of the Mexican immigrant community of El Paso, Texas, Mario T. García considers the role of some of the women in El Paso's border economy. Working predominantly as domestics and laundresses, Mexican women also found employment in a variety of other jobs, serving as clerical workers and as seamstresses in El Paso's garment industries. Like their male counterparts, Mexican women encountered job and wage discrimination. Indeed, the intersections of class, race, and gender formed the basis for positioning Mexican female workers in the most exploited sector of the labor market—not only in El Paso but in other Mexican immigrant communities as well.

STUDY QUESTIONS

1. What various kinds of work did Mexican immigrant women perform in El Paso?

2. Comparing this reading with the preceding one by Smith, do you think there was a sexual division of labor in Oklahoma's and El Paso's job markets? Explain.

[S]ome Mexican women found employment and became a significant portion of the Mexican working class of El Paso. Because entire families as well as single men had arrived from Mexico, many females, especially daughters or other young female relatives, had to find work to augment the earnings of the men. Moreover, some women had lost their husbands and consequently had become the main source of income for their children. A sample of 393 El Paso households from the 1900 manuscript census reveals that almost one-fifth (17.11%) of Mexican households contained a working woman. American women also had to enter the labor force and the census sample recorded 11.21 percent of American households with a female worker. Mexican women who worked, according to the census sample, were unmarried daughters, wives with no husbands, or single women. Married Mexican women, on the other hand, both foreign and native born, within a nuclear or an extended family, did not work outside the home. In no case in the sample did a woman with an employed husband have a job. Because both the census and city directories failed to count many Mexicans it may well be that a larger percentage of Mexican women, including married ones, worked, especially at part-time labor and laundry or sewing. In any event, fewer married women appear to have had jobs than unmarried ones. Age and fertility help explain this condition. In the 1900 sample, more than three-fourths of married Mexican immigrant women were between fifteen and forty years of age, a period when women generally gave birth and had children at home. Indeed, more than three-fourths of all married Mexican immigrant women in El Paso, based on the sample, had children twelve years of age or under or children listed as attending school; of these, more than one-third had children five years of age and under. If having children kept married women in the home, so too, apparently, did the attitude of many Mexican men, who resented women, especially wives, working or wanting to work. Most males believed that their work was a man's duty but that women's consisted of raising children and keeping house. As one working-

From Mario T. García, *Desert Immigrants: The Mexicans of El Paso, 1880–1920*, pp. 74–78. Copyright © 1981, reprinted by permission of Yale University Press.

class newspaper in Mexico during the age of Porfirio Díaz emphasized: "To be a wife is to be a women preferably selected amongst many other women, for her honesty, for her religiousness, for her amiability, . . . for her industriousness [and]) for her docility."

Nevertheless, despite such attitudes the Mexican family in the United States did not remain static. Over the years more Mexican women, especially daughters, became wageworkers to augment the family income. Also, as the economy expanded, El Paso and southwestern industries and services began to recruit more Mexican women workers. The increase in Mexican female wageworkers in El Paso by 1920 can be seen in census figures for that year. The census reported that 3,474 foreign-born females, almost all Mexicans, ten years of age and older were engaged in a gainful occupation. Foreign-born female wageworkers represented half of all females ten years and over who held jobs in El Paso. Most female workers in El Paso (3,112 females, or 45% of all employed women) did "women's work." The two largest occupations, familiar to women in Mexico, were servant (1,718) and laundress (710), where the majority of Mexican working women could be found. Owing to deficiencies in skills and schooling, as well as to prejudice against them, few Mexican women, unlike their American counterparts, were in such skilled professional occupations as teaching, nursing, or office work. The table shows the number and percentage of Spanish-surnamed women listed as domestics and laundresses in the city directories of 1889, 1910, and 1920.

Victor S. Clark, a Bureau of Labor inspector, noted in 1908 that Mexican "immigrant women have so little conception of domestic arrangements in the United States that the task of training them would be too heavy for American housewives." Yet domestic work proved to be the most readily available source of jobs for Mexican women. Still, Clark correctly recognized that women from preindustrial cultures might have difficulty adjusting to the new electrical devices of middle-class American homes, although he failed to understand that the employment of Mexican maids saved southwestern housewives from having to buy the new appliances. Mexican domestics did their work by hand. Elizabeth Rae Tyson, who grew up in El Paso, remembered the extent of Mexican maids used by American families. "Owing to the large Mexican majority," she recalled,

> almost every Anglo-American family had at least one, sometimes two or three servants: a maid and laundress, and perhaps a nursemaid or yardman. The maid came in after breakfast and cleaned up the breakfast dishes, and very likely last night's supper dishes as well; did the routine cleaning, washing and ironing, and after the family dinner in the middle of the day, washed dishes again, and then went home to perform similar service in her own home.

An examination of the city directories, listing both home and work addresses, indicates that the Mexican maids left their homes in the barrios in the morning to work in American neighborhoods during the day and then returned in the afternoon or evening to the Mexican districts. In some cases Mexican domestics had living quarters with their employers. One newspaper account reported that the hours of "house girls" went from seven in the morning to five in the afternoon, and in 1907 they received from $3 to $6 per week for this. Most, apparently, were hired by American middle-class families.

Mexican women, besides working as servants, found other employment opportunities. Many worked as washerwomen, either in American homes or in their own as well as in the various laundries of El Paso. In laundries they learned such other skills as the use of sewing machines and received from $4 to $6 a week. In 1917 the largest in the city, the El Paso Laundry, employed 134 Spanish-surnamed workers out of a total of 166, and Mexican women, mostly doing collar and flatwork, comprised what appears to have been more than half the Mexican employees. That same year the Elite Laundry had 76 Spanish-surnamed female workers out of a total of 128. Another of the larger laundries, the Acme, employed 75 Spanish-surnamed females out of 121 employees in 1917. The same pattern prevailed in the smaller laundries. For example, the Post Laundry had 33 Spanish-surnamed women in their work force of 49. While many of these laundresses lived in El Paso, some came from Ciudad Juárez. The daughter-in-law of Frank Fletcher, who owned the Acme Laundry, remembers that when she arrived in 1926, a laundry truck picked up the Mexican women at the border, took them to work, and returned them in the evening to the international bridge. The use of non-resident Mexican women limited already low wages.

In addition to service jobs some Mexican women labored as production workers, especially in El Paso's early garment factories. In 1902 Bergman's factory, which turned out shirts and overalls, reported that it had 3 American women and a large number of Mexican females. Yet, according to a newspaper account, Bergman concluded that he could get more and better work out of his Americans and consequently paid them $10 to $ 14 a week while the Mexicans received no more than $9 a week. Several years later, in 1919, the El Paso Overall Company advertised in a Spanish-language newspaper that it needed Mexican women for sewing and for general work. Mexican women likewise worked in the Kohlberg Cigar Factory. Mostly boxing cigars, 22 Mexican women out of 113 employees labored in the plant in 1917. Some women also found jobs as clerks and sales personnel in the downtown stores. A *Times* ad in 1905 read: "Wanted—5 experienced American and Spanish salesladies." The Mexican newspaper, *El Día*, in 1919 praised Panchita Salas for her "work and charm" at the El Globo Department Store run by the Schwartz family. That same year the White House Department Store, one of El Paso's largest, publicized in *La Patria* that it

Number and Percentage of Spanish-Surnamed Domestics and Laundresses, 1889, 1910, 1920

	Year	Number	Percentage of total workers (Mexican and American)
Domestics	1889	61	49.73
	1910	447	65.37
	1920	1,528	76.18
Laundresses	1889	40	34.90
	1910	220	64.48
	1920	516	92.17

Source: *El Paso City Directories*, 1889, 1910, 1920. The 1890 city directory was not used, because no copies for that year could be found. The discrepancy between the 1920 census figures and those of the city directory is probably the result of a more limited survey by the city directory.

Mexican women workers relaxing during their leisure hours

needed young women clerks in all its departments. Still other Mexicans worked as cooks or dishwashers in restaurants. In more unfortunate cases Mexican women sold food on the streets of Chihuahuita.

Finally, as in other societies, some women inhabited the saloons and gambling halls of the red-light district. The *Lone Star* in 1885 expressed shock over a twelve-year-old Mexican girl's activities. "It is rumored," the newspaper sermonized, "that she is a prostitute and most any hour of the day she can be seen in the streets with different men." When the city government enforced an ordinance in 1903 to move the district farther from the center of El Paso, the *Times* reported that many of the prostitutes "proposed to go across the river, among the number being Mexicans, which include the dance hall girls." Two years later, when Lou Vidal attempted to open his dance hall, police raided and arrested his employees, which included dance hall girls María González, Josefa González, Lola Beltrán, and Senida García.

FURTHER READING

Robert Archibald, *The Economic Aspects of the California Missions* (Washington, D.C.: Academy of American Franciscan History, 1978).

Mario Barrera, *Race and Class in the Southwest: A Theory of Racial Inequality* (Notre Dame: University of Notre Dame Press, 1979).

Edward D. Beechert, *Working in Hawaii: A Labor History* (Honolulu: University of Hawaii Press, 1985).

Albert Camarillo, *Chicanos in a Changing Society: From Mexican Pueblos to American Barrios in Santa Barbara and Southern California* (Cambridge, Mass.: Harvard University Press, 1979).

Leonard A. Carlson, *Indians, Bureaucrats, and Land: The Dawes Act and the Decline of Indian Farming* (Westport, Conn.: Greenwood Press, 1981).

Sucheng Chan, *This Bittersweet Soil: The Chinese in California Agriculture, 1860–1910* (Berkeley and Los Angeles: University of California Press, 1986).

Bong-Youn Choy, *Koreans in America* (Chicago: Nelson-Hall, 1979).

Douglas Henry Daniels, *Pioneer Urbanites: A Social and Cultural History of Black San Francisco* (Philadelphia: Temple University Press, 1980; Berkeley and Los Angeles: University of California Press, 1990).

Philip Durham and Everett L. Jones, *The Negro Cowboys* (New York: Dodd, Mead, and Co., 1965).

Chris Friday, *Organizing Asian American Workers: The Pacific Coast Canned-Salmon Industry, 1870–1942* (Philadelphia: Temple University Press, 1994).

Evelyn Nakano Glenn, *Issei, Nisei, Warbride: Three Generations of Japanese-American Women in Domestic Service* (Philadelphia: Temple University Press, 1986).

Clarence E. Glick, *Sojourners and Settlers: Chinese Migrants in Hawaii* (Honolulu: University of Hawaii Press, 1980).

Albert L. Hurtado, *Indian Survival on the California Frontier* (New Haven: Yale University Press, 1988).

Yuji Ichioka, *The Issei: The World of the First Generation Japanese Immigrants, 1885–1924* (New York: Free Press, 1988).

Masakazu Iwata, *Planted in Good Soil: A History of the Issei in United States Agriculture* (New York: Peter Lang, 1992).

Cardell K. Jacobsen, "Internal Colonialism and Native Americans: Indian Labor in the United States from 1871 to World War II," *Social Science Quarterly 65* (1984): 158–171.

Rudolph Lapp, *Blacks in the Gold Rush* (New Haven: Yale University Press, 1977).

Bruno Lasker, *Filipino Immigration into Continental United States and to Hawaii* (Chicago: University of Chicago Press, 1931; New York: New York Times and Arno Press, 1969).

Karen Isaksen Leonard, *Making Ethnic Choices: California's Punjabi Mexican Americans* (Philadelphia: Temple University Press, 1992).

David Montejano, *Anglos and Mexicans in the Making of Texas, 1836–1986* (Austin: University of Texas Press, 1987).

Donald L. Parman, *The Navajos and the New Deal* (New Haven: Yale University Press, 1976).

Vicki L. Ruiz, *Cannery Women, Cannery Lives: Mexican Women, Unionization, and the California Food Processing Industry, 1930–1950* (Albuquerque: University of New Mexico Press, 1987).

Ronald Takaki, *Pau Hana: Plantation Life and Labor in Hawaii* (Honolulu: University of Hawaii Press, 1983).

Ronald L. Trosper, *Earnings and Labor Supply: A Microeconomic Comparison of American Indians and Alaska Natives to American Whites and Blacks,* Social Welfare Research Institute, Publication No. 55 (Boston: Social Welfare Research Institute, Boston College, 1980).

CHAPTER 5

Family

In one sense, dividing human history along a gender line leads to distortion, for despite obvious differences between the sexes, the lives of men and women are inextricably intertwined. Nonetheless, scholars in recent years have separated out women as a distinct topic for inquiry, recognizing that the written narratives labeled "history" all too often have meant a discussion of only men's activities. The neglect of women of color is especially acute in light of the tendency of many American historians to slight the past of minority groups generally and to concentrate on the "mainstream" doings of Euro-Americans.

The readings in this chapter focus on women and families among westerners of color—specifically, Native Americans, Japanese Americans, Mexican Americans, and African Americans. Terry P. Wilson traces the changing lives of the females within a single Indian tribe during the reservation and postreservation periods. Yuji Ichioka focuses on immigrant Japanese and the development of Japanese-American family life. Richard Griswold del Castillo briefly sketches four patterns of Mexican-American family life. And Maya Angelou tells the story of her teenage pregnancy and the support she received from her family during this difficult period, in the process illustrating the close bonds among members of an African-American family.

FOR ANALYSIS AND DISCUSSION

1. How did the wealth derived from oil production affect women's status and power within the Osage tribe?

2. Compare and contrast the manner in which Japanese women immigrated to the United States with the experience of Japanese men, as well as that of female European immigrants.

3. What factors account for the differences in the four types of Mexican-American families discussed in the Griswold del Castillo essay?

4. Compare the teenage pregnancy of Maya Angelou with the experiences of someone you know who has become pregnant.

5. Describe some commonalities in the experiences of the different groups of women examined in this chapter.

6. Compare and contrast the position and activities of the women discussed in this chapter's selections with gender relations in your own family.

 # Osage Women, 1870–1980

TERRY P. WILSON

Despite the fact that more than two-thirds of the nation's Native American tribes were originally matrilineal and matrilocal*, historians and social scientists have scarcely noted Indian women in their studies. This omission can be partially explained by the male-dominated Western European thinking that saw Indian males as much more significant than females. In this selection about the Osage tribe, however, women are the focus. Terry P. Wilson highlights the importance of tribal women in a traditional society and the ways in which their roles and status changed with the passage of time and through their interrelationships with non-Indians.

It should not be presumed that the experiences of the Osage women were typical of Indian women generally. Each tribe's individual culture and history render generalizations difficult. Yet there are some aspects of the Osage women's saga that were probably shared by most other western Native American women. The issue of intermarriage with white men, for example, confronted most native women. Because white women were in short supply on the frontier, Indian women served as a ready alternative. The intermarriage of white males and Indian females and the birth of mixed-race offspring posed social and political problems within many tribes.

When the Osages in the twentieth century grew wealthy from their oil-rich and natural-gas-rich lands, the royalties were split equally among all living tribe members, and Osage women became especially desirable to non-Indians as mates. Tribal governance was vitally affected by the presence of intermarried citizens and mixed-bloods. Osage women themselves found new empowerment as holders of "headrights"—shares in the mineral estate—and increasingly took part in tribal politics. Even if divorced or widowed, they remained powerful because they retained their headright incomes. By the last quarter of the twentieth century, the women of the tribe occupied a position as significant in most cases as their male counterparts.

STUDY QUESTIONS

1. What role did Osage women play in tribal politics?

2. How did the lives of Osage women change after oil brought wealth to their people?

---

* *Matrilineal* refers to a society that traces descent and inheritance through the mother's line, and *matrilocal* pertains to a society in which men, upon marriage, live with their wives' families.

3. Discuss the issues raised in Osage tribal affairs by the practice of interracial marriage and the presence of mixed-race children.

Indian women and men both seem trapped somewhere between caricature and stereotype. Reduced to the status of ethnographic specimens by anthropologists, lumped together and described as a barrier to the advance of Anglo-American frontiersmen by historians, and portrayed as savage villains in countless westerns by moviemakers, Native Americans rarely emerge as more than cardboard figures. . . .

While Indian men race across movie and television screens on horseback, brandishing bows and arrows, or swoop down upon the courageous defenders of forts and wagon trains, their women—dull-countenanced squaws—remain behind the action. Rarely does the Native American female emerge from the background scenes of cinematic epics to speak or otherwise participate in the action. Scholars have done little better. Historians in particular have concentrated on the deeds of the men, while largely neglecting their wives, mothers, and daughters. . . .

A clear image of the Indian women, past and present, remains elusive. Most of the available written sources regarding Indian history and culture dwell much more extensively with males than females. When the latter are mentioned, the information virtually always provides a narrow perspective, describing the role of women as marital objects, mothers, or divorcees. A balanced description of Indian women, therefore, is difficult, as much of the historian's analysis must be inferred from scanty and slanted sources. Perhaps the very difficulties of research constitute sufficient reason to attempt a study of Native American women before their history is irrevocably obscured. The partial picture represented by these observations of the Osage women of Oklahoma between the 1870s and 1970s may instigate a desire on the part of others to produce a fuller story.

The Osage traced their heritage by patrilineal descent, that is through the male line; but they lived according to a matrilocal arrangement, the husbands residing with their wives' families. Some other tribes practiced both matrilineal descent and matrilocal living. The combination of patrilineal descent and matrilocal living, however, occurs so infrequently among Native Americans that most anthropologists believe that the Osage were originally patrilocal, but changed to matrilocal living as a result of societal upheaval connected with European contacts before 1800. This theory gains credence

"Osage Indian Women during a Century of Change, 1870–1980," by Terry P. Wilson from *Prologue: Journal of the National Archives* 14 (1982), pp. 185–189, 191–194, 196–220. Reprinted by permission of Prologue.

from the fact that husbands retained their original status within their clans, even if they lived apart, and their children also became members of the paternal clans.

The clans carefully protected young women, seeking to preserve the pubescent girls' virginity until marriage. Older women acted as *duennas*. Their presence was generally sufficient to protect their charges, since powerful taboos existed against anyone interfering with those performing this function. As tribal custom weakened during the agency period, the chaperons prevented the advances of disrespectful young men, even to the extent, if necessary, of wielding the utility knives they usually carried. Apparently, visiting warriors from other tribes constituted the greatest worry for the *duennas*. Fearing unknown magical conjurations, the ever-cautious women would stow their adolescent charges in two or three large dwellings, allowing no one to approach these woodland hideaways. The girls' urine was spirited away in vessels especially made for the purpose, mixed with the ashes of the sacred willow, and spilled a long distance from camp to nullify the powers of any alien love charms.

Such extreme procedures were a measure of the worth placed on marriageable females by their clansmen. The Osage numbered twenty-four clans, which for ceremonial, social, and political purposes were divided into moieties representing earth and sky. Marriage was arranged according to the moiety exogamy; that is, males and females mated outside their own clan groupings. Certain families, prestigious by reasons of wealth and birth, tattooed the spider symbol on the backs of the hands of their young women. Despite the social stratification indicated by this and other practices, marriage was not seen as a political event—a joining of powerful clans or families. Rather, the restrictions placed on Osage women protected them for mating with the best young men so that the tribe could prosper by the pairs' offspring. Instances of particularly renowned warriors taking two, three, or more wives were not unknown, and it was fairly common practice for noteworthy husbands to exercise marital claims on some or all of the younger sisters of his wife. By the early 1800s, following extended relations with Euro-Americans, the status of men had changed; the ability to obtain trade goods now loomed larger than birth in determining fitness for marriage.

The foregoing might indicate that Osage women, at least those of marriageable age, were mere chattels in tribal society. Although it is difficult to make authoritative statements in regard to traditional custom, the status of women certainly involved more than being docile subjects for male marital plans. Families and clans representing women in negotiations could and did turn down would-be suitors and their families. Once married, an Osage man presented his wife with a *mon-sha-ken,* or burden strap, made of uncured buffalo skin. Each wife possessed two such straps (one used solely for ceremonial purposes), both of which served as symbols of virtue and of the prerogatives of an essential member of the family and tribe. The burden strap did not signify that Osage women were drudges, a stereotyped image of Indian females "completely without foundation," according to one study that pointed out the division of labor practiced by most tribes. White observers viewing Native American women toiling in the fields, while their husbands and sons seemed to frolic about hunting and fishing, concluded that Indian males shunted all the hard tasks onto their wives. It did not occur to the onlookers that hunting and fishing were not leisure activities for Indians, but quite serious means of sustaining life. Most outsiders failed to realize that Indian women were in charge of certain important duties, varying from tribe to tribe, just as the men had specific responsibilities. For example, the month of April corresponds to the Osage Planting Moon, the women's moon. Men aided in the sacred planting of the corn *under the direction* of the women. The two sexes complemented one another's lifestyles in many ways—if not on a plane of perfect equality, certainly on one of mutual respect.

Their traditional ways underwent a series of severe modifications beginning with the initial contacts of the Osage with Euro-Americans in the seventeenth century. The tribe controlled a large area of land along the Mississippi River and its tributaries in present-day Missouri and Arkansas until 1839, when the pressure of white settlements caused them to cede their territory in return for a reservation in southern Kansas. Three decades later, the advance of bumptious Anglo-American frontiersmen and farmers forced another move, this time southward into Indian territory. Unsympathetic to his departing Osage neighbors, one white squatter wrote to his congressman: "Mr Clarke, hurry up the removal of these lazy, dirty vagabonds. . . . It is folly to talk longer of a handful of wandering savages holding possession of a land so fair and rich as this. We want this land to make homes. Let us have it.". . .

. . . [T]he presence in 1800 of mixed-blood faces "like gypsum-rubbed deerskin rather than the bronze" of the full-bloods suggests a . . . serious tribal transformation, one in which women played an essential role. According to the agency physician, full-bloods outnumbered mixed-bloods by a ratio of 2,701 to 280 when the Osage moved to Indian Territory in the mid-1870s. In the beginning, most of the women who lived with or married white men, almost always French, were lured by presents and promises. Many were widows with little chance of remarriage or were women born of unwed parents, relegated to the lower classes and considered unacceptable as mates by prestigious families. During the last quarter of the nineteenth century, the percentage of mixed-bloods increased so rapidly that by 1900 it equaled that of the full-bloods. Fifty years later, the latter represented a scant 9 percent of the tribe's population of five thousand. Most of the persons within the mixed-blood community were products of marriages between Indian women and white men. The white husbands, referred to as "intermarried citizens," composed, along with the mixed-bloods, a separate designation "the Half Breed Band," in 1870 when the tribe was negotiating its removal from Kansas.

Once ensconced on the reservation, mixed-bloods and full-bloods alike experienced the effects of the government's program of "civilization" and education. Through a variety of blandishments, cajolements, and pressure, subtle or otherwise, the Osage were to be . . . assimilated into the mainstream of Anglo-American society, willingly or unwillingly. . . . Apparently the Osage were somewhat capable of successfully resisting progress toward "civilization." Their agent in the late 1890s, William J. Pollock, described the tribal mixed-bloods "as civilized and as competent to care for themselves as any community of white people . . . while the large majority of the full-bloods still cling as near as possible to their ancient customs and traditions. . . . The females wear blankets, a short skirt, leggings, and moccasins, with their hair hanging loosely down their backs. The brighter and gayer the colors of their blankets the better dressed they imagine themselves."

If Agent Pollock believed he could discern a difference in the degrees of acculturation reached by mixed-bloods and full-bloods, others in government service were certain they saw similar distinctions between male and female Indians. In 1890, Merial A. Dorchester, a special agent in the Indian School Service, submitted a report to the commissioner of Indian affairs on the status of women in the western tribes. "It is a truism," she wrote, "that in order to reach any heathen people the mothers and homes must be interested first. It is also just as much a truism . . . that the Indians as a whole are still pagan, and the women most conservatively pagan of all." Dorchester noted that ridicule, a powerful weapon in any culture, was "multiplied and intensified . . . in Indian society, and [that] the squaws understand best when and how to use this weapon most successfully." She blamed particularly "the mothers who keep up the old superstitions and laugh down modern ideas and customs.". . .

Given their perception of Indian women, the government civilization experts could not ignore the education of Native American girls. The Sisters of Loretto, a Catholic order, had established a mission school for Osage girls in 1847. After removal to Indian Territory in 1872, the first government boarding school was built; it remained open until 1921, when the children were transferred to public institutions. Two Catholic boarding schools, St. John's for girls and St. Louis's for boys, were opened in 1887 and continued operating until 1915 and 1948. The off-reservation boarding schools, selecting only the more promising Osage youth from the local classrooms, constituted "higher education" for tribal scholars until the 1920s. Recruiting female students for any of the schools proved troublesome. Osage parents were reluctant to release their male progeny to follow the white man's educational path. They came to view that process as inevitable, however, since the traditional employments . . . of men as warriors and hunters were no longer feasible lifetime pursuits. Girls, on the other hand, could expect to continue to fill their traditional roles as wives, homemakers, and agricultur-alists.

The boarding schools carefully identified female and male activities with distinctly separate, and not necessarily equal, role models. Merial Dorchester charged that Indian girls were not accorded "an equal, chance with the boys out of school hours, and in some places the girls are neglected even in the school room" Boys' uniforms were better made than those issued the girls, according to Special Agent Dorchester. She also complained that girls were usually restricted to a high-fenced pen, while the boys ranged all over the school grounds. This was true at the Osage reservation boarding school, where the fencing was strengthened on several occasions to prevent run-aways and unauthorized visits by parents. There is a hint of latter-day women's liberation sentiment in Dorchester's report. Not content with pointing out the inequity of the school's paying boys, but not girls, for labor performed, she insisted that the former "would enjoy a military drill . . . as [much as] the boys."

She need not have worried about the Osage reservation school's dedica-tion to equal doses of disciplined activities for girls as well as boys. A chart showing chore and industrial details for the last three months of 1894 reveals a strict schedule, at least on paper, for the young women. Six teams of seven girls each rotated in performing four types of tasks: dishwashing for the girls' dining room, dishwashing for the boys' dining room, bedmaking, and sweeping. These chores occupied the morning hour between seven and eight o'clock and an unspecified period following each meal. Industrial details were also assigned daily so that each girls' team spent 2 1/2 hours at these tasks either in the morning (9:00–11:30 or in the afternoon (1:30–4:00). The young Osage girls worked for month-long stints under the varying supervision of the school's seamstress, cook, laundress, or matron. Apparently the school was complying with a request made ten years earlier by the Osage agent who urged that the girls "be instructed carefully and thoroughly in *all* branches of housekeeping . . . including . . . cooking and dairy work.". . .

The schools rarely deviated from these and similar methods in turning out Osage imitations of white society. Concomitant with harsh regimenta-tion, the Indian Office's educational system attempted to remove the stu-dents physically from their tribes. Reservation boarding schools were considered an advance over day schools, and off-reservation schools were seen as the ideal method for divorcing Indian children from the supposedly devitalizing influence of their families and friends. Children were encouraged to stay away from home for as long as possible. Even visits for holidays were grudgingly granted, the government educators preferring that their charges live with white families during the summer months, perfecting their English, learning industrious habits, and generally working themselves into a new lifestyle. In 1900 Agent Pollock praised Nannie She-ah-ku's decision not to return to the Osage agency following her graduation from an off-reservation-boarding school when she took a position with the Bureau of Indian Affairs (BIA) school system.

Not surprising then, given the government goals, was the emphasis attached to the fate of returned students. In 1891 Charles Meserve, Haskell Institute's superintendent, wrote the Osage Agency requesting information on the moral status of returned female students. Unfortunately the reply, if one was made, is not extant. Six years later, however, the Osage agent wrote Washington that returned female students "generally find the pressure put upon them by parents and other relatives too heavy to resist, and almost without exception, drop into the old conditions."

By the "old conditions," the agent meant taking up the blanket, that is, returning to Osage tradition, especially in regard to marital custom. Merial Dorchester called the practice of early marriage "perhaps the most formidable obstacle to the education of these girls. . . . While all life, animal as well as vegetable, matures more rapidly here [among the Indians], still maturity of life among the Indian girls is forced to the extreme. Marriages often occur at twelve or fourteen years of age." The Osage clashed often with their agents over the questions of youthful marriages, plural relationships, divorces, the selling of girls as brides, and the matter of acceptable wedding ceremonies. Among themselves, the tribesmen pondered all these concerns and the additional worrisome issue of intermarriage with members of the surrounding white community.

Other tribes on reservations in Oklahoma and Indian territories faced similar problems. The Osage's struggles with shifting societal and cultural modes, however, were exacerbated by a factor not usually considered a burden—wealth. The Osage received a per capita yearly stipend of $200 from the forced sale of their Kansas reservation. This represented a more than substantial family income for the tribesmen who also received money from grazing leases to Texas cattlemen. Agent Pollock regarded this largess as a baneful influence keeping the Osage in idleness, "their next worst enemy" to drinking, which, he complained, "constituted their sole employment, along with eating, visiting, dancing, and recount[ing] their feats and greatness in former times." Other agents were equally outraged by the tribe's unearned ease and, what they gradually perceived as a more dangerous threat to the Osage, the plague of whiskey peddlers, thieves, confidence men, and other similar elements that infested the reservation. An already bad situation worsened during the first decades of the twentieth century, when the Osage, following the success of an 1897 exploratory drilling, found themselves beneficiaries of an oil bonanza, which by the 1920s, caused them to be billed as the richest group of people on earth. The rush to relieve the tribe of its excess monies led the noted Osage historian, John Joseph Mathews, to characterize the resultant hustle as "the great frenzy." The tribe's women, traditionally treasured as marital partners, became still more valuable as the size of their dowries increased by quantum leaps.

When the Osage first arrived at their Oklahoma reservation, the marriage patterns of the tribe already showed the effects of long association with Euro-Americans. The large number of mixed-bloods attested to one aspect of change; another was manifested in the modifications of the wedding ceremony itself. Mathews's nearly poetic word picture carefully explaining the rich symbolism of the rituals compares closely with many of the details offered by an 1876 newspaper account of a reservation wedding, while contrasting widely with the latter's journalistic skepticism regarding the sincerity of the rites. In both narrations, there is emphasis placed on the "arranged" nature of the marriage. The kinsmen of the prospective groom, especially the parents and uncles, chose a suitable bride, a personage not necessarily acquainted with her future husband. Following the initial selection and negotiation, a feast was prepared by the groom's female relatives; if the young woman's family accepted the food, the match was made.

During the era before contact with the white man, four full days of feasts and talks might ensue, but by 1876 this measured, unhurried sequence had been telescoped into two days. Gifts of horses were tendered by the groom's male relatives to the bride's kinsmen. Given the importance of horses in the Osage economy, this aspect of the marital contract possessed considerable importance. Mathews, stressing what he termed "the Olympian indifference" of the Osage toward wealth, described how the groom's men picked their best horses, ridiculing and scorning any of their number who offered an inferior animal on such an auspicious occasion. Meanness of spirit at this juncture could have serious consequences, as any one of the bride's family could refuse a gift horse, thus bringing the proceedings to a halt. In 1905 a Pawhuska newspaper commenting on the custom suggested that "from a white man's standpoint the whole thing appears to him to be a holdup."

On the day of the wedding, the bride was placed on a horse and led by an aunt, preferably her father's sister, to the groom's lodge, and her coming was announced by a rifle shot. In the old days the wedding participants, male and female, on the woman's side staged a footrace between the respective camps of bride and groom for prizes offered by the latter's relatives. By the 1870s, horseraces held after the wedding replaced this practice. The father of the groom received the bride on a red blanket (a buffalo robe, formerly) held at the four corners by her kinsmen. She was carried to the family's lodge and completely redressed, along with her attendants, exchanging clothes with the groom's sisters and cousins. Finally, the town crier or kettle tender . . . was instructed to summon the groom, who entered a large communal lodge to find his bride surrounded by the entire wedding party sitting before an elaborate feast. Once seated next to her, the man and woman were considered officially wedded. The next day, after spending the night in his lodge, the new husband and wife were escorted on horseback by the latter's kinsmen to their dwelling place, where a new lodge was presented to the couple.

Wealth brought in by the oil wells, the opposition of BIA officials, and the influence of Christian missionaries combined to continue the process of change in the Osage wedding ceremony. By the turn of the century, most of the full-bloods still entered marriage through the traditional practice; "but the mixed bloods," reported Agent Pollock, "now marry according to civilized custom." A decade later a new agent wrote Washington that more and more full-bloods were either marrying by Christian rite or undergoing a church ceremony in addition to the Osage custom. The elaborate traditional ritual was observed less and less often, and had virtually disappeared after World War II. During the late 1970s, the old ceremony resurfaced and has been utilized by a few young Osage couples anxious to rekindle their cultural heritage. . . .

Before the declaration of Oklahoma statehood in 1907, the BIA had no legal grounds for interfering with Osage or other Indian marriages and divorces in Oklahoma and Indian territories. There was no general statutory enactment regarding these matters, so tribal authority was paramount. In cases where one party was white, U.S. law could be invoked. Agent Laban Miles was instructed to encourage "solemnizing" marriages with Christian rites during the early 1880s. Miles was especially concerned with the activities of some mixed-bloods who were married according to territorial law, and then divorced without legal formality and remarried. There were also instances of Osage tribal marriages, divorces, and remarriages well outside the bounds of Anglo-Saxon jurisdiction. Washington advised Miles that Indian marriages were subject solely to tribal law, and, since divorce was not covered, "the contracting parties have no remedy." After November 31, 1881, the problem was eliminated when the Osage inaugurated their own constitution modeled on those devised by the Five Civilized Tribes. The new tribal government's judicial system included provision for judges to grant divorces as well as marriages, an authority frequently exercised, to the consternation and dissatisfaction of Osage agents. The constitution was abrogated in March 1900 causing a seven-year legal hiatus which ended only when statehood brought the Osage under the authority of Oklahoma statutes.

As the wealth from their developing petroleum fields continued to increase, the tribe was faced with a great deal of unwanted notoriety. Each gusher, and consequently larger royalty payment, was trumpeted in newspapers of Osage and surrounding counties. The resultant publicity spread beyond the new state's boundaries, bringing to Pawhuska, the county seat, a cosmopolitan flavor known only to other mineral-based boomtowns. Just before statehood was granted in 1906, the reservation area was divided among the 2,229 Osage allottees, who also shared equally in the oil royalties paid to the tribe as a whole. By the year 1920, an Osage family of five was receiving an income exceeding $40,000 yearly from mineral rights alone. That amount increased steadily during the decade of the 1920s as oil production expanded.

While these riches spawned an ingenious variety of frauds and crimes aimed at dispossessing individual tribesmen of their wealth, marrying into the tribe seemed the least taxing way of making a fortune from an Osage connection. The following letter was unique for its exceptional candor, if not in its sentiment, which was widely shared.

Joplin, Mo. 10/16/07

INDIAN AGENT,
  Pawhuska, Okla.
DEAR SIR:–
  I am a young man with good habits and none of the bad, with several thousand dollars, and want a good indian girl for a wife. I am sober, honest industrious man and stand well in my community.
  I want a woman between the ages of 18 and 35 years of age, not a full blood, but prefer one as near white as possible.
  I lived on a farm most of my life and know how to gets results from a farm as well as a merchantile business. Having means it is natural I want some one my equal financially as well as socially. If you can place me in correspondence with a good woman and I succeed in marrying her for every Five Thousand Dollars she is worth I will give you Twenty Five Dollars. If she worth 25,000 you would get $125 if I got her.
  This is a plain business proposition and I trust you will consider it as such. You have every facility to know them and help me. Now will you? General Delivery. C. T. Plimer
P. S. —
  I will furnish them with every facility to investigate me as to what I am worth, my standing, etc. I am not a pauper or worthless being, but what I claim but believe marriage is as much of a business matter as anything else, or else it is likely to be a failure.

C. T. Plimer. . .

Osage women and men continued to be victims of their own affluence through the 1920s. Sometimes the sudden wealth was employed to provide educations, start businesses, especially stock raising and farming, and broaden the perspectives of the tribespeople, but more often the oil revenues brought trouble. Despite the watchful eye kept on the Osage and their fortunes by the BIA, the Department of the Interior, and government-appointed guardians (and sometimes due to the connivance of the last-mentioned), the Osage men and women continually fell prey to the machinations of human predators. In 1926 the actions of one group of conspirators were disclosed revealing a plot so bizarre and bloody that it made headlines nationally and internationally, leading eventually to the enactment of a federal law to protect the Osage and their wealth.

No one knows precisely when the scheme was contrived, nor have all the details been uncovered even today. Sometime after the signing of the

Armistice that brought the doughboys home from the European battlefields of the First World War, a longtime Osage County dweller, William K. Hale, had an idea. Among the returning veterans was Hale's nephew, Ernest Burkhart, who had married an Osage woman, Mollie Kyle, after moving to Fairfax from his native Texas in 1919. Hale and Burkhart conceived a simple plan: they would have the latter's wife's relatives killed so that Mollie Burkhart would inherit their headrights and properties, thus placing a fortune under the conspirators' control. Mollie's mother, Lizzie Q. had other daughters and numerous relatives, whose deaths would make the schemers wealthy. Before the conspiracy had run its course, between twenty and thirty Osage were killed as a direct or indirect result of the uncle's and nephew's greed.

Although the killings began in 1921, the pattern did not become apparent until 1926, when a grand jury heard testimony sufficient to indict Burkhart, Hale, and a cross section of Oklahoma outlaws hired to commit the murders. State and federal authorities had investigated the murders for months before calling a grand jury. Hale was among the loudest and most demanding in his calls for bringing to an end what newspapers as far removed as the *New York Times* termed "The Osage Reign of Terror." As a highly respected rancher, banker, and businessman whose prominence and influence had earned him the sobriquet, "King of the Osage Hills," he had expressed shock and dismay over the murders on a number of occasions. His implication in the intricate workings of the multiple murder plot surprised his fellow citizens, Indian and white, in Fairfax and throughout Osage County. Hale had covered his tracks well, employing various local outlaws to kill his nephew's kinsmen. It is doubtful that his eventual conviction in 1929 after three trials would have been possible had not the Federal Bureau of Investigation convinced Ernest Burkhart to confess to his own and his uncle's part in the conspiracy.

When the litigation surrounding the case had scarcely begun, the savagery of the murders had moved the federal government to enact legislation to discourage similar crimes. No person convicted of having taken the life of an Osage Indian "or procuring another" to do so would "inherit from or receive any interest in the estate of the decedent, regardless of where the crime was committed and conviction obtained." Excepting those already married at the time the law was passed, none but heirs of Indian blood could inherit from deceased Osage whose Indian blood quantums were one half or more. The atmosphere of conspiracy so permeated the thinking of local officials that the tribal attorney insisted that "every sudden death of an Osage Indian" be investigated for the possibility of "foul play."

Despite the publicity brought to bear on the Osage by sensational cases such as those involving . . . Lizzie Q's family, the tribe continued to experience grave difficulties from mixed marriages. Attention was focused generally on tribal women rather than men. Probably the male members of the tribe presumed that their own less common marriages to non-Indian women did not constitute a pattern of mésalliances as did those of the women, and thus were not a threat to the established social, economic, and political order. The resulting mixed blood offspring, already very much in evidence before the turn of the century, composed a group somewhat more palatable to the tribesmen (at least they were racially and culturally part Osage) than did the intermarried citizens. Long before the oil boom brought the tribe enormous wealth, the Osage viewed these white men as self-seeking interlopers, dangerously subverting of the tribe's best interests.

In 1881, efforts to maintain a semblance of tribal sovereignty through the adoption of a constitution ended in failure. The inability of the government to protect its constituency and solve the internal political impasse resulting from the growing strength of the mixed bloods and intermarried citizens caused the Department of the Interior to abrogate the Osage constitution in August 1900. Both before and after that occurrence, the Osage continually struggled to control those adopted by the tribe by virtue of marriage. They were condemned by one Indian agent who noted that they were "as fruitful of trouble . . . as all others combined." Perhaps the most direct action taken by the Osage national government was the imposition of a $250 fee levied on any white man marrying an Osage woman. The paucity of records regarding the activities of the constitutional government does not reveal the precise year this enactment was made nor how seriously it was observed, but simply that it was enforced to an extent for an indeterminate period of time. Certainly its passage symbolized the great concern felt by the Osage over this question, but did not constitute an effectual resolution of the problem.

The influence of intermarried citizens on their spouses proved a serious handicap for Osage women when they insisted upon an equal share of responsibility and rights in tribal government. In 1906 the Osage Allotment Act provided for a tribal council consisting of a principal chief and eight council members. Subsequent amendments established four-year terms for these positions, which were voted upon by males of the tribe over the age of twenty-one whose names appeared on the annuity rolls. Thus, the council, which operated without a constitution, bylaws, or corporate charter, and accepted as officeholders and voters only those with shares in the mineral estate, functioned as a board of directors of a corporation.

As in the case of the older constitutional government of the tribe, the politics of the Osage Council revolved around the mixed-blood/full-blood factions and their differences. Until 1916 the full-bloods dominated the council, because there existed an unwritten precedent that no more than two mixed-bloods could serve on the council simultaneously. The growing, and increasingly obvious discrepancy of population in favor of the mixed-bloods led to the abandonment of this arrangement. For the sake of appearances, however, the chief and assistant chief were always chosen from among the full-bloods until relatively recent times.

Female participation in tribal elections as voters and officeholders was tied directly to the factionalism just described and the problem of intermarried citizens. Traditionally, women had not played a significant role in Osage government and politics. Before the present century, there was only a single recorded exception, Rosana Choteau. "Mother Choteau" held the position of second chief of the Beaver Band of Osage during the 1870s for an unrecorded length of time. In 1875, appearing before a Senate investigating commission, she was asked how she became a chief.

> They elected me second chief; I had an uncle who had always been chief; six months after he died I came to the agency to buy a little provision. I camped. . . . The band was counciling to elect a chief in my uncle's place, I sat among the women; did not think they were voting for me. They called me out to the camp. I went there and sat down. They had four sticks, representing three men and myself to be voted for. They called me in, gave me my stick and threw the others away, and gave me my uncle's place; said they preferred me. I cried and told them I hope they would take pity on me and pick out one. They talked it over and said we have done, made you, it is finished. I have been second chief since that time. This was about one year ago.

Questioned also about progress the Osage had made in "becoming civilized," Choteau replied that her band "has improved the past year. . . . We went to where we now live about the spring of 1872 . . . [We] all had Indian clothing, now most of the young women wear dresses . . . and are trying to be civilized. I am half blood." This last statement might offer a partial clue as to why the Osage chose this particular woman as chief; yet those qualities that rendered Rosana Choteau exceptional remain obscure. When queried on the point of whether it was customary to elect women chiefs, she answered sparingly, "It is not, I am first one and I expect to be the last one. I think my band obey me better than they would a man."

A lengthy hiatus stretched between the tenure of the first and only female Osage chief and the 1920s, when tribal women began demanding the right of suffrage. During that period, Osage women experienced the heady sensation of new-found freedom of action stemming from the tribe's rapidly accumulating wealth. The acculturating effects of having been made equal shareholders in the petroleum bonanza and earlier tribal annuities were nowhere more apparent than in the changed status of divorced and widowed women. Traditionally such tribe members could not have established or maintained independent households, but by 1900 a number had done so. Most Osage women had then become liberated from forced dependence on male financial support. The next step was political equality.

On March 30, 1922, two mixed-blood sisters, Corine and Leona Girard, original allottees aged twenty-seven and twenty-four respectively, appealed to the BIA Washington office for help in obtaining voting rights for Osage women in tribal elections. They argued that many female allottees had been educated at the St. Louis Mission School, Carlisle Indian School, and at "scholarly public schools and other institutions of learning." They suggested that "the standard of intelligence among the women is equally as high, if not higher, than that of the men." The Girard sisters noted that, according to the 1906 Osage Allotment Act, each Osage woman possessed the same property rights and economics stake as the men, and concluded that "if a few Osage women were elected members of the council, such addition to the Council would prove beneficial to the Tribe as a whole." In reply Assistant Commissioner of Indian Affairs E. B. Meritt acknowledged the Girards' remonstrances as valid and informed them that the BIA had urged the Osage Tribal Council to amend its regulations to allow female allottees to vote and run for office. At an April 18 session, the council chose to defer the matter, voting to affirm a resolution whose wording must have infuriated the Girards and other activist tribal females: "Whereas, at this time it is not deemed to be in the best interests of the Osage Tribe to permit the women members of said Tribe to vote [the Council will not accede to the Indian Office's suggestion as] . . . it has always been the custom for only male members over 21 to vote. . . ."

Another twenty years elapsed before the Osage Council could be induced, reluctantly, to change its stance. Tribal women, although barred from the franchise, did participate in Osage politics. In 1927 at a Pawhuska political gathering to discuss oil leasing. Chief Bacon Rind was reported "eulogizing the female members of the tribe for their keen interest in the meetings and the way they turned out in large numbers." In spite of the somewhat patronizing tone of his remarks, Bacon Rind and the other Osage men generally recognized the legitimacy of the women's involvement in tribal politics and probably would have extended suffrage rights much earlier had the political scene been less divisive. In the fall of 1941, James G. Blaine, Jr., an Osage full blood, was named president of a newly organized tribal political party. Inaugurated as the American Party, the new group announced its plans to urge an extension of the franchise to females and unallotted members of the tribe of both sexes. Maggie Goode was selected to be vice president of the party, and Agatha Conway was chosen as secretary, while thirteen other women sat on the advisory board.

Agitation for women's suffrage and enfranchisement of unallotted members of the tribe had reached the required level of pressure. Activities of the American Party were coupled with strongly worded messages from the commissioner of Indian Affairs to the council, which finally granted to Osage female allottees, and all tribal members holding full or fractional headrights, voting privileges and the right to run for council seats. Two full blood councilmen opposed the move because they believed it would enhance the power of the mixed-blood voting strength and give the white husbands of Osage women undue influence through their wives. The Osage women voted in the 1942 council elections in undisclosed numbers. Over five hundred were enfranchised that year, of whom nearly four hundred were less than one-half Osage according to their blood quantums.

Women's names appeared frequently on the ballots running for seats on the council during the 1950s and 1960s, but none were elected. It was the mid-1970s before a mixed-blood Osage woman, Camille Pangburn, took her elected seat on the council. Asked about the significance of becoming the first female council member, she suggested that "it was a precedent that had to be changed. . . . I think the fact that I was probably pretty well known . . . helped." Pangburn was referring to her part in overseeing the distribution of a 1973 federal judgment, which caused her to interact by mail, telephone, and personal interview with a large part of the tribal membership. Additionally she had served as secretary to the council for several years prior to seeking tribal office. Pangburn revealed that she had some trepidations about entering the electoral race and "discussed it with some of the older tribal women [because] . . . I didn't want to do anything that would go against tribal tradition." Some Osage political observers feel that Pangburn's election will pave the way for the subsequent elections of more females, while others stress the fact that she was elected in spite of being a woman, primarily on the basis of her experience and high visibility.

In still other ways the tribal accretions of wealth and their equal distribution among males and females helped shape the model of the twentieth-century Osage woman. The Girard sisters cited the fact that many tribeswomen had received good educations. Once survival dictated the necessity for gaining knowledge of the world of the white majority, many Osage women used their financial advantages to good and sometimes dazzling effect. The pages of the Pawhuska and other Osage County newspapers carried stories with accompanying pictures portraying the social prominence of some mixed-blood women. The September 13, 1925, edition of the *Daily Journal-Capital* informed its readers that Isabel Rogers had decided to matriculate at the exclusive Chevy Chase (Maryland) School for Girls. Some months later the society page heralded the selection of Catherine Revard as one of the princesses at a special pageant opening the 1926 Southwestern Exposition and Fat Stock Show in Fort Worth, Texas. According to the society editor, "Miss Revard being a descendant of Osage Indian and French blood, carries with it a distinctive touch of interest."

Fine clothes and social prominence did not comprise the whole of the tribal female's ambition. During the spring of 1919, a special ceremony was held in the Indian community of Pawhuska honoring Angela Gorman, a young Osage who had just completed a year's study in New York training her voice for opera. She was given the name, Klu-ah-er, Eagle Maiden, a cognomen chosen from her family's clan designation, and was quoted afterward as saying that she "must prove the qualities of my ancestry as well as be the pioneer blazing the trail for other girls of her tribe. . . ." While many Osage women might have been momentarily inspired by Angela Gorman's example, probably no one anticipated that worldwide fame in the arts would come for a member of the tribe three decades later. Born in Fairfax, Maria Tallchief, a half blood whose father was a tribal councilman, became in the decade of the 1950s what some called "the finest American-born classic ballerina the twentieth century has produced." A sister, Marjorie, joined a handful of other Oklahoma Indian women, some of them Osage, in following her into careers in ballet, although none achieved the same level of prominence.

As the roaring twenties quieted into the sobering thirties and forties, the Osage adapted themselves to a less frenetic lifestyle. No longer objects of greedy white men's desires, the women, especially full-bloods, more often married members of the tribe. Arranged matches were quite common in the 1930s and for some time thereafter among the rural full-bloods, and divorces became less common. In 1936 the agency superintendent reported that "family conditions among the Osage compare favorably with the average small town or rural community." Certainly the lifestyles of Indian and white in Osage County tended more and more toward parallels than contrasts as the tribe continued its existence into the second half of the twentieth century. The Osage, however, cherished the differences that distinguished them from their Anglo-Saxon neighbors. The Klash-kah-she Club, an Osage women's altar society in Pawhuska, provides a good example. Begun in the 1920s by Sister Mary Magdelene of the Loretta Order, the all-Indian organization functions very similarly to its all-white counterparts, yet provides the women with a special sense of identification and removes any tensions which might result in an interracial grouping.

Much has changed for the Osage tribe and its women since coming to Oklahoma a century ago. The status of women underwent some serious modifications concomitant to the changes taking place within the whole tribe. Judged by white observers to be the most conservative elements opposed to the planned acculturation programs, the Osage women emerged in the 1920s as the group that best utilized the petroleum-based wealth of the tribe to pursue educational and cultural goals. They retained their importance as desirable marital partners, thanks to the oil bonanza, but gained new independence when divorced or widowed. The most dramatic alteration in their position within the tribe, also partially the result of sharing as equal partners in the tribal revenues, was the women's successful struggle to share in the political governance of the Osage tribe.

Perhaps the scene at Indian dances best describes the current status of Osage women within tribal society and the degree to which they have experienced the effects of acculturation. At the I'N-Lon Schka ceremonial dances held each June since the 1880s, only men were allowed to participate until the 1940s, when women were admitted. During the 1970s, as greater numbers of women and men (particularly the young) have taken part in such tribal cultural events, reenforcing their self-realization of "Indianness," it was not uncommon to see Osage females don shawls over their street clothes and join the dancers, always careful to stay at the outer edges of the ceremonial circle, as prescribed by tradition. Whatever misgivings or doubts that Osage women might harbor regarding the propriety and wisdom of their changed lives, they can join an Indian poetess in asserting that "it is our faith which holds up half the sky."

The Japanese Immigrant Family, 1900s–1920s

YUJI ICHIOKA

Most of the Asian immigrants who arrived in America before the 1940s were men in their prime working years. Only relatively small numbers of women from China, Japan, Korea, and the Philippines and no more than a dozen women from India settled in Hawaii and the continental United States.

A majority of the approximately 9,000 Chinese women who set foot on the Pacific coast between 1850 and 1875 were forced into prostitution, though some escaped that fate by running away, marrying one of their customers, earning and saving enough money to buy their freedom, or being rescued by Euro-American women missionaries. Because of the scarcity of complete families, few Chinese-American children were born; they numbered about 500 in 1870 and 9,000 in 1900.

The history of female Japanese immigrants differed from the experiences of their Chinese counterparts. Although Japanese prostitutes were also brought to America from the earliest days of Japanese immigration, the Tokyo government, concerned about Japan's international image, took forceful measures to end that traffic. Most of the 30,000 or so women from Japan who entered the country after 1908, when the Gentlemen's Agreement—an unwritten understanding between the Japanese and American governments to curb the influx of Japanese laborers—went into effect, came as wives or "picture brides." The latter had entered arranged marriages, facilitated by an exchange of photographs, with Japanese men living and working in the United States. Their immigration ended in 1920 when the Japanese government, once again responding to anti-Japanese agitation in American society, ceased issuing passports to them.

As Yuji Ichioka shows in the following reading, during the dozen years when they could enter freely, these women helped to establish family units that became instrumental in shaping Japanese immigrant communities throughout the American West and in Hawaii.

STUDY QUESTIONS

1. Do you think that the "picture bride" system of finding a female marital partner was unusual? If so, why? If not, why not?

2. What qualifications did Japanese immigrants living in the United States have to meet before they could send for brides? Why?

Between 1900 and 1920 many [Japanese immigrant] men summoned wives from Japan. In 1900 there were only 410 married women in immigrant society. This number increased to 5,581 by 1910 and leaped to 22,193 by 1920. These women enabled many immigrant men to enjoy a settled family life which socially reinforced the economic foundation of permanent settlement. Married women entered immigrant society in one of three ways. Some wives who had been left behind in Japan were summoned by their husbands. Other women married single men who returned to Japan to seek brides. These women came to the United States with their spouses. Two factors limited the number of bachelors who returned to Japan to seek brides. Few could afford the time and expense of such a trip, which included the heavy outlays for marriage required by Japanese social custom. Some returnees faced the possibility of being inducted into the military. All Japanese men living abroad enjoyed deferments, but lost their deferred status if they returned for more than thirty days. The time spent in finding an appropriate bride, in entering into a formal engagement, and in getting married often exceeded a month.

Thus many bachelors resorted to the so-called picture-bride practice, the third way by which women entered immigrant society. The picture-bride practice did not diverge sharply from traditional Japanese marriage custom. In Japan, marriage was never an individual matter, but always a family affair. Heads of household selected marriage partners for family members through intermediaries or go-betweens. An exchange of photographs sometimes occurred in the screening process, with family genealogy, wealth, education, and health figuring heavily in the selection criteria. Go-betweens arranged parleys between families at which proposed unions were discussed and negotiated. Although at such meetings prospective spouses normally met each other for the first time, it would be unusual for them to talk to each other. After all, the meetings were for the benefit of the heads of family, and not designed for future couples to become acquainted with each other. If the families mutually consented, engagement and marriage ensued.

Edited with the permission of The Free Press, a Division of Macmillan, Inc. from *The ISSEI: The World of the First Generation Japanese Immigrants 1885–1924,* by Yuji Ichioka, pp. 164–175. Copyright © 1988 by The Free Press.

In general, the picture-bride practice conformed to this marriage custom. Single immigrant men had brides picked for them by their parents or relatives. Along with photographs of themselves, the men forwarded information about their lives in America, which go-betweens used in negotiations with parents of eligible daughters. The practice deviated in only one important respect from conventional marriages: bridegrooms were physically absent at wedding ceremonies. Still, the practice satisfied all social and legal requirements governing marriage in Japan. Marriages were legal as long as husbands fulfilled a simple bureaucratic condition: they had to enter the names of their brides into their own family registries. By meeting this requirement, men became legally betrothed no matter where they resided. That they had never laid eyes upon their brides nor had participated in wedding ceremonies was of no consequence. In accordance with this practice, the majority of wives who entered immigrant society between 1910 and 1920 came as picture-brides.

To control the entry of married women, Japanese consulates set rigid standards. The fundamental yardstick was economic. Only men who had

Japanese "picture brides" disembarking at San Francisco, 1919

proven means of supporting families were qualified to summon wives. All laborers were ineligible until 1915. Rare exceptions were made for those in urban occupations—for example, butlers, waiters, and cooks—if they commanded high wages and could provide proof of continuous employment and savings of at least $1,000. Businessmen and farmers were eligible, but they had to meet specific criteria. A businessman had to have an annual gross income of $1,200 or more, a farmer had to have an annual profit of $400 to $500, and both had to have savings of at least $1,000 as well. In 1915 the Japanese government modified its requirement to make laborers eligible. Effective July 1, 1915, all male residents of the United States, including laborers, became eligible to summon wives, provided they had savings of $800. To reduce the possibility of fraud, Japanese consuls required that men who applied to bring over their wives had to submit bank deposit books as proof that this sum had been in their accounts for no less than five months preceding the date of applications.

Women had to satisfy specific government regulations too. If they were picture-brides, their names had to be entered into their husbands' family registries six months prior to their passport applications. This requirement, Japanese officials believed, impeded procurers from obtaining prostitutes disguised as picture-brides. After 1915 picture-brides also had to meet an age regulation. They could not be more than thirteen years younger than their spouses. This age limit was set on the premise that too wide a disparity was not conducive to harmonious marriages. If there were extenuating circumstances, however, the regulation was waived. All Japanese emigrants had to pass physical examinations at ports of embarkation. American immigration statutes prohibited the admission of bearers of contagious diseases. Immigration inspectors were especially alert for those afflicted with trachoma and hookworm, two fairly common diseases in Japan. Aware of American regulations, the Japanese government administered physical examinations to all departing women to make sure that they had neither.

No single motive explains why Japanese women came to the United States. In the case of married women who had been left behind in Japan, they responded to their spouses' summons to join them. Most picture-brides simply obeyed parents. Betrothed by parental arrangement, they, too, came to join their spouses. To refuse would have been an act of filial disobedience, a grave moral offense. Economic motives no doubt were also involved. Some daughters became picture-brides to help their families through hard times or to put a younger sibling through school. By working in this country, they expected to be able to remit money to their families. For women who found themselves in social predicaments, marriage with men abroad offered an avenue of escape. For such women life in America held out hopes for a new beginning, a future in a country which evoked images of material comfort unimaginable at home. Some women came for even more fundamental economic reasons—they lacked sufficient food, clothing, and shelter.

Regardless of motives, all women were beset by common problems as soon as they landed. Their first encounter with America was the ordeal of passing through the labyrinth of the immigration station. Most women arrived as third-class steerage passengers for whom an immigration inspection was a grim experience. Inspectors examined them more scrupulously than first- or second-class passengers. Advance briefings about what to expect did not allay anxieties. Many questions worried the women no end. Were their papers in order? Each wife had to have a valid passport, a certified copy of her husband's family registry, and a health certificate. Would she pass the physical examination? That she had been found free of trachoma and hookworm in Japan was no guarantee she would. Would her husband be at the immigration station to welcome her? Some wives did not know. All husbands had to appear in person to receive wives. Picture-brides gazed upon their spouses for the first time in the station. Such anxieties were compounded by fear of the unknown and by lack of knowledge of English.

Wives were matched up with husbands at the immigration station. Immigration officials required husbands to present documents to avert mix-ups. First, they had to have certificates issued by the Japanese consulates which attested to their identity and occupation. Second, they had to have additional proof of employment. Farmers had to show land titles or lease agreements, businessmen had to show commercial licenses, and salaried workers had to produce letters signed by employers. Third, they had to have bank deposit books as evidence of their ability to support wives. If everything was in order, officials released wives into the custody of husbands. Prior to 1917, the American government did not recognize picture-bride marriages, so that pictures-brides and their spouses had to be remarried in a ceremony in order to be considered legally married in the United States. Group ceremonies were conducted in the immigration station at the beginning; later they were held in hotel lobbies or churches by special arrangement with immigration authorities. In 1917 the State Department granted legal recognition to picture-bride marriages, allowing picture-brides and their spouses to dispense with this second wedding ceremony.

Many picture-brides were genuinely shocked to see their husbands. Sometimes the person was much older than he appeared in his photograph. As a rule husbands were older than wives by ten to fifteen years, and occasionally more. Men often forwarded photographs taken in their youth or touched up ones that concealed their real age. No wonder some picture-brides, upon sighting their spouses, lamented dejectedly that they had married "an old man." Husbands appeared unexpectedly different in other ways. Some men had photographs touched up, not just to look youthful, but to improve their overall appearance. They had traces of facial blemishes and baldness removed. Picture-brides understandably were taken aback because such men did not physically correspond with their photographs at all. Suave, handsome-looking gentlemen proved to be pockmarked country bumpkins.

A few disillusioned picture-brides declined to join their husbands and asked to be sent back to Japan. Others who had married distant relatives or men they had known in their villages as young girls were disappointed, perhaps, but not crestfallen.

Almost all women landed wearing Japanese kimonos and sandals. As a part of their initiation into American society, it was common for husbands to take their wives to a clothing store to outfit them in a set of western clothes. Of all the strange items of apparel, corsets were the most uncomfortable. Newly outfitted women had trouble breathing while wearing something so constricting. Western-style shoes were no less uncomfortable. The enclosed, pointed toe of shoes, particularly of fashionable, high-lace boots, were not suited for Japanese women whose feet, shaped since childhood by open slippers and sandals, were wide and flat. Pointed shoes were painful to wear and impossible to walk in at first.

Other more serious problems lay in store. Besides sending touched-up photographs, Japanese immigrant men were sometimes disingenuous in other ways. To enable parents or relatives to find brides easily, they often exaggerated their own attractiveness as future husbands. Keepers of small Japanese-style inns or boardinghouses referred to themselves as hotel operators. In Japan, the work "hotel" connoted something much larger than either, conjuring up images of modern, multistoried brick or concrete structures. Similarly, sharecroppers passed themselves off as landowning farmers, small shopkeepers as big merchants, hotel bellboys as elevator engineers, railroad section foremen as labor contractors. A female reader of the *Shin Sekai* once wrote that, if the newspaper ever printed the letters men forwarded to Japan in seeking picture-brides, the men would have to cringe in shame. She believed that these letters were devoid of sincerity. A few men were culpable of more than hyperboles; they relayed utterly false information about themselves. A picture-bride in one case discovered that her husband was an itinerant gambler instead of being the landowning fruit grower he had claimed to be. Picture-brides had no way of verifying information about their spouses. In general, they believed what they heard from go-betweens until they arrived in the United States and learned otherwise.

Women quickly came into contact with American realities through work. The majority went into rural areas. Scattered throughout the western United States, many entered labor camps operated by their husbands. Alternatively, women entered farmlands on which their husbands tilled the soil as share or cash tenants. This was especially common in California where Japanese immigrant agriculture flourished the most. In urban areas, women entered small businesses in which their husbands were engaged: laundries, bathhouses, bars, markets, restaurants, boardinghouses, and poolhalls. Or they became domestic servants, seamstresses, or cannery workers. But no matter where they ended up, a life of unending labor was their lot. Ideally, Japanese women were supposed to confine themselves to the home as "dutiful wives and intelligent mothers" (*ryōsai kenbo*). Very few immigrant women could afford to limit themselves to these two roles. Economic realities forced the majority to assume a third role as workers whose labor was indispensable in the operation of labor camps, farms, and small businesses.

Living and working conditions generally were primitive. In rural areas women had to draw water for cooking, washing, and bathing from wells. Kindling wood was the source of heat. Frequently, women had to cook for large gangs of workers employed by their husbands. Makeshift wooden shacks on farms and small rented rooms in towns usually served as initial living quarters. Working from dawn to dusk left little time to socialize, even less to devote oneself to the leisure arts or to learn English. Women were compelled to work in order to survive, a reality which made them aware of the hyperboles and falsehoods their husbands had told before marriage.

This harsh reality was behind marital scandals known as *kakeochi* or desertion of husbands by wives. The immigrant press regularly printed *kakeochi* notices. A typical notice announced that a married woman and a "scoundrel," both named specifically, had "disappeared," meaning that they had absconded together. The notice included their physical description, place of origin in Japan, and even photographs. Husbands who had been deserted, or local immigrant organizations, placed these notices in the immigrant press and offered rewards for information leading to the discovery of the guilty parties. The *Shin Sekai* ran a typical notice in 1909 submitted by Kojima Aizō of Walnut Grove announcing that his wife, Tsuta, had fled with Miki Jōkichi. A native of Wakayama Prefecture, Miki was described as 33 to 34 years old, 5 feet 2 inches, 115 pounds with dark complexion and a scar at the nape of his neck. A native of Yamaguchi Prefecture, Tsuta was described as 28 years old, 5 feet, 110 pounds, with fair complexion. The notice stated that the two had vanished together on December 12. Kojima offered a reward of $25 to any party furnishing information as to their whereabouts. . . .

Desertion stories appeared in the immigrant press as often as *kakeochi* notices. As early as April 1908, the *Shin Sekai* reported the case of Odawara Toshiko, who ran away from Sacramento to Stockton with her paramour. In 1914 the *Taihoku Nippō* of Seattle carried a story about Nishizaki Juta who was depicted as a moral derelict. He had seduced the wife of Hashimoto Yoshirō of Tacoma, and harbored her secretly until the local Japanese association uncovered his hideaway and had them arrested. Legal charges were dropped once Nishizaki agreed to pay Hashimoto $600. . . .

All stories contained variations of the desertion theme. The detail differed depending upon the story. A picture-bride deserts right after arriving; another deserts after living with her husband for a spell. An older married woman leaves her husband and children, while another takes her infant with her. A woman and her paramour plot to steal her husband's hidden money before absconding together. A woman is caught and sent back to Japan, while another is placed in a church-operated women's home. The men with whom women run off range from young laborers to roving city salesmen, to partners in their husbands' farms or businesses, and even to professional gamblers. Most stories are written in a tragic vein; a few have elements of the comic. All have didactic overtones. . . .

The publication of *kakeochi* stories and notices by the immigrant press was also a means of social control. The publicity exposed to public shame those women who deserted their husbands. Branded as "adulteresses" or "immoral hussies," women who deserted were ostracized and inevitably forced to move to new locales. The *Nichibei Shimbun* printed two notices in July, 1913, one announcing that Omoto Mine had deserted her husband in Alameda, and another that Furube Shizue had left her husband in Oxnard. Both women fled eastward to Utah. Remote places, however, were not always safe havens, as a Stockton man found out when he deserted his own wife and ran away with another man's. The two were apprehended in Medford, Oregon, as they were heading for Seattle, by local Japanese residents who recognized them.

Complementing the immigrant press were the Japanese associations which acted as the moral watchdogs of Japanese communities. Association leaders became alarmed in 1916 over the rate of desertion. As evidence of a rising rate, the *Nichibei Shimbun* reported that the local association of San Francisco had received an inordinate number of *kakeochi* notices from other associations. In the spring, secretaries of local associations affiliated with the Japanese Association of America deliberated on the problem of desertion at their annual meeting. They described the state of marriages within the jurisdiction of their association, and to account for marital failures, enumerated such factors as the drinking and gambling habits of husbands, the disillusionment of picture-brides, and the gaps in age and education among spouses. To the horror of the assembled males, a few cases were cited in which picture-brides had had affairs with seamen or other men aboard ships en route to the United States. This prompted the Japanese Association of America to issue a guide to the United States for women and to have it distributed at ports of embarkation in Japan. . . .

All Japanese associations treated absconding couples as outcasts. The Western Idaho Japanese Association is a case in point. In September 1923 this association received a letter from the North American Japanese Association of Seattle notifying it that Araeda Asako had absconded with Amano Sanji. She had deserted her sick husband, Araeda Aiji, and her child. Photographs of her and her paramour were enclosed. The Seattle association asked the Idaho association to be alert to their possible appearance in its jurisdiction and to have no dealings with them until Asako returned to her husband and Amano made proper restitution. . . . Japanese associations . . . refused to have any dealings with absconding couples. The network of associations made it well-nigh impossible for such couples to escape detection, even when they left one state and settled down in a Japanese community in another. If they wished to elude social ostracism altogether, they had no choice but to resettle in a place where there were no Japanese.

Marital estrangement was at the bottom of desertions. No woman took desertion lightly. Living in an alien land reinforced the traditional subordinate role of Japanese women. With little or no knowledge of the English language and of American society, wives had to depend upon their husbands for almost everything. This dependency, coupled with the threat of public exposure, inhibited desertion. As a general rule, therefore, women who deserted had to be those who were very desperate. Becoming a social outcast, to them, was better than enduring conjugal relations which had degenerated to an insufferable level. . . .

Notwithstanding all the hardships Japanese immigrant women had to endure, the majority did not desert their husbands, and thus enabled many men to enjoy a settled family life. The emergence of the Japanese immigrant family was reflected in the dramatic increase in the number of American-born, or Nisei, children between 1900 and 1920. At the turn of the century, there were only 269 children; by 1910 the number grew to 4,502, and by 1920 it multiplied more than sixfold to 29,672. Most women gave birth to these children through midwifery. Nearly every Japanese settlement had midwives. If a settlement did not have one, women relied upon those who worked in neighboring communities. Many pregnant women in the Imperial Valley, for example, entered Los Angeles maternity clinics that were staffed with midwives. In isolated rural areas, husbands served as midwives or women gave birth unassisted, even cutting and tieing the umbilical cord themselves. Most women never had prenatal or postnatal care. They worked until a few days before delivery and resumed work shortly after. The birth of Nisei children accelerated the transformation of Japanese immigrants from sojourners to permanent settlers as the Issei (immigrant) generation eventually identified its own future with that of its children in America. In sum, the entry of women into immigrant society was integral to the process by which Japanese immigrants sank roots in American soil.

In 1919 the agitation against the picture-bride practice emerged in California. Senator James D. Phelan, anticipating his 1920 reelection campaign, started the agitation in March. Japanese women were easy targets. Phelan and others attacked the picture-bride practice as an uncivilized "Asiatic" custom, a throwback as it were to barbarism by which women were married off without regard to love or morality. They alleged that the practice violated the Gentlemen's Agreement which had been negotiated to curtail labor immigration from Japan. Deviously undermining the agreement, Japanese female laborers were entering the United States under the guise of being "homemakers." To make matters worse, these women produced children, enabling Japanese immigrants to circumvent the 1913 California Alien Land

Law. Exclusionists charged that the Japanese were buying agricultural land in the name of their offspring who were American citizens. Lastly, they saw the increasing number of Nisei children as dangerous increments to the Japanese population because the children, like their parents, could never be assimilated into American society. . . . Judging the situation to be truly grave, Consul Ota Tamekichi wired the Foreign Ministry on October 5 and recommended that it cease issuing passports to picture-brides. . . .

. . . Consul Ota called a meeting of the executive board of the Japanese Association of America. He asked the board members to declare publicly that they were opposed to the picture-bride practice. . . . The executive board agreed with him, and on October 31 issued a press release in English which declared that the practice "should be abolished because it is not only in contravention of the accepted American conception of marriage, but is also out of harmony with the growing ideals of the Japanese themselves.". . .

As soon as the press release became public, a veritable storm of criticism came down upon the Japanese Association of America. . . . On December 6 the Foreign Ministry informed the Japanese ambassador to the United States of its decision to cease issuing passports to picture-brides effective March 1, 1920.

Japanese immigrants did not acquiesce quietly in this decision. Many local associations, both in and outside of California, convened emergency meetings at which local residents adopted protest resolutions. . . . In 1920 there were still 24,000 single, adult males within immigrant society, the overwhelming majority of whom were laborers. These laborers were single, not because they preferred bachelorhood, but because they had not been able to meet the $800 requirement. Now they were doomed to perpetual bachelorhood.

Chicano Families in the Southwest, 1910–1945

RICHARD GRISWOLD DEL CASTILLO

The Mexican-American family, much like families in other ethnic groups, functions as the central social institution in Chicano communities. It provides economic, social, and cultural support to both immigrants and Americans of Mexican ancestry. Despite its importance, the Mexican-American family has been discussed largely in essentialist terms—bordering on stereotype—as a traditional, unchanging extended network characterized by patriarchal (father-dominated) control. *La familia*, the family, has become a metaphor for traditional Chicano culture from both a Chicano and a non-Chicano perspective.

The problem with this simplistic view is that there is no such thing as *the* Chicano family. In reality, *la familia* is neither monolithic nor unchanging. There are many variations in its pattern, representing both continuity and change, tradition and innovation, stability and tension. Chicano families have survived over the years because they have adapted to changing conditions.

In the following selection, Richard Griswold del Castillo notes how Chicano families evolved during an era of significant change—1910 to 1945, a period characterized by sizable immigration to the United States from Mexico, ongoing urbanization and industrialization, continuing acculturation, severe economic depression, and world war. He also briefly discusses how the internal dynamics of Chicano families differed among four segments of the Mexican-ancestry population.

STUDY QUESTIONS

1. What factors explain the different forms of *la familia*?

2. In what ways have Mexican-American families adapted to changing circumstances?

After 1900 three tendencies became more pronounced in the American Southwest: rapid industrial and commercial growth, progressive urbanization, and large-scale Mexican immigration. . . . [T]he most pervasive force

Text excerpted from Richard Griswold del Castillo, *La Familia: Chicano Families in the Urban Southwest, 1848 to the Present,* 1984, pp. 93–94, 96–98, 100–102, 104–106. University of Notre Dame Press.

making for continuity in family life was the grinding poverty endured by the majority of Mexican families whether immigrant or native-born. The basic problems which had influenced Mexican-American family life in the previous century, those of marginalization, discrimination, and economic insecurity, remained. Overcrowding in large cities, the massive influx of new immigrants and migrants, the proliferation of low-paying industrial jobs, the impact of new technologies, the superheated nationalism and nativism spawned by World Wars I and II, and the economic disasters of the Great Depression all affected the daily lives of Mexican-American families. . . .

Rapid industrial growth in various regions of the historical Southwest after 1880 had the effect of intensifying the dependency of families on wage-paying jobs and of removing them from agricultural ties. Industrial growth was greatest in California and Texas and much slower in Arizona and New Mexico. . . . During this period there was an increasing specialization in laboring occupations, and large numbers of Mexican laborers entered the industrial work force. . . . Industrial growth and the specialization of labor meant that Mexican-American wage earners, as heads of families, were increasingly integrated into the urban economy, much more so than had been true in the previous century. This also meant that they and their families were subject to technological unemployment and more intense job competition. . . .

Mexican-American family history during this period continued to be characterized by persisting regional, socioeconomic, and generational differences. Conceivably there were at least four different kinds of family experience corresponding to complexities in the social and economic life, although more can be imagined.

The families of the working-class Mexican immigrants in the cities were predominantly monolingual Spanish-speaking, and hence not acculturated. They were the most disadvantaged segment of Mexican-American society. A very small but socially and politically important portion of Mexican immigrant families were from the middle and upper classes in Mexico. They brought with them the cultural ideals of their class but usually, owing to their social status, accommodated themselves more easily to American society than did the working-class immigrant. The native-born families of laboring and semiskilled occupations were the core populations who lived in the urban barrios. They lived alongside the Mexican immigrant working class and shared, for the most part, the social and economic world of the immigrant, although they had the distinct advantage of being bilingual and more accustomed to life in the United States. The upper-class native-born families, of which the Hispano aristocracy in New Mexico was the most visible element, had their own familial environment. Usually they lived apart from the working classes and had values which shadowed those of the majority middle class. Sometimes they joined with the Mexicano upper-class immigrant families in social and political activities. Within this group the Hispano upper class considered themselves to be set apart by their Spanish heritage from the Mexican-born and Mexican-heritage populations and probably were more a part of American society than any other group. . . .

. . . [T]he middle- and upper-class families of this period . . . tended to be more acculturated than the families of the working class. In these families, "Both Mexican and American cultures co-existed." They had their own circle of clubs, schools and churches. Bilingualism within the family was more pronounced and social controls over girls' activities were more strict. While patriarchal family values pervaded all strata of Mexican society, . . . the "Ricos" and "Los de Clase Media" (rich and middle class) contradictorily tended to emphasize the theoretical equality of men and women within marriage. Thus, "For the 'Ricos' the woman was equal but marriage was still her personal 'salvation'." In practice the middle- and upper-class women had more freedom than working-class women, but this was due primarily to their class position. Otherwise "emotionally and intellectually she was reared to 'please, comfort and know her place. . . .' "

One of the main differences between the ambience surrounding the lives of these middle- and upper-class families and that of the working class lay in the area of security. The more affluent Mexicanos felt more confident in their daily lives, while insecurity pervaded the lives of the poor. . . . Among the Mexicano upper classes fewer women and children worked outside the home since there was no economic necessity for them to do so. And in any case it was regarded as being degrading to the family's honor to have them employed for wages outside the home. . . .

The bulk of the [existing] historical and social scientific literature . . . documents the problems of the laboring-class Mexican immigrants as part of a national concern over the effects of unlimited Mexican immigration into the United States. In the arena of family life the tendency was to focus on the social disorganization and pathologies suffered by family members. . . . [T]his emphasis obscures more positive aspects of family experience. Instances of poverty and family disorganization mask the fact that for many working-class Mexicanos and Chicanos life within families continued to be a source of support and succor within an oppressive environment. Conceptually what is significant are the strategies these families used to survive despite hardships. . . .

[R]egardless of urban location the conditions surrounding the family life of Mexican immigrant laborers were oppressive: overcrowding, high rates of infant mortality, substandard housing, malnutrition, juvenile crime, and economic insecurity were prominent features among . . . Mexican workers. . . . One of the effects of poverty and migration on family life was to produce orphans that could not be cared for by kin or families. In the nineteenth century the tendency was for families to take in orphaned or unwanted children. The increasing numbers of Mexican-heritage orphans being institutionalized within Los Angeles indicated that the extended-family network was breaking down. . . .

In Los Angeles the large family was not economically advantageous, since the kinds of industrial jobs available did not employ child labor. Still, children worked part-time after school in a number of low-paying jobs. A study of 788 Mexican families in Southern California in 1929 reported that one-fourth of the children had part-time jobs but there was no correlation between a family's income and the numbers of children. In comparison to . . . San Antonio, the Spanish-speaking families of Los Angeles had a higher income, averaging $1,500 a year. But this was still at or below the poverty level for a family of four. . . .

. . . [T]he Mexican families of Los Angeles experienced a great deal of transiency, a continuation of patterns begun in the previous century. Less than 21 percent of the skilled and unskilled workers and their families continued to live in Los Angeles during the period 1921–1928. Transiency was related to the proximity of the Mexican border, which made it easy for Mexicanos to travel back and forth according to the economic cycle. In addition a large number of Mexicans in the city moved on to the agricultural areas, lured by higher wages and the opportunities for family income as farmworkers. . . . Los Angeles' barrio "functioned as a depot or 'stepping stone' for Mexican immigrants recruited to work in the Midwest and other areas of the Southwest."

It seems likely that the conditions surrounding family life for the native-born adults of long residence in the Southwest were better than for the Mexican immigrants, if only because they were more likely to be fluent in English and hence be more able to get better-paying jobs. There were only a few studies of the Mexican-American native-born, as a group separate from the Mexican immigrant, during the 1920s or 1930s.

A special census report published in 1933 provides a rough outline of the major characteristics of the native-born Mexican-heritage families. Nationwide, the natives were more likely to live in rural regions than was true for immigrants. Fifty-five percent of all Mexican immigrants lived in urban settings, while only 41 percent of the natives lived in cities in 1930. The families of the native-born were a minority of the Spanish speaking in all the largest cities of the Southwest, ranging from 16 percent in Los Angeles to 33 percent in San Antonio. Compared to the immigrant families, the natives were more likely to own their own homes, but there was little difference between the two groups with respect to the values of these dwellings. Roughly the same proportions of Spanish speaking, regardless of nativity, lived in substandard ($1,500 and below), middle-class ($3,000 to $4,999) and affluent ($10,000 and over) housing, which suggests that the native families were not necessarily better off than the immigrants. The native-born had a smaller family size, fewer employed adults per household, and lower proportions of lodgers than did the Mexican-immigrant families. Overall, however, the differences in living conditions were not as great as the similarities. . . .

Even though many Hispano migrants in the cities may have retained their familial ties to relatives back home, and this became easier to do with the construction of modern roads and telephones, there were differences between their family lives and those of the rural villagers they left be-

A Mexican-American family in New Mexico sharing tight bedroom quarters, 1943.

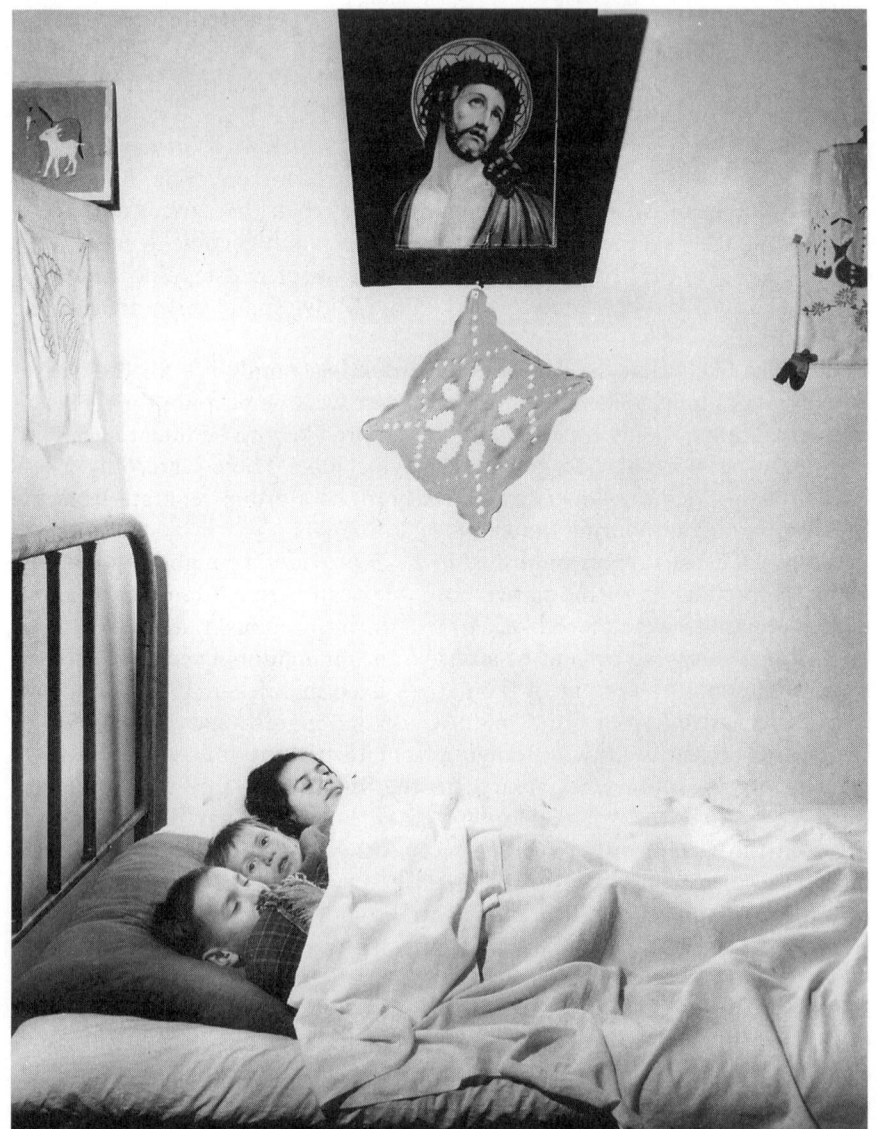

hind. . . . One old-timer [has] lamented, "The younger generation, finding the strangers' customs new and attractive, began to adopt them and forget their own. The quiet reserve and respect has gone. . . . The old Spanish courtesy and hospitality has also changed, to the regret of the elders, who have found it hard to get accustomed to the new ways. . . . The land of *Poco Tiempo* has become the land of haste and hurry.". . .

Hispano family life was characterized by a mixture of urban and rural patterns. Community social controls, fiestas, dances, and religious celebrations commingled with periodic unemployment, public relief, and transiency. . . . [P]overty acted as a buffer preventing a more rapid change in family life. . . . [T]he sense of extended-family solidarity was stronger for Hispanos who had ancient roots in the region. . . . [T]he Hispano immigrants in Albuquerque probably felt less *anomie* and had less social disorganization in their lives than did the Mexican immigrants farther to the south in Las Cruces and El Paso. . . . [T]he urbanization of Hispanos resulted in more ethnic exogamy (with Anglo-Americans), more educational opportunities for children, and increased juvenile delinquency. At the same time there was a tendency for Hispanos to retain their traditional Catholic religious affiliations. No clear pattern of Protestant or secular marriages emerged among the urbanizing Hispanos.

Hispanos, the long-term residents from established families, should have been more likely to experience upward socioeconomic mobility than would Mexican immigrants. A few examples of Anglo-Hispano joint business ventures in the nineteenth century would seem to promise greater upward mobility in the twentieth century for Hispanos. A study of upper-class Hispano families in urban areas of New Mexico found that skin color was an important feature of their status. Individuals with lighter complexion were more often monolingual English speaking, even while retaining a pride in their Spanish heritage. But before World War II limited evidence for urban areas of New Mexico indicates that remaining linguistic, cultural, and educational barriers prevented most Hispanos from achieving middle-class status. The 1907 *Albuquerque City Directory* did not list any Spanish-surnamed professionals, and few Hispanos were able to afford a college education until the G.I. Bill of World War II. Most of the economic and educational progress of the New Mexican Hispanos occurred after that war.

Thus it appears that in many respects the working-class Hispano family experience may well have resembled that of the Mexican immigrant. Large numbers of Hispanos were themselves uprooted migrants who had been forced to leave their traditional village cultures. In the cities they were subject to the same kinds of discrimination, job competition, and poverty as were the Mexican immigrants of San Antonio and Los Angeles. Once in the urban environment, both Hispanos and Mexican immigrants retained strong ties to their family and kin back home. And Hispano urban dwellers, because of low wages, were forced to pursue a migratory existence, often competing with Mexicano migrant labor.

The Immaculate Pregnancy: Maya Angelou as Teenage Mother, 1946

MAYA ANGELOU

The story of a teenager's pregnancy is rarely told with the insight and understanding evident in this selection from poet and theatrical performer Maya Angelou's autobiography; it is a remarkable portrait of an adolescent's difficult transition from her awkward years and uncertainty over her sexuality to her acceptance of her infant and her role as a mother. The understanding and compassion of her own mother, brother, and stepfather are no less remarkable. Some scholars maintain that such support and humanity are typical of African-American families.

During World War II, Angelou and her brother had left their grandparents in Stamps, Arkansas, to live with their father, and later their mother, in San Francisco. Angelou became better acquainted with both parents, learned Spanish, enjoyed the benefits of residing in a large metropolis, and fought discrimination to become one of the city's first black female streetcar attendants. In subsequent years she danced, acted in, produced, and directed theatrical productions. Angelou has been active in civil-rights organizations and has written poetry as well as several autobiographical accounts; this selection is excerpted from the first volume, *I Know Why the Caged Bird Sings*.

STUDY QUESTIONS

1. How did the author's mother and stepfather react when she finally told them that she was pregnant?

2. Compare the author's parents' reaction to what you think your own parents' response might be if confronted with a similar situation.

3. How did the author's mother teach her to trust her own instincts about taking care of her newborn child?

The little pleasure I was able to take from the fact that if I could have a baby I obviously wasn't a lesbian was crowded into my mind's tiniest corner by the massive pushing in of fear, guilt and self-revulsion.

For eons, it seemed, I had accepted my plight as the hapless, put-upon victim of fate and the Furies, but this time I had to face the fact that I had

Text excerpted from Maya Angelou, *I Know Why the Caged Bird Sings*, 1970, pp. 241–246. Random House, Inc.

brought my new catastrophe upon myself. How was I to blame the innocent man whom I had lured into making love to me? In order to be profoundly dishonest, a person must have one of two qualities: either he is unscrupulously ambitious, or he is unswervingly egocentric. He must believe that for his ends to be served all things and people can justifiability be shifted about, or that he is the center not only of his own world but of the worlds which others inhabit. I had neither element in my personality, so I hefted the burden of pregnancy at sixteen onto my own shoulders where it belonged. Admittedly, I staggered under the weight.

I finally sent a letter to Bailey, who was at sea with the merchant marines. He wrote back, and he cautioned me against telling Mother of my condition. We both knew her to be violently opposed to abortions, and she would very likely order me to quit school. Bailey suggested that if I quit school before getting my high school diploma I'd find it nearly impossible to return.

The first three months, while I was adapting myself to the fact of pregnancy (I didn't really link pregnancy to the possibility of my having a baby until weeks before my confinement), were a hazy period in which days seemed to lie just below the water level, never emerging fully.

Fortunately, Mother was tied up tighter than Dick's hatband in the weave of her own life. She noticed me, as usual, out of the corner of her existence. As long as I was healthy, clothed and smiling she felt no need to focus her attention on me. As always, her major concern was to live the life given to her, and her children were expected to do the same. And to do it without too much brouhaha.

Under her loose scrutiny I grew more buxom, and my brown skin smoothed and tight-pored, like pancakes fried on an unoiled skillet. And still she didn't suspect. Some years before, I had established a code which never varied. I didn't lie. It was understood that I didn't lie because I was too proud to be caught and forced to admit that I was capable of less than Olympian action. Mother must have concluded that since I was above out-and-out lying I was also beyond deceit. She was deceived.

All my motions focalized on pretending to be that guileless schoolgirl who had nothing more wearying to think about than mid-term exams. Strangely enough, I very nearly caught the essence of teenage capriciousness as I played the role. Except that there were times when physically I couldn't deny to myself that something very important was taking place in my body.

Mornings, I never knew if I would have to jump off the streetcar one step ahead of the warm sea of nausea that threatened to sweep me away. On solid ground, away from the ship-mounted vehicle and the smell of hands coated with recent breakfasts, I regained my balance and waited for the next trolley.

School recovered its lost magic. For the first time since Stamps, information was exciting for itself alone. I burrowed myself into caves of facts, and found delight in the logical resolutions of mathematics.

I credit my new reactions (although I didn't know at the time that I had learned anything from them) to the fact that during what surely must have been a critical period I was not dragged down by hopelessness. Life had a conveyor-belt quality. It went on unpursued and unpursuing, and my only thought was to remain erect, and keep my secret along with my balance.

Midway along to delivery, Bailey came home and brought me a spun-silver bracelet from South America, Thomas Wolfe's *Look Homeward, Angel*, and a slew of new dirty jokes.

As my sixth month approached, Mother left San Francisco for Alaska. She was to open a night club and planned to stay three or four months until it got on its feet. Daddy Clidell was to look after me but I was more or less left on my own recognizance and under the unsteady gaze of our lady roomers.

Mother left the city amid a happy and cheerful send-off party (after all how many Negroes were in Alaska?), and I felt treacherous allowing her to go without informing her that she was soon to be a grandmother.

Two days after V-Day, I stood with the San Francisco Summer School class at Mission High School and received my diploma. That evening, in the bosom of the now-dear family home I uncoiled my fearful secret and in a brave gesture left a note on Daddy Clidell's bed. It read: *Dear Parents, I am sorry to bring this disgrace on the family, but I am pregnant, Marguerite.*

The confusion that ensued when I explained to my stepfather that I expected to deliver the baby in three weeks, more or less, was reminiscent of a Molière comedy. Except that it was funny only years later. Daddy Clidell told Mother that I was "three weeks gone." Mother, regarding me as a woman for the first time, said indignantly, "She's more than any three weeks." They both accepted the fact that I was further along than they had first been told but found it nearly impossible to believe that I had carried a baby, eight months and one week, without their being any the wiser.

Mother asked, "Who is the boy?" I told her. She recalled him, faintly.

"Do you want to marry him?"

"No."

"Does he want to marry you?" The father had stopped speaking to me during my fourth month.

"No."

"Well, that's that. No use ruining three lives." There was no overt or subtle condemnation. She was Vivian Baxter Jackson. Hoping for the best, prepared for the worst, and unsurprised by anything in between.

Daddy Clidell assured me that I had nothing to worry about. That "women been gittin' pregnant ever since Eve ate that apple." He sent one of his waitresses to I. Magnin's to buy maternity dresses for me. For the next two weeks I whirled around the city going to doctors, taking vitamin shots and pills, buying clothes for the baby, and except for the rare moments alone, enjoying the imminent blessed event.

After a short labor, and without too much pain (I decided that the pain of delivery was overrated), my son was born. Just as gratefulness was confused in my mind with love, so possession became mixed up with motherhood. I had a baby. He was beautiful and mine. Totally mine. No one had bought him for me. No one had helped me endure the sickly gray months. I had had help in the child's conception, but no one could deny that I had had an immaculate pregnancy.

Totally my possession, and I was afraid to touch him. Home from the hospital, I sat for hours by his bassinet and absorbed his mysterious perfection. His extremities were so dainty they appeared unfinished. Mother handled him easily with the casual confidence of a baby nurse, but I dreaded being forced to change his diapers. Wasn't I famous for awkwardness? Suppose I let him slip, or put my fingers on that throbbing pulse on the top of his head?

Mother came to my bed one night bringing my three-week-old baby. She pulled the cover back and told me to get up and hold him while she put rubber sheets on my bed. She explained that he was going to sleep with me.

I begged in vain. I was sure to roll over and crush out his life or break those fragile bones. She wouldn't hear of it, and within minutes the pretty golden baby was lying on his back in the center of my bed, laughing at me.

I lay on the edge of the bed, stiff with fear, and vowed not to sleep all night long. But the eat-sleep routine I had begun in the hospital, and kept up under Mother's dictatorial command, got the better of me. I dropped off.

My shoulder was shaken gently. Mother whispered, "Maya, wake up. But don't move."

I knew immediately that the awakening had to do with the baby. I tensed. "I'm awake."

She turned the light on and said, "Look at the baby." My fears were so powerful I couldn't move to look at the center of the bed. She said again, "Look at the baby." I didn't hear sadness in her voice, and that helped me to break the bonds of terror. The baby was no longer in the center of the bed. At first I thought he had moved. But after closer investigation I found that I was lying on my stomach with my arm bent at a right angle. Under the tent of blanket, which was poled by my elbow and forearm, the baby slept touching my side.

Mother whispered, "See, you don't have to think about doing the right thing. If you're for the right thing, then you do it without thinking."

She turned out the light and I patted my son's body lightly and went back to sleep.

FURTHER READING

Robert R. Alvarez, Jr., *Familia: Migration and Adaptation in Baja and Alta California, 1800–1975* (Berkeley and Los Angeles: University of California Press, 1987).

Maya Angelou, *I Know Why the Caged Bird Sings* (New York: Random House, 1970; New York: Bantam Books, 1971).

Gretchen Bataille and Kathleen Mullen Sands, *American Indian Women: Telling Their Lives* (Lincoln: University of Nebraska Press, 1984).

Gae Whitney Canfield, *Sarah Winnemucca of the Northern Paiutes* (Norman: University of Oklahoma Press, 1983).

Norma Kidd Green, *Iron Eye's Family: The Children of Joseph LaFlesche* (Lincoln: University of Nebraska Press, 1969).

Jonathan D. Greenberg, *Staking a Claim: Jake Simmons and the Making of an African-American Oil Dynasty* (New York: Atheneum, 1990; New York: Plume, Penguin Books, 1991).

Richard Griswold del Castillo, *La Familia: Chicano Families in the Urban Southwest, 1848 to the Present* (Notre Dame: University of Notre Dame Press, 1984).

Mary Paik Lee, *Quiet Odyssey: A Pioneer Korean Woman in America,* ed. with an Introduction by Sucheng Chan (Seattle: University of Washington Press, 1990).

Karen Isaksen Leonard, *Making Ethnic Choices: California's Punjabi Mexican Americans* (Philadelphia: Temple University Press, 1992).

Pardee Lowe, *Father and Glorious Descendant* (Boston: Little, Brown, 1943).

Patricia Preciado Martin, *Songs My Mother Sang to Me: An Oral History of Mexican American Women* (Tucson: University of Arizona Press, 1992).

Alfredo Mirande and Evangelina Enrique, *La Chicana: The Mexican-American Woman* (Chicago: University of Chicago Press, 1979).

Gene Oishi, *In Search of Hiroshi: A Japanese-American Odyssey* (Tokyo: Charles E. Tuttle Co., 1988).

Anna Moore Shaw, *A Pima Past* (Tucson: University of Arizona Press, 1974).

C. Matthew Snipp, *American Indians: The First of This Land* (New York: Russell Sage Foundation, 1989).

Monica Sone, *Nisei Daughter* (Boston: Little, Brown, 1953; Seattle: University of Washington Press, 1979).

Victor Villasenor, *Rain of Gold* (Houston: Arte Publico Press, 1991).

Jade Snow Wong, *Fifth Chinese Daughter* (New York: Harper & Row, 1945; Seattle: University of Washington Press, 1989).

Sylvia Junko Yanagisako, *Transforming the Past: Tradition and Kinship Among Japanese Americans* (Stanford: Stanford University Press, 1985).

CHAPTER 6

Community

O ne way in which to depict peoples of color as agents of history, and not simply as victims of oppression, is to show how they organized to ensure their survival and to counter the devastating impact of multiple forms of discrimination. The four readings in this chapter describe situations several centuries apart. Nevertheless, all demonstrate how community organizations, though assuming many different forms, often performed the same functions to fulfill basic human needs. And all reveal that women, as well as men, devoted their energies to this effort.

The chapter opens with a description by Bruce W. Miller of the social organization of Chumash Indian villages along the central California coast. In the second reading, the lens shifts northeastward as Lynda Fae Dickson tells how black women in Denver formed a large number of clubs in the period c. 1890–1930. These establishments not only offered their members opportunities to socialize but also served as vehicles for community uplift and group self-empowerment. Jon D. Cruz then examines how male Filipino immigrants in Washington State infused the clubs they founded with the nascent nationalism that had developed in the Philippines by the turn of the century. In so doing, they preserved a sense of history as they tried to carve a place for themselves in American society. Undocumented Mexican workers, who cross the 2,000-mile U.S.-Mexico border without proper papers, are perhaps the most exploitable and exploited people of color in the American West today. In the final selection, Chicano activist Bert Corona recounts how he worked with these people to gain a measure of protection for them, despite their uncertain status.

FOR ANALYSIS AND DISCUSSION

1. In each of the widely different settings featured in the readings, on what basis did people establish ties to enable them to work together?

2. Why did the people in each case feel a need to form a community?

3. What ends did they hope to achieve by grouping together?

4. More often than not, poor and oppressed people are depicted as passive victims of their fate. Do the readings in this chapter change that picture? If so, how?

5. Among the groups discussed in this chapter, can you tell what relationship might have existed between racial and ethnic identity on the one hand, and class consciousness on the other hand?

Chumash Village Life and Social Organization

BRUCE W. MILLER

Because each Indian tribe or tribelet has had its own singular culture, it may be seen as misleading to include only one reading here on the traditional lifestyle of Native Americans. But the California Chumash described in this first selection are typical of other California Indian peoples in that they have had abundant food sources and a system of governance based on the power of a single chief. Considering the widespread erroneous belief among many scholars that Indians historically have had no sense of property, Miller's emphasis on the Chumash's territoriality is especially noteworthy.

The reader must be cautioned, however, against accepting at face value a modern scholar's sense of "otherness" as conveyed through the detailing of what seems to him the mysterious traditions of a people's daily life. For example, calling Chumash birthings primitive may distort our view of these Indians; indeed, the childbirth process worked efficiently, and there was probably a spiritual reason for breaking the baby's nose—a practice that, if not properly understood by the researcher, might be interpreted as an example of the needless "savagery" of a "primitive" people. In other words, describing people of other cultures and other historical times with today's social-scientific language might lead to unconsciously pejorative and highly ethnocentric conclusions.

STUDY QUESTIONS

1. What were the Chumash people's principal means of providing themselves with food, clothing, and shelter?

2. Compare the Chumash form of governance with Euro-American forms of government.

3. What are the most striking differences between the Chumash way of life and non-Indian rural life in small farming communities?

The village was the focal point of daily activity and the spiritual center of Chumash life. Many important activities took place in the village setting; the preparation of food, the manufacture of crafts, most games and sports, and the most significant ceremonies. There is little doubt that the Chumash took care in selecting a site to live and when living there took pride in its up-keep.

Along the coast between present day Ventura and Goleta, the Chumash were most numerous. Many villages were permanently occupied although their population may have varied with the season depending on food resources. Shisholop, the village at the present site of Ventura, was reported to have had 400 people and 30 houses. Up the coast ranged fifty or more villages, some as large as 1000 inhabitants and 100 or more houses. Estuaries and sloughs at the mouths of creeks were favorite coastal village sites. On the Islands, particularly Santa Cruz and Santa Rosa, the villages tended to be near the shoreline rather than the mountainous interior. The Inland Chumash, living in an arid region and at a higher altitude were probably more nomadic, with less permanent and smaller villages due to their smaller food base.

Large or small, villages were planned around the same principles. The "design" of a village would include houses, including the chief's house, pathways leading between houses forming a kind of street in some larger villages, and a sweat house. Another important feature of the village was the storehouse or granary which might be located near the chief's house or in a dry, well trafficked area away from rodents. To one side of the village was a flat cleared playing field for games, a ceremonial ground with a sacred enclosure called a *siliyik* and on high ground but within the environs of the village there was usually a cemetery.

The largest and best situated house in a village would be the house of the chief. It might hold his immediate family and his extended clan, usually sons and their families. Every village had at least one chief. The Chumash called him *Wot* and he was the moral authority over his people, dispensing justice as he saw fit. Some villages were reported to have more than one leader and some areas of the coast were so heavily populated that the chiefs of several villages would form a council with one being made *paqwot* or "big chief."

Still there were limits on the authority of the chief. Even though he ruled for life the village had final approval on his decisions such that in some ways his role was that of a figurehead. He was in charge of the ceremonial objects and costumes which were kept in a special place until the festivals. He also arranged for, furnished and paid the personnel who gave the ceremony and performed the dances.

The position of chief was inherited patrilineally and both men and women have been reported by Cabrillo and others as being *Wot*. A daughter might inherit the reins of power and thus continue the bloodline's high position.

The chief exercised his power over many areas of daily life, such as the gathering and dispensing of food and the allotment shelter. One of the duties of the chief was caring for the poor. It was also his duty to feed and entertain visitors, hence many Spanish diary accounts featured notes on the important people of a village and scant information on the poorer or less powerful members of the tribe.

Another duty of the chief was to declare war and to plan battles. These battles were generally for revenge, not for conquest. The reason for a war might stem from an insult from one village to the other, or from one chief to another. Perhaps the untimely death of a woman of one community who had married into another might bring on suspicions and accusations of unjust treatment from one community to another. Wars were fought for territorial reasons; one village invading the other's hunting or acorn gathering area was an often stated reason. Black mischief and petty theft were also said to be just reasons for war. The Chumash were not easily angered although they did have a strong sense of territory and would protect it when necessary.

Sometimes mock or formal battles were fought to settle a dispute. This civilized form of warfare usually involved a challenge as to the time and place a battle was to be fought. The Indians would arrive in full paint and wargear—bows, arrows, wooden spears with stone points and heavy wooden war clubs. Chert knives were used for fighting at close quarters. The Chumash would then throw feathers in the air and exchange war cries. Then one warrior would step forward and fire off a quiverful of arrows and when finished the other side would send someone forward to do the same. This continued until one or more were wounded or killed and the battle decided in favor of the side that held the field. In this way both sides satisfied their honor.

The Chumash were monogamous with the exception of the village chief who could have more than one wife. Marriages were simple with a few words exchanged. The only grounds for divorce was adultery although separation and infidelity were apparently common. Sexual relations of the Chumash were expansive even shocking by Europeans standards.

Births were primitive although they were significant enough to be attended by a shaman and verbally recorded by the village messenger. The pregnant woman would deliver the baby on her own into a hole filled with straw. She would then clean the newborn infant of the amniotic sack and blood, cutting the umbilical cord with a knife. She would then immediately break the cartilage in the nose of the infant to flatten it in accordance with custom.

Chumash society was a classed society with upper, middle and lower groups. A person's class depended on family relationships, on knowledge and skills, and on wealth. Most people, as would be expected, fell into the middle class. These were the people who were working members of society in good health and with skills such as basket making and hunting. Members of the village from the most important craft specialist groups, the shaman-doctors, the astrologer priests and the brotherhood of the canoe belonged to the upper class and were privileged in both position and wealth. They made up the ruling group and among them were all the important people: the *Wot,* the *Paha* who was an assistant to and appointed by the chief as master of ceremonies at festivals and the *Ksen* who was a messenger to the chief and reported directly to him. The *Ksen* would often travel from village to village collecting news and important information such as births and deaths. In one sense he was the eyes and ears of the chief.

The poor Chumash, the lower class, were no doubt those of lesser abilities, the layabouts, the unskilled and the infirmed who didn't have family clans to help them.

The Chumash society was further stratified by craft guilds. There is evidence that a number of guilds existed—canoe builders, basketry makers, bead making, hunting, woodworking and weapon makers to name some of the most obvious. It is thought that among them, the brotherhood of the canoe was probably the most powerful. These guilds operated on a profit motive and were very much like extended families.

Craft specialization encouraged the manufacture of more goods than could be used in one locale. This in turn led to an increase in trading between villages and between tribes, an activity that was common and on going throughout the year. With the easy flow of goods, local economies thrived and the Chumash way of life was not only sustained but flowered.

 # African-American Women's Clubs in Denver, 1890s–1920s

LYNDA F. DICKSON

Lynda Fae Dickson's doctoral dissertation examines the black women's clubs of Denver from a holistic, broad-based perspective and from the vantage point of a specific urban locale. African-American ideology at the turn of the century, emphasizing self-help, racial solidarity, and respectability, and the politics of race relations in Denver provided the context for the clubs' development and for Dickson's analysis. By 1890 Denver's black female population of 1,343 was sufficiently large and assertive to form community-based clubs dedicated to "racial uplift."

These clubs' social and cultural activities mirrored similar efforts on the part of African-American residents of San Francisco and other western as well as eastern cities in the early twentieth century. In San Francisco, journalist Delilah Beasley (author of the first history of blacks in the American West, *Negro Trail Blazers of California,* published in 1919), and in Chicago, activist Ida B. Wells, engaged in efforts nearly identical to those of Denver's club women. In the Rocky Mountain city, African-American club women established their own home for "deserving" young ladies and in 1916 began operating a children's day-care nursery that compared in some respects with Chicago's famous settlement house, Hull House.

Black club women of Denver assisted the city's less fortunate African-American residents in a variety of ways and acquired considerable political and organizing skills through their cooperative efforts. In addition to these collaborative enterprises, these women were active in the State and National Associations of Colored Women—organizations that were associated with their local clubs. Thus their work reflected important political and racial goals as well as social and cultural themes.

STUDY QUESTIONS

1. What does the author mean by the statement that the club movement among Denver's black women was "in part, a defensive reaction to white hostility and exclusion"?

2. What functions did the clubs serve? What goals did they aim to accomplish?

By 1890, Denver had become a miniature version of the larger urban areas in the East. The elite closed themselves off in the Capitol Hill area, surrounding themselves with beautiful homes, lawns, and educational, recreational, and religious facilities; the middle-class merchants huddled around the central business district; while the poor whites, the Chinese, the Italians, and the blacks sliced off portions of the poorest district (along the South Platte). Each group went about the business of establishing its own communities and remained ignorant of the others' way of life.

The development of Denver's black community represented a microcosm of those found in Chicago, Boston, Philadelphia, and New York. Its early migrants were mostly southern, upwardly mobile, often skilled and educated. Blacks as a proportion of the total population were never more than 4 percent before 1930. The dominant group tolerated them while their numbers remained small, but intolerance increased as their numbers grew. They were residentially segregated, living in the worst areas of the city. There was a large number of females initially due to greater opportunities for them in domestic employment in urban areas. The early immigrants' attitude toward the later influx of southern migrants was to blame increased racism on the

---

"The Early Club Movement among Black Women in Denver, 1890–1925," (Ph.D. diss., University of Colorado, Boulder, 1982), edited excerpt from pp. 80–81, 114–118, 129–131, 182–188, 191–202, and 203–209. Reprinted by permission of Lynda F. Dickson.

greater number of "backward" Negroes from the rural South, leading to the establishment of a class system within the black community—a distorted facsimile of that found in the broader community. . . .

Social and demographic statistics on blacks in Denver during the 1890–1925 period do not tell the whole story. Based on the social class structure that developed within black communities generally, for which Denver is an example, there are indications that more than 10 percent might have been middle class. For our purposes this is important, since we are ultimately looking for the preconditions . . . for club development: a sizable black population, educated women with leisure time, and unmet needs of the poor. It appears that these conditions existed in Denver, the one exception being that it is questionable how much leisure time the early black club women had to devote to club activities. But they did make efforts to compensate for the lack of time. . . .

[Members of] Denver's black community, like those in other urban areas, believed that in order to improve their condition, they must rely upon themselves. Organized efforts at self-improvement ranged from activities within churches, fraternal organizations, and women's groups to independent efforts by concerned individuals. All attempted to alleviate economic needs, unemployment, and inadequate recreational activities for youth, as well as to obtain civil rights.

As is generally the case, the earliest organizational efforts took place within churches. Zion Baptist Church was organized in 1865 under the leadership of the Reverend William Norris. Three years later, Shorter African Methodist Church was established, largely through the efforts of Mrs. Mary E. Smith, who came to Denver in 1863. She obtained many a dollar for her church by entering gambling houses and passing a collection box among poker players.

Denver's black churches played a significant role in creating an internal support system within the community. Though much of the mutual aid efforts was not recorded, one resident of the Denver Association for the Aged recalled that when members of the community met with some misfortune, the churches would pitch in. If they heard of a family in need, church members, especially women, would care for the children, bring food, take up collections, and so on. Much of the support provided was of an informal nature.

The churches also served an important social function for the community. They often sponsored picnics, young people's hikes, birthday parties, plays, and concerts. But as Ira De A. Reid found, the churches were often so preoccupied with raising funds for their own maintenance that they could not financially support extensive community programs. At the time of Reid's study [1929], all seventeen churches in the community were in debt and struggling to raise funds. Within two months eleven affairs for the two churches were held in members' homes. These may help to explain why churches often appeared to provide more social outlets than actual community support. Women's clubs had similar problems. . . .

The local club movement was, in part, a defensive reaction to white hostility and exclusion, as manifested in the dominant image of black women as immoral, promiscuous, and lacking the proper skills for family maintenance. But while major club efforts were directed toward improving the image of black womanhood, the broader purpose was ultimately to assist in the elevation of the race. As the president of the Colorado Association of Colored Women's Clubs stated in her address at the sixth annual convention in 1909: "The responsibility [is] on women [to lift] . . . a downtrodden race above the rockies of prejudice." The purpose, in fact, of the State Association was, among other things, to "assist and to promote higher social and better moral conditions of our race." Thus, the club movement was part of the self-help, racial-unity effort among blacks during the late nineteenth and early twentieth centuries.

While the above factors are helpful in pointing to the link between the local movement and broader ideology, it is also necessary to describe the local conditions conducive to the "spirit of clubdom" that prevailed by the turn of the century. . . . Denver was in the process of rapid growth, and increasing numbers of blacks, along with other racial groups, flocked to the Queen City in hopes of improving their lot. Thus, by 1890 a distinct black community had emerged. Because of the (albeit limited) opportunities that existed—largely through providing services to this community—a prosperous, if small, middle class soon appeared. It is from this class that the leaders of the club movement came. Many were recent immigrants from larger urban areas who had been exposed to and recognized the potential of women's club efforts in helping the less fortunate among blacks.

Mrs. Elizabeth (Piper) Ensley was one such person. She had studied abroad during the 1870s. Upon returning to the United States, she established a circulating library in Boston, where she became a public school teacher. In 1882 she married Horwell N. Ensley and moved to the District of Columbia, where they joined the faculty of Howard University. They later moved to Mississippi and she taught for a period at Acorn University. The Ensleys moved to Denver in the early 1890s, where she quickly became active in club work. She was one of the founding members of the Woman's League, which was organized around 1894, and served as Denver's correspondent to the *Woman's Era,* the official journal of the National Association of Colored Women. Then in 1904 she founded the Colorado Association of Colored Women's Clubs, an idea that had begun to form as early as 1896, when Mrs. Ida DePriest, another early club mover, suggested the possibility of such an organization to the National Association that year. . . .

A tremendous amount of cooperation was required of club members, particularly in fund-raising activities. When the clubs sponsored a bake sale, for example, the picture that no doubt comes to mind is that of each member contributing a cake, pie, or some other item, but this was rarely the case. Much more likely, each member donated an ingredient for the baked goods. Thus, while occasionally one finds statements such as "Mrs. Gatewood donated a cake," more frequently are references such as ". . . Cannon [donated] sugar, . . . Caldwell [donated] six eggs, . . . Waldon [donated] one pound of butter. . . ." If a member had nothing to contribute, she usually volunteered to collect the ingredients and do the actual baking.

Club work involved a commitment to, and active participation in, a wide range of activities. While there were individual members who were perhaps more "committed" than others, the successful functioning of the clubs called for considerable teamwork, and this teamwork extended beyond the individual clubs. . . .

To be a "Federated Woman" meant more than actively participating in one's own club. There was definite expectation that assistance be provided to other clubs in their various endeavors. Whether the club women were committed to mutual support in order to accomplish more for their communities or simply adhered to the philosophy of "you scratch my back, I'll scratch yours" is debatable, but whatever the reasons, there are numerous indications that the clubs cooperated with each other on both formal and informal levels. The minute books still available continually refer to communications received from other clubs, in the form of notices of events, invitations, solicitations, or simple greetings. In many instances only passing reference is made to a "communication" received from another club, with a notation that the secretary would respond to the request, but even these unspecified correspondences are valuable, for not only do they indicate that the clubs kept in touch with each other, but they also provide a sense of the number of different clubs that existed during a given time period, as well as some clue as to which clubs were the most active.

Taka Art Club's minutes for the period 1916 to 1920, for example, contain numerous references to communications received from Carnation Art, Self-Improvement, Pond Lily, and Twentieth Century clubs—the last club being referred to no less than twenty times, suggesting that it was extremely active during this period. But there was also correspondence from the Golden West, Progressive Art, Martha Washington Study, Dumas Reading and Literary, Searchlight, Garden Study, Emerald, and Sojourner Truth clubs. . . . Specific references to activities with other clubs for the same period include an invitation to assist the Twentieth Century Club in its dinner to benefit an Easter rally (1914); a request to join other clubs in giving a prize for civic pride (1915); invitations to attend entertainment given by the Twentieth Century Club (1915, 1916, 1918); numerous requests to sell tickets for various activities sponsored by the Self-Improvement Club; a request to send a representative for a program given by Carnation Art (1916); and a request to assist Pond Lily in providing entertainment to raise funds for artificial limbs for an inmate at the County Hospital (1915). . . .

Another indication of cooperation between clubs on a more formal basis was the establishment of the Denver Federation of Colored Women, organized in 1903 by Mrs. Alice Webb. Mrs. Webb had envisioned a non-profit organization whose primary purpose was to raise the cultural standards of colored girls and women. Believing that this could best be accomplished through the combined efforts of many clubs, she asked Pond Lily, Taka Art, Carnation Art, and the Self-Improvement clubs to join her. In 1908 this organization changed its name to the City Federation of Colored Women's Clubs, and the four charter clubs were joined by the Woman's League, Margaret Murray Washington Art, Sojourner Truth, Twentieth Century, and Sunshine clubs. The City Federation then became affiliated with the State and National Associations.

The City Federation met once a month, with one club serving as hostess. Each club sent five representatives to these meetings, and they in turn reported back to their own clubs the planned activities of the City Federation and the specific contributions each club was to make toward these efforts. The City Federation focused on issues and activities of a somewhat broader scope than did the individual clubs. In 1914, for example, a proposition for a sanitarium was discussed. Each club was asked to contribute five dollars per month to benefit the facility. The sanitarium was mentioned a number of times after this, and it was apparently still in existence in 1927.

Another undertaking of the City Federation was a drive to benefit the poor and needy in the South. Individual clubs were asked to bring in clothing and other items, as well as to contribute money for the cause. Several members of Taka Art volunteered either to raise or to give ten dollars toward the cause. Other forms of individual contributions included volunteering to buy boxes, pack, and send the collected items.

The City Federation, under the auspices of national guidelines, also initiated "Reciprocity Day," a major cooperative effort that occurred on an ongoing basis among clubs. Reciprocity Day was held on the second Wednesday in March of each year (the same date chosen by all federated clubs across the country). Clubs used this day to get together and engage in an exchange of ideas, exhibits, arts and crafts, and home economic tips. Each club shared responsibility for preparing the program, usually working through a reciprocity committee. The minute books of the various clubs indicate the specific duties of each club toward making Reciprocity Day a success. In 1924, for example, Carnation Art and the Emerald Club were to sponsor a bake booth, while Taka Art was to provide the butter and salad for the meal. . . .

The concept of a club home for which several clubs would be responsible was first suggested by Mrs. Georgia Contee of the Self-Improvement Club, who recognized the need for a place where colored girls coming to Denver might stay. This appeared to be too large an undertaking for one club, so the Self-Improvement Club invited the presidents of the various women's clubs in Denver to a meeting, asking whether they would be interested in contributing to the establishment of such a home. . . . Seven clubs responded to the challenge—Taka Art, Pond Lily, Carnation Art, Self-Improvement, Progressive Art, Sojourner Truth, and Twentieth Century—and these became known as the Negro Woman's Club Home Association.

The decision to become a part of the association was no doubt a difficult one for many of the clubs, as illustrated in the case of the Carnation Art Club. Carnation Art members split over the issue to such a point that all officers resigned, with the exception of Mrs. Ada Webster (then club secretary). Mrs. Webster, along with six remaining members, kept the club alive. Under Webster's leadership, Carnation Art joined the association, raised the necessary funds for its share in getting the home started by hosting a large chitterling dinner, and ultimately became the second club to pay off its shares of stock in the home—no small feat given the small size of its membership. . . .

During the next few months the association met regularly to make plans for the home. Each club was asked to submit an idea for "the ideal club

African-American Women in Denver

home." The suggestion offered by Mrs. Ross of Taka Art (which was later submitted to the association as Taka's suggestion) was:

> The home should take up all lines of charity, rescue nursery, employment. . . . A committee [should be established] to look into the matter of educational rights. . . . A committee to look after Colored children who have been arrested to see that they are given a fair trial—[and] . . . anything else that might help humanity. . . .

Taka Art had made the suggestion in April that it might be a good idea for the association to begin a campaign in July to raise funds. The association evidently accepted the suggestion, for Carnation Art's minutes indicate that a mass meeting was held in July at Shorter Chapel, during which the association introduced its plan to the public. Various speakers were invited to discuss the subject of the home, and ice cream and cake were served to the public free of charge.

One can well imagine the sense of accomplishment the seven clubs no doubt felt when, on December 16, 1916, they moved into the modern, two-story brick structure at 2357 Clarkson Street. The home, which consisted of eight rooms, was incorporated for five thousand dollars, with each club buying equal shares of stock at ten dollars per share. The aim of the new home was the maintenance of a dormitory for "deserving" girls and a day nursery for children. The upper floor of the building was used for the dormitory, while the lower floor housed the nursery. . . . Not only was considerable time and effort devoted to raising money to purchase shares of stock, but the clubs were also responsible for soliciting sustaining members—either individuals or groups who would pay a twelve-dollar sustaining fee—as well as associate members, who paid six dollars per year toward the maintenance of the home.

Before leaving the issue of fund raising, it is pertinent to point out that the association, consisting of seven clubs, itself became a federated club and joined the City, State, and National Association of Colored Women's Clubs. This means that members in the individual clubs were required to pay weekly club dues; the club in turn paid city, state, and national dues. When these dues are added to the numerous collections taken up during the meetings for one purpose or another regarding the home, combined with the collections made to charity, contributions to the YWCA and other organizations to which the clubs were expected to contribute, it is little wonder why one irate member of Carnation Art suggested, "Why not raise the club dues rather than nickel-and-dime-ing us to death?" It also becomes a bit more understandable why not all the Denver clubs wholeheartedly embraced the idea of becoming part of the Club Home Association.

In addition to raising money for the home, the clubs also contributed whatever the home needed, ranging from dishes and other utensils, milk, bread, and even clothing for the children in the nursery, to buying sheeting for the exterior of the building, screens for the windows, and rakes for the yard. Yet perhaps more important than any of the above contributions was the amount of time spent in the home. Mrs. Harvey of the Pond Lily Club recalls that she "changed many a diaper" and "cooked many a meal" for the home. Other members recall working to keep the facility clean and running smoothly. . . .

Given the amount of time and energy that it took to get the home established and functioning, it comes as little surprise that the Board of Directors ran a very tight ship. The one available minute book for the association covering the period 1919 to 1922 clearly suggests that every aspect of the home's operation was taken seriously—from establishing rules for the dormitory and nursery and having the cupboards repaired, to hiring and firing a yard man. The secretary maintained meticulous accounts of each transaction occurring in the home, and every action taken by the Board was put in motion form, including motions to pay the insurance on the home, to purchase staples, and to give a member ten dollars to buy meat.

By far the most important individual in the home was the matron. She was responsible for endless tasks, especially the running of the dormitory. In particular, she had to see to it that the rules relating to the dormitory were kept. But of equal importance, she was to "make the home comfortable and at all times, take the place of mother for the girls entering the home." For all of these responsibilities, the matron's salary was forty dollars a month in 1920.

Young working girls could rent a room in the dormitory, including kitchen privileges, for $1.25 per week (the price was increased to $1.50 in 1920, and $2.00 in 1924). The "inmates"—as the residents were called— were governed by strict rules, which were upheld by the matron: they were not allowed to bring furniture, boxes, trunks, or pictures into the home; lights were to be out by 10:30 P.M.; all washing and ironing were to be done in the laundry room during specified days and hours, at $0.25 per person, and electric irons were prohibited in the building. Girls were responsible for making their own beds and keeping their portion of the room tidy, and they were "absolutely prohibited" from lounging on vacant beds. To use the kitchen, arrangement had to be made with the matron, and they had to, at all times, use the dining room for lunch, use club dishes, and leave the kitchen and dining room clean.

The rules clearly indicate the club women's desire to instill proper manners and morality in the girls. Specific requirements concerning the washing of dishes ("must use pan instead of sink; must use soap when washing dishes"), or personal grooming ("arrangement of toilet, including the straightening of hair, must be done in one's room"), or entertainment of "company" ("must use the parlor and matron must be present") were rigidly upheld. . . .

Both the nursery and the dormitory continued to prove successful, and in 1921 the association's report to the State Board of Charities and Corrections indicated that the home had four paid officers (one man and three women—they had hired a second matron by this time; it is unclear who the third woman was). The nursery had cared for thirty children, and the dormitory had nine girls in residence.

The home also allowed various community organizations to rent its facilities for entertainment, stipulating that these could not be card parties, dancing parties, or political meetings. The women's clubs began holding their weekly meetings there, paying the nominal fee of $0.50 per meeting. Three dollars per entertainment for other organizations was the fee charged. In this way, the association contributed to the home's income and became a community center in the process. . . .

Another major activity that began in 1921 was the establishment of a health clinic in the home. The association had earlier recognized the need to relieve the congestion at the clinic located at Twenty-sixth and Lawrence streets, as well as the inconvenience that the use of this clinic posed to mothers who had to take their children a long distance. But it also knew that it must have the cooperation of the community if the clinic was to be a success. Thus, some members of the board visited doctors in the area to determine whether they would be willing to cooperate, while others visited the homes of mothers to get assurance that they would in fact use the clinic. After getting the support of both groups, the association officially opened the clinic in 1922. . . .

As community needs changed, so did the home. For example, the YWCA had sponsored a building fund during the early 1920s, and once the new building was completed, there was less of a need for the dormitory. But at the same time, there was a growing need to expand the nursery. Thus, the dormitory was eliminated and the association devoted most of its energies toward maintenance of the nursery.

The association was also interested in cases of discrimination in Denver. In one instance, the chairman of the house committee told of the arrest of one of the girls in the home, indicating that the whole affair was "deplorable, inasmuch as the girl was innocent of the charge, and she was humiliated in having to ride in the patrol car and being roughly treated by the officers." In 1923, a member of the board recommended that a letter be written to (then Governor) Sweet, commending him on his "splendid attitude" on ending segregation of public schools in Denver. Also during 1923, a member of the board was appointed to investigate a report that the community lodging house denied service to colored people. In cases where there was little that could be done, the association nevertheless expressed concern, as indicated in the report made of a girl to be hanged in Washington, D.C. Members were asked to pray for the commutation of her sentence, and the president urged all who could to attend a prayer meeting to be held in the home.

Each activity of the association—whether participation in Community Chest drives, assisting the YWCA, sponsoring fund raisers for the home, or putting on Christmas parties for the children in the nursery—required sincere commitment from each club. Their specific contributions ranged from buying shares of stock, soliciting sustaining members, and making donations to the home, to devoting time and energy toward the maintenance of the home. But as in most instances where members must spend a considerable amount of time together, occasional conflicts arose, stemming from personality clashes as well as club differences. In 1920, for example, an oversight on the part of the secretary led the president (Isabelle Stewart) to reprimand her severely, calling on the other members to find out what could be done with a secretary who neglected her duties. As the president put it, "That's what's wrong with the Association now; the Secretary had been too lax and left too many things undone." The president then indicated that she herself had been mistreated by the association, citing as an example the omission of her name by the social committee chairman in an article in the newspaper concerning payment of the mortgage on the home. She then submitted her verbal resignation, stating before taking her seat, "My superiors won't insult me; my inferiors can't insult me."

This evidently precipitated a later argument between the president and the social committee chairman (Mrs. Abernathy) on the issue of who was really the initiator of the idea for the club home. Mrs. Stewart produced a book which she claimed was the 1914 year book of the Self-Improvement Club, from which she read, saying that she wished to prove that Mrs. Contee was in fact the originator of the idea for the home. Mrs. Abernathy questioned the authenticity of the book, and an argument ensued, during which Mrs. Abernathy was told to "shut up" so the issue could be settled. The association members eventually credited Mrs. Contee with the idea for the home, and Mrs. Abernathy resigned, as did the secretary who had been accused of neglecting her duties.

In spite of these differences, the clubs managed to stick together rather than letting personal grudges and club allegiances destroy what they had worked so hard to accomplish. Three of the seven clubs eventually disbanded and in that way left the association, but the remaining ones—Pond Lily, Self-Improvement, Carnation Art, and Taka Art—still compose the Negro Woman's Club Home Association. The nursery changed its name to the George Washington Carver Day Nursery in 1946 and is now housed in a modern building in Denver.

Filipino-American Community Organizations in Washington, 1900s–1930s

Jon D. Cruz

The 1990 U.S. census of population shows that Filipino Americans now compose the second-largest Asian-American group in the nation, numbering more than 1.4 million. Although a majority have come only since the liberalization of U.S. immigration laws in 1965, the history of Filipinos in the United States goes back to the beginning of this century and can best be understood within the dual contexts of American rule over the Philippine Islands from 1898 to 1946 and of race relations in the American West.

Agents of Hawaii's sugar plantations tried hard to recruit workers from the Philippines before 1910, but Filipinos did not arrive in sizable numbers in the islands or on the mainland until the 1920s. By then, agricultural production both in Hawaii and along the Pacific coast had become highly capitalized, using large tracts of land to grow crops for sale in the national and world markets. But whereas Hawaii's plantation owners even today concentrate on cultivating sugarcane and, to a small extent, pineapple and coffee, farm operators in the Pacific coast states produce hundreds of specialty crops.

One salient feature of modern "agribusiness" in the American West is its dependence on a migratory labor force that can move with the harvests. From the 1920s to the 1970s, Filipinos, Mexicans, and Mexican Americans formed the backbone of this harvest labor supply. As the Filipino farmworkers aged, however, they were not replaced by new immigrants, for Filipino immigrants today are largely well-educated professionals or the dependents of those who came in earlier times.

Despite the unsettled nature of their lives as migrant farm laborers and cannery workers during their first half-century in the American West, Filipinos in Washington State and elsewhere started many clubs that tied their communities together socially. As Jon D. Cruz argues, their ability to organize was the key to their survival in a hostile environment.

Study Questions

1. Why did Filipino immigrants feel a need to form clubs?

2. What functions did these associations serve?

FILIPINO COMMUNITIES IN
WASHINGTON STATE

Filipinos arrived in Washington State during the first decade of the twentieth century. While the Filipino-American population of Washington is dwarfed by the numbers found in California and Hawaii, this Pacific Northwest state is representative of the conditions on the U.S. mainland that gave rise to and shaped the early Filipino-American communities. It also offers experiences and conditions that were unique.

I shall examine the ways in which Filipinos in the state of Washington accommodated themselves to the tensions and hardships encountered in their various struggles to gain a foothold in American society while resisting dehumanizing forces and demeaning barriers in a society that kept them politically alienated and economically marginalized. I shall highlight how Filipino Americans devised collective responses to make some of the sweeping forces of history more manageable and tolerable.

According to Dorothy Cordova, the U.S. government recruited forty Filipino men directly from the Philippines in 1903 to help lay cable in the Pacific Ocean and off Alaska. Some of these men remained and settled in Seattle. By 1910, seventeen Filipinos were officially counted as residents in the state. Ten years later, there were an estimated 1,000. By 1930 the numbers had swelled to approximately 35,000, reflecting the massive influx of a predominantly male immigration wave of agricultural laborers, students, adventurers, and even some military personnel.

Disenchanted by aborted hopes, funneled into unskilled labor, trapped in perpetual subsistence dictated by seasonal agricultural and salmon canning cycles, and living and working within a gender-skewed context with few Filipina women present, it seemed highly unlikely that such a predominantly male population could form strong and lasting cultural and community organizations. But they did soon after their arrival. In virtually every area along the western United States where Filipinos labored in large numbers (California, Oregon, Washington, Idaho, Colorado, and Alaska), they established social clubs and community organizations that gave them a social presence. Some organizations, such as fraternal lodges and labor unions, even spanned great geographic distances.

TYPES OF FILIPINO ORGANIZATIONS
AND THEIR FUNCTIONS

The very first settlers managed to develop "clubs" or "associations" in Seattle, Mason and Kitsap counties, and the Green River, Puyallup River, and Yakima valleys long before they bought or leased buildings under their col-

---

"Filipino American Community Organizations in Washington," printed with permission of the author, Jon D. Cruz.

lective names. These associations were the first signs that Filipinos were taking concrete steps toward establishing permanent settlements and took three general forms: umbrella community organizations, smaller groups based on limited and, in some cases, restricted membership, and labor unions.

Umbrella community organizations attempted to provide a broad social framework for all the Filipinos in a given locale. Such organizations often adopted names that marked them off geographically—such as the Filipino Community of Yakima Valley, Inc. or the Filipino Community of Puget Sound, Inc. (the name adopted by Filipinos from the Green River and Puyallup River valleys). Such names solidified a sense of place and became part of the Filipino immigrants' identity. By design, these organizations attempted to embrace and include as many Filipinos as possible residing in a designated area.

There were also a host of smaller organizations based on specific identities with more distinctive membership requirements. This was especially the case in the greater Seattle area, which had the population diversity making such pluralism possible. These groups ranged from very informal to highly formal. An informal group might consist of individuals who came from a Philippine region (e.g., Luzon), province (e.g., Pangasinan), or even a particular town (e.g., San Nicolas), whose members met occasionally. Camaraderie rather than a specific organizational mission characterized such tightly knit social groups. At the other extreme were very formal organizations, such as fraternal lodges. While lodges also provided camaraderie, they espoused more explicit ideologies. Transplanted from the Philippines, the lodges possessed a significant history, well-defined leadership, a highly organized internal structure with a hierarchical ranking system among members, and a clearly articulated mission supported by written articles of governance and codes of conduct. These groups were not designed to be inclusive of all Filipinos; rather, they achieved internal solidarity through restricted membership.

Labor unions were a third type of organizations. In the 1930s, Filipinos in the greater Seattle area were involved in the struggle to forge a union that would include both cannery workers and farm laborers, binding workers from Alaska to California and across the Pacific to Hawaii.

From the outset, a primary goal of the fledgling community organizations was to raise enough capital to obtain a building for a Filipino community center. The centers had two purposes: they provided a place for community social functions, and they signified to the community at large that Filipinos desired public recognition as contributing citizens. Filipinos were barred from mainstream civic organizations and political bodies; their establishment of a physical community center was, in part, a claim to participation in the larger society, but on their own terms as Filipino Americans.

The arduous task of raising funds to buy or build a community center took place in an antagonistic social climate that sought to drive Filipinos from American soil. Because Filipinos were never affluent, raising the capital often took many decades. The only source of capital came from the community members themselves, and devising strategies to secure an ongoing trickle of contributions was a central task of the leaders of each community year after year. Interestingly, the more rural and smaller communities of the coastal valleys and the inland Yakima Valley were more successful in this collective enterprise, managing to construct centers by the early 1950s. The Filipino Community of Seattle, Inc., with its greater numbers, diversified population, and dozens of small organizations, did not obtain a community center until 1965.

SEATTLE

Nestled on the inland waters of Elliott Bay and close to several agricultural valleys, Seattle was a multiethnic, multiracial urban center with an already established population of Chinese and Japanese Americans. As a key West Coast port city, it served as a point of entry for Filipinos arriving from Hawaii as well as directly from the Philippines. In Seattle, Filipino migrant and itinerant laborers could reconnoiter and reestablish contacts after returning from their seasonal forays in the agricultural hinterlands of the entire West Coast. Seattle was the hub for Filipinos who worked in the booming salmon canneries scattered along coastal British Columbia and Alaska. As the Northwest's major metropolitan area, Seattle provided a broad range of domestic service and menial jobs that enabled many to subsist when seasonal agricultural and cannery work was not available.

In addition, the University of Washington, also in Seattle, was one of the most desired schools among young Filipino students who sought higher education in the United States. As the social and economic climate of the late 1920s and early 1930s made it increasingly difficult for Filipino students to pursue higher education, many of them became involved in community organizing. Time and again ex-students surfaced as initiators and key leaders in many of the Seattle-based organizations. Though forced to abandon their plans for higher education, the ex-students' fellow immigrants continued to look up to them for organizing skills and community leadership.

Seattle's proximity to Alaska helped to make the city the home base for the first major unionizing activities of Filipinos who worked in the salmon canning industry. By the mid-1930s, Filipinos had become the backbone of the labor force in the canneries. The labor movement became increasingly attractive to Filipinos as they devoted more and more energy to secure a stable livelihood. During this period, cannery workers and agricultural laborers developed a sense of solidarity and combined their struggles, partly because many of the same Filipinos who worked in canneries were also agricultural laborers.

As the number of Filipino laborers increased, their exploitation became more apparent, but they also responded strategically and effectively. The once unassuming and compliant Filipino labor force was transformed in 1933 into a militant and organized entity with the establishment of the Cannery Workers' and Farm Laborers' Union (CWFLU), headquartered in Seattle. Prior to unionization, Filipinos were especially economically dependent on the whims of employers. Furthermore, they were culturally isolated and politically unprotected. Employers and labor contractors took advantage of the workers, whose earnings were whittled down by being overcharged for food, clothing, and housing. Prostitution and gambling were used to retrieve labor costs; they also functioned as forms of labor control. In some cases, contractors absconded with the seasonal wages of a whole Filipino crew. Through unionization, Filipinos were able to ward off some of the most exploitative methods used by employers and unscrupulous labor contractors who had exerted control over them during the preceding decade.

Unionization also allowed Filipino workers to established relationships with, and garner recognition from, the larger national labor movement. For the first time, Filipinos were able to take advantage of the emerging institution of collective bargaining. Their new-found security contributed, in turn, to the stability of families, community organizations, and Filipino settlements in general.

In Seattle, community organizations sprang up on several fronts. In the mid-1920s, groundwork was laid for what would eventually become the Filipino Community of Seattle, Inc. Students, small businessmen, and laborers each helped to organize their peers. In the late 1920s Filipino students sought help from Seattle-area Filipino businessmen in their attempt to acquire a building for a Filipino Students' Clubhouse. Fund-raising activities were undertaken, but within a year the goal to obtain a building site for students only was superseded by plans for a more general Filipino community center, which resulted in a new organization in 1933, the Seattle Filipino Community Clubhouse. When the Philippines was granted commonwealth status in 1935, key leaders in Seattle formed the Philippine Commonwealth Council of Seattle. When the Philippines became independent in 1946, the organization again changed its name, to the Filipino Community of Seattle and Vicinity, but only in 1965 was a community center obtained.

Events that provided and rekindled feelings of solidarity in the face of frustration were very important. One such event was the celebration of Rizal Day. José Rizal was a Filipino writer, nationalist, and revolutionary leader. Infusing the genre of the European novel with an emergent nationalist anticolonial sensibility, Rizal's writings were scathing indictments of the spiritual feebleness, the religiously clothed racism, and the brutal hypocrisy of the Spanish colonial regime. So effective were his invectives that he was executed in 1896 for subversion. His death helped solidify anticolonial grievances among Filipinos of all classes, who launched a revolution against the Spanish colonial regime. The United States, also at war with Spain, took advantage of the situation and forced Spain to cede the Philippines to the United States.

An ensuing American military campaign subjugated the Filipinos. The Philippine-American War officially ended in 1902, but mopping-up campaigns continued for some years.

As an organizing strategy, Rizal Day commemorated a significant though painful event while providing Filipinos everywhere with a chance to draw together. Among the Seattle population were many students coming to terms with the likelihood that their plans for education and career enhancement in the classrooms of America's universities would be nipped in the bud. It is against this backdrop that the more educated Filipinos in Seattle found Rizal Day an appropriate vehicle for rallying their compatriots, to galvanize their collective will, to salvage a sense of personal and racial worth, and to protect themselves and their emergent communities.

Filipino lodges were similarly important in laying the groundwork for community organizations in Seattle. The spirit of solidarity behind the loose coalition of students, businessmen, and laborers who formed the Rizal Day Committee was even more tenacious in the Filipino fraternal lodges, which, due to their cultural and historical origins, tapped a deeper ideology. Developed in the Philippines during the last three decades of the nineteenth century, the lodges were the outgrowth of secret revolutionary societies that were both responses to and a stimulus for the anticolonial revolts culminating in the Philippine Revolution, which took place during the last decade of the nineteenth century. Aspirations for independence were crushed with the American annexation of the Philippines, but this multiclass and transregional sense of Filipino solidarity remained in the form of the fraternal lodges, which Filipinos brought with them when they immigrated to the United States. The lodges perpetuated the collective identify and cultural and political ideologies that were encoded in mutual assistance and helped prepare the social ground for organizational activities among the immigrants. Regional relationships were also consolidated through the lodges; many of the farmers of the Green River and Puyallup valleys were very active in the fraternal lodges based in Seattle, some assuming leadership posts.

Three fraternal organizations—Gran Oriente Filipino, Legionarios del Trabajo, and Caballeros de Dimas Alang—took hold in the greater Seattle area. The names of the lodges capture the spirit of unified nationalism (Gran Oriente Filipino), revolutionary symbolism (shortly before Rizal's death, he adopted the underground name of Dimas Alang), and the dignity of labor (Legion of Workers). Headquartered in California, each fraternal organization managed to establish several lodges in Seattle. The revolutionary and resistance-based consciousness transplanted with the cultural sensibility of lodge members in Seattle is captured on the pages of Fred Cordova's pictorial history, *Filipinos: Forgotten Asian Americans*, in the words of Teodulo Ranjo:

> It was a civic organization, mainly fostering the idea of the dreams of the "Katipuneros". . . our forefathers who fought for our independence. . . .

> It was a patriotic organization. . . . Our rituals were in Tagalog. . . . It was a secret organization, an organization for the help of the Filipinos. We wanted to carry on the deeds of our revolutionaries.

The lodges, of course, did not function as revolutionary organizations in the United States. Nevertheless, the collective solidarity forged in an earlier revolutionary era was not irrelevant; it was transformed and redeployed by Filipinos within a context of profound cultural alienation. Transmitted through these semireligious and highly ritualized social organizations, Filipinos cultivated the principles of Filipino brotherhood. Women's auxiliaries were also formed, especially after the late 1940s, when some men were able to secure more stable livelihoods and to form families, either through marriages with Caucasian women or by returning with Filipina wives from the Philippines. Lodges also affirmed social bonds through a wide range of intimate as well as community events, including the celebration of holidays, births, marriages, and beauty contests. The merger of deeply personal and community ties was especially apparent at the death of a fellow countryman, always a key event that drew the brotherhood together and reminded members of their special bonds. The lodges played a central role in the funeral by collectively sharing grief and shouldering the financial burden of mortuary and burial expenses. If any Filipino organizations functioned like the traditional—but biologically absent—extended family, it was these fraternal organizations.

As a civic organization, the lodges were intellectually influenced by the European Enlightenment's free thinking and practical knowledge. Members attempted to follow a clearly delineated moral code of conduct, embraced religious principles, and were governed by a closed and cultish set of rituals. Modified on American soil, the spirit of solidarity cultivated by the lodges while under colonialism was readapted to, and enlisted in, the struggle for personal dignity, a sense of place, and the central importance of community. Of all the Filipino-American organizations, the lodges probably came the closet to binding their members together and providing participants with what the sociologist Robert Bellah has called a civil religion.

Seattle's diversified population and its capacity to draw Filipinos of all ranks, especially intellectuals and aspiring university students, made possible the unique transformation of historical sensibilities to underpin Filipino organizations. The same cultural sensibility is found in the motivations behind the use of Rizal Day to rekindle solidarity and the cultural activities of the more cohesive Filipino lodges. Certainly each organization had its own distinct activities, but their cultural overlap helped prepare the ground for the succeeding stages of community building in the Seattle area. And community cohesion became increasingly crucial as the economic depression of the 1930s endangered jobs, eroded civil rights, and subjected Filipinos to institutional racism, sporadic assaults, and organized violence.

GREEN RIVER VALLEY

Filipinos also settled in the large and long Green River Valley of southern King county. South of Seattle is a string of small cities and towns—Renton, Tukwilla, Kent, Auburn, Algona, Pacific, Sumner, and Puyallup—that stretch from the metropolis's outskirts toward the foothills of the Cascade Mountains. Surrounding these towns in the 1920s were dozens of prosperous and productive truck farms operated by Japanese Americans and Italian Americans. Filipinos worked as laborers on these farms during the spring and summer seasons.

According to "old timers," who serve as self-appointed community historians, Filipinos began to settle in this area around 1915. By the late 1920s they had formed a number of organizations that covered the large and sprawling area between Tacoma and Seattle. These culminated in the formation in 1948 of the Filipino American Community of Puget Sound. Like all other umbrella community organizations, its primary goal was to acquire a community center, which materialized in seven years.

During the Second World War, some of the Filipinos residing in the valley were able to change their status from farm laborers to farmers. Facing incarceration at the nearby Puyallup Fairgrounds, Japanese-American farmers requested Filipinos to operate their farms and small businesses. Other Filipinos were asked by the U.S. government to manage farms. Rather than being drafted into military service, some Filipinos were granted deferments to work in agriculture, a key economic sector. After being farm operators (instead of migrant stoop laborers), many Filipinos continued to lease land as small independent truck farmers after the Second World War.

Filipinos also secured railroad jobs. Auburn had a major railroad maintenance yard. Some Filipinos worked as section hands in all-Filipinos crews to maintain and repair rail lines (work previously done by Italian Americans), while other Filipinos worked in the railroad yard, where their primary task was to clean out boxcars and ready them for their next loading. They were frequently called upon to clean up after train accidents and derailments. Railroad employment enabled them to become unionized wage laborers with retirement benefits—highly unusual for Filipino workers anywhere in the United States at that time. Understandably, the valley Filipinos, with a history of migrant work, seized these jobs when they became available. The formation of Filipino nuclear families in the smaller towns of Kent, Auburn, Algona, Pacific, and Sumner was made possible by the new stability offered by railroad employment.

Like their counterparts in other areas, the valley Filipinos raised a significant amount of money through bingo, raffles, dances, dinners, queen contests, and beauty contests. One of their most successful fund-raising events was the annual queen or beauty pageant. Contestants—entering usually at the request of parents or other very close family friends—had to sell as many tickets as possible. In this manner, the queen and her numerous runners-up all contributed to an event that was based less on beauty than the need to raise money for the organization. All of the Filipino community umbrella organizations began resorting to this particular strategy by the early 1950s, which reflected an underlying demographic change: the appearance of nuclear families, second-generation daughters, and new immigrant families who had obtained citizenship through service in the U.S. military.

YAKIMA VALLEY

Filipinos began settling in the Yakima Valley around 1918–1920. The main work available to them was agricultural labor. By the late 1920s there were many who worked on truck farms, in orchards, and in packing houses. Some even leased plots for independent farming. The concentration in agricultural labor presented Filipinos with a very restricted set of options. Filipinos in Seattle and the other valley communities on the western side of the Cascade Mountains had a variety of jobs that were not readily available to the Yakima Valley Filipinos, who desired a more settled livelihood. If Filipinos were going to settle in the Yakima Valley, they had to secure work within agriculture; Yakima was a single-economy region.

By 1927 Filipinos had engendered the resentment of whites who viewed them as competitive sources of labor. So deep was the anti-Filipino animosity that mob attacks took place that same year. Filipinos were attacked wherever vigilante groups encountered them. Some Filipinos were even assaulted in their homes, while others were forcibly rounded up and placed on outbound trains. Having invested in their small truck farms, Filipinos refused to allow themselves to be pushed out.

As the national depression deepened and jobs disappeared, even more Filipinos came to Yakima because farming enabled them to survive. The lack of options, the total dependence on farming, and the desire to stay, even in the face of intense hostilities, forced the Yakima Filipinos to organize. By 1935, they had successfully pooled their resources to create the Filipino Marketing Cooperative. However, with the passage of the Tydings-McDuffie Act of 1934, which had granted commonwealth status to the Philippines, Filipinos had been reclassified as aliens. Under pressure from local growers, Washington's 1921 Alien Land Law, initially targeting mainly Japanese, was amended in 1937 to apply to Filipinos. The result made it illegal for Filipinos to own, lease, or rent land; the amended law prevented even sharecropping. Thus their newly found cooperative was deemed invalid, and twenty-one Filipino farmers were jailed.

Blocked from pursuing their only option for livelihood, Filipinos responded by forming the Filipino Community of Yakima, Inc. As part of their struggle, Filipinos undertook an intensive letter-writing campaign in 1938 to President Franklin D. Roosevelt, other administration officials, the resident commissioner of the Philippines, and President Manuel Quezon of the Philippine Commonwealth. With the support of the Native American

Yakima Tribal Council, Filipinos vigorously protested the state's amended Alien Land Law, publicized their local plight, obtained broader support from Philippine Commonwealth representatives, and called for investigations by additional state and federal agencies. Securing such attention helped stiffen their resistance to state laws aimed at dislodging members of the Filipino community from their economic base in farming.

Denied opportunities within agriculture, the Filipino community of Yakima might have ceased to exist were it not for another option: they turned to the Yakima Indian tribe whose members had leased land on an informal basis to Filipinos for more than a decade. The Filipino community's appeal to the tribal council was accepted favorably, and land leases were granted in 1941. The onset of the Second World War, however, transformed the situation. As the Philippines became a wartime ally of the United States, local anti-Filipino animosities lessened, and Filipinos were able to continue farming without restrictions.

Unlike the other Filipino-American community organizations in Washington State, the formation of the Filipino American Community of Yakima, Inc. was a distinct political response, with the immediate goal of gaining the release of the Filipino farmers jailed under the state's Alien Land Law. Since the identity of this community was structurally rooted in the material limits placed upon Filipino livelihood, its members had little recourse other than to engage in highly conscious, formal political struggles to ensure their future as a community. While this can be said about all the early Filipino attempts to form communities, the specific circumstances in Yakima were unique.

THE DYNAMICS OF FILIPINO COMMUNITY FORMATION

Filipinos could not escape the social, political, economic, and cultural conditions that shaped their lives. Their efforts to build communities, and the forms and modes of organization they drew upon, were strategic responses to difficult conditions. These responses were always a blend of unique cultural sensibilities and available local resources. Communities were not simply the outcome of individuals who happened to cluster in a particular geographic location; rather, community formation involved far more complex dynamics.

Communities provide avenues for people to establish networks with others with whom they identify and to reflect on shared circumstances; they make possible a supportive social milieu that promotes efforts to bring collective meanings and interests into sharper focus; they foster opportunities to define, clarify, and prioritize perceived needs; and they facilitate the mobilization of resources in the broadest sense, including the strengthening and maintenance of emotional and psychic bonds, the pooling of economic assets, the organization of cultural activities, and the designing of political strategies to protect and promote the community's well-being. Thus community building takes various forms, operates through many interlocking activities, and is far more than simply a means for people to socialize.

There is another way to view the range of community organizations that Filipinos established. As some have argued, organizations—even the small ones with just a handful of members—helped provide the earliest immigrants with a substitute for the extended families so central to Philippine culture. In the homeland, the extended family offered emotional support, helped individuals develop and retain a collective identity, provided a framework within which moral values could be inculcated and reinforced, prevented the isolation of the individual, and made available a collective storehouse of help and solutions for those in crisis. Furthermore, families are the primary social moorage that anchors individuals to the cycle of birth, maturity, marriage, and death. In short, extended families develop, watch over, protect, guide, and constrain their members. The fledgling organizations established by the first wave of Filipinos in Washington State performed many of these functions for those who had been torn from their extended families.

When Filipinos took up the tasks of developing community organizations, however, it was not just the need for a surrogate family and kinship structure that they sought to fulfill. They also had to adapt to external pressures. Social conditions were harsh, exploitative, demeaning, and, in some cases, violent. Familylike as they were, organizations provided the basis for reactive and defensive as well as proactive and offensive cultural strategies. Organizations served as the trenches in which Filipinos could seek cover and regroup to protect themselves from the ravages of a society that had beckoned them with promises but delivered little more than a poverty-level livelihood at the margins of American society. Organizations ensured their survival as a people with an identity, a culture, a purpose, a history, and a place—as Filipino Americans.

The Filipino organizations in Washington State remain vibrant to this day. A handful of those who helped to establish Filipino-American communities are still alive; they continue to be active in what they helped launch approximately seventy years ago, binding the present to the past.

Organizing Undocumented Immigrants, 1960s–1970s

BERT CORONA, AS TOLD TO MARIO T. GARCÍA

Unlike many other ethnic groups living in the United States, Mexicans have immigrated into the country steadily since the turn of the present century. Owing to Mexico's proximity, earlier patterns of northward migration, persistent economic dislocation within Mexico, and a steady demand for cheap labor in the American Southwest, hundreds of thousands of Mexicans have entered and continue to enter the country. For several decades, many have come without "papers," as "undocumented workers"—a more proper term than the pejorative "illegal aliens."

These workers have served as a hard-working labor force, performing the "dirty work" in industries, farms, restaurants, the homes of wealthy people as well as of middle-class professionals, and countless other jobs that Euro-Americans find undesirable. In the light of their undocumented status, they are highly vulnerable and consistently exploited. They live in constant fear of apprehension and deportation by the Immigration and Naturalization Service in conjunction with the Border Patrol.

To secure a degree of protection for these workers, long-time labor and community organizer Bert Corona in 1968 helped to establish La Hermandad Mexicana in Los Angeles. He organized the workers and took steps to develop leadership within their ranks, giving them a sense of community and a better understanding of their rights under the U.S. Constitution. La Hermandad has grown considerably since then and now has branches throughout the nation. One of its most important roles in recent years has been assisting those "undocumented" people who qualify for amnesty under the 1986 Immigration Reform and Control Act. This law contains certain English-language and civics requirements that applicants must meet before they can regularize their status and become permanent U.S. residents.

STUDY QUESTIONS

1. In what sense did the workers whom Bert Corona organized become a community?

2. How has La Hermandad tried to help undocumented workers?

When some of us decided to organize the undocumented in Los Angeles, we were fortunate that we didn't have to invent the wheel. We had the advantage of a group in the San Diego area that since the early 1950s had attempted to do precisely the same thing. This was La Hermandad Nacional Mexicana (the Mexican Brotherhood) led by Phil and Albert Usquiano, two trade union leaders in San Diego. The Hermandad was an organization of Spanish-speaking Mexican immigrant workers. It had chapters in San Diego, National City, Oceanside, and Escondido. The members were for the most part members of the Carpenters' Union and Laborers' Union.

The Hermandad had been formed due to the efforts of the INS (Immigration and Naturalization Service) after World War II to cancel the work visas of many Mexicans working in the San Diego area but living in Tijuana. In fact, these workers had acquired the right to live in the United States as permanent residents, but due to housing shortages during and after the war years, they had been forced to raise their families on the other side of the border. The INS threatened not only their jobs but their hopes to reside in the United States.

The Hermandad was formed around 1951 to protect their rights, and it succeeded in many cases. During the 1960s, the Hermandad in these towns formed strong chapters of MAPA (Mexican American Political Association). We knew of the Hermandad and respected its work. Consequently, when we moved back to Los Angeles to work with the undocumented, we simply extended La Hermandad Nacional Mexicana to this area beginning in 1968.

In Los Angeles we opened our first Hermandad office on West Pico Boulevard near Vermont Avenue. This was a big immigrant area. Our most immediate task was to provide some assistance and protection to the undocumented due to the deportation pressures being exerted by the INS and the Border Patrol. We began to pass out cards and leaflets informing the people that we were there to counsel them at no charge regarding their status, and we told them how to protect themselves against deportation.

People showed a lot of interest. They were not aware that they had rights under the Bill of Rights of the U.S. Constitution. These rights pertained to resisting arrest without warrants for merely looking like a class of people whom the INS and Border Patrol defined as "illegal." We informed them that they did not have to incriminate themselves since they were protected by the Fifth Amendment. We also told them that, according to the law, they did not have to give any information other than their names and addresses to the INS or Border Patrol, if apprehended. That was it. They didn't have to give any information on which they could be deported. They had the right to call an attorney and to be released on bail.

Text from Bert Corona and Mario T. García, *Memories of Chicano History: The Life and Narrative of Bert Corona,* edited typescript, University of California Press—not yet published.

The INS, needless to say, became quite upset over our counseling of immigrants. Officials felt that we were impeding their ability to enforce the law and to do their job properly. Up to this time, the INS's practice had been that people could be deported merely by the determination that they were here illegally. This determination could be made by the apprehending officer or by obtaining an admission from those apprehended that they were illegal. What was happening was that those arrested were being given what was called "voluntary departure." In effect, they were not given access to their constitutional rights. Instead, they were being pressured to admit their status, taken to the border, and released to return to Mexico without a hearing or a trial.

Mexican-American labor organizer, Bert Corona

Out of some 700,000 recorded voluntary departures at this time, only about 100 had been given the right to legal counsel. The rest had been unjustly induced to sign voluntary departure [forms]. This is how the INS covered its tracks. But the methods it used to obtain such departures ranged from physical threats to actual beatings.

To counter these illegal and unjust acts, we took the federal government to court. We counseled immigrants to request a hearing where they could be entitled to a lawyer. We began to request that copies of appropriate records, such as birth certificates, be given to those people who claimed they had been born here. We won a number of these cases. We appealed the cases that we lost and usually won [on appeal] based on facts that revealed that persons had been falsely arrested with no proof that they were illegal. We also aided immigrants in processing their applications to legalize their status and to obtain permanent residency.

We felt that we were playing a legitimate adversarial role with regard to the INS in representing the right that people have to stay here or to be given the right to prove they merited staying here. Our position was that the INS had developed an illegal policy based on its unproved premise that the bulk of the Spanish-speaking people who walked the streets were here illegally and therefore had no right to constitutional appeals or defenses. We disagreed. The U.S. Supreme Court had ruled that *every* person in the United States, regardless of [his or her] citizenship status, is covered and protected by the U.S. Constitution no matter how [he or she] had entered the country. Once they're here they're covered by the Constitution, including the Bill of Rights, especially the Fourth and Fifth amendments, which include the right to an attorney and the right to a reasonable bail. With the help of our attorneys we were able to establish that the INS's policy was unconstitutional and a violation of American standards of justice. Unfortunately, this did not deter continued violations and deportations.

As a result of our efforts and our partial success in helping people stave off deportation, the Hermandad grew rapidly. By 1971 we had developed a very large membership in the West Pico area. We attracted people from all over Los Angeles County as well as Orange County. We had meetings every night to inform people of their rights. Our meetings began to overflow, and we had to find larger meeting places. By 1972 we had several thousand members. Besides forming additional chapters in the greater LA area, such as in the San Fernando Valley and East Los Angeles, we also began to expand nationally. One year later we opened new offices in San Diego, Oakland, San Antonio, Chicago, New York, and Seattle.

Our activity led the federal government in 1974 to subsidize other community-based organizations, some of them church affiliated, that advised immigrants of their rights through bloc grant programs. Although we qualified for federal subsidies, the Hermandad never accepted such support in order to preserve our adversarial role with the government. We also refused such grants because they were based on the recipients' cooperation with the INS on the belief that the INS was a legitimate agency enforcing the law of the land. We, of course, delegitimized the INS because of its refusal to guarantee the constitutional rights of immigrants. To this day the Hermandad has never received a penny from the federal government or from the state of California for doing immigrant defense work. This leaves us free to criticize the INS and to propose changes in immigration laws to make them more reasonable and just without compromising ourselves.

The Hermandad is not too dissimilar from earlier Mexican immigrant organizations. It is largely staffed by volunteers, many of them members of immigrant families, both men and women. We also have a number of young Chicano students, members of MEChA (Movimiento Estudiantil Chicano de Aztlán) groups on campuses who have helped us. Other volunteers include social workers, law students, nuns, priests, and pastors. We have no paid staff. Members of the Hermandad pay fifteen dollars a year, but this comes nowhere close to covering the costs of the legal and other services we provide. We count on volunteer work. If we have money, it is divided, ranging from ten to fifty dollars a week, to assist some of our volunteer families.

The Hermandad is very similar to the earlier Mexican mutual benefit societies. Some of the current immigrants have relatives who had arrived earlier, and they know that such societies had existed to assist immigrants. In these mutual aid societies, immigrants paid a small fee every week or every payday. If they suffered any calamity, such as their house burning down or a death in the family, it was through their contributions to the society that they could secure assistance. The societies functioned like insurance companies. They also defended immigrants unjustly accused of crimes such as murder or theft. These *logias* or *sociedades de beneficial mutua* were often the only means by which immigrants could defend themselves and get help. The societies, even though they represented an adaptation to life in the United States, were not unknown in Mexico. In small villages there, some forms of mutual assistance existed.

We applied this concept of the mutual benefit society to the Hermandad. We needed and wanted the participation of our members. We needed voluntary services in maintaining our headquarters, in gathering food and clothing, and in public demonstrations against the INS and Border Patrol. We were an extended family which looked after the needs of all its members. Our general meetings were family based, where all family members attended and participated. These were educational meetings where we talked about how the immigration laws are affecting our people, about the policies of the local police, housing, schools, and other relevant matters. We also sponsored picnics and potlucks. This social activity was very important since social life for immigrants, outside of the family, was very restricted.

FURTHER READING

Edwin B. Almirol, *Ethnic Identity and Social Negotiation: A Study of a Filipino Community in California* (New York: AMS Press, 1985).

Robert N. Anderson, Richard Collier, and Rebecca F. Pestano, *Filipinos in Rural Hawaii* (Honolulu: University of Hawaii Press, 1984).

Lowell John Bean, *Mukat's People: The Cahuilla Indians of Southern California* (Berkeley and Los Angeles: University of California Press, 1972).

Kendall A. Blanchard, *The Ramah Navajos: A Growing Sense of Community in Historical Perspective* (Window Rock, Ariz.: Navajo Parks and Recreation Research Section, Navajo Tribe, 1971).

Lawrence P. Crouchett, Lonnie G. Bunch III, and Martha Kendall Winnacker, *The History of the East Bay Afro-American Community, 1851–1977* (Oakland: Northern California Center for Afro-American History and Life, 1989).

Arnoldo De Leon, *Ethnicity in the Sunbelt: A History of Mexican Americans in Houston* (Houston: Mexican American Studies Program, University of Houston, 1989).

Arnoldo De Leon, *The Tejano Community, 1836–1900* (Albuquerque: University of New Mexico Press, 1982).

Lynda Fae Dickson, "The Early Club Movement Among Black Women in Denver, 1890–1925" (Ph.D. dissertation, University of Colorado, 1982).

Richard Griswold del Castillo, *The Los Angeles Barrio, 1850–1890: A Social History* (Berkeley and Los Angeles: University of California Press, 1979).

Hazel W. Hertzberg, *The Search for an American Indian Identify: Modern Pan-Indian Movements* (Syracuse: Syracuse University Press, 1971).

Arthur E. Hippler, *Hunter's Point: A Black Ghetto* (New York: Basic Books, 1974).

Yuji Ichioka, *The Issei: The World of the First Generation Japanese Immigrants, 1885–1924* (New York: Free Press, 1988).

Bruce La Brack, *The Sikhs of Northern California, 1904–1975* (New York: AMS Press, 1988).

Rose Hum Lee, *The Growth and Decline of Chinese Communities in the Rocky Mountain Region* (New York: New York Times and Arno Press, 1979).

Sandy Lydon, *Chinese Gold: The Chinese in the Monterey Bay Region* (Santa Cruz: Capitola Book Co., 1985).

Russell M. Magnaghi, "Virginia City's Chinese Community, 1860–1880," *Nevada Historical Society Quarterly* 24 (1981): 130–157.

S. Frank Miyamoto, *Social Solidarity Among the Japanese in Seattle* (Seattle: University of Washington Press, 1939, 1981, 1984).

John Modell, *The Economics and Politics of Racial Accommodation: The Japanese of Los Angeles, 1900–1942* (Urbana: University of Illinois Press, 1977).

Ricardo Romo, *East Los Angeles: History of a Barrio* (Austin: University of Texas Press, 1983).

Robert H. Ruby and John A. Brown, *The Spokane Indians: Children of the Sun* (Norman: University of Oklahoma Press, 1970).

Thomas E. Sheridan, *Los Tucsonenses: The Mexican Community in Tucson, 1854–1941* (Tucson: University of Arizona Press, 1986).

Mischa Titiev, *The Hopi Indians of Old Oraibi: Change and Continuity* (Ann Arbor: University of Michigan Press, 1972).

Patricia Zavella, *Women's Work and Chicano Families: Cannery Workers of the Santa Clara Valley* (Ithaca, N.Y.: Cornell University Press, 1987).

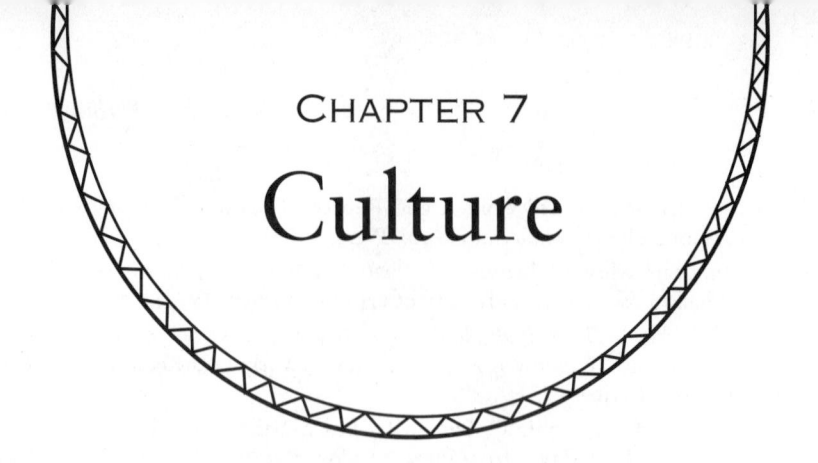

CHAPTER 7

Culture

There is no satisfactory way to convey fully the rich diversity of west-ern America's cultures. The selections in this chapter make no pre-tense to be comprehensive; rather, they are meant to spotlight select parts of the colorful human mosaic that composes the population of the western states, including Hawaii and Alaska. The very notion of culture, moreover, is susceptible to various interpretations and is perceived quite differently by individuals and groups.

The four readings in this chapter survey different forms of cultural conflict. Native American tribal life traditionally was not separable into religious and nonreligious spheres; rather, spirituality was literally a part of living on a daily basis. But after Native Americans came into contact with non-Indians and their various Christian denominations, this perva-sive spiritually was drastically modified, as the first selection shows. A different kind of cultural clash is explored in the second reading. Mexico and the United States share a border and dissimilar cultures, which meet, partially merge, and continually wage war over language, custom, poli-tics, food, marriage, architecture, and many other aspects of the south-western lifestyle. Asian immigrants, particularly Chinese, Japanese, and Koreans, set up language schools in the late nineteenth and early twenti-eth centuries to inculcate not only their ancestral languages but also their homelands' cultural values in their American-born children. But the host society saw these schools as "proof" of Asian unassimilability and, in the case of Hawaii, tried to close them down, as the third selection reveals. The final piece probes the musical genius of Count Basie. Basie's blues captures the African American's problematical place in American society and resonates with racial dissonances—as does every aspect of culture in the American West.

FOR ANALYSIS AND DISCUSSION

1. Were there any clashes between the traditional tribal spiritual beliefs of Native Americans and the tenets of Christianity? If so, what were they? How did each side accommodate the other?

2. How have differences between Mexicans and "Anglos" influenced Mexican identity in the U.S.-Mexican border region?

3. To what extent did Hawaii's Japanese-language schools affect the relationship between Japanese immigrants and Euro-Americans?

4. What are the most arresting observations that Count Basie made about life in the West?

5. What cultural aspects of American society seem most significant when you analyze the experiences of peoples of color in the United States?

6. Do you have any sense of your cultural identity? If so, try to describe the key characteristics that define your cultural identity.

 # Religion and American Indians in the Northwest, 1850s–1890s

CLIFFORD E. TRAFZER AND MARGERY ANN BEACH

Native American spiritualism is a daunting subject to plumb, and one plagued by trivialization and misunderstanding. Filmmakers, New Age philosophers, and self-styled shamanic healers in various ways have all diminished the richness and complexity of Indian spiritual belief systems. Social scientists have analyzed tribal worldviews with mixed results, and until the past fifteen to twenty years, most historians have ignored or misinterpreted native peoples' religious experiences. Some observers seem incapable of perceiving the myriad spiritual forms in tribal lives except through the distorting ethnocentric lens of their Judaic-Christian backgrounds, and as a result they have dismissed Indian religions as pagan, hopelessly animistic,* and obviously incorrect. Others project their own modern secularism and skepticism when trying to understand Indian spiritual life and to place it in historical perspective.

Grasping the full significance of what many Native Americans characterize as the sacred hoop of life is no easy task. Most Indian and non-Indian people today have been reared in a religious tradition that draws a sharp distinction between the sacred and the worldly, a dichotomy that seems not to have been made with the same rigor in tribal societies. Further complicating the process of understanding the native peoples' spiritual beliefs is the genesis of new Indian religious experiences, growing out of the military domination and forced cultural change that were the products of European and Anglo-American invasions. A tradition of prophets preaching and predicting an Indian millennium originated early in the history of the conquest of America. In this selection Clifford E. Trafzer and Margery Ann Beach tell the story of Smohalla, a Shahaptian from the Columbia River region, one of a long line of messiahs. Like other prophets, he emphasized to his reservation constituencies a return to the Indians' traditional ways and urged resistance to the white man's program of acculturation.

Animistic refers to the belief that nature and natural objects possess the soul of gods whom humans must propitiate, or please, in order to gain some control over and understanding of nature.

STUDY QUESTIONS

1. What was the central tenet of Smohalla's spiritual message?

2. In what ways were Smohalla's teachings "political"?

3. How did the Washani faith affect the history of Native American tribes in the Northwest?

The young woman's body was dressed in a white deerskin, and she lay in state for three days while the Wanapum Indians and their neighbors danced, sang, and mourned her death. She was the eldest child of Smohalla, an important Indian religious leader of the middle Columbia River. Smohalla's power had failed him, and his daughter had died. She was buried in a canoe upstream from his village at Priest Rapids on a sandy hillside overlooking the river. Smohalla remained at his daughter's grave for a few days, praying and singing, until some villagers returned to the cemetery to urge their leader to return to his home. When they arrived at the grave, they found Smohalla dead. His body was returned to his longhouse, where it was washed and dressed in fine buckskin. Strips of otter fur adorned his grey braids, and in the traditional manner, his face was painted yellow. Once the body had been properly prepared, the people assembled to begin the funeral ceremony honoring one of the greatest leaders of the Washani faith.

Men gathered on one side of the body, and the women on the other. Hand drums and hand bells were used to keep time, as the people sang funeral dirges throughout the night. The next morning the singing stopped abruptly, as Smohalla's body twitched and his hand removed the hide covering his face. Smohalla opened his eyes, rose to his knees, but he did not speak. The people were stunned, and they quickly left Smohalla's mat lodge. Two days later, Smohalla instructed one of his ten wives to gather the people together at a site on the Columbia River known as Water Swirl Place, where he would tell them of his visit to the "land in the sky" and of the message he had received from *Nami Piap,* God, the Creator.

Smohalla's experience was not unique, for there had been other Northwestern Prophets who had died, traveled to heaven, and returned from the dead with a message from God. The messages were usually similar, generally demanding that the Indians return to their old ways, live a righteous life, and reject the political, social, and religious practices of whites. Through these messengers, God also warned Indians that the world would end soon, but

From "Smohalla, the Washani, and Religion as a Factor in Northwestern Indian History," by Clifford E. Trafzer and Margery Ann Beach, *American Indian Quarterly* 9 (1985), pp. 309–313, 315–322. Reprinted by permission of American Indian Quarterly.

that those Indians who had kept the old ways would be resurrected and their traditional lands and lifeways restored. During the eighteenth century, for example, a Wanapum Indian named Shuwapsa emerged as a prominent holy man among the Plateau Indians. He had instructed the people to live in peace, share the earth's bounty, and thank God for all things, particularly food. He was one of many prophets among the Plateau Indians, and thus, Smohalla, the charismatic Wanapum *yantcha* or spiritual leader, "was just one prophet in a whole series of Washani dreamers." He was, however, the most important religious leader in the Inland Northwest during his day. His ascendency coincided with an era characterized by white expansionism, armed conflict, and forced removal to reservations. . . . Through the dance and songs, Smohalla formalized traditional Plateau Indian beliefs, adding structure, ceremony, and ritual to the ill-defined old Washani faith. Smohalla's doctrines, and those of the Washani religion, emerged as significant factors in Northwestern history during the mid to late nineteenth century. Religion had long played a central role in the cultural traditions of the Plateau Indians, and it became an even greater factor within the Indian communities in response to white expansionism, violent conflict, and government Indian policies. . . .

A hunchback at birth, Smohalla was not an impressive character, and he certainly did not reflect the image held by whites of a great Indian leader. According to whites who met the *yantcha*, Smohalla was "peculiar" and "not prepossessing at first sight." He was considered "to be a rather undersized Indian with a form inclining toward obesity.". . . What Smohalla lacked in appearance, however, he made up for many fold as an accomplished orator who, "when aroused," was full of fire.". . . Added to this was Smohalla's ability to predict future events, including eclipses, storms, earthquakes, salmon runs, and other natural phenomenon. Today, Smohalla would be considered a psychic, but to the people of his time, he was a medicine man and doctor who received his power directly from *Nami Piap.*

Smohalla was born at the village of Wallula on the east bank of the Columbia River sometime between 1815 and 1820. Little is known of his youth, except that he grew up on the Great Columbia Plateau during a turbulent period which saw the rise and decline of the Hudson's Bay Company, the establishment of Catholic and Protestant missions, the ever-increasing migration of *suyapo* (white people), and the spread of infectious diseases. . . . Smohalla learned at an early age about traditional Indian spiritual beliefs which revolved around many general concepts, including that *Nami Piap* had created the earth, that particular Indians were chosen to use certain lands, and that the Mother Earth provided sustenance through the roots, berries, game, and fish. Smohalla learned that a holy covenant existed between God and man, and that in order to maintain this relationship, the Indians were not to disturb the earth by dividing it into parcels, by farming, or by selling any portion of land. Early in his life, Smohalla learned of the spiritual relationship between *Nami Piap,* man, and the natural world. The Indians often gave thanks to God for *nasau,* the salmon, *camash,* the nutritious camas root, *skolkol,* an early spring root, and a host of other foods. From his parents and his extended family, Smohalla received a basic education which included a good measure of instruction about the life-giving products of the earth. . . .

While Smohalla was a young man living at Wallula, he experienced his first major religious revelation. Depressed over the fact that many Indians were increasingly becoming more white-like in their attitudes and beliefs, the young Wanapum decided to pray about this social trend which had placed a wedge between "progressive" and "traditional" Indians. . . . Smohalla meditated, fasted, and awaited the arrival of his *wot,* his guardian spirit power, which would help him with his problems. According to Smohalla's nephew, Puck Hyah Toot, Smohalla died on the mountain of La Lac, and his spirit traveled to the "land in the sky." When Smohalla arrived in the land of the dead, he was not permitted to remain but was told to return to his people with an important message from the spirit world. Like other Indian prophets before him, Smohalla was given a holy mission to preach a rejection of white culture and a return to Indian social, economic, political, and religious traditions. Following his religious experience, Smohalla changed his name from one that is forgotten today, to *Shmoquala,* meaning dreamer, teacher or preacher. Smohalla's experience enhanced his reputation as a seer and Prophet among his own people and among many others of the Columbia Plateau. . . .

Between 1858 and 1860, following the disastrous attempt by the Plateau tribes to stand against the United States Army, Smohalla moved his small band up the Columbia River to a fishing area known as Priest Rapids. There, the Prophet built a small village, living in a large A-framed mat lodge with his ten wives and one daughter. Smohalla had chosen his daughter to succeed him as the keeper of the faith, but even before the girl had gone on her *wyak,* or vision quest, she became ill with disease and died. Neither Smohalla's medicine nor that of the other religious leaders could save the girl and she died. While sitting at his daughter's grave praying, singing, and mourning, Smohalla had his second and most significant religious revelation. He died and once again traveled to the spirit world where God taught him a sacred *washat* or dance and numerous religious songs. The dance and songs formed the basis of a religious revival of the old Washani faith and a renewed interest among many Indians in traditional spiritual beliefs. When Smohalla awoke from his comatose state, he found himself lying within his own lodge. His apparent resurrection frightened his followers, who left the funeral and spread the word that Smohalla had returned from the dead. . . .

Smohalla explained that *Nami Piap* had not permitted him to remain in the land of the dead, because the Wanapum was to return to the earth and teach the people a special *washat,* and over 120 songs to add to the old

Washani songs. Smohalla had been told by *Nami Piap* to "teach the Wana-pums and others to be good, do good, and live like Indians. . . ."

Smohalla and other religious leaders on the Plateau taught that God had created the earth, heavens, and all things. The Creator had then "called forth all animals, birds, and plants." The salmon was first among all animals while the small huckleberries were created last. Thus, Smohalla reasoned, "it is in this order that salmon and food roots are taken as Communion at the feasts of thanksgiving to the Creator." The Indians believed that since God had provided life-giving foods, then they were obliged to offer thanks for the bounty. During the harvest of salmon, roots, and berries, the Indians were instructed to perform specific ceremonies of thanksgiving, and they were instructed never to "taste the first food without performing the first-food ceremonies.". . .

Smohalla had taken traditional Washani beliefs of the Plateau Indians and had formalized the faith through a ceremony which Smohalla said had been given to him by God. This claim had a powerful effect on the Indian communities, because Smohalla's experience was very much in line with the spiritual traditions of the Plateau tribes. Smohalla emphasized the sacredness of the earth, sky, plants, water, animals, and other aspects of the natural world. Smohalla added to the Washani religion an organized ceremony complete with prescribed procedures, paraphernalia, instruments, dance, songs, and prayers. Smohalla was a militant in his religion, demanding a religious crusade against white culture, but unlike Tenskwatawa, the Shawnee Prophet, and other Indian spiritual leaders before and after him, Smohalla did not advocate the violent extirpation of the whites. He did, however, demand a rejection of the white work ethic, the reservation system, Christian religion, and American Indian policies. By such teachings Smohalla emerged as a prominent leader among the Indians and as a targeted enemy of the Christian-minded agents of the Indian Bureau and the War Department. Smohalla's teachings served as a justification for the forced removal of Indians to reservations where the so-called Dreamers could be Christianized and civilized. . . .

In spite of Smohalla's message and the teachings of other spiritual leaders, many Plateau Indians lived on the reservations and some became Christians. Thus, a major division occurred within the Indian communities of the Northwest, as Christian, reservation, treaty Indians stood in marked contrast to non-Christian, non-reservation, and non-treaty Indians. The most glaring example of this social schism emerged among the Nez Percés, particularly after 1863, when a part of the tribe signed a treaty relinquishing to the government 6,932,270 acres of their reservation. Of the 52 Indians who agreed to the "Thief Treaty," all were either Christians or openly sympathetic to Chief Lawyer and his faction of the tribe. However, not one of the anti-treaty Indians signed the treaty which left the tribe a reservation one-tenth the size of the original one. The actions of the treaty Nez Percés, government agents, miners, and ranchers put the Nez Percé on a course that ultimately ended in bloodshed.

In response to the extreme pressures of governmental policies, white expansion, and tribal factionalism, many Nez Percés and their Palouse neighbors turned inward toward their traditional spiritual beliefs. To some degree, all of them were influenced by the teachings of Smohalla and some of them practiced derivatives of the Washani faith, categorized by whites as the "Dreamer Religion." Representatives of the government characterized Washani religious followers as practicing the "new-fangled religious delusion.". . . . The tension between the Indian traditionalists and the government agents reached an impasse when General Oliver O. Howard and Nez Percé Agent John B. Monteith ordered the non-treaty Nez Percés and Palouses to move onto the Nez Percé Reservation. . . . The Indians responded by enunciating again the precepts of their religion. To speak of surrendering the earth—the soil that held the bones of their ancestors—was to speak of a sacred topic. . . . The Prophet knew many of the Nez Percés and may well have directly influenced some of them. However, Smohalla never advocated violence or an Indian confederacy, but he many have had an indirect hand in influencing the non-treaty Nez Percés. . . .

Smohalla had long preached against cultivating the ground and raising crops, and the Prophet once explained his position by stating:

> You ask me to plow the ground! Shall I take a knife and tear my mother's bosom? Then when I die she will not take me to her bosom to rest.
>
> You ask me to dig for stone! Shall I dig under her skin for her bones? Then when I die I cannot enter her body to be born again.
>
> You ask me to cut grass and make hay and sell it and be rich like white men! But how dare I cut off my mother's hair?

Smohalla was a strong advocate of a traditional way of life among the Indians, and he urged his followers to remain on the land and not to remove to the reservations. . . .

While the Nez Percés and Upper Palouses prepared to move onto the reservation, Howard traveled to the lower Snake River to council with a number of Indians, including Smohalla and his close friend, the Palouse headman, Thomash, Howard feared a general rebellion among the Indians because of "a craze that spread from tribe to tribe, and swept many of the peaceable and friendly Indians from the moorings of common sense and prudence." Howard and other officers accused Smohalla of teaching a "fanaticism" that was "calculated to appeal to the Indians and stir them up against the whites, and unite them in rebellion." Rumors had spread within the white communities that Smohalla and a host of "dreamers, and prophets" contemplated "a general uprising" that would spread across the land "like wild fire." In late May, 1877, Howard met with Smohalla and representatives from the Palouse, Cayuse, Wanapum, and Walla Walla Tribes in an attempt to quiet the Indians and to explain the government's position.

Howard camped near Smohalla's first home at Wallula and invited the chiefs to visit him. Smohalla entered Howard's camp "bedecked with paint and feathers." The Prophet's "cavalcade filed in with all the pomp and circumstance characteristic of Indian conceit." Howard later wrote that Smohalla "could not be exceeded by any earthly potentate in assumption of power or importance of manner." The Prophet stated that he wanted peace with the whites, but he wished for his band the right "to roam at large whenever and wherever they pleased." Smohalla caused no trouble during his conference with Howard, but Thomash "was wild and fierce to the last." Thomash, a prominent Palouse Indian and Washani leader from the Snake River village of Sumuyah, chastised Howard for "sending troups to Wallowa, and denounced the actions and wishes of the United States government

A Nez Percé medicine dance featuring Two Moons, principal tribal shaman in 1900

in unmeasured terms." Thomash left the council angry, but like Smohalla, he met with Howard again on June 8, 1877, at Fort Simcoe.

Smohalla, Thomash, and a host of others were present at the Simcoe Council, when Howard announced that the government required that the Indians "shall all come on this [the Yakima] or some other of its reservations." None of the leaders liked this talk, and Smohalla reportedly "seemed to be out of his place and was ill at ease." The Prophet was nervous when he spoke, and he perspired profusely as he explained his position in terms of what he had learned from God. According to Dr. G. B. Kuykendall, a physician stationed at the fort, "Smohalla's talk was quite rambling . . . aimed to impress those present that he was a great teacher and leader." Smohalla knew that Howard wanted all of the Indians to move onto the reservation, and despite his objection to doing so, Howard reported that Smohalla agreed to move onto the Yakima Reservation and Thomash onto the Umatilla Reservation. Smohalla probably agreed to move onto the reservation as a delay tactic, since he knew that trouble was brewing in the Nez Percé country. On June 13, 1877, three young warriors triggered the Nez Percé War. After the war commenced, Smohalla, Thomash, and other followers of the Washani abandoned any idea of relocating to the reservation, knowing that troops would be committed to the Nez Percé theater of war. . . .

. . . Smohalla maintained strict neutrality, and he never joined in the war efforts, primarily because he adhered to nonviolent religious precepts. Nevertheless, agents, soldiers, settlers, and ranchers suspected "that Smohalla had been in back of a great deal of disquietude and unrest among the 'wild' Indians." Although Smohalla was innocent of inciting the tribes, a group of white men formed a lynch mob and planned to hang the Prophet while he was encamped on the Yakima Reservation. Smohalla fled the reservation by cover of darkness and hid in the mountains along the Columbia River. Furthermore, General Howard feared that Smohalla would lead a religious crusade against the whites, while others argued that the "treacherous deceptive old rascal" busied himself "secretly helping to keep up the strife . . . sending his young men out on the war path, while he was skulking in the mountains." Smohalla was accused of "harboring all the renegades and disaffected of all the surrounding tribes," but there is no evidence to support this assertion. These false perceptions about Smohalla and the other Washani followers created an image that the non-Christian Indians constituted a real threat to white security. This image formed the basis of a justification for the wholesale removal of the Indians off the land. . . .

Following the Nez Percé War, Smohalla "resisted all inducements offered by the government to settle on some reservation." The Prophet urged people to practice peaceful resistance and to place their lives in the hands of *Nami Piap*, who promised he would deliver those who danced and sang the *washat* ceremony. On the lower Snake River, Thomash followed the precepts of Smohalla's teachings. However, Thomash and Smohalla disagreed about the application of the Indian Homestead Act of 1874 which offered 160 acres on the public domain to any Indian who filed for a homestead. In 1878 Thomash filed claim to his land on the Snake River where his family and his ancestors had resided for years and where his family continued to reside until the early 1960's when "the law" moved them to the Yakima Reservation.

Much to the chagrin of Smohalla, some of his other followers filed for homesteads. In 1878 Big Thunder, chief of the Palouses at the confluence of the Snake and Palouse Rivers, told General Howard that "they wished to remain where they were" and to take up lands in severalty. Howard urged Big Thunder to file claims under the Indian Homestead Act, because "it was right to do so, and that was just what the great father in Washington wanted all Indians to do." The very policies advocated by President Rutherford B. Hayes were those abhorred by Smohalla. According to Smohalla, *Nami Piap* had told the Prophet that "lands were never to be marked off or divided." According to Smohalla, "Those who cut up the lands or sign papers for lands will be defrauded of their rights and will be punished by God's anger." Thus, Indians who filed homesteads broke a fundamental law of God. Added to this was the necessity of Indian homesteaders to improve their lands which Smohalla felt was against God's law. Around 1890, Captain E. L. Huggins visited the Prophet and reported that Smohalla put it this way: "My young men shall never work. Men who work cannot dream, and wisdom comes to us in dreams.". . .

Despite the fact that Smohalla never filed claim to his land on the banks of the Columbia River, he remained on the land and refused to move to the Yakima Reservation. Under the terms of the Yakima Treaty, the government was required to pay the Indians for any improvements before the people were compelled to surrender their land and property. Thus, Yakima agent James Wilbur never succeeded in his attempt to force Smohalla and his band onto the reservation. Smohalla continued to reside at his village at Priest Rapids until his death in the 1890s. During all of that time he never wavered from his beliefs and the ceremony given to him by *Nami Piap*. He passed on his religion to his son, Yoyoni, and his nephew, Puck Hyah Toot, who in turn passed on remnants of the faith to other followers of the Washani religion. Smohalla was one of many religious leaders in the Inland Northwest during the turbulent era of the late nineteenth century, but he was the most important *yanchta* in the region. Yet far more important than Smohalla or the changes he brought to the old religion was the influence of the Washani faith on the course of history. In response to white expansion and the pressures of a new economic, political, social, and religious order, the Plateau Indians turned inward and sought security in their own belief systems. Smohalla's afterlife experiences and his beliefs about land, animals, and spirits made little sense to nineteenth century white Americans. But since his faith was built on the precepts of the old Washani, his teachings made a great deal of sense to the Indians. Thus, his beliefs and those of Joseph, Toolhoolhool-zote, Husishusis Kute, and others were very much alike. And these ideas—shared by all the principal chiefs of the non-Christian Indians—had a profound influence on the course of Northwestern history.

Mexican-American Identity and Culture

AMÉRICO PAREDES

The U.S. conquest of Mexico's northern borderlands in the 1840s produced not only a new political border but a new cultural one—a cultural frontier that intersected Mexican and Euro-American cultures. This frontier is best illustrated by the unique border culture flourishing along the almost 2,000-mile boundary between the United States and Mexico. Américo Paredes, the dean of Mexican-American intellectuals and one of the foremost scholars of border culture, discusses the historical development of frontier culture in the Lower Rio Grande Valley border area of Texas as expressed in the folklore of both Mexican Americans and Euro-Americans.

He notes that the intersection of Mexican-American and Euro-American cultures has led to conflict as well as cultural synthesis. *Corridos*—Mexican-American folksongs—express well this dual character of border culture. Particularly important in Paredes's analysis is the notion of a changing Mexican-American culture and identity. Implicitly challenging the stereotypical view that sees Mexican Americans as members of a static, traditional culture, Paredes stresses change, adaptation, and innovation in the production of a dynamic cultural presence, as well as an evolving ethnic identity.

STUDY QUESTIONS

1. How does the emergence of a border culture counteract the image that cultures are static and unchanging?

2. What characteristics did some of the heroes in this border culture possess?

Conflict—cultural, economic, and physical—has been a way of life along the border between Mexico and the United States, and it is in the so-called Nueces-Río Grande strip where its patterns were first established. Problems of identity also are common to border dwellers, and these problems were first confronted by people of Mexican culture as a result of the Texas revolution. For these reasons, the Lower Río Grande area also can claim to be the source of the more typical elements of what we call the culture of the border.

The Handbook of Middle American Indians divides northern Mexico into four culture areas: (1) Baja California; (2) the northwest area—Sonora and south along the Pacific coast to Nayarit; (3) the north central area—Chihuahua, Durango, and some parts of Coahuila; and (4) the northeast area—Tamaulipas, most of Nuevo León and the lower-border areas of Coahuila, ending a few miles upriver from Ciudad Acuña and Del Río.

The culture of the border is not only historically dynamic but has its regional variations as well. Because it is difficult to generalize on so vast an area, this essay focuses on one region, the northeast. It sometimes is referred to as the Lower Río Grande Border or simply, the Lower Border. In a strictly chronological sense, this region may claim priority over the other areas. If we view a border not simply as a line on a map but, more fundamentally, as a sensitized area where two cultures or two political systems come face to face, then the first "border" between English-speaking people from the United States and people of Mexican culture was in the eastern part of what is now the state of Texas. And this border developed even before such political entities as the Republic of Mexico and the Republic of Texas came into being. Its location shifted as the relentless drive south and west by Nolan, Magee, and their successors pushed a hotly contested borderline first to the Nueces and later to the Río Grande.

Certain folklore themes and patterns spread from the Nueces–Río Grande area to other parts of the border as cultural conflict spread. That a distinctive border culture spread from the Nueces–Río Grande area to other border regions (as well as to other areas of the West) is a thesis explored by Professor Walter Prescott Webb in *The Great Plains*. In the chapter "The Cattle Kingdom," Webb sees his "kingdom" as developing a peculiar "civilization." This "cattle culture" was the result of a union of northern Mexican ranchero culture, including techniques of raising cattle and horses, with new technological improvements brought in by Anglo Americans, especially such things as revolvers, barbed wire, and lawyers versed in the intricacies of land titles.

Text excerpted from Américo Paredes, "The Problem of Identity in a Changing Culture: Popular Expressions of Culture Conflict along the Lower Rio Grande Border," in *View Across the Border: The United States and Mexico*, ed. Stanley R. Ross, 1978, pp. 68–78. The Weatherhead Foundation.

Much has been written about the blending of cultures in the southwestern United States, though less has been said about the impact of United States culture on northern Mexico. The number of books written about the influence of Mexican (or Spanish) architecture in the southwestern United States, if placed one beside another, would fill an extremely long bookshelf. Even more has been said and written about Mexican foods in the United States, an interest also manifest in the number of "Mexican" restaurants in almost any American town or city, patronized for the most part by WASP [white Anglo-Saxon Protestant] Americans. The ultimate in Mexican food in the Southwest and other areas are the quick-service chains that now sell tacos the way other chains sell hamburgers and hot dogs.

"Mexican food" is of course defined as tamales, tacos, enchiladas, chalupas, nachos, tostadas, frijoles refritos, and delicacies of that sort. What is rarely noted is that for the border Mexican of the past couple of centuries these foods have been almost as exotic as they are to the WASP American. One of the popular etymologies given for "greaser," an epithet applied by Anglo Americans to Mexicans, is that the term arose when the Anglos first encountered Mexicans in the Nueces–Río Grande area and were struck by the greasiness of Mexican food. O. Henry has enshrined this stereotype in his poem "Tamales," according to which "Don José Calderón Santos Espirition Vicente Camillo Quintana de Ríos de Rosa y Ribera" takes revenge on the Texans for having killed his grandfather at San Jacinto by selling greasy tamales to Anglos:

> What boots it if we killed
> Only one greaser,
> Don José Calderón?
> This is your deep revenge,
> You have greased all of us,
> Greased a whole nation
> With your Tamales . . .

The author of "The Little Adobe Casa," a parody of "The Little Sod Shanty on My Claim," has a much better idea of the border Mexican's fare, perhaps based on more direct experience than O. Henry's. The singer lives in Mexico, where "the Greaser roams about the place all day." Still, he keeps hoping that some "dark eye mujer" will consent to be his wife. Meanwhile,

> My bill of fare is always just the same
> Frijoles and tortillas
> Stirred up in chili sauce
> In my little adobe casa on the plains.

Frijoles, chiles, and tortillas were the standard fare along the border, as everywhere else in Mexico, except that the tortillas were more likely to be made of flour than of *nixtamal* [cooked maize], while the frijoles were never refried but boiled and mashed into a soupy stew—*caldudos*. Tamales were eaten once a year, at Christmas after the yearly hog was killed; and a taco was any snack made of a rolled tortilla with some kind of filling. For a more varied daily menu there might be rice with chicken or dried shrimp, beef either fresh or dried, as well as almost any other part of the steer. And for a real treat there was *cabrito* [goatmeat].

Bigfoot (El Patón) Wallace, who was captured by Mexican troops after the Mier Expedition, used his alleged sufferings in captivity as an excuse for the barbarities he committed against Mexican civilians when he was a member of Hays's Rangers during the Mexican War. One of the examples of his mistreatment at Mexican hands is mentioned in John Duval's romanticized biography of Wallace. Wallace complained that after being captured, and during the time he spent along the Río Grande, all he ever was given to eat were beans, tortillas, and roast goatmeat. Nowadays, many of Wallace's fellow countrymen journey all the way from central Texas to "in" eating spots on the Río Grande, to satisfy their craving for beans, tortillas, and roast goatmeat. But perhaps Bigfoot found border Mexican food too greaseless for his taste; he probably missed his sidemeat and the rich gravies he was accustomed to sopping his biscuits in.

A better case for the blending of Anglo-American culture with that of the northern Mexican ranchero may be made in respect to the more practical elements of the "cattle culture." Cattle and horses, as well as land, were Mexican to begin with; and when the Anglo took them over he also adopted many of the techniques developed by the ranchero for the handling of stock. The vocabulary related to the occupation of the vaquero also became part of

A Mexican-American vendor dispensing his wares at an outdoor chili stand in San Antonio, Texas, c. 1889

the blend. These things also have merited the attention of scholars and popular writers alike, especially those interested in the process whereby the rough Mexican ranchero was transformed into the highly romanticized American cowboy. All these subjects, from food and architecture to the birth of the cowboy, have attracted interest mainly from the viewpoint of their impact on the culture of the United States. My own interest in the cowboy has been a bit more intercultural, I believe, and it has focused on the manner in which an ideal pattern of male behavior has been developed interculturally along the border, subsequently to influence the male self-image first in the United States and later in Mexico. I refer to the familiar figure of popular fiction and popular song—the mounted man with his pistol in hand. Take the Mexican ranchero, a man on horseback par excellence, add the six-chambered revolver, and you have the American cowboy of fiction and popular legend—the ideal figure of many an Anglo male. The cowboy as a *macho* image was carried by the Texan, along with other elements of the "cattle culture," to other areas of the border, as well as to other parts of the West. The idea of the cowboy as the American *macho* becomes so pervasive that it can influence the private and public life of Theodore Roosevelt, as well as the scholarly writings of historians like Walter Prescott Webb. Finally—aided in the last stages of the process by such books as Webb's *The Texas Rangers*—the cowboy has his apotheosis in Hollywood. The impact on a people of an idea or an ideal may be gauged by its influence on the folksongs of that people. Thus, it is worth noting that by 1910 the work of John A. Lomax, the great collector of North American folksongs, was beginning to make Americans see the cowboy as the national image and find the essence of the North American spirit in the cowboy, as expressed in the cowboy's songs. At that time the Mexican Revolution was just getting under way, and it would be almost a generation before romantic nationalists in Mexico would discover the essence of *mexicanismo* in the *corridos* of the Revolution.

The cowboy had influenced the border Mexican long before, and in a very direct way, because "cowboy" began as the name of the Anglo cattle thieves who raided the Nueces–Río Grande area in the late 1830s, and who, revolver in hand, began the dispossession of the Mexican on the north bank of the Río Grande. Understandably, the border Mexican developed a fascination for the revolver as a very direct symbol of power; he had learned the power of the pistol the hard way. Mexicans lent the image of the vaquero to their neighbors to the north, and the image returned to Mexico wearing a six-shooter and a Stetson hat. The cowboy *macho* image influenced the Revolution, in men such as Roberto Fierro; but it was after the Revolution that the cycle was completed, with the singing *charros* of the Mexican movies. And it was at about this same time that anthropologists and psychoanalysts discovered *machismo* in Mexico and labeled it as a peculiarly Mexican way of behavior.

But life along the border was not always a matter of conflicting cultures; there was often cooperation of a sort, between ordinary people of both cultures, since life had to be lived as an everyday affair. People most often cooperated in circumventing the excessive regulation of ordinary intercourse across the border. In other words, they regularly were engaged in smuggling. Smuggling, of course, has been a common activity wherever Mexicans and North Americans have come in contact; and this goes back to times long before Mexico's independence, when Yankee vessels used to make periodic smuggling visits to the more out-of-the-way Mexican ports. The famous Santa Fe Trail, begun about 1820 between Santa Fe and Independence, Missouri, may be considered one of the largest and most publicized smuggling operations in history. But even earlier, smuggling had been fairly general from the United States into Texas. The fact that the United States had consumer goods to sell and that Mexicans wanted to buy made smuggling inevitable, and many otherwise respected figures in the early history of the Southwest seem to have indulged in the practice. Smuggling could even be seen in those early days as a kind of libertarian practice, a protest against the harsh customs laws of the colonial times that throttled Mexico's economy. So, smuggling was not peculiar to the Nueces–Río Grande area, while the romanticizing of the smuggler as a leader in social protest was not limited even to the border areas as a whole. One has only to remember Luis Inclán's *Astucia*, where tobacco smugglers in interior Mexico are idealized as social reformers of the gun and hangman's noose. (It is worth mentioning, however, that Inclán's hero sends to the United States for *pistolas giratorias* to accomplish his pre–Porfirio Díaz version of iron-fisted law and order.)

Borders, however, offer special conditions not only for smuggling but for the idealization of the smuggler. This sounds pretty obvious, since, after all, political boundaries are the obvious places where customs and immigration regulations are enforced. But we must consider not only the existence of such political boundaries but the circumstances of their creation. In this respect, the Lower Río Grande Border was especially suited for smuggling operations.

To appreciate this fact, one has only to consider the history of the Lower Río Grande. This area—presently Tamaulipas and the southern part of Texas—was originally the province of Nuevo Santander. Nuevo Santander differed from the other three northernmost provinces of New Spain—New Mexico, Texas, and California—in an important way. It was not the last to be founded, its settlement having preceded that of California by some twenty years. But it was the least isolated of the frontier provinces. Great expanses of territory separated the settlements in New Mexico and California from the concentrations of Mexican population to the south. The same was true of the colony of Texas until 1749. It was in that year that Escandón began the settlement of Nuevo Santander, and one of the aims of settlement was precisely to fill the gap between the Texas colony and such established population centers to the south as Tampico and Monterrey.

So from their very first days of settlement, the colonists of Nuevo Santander lived an in-between existence. This sense of being caught in the middle was greatly intensified after 1835. As citizens of Mexico, the former *neosantanderinos*—now *tamaulipecos*—faced an alien and hostile people to the north. As *federalistas*, they also had to contend with an equally hostile *centralista* government to the south. For the people of the Lower Río Grande, the period from the mid 1830s to the mid 1840s was marked by cattle-stealing raids by Texas "cowboys" from north of the Nueces and incursions of Mexican armies from the south. It would be difficult to find parallels to this situation in the other frontier provinces; however, the bitter hatreds that developed in the Nueces–Río Grande area during that bloody decade were soon diffused to other areas of the Southwest, along with other elements of the "cattle culture."

The Treaty of Guadalupe Hidalgo settled the conflict over territory between Mexico and the United States, officially at least. It also created a Mexican-American minority in the United States, as has often been noted. But it did not immediately create a border situation all along the international line. The *nuevomejicano* in Santa Fe, the *californio* in Los Angeles, and the *tejano* in San Antonio were swallowed whole into the North American political body. The new border—an imaginary and ill-defined line—was many miles to the south of them, in the uninhabited areas that already had separated them from the rest of Mexico before the war with the United States. The immediate change in customs demanded of *tejanos*, *californios*, and *nuevomejicanos* was from that of regional subcultures of Mexico to occupied territories within the United States.

Such was not the case with the people of the Lower Río Grande. A very well-defined geographic feature—the Río Grande itself—became the international line. And it was a line that cut right through the middle of what had once been Nuevo Santander. The river, once a focus of regional life, became a symbol of separation. The kind of borderline that separates ethnically related peoples is common enough in some parts of Europe; but in the earliest stages of the border between Mexico and the United States, it was typical only of the Lower Río Grande, with some exceptions such as the El Paso area. Here a pattern was set that would later become typical of the whole border between Mexico and the United States. Irredentist movements were shared with other occupied areas such as New Mexico, though the Cortina and Pizaña uprisings of 1859 and 1915 respectively were strongly influenced by the proximity of the international boundary. More to our point was the general flouting of customs and immigration laws, not so much as a form of social or ethnic protest but as part of the way of life.

When the Río Grande became a border, friends and relatives who had been near neighbors—within shouting distance across a few hundred feet of water—now were legally in different countries. If they wanted to visit each other, the law required that they travel many miles up or down stream, to the nearest official crossing place, instead of swimming or boating directly across as they used to do before. It goes without saying that they paid little attention to the requirements of the law. When they went visiting, they crossed at the most convenient spot on the river; and, as is ancient custom when one goes visiting loved ones, they took gifts with them: farm products from Mexico to Texas, textiles and other manufactured goods from Texas to Mexico. Legally, of course, this was smuggling, differing from contraband for profit in volume only. Such a pattern is familiar to anyone who knows the border, for it still operates, not only along the Lower Río Grande now but all along the boundary line between Mexico and the United States.

Unofficial crossings also disregarded immigration laws. Children born on one side of the river would be baptized on the other side, and thus appear on church registers as citizens of the other country. This bothered no one since people on both sides of the river thought of themselves as *mexicanos,* but United States officials were concerned about it. People would come across to visit relatives and stay long periods of time, and perhaps move inland in search of work. After 1890, the movement in search of work was preponderantly from Mexico deep into Texas and beyond. The ease with which the river could be crossed and the hospitality of relatives and friends on either side also was a boon to men who got in trouble with the law. It was not necessary to flee over trackless wastes, with the law hot on one's trail. All it took was a few moments in the water, and one was out of reach of his pursuers and in the hands of friends. If illegal crossings in search of work were mainly in a northerly direction, crossings to escape the law were for the most part from north to south. By far, not all the Mexicans fleeing American law were criminals in an ordinary sense. Many were victims of cultural conflict, men who had reacted violently to assaults on their human dignity or their economic rights.

Resulting from the partition of the Lower Río Grande communities was a set of folk attitudes that would in time become general along the United States–Mexican border. There was a generally favorable disposition toward the individual who disregarded customs and immigration laws, especially the laws of the United States. The professional smuggler was not a figure of reproach, whether he was engaged in smuggling American woven goods into Mexico or Mexican tequila into Texas. In folklore there was a tendency to idealize the smuggler, especially the *tequilero,* as a variant of the hero of cultural conflict. The smuggler, the illegal alien looking for work, and the border-conflict hero became identified with each other in the popular mind. They came into conflict with the same American laws and sometimes with the same individual officers of the law, who were all looked upon as *rinches*—a border-Spanish rendering of "ranger." Men who were Texas Rangers, for example, during the revenge killings of Mexicans after the Pizaña uprising of 1915* later were border patrolmen who engaged in gun-

---

* The uprising occurred on the Lower Río Grande Border and involved a group of Texas-Mexican rancheros attempting to create a Spanish-speaking republic in South Texas. Pizaña endeavored to appeal to other United States minority groups. [Editor's note] battles with *tequileros*. So stereotyped did the figure of the *rinche* become that Lower Río Grande Border versions of "La persecución de Villa" identify Pershing's soldiers as *rinches*.

A *corrido* tradition of intercultural conflict developed along the Río Grande, in which the hero defends his rights and those of other Mexicans against the *rinches*. The first hero of these *corridos* is Juan Nepomuceno Cortina, who is celebrated in an 1859 *corrido* precisely because he helps a fellow Mexican.

> Ese general Cortina
> es libre y muy soberano,
> han subido sus honores
> porque salvó a un mexicano.

> That general Cortina is quite sovereign and free;
> The honor due him is greater, for he saved a Mexican's life.

Other major *corrido* heroes are Gregorio Cortez (1901), who kills two Texas sheriffs after one of them shoots his brother; Jacinto Treviño (1911), who kills several Americans to avenge his brother's death; Rito García (1885), who shoots several officers who invade his home without a warrant; and Aniceto Pizaña and his *sediciosos* (1915). Some *corrido* heroes escape across the border into Mexico; others, like Gregorio Cortez and Rito García, are betrayed and captured. They go to prison but they have stood up for what is right. As the "Corrido de Rito García" says,

> . . . me voy a la penitencia
> por defender mi derecho.

> I am going to the penitentiary because
> I defended my rights.

The men who smuggled tequila into the United States during the twenties and early thirties were no apostles of civil rights, nor did the border people think of them as such. But in his activities, the *tequilero* risked his life against the old enemy, the *rinche*. And, as has been noted, smuggling had long been part of the border way of life. Still sung today is "El corrido de Mariano Reséndez" about a prominent smuggler of textiles into Mexico, circa 1900. So highly respected were Reséndez and his activities that he was known as "El Contrabandista." Reséndez, of course, violated Mexican laws; and his battles were with Mexican customs officers. The *tequilero* and his activities, however, took on an intercultural dimension; and they became a kind of coda to the *corridos* of border conflict.

The heavy-handed and often brutal manner that Anglo lawmen have used in their dealings with border Mexicans helped make almost any man outside the law a sympathetic figure, with the *rinche* or Texas Ranger as the symbol of police brutality. That these symbols still are alive may be seen in the recent Fred Carrasco affair. The border Mexican's tolerance of smuggling does not seem to extend to traffic in drugs. The few *corridos* that have been current on the subject, such as "Carga blanca," take a negative view of the dope peddler. Yet Carrasco's death in 1976 at the Huntsville (Texas) prison, along with two women hostages, inspired close to a dozen *corridos* with echoes of the old style. The sensational character of Carrasco's death cannot be discounted, but note should also be taken of the unproved though widely circulated charges that Carrasco was "executed" by a Texas Ranger, who allegedly shot him through the head at close range where Carrasco lay wounded. This is a scenario familiar to many a piece of folk literature about cultural conflict—*corridos* and prose narratives—the *rinche* finishing off the wounded Mexican with a bullet through the head. It is interesting to compare the following stanzas, the first from one of the Carrasco *corridos* and the other two from a *tequilero* ballad of the thirties.

> El capitán de los rinches
> fue el primero que cayó
> pero el chaleco de malla
> las balas no traspasó.

> The captain of the Rangers was the first one to fall.
> But the armored vest he was wearing did not let the bullets through.

> En fin de tanto invitarle
> Leandro los acompañó;
> en las lomas de Almiramba
> fue el primero que cayó.

> They kept asking him to go, until Leandro went with them;
> In the hills of Almiramba, he was the first one to fall.

> El capitán de los rinches
> a Silvano se acercó,
> y en unos cuantos segundos
> Silvano García murió.

> The captain of the Rangers came up close to Silvano;
> And in a few seconds Silvano García was dead.

Similar attitudes are expressed on the Sonora-Arizona border, for example, when the hard-case hero of "El corrido de Cananea" is made to say,

> Me agarraron los cherifes
> al estilo americano,
> como al hombre de delito,
> todos con pistola en mano.

> The sheriffs caught me, in the American style,
> As they would a wanted man, all of them pistol in hand.

The partition of Nuevo Santander was also to have political effects, arising from the strong feeling among the Lower Río Grande people that the land on both sides of the river was equally theirs. This involved feelings on a very local and personal level, rather than the rhetoric of national politics, and is an attitude occasionally exhibited by some old Río Grande people to this day. Driving north along one of today's highways toward San Antonio, Austin, or Houston, they are likely to say as the highway crosses the Nueces, "We are now entering Texas." Said in jest, of course, but the jest has its point. Unlike Mexicans in California, New Mexico, and the old colony of Texas, the Río Grande people experienced the dismemberment of Mexico in a very immediate way. So the attitude developed, early and naturally, that a border Mexican was *en su tierra* in Texas even if he had been born in Tamaulipas. Such feelings, of course, were the basis for the revolts of Cortina and Pizaña. They reinforced the borderer's disregard of political and social boundaries. And they lead in a direct line to the Chicano movement and its mythic concept of Aztlán. For the Chicano does not base his claim to the Southwest on royal land grants or on a lineage that goes back to the Spanish conquistadores. On the contrary, he is more likely to be the child or grandchild of immigrants. He bases his claim to Aztlán on his Mexican culture and his mestizo heritage.

Conversely, the Texas-born Mexican continued to think of Mexico as "our land" also. That this at times led to problems of identify is seen in the folksongs of the border. In 1885, for example, Rito García protests illegal police entry into his home by shooting a few officers of Cameron County, Texas. He makes it across the river and feels safe, unaware that Porfirio Díaz has an extradition agreement with the United States. Arrested and returned to Texas, according to the *corrido,* he expresses amazement,

> Yo nunca hubiera creído
> que mi país tirano fuera,
> que Mainero me entregara
> a la nación extranjera.

> I never would have thought that my country would be so unjust,
> That Mainero would hand me over to a foreign nation.

And he adds bitterly,

> Mexicanos, no hay que fiar
> en nuestra propia nación,
> nunca a vayan a buscar
> a México protección.

> Mexicans, we can put no trust in our own nation;
> Never go to Mexico asking for protection.

But the *mexicanos* to whom he gives this advice are Texas Mexicans.

An even more interesting case dates back to 1867, the year Maximilian surrendered at Querétaro. A few days before this event, on May 5, Mexicans celebrated another event just as historic, the fifth anniversary of the defeat of the French at Puebla by Mexican troops under Ignacio Zaragoza. The little town of San Ignacio, on the Texas side of the river, celebrated the Cinco de Mayo with a big festival at which a local *guitarrero* sang two of his songs, especially composed for the occasion. One was "A Zaragoza," in praise of the victor over the French at Puebla; the other was "A Grant," in praise of Ulysses S. Grant, the victor over the Confederacy. The same set of symbols—flag, honor, country—is used in both songs.

Japanese-Language Schools in Hawaii, 1890s–1920s

JOHN N. HAWKINS

More male Japanese immigrants formed families in the United States than did any other Asian immigrant group. Thus American-born youngsters of Japanese ancestry outnumbered children of Chinese, Korean, Filipino, or Asian Indian descent during the early decades of this century. When these Japanese-American children started attending public schools, learned English, and behaved more and more like their Euro-American peers, their parents tried strenuously to teach them the cultural values and norms of the homeland. One widely used instrument was privately supported Japanese-language schools staffed by teachers trained in Japan. These instructors used textbooks published in Japan and ran their classrooms with the strictest discipline.

As members of the host society began to view these institutions with suspicion, however, calling them tools of an increasingly militaristic Japanese imperial government, officials in Hawaii and the Pacific coast states sought ways to control or even eliminate the schools. But the immigrants fought back, in the process making Asian-language schools an arena in which battles over conflicting cultures were waged.

STUDY QUESTIONS

1. Why did Japanese immigrants establish Japanese-language schools?

2. Why were officials in Hawaii suspicious of these schools?

3. What was the outcome of the battle over the Japanese-language schools in Hawaii?

In culturally diverse societies, national language policy, especially as it relates to the function of schooling, is one of the most complex and at times emotionally-charged educational issues. . . . [This] study will focus on the political struggle of the Japanese immigrant community in the early twentieth century to maintain their autonomous Japanese-language schools in the face of strong opposition from the Hawaiian Territorial Government, controlled by the *haole* (white) elite. . . .

Following a major period of Japanese immigration to Hawaii in the late 19th century and the subsequent rise of a new second generation, the Japanese community developed independent, private language schools which were designed to promote a sense of community through the study of Japanese culture and language, as well as to perpetuate Japanese culture and values. The first schools were founded in the late 1800s on Maui and in Honolulu by both Buddhist and Christian representatives. Although initially the schools were strongly tied to formal religious organizations, independent schools eventually dominated. Of the 181 Japanese-language schools established in Hawaii by 1934, 76 percent were independent, 22 percent Buddhist, and 2 percent Christian. . . . Children in these early schools observed major Japanese holidays and were at those times absent from the American public schools, which according to law they were required to attend. They bowed to the Emperor's picture, sang the Japanese national anthem, and studied the Imperial Rescript on Education. This type of instructional activity continued down to 1915. As a result of increasing criticism by American educational authorities, from 1916 onward most schools made efforts to discard the image of being a separate educational track. They changed their names from Japanese Elementary Schools to Japanese Language Schools and discontinued use of Japanese Ministry of Education instructional materials; a period of curricular reform began.

An umbrella organization, the Japanese Education Association, was founded in 1914 and included both Christian and Buddhist representatives. . . . [I]n 1915 a distinguished group of Japanese educators met to formulate a revision plan. . . . [I]n 1916, Japanese Consul General Rukuro Moroi spearheaded a Central Educational Association which worked in cooperation with the Territorial Government to standardize the curriculum. . . . [T]he revised texts that appeared after 1916 were "Hawaiianized versions" of the previous materials. These revisions made by the Japanese schools can be seen as a political strategy to relieve the pressure from American authorities. Concomitantly, the revised curriculum may also be viewed as a reflection of the changing world view of the Japanese immigrants toward themselves, from sojourners to settlers with a political and economic status in Hawaii.

From John N. Hawkins, "Politics, Education, and Language Policy: The Case of Japanese Lanaguage Schools in Hawaii," *Amerasia Journal* 5:1 (1978), pp. 39–40 and 42–54. Reprinted with permission of Amerasia Journal.

Apart from the criticism directed against the curriculum, the schools drew little attention from authorities in the Territorial Government and expanded steadily. By 1917, the majority of Japanese school-age children attended the public schools during the day and the Japanese-language schools in the late afternoon and on weekends. The end of World War I brought a high degree of national chauvinism to Hawaii which, coupled with rising suspicion of the Japanese community in the 1920s (related in some measure to Japan's actions in China), created conditions for the conflict around the issue of control and regulation of the language schools. An additional factor raised repeatedly by the *haole* elite was the role played by Japanese strike leaders in the 1909 and especially the 1920 sugar plantation strikes. Even though the latter strike was broken and the leaders publicly humiliated the specter of a unified and mobilized Japanese labor force alarmed Hawaii's dominant groups, who viewed the language schools as an institutional organizational base of un-Americanism. . . . [and feared] that the Japanese were getting out of hand economically and politically. The Buddhist temples and the language schools were considered the most dangerous manifestation of this trend.

Throughout the struggle over regulation of the schools, Japanese supporters of the schools . . . maintained that the basic problem was the religious differences between Buddhist and Christian communities. Supporters of regulatory legislation, however, argued that religion had nothing to do with the struggle and instead stressed institutional and pedagogical problems related to the language schools. Despite some outward displays of religious tolerance, the record of *haole* antagonism toward non-Christian religions coupled with anti-foreign sentiment during this period made it easier for government officials and American educators to attack the language schools. The Territorial Government could and did interfere often on educational matters, and educational agencies in Hawaii increasingly saw the Japanese-language schools as obstacles to their attempts to inculcate American values and attitudes in Japanese as well as other ethnic groups (especially Chinese and Koreans, who also maintained separate language schools).

By 1919, legislation and proposals began to appear, calling for the certification of teachers on the basis of "ideals of democracy and knowledge of English." This represented the first of several moves to monitor and limit the number of Japanese teachers (the majority of whom spoke only Japanese) and thereby further regulate the schools. . . . Other legislation was introduced to abolish the schools entirely, but such efforts were haphazard and immediately opposed by leaders in the Japanese community. . . . The Japanese community was warned that such an attitude might result in further regulatory legislation. In fact, the Japanese response was quite temperate and consisted of petitions, mass meetings, . . . and a formal request from the Japanese Education Association . . . to officials requesting that the bills be withdrawn. . . . Consequently, till 1920 all such acts . . . were either tabled or defeated. . . . A "veritable flood of petitions" was sent to the legislature, Japanese workers on the plantations threatened to leave their jobs, and even the Chinese and Korean communities supported efforts to defeat the measures.

Both sides had, however, made their positions clear. The Territorial Government realized that a planned, concerted effort was required to obtain control of the language schools. The Japanese community had, on the other hand, realized that only through effective mobilization could they influence educational decision making. The lines were thus drawn between those (including some Japanese) who increasingly favored control or abolition of language schools—accompanied as rapidly as possible with total assimilation of the Japanese into American society—and those, primarily in the Japanese community, who argued for cultural preservation and saw the language schools as the principal vehicle to achieve this goal. . . . [T]he Governor . . . invite[d] the United States Commissioner of Education to investigate all public and private schools in the Territory in order to build a base for elimination of the private language schools. The 1920 labor strike also had the effect of inflaming opinion against the Japanese. . . .

[T]he Territorial Attorney General, Harry Irwin, drafted a proposal which was presented at a special session of the Territorial legislature on 20 November 1920. This proposal urged the total abolition of all foreign-language schools and was the harshest legislation yet presented. The response by moderate members of both the Territorial Government and the Japanese community was a compromise proposal known as Act 30. This measure . . . led to an open struggle and eventually a complicated legal battle over the issue of control of the Japanese-language schools.

Educational officials, government authorities, and other leading members of the Territory of Hawaii set the stage for the legislative struggle that was to follow by a variety of both direct and indirect means. Direct efforts were made to remove the financial base of the language schools. . . . An annual government report issued in 1919 stated: "There can neither be national unity in ideals nor in purpose unless there is some common method of communication through which may be conveyed the thought of the nation. All Americans must be taught to read and write and think in one language; this is a primary condition to that growth which all nations expect of us and which we demand of ourselves.". . .

Supporters of the language schools at this time were represented primarily by the Hawaii Kyoiku Kai (Hawaii Education Association, also known as Japanese Education Association) founded in 1914. The Association had been forewarned of the potential dangers of stressing cultural preservation and language integrity by Japanese Consul General Arita. In 1916, the Association began to revise the curriculum to remove clauses overtly stressing Japanese citizenship. A parallel move to separate the language schools from religious affiliation also took place. However, these compromise actions had little effect as several bills introduced in 1919–1920 proposed either the abolishment or regulation of the language schools. The Japanese community responded with a series of volatile mass meetings during which race discrimination was denounced, petitions were drawn up and presented to a wide range of government authorities . . . and appeals were made through the Japanese-language newspapers . . . to the community to fight the legislation. . . .

In the face of such widespread mobilization by the Japanese, Territorial Government officials, especially the Office of the Superintendent of Public Instruction, did not expect to successfully promote legislation that would entirely abolish the language schools. They were successful, however, in introducing and eventually signing into law the compromise measure, Act 30. The committee which drafted the measure included both moderate government officials and moderate members of the Japanese community. The Act stated that the government and the Office of the Superintendent of Public Instruction would be allowed to: "Regulate and not to prohibit the conducting of foreign language schools and the teaching of foreign languages; but to regulate the same so that the Americanism of the pupils be promoted." The measure thus satisfied a broad segment of both communities, the *haole* elite who were concerned about the Americanism of Japanese youngsters, and the Japanese community who were now assured that the schools would not be eliminated but only "regulated." However, in a move that retriggered the conflict, American members of the committee proposed and added a clause to Act 30 that restricted the student enrollment in language schools to students who had reached the third grade of the public schools. The Japanese members of the committee first opposed this action and then reluctantly agreed to support the entire document. . . . [T]he Act was signed into law and became effective 1 January 1923.

Dissension in the Japanese community took place over the course of what future action, if any, ought to be taken. The possibilities ranged from complete acquiescence to mass protest and violence. One group, supported and encouraged by the Japanese Consul General and several prominent members of the Japanese community, urged the community not to fight the issue at this time but to assure government officials that they would Americanize as quickly as possible and reorganize the language schools accordingly. They argued that only through this method could the language schools be saved from complete elimination. . . .

The forces in the community opposed to the Act realized that the dissension over the issue of litigation seriously retarded the momentum that had built up since the Territorial Government began introducing regulatory legislation. The range of opinion was wide. One prominent Buddhist priest . . . commented that the cultural differences between Japanese and Americans were simply too great and probably irreconcilable. For this reason he opposed control or elimination of the language schools on the grounds that it would be disastrous to the cultural integrity of Japanese in Hawaii. . . . Others were more hopeful that a less extreme position could be found. The Japanese Society of Hawaii, a large umbrella organization of Japanese public opinion, met several times and reached the conclusion that further protest was necessary; that the language schools should be supported. At the same time, their argument shifted to emphasize the positive role the schools could play in creating good American citizens (not necessarily "Americanized," however). Moreover, they took the position that if the schools were eliminated, social disorder could result, especially among Japanese youth.. . . The Japanese media (primarily the *Hawaii Hochi* and *Hawaii Shinpo*) directed their attention to the Japanese community itself. In a series of articles from February to May 1923, the *Hawaii Hochi* encouraged the community to fight the legislation and stand up for their rights. Writers played on the theme of "manhood" and derided those who succumbed to the Territorial Government's actions as "weak Japanese.". . . Editorials encouraged Japanese labor to apply pressure on the Sugar Planter's Association and reminded the Association of the 1920 strike and the potential danger of a similar strike over the school issue. The paper urged a frontal assault against the Territorial Government, extending from formal litigation to pressure on the labor community and the educational establishment. All of these plans sufficiently alarmed the Government, the *haole* elite, and the sugar plantation owners for whom the labor strike of 1920 was still a fresh memory. . . . The combined threats of labor unrest (in actuality more in the minds of the *haole* elite than most Japanese), youth violence, and social instability within the Japanese community had the effect of weakening support for Act 30 and regulation of the language schools in general.

Although the initial response of the Japanese community toward the idea of formal legal action was not widespread (only eleven out of one hundred and thirty language schools voted to join a lawsuit), a test case was entered. As litigation proceeded and community pressure grew in favor of fighting the Act, more schools joined, so that by August 1923 eighty-seven supported the test case.

Prior to the signing of Act 30, the legal firm of Lightfoot and Lightfoot, representing the Japanese Society of Hawaii, filed a brief with the Governor's office challenging the constitutionality of the new regulations. The Hawaii Circuit Court tried the case, and the constitutionality of Act 30 was upheld by Judge James Banks. . . . [B]y 1925, eighty-four of a hundred and forty Japanese-language schools [had] joined the litigants. The Japanese community was able to raise over $25,000 to fight the case. On 21 February 1927 the United States Supreme Court finally decided in favor of the Japanese-language schools. The judgment of the Court was particularly harsh toward Territorial officials. After detailing the various attempts to control the language schools, the court ruled: ". . . all are parts of a deliberate plan to bring foreign language schools under a strict governmental control for which the record discloses no adequate reason." Both parties avoided the religious issue and focused instead on loyalty, stability, and threats to the state. The seven year effort to preserve the schools and to maintain autonomous control over the curriculum and administration was successful. This was an impressive example of a clearly subordinate group effectively mobilizing available resources, coping with a damaging split in the mobilization effort, and finally emerging victorious.

 # Count Basie and Western Swing, 1920s–1930s

WILLIAM 'COUNT' BASIE, AS TOLD TO ALBERT MURRAY

Ragtime, jazz, blues, and other African-American musical forms constituted alternative ways of conceiving and playing music; the urban resorts and settings from which they emerged also represented alternative lifestyles in the United States. From the end of the nineteenth century onward, Kansas City, Missouri, was known for its ragtime music. The famous Lincoln Theatre and Dance Hall, Yellow Front Saloon, Subway Club, Reno Club, and Booker T. Washington Hotel were centers of African-American music and life in the 1920s and 1930s. What was known at that time as western swing was popularized by the bands of Bennie Moten, Walter Page and the Blue Devils, and William "Count" Basie.

In the mid-1930s this music gave a new impetus and a unique rhythmic pulse to the swing fad. From Red Bank, New Jersey, Basie went West with the Gonzelle White Company. In the following selection, he mentions some of the stereotypical notions about the West that visitors discarded after experiencing the region themselves. As music came to play an increasingly important role in Basie's life, he decided to remain in Kansas City. Basie also describes how he met other entertainers and visited the clubs and night spots for which Kansas City was known.

STUDY QUESTIONS

1. In what ways did African-American music shape black culture in the United States?

2. What did Count Basie mean when he said that he was "becoming more and more tied up with music itself and less and less concerned with show business and entertainment in general"?

On my first trip to Kansas City with Gonzelle White, we stayed at the Eastside Hotel on Eighteenth Street, and we played at the Lincoln Theatre on Eighteenth and Lydia. Our opening was reported in the Chicago *Defender* on July 16 by Charles O'Neal in his regular column, "In Old Kaysee.". . .

It was during the time that the Gonzelle White show was playing at the Lincoln that I first met Piney Brown. There were all these girls in the show, and Piney was the man-about-town in Kansas City in those days, and by the way, he was the nicest guy you'd ever want to meet in the world. When you were with him, you never had to worry about anything, because he always took care of the bill.

I had already heard about him, and when he came by the theater and said he wanted to meet the show girls, I already knew who he was. So right away I said to myself, "I got to figure a way to get in on this action." Because I knew he had a little club down the street (Twelfth Street) that looked like it might be a little more expensive than I could afford. So I told him, "Why don't you invite us over to the club, and we'll come by there."

Then I went and told a couple of the girls.

"This rich gentleman out here would like to meet you." And they looked at me as if to say, "What's this?" And I said, "Oh, he is a very nice guy. Everybody knows him. His name is Piney Brown."

I think he also sent some little things backstage to them from the restaurant, and also a little taste, of course, a little something to sip. Then, after the show, he came and took them across the street, and I went along with them. That's how I got to meet him and began to get to know him, and he was definitely somebody worth knowing.

It was also during this time that I just met Ellis Burton. He was the one who ran the Yellow Front Saloon. Incidentally, I was actually the one who started calling him the Chief. But not at that time, because I didn't know him that well then. I met him because we were living at the Eastside Hotel, right across the street from the Lincoln, and his place was right down the street where Elmer Williams and I had discovered all that action when we were on the burlesque circuit. I used to go down there all the time. That was one of the first places in Kansas City where I got a chance to sit in on piano a few times.

There were a lot of joints right there in that same area, and I got a chance to play in several and meet some of the musicians around town. That was how I began meeting people like Baby Lovett, the drummer; and some people claim that I also played the organ in church a couple of Sundays. I don't actually remember playing organ in church at that time, but I know for certain that I did so later on.

The Eastside Hotel had a little restaurant on the street level, and the rooms were upstairs. The food in that restaurant was very good, and I also used to go to a Greek restaurant across the street. Another place I was introduced to during that time was Marie's on Hyde. It was right across the street corner from the stage door of the Lincoln. I remember that there was a little porch to that house, which I remember was next door to Watkin's Funeral Home. Marie had the best brew in town. When Prohibition went out, Marie's was one of the first places in that part of Kansas City to have a bar.

After we closed at the Lincoln, we cooled it around Kansas City for a while. Then we got a chance to go down to Tulsa, which was very exciting to me because at that time I had gotten it in my mind that Oklahoma was the wild West. I thought there would be a lot of cowboys and Indians like in the Western moving pictures that I remembered from all the way back to the time when I was working in Mr. McNulty's theater in Red Bank, and I was so excited about seeing all of that in real life that I stayed awake looking out of the train window all night.

I actually expected to see cowboys and Indians riding across the plains outside. I don't think I said anything to anybody else about any of that because I'm pretty sure that they would have made fun of me for still being such a kid. But actually, I sat awake looking out that window all night, and I was never as disappointed in all my life as I was when I finally nodded off and woke up. The train pulled into Tulsa, and I saw that great big city station. I was ready to turn around and go back to Kansas City. I didn't see any cowboys and Indians anywhere! There really wasn't all that much difference between Tulsa and Kansas City, or even St. Louis, so far as city streets and lights and automobiles were concerned. . . .

It was while we were in Tulsa playing at the Dreamland Theatre that I woke up late one morning hearing the Blue Devils for the first time. And it was also while I was still in Tulsa that time that Seminole, that bad left-handed piano player from back east, came in and broke up a nice little thing I had going for myself in a great little back-alley joint. There was no battle or anything like that. They just brought him around there and invited him to sit in, and when I heard him, I knew I was out. . . .

When I came back into Kansas City after spending the time I spent with the Blue Devils, I got my old job playing organ for the silent movies at the Eblon Theatre again, and it was during this time that I began to work and finagle my way into a few of the things that were going on around town.

I think I must have gone back to my little bunk at Temple's place back up in the alley off Eighteenth Street for a while, because I'm pretty certain that I had left a few of my belongings around there when I cut out for Oklahoma. Not that I had a lot of property to be leaving anywhere. I was traveling pretty light in those days. But that's where I left whatever I had to leave. And naturally, I also went back to all of that good home cooking old Temple used to do. I didn't ever live at the Eastside Hotel anymore. . . .

Meanwhile, without really being aware of the big change I was making, I was becoming more and more tied up with music itself and less and less concerned with show business and entertainment in general. Of course, it was all a part of the same world, but after playing with those Blue Devils, being a musician was where it was really at for me. I was still playing the organ at the Eblon, and that was still show biz, and as much as I still enjoyed it, the music scene was what Kansas City was really all about. . . .

My next room after Temple's was in the Booker T. Washington Hotel, right across Eighteenth from the Eblon. It was right on the main drag then. It was only a few steps down the block to Jones Pool Hall, Lincoln Dance Hall, and the barbershop. The Subway Club was at Eighteenth and Vine. Piney Brown's place was at Eighteenth and Highland. Street's hotel was on the corner of Eighteenth and Paseo, and in the next several blocks beyond Paseo there were all those bars and restaurants and cabarets and other different joints that Elmer Williams and I had stumbled upon.

At first I didn't have nerve enough to go into the pool hall because that had seemed to be a bit out of my range ever since I used to sit and look out at it from the Eastside Hotel back before I worked up enough confidence to cross Paseo. Then I finally did start going into the pool hall, and then I also began to get hold of enough money to use the barbershop that was in the same building. Up to that time the barbershop I went to was the one right across the street from the Eastside Hotel, where Harry Smith had taken me. . . .

There were matinees at the Eblon on Saturdays and Sundays. But during the week I used to go to work around six o'clock, and by ten-thirty the last show was over. So I was on my own, and there were all those wonderful joints and all that live music, and I used to go into a few of them. Not really a lot of them. The main one I actually remember hanging out in the most was the Yellow Front Saloon, which was run by Ellis Burton, also known later on as the Chief, who, as anybody who was there will tell you, was the greatest friend the musicians ever had in that town. He used to take care of musicians just like they were all members of a big family.

If you were out of work and showed up in his place and wanted to gig, he would give you a break. Because there was no regular house band, and he didn't book anybody for a definite period of time or anything like that. There was a good piano and a set of drums, and if you wanted to sit in and pick up a little change, it was pretty wide open.

The Yellow Front Saloon was at Eighteenth and Lydia, near the Phyllis Wheatley Memorial Hospital, and sometimes, when things were really jumping in the joints in that neighborhood, you could come in there and there would be musicians leaning out of the windows of the hospital, playing their horns. I'd never seen and heard anything like that in my life. Kansas City was a musicians' town, and there were good musicians everywhere you turned. Sometimes you just stayed at one place, and sometimes you might hit maybe two or three or more, but you could never get around to all the jumping places in that town in one night. There were just too many.

Sometimes I used to go by and listen to Joe Turner singing the blues. The first time I met Joe he was working down on Independence Avenue. He was the bartender down there in a basement joint where they used to serve whiskey by the dipper. Big Joe was the singing bartender. He would sing his numbers right behind the bar while he was mixing drinks. He'd be hollering the blues and dipping that good taste, and also taking special care of all the cats he knew. He was in charge of that whole basement down there.

Later on, he was working for Piney Brown at Piney Brown's Sunset on Twelfth Street with Pete Johnson, playing piano with Murl Johnson, and sometimes Baby Lovett on drums. And they were something. When I heard him that first time, I said to myself, Jesus, I *never* heard nothing like this guy. He was *the* blues singer in that town. Anybody who came to Kansas City talking about singing some blues had to go listen to *him*.

And Pete Johnson was the piano player. I liked Pete an awful lot. I was mostly interested in the blues, and Pete was really playing the blues and swinging the blues. He was really doing it. And another guy by the name of Everett Johnson was also playing the blues and singing. They were playing a lot of blues and boogie-woogie, and I really tried to get with it, and I really haven't gotten it yet. I still haven't gotten it like I really wanted to get into it. But those guys could really play it. Old Pete and Albert Ammons and those guys could get down with it .

Count Basie and his band

I've been asked what I had going for me in a town with all those piano players like that around, and I say luck. That's what. And enough sense to stay out of the way of Pete and those guys.

I don't think I ever played up at the Lincoln Dance Hall. But sometimes I used to sit in at the Subway Club. I remember working down there with a drummer named Merle something, unless I'm confusing his with the Murl that used to play with Pete Johnson. But I didn't hang around there too often, because the Subway also used to be one of Mary Lou Williams's stopping-off places, and I always used to get out of her way. Anytime she was in the neighborhood, I used to find myself another little territory, because Mary Lou was tearing everybody up.

It was while I was working at the Eblon Theatre that second time and living at the Booker T. Washington Hotel that I got to meet the great Fletcher Henderson. When he came to town and worked at the Pla Mor Ballroom for about a week, he was also staying at the Booker T., and he used to come into a little candy stand near the theater. He heard me on the organ and wrote out a few little things he wanted me to play. I never will forget that. He said he had a little something for me to play down there, and he gave me an envelope with the music on it and went on to work. Then that night, when he came back to the hotel and saw me, he asked me about it.

"Did you play it?"

"I didn't," I said.

"Why not?"

"There were too many sharps in there," I said. I wasn't about to mess with all them sharps.

I remember another little caper I used to pull while I was living at the Booker T. Washington Hotel. Sometimes I used to sneak back into the Eblon and have a little after-hours party with a few of my friends. Somehow I found a way to get back in there after Jap Eblon had closed up. I used to wait until I was pretty sure he had plenty of time to get all the way across town to wherever he lived, and then I would take my little party in there and get my little quiet thing going.

But finally one night, there was a little surprise waiting for me. I don't know how many of us there were in there that night. Sometimes I'd take one other couple and sometimes maybe two, never a crowd or anything like that; and we would stay for about an hour or something like that. But when I started closing the organ up this particular night, a very familiar, very loud voice yelled out and shocked the hell out of me.

"What the hell are you stopping for?"

I knew exactly who it was, and all I could do was stand there thinking, Oh, Lord, I done lost my job.

"Ain't no use stopping now," he said, and then he said, "Come on up here."

He was way up in his office looking out through the window that opened out on the auditorium, and when I got up there, he called me a few little well-chosen names, and I just listened and waited. Then he smiled.

"You want a drink?"

I thanked him and took it.

"What did you stop for?"

I don't know what I answered.

"So you found a way to get in there? And you don't have to tell me how long you been doing it, because I been up here catching you for some time now."

FURTHER READING

Paula Gunn Allen, *The Sacred Hoop: Recovering the Feminine in American Indian Traditions* (Boston: Beacon Press, 1986).

Red Callender and Elaine Cohen, *Unfinished Dream: The Musical World of Red Callender* (London: Quartet Books, 1985).

Guillermo E. Hernandez, *Chicano Satire: A Study in Literary Culture* (Austin: University of Texas Press, 1991).

Marlon K. Hom, *Songs of Gold Mountain: Cantonese Rhymes from San Francisco Chinatown* (Berkeley and Los Angeles: University of California Press, 1987).

Nicolas Kanellos, *A History of Hispanic Theater in the United States: Origins to 1940* (Austin: University of Texas Press, 1990).

Jane B. Katz, ed., *This Song Remembers: Self Portraits of Native Americans in the Arts* (Boston: Houghton Mifflin Co., 1980).

Elaine H. Kim, *Asian American Literature: An Introduction to the Writings and Their Social Context* (Philadelphia: Temple University Press, 1982).

Stephen J. Kunitz, *Disease, Change, and the Role of Medicine: The Navajo Experience* (Berkeley and Los Angeles: University of California Press, 1983).

Shirley Geok-lin Lim and Amy Ling, *Reading the Literatures of Asian America* (Philadelphia: Temple University Press, 1992).

Américo Paredes, *"With His Pistol in His Hand": A Border Ballad and Its Hero* (Austin: University of Texas Press, 1958).

Nathan W. Pearson, Jr., *Goin' to Kansas City* (Urbana: University of Illinois Press, 1987).

Manuel Pena, *The Texas-Mexican Conjunto: History of a Working-Class Music* (Austin: University of Texas Press, 1985).

Ronald Riddle, *Flying Dragons, Flowing Streams: Music in the Life of San Francisco's Chinese* (Westport, Conn.: Greenwood Press, 1983).

Ross Russell, *Jazz Style in Kansas City and the Southwest* (Berkeley and Los Angeles: University of California Press, 1971).

Stephen H. Sumida, *And the View from the Shore: Literary Traditions of Hawaii* (Seattle: University of Washington Press, 1991).

Fred Voget, *The Shoshoni-Crow Sun Dance* (Norman: University of Oklahoma Press, 1984).

Walter L. Williams, *The Spirit and the Flesh: Sexual Diversity in American Indian Culture* (Boston: Beacon Press, 1986, 1992).

CHAPTER 8

Interactions

R ace relations in the United States are usually viewed narrowly, in terms of the interactions between blacks and whites, African Americans and Euro-Americans. But the history of the American West demonstrates that a more sophisticated approach is needed. Such an approach would take into account relations between and among other racial groups and would recognize that, beyond the usual groupings of Native, African, Mexican, Asian, and European Americans, there are important divisions *within* these groups. Moreover, some communities do not fit readily into the prevailing categories.

Donald Grinde and Quintard Taylor's study of blacks in the Indian Territory (present-day Oklahoma), Karen Leonard's work on Punjabi-Mexican Americans, and Tomás Almaguer's piece on Mexican and Japanese immigrant farmworkers all present neglected aspects of western American history that defy conventional ideas concerning race relations. These three selections suggest the infinite possibilities in western American historiography and underline the need to abandon preconceived notions about peoples of color.

FOR ANALYSIS AND DISCUSSION

1. Why is the conception of American race relations in black and white terms inadequate?

2. What new patterns of interaction are evident when you consider peoples of color besides blacks in the American West?

3. Why is Oklahoma's territorial history significant in the study of race relations in the American West?

4. What circumstances gave rise to "Mexican Hindu" families? Why are such families a phenomenon that may not last beyond two generations?

5. What factors made it possible for Japanese and Mexican farmworkers to cooperate with each other in Oxnard in 1903? Why was this cooperation so rare?

Slaves, Freedmen, and Native Americans in Indian Territory (Oklahoma), 1865–1907

DONALD A. GRINDE AND QUINTARD TAYLOR

Viewed from the vantage point of ethnic relations, the history of Indian Territory (Oklahoma) reverses popular views of the history of the American West. There Native Americans and African Americans outnumbered whites until well into the late nineteenth century. Moreover, internal developments among the territory's different peoples played an important part in their affairs, along with such external factors as migration and white racism. For example, although the Creeks, Seminoles, Cherokees, Chickasaws, and Choctaws—the so-called Five Civilized Tribes—held black slaves, they treated them differently (both before and after emancipation) than white slaveowners treated theirs.

Some black residents of Indian Territory were quite acculturated, speaking Native American languages and enjoying a way of life similar to that of nonblacks there, though often residing in their own communities. As late as 1870, African Americans outnumbered whites in the territory. And far from helpless victims, these blacks had considerable power and independence. They commonly acted as interpreters between whites and Native Americans, as a result of their linguistic skills; voted in elections; and served on councils of the Five Civilized Tribes. Relations between these acculturated African Americans and black newcomers from the South became strained at times, and the tensions complicated local debates over race, citizenship, and homesteaders' rights.

Expanding white and black settlement, technology in the form of the railroad, and eventually Oklahoma's statehood (in 1907) changed daily life forever, especially relations among Native Americans, blacks, and whites. But Oklahoma's unique history lives on, revealing a high level of cooperation among its peoples in the nineteenth century. Only following emancipation and increased white and black settlement did disfranchisement and segregation become the law of the land.

STUDY QUESTIONS

1. In what ways is the acculturation of blacks living among Oklahoma's Native Americans revealed?

2. How did the Civil War affect black–Native American relations?

3. Why were Native Americans defined as whites in Oklahoma's constitution, and what consequences did this designation have?

Indians and blacks have interacted frequently and for the most part positively during the course of the past three centuries. There were numerous instances of interracial cooperation and assimilation during the 18th and much of the 19th centuries as indicated in the writings of historians Kenneth Porter, Daniel Littlefield, Lawrence Foster, and others. However, this positive interaction was not the case in post–Civil War Indian Territory. Racial antagonism, intensified by the abolition of slavery among the Five Civilized Tribes—the Seminoles, Creeks, Cherokees, Chickasaws, and Choctaws—and the new pressures brought on by the influx of land-hungry non-Indian settlers, combined to create bitter hostility and in a few instances violent clashes between the two peoples who had previously lived in relative harmony.

The evolution of this changing Indian-black relationship can be traced to the Civil War. The war terminated the previous association of the Five Civilized Tribes with the federal government and permanently altered the status of blacks living in Indian Territory. After the war began tribal leaders futilely attempted to maintain neutrality between the Union and the Confederacy. However, formidable pressures propelled the nations toward the South. Indian slaveholders felt threatened by a Union victory. Most of the Indian agents operating in the territory prior to the war were Southerners or slavery sympathizers, who used their influence to win support for the Southern cause. Indian nations were also enticed by the Confederacy's promise of more favorable treaties and the federal government's unexpected abandonment of military outposts in the territory. By mid-October 1861, the Confederacy had negotiated treaties with each of the five Indian nations.

Despite circumstances favoring an Indian-Confederate alliance, significant segments of the tribal populations supported the Union cause. Some Indian leaders felt obligated by previous treaties with the federal government. Many Native Americans were angered that pro-Confederate treaties committing entire Indian nations were frequently ratified without full consent of tribal leaders. At least some Indians were against slavery and saw the war as an opportunity to end the "peculiar institution." Before 1861 antislavery Creeks and Seminoles allowed fugitive slaves from surrounding states to reside in their lands while some Cherokees maintained the Keetoowah Society, a secret abolitionist organization, among an Indian people generally favorable toward black servitude. These groups remained loyal to the Union.

Intratribal divisions over slavery, fidelity to the United States, and attempts by both the Union and the Confederacy to exploit intratribal dissension quickly brought the fighting to Indian Territory. Large numbers of Creeks, Seminoles, and Cherokees who remained loyal to the Union fled the

From Donald A. Grinde, Jr., and Quintard Taylor, "Red vs. Black: Conflict and Accommodation in the Post Civil War Indian Territory, 1865–1907," *American Indian Quarterly* 8 (1984), pp. 211–225. Reprinted by permission of American Indian Quarterly.

Territory. Indian regiments organized by both sides fought bloody battles or engaged in guerrilla warfare in an attempt to obtain control of the land and people. Ultimately, pro-Union forces dominated the area and by June 23, 1865, the Confederate Indian Commander, Stand Watie, surrendered to Union troops ending the Civil War in Indian Territory.

Citing widespread Indian support of the Confederacy, the United States government declared all previous treaties with the five Indian nations nullified. New treaties negotiated in 1866 abolished slavery, required the tribes to cede the western half of their land to the government, and called for reorganized tribal governments. Federal authorities used these new treaties to punish pro-Confederate Indians and to obtain additional concessions from and greater authority over each of the five nations.

The most significant accomplishment of the treaties was the liberation of 7,000 black slaves. With emancipation the federal government allowed the five nations to individually decide if, and in what manner, they would incorporate these freedmen. Creek and Seminole Indians made their former slaves tribal citizens with full civil and political rights. Cherokee slaveholders freed their slaves in 1863 in accordance with President Lincoln's Emancipation Proclamation; however, under the provisions of the post-war treaty only those freedmen and free blacks residing in the Cherokee nation before the war and who remained in 1866 were declared citizens and entitled to vote and hold office. All other Cherokee freedmen wanting citizenship had to return to the nation within six months of the treaty signing. Consequently, a number of former Cherokee slaves who had fled during the war but returned after 1867 were not allowed citizenship. This category of non-citizen "intruders" often included husbands, wives, and children of Cherokee citizens. Despite legislative attempts by some tribal leaders such as Chief Lewis Downing, the National Council, the Cherokee national legislature, rejected these measures and called on federal authorities to eject the intruders.

Of the five Indian nations, the Chickasaw and Choctaw dealt most severely with their freedmen. Both nations enacted "Black Codes" similar to those in Southern states which determined wages ex-slaves received for various jobs and forced newly freed blacks to find employment or be jailed. Neither nation permitted the return of former slaves who left during the war, nor did they allow the remaining freedmen to vote or hold office, a right supposedly guaranteed by the 1866 treaty. For a brief period some Choctaws and Chickasaws resorted to violence to drive out unwanted blacks. During and immediately following the war, colonies of ex-slaves from Texas settled north of the Red River on tribal lands. The Choctaws and Chickasaws attributed the sharp increase in cattle rustling to these ex-slaves and believed their continued presence would encourage larger numbers of freedmen to migrate from neighboring states. Consequently, Indian vigilantes seized and whipped blacks who were not known in the area, broke up their settlements and forced most of these Afro-Americans out of their nations.

Choctaw and Chickasaw treatment of their ex-slaves precipitated a bitter controversy over proceeds from the Leased Lands District. The District, an area of Choctaw and Chickasaw land west of the ninety-eighth meridian, was leased to the United States for settlement by other Indian tribes. The two nations had originally been promised $800,000 for the district but because of their support of the Confederacy, leasing fees were reduced to $300,000. The treaty of 1866 gave the tribes the option of adopting the freedmen and receiving $300,000 for the Leased District or having the ex-slaves granted the proceeds after being removed by the government to the District. Tribal leaders favored adoption for disparate reasons; some argued that freedmen could be utilized as laborers; others feared that if former tribal slaves were colonized in the Leased District, ex-slaves from Southern states might settle there creating a formidable black nation adjacent to the borders of the Choctaw-Chickasaw country. Yet a majority in the two nations called for removal despite the apparent financial loss. Although they presented petitions to Congress demanding the immediate expulsion of the ex-slaves, no federal action was taken. For the next twenty years freedmen residing in the Choctaw and Chickasaw nations had no clearly defined legal status. Although they had lived in Indian Territory before the war, they were treated in much the same manner as temporary non-Indian aliens. After realizing the federal government would not remove the freedmen, the Choctaws, in 1883, reluctantly passed a law adopting them as citizens. The government in return gave the tribe $52,000, their share of the Leased District money. But the Chickasaws refused to alter the status of their freedmen and were denied any proceeds from the District.

By 1870 Indian Territory had 68,152 residents. Native Americans constituted 87% of that population while 6,378 blacks and 2,407 whites comprised the remainder. Although the six thousand Afro-Americans included blacks emancipated before the Civil War and freedmen from neighboring Texas, Arkansas, and Missouri, the overwhelming majority of the persons of African descent were former slaves in the various Indian nations.

Their fate in post–Civil War Indian Territory was determined by two factors: the attitudes of individual Indian nations toward them and, to a lesser extent, the ambiguous role of the federal government as their protector and benefactor.

Culturally, these freedmen resembled Indians among whom they lived rather than ex-slaves in the defeated Confederacy. They spoke the various Indian languages, ate Indian foods, wore Indian clothing, and followed local religious customs. They organized small communities patterned after those of the Indians. The major exception in this process of acculturation was the ability of most freedmen to speak English as well as their Indian language, while the majority of Indians conversed solely in their indigenous language. Some Indians and blacks saw this as an advantage in that freedmen could serve as interpreters between Native Americans and whites; other Indians were distrustful of freedmen for the same reason.

The level of acceptance and assimilation of the ex-slaves varied with the five nations, but generally paralleled tribal attitudes toward slavery, the Confederacy, and adoption of freedmen; Seminoles and Creeks were the most liberal, the Cherokees moderate, and Choctaws and Chickasaws the most conservative. All five civilized tribes extended certain privileges and protection. Each allocated lands for cultivation and there is little indication of a systematic attempt to give the poorest farm lands to the freedmen. For example, most of the Creek and Seminole freedmen allotments were along the river bottoms, choice lands for cotton production. Theoretically, the new tribal constitutions guaranteed freedmen full protection of person and property, as well as civil and criminal protection in the courts, but local prejudice, especially among the Cherokees, Choctaws and Chickasaws, may have limited those liberties. . . . For much of the post-war period former slaves, regardless of their citizenship status, were allowed to reside without molestation in the Indian nations, including the Chickasaw and Choctaw lands where many tribal members zealously labored for their removal.

Tribal attitudes toward freedmen were also reflected in the level of political participation by ex-slaves, educational opportunities, and social interaction, particularly the instances of intermarriage. Ex-slaves were far more politically active among the Creeks and Seminoles than in the other nations. After 1866 Seminole Nation blacks were afforded full political rights. By 1875 the Seminole legislative body—the National Council—which was composed of three representatives from each of the nation's fourteen towns, included six freedmen representing the two towns of Seminole freedmen. A similar political situation existed in the Creek Nation where freedmen representing four of the forty-six towns sat in each house of the legislature. Creek freedmen usually voted in a bloc and formed an alliance with one of the major tribal political parties, the Sands Party. That party narrowly won the election of 1875 with the help of freedmen voters. One freedman, Jesse Franklin, was elected a judge in the tribal Supreme Court in 1876. . . .

Cherokee freedmen voted in their nation's elections. Although there were attempts at bloc voting, freedmen in most elections divided their votes between the Union Party and the National Party, the two major political factions. In 1875 Joseph Brown became the only freedman elected to the National Council. Six years later both the Union and National parties nominated freedmen for the Council at their political conventions; however, neither candidate was elected. As with Creek freedmen, a few Cherokee ex-slaves became entrepreneurs. . . .

Unfortunately, Choctaw and Chickasaw freedmen existed in a decidedly more adverse social milieu. They were not afforded the political freedom or economic mobility of their Creek, Cherokee or Seminole counterparts. The Choctaw did not allow their former slaves to become tribal citizens until 1883, and tribal constitutional guarantee notwithstanding, discouraged voting and disallowed office holding or other participation in government after that date. The Chickasaw steadfastly refused to adopt their freedmen and made no attempt to encourage their prosperity or continued residence in the nation.

Seminole and Creek tribal governments put few obstacles in the path of freedmen who sought education. Seminole tribal funds supported four schools in 1870, two of which were for Indian children and two for black children. By 1877 the Creek tribe had established three boarding schools; one for Creek Indian males, another for Creek Indian females and a third for freedmen. Creek freedmen seemed particularly anxious that their children be educated and utilized their considerable political strength at the local level and lobbying efforts at the national level to secure that education.

The Cherokee nation placed greater emphasis on education than any of the other tribes and consequently its educational system was more advanced than any of its Indian neighbors during the pre–Civil War era. However, the war disrupted that system and schools were not re-established until 1870. The Cherokees did not prevent the children of their former slaves from acquiring an education. By 1872 fifty-seven schools were in operation including three for freedmen. Two years later tribal educational appropriations had increased to support sixty-five schools with seven reserved for black children. A high school for Cherokee freedmen was established in 1890.

The Choctaw nation denied schooling to its freedmen until 1887. After that date the nation provided one boarding school, the Tuskalusa Colored Academy, for freedmen. The Chickasaw nation did not allocate tribal funds for the education of its freedmen. Educational opportunity for these ex-slaves was limited to five schools maintained by the Freedmen's Bureau between 1867 and 1869. After that date freedmen desiring an education had to emigrate from the nations.

The extent of Indian-black social interaction was clearly the most significant gauge of post-war acceptance and assimilation of the former slaves in Indian territory. In this regard Seminoles and Creeks were again the most progressive. Blacks and Indians in these nations intermingled freely until the 1890s. There were no laws against intermarriage between Creeks or Seminoles and freedmen, and indeed, among the latter intermarriage had been frequent before the Civil War. . . .

The Choctaw and Chickasaws harbored the greatest animosity toward their former slaves. Not surprisingly, this aversion prevented all but the most minimal social interaction between Chickasaws and Choctaws and their freedmen. While intermarriage with whites was accepted, and in many instances welcomed as strengthening the tribes, both nations discouraged intermarriage between blacks and Indians and the Choctaws passed a law in 1885 making it a felony.

Reconstruction in Indian Territory ushered in innumerable changes in the relationship of the Five Civilized Tribes to the federal government. Some of these changes seemed initially insignificant but ultimately had a detrimental impact on the autonomy of the nations. Each tribe was required to relinquish control of the sparsely settled western portion of their lands. This region, eventually called Oklahoma Territory, was opened to settlement by other Indian tribes, and in 1889, non-Indians. In addition, the nations were compelled to grant rights-of-way to railroads seeking to cross their lands, concessions that exposed Indian Territory to hordes of uninvited outsiders.

Whites who established homesteads on tribal lands, frequently in defiance of Indian or federal laws, were the largest non-Indian group to enter the territory. By 1885 some of the largest landholders in the Cherokee Nation were non-citizens who seized their lands. But the ranks of non-citizens were swelled by whites and blacks who came at the invitation of Indian capitalists and landholders, to develop the coal and timber resources of the region or to work as sharecroppers on Indian farms. . . .

By the 1880s large-scale railroad construction commenced across Indian Territory with construction crews creating virtual instant cities such as Tulsa and Ardmore. Other non-Indian towns became important shipping centers for coal, timber, cattle and agricultural products. Nearly all of these towns

Choctaw Light Horsemen policing tribal lands and people at Antlers, Indian Territory in 1893

were unincorporated, had no legal standing in the Indian nations, and were populated by non-Indian interlopers. Immigration increased after oil was discovered in the Cherokee Nation in 1889. By 1890, 109,393 whites and 18,636 blacks comprised 72% of the total territorial population of 178,097. Less than twenty-five years after the Civil War, the Indian had become a minority in his own land.

Black immigrants in Indian Territory, while small in comparison to white newcomers, nevertheless tripled the area's Afro-American population. Their arrival substantially altered the status of the territory's freedmen and the course of race relations in the region. While the majority of blacks in the Territory in 1870 were ex-slaves of the Indians, most blacks residing there in 1890 came from neighboring states. These newcomers, contemptuously called "state Negroes" by established residents, moved into every Indian nation. Frequently Afro-Americans, like some of their white counterparts, were invited into the territory as laborers, drovers or tenant farmers for Indian landholders. Others came with railroad construction gangs or oil drilling crews, and stayed once the work was completed. . . . [T]he majority of the "state Negroes" settled in the nations and began farming because they realized tribal and federal officials were powerless to remove them.

Freedmen native to Indian territory initially disliked the black immigrants. They, like the Indians, feared being inundated by outsiders who could eventually dominate the region politically and economically. But they were also disdainful of state Negroes calling them *watchina,* meaning "white man" with the connotation of "white man's Negro." Indian freedmen feared being identified with black newcomers, and saw "state Negroes" as more accommodating and submissive to the racial hierarchy. One Creek freedman explained: "It was those state niggers from Texas that spoiled it for us, bowing and scraping and scratching their head." Choctaw and Chickasaw freedmen, themselves socially isolated from their former masters, refused to intermingle with "state Negroes." Creek freedmen briefly imposed social sanctions against marriage with blacks from neighboring states. However, these distinctions broke down in the face of increasing hostility of both Indians and whites toward Indian freedmen and by extension, all blacks.

"State Negroes" migrating to Indian territory came for reasons similar to those of white settlers. . . . However, black immigrants also recognized the absence of rigidly drawn racial caste lines so prevalent in Southern states. They pointed to the benign nature of African slavery among the Indians and hoped the region, a major refuge for fugitive slaves before the Civil War, would continue as such for Afro-Americans fleeing political and economic repression in the postwar South.

The black state movement of the 1880s intensified Indian fears of a rapidly expanding black population in or near their territory. Many freedmen in the postwar South, basing their claims on statements by Union leaders during the Civil War, hoped the federal government would set aside the western portion of Indian Territory (Oklahoma) for exclusive Afro-American settlement. Federal officials discarded the colonization scheme after the war, but a small group of black leaders tenaciously adhered to the belief that all or part of the territory would eventually be reserved for Southern freedmen and urged Afro-American migration there to pressure the government to act. Hannibal Carter and James Milton Turner organized the Freedmen's Oklahoma Immigration Association in 1881 to encourage black migration into the Oklahoma district. In 1889, two black Kansas politicians, W. L. Eagleson and Edwin P. McCabe, joined the campaign to establish black political hegemony in the region. McCabe, a former auditor of Kansas, emerged as the leader of this movement. He relocated in Logan County, Oklahoma Territory in 1889 and was elected the first treasurer of the county. One year later he founded Langston City, an all-black town near Guthrie. McCabe, through his newspaper, the *Langston City Herald*, encouraged Southern blacks to settle in Oklahoma and personally lobbied President Benjamin Harrison requesting an appointment as territorial governor to advance his colonization plans.

The all-black state campaign failed for a number of reasons. Despite elaborate efforts to encourage black immigration to Oklahoma, white settlers vastly outnumbered blacks. Whites were the majority in virtually every district and ridiculed or ignored black claims to the Territory. . . . Nationally prominent Afro-American leaders such as Frederick Douglass opposed both the idea of an all-black state and of blacks migrating en masse from the South.

Recognizing the futility of the black-state movement, McCabe and other leaders began establishing all-black towns where Afro-Americans could reside without fear of physical molestation or political control by whites. Twenty-nine towns and one colony were founded between 1889 and 1900. Four towns and the colony were in Oklahoma Territory while twenty-five towns were in Indian Territory. Two of the largest towns, Boley and Clearwater, were both in Indian Territory. The number of all-black towns reflected the success of McCabe's appeals, and the unwillingness of the federal government and inability of the Indian nations to block these efforts.

While these towns symbolized freedom and self-determination for blacks, they were to Indians glaring examples of continued encroachment upon tribal lands by non-Indians. Not surprisingly, resentment of these intruders increased in proportion to their growing population. Chickasaws and Choctaws had always based their anti-black policies on the assumption that a more liberal policy would lead to political and even physical domination by their ex-slaves. Continued settlement by Texas and Arkansas blacks on tribal lands simply exacerbated Indian fears. In 1891 the Choctaws responded by driving most "state Negroes" out of the nation and passed a law subjecting anyone employing a black servant to a $50 fine. The same year Cherokee animosity toward blacks in that nation caused over 200 to emigrate from Indian Territory.

By 1890 even Creeks, long noted for racial tolerance, were beginning to display antipathy towards blacks—freedmen and "state Negroes." L. C. Perryman, a Creek chief, filed a protest with federal officials when Afro-American troops were stationed in his nation. A "race war" between Creeks and blacks was reported by a local newspaper in November, 1889. By 1898 interracial tension had become serious enough to warrant a discussion by Dew M. Wisdom, U.S. Indian Agent for the Territory, in his annual report to the Commission of Indian Affairs. . . .

Indian-black tension increased during and immediately following tribal allocation, the federally mandated and supervised process of dividing communally owned tribal lands among individual tribal members. In 1893 Congress created the Dawes Commission to negotiate agreements with the Five Civilized Tribes to terminate their existence as separate nations. Each tribal member would receive an allotment of land (usually 160 acres) with the remainder returned to the federal government. In 1896 Congress directed the Commission to make rolls for each of the tribes that included Indians and freedmen who were tribal citizens. For the first time in tribal history, non-Indians were determining Indian citizenship and were awarding sections of lands on that basis.

The Dawes Commission attempted to insure equitable land allotments to Indian freedmen even though the Chickasaws vehemently refused to recognize freedmen as tribal members and the Choctaws withheld recognition nearly twenty years after the war. Thirty-six percent of the allottees in the Creek nation were freedmen, including a sizeable number probably not descendants of Indian Territory ex-slaves, but recent arrivals who had intermarried or who simply took up residence. Their ability to get on the rolls caused Pleasant Porter, a Creek Chief to satirically remark, "Our freedmen have increased wonderfully. . . . They come forth from the four quarters of the earth and employ a lawyer here to assist them, and they and the lawyer will get up the proof that slides them through.". . .

By 1907, the date of unification of Indian and Oklahoma Territories and their admission to the Union as Oklahoma, the five tribes had lost political and economic control of the region promised exclusively to them by the federal government in 1830. They had witnessed the land's inundation by white and black settlers and heard the newcomers' demands that the region be given to them with little regard for the fate of the Indian residents. Native Americans reacted with hostility and bewilderment as their lands, tribal authority, and ultimately, tribal existence, were systematically dismantled by the federal government. Much of this hostility was directed at blacks, both freedmen and "state Negroes."

Historians have frequently assumed that the increasing Indian hostility to persons of African descent resulted primarily from the rapid influx of whites, particularly white Southerners between 1889 and 1907. While this undoubtedly had a major effect, Indian attitudes towards blacks were also shaped by internal factors. Since the treaties of 1866, many Indians felt the federal government viewed the freedmen, to use the words of Angie Debo, as "special favorites." They bitterly spoke of the Reconstruction requirement that Indians divide their lands with their ex-slaves, a requirement not imposed on white ex-slaveholders. Throughout the 1870s and 1880s they feared the government would redesignate part or all of the Indian Territory as an area for exclusive Afro-American settlement. They were incensed by the Dawes Commission demand that freedman be considered for land allotments and their eligibility be determined by the Commission rather than tribal governments.

Indian leaders feared being overwhelmed by freedmen and "state Negroes" in their own nations and reacted by increasing their social distance as the black population grew. Unlike whites who entered Indian tribes mainly through intermarriage, black tribal membership was augmented through the post–Civil War adoption of ex-slaves, the marriage of "state Negroes" to either Indians or freedmen and the high birth rate among both "state Negroes" and freedmen as compared with Native Americans. By 1908 the Dawes Commission estimated that freedmen comprised 42% of the Chickasaw, 36% of the Creek and 31% of the Seminole allottees. Even allowing for the liberal interpretation of tribal membership by the Dawes Commission, these figures show the extensive black components of each tribe. . . .

. . . In 1894 the editor of the *Cherokee Advocate* urged his fellow countrymen to resist the growing number of black newcomers. He implored, "Be men and fight off the barnacles that now infest our country in the shape of non-citizen free Arkansas niggers and traitors." Creek tribal members complained that many individuals "on the rolls" were not their ex-slaves. Creek parents were especially concerned about the increasing enrollment of non-Indian youngster in their schools. . . .

Creek fears were not unwarranted. Even though the five tribes paid the entire administrative cost of the territorial school system and a disproportionate share of its maintenance, Indian enrollment in 1904 was 10,041 or 15% of the total. Black enrollment of 11,556 had surpassed Indian enrollment for the first time and white enrollment was 54,853.

Finally Indians resented black attempts to colonize their lands (just as they resented white colonization efforts) and were fearful of black, particularly freedmen, duplicity in schemes to obtain their property. Bold pronouncements of the black political takeover of neighboring Oklahoma Territory by such immigration advocates as Edwin McCabe and organizations like the Freedmen's Oklahoma Immigration Association were not viewed sympathetically by Indians as black attempts at self-determination, but rather as thinly veiled devices to open Indian lands to additional non-Indian settlement and further erosion of tribal authority.

In decided contrast to the attitudes of most Indian leaders, freedmen during the post–Civil War period welcomed adoption by Indian nations because it allowed them to become economically self-sufficient either through farming small plots or entrepreneurial activities. They favored adoption because it gave them political and legal status in the nations, afforded them the protection of their civil rights and personal property, and in the instance of the Seminoles and Creeks, entitled these ex-slaves to share in tribal funds. Most freedmen saw themselves as Indians culturally, if not racially, and eagerly accepted the opportunity to remain in the religion to prosper with the tribes.

Their overall regard for Indian culture and the Indian nations, however, did not prevent freedmen from aggressively supporting or defending their interests if they perceived those interests threatened. Realizing significant elements in each tribe were opposed to adoption including the majority of Cherokees, Choctaws and Chickasaws, these ex-slaves appealed to the federal government in disputes with tribal leadership.

During the 1870s and the early 1880s most freedmen in Indian Territory enjoyed substantial economic freedom, and in the case of the Creeks and Seminoles, political influence as well. However, by the late 1880s the influx of white and black settlers permanently altered their status. Whites, and increasingly Native Americans as well, categorized them as blacks rather than Indians and treated them in much the same manner they treated "state Negroes." Conversely, blacks from outside the Territory resented what appeared as unwarranted aloofness on the part of the freedmen and their unwillingness to strive for common "race goals."

Yet "state Negroes" who entered the territory, often illegally, must share responsibility for altering Indian attitudes and actions towards freedmen and by extension, all blacks. Their increasing presence and the desire by some leaders to control all or part of the region caused a backlash among Indians. Indeed, some immigration leaders felt entitled to Indian lands and displayed little concern for the effect of these proposals on Native Americans. Other "state Negroes" took advantage of lax citizenship requirements and became tribal members solely to obtain Indian lands. Hundreds of "state Negroes" settled on Indian lands without even the pretense of joining the tribes. While it is clear that a large number, perhaps the majority of "state Negroes," sought to live free of the racial proscriptions existing in neighboring Southern states, and accommodated themselves to Indian rule, others took advantage of the weakness and inconsistency of tribal and federal authority for personal gain.

By 1907 Oklahoma and Indian Territories entered the Union as the State of Oklahoma. The new constitution reserved the terms "colored" and "colored race" to singularly apply to persons of African descent. The term "white race" referred to all other persons including Indians. It specifically guaranteed Indians but not blacks the right to vote and its stipulations regarding segregated schools implied a special and inferior status for Oklahoma blacks. Indians acquiesced in this political subjugation of black citizens for a number of reasons. They, as well as many whites, had long feared the increasingly visible and vocal black community. Native Americans had over the years incorporated a number of beliefs about black racial inferiority. Political differences were also a factor as the majority of Indians were Democrats and most of the black Republicans. But most crucial was the belief that Afro-Americans in general, and particularly Indian freedmen, had helped bring about the postwar economic and political demise of Native Americans in Indian Territory.

By 1907 Indians had little political power to stop the emerging segregation system even had they desired to do so. However, a number accepted it as an accomplished, if not desirable, reality. The land that forty years earlier had been ruled by Indians and sought by blacks as a refuge had now been converted into a bastion of white supremacy. Ironically, that conversion was unwittingly assisted by the attitudes and actions of both Indians and blacks.

The 1903 Oxnard Sugar Beet Workers' Strike

TOMÁS ALMAGUER

Many owners of manufacturing industries, railroads, farmland, timberland, and other economic resources in the American West hired multiethnic work forces. Whenever possible, however, employers kept the different ethnic groups apart, dealing with each one through intermediaries known as labor contractors, bosses, or *padrones*. These men rounded up the requisite number of workers, transported them to the work sites, provisioned them, and even supplied them with recreation, mainly in the form of gambling and prostitution. The labor contractors collected a commission from each worker but made most of their profits through the high prices they charged for the food and recreational vices they provided.

Because of language and cultural barriers, the workers from the various ethnic groups interacted little, even when they toiled alongside each other. But there were a few exceptions, as in the case of the joint strike undertaken by Mexican and Japanese beet workers in Oxnard, California, in 1903. Tomás Almaguer's study of this important event in the history of peoples of color in the American West shows how the two groups transcended their differences and worked in solidarity.

Most significantly, when the American Federation of Labor agreed to give a charter to the local union that the Mexican and Japanese workers had formed only if Japanese were barred from membership, the Mexican members refused to accept this discriminatory condition, declaring, "We would be false to them [the Japanese] and to ourselves and to the cause of unionism if we now accepted privileges for ourselves which are not accorded to them." This sense of interethnic brotherhood was not seen again until the 1930s, when the International Longshoremen and Warehousemen's Union organized workers of many different backgrounds along the Pacific coast and in Hawaii.

STUDY QUESTIONS

1. What social impact did the new Ventura County sugar beet industry have upon Oxnard?

2. Why was the cooperation between Japanese and Mexican sugar beet workers at Oxnard historically significant?

3. Discuss the accomplishments as well as the failures of the Japanese-Mexican Labor Association in 1903.

In February 1903 over 1,200 Mexican and Japanese farm workers organized the Japanese-Mexican Labor Association (JMLA) in the southern California community of Oxnard. The JMLA was the first major agricultural workers' union in the state comprised of different minority workers and the first to strike successfully against capitalist interests. . . . Emerging as one of the many "boom towns" in California at the turn of the century, Oxnard owed its existence to the passage of the 1897 Dingley Tariff Bill, which imposed a heavy duty on imported sugar, and the introduction of the sugar beet industry to Ventura County. The construction of an immense sugar beet factory in Ventura County by Henry, James, and Robert Oxnard, prominent sugar refiners from New York, drew hundreds into the area and led to the founding of the new community. The sugar beet factory quickly became a major processing center for the emerging U.S. sugar beet industry, refining nearly 200,000 tons of beets and employing 700 people by 1903.

The developing Ventura County sugar beet industry had an important social impact on the new community. One major repercussion was the racial segregation of Oxnard into clearly discernible white and non-white social worlds. The tremendous influx of numerous agricultural workers quickly led to the development of segregated minority enclaves on the east side of town. The Mexican section of Oxnard, referred to as "Sonoratown," was settled by Mexican workers who migrated into the area seeking employment. Arriv-

From Tomás Almaguer, "Racial Domination and Class Conflict in Capitalist Agriculture: The Oxnard Sugar Beet Workers' Strike of 1903," *Labor History* 25 (1984), pp. 325–350. Used by permission of Labor History.

ing in the early 1900s, the Mexican population was viewed by the Anglo population with disdain. . . .

Also segregated on the east side of town, adjacent to the Mexican colonia, was the "Chinatown" section of Oxnard. This segregated ethnic enclave was even more despised by the local Anglo population than "Sonoratown." . . . Despite widespread anti-Oriental sentiment in the local community, the Asian population grew to an estimated 1,000 to 1,500 people in less than a decade after the founding of Oxnard. . . .

The Anglo residents on the west side of town, in contrast, were comprised of "upstanding" German and Irish farmers and several Jewish families. "While the east side of town was a rip-roaring slum," according to one local historian, "the west side was listening to lecture courses, hearing WCTU [Women's Christian Temperance Union] speakers, having gay times at the skating rink in the opera house, [and] putting on minstrel shows . . .".

The development of the sugar beet industry in Ventura County led to a precipitous increase in the demand for seasonal farm laborers in Oxnard. Initially, sugar beet farmers in Oxnard relied upon Mexican and Chinese contracted laborers. The decline in the local Chinese population and the utilization of Mexicans in other sectors of agriculture, however, led to the recruitment of Japanese farm laborers to fill this labor shortage. Japanese farm laborers were first employed in the Oxnard sugar beet industry in 1899. By 1902 there were nine Japanese labor contractors meeting nearly all the seasonal need for farm laborers in the area.

In the spring of 1902, however, a number of prominent Jewish businessmen and bankers in Oxnard organized a new contracting company, the Western Agricultural Contracting Company (WACC). . . . [Its] initial purpose . . . was to provide local farmers with an alternative to the Japanese labor contractors in the area. Anglo farmers and the American Beet Sugar Company feared that these contractors would use their control of the local labor market to press for wage increases and improvements in working conditions. Under the leadership of Japanese contractors, Japanese farm laborers had already engaged in work slowdowns and strikes to secure concessions from Anglo farmers elsewhere in the state. . . .

Undermining the position of Japanese labor contractors and gaining control of approximately 90% of the contracting business by February 1903, the WACC forced all minority labor contractors to subcontract through their company or go out of business. Through this arrangement, minority contractors and their employees were both forced to work on terms dictated by the WACC. The commission formerly received by minority contractors was reduced severely through this subcontracting arrangement and they could no longer negotiate wages directly with local farmers. The minority farm laborers employed on this basis also were affected negatively. In addition to paying a percentage of their wages to the minority contractor who directly supervised them, they also paid a fee to the WACC for its role in arranging employment. Furthermore, the WACC routinely required minority workers to accept store orders from its company-owned stores instead of cash payment for wages. Overcharging for merchandise at these stores was common. . . .

Most of the Japanese farm laborers and labor contractors working in Oxnard were extremely dissatisfied with having to subcontract through the WACC. Mexican farm laborers in the area and the other numerous minority laborers recruited from other parts of the state also expressed displeasure with the new system. . . .

The grievances of these disgruntled workers provided the key impetus for forming a union comprised of Japanese and Mexican farm workers and contractors in Oxnard. At a . . . meeting held on February 11, 1903, approximately 800 Japanese and Mexican workers organized the Japanese-Mexican Labor Association, electing as officers Kosaburo Baba (president), Y. Yamaguchi (secretary of the Japanese branch), and J. M. Lizarras (secretary of the Mexican branch). Among the charter members of the JMLA were approximately 500 Japanese and 200 Mexican workers. The decision to form this union and challenge the WACC marked the first time the two minority groups successfully joined forces to organize an agricultural workers' union in the state. This was no minor achievement, as the JMLA's membership had to overcome formidable cultural and linguistic barriers. At their meetings, for example, all discussions were carried out in both Spanish and Japanese, with English serving as a common medium of communication. . . .

The major purpose of the Japanese-Mexican Labor Association was to end the WACC's monopoly of the contract labor system in Oxnard. By eliminating the WACC's control, the JMLA sought to negotiate directly with local farmers and to secure better wages. Since the formation of the WACC, the prevailing rate of $5.00 to $6.00 per acre of beets thinned had been reduced to as low as $2.50 per acre. The new union wanted to return to the "old prices" paid for seasonal labor. By eliminating the WACC from the contracting business, the JMLA also sought to end the policy of enforced patronage. . . .

In order to secure their demands the JMLA membership agreed to cease working through the WACC and their subcontractors. This decision was tantamount to call for a strike. In striking the JMLA threatened seriously the success of the local sugar beet crop because its profitability rested on the immediate completion of the thinning operation. This labor-intensive process required that workers carefully space beet seedlings and allow only the strongest beet plants to remain. Unlike the harvest, where timeliness was not as crucial, beet thinning required immediate attention in order to ensure a high-yield crop.

Although the JMLA was largely concerned with wages and the policy of enforced patronage, there is evidence that the leadership of the union saw their struggle in broad class terms. . . . Eloquent testimony of the JMLA's position is captured vividly in one news release issued by the Japanese and Mexican secretaries of the union. In putting forth the union's demands, Y. Yamaguchi and J. M. Lizarras wrote:

> Many of us have families, were born in the country, and are lawfully seeking to protect the only property that we have—our labor. It is just as necessary for the welfare of the valley that we get a decent living wage, as it is that the machines in the great sugar factory be properly oiled—if the machines stop, the wealth of the valley stops, and likewise if the laborers are not given a decent wage, they too, must stop work and the whole people of this country suffer with them. . . .

Reacting to the organization of the JMLA, the American Beet Sugar Company made clear that it would do everything in its power to insure that the new union did not disrupt the smooth operation of the sugar beet industry in Oxnard. It immediately informed the union that the company was fully in support of the WACC. . . .

By the first week in March, the JMLA had successfully recruited a membership exceeding 1,200 workers or over 90% of the total beet workforce in the county. The JMLA's recruitment drive resulted in the WACC losing nearly all of the laborers it had formerly contracted. The growing strength of the JMLA greatly alarmed beet farmers in the area, for nothing like the new union had been organized in Ventura County or, for that matter, anywhere else in southern California.

One of the first public displays of the JMLA's strength was exhibited at a mass demonstration and parade held in Oxnard on March 6, 1903. . . . Unwilling to allow this exhibition of strength to go unchallenged, the WACC initiated an effort to undercut the solidarity of the JMLA and regain its position as the major supplier of contracted labor in Oxnard. During the second and third week of March, the WACC helped form an alternative, minority-led union. In supporting the organization of the Independent Agricultural Labor Union (IALU), the WACC sought to undercut the organizational successes of the JMLA and use the IALU to help regain its former dominance. . . .

Immediately after its foundation, the IALU began working in conjunction with the WACC to meet the pressing labor needs of local farmers. These efforts were, of course, seen by the JMLA as a strikebreaking tactic. . . . [A]n outburst of violence occurred a few days after the IALU was organized.

Occurring on March 23, 1903, in the Chinatown section of Oxnard the violent confrontation was triggered when members of the JMLA attempted to place their union banner on a wagon loaded with IALU strikebreakers being taken to a ranch of a local farmer. . . . One newspaper described the ensuing confrontation in the following way: ". . . [A] fusillage of shots was fired from all directions. They seemed to come from every window and door in Chinatown. The streets were filled with people, and the wonder is that only five persons were shot." When the shooting subsided, two Mexican and two Japanese members of the JMLA lay wounded from the erupting gun-fire. . . . Another Mexican, Luis Vasquez, was dead, shot in the back.

Responsibility for the violent confrontation was placed on the JMLA. The Los Angeles *Times,* for example, reported that "agitation-crazed striking Mexicans and Japanese" had attacked "independent workmen" and precipi-tated a "pitched battle" in which dozens had been wounded and "thousands gone wild.". . . Although more restrained than the *Times*, the Oxnard *Courier* also blamed the union for precipitating the confrontation. . . . The only weekly that did not directly blame the JMLA was the Ventura *Indepen-dent.* . . .

Outraged over the biased coverage of the March 23rd confrontation the JMLA issued its own public statement. It was subsequently published in only two newspapers: the Los Angeles *Herald* and the Oxnard *Courier*. The newspaper that the JMLA was principally responding to, the Los Angeles *Times*, refused to publish the following release:

> . . . [W]e assert, and are ready to prove, that Monday afternoon and at all times during the shooting, the Union men are unarmed, while the nonunion men sent out by the Western Agricultural Contracting Com-pany were prepared for a bloody fight with arms purchased, in many cases, recently from hardware stores in this town. As proof of the fact that the union men were not guilty of violence, we point to the fact that the authorities have not arrested a single union man—the only man actu-ally put under bonds, or arrested, being deputy Constable Charles Arnold. Our union has always been law abiding and has in its ranks at least nine-tenths of all the beet thinners in this section, who have not asked for a raise in wages, but only that the wages be not lowered, as was demanded by the beet growers. . . .

Shortly after the shooting, Charles Arnold was arrested for the murder of Vasquez, and a coroner's inquest held to determine his guilt or innocence. The conflicting testimony of 50 eyewitnesses was heard at the inquest. . . . Testifying against Arnold were a number of Mexican witnesses claiming to have seen Arnold fire at JMLA members. Among these witnesses was Manuel Ramirez, a victim of the shooting, who testified that it was a Japan-ese strikebreaker in the WACC wagon who had shot him in the leg. Despite the evidence presented to the all male Anglo jury, . . . Arnold was cleared of any complicity in the death of Luis Vasquez.

Outraged at what they believed to be a gross miscarriage of justice, mem-bers of the JMLA stepped up their efforts to win the strike. Following the March 23rd confrontation, the union took the offensive and escalated mili-tant organizing activities. . . .

. . . [T]he JMLA organized laborers being brought to Oxnard and suc-ceeded in winning them over to the union's side. In doing so, the union sta-tioned men at the nearby Montalvo railroad depot and met the newly recruited laborers as they arrived in the county. In one incident reported by the Ventura *Free Press,* a local rancher attempted to circumvent JMLA organizers by personally meeting incoming laborers and scurrying them off to his ranch. Before arriving at his ranch, however, the farmer was intercepted by a group of JMLA members who unloaded the strikebreakers and convinced them to join the union. . . .

The success of the JMLA in maintaining their strike lead to a clearcut union victory. In the aftermath of the violent confrontation in Chinatown, representatives of local farmers, the WACC, and the JMLA met at the latter's headquarters in Oxnard to negotiate a strike settlement. . . . The JMLA negotiating team was led by J. M. Lizarras, Kosaburo Baba, Y. Yamaguchi, J. Espinosa, and their counsel, W. E. Shepherd. Also representing the union were Fred C. Wheeler and John Murray, socialist union organizers affiliated with the Los Angeles County Council of Labor, the California State Federation of Labor, and the AFL.

J. M. Lizarras forcefully presented the JMLA's demands at the initial meeting. Insisting that the union wanted to bargain directly with local farmers, Lizarras threatened that the union would take all of their members out of the county, thereby ensuring the loss of the entire beet crop, if their demands were not met. . . .

. . . [T]he WACC partially acceded to the JMLA's demand to negotiate contracts directly with local farmers. The WACC offered the JMLA the right to provide labor on 2,000 of the 7,000 acres of farm land it had under contract. In return, the WACC requested that the JMLA order its men back to work and agree not to unionize men working for the WACC on the remaining farm land. This offer was flatly rejected by JMLA negotiators, who insisted that they would not end their strike until the WACC's monopoly was broken and all farmers agreed to contract directly with them. . . .

. . . [T]he union firmly stood by its demand and gained the first important concession in the negotiations. It was an agreement from the farmers' committee to establish a minimum wage scale of $5.00, and a high of $6.00, per acre for the thinning of beets by union laborers. This was nearly double what the WACC was paying laborers before the strike.

On March 30, 1903, the tumultuous Oxnard sugar beet workers' strike ended with the JMLA winning a major victory. The agreement reached included a provision forcing the WACC to cancel all existing contracts with local sugar beet growers. The only exception to this was the 1,800 acre Patterson ranch. . . . [T]he WACC relinquished the right to provide labor to farmers owning over 5,000 acres of county farm land. . . .

The issue of admitting Mexican and Japanese workers to the trade union movement became an important issue in both northern and southern California after the JMLA victory. . . . The official attitude of organized labor toward the JMLA was, from the very beginning, mixed and often contradictory. Certain local councils, for example, supported the JMLA and further organizing of Japanese and Mexican workers. This tendency, led by prominent union socialists, also supported organizing all agricultural workers and including farm labor unions in the AFL. Most union councils and high-ranking AFL officials were, on the other hand, opposed to any formal affiliation with the JMLA. This position was based, in part, on organized labor's anti-Asian sentiment and its general opposition to organizing agricultural laborers. . . .

. . . Although the AFL convention of 1894 formally declared that "working people must unite to organize irrespective of creed, color, sex, nationality or politics," the reaction of the Federation leadership to the JMLA belied this stated purpose. Following the JMLA victory in March 1903, J. M. Lizarras—Secretary of the Mexican branch of the union—petitioned the AFL Executive Council for a charter making the JMLA the first agricultural laborers' union to be admitted into the AFL.

Upon receiving the JMLA's petition, which was submitted under the name of Sugar Beet and Farm Laborers' Union of Oxnard, Samuel Gompers granted the union a charter but stipulated a prohibition on Asian membership. . . .

Gompers' refusal to grant an AFL charter allowing Japanese membership was vehemently denounced by the Mexican branch of the JMLA. Outraged at Gompers' action, the Mexican membership of the union directed Lizarras to write Gompers what is undoubtedly the strongest testimony of the solidarity reached between the Mexican and Japanese farm workers of Oxnard. On June 8, 1903, Lizarras returned the issued charter to Samuel Gompers with the following letter:

> . . . We beg to say in reply that our Japanese brothers here were the first to recognize the importance of cooperating and uniting in demanding a fair wage scale . . . They were not only just with us, but they were generous when one of our men was murdered by hired assassins of the oppressor of labor, they gave expression to their sympathy in a very substantial form. In the past we have counseled, fought and lived on very short rations with our Japanese brothers, and toiled with them in the fields, and they have been uniformly kind and considerate. We would be false to them and to ourselves and to the cause of unionism if we now accepted privileges for ourselves which are not accorded to them. We are going to stand by men who stood by us in the long, hard fight which ended in a victory over the enemy. We therefore respectfully petition the A.F. of L. to grant us a charter under which we can unite all the sugar beet and field laborers in Oxnard, without regard to their color or race. We will refuse any other kind of charter, except one which will wipe out race prejudices and recognize our fellow workers as being as good as ourselves, I am ordered by the Mexican union to write this letter to you and they fully approve its words.

In refusing to join the AFL without the Japanese branch of the union, the JMLA ultimately closed the door to any hopes of continuing its union activities in Oxnard. The AFL decision not to admit all members of the JMLA undoubtedly contributed to the union eventually passing out of existence. . . . For years after the Oxnard strike, AFL hostility towards organizing Japanese workers and farm laborers persisted. Not until 1910 did the AFL Executive Council attempt to organize farm workers as an element of the Federation. These efforts, however, accomplished very little.

California's Punjabi–Mexican Americans, 1910s–1970s

KAREN LEONARD

Though popularly called Hindus, most of the men who immigrated to the United States from India during the first two decades of the twentieth century were adherents not of Hinduism but of the Sikh religion. They came from Punjab province in the northwestern corner of the South Asian subcontinent. Many of the early arrivals had drifted into Washington State from the Canadian province of British Columbia, where strong anti-"Hindu" feelings had developed within a half-dozen years of the Punjabis' arrival.

Those who found their way to California became farmworkers and, to a lesser extent, tenant farmers. Some worked in lumber mills and as section hands maintaining railroad tracks. Their immigration ended when Congress passed the Immigration Act of 1917, which barred immigration from a specified zone of the globe encompassing most of Asia, including India.

As in the case of other Asian groups, few women immigrated from India before World War II. Antimiscegenation laws—laws barring the marriage of a white person and a member of another race—prevented the Punjabi men who remained in the United States from marrying Euro-American women. As a result, several hundred of them working in the Imperial Valley in the southern-most part of California adjoining Mexico married Mexican or Mexican-American women and formed biethnic families whose members called themselves Mexican-Hindus. The internal social dynamics of these families have been documented by Karen Leonard.

As an increasing number of immigrants arrived from India after U.S. immigration laws were liberalized in 1965, the newcomers quickly exceeded the "Mexican-Hindus" in number, but the latter are endeavoring to retain their distinct identity. During the early decades of the twentieth century, Filipinos were the only other Asian immigrants who married or acquired common-law spouses across racial lines in noticeable numbers.

STUDY QUESTIONS

1. Why did Punjabi men from India marry Mexican and Mexican-American women?

2. What were the characteristics of Punjabi-Mexican marriages?

3. How did the 1965 liberalization of immigration laws affect the "Mexican-Hindus"?

The end of British colonial rule in India and the birth of two new nations—India and Pakistan—was celebrated in California in 1947 by immigrant men from India's Punjab province. Their wives and children celebrated with them. With few exceptions, these wives were of Mexican ancestry and their children were variously called "Mexican-Hindus," "half and halves," or simply, like their fathers, "Hindus," an American misnomer for people from India. . . .

. . . Men from India's Punjab province came to California chiefly between 1900 and 1917; after that, immigration practices and laws discriminated against Asians and legal entry was all but impossible. Some 85 percent of the men who came during those years were Sikhs, 13 percent were Muslims, and only 2 percent were really Hindus.

Marriages between Punjabis and Mexicans began in the second decade of the twentieth century. Most descendants of these Punjabi-Mexican couples continue to refer to themselves as Hindus, and they are very proud of their Punjabi background. Yet most descendants are Catholic, and while most are bilingual, they speak English and Spanish, not Punjabi. An understanding of the ethnic choices made by the Punjabi-Mexican descendants requires an excursion into the history of their community.

For decades, farming families had been sending sons out of the Punjab to earn money. Punjabis constituted a disproportionate share of the British Indian military and police services throughout the British Empire, in the Middle East, Africa, Southeast Asia, and the China treaty ports. Many of those who ended up in California had served overseas in the British Indian army or police in China and crossed the Pacific for the better wages in railroad, lumbering, and agricultural work. On arrival in California, a few sold tamales from carts in San Francisco, but the majority began as migrant laborers, moving in groups around the state with a "boss man" who knew English and made contracts with employers.

From "California's Punjabi–Mexican–Americans," by Karen Leonard, pp. 612–623. This article appeared in the May 1989 issue and is reprinted with permission of *The World and I*, a publication of *The Washington Times Corporation*, copyright © 1989.

Work and settlement patterns varied regionally in California, depending on the types of crops grown and the nature of the local population, both in terms of numbers and racial or ethnic composition. Intending to return to India, only a handful of men had brought their wives and families; soon it was not possible to bring them. In northern California's Sacramento Valley, Punjabis tended to work in gangs, and were called "Hindu crews." Most of the Punjabi men there remained bachelors, at least in part because there were no local women whom they could legally marry. California's [anti-]miscegenation laws made marriage with women of other races difficult. In the southern Imperial Valley, however, the Punjabis met and married Mexican or Mexican-American women, whom Americans considered racially the same as the Punjabis.

Located along California's Mexican border inland from San Diego, the Imperial Valley was a desert until the first decade of the twentieth century, when engineers tamed the Colorado River and the Imperial Irrigation District was organized to ensure the systematic delivery of water to cultivators. The valley was a raw, rough place, where predominantly male immigrants developed capital-intensive, labor-intensive, predominantly large-scale agriculture. Native-born whites were the largest group, but the 1920 census shows many other groups represented. Especially numerous were Mexicans, Japanese, and African [Americans], followed by Canadians, Swiss, Germans, English, Greeks, Italians, Irish, and Portuguese. There were smaller numbers of Chinese and Punjabi immigrants.

Asian farm laborers had a hard time working their way up California's agricultural ladder. The Punjabis were largely illiterate and faced strong initial prejudice, partly due to the distinctive turbans and beards of the Sikhs. The 1920 State Board of Control termed them the "most undesirable" of Asians. Initially the men from India were not wanted in the Imperial Valley even as laborers—there were alarmed headlines when they were brought in to pick the cotton crop in 1910—and only a few years later their movement up from the labor category to become landowners aroused more apprehension. Contemporary sources express clearly the thinking of the time—that various national and ethnic groups filled different niches in the economic system. Writers constantly compared the "Hindus" to others involved in agricultural labor, and usually placed them, with the Mexicans, at or near the bottom in the rural stratification system.

Asians—Chinese, Japanese, and Punjabis—were among the pioneers in the Imperial Valley and some of them moved rapidly from labor to tenancy to ownership. Yet from the first they encountered prejudice, expressed first through "custom" and finally through law. The ranchers or growers, the shipping agents, and the bankers—those who dominated the rural economy—were white and viewed the Japanese in particular as threats to their livelihood. In 1913, the first version of California's Alien Land Law decreed that those ineligible for U.S. citizenship could neither lease for more than three years nor own agricultural land. (The law was strengthened in subsequent years to bar even leasing.) Since only whites and people of African descent were eligible for citizenship, Asian immigrants could not lease or own agricultural land.

Initially, the Punjabis did have access to American citizenship, being of the Caucasian race, and nearly sixty men became citizens. But in 1923, the Punjabis were ruled ineligible for citizenship because of their race—the Supreme Court in that year pronounced them Caucasian, but not "white" in the poplar meaning of the term. So, early on, perceived race or ethnicity was a factor determining access to resources for the Punjabi immigrants in California.

The Punjabi men were united by the Punjabi language and its regional culture as they moved into the California economy. Although the men came from three different religions, partnerships that formed to lease and farm agricultural land included Sikhs, Muslims, and Hindus in the Imperial Valley; local associations did the same. The Sikh temple founded in 1912 in Stockton, California, included Muslim and Hindu men in its political and social activities. The men worked together and formed social, religious, and political institutions in California. They were self-identified and identified by others as "Hindus."

The kind of racial/ethnic perceptions and laws that impeded Punjabi access to agricultural land also helped determine their choice of spouses. Many of the men had been married in India and had families there, but those who decided to stay in California faced a difficult choice. U.S. immigration laws, increasingly hardened against Asians, prevented them from bringing their wives; the same laws prevented the men from visiting India and returning, since they could not be readmitted legally. Their choice was to live as bachelors or to marry local women.

Eighty-five percent of those who wanted women to live with them, cook and clean for them, and bear their children turned to Mexican and Mexican-American women. About one-third of the Punjabi men who settled in California married; the first recorded marriages occurred in 1916 and 1917 in the Imperial Valley. Eventually, there were almost four hundred of these biethnic couples clustered in California's agricultural valleys. Some 250 couples lived in the Imperial Valley in the south, some ninety couples lived in the Sacramento Valley in the north, and some fifty couples lived in the Central Valley around Fresno.

The Punjabi men chose women of Mexican ancestry for many reasons. Mexican women were thought to resemble Punjabis physically, and many were beautiful. Perhaps most important, Mexican women were accessible in southern California (in the central and northern areas of the state most of the Punjabi men remained bachelors). Mexican families picked cotton in the fields farmed by the Punjabi men. Mexicans and Punjabis shared a rural way of life; with similar types of food, furniture, and so on, they had a similar material culture. Furthermore, Mexicans and Punjabis shared an initially lower-class status.

These marriages were more than a matter of individual choice, however, for the fact was that [anti-]miscegenation laws prohibited marriages across racial lines in California until 1948. Most California county clerks saw the Punjabi men as colored, or "brown," the word they used most often on the marriage license to describe the men's race. Thus the women the Punjabis married also had to be perceived as "brown," and that generally meant women of Mexican ancestry.

Ethnic similarities between the men and women were most striking at the time these marriages began to occur. Like Mexicans, Punjabis were discriminated against by white society. At least half of the women, like the men, were pioneers in a new country and came from a group entering the agricultural economy as laborers. A wave of Mexican migration into the United

Two Punjabi brothers with their Mexican wives and relatives

States was just beginning in the decade of the 1910s, fueled by the Mexican Revolution and its attendant political and economic turmoil.

In Texas and California, where cotton was being cultivated by Punjabi men with the help of Mexican immigrant laborers, the growing number of biethnic couples began to constitute a biethnic community with certain characteristic features. The women were usually much younger than their husbands—the men were typically in their thirties and forties, and the women were in their teens and twenties. The women were almost all Catholic, but most marriage ceremonies were civil. The signatures of brides and grooms alike testify to a low level of literacy. Husbands and wives spoke to each other in rudimentary English or Spanish. Punjabi men learned Spanish to deal with Mexican agricultural laborers and to speak to their wives. Some Punjabi men adopted Spanish names or nicknames: Miguel for Magyar, Andreas for Inder, Mondo for Mohamed.

The Punjabi-Mexican marriage pattern soon became well established. The first brides recruited other women, their relatives and friends, for marriages with Punjabi men. Sisters with small children who had been deserted or widowed were called from Mexico to marry Punjabis. The men traveled too. A Sikh from the Imperial Valley took the train to El Paso, Texas, looking for the nieces of a Mexican woman working for him. He knocked on the wrong door, and the mother and three daughters on the other side mistook him at first for a Turk because of his turban. But in a few days, he and his new bride, her mother, and sisters were on the train back to El Centro. The Sikh's partners married the other sisters and eventually the mother also married a Punjabi Sikh. This was a typical pattern—many sets of sisters or female relatives married business partners and formed joint households along the irrigation canals and country roads.

The birth of children brought a stronger sense of community and a shift of domestic power to the women. Almost without exception, the children were given Spanish names. (Rarely, a father filed an affidavit of correction later, giving a son a Punjabi name. Some divorce cases showed that names were a source of conflict: The fathers used Punjabi names for their children, the mothers, Spanish.) Another strengthening of the women's network came with the appropriation of the *compadrazgo* system of fictive kinship, which drew upon relatives and friends as religious sponsors in the Catholic church. Punjabi men stood as godfathers to each other's children in this basically Catholic system, but it was the women who were central to it.

How were children, given names like Maria Jesusita Singh, Jose Akbar Khan, and Armando Chand, socialized, and how did they think of themselves? Contrary to Yusuf Dadabhay's theory that the Punjabis assimilated to American culture by way of the Mexican-American subculture, the Punjabi-Mexican families did not participate in activities with Mexican-Americans nor were they well received by members of that community. Mexican men opposed these marriages, and there were some early instances of violence between Punjabis and Mexicans over them. While some Punjabi men were close to their Mexican relatives by marriage, most were not.

These biethnic families formed communities of their own, and families visited across county and state lines (there were small numbers of Punjabi-Mexican families in Arizona, Texas, New Mexico, and Utah, too). The partnerships and friendships of the Punjabi men were the basis of these interactions, but there was a double structure; often the wives of given sets of business partners or friends were sisters or related to each other in some other way. So both male friendships and female kinship structured family life.

Yet it was clearly the mothers who socialized the children. The children spoke to their mothers in Spanish and to their fathers in English and/or Spanish. A few of the boys who worked in the fields with Hindu crews learned some Punjabi; sometimes these boys were Mexican stepsons. Most of them were raised as Catholics, and the fathers left this to the mothers and encouraged it. The fathers had neither the time nor the training to teach their children about Sikhism, Islam, or Hinduism. The children had godparents who sponsored them at baptism, confirmation, and marriage in the Catholic Church—even though most godfathers were from the community and were Sikhs, Muslims, or Hindus. These children met with prejudice from both Anglos and from Mexicans—they were called "dirty Hindus" and "half and halves." Their favorite day was Sunday, when Punjabi men and their families got together for talk, play, and a dinner of chicken curry and roti (bread). They liked going to the Stockton Sikh temple or working the migratory labor route, because they could meet others like themselves.

The fathers transmitted little of Punjabi culture to their wives and children, save in the domains of food and funeral practices. Cooking in the homes drew from both Mexican and Punjabi cuisine and the men taught their wives to cook chicken curry, roti, and various vegetables curries. Today, the Rasul family in Yuba City runs the only Mexican restaurant in California that features chicken curry and roti. Another important retention of Punjabi culture was the disposition of the body upon death. Sikhs insisted upon cremation, then uncommon in North America, and Muslims carried out orthodox burial ceremonies for each other (through the plots in which they are buried in rural California are termed "Hindu plots"). The wives, however, were buried in the Mexican Catholic sections of local cemeteries, as were the children.

Most of the Punjabi descendants refer to themselves as Hindu or East Indian today. When they talk about being Hindu, these descendants do not mean objective criteria that link them to India or the Punjab—attributes such as those an anthropologist might list. They are fundamentally ignorant of Punjabi and Indian culture. For example, while most of the men who founded these families were actually Sikhs, not Hindus, their descendants (and even the descendants of Muslim Punjabis) proudly claim to be Hindu.

These descendants are almost all nonspeakers of Punjabi and have no sense of the Punjab's distinctive regional culture. They have a sense of place and history, however, and they possess a heritage that is distinctly Punjabi nonetheless.

One of the reasons descendants claim more strongly to be Hindu rather than Mexican is a negative one—to be Mexican in California's agricultural towns is to affiliate with the laborer, not the landowner, class—but there are other, positive reasons for claiming to be Hindu. There is some identification with place and locality in the spatial sense, a belief that California's agricultural valleys resemble the Punjabi homeland (certainly the fathers promulgated this view). There were other perceptions (or creations) of similarities that the men expressed about their new lives and that their descendants continue to voice. These other perceived similarities, the senses in which the descendants in California today feel themselves to be Punjabi, to be Hindu, include their place in the political system and their ideas about Punjabi and Mexican material culture, language, and religion.

The original Punjabi immigrants found the physical landscape of California similar to that of the Punjab; the political landscape and their place in it also struck them as similar to that in British India. The men's resentment at being colonial subjects as well as their resentment at being deprived of legal rights in the United States is strongly evident in all contemporary accounts. The Punjabi men organized the militantly nationalist Ghadar Party in California to fight against the British back in India; they contributed money, and some of them went back to participate in Ghadar party activities there. They fought hard for political rights here, too, organizing groups and supporting lobbyists to gain U.S. citizenship. They interpreted both their past and present as a struggle for one's rightful place in society, particularly a place on the land, a very important component of Punjabi identity.

This interpretation has continuing meaning to their children, most of whom still live and work in agricultural valleys in California. They too feel strong resentment for being looked down upon as "half and halves," for being pushed into the Mexican and black schools, and, most of all, for not having the land today that their fathers "really earned" but were unable to acquire easily because of the Alien Land Law. Passionate resistance to the political authority that subordinated them linked the fathers to each other in the past, and it links their descendants to their fathers and to each other today.

Central to the sense of continuing Punjabi identity is the question of how the marriages with Mexican women—women perceived today by new Indian immigrants as decidedly different from them—are viewed. Rather than emphasize (or even mention) the [anti-]miscegenation laws that played a major role in determining their choice of spouses, the men and their descendants, when interviewed, talk about commonalities between the Punjabi men and Mexican women. They do not argue that they occupied the same space in the social landscape; that would go against the general Punjabi sense of superiority to Mexicans that carried over from their landowner status in the Punjab. They do argue that there were similarities of physical appearance and even of language ("Spanish is just like Punjabi, really"); they argue also that Mexicans and Punjabis shared the same material culture. As Moola Singh of Selma, California, who has thirteen children from three marriages with Mexican women, says:

> I never have to explain anything India to my Mexican family. Cooking the same, only talk is different. I explain them, customs in India same as in Mexico. Everything same, only language different. They make roti over there, sit on the floor—all customs India the same Mexico, the way of living. I went to Mexico two, three times, you know, not too far; just like India, just like it. Adobe houses in Mexico, they sit on floor there, make tortillas (roti, you know). All kinds of food the same, eat from plates sometimes, some places tables and benches. India the same, used to eat on the floor, or cutting two boards, made benches.

The women came from a similar material culture, it seems, but what about the religious differences? The men and their descendants state repeatedly that all religions are the same, a view again in sharp contrast to that expressed by more recent immigrants from India. The statements take different forms: The Sikh religion is just like the Catholic one; Sikhism is a composite of Islam, Hinduism, and Christianity; the Granth Sahib is just like the Bible; all gods are the same, but they are called different names because languages are different; Sikhism has the ten cruz, or ten crosses which are the ten gurus; the founding Sikh guru preached just what is in the Old Testament; Sikhs have all the commandments Catholics have; one can be Muslim and Catholic or Sikh and Catholic at the same time.

Ignoring religious differences now significant in India, these statements stress similarities between the Indian religions and Christianity, frequently using metaphors and analogies to erase distinctions. While there were many vigorously contested matters between pioneer Punjabi husbands and Mexican wives, the children's religious training was not one of them. The men wanted to inculcate respect for Sikhism, Hinduism, or Islam, while they encouraged their children to practice Catholicism (or whatever form of Christianity their wives practiced).

Even as the Punjabi men talk about the similarities between their homeland and California, upon which they base their continuing collective identity—geography and landscape, the struggle for one's rightful social and political place, wives from a background materially and culturally similar to their own—they also talk about things that are different, particularly social practices that were not appropriate to their new country. Most mention behaviors conditioned by caste and religion back in India, but they usually behave or advocate behaving differently in California. While they point out the Untouchables in their midst (most immigrants were Jat Sikhs, a landowning caste), the Untouchables socialize with the others on a daily basis—chatting, for example, in Holtville Park during the midday rest. The Punjabi men also remark on prohibited Sikh-Muslim-Hindu interactions in India, but men from all three religions generally work, eat, and socialize together in California. When talking to their wives and children about religion, . . . the husbands reconceptualize differences as similarities at a higher analytic level.

The original Punjabi immigrants refused to transmit elements of Punjabi culture that they judged inappropriate in the United States, according to their children. Many fathers felt that the immigration laws and other discriminatory policies against Asians had made it useless to teach the children Punjabi, or even to tell them about Punjabi society. Social practices from the Punjab, life cycle ceremonies, and caste and religious distinctions and observances, were consciously discarded; when interviewed, several children remarked on their father's refusal to talk to them about the Punjab, refusals justified by the uselessness of such knowledge and by the need to become American. Of course, some fathers resurrected the ghosts of caste, sect, and region from their pasts as their children began to date and marry. But since they had not taught their wives and the children the importance of these distinctions earlier, their concerns came too late. As one indignant wife defended her daughter's right to date someone: "We're all Americans here—what is this caste thing?"

The children grew up, therefore, with a collective identity that drew upon two cultural traditions, and they drew upon both in making ethnic choices. There were occasions for choice, some posed by the individual life cycle. As they grew up and began dating (parents permitting), they could date and marry older Punjabi men, Anglos, Mexican-Americans, or others like themselves. Most married Anglos or Mexican-Americans. They could profess Christianity (most) or Islam (a few), or they could feel themselves to be both Christian and Sikh, Muslim, or Hindu at the same time (many).

As they left the Imperial Valley and other places where they were known, they were given new labels. One man had been called Mexican-Hindu all his life by everyone, including state authorities in the Imperial Valley. Working near Sacramento when the United States entered World War II, he enlisted in military service there, giving his race as "Hindu and Mexican." The clerk listed him as Caucasian despite his protests; this was a shock to him, an introduction to a wider world, and in some sense, a loss.

Other ethnic choices [have been] posed by external circumstances. . . . The arrival of many new South Asian immigrants after the 1965 liberalization of U.S. immigration law has changed the context dramatically, and the descendants of the old-timers have had to sharpen and defend their ethnic choices. Thousands of the newcomers—most of them—are educated professionals coming from all over South Asia. Some, however, are Punjabi villagers much like the earlier immigrants, coming from the very same villages and settling in the same rural areas of California where descendants of the pioneers reside. . . .

. . . [B]y the mid-1970s, the two groups were diverging fast; the newcomers disapproved of and minimized the Punjabi-Mexican marriages that had occurred and would not acknowledge the descendants' claims to membership in the same community. One anthropologists reports that Punjabi wives objected to the other wives cooking in the gurdwara [temple], suspecting that the food was being poisoned. Even if the story is untrue, it is significant that it is being told, and the fact is that few Punjabi-Mexican descendants visit the gurdwara for any reason today.

In both the Stockton Sikh temple and the Muslim mosque started in Sacramento in 1947, the old and new immigrant communities jostle uneasily. Spanish-Pakistani descendants do not like the practice of gender segregation instituted by the new immigrants from Pakistan, and the old Sikhs and their descendants find new practices in the Sikh temple similarly objectionable. . . .

. . . [T]he pioneer immigrants and their descendants have adopted new ways appropriate to their new country, and they view the reimposition of South Asian customs as unwelcome and backward-looking. As the new Punjabi immigrant population has increased, tension over such issues has increased as well.

In 1974, the Punjabi-Mexicans initiated their Old-Timers' Reunion Christmas Dance, billing it as a reunion for descendants of the Punjabi pioneers and publicizing it to bolster their claims of South Asian descent. Yet from the first, the dance betrayed the double ethnic identity of its sponsors, featuring mariachi bands and exuberant dancing, and including Mexican-American friends and relatives. In 1979, the new immigrant Sikh community began its annual Sikh Parade, a militant-looking march through Yuba City by hundreds (some say thousands) of Sikh men, women, and children in Punjabi dress led by bearded, turbaned men with drawn swords. This first parade aroused local apprehension and prejudice. . . .

The descendants' strategy now is to claim not only to be real Hindus, but better Americans than the newcomers. They draw attention to the differences between their fathers and the new Punjabi immigrants. These differences begin with physical appearance and manner of self-presentation: They say their fathers were big men, commanding, proud, and light-skinned, while the newcomers are small, obsequious, deferential, and dark-skinned. (This may have some basis in reality: Many of the pioneers had served in the British military and police services, which had such physical requirements for enlistment.) Attitudinal and behavioral differences—ways in which the newcomers are *not* becoming American as the old-timers did—are stressed as well.

The descendants of the Punjabi pioneers now avoid the Sikh Parade. They still hold their annual Christmas dance, but its character has changed. The dance has broadened its constituency to include all who went to school with the founders of the dance in Yuba City; it is now called the Old-Timers' Dance and the organizing committee is primarily Mexican-American. . . .

The ethnic choices made by the Punjabi-Mexican-American pioneers remind us sharply that collective social identity entails some form of self-definition founded upon a marked opposition between "we" and "others." Changing contexts, changing local configurations of "we" and "others," stimulated the "old Hindus" and their descendants to make ethnic choices to reconstruct their sense of place and society as they made this land their own. The contribution of the Punjabi-Mexican-American families of California, chicken curry and tamales aside, ultimately lies in their demonstration of the flexibility of ethnicity, both its grounding in a specific political economy and its responsiveness to situational factors that allow individuals and groups to make ethnic choices.

FURTHER READING

Robert L. Bee, *Crosscurrents Along the Colorado: The Impact of Government Policy on the Quechan Indians* (Tucson: University of Arizona Press, 1981).

Monroe Lee Billington, *New Mexico's Buffalo Soldiers, 1866–1900* (Niwot, Colo.: University Press of Colorado, 1991).

Sherburne F. Cook, *The Conflict Between the Californian Indian and White Civilization* (Berkeley and Los Angeles: University of California Press, 1976).

Ramón A. Gutiérrez, *When Jesus Came, the Corn Mothers Went Away: Marriage, Sexuality, and Power in New Mexico, 1500–1846* (Stanford: Stanford University Press, 1991).

William T. Hagan, *United States–Comanche Relations: The Reservation Years* (New Haven: Yale University Press, 1976; Norman: University of Oklahoma Press, 1990).

Ronald C. Johnson, "Offspring of Cross-Race and Cross-Ethnic Marriages in Hawaii," in *Racially Mixed People in America*, ed. Maria P. P. Root (Newbury Park, Calif.: Sage Publications, 1992).

Karen Isaksen Leonard, *Making Ethnic Choices: California's Punjabi Mexican Americans* (Philadelphia: Temple University Press, 1992).

Amy Iwasaki Mass, "Interracial Japanese Americans: The Best of Both Worlds or the End of the Japanese American Community?" in *Racially Mixed People in America*, ed. Maria P. P. Root (Newbury Park, Calif.: Sage Publications, 1992).

Douglas Monroy, "Anarquismo y Comunismo: Mexican Radicalism and the Communist Party in Los Angeles During the 1930s," *Labor History* 24 (1983): 34–59.

Robert K. Thomas, "Pan-Indianism" in *The American Indian Today*, ed. Stuart Levine and Nancy O. Lurie (Baltimore: Penguin Books, 1968).

Michael C. Thornton, "The Quiet Immigration: Foreign Spouses of U.S. Citizens, 1945–1985," in *Racially Mixed People in America*, ed. Maria P. P. Root (Newbury Park, Calif.: Sage Publications, 1992).

Arthur L. Tolson, *The Black Oklahomans: A History, 1541–1972* (New Orleans: Edwards Print Co., 1972).

Terry P. Wilson, "Blood Quantum: Native American Mixed Bloods," in *Racially Mixed People in America*, ed. Maria P. P. Root (Newbury Park, Calif.: Sage Publications, 1992).

CHAPTER 9

Racism

The following selections on racism directly address a theme that is evident throughout this book: that white racist ideology and institutions have profoundly affected Native, African-, Asian-, and Mexican-American life and society from the Canadian boundary to the Mexican border. Although central to the history of the American West, racism is often presented as something exceptional, involving only one group in a few contiguous states, rather than as the rule. In fact, similarities in the methods and results of discrimination against peoples of color are more than coincidental; they form part of an overall pattern of oppression. Racial theories have been intertwined with political, economic, and legal factors to prevent each group from attaining material and social progress. Even laws designed to equalize relations have often elicited a response that has led to greater inequality.

But discrimination based on alleged racial differences denies members of oppressed groups dignity and civil rights; neglect of their histories and struggles for political power, of their economic opportunities, and of their equal protection under the law distorts the history not only of the groups themselves but also of the American West. As this chapter's readings by Elmer Rusco; Gilbert Gonzalez; the staff of the Asian American Studies Center at the University of California, Los Angeles; Robert Bullard and Donald Taylor; and Orlan Svingen show, racism in the form of racial epithets, physical expulsion, job discrimination, segregation in housing and schools, antimiscegenation laws, and disfranchisement has prevented many westerners from appreciating the common humanity of the descendants of slaves, immigrants, and indigenous peoples.

FOR ANALYSIS AND DISCUSSION

1. How does the history of blacks in Nevada compare with the history of African Americans in other states?

2. In the creation of "Mexican schools," what arguments were used to justify segregation?

3. Why did Euro-Americans fear interracial marriages so much that various states passed antimiscegenation laws?

4. How did discrimination affect housing patterns in Houston, Texas?

5. What arguments and methods were used to disfranchise Native Americans in Montana?

6. Have there been any changes in the methods employed to discriminate against peoples of color for the last one hundred years? If so, describe the changes.

African Americans in Nevada, 1860s–1920s

ELMER R. RUSCO

The history of blacks and of race relations in the American West has paralleled developments in the South, insofar as the Civil War and Reconstruction years brought significant new opportunities for African Americans. However, conditions worsened for blacks at the end of the nineteenth century in Nevada as well as in California and the South. The first half of the twentieth century was characterized by society's reluctance to accord blacks those liberties, civil rights, and economic opportunities guaranteed to European immigrants and their descendants.

Elmer Rusco's history of blacks in Nevada in the nineteenth century is a rare study of race relations and African-American enterprise in a state in the Far West. Besides blacks' migration, social life, and employment, Rusco chronicles the state of race relations and the end of the relative equality that had existed in the early years of the territory's and the state's history. Until the mass migration of blacks to the Pacific coast, and until the Supreme Court's famous 1954 decision (in *Brown* v. *Board of Education of Topeka*), ending racial segregation in public schools, which provided the climate for further vital developments in civil rights, Nevada was known as one of the most inhospitable states for African-American residents in the American West.

STUDY QUESTIONS

1. Why did black Nevadans create institutions of their own?

2. In what areas of life did black Nevadans face racism in the nineteenth century?

3. In what sense did black Nevadans experience a "decline" after 1880, and why?

White Nevada's racist beginning, the partial erosion of that racism, the role black Nevadans played in this improvement, and the economic progress that Nevada's black community made in the late 1860s and 1870s have been noted . . . A number of black Nevadans felt that the progress

From *"Good Time Coming?": Black Nevadans in the Nineteenth Century* by Elmer R. Rusco, pp. 192–200, 202–214. Copyright © 1975 by Greenwood Press, an imprint of Greenwood Publishing Group, Inc., Westport, CT. Reprinted with permission.

would continue and that there was a "good time coming." Instead, all the available evidence points to a reversal of the trends at the end of the nineteenth century and the beginning of the twentieth century, the result of a revival of white racism. Not until the late 1950s would a new wave of opposition to racism develop; when it did, some black people described Nevada as "the Mississippi of the West" and demanded laws to end private discrimination. While precise measures . . . are lacking, it appears that the status of black Nevadans vis-à-vis white Nevadans was lower in the 1950s than it had been in the 1870s, particularly in an economic sense . . .

Apparently blacks did not experience substantial discrimination in the application of criminal laws in the nineteenth century in Nevada. Although there may have been a tendency to apply criminal laws more harshly against blacks than against whites in some cases, there is no evidence of an unusually high number of convictions of blacks. Neither is there evidence of a white fear of black criminality or of black protests against the application of the criminal laws to them; their efforts to change discriminatory laws were persistent, however. While protection against violence was not well established for whites in nineteenth-century Nevada, especially in the early 1860s, it does not seem that blacks had to go without protection from law enforcement officers or were mistreated by such officers, as a general rule. (This is in contrast with the experience of Indians and Chinese, who often suffered violence from whites in early Nevada and who often found law enforcement officers participating in the violence.) . . .

In the 1860s blacks quite actively protested the legal discriminations against them. But by the 1870s, there were reports by blacks and others that indicated that they were no longer being discriminated against. M. Howard reported after the great fire of 1875 in Virginia City that the relief committee, which was providing aid for the victims, did not discriminate against blacks: "All that is necessary for any one to do; who is in want, is to apply to the Relief Committee, prove themselves worthy and their wants are at once attended to, whether in the shape of provisions bedding, clothing or fuel.". . .

One of the most optimistic reports on the treatment of blacks in the 1870s in Nevada was contained in a long letter from "Whiskiyou," a correspondent of the *San Francisco Elevator*, written in 1874 from Elko. . . . After reporting that Elko had accepted black students in its public schools without the necessity of legal action and that a black had recently served on a criminal jury there, he asserted that there was no necessity for "any additional Civil Rights Bill" because blacks already had all the rights they wanted. . . .

. . . [As] discrimination against blacks declined in the late 1860s and 1870s in tandem with the elimination of most racist laws, . . . it seems that there was black economic advance; although only some of the black community engaged in business that could attract white trade, those who did found that whites would frequent them. Barbers were typical of this development.

There were far more of them than would have been possible if they had been confined to serving the black community alone, and a number of them obviously were prosperous. For this reason leaders of the black community, such as Thomas Detter, often came from the ranks of the barbers. At the end of the 1870s, it must have seemed to many black Nevadans that, although the average black man or woman was engaged in unskilled labor which did not pay well or have high status, there were paths to a different and better economic life open to them. By the turn of the century, both the absence of discrimination and the economic development had apparently come to an end; black Nevadans were once more in the depressed status they had known in the 1850s and early 1860s in the West, although this time the laws were not overtly racist. If what happened in Nevada also occurred elsewhere in the West and North, the implications for understanding the current status of black Americans are substantial. It is well known that the last part of the nineteenth century brought a checking of previous progress for the bulk of the black population of the country—those who lived in the South. If this also happened in the rest of the country, the negative effects on black people must have been overwhelming. . . .

One thing that happened to black Nevadans after about the middle of the 1880s was that the economic decline that caused a drop in white population was evidently felt even more severely among the black population. Between 1880 and 1890, chiefly as a result of the failure of mining in several areas, notably what had been the state's most prosperous area, the Comstock, the total population of the state declined by 23.9 percent, and there was another decline of 10.6 percent between 1890 and 1900. The black population also dropped during this period, from 396 people in 1880 to 242 in 1890 and 134 in 1900, declines of 38.9 and 44.6 percent. The black populations in Virginia City and Carson City, which had been large enough to sustain various community organizations, dropped to quite low levels. . . . As a result, there must have been extensive changes in the community, and there can have been little continuity between the black population of nineteenth-century Nevada and that of the twentieth century. After 1900 the black population increased again, although it did not exceed 700 until the 1940s, but the new people must have had few personal ties with their predecessors of the previous century. . . .

Rising white hostility to blacks can be inferred from several sorts of facts. There appears to have been an increase in derogatory terms applied to blacks when newspapers reported news about them. The use of such terms appears to have been routine for several decades in contrast with the situation in the nineteenth century. Then, Republican-oriented newspapers, the most influential segment of the press in early Nevada, had avoided derogatory terms for the most part although Democratic-oriented papers were more inclined to refer to "niggers." After 1900, routine news about blacks often involved the use of terms denoting their inferior status. For example, in 1901 a newspaper reported the birth of a child to a black couple with this headline: "Dar's a New Coon in Town.". . .

Blacks were excluded from some Nevada communities at various times during the twentieth century and were forced out of other communities. Evidently this development, for which there is no known nineteenth-century precedent (although there was similar treatment of the Chinese), reflected a rising white Anglo-Saxon Protestant ethnocentrism directed against various non-WASP groups. . . . In Reno in 1904 Police Chief R. C. Leeper openly carried out a policy of arresting all unemployed blacks and forcing them to leave the city, and the policy was endorsed firmly by both daily newspapers. On November 16, 1904, the *Reno Evening Gazette* reported that the police were conducting a "general round up of the idle and vagrant negroes of the city" and that these persons were "being expelled from the city.". . .

It is not known how widespread the policy of forcing blacks out of Nevada cities was, but in 1914 a newspaper in eastern Nevada reported that "all along the Southern Pacific railroad the Nevada towns are making war upon unemployed negroes. The attacks are directed principally against unemployed blacks in the restricted districts.". . .

In the 1920s, there were Ku Klux Klan groups in several Nevada towns, and two organizations were chartered in the state. In December 1922 the newspapers began to note rumors of Klan organization in Elko. . . . In 1925 two rival Klan groups incorporated in the state and engaged in litigation over the use of the name "Ku Klux Klan."

The discrimination against not just nonwhites but non-Anglo-Saxon Protestant whites that developed in twentieth-century Nevada was more extreme than anything recorded for the nineteenth century. A particularly interesting example of this is the residential and occupational segregation rigidly established by company policy in the copper-mining towns of Ruth, McGill, and Kimberly in the Robinson district of eastern Nevada after about 1905. Employees of English, Irish, German, or Scandinavian ancestry were considered "whites" and were assigned the better jobs and better housing in these communities; all others were considered "foreigners" and relegated to an inferior status. Although the "foreigners" included some Japanese, the Austrians, Greeks, Italians, Serbians, and other white but non-WASP groups were lumped together as nonwhite. . . .

In Reno in the 1930s and 1940s Mrs. Alice Smith, a black founder of the Reno-Sparks branch of the NAACP, remembered that "in the windows of restaurants you would see a little sign that stated 'No Negroes allowed,' 'No Colored Trade Solicited' and the most attractive and impressive and aggravating one also, to me was a sign that was on east Fourth Street on a restaurant and it read like this: 'No Indians, dogs or Negroes allowed.' " When the civil rights movement began in Nevada in the late 1950s, the state had been dubbed the "Mississippi of the West" and it was clear that there was widespread discrimination against blacks in public accommodations, employment, and housing.

It seems also that blacks in twentieth-century Nevada occupied an inferior economic status to that achieved in the 1870s and 1880s. The main reason for this was the decline of . . . the black middle class of the nineteenth century; this decline, in turn, must have been due chiefly to the loss of white customers for black professionals and businessmen.

While census data are not very adequate for Nevada blacks in 1890, they show that there were no professionals in the state and that fifty-six percent of black persons ten years of age or older engaged in gainful occupations were in domestic and personal service.

There is a substantial literature that documents the decline in economic standing of blacks in the South in the 1890s; partly because the overwhelming majority of blacks in the country were still in the South at that time, little attention has been paid to what must have been a similar process in the North (including the West). There is also ample documentation of the exclusion of blacks from the craft unions at the end of the nineteenth century, but again the implications for northern blacks have been given less attention than the implications for southern blacks. Northern politicians had little difficulty, for the most part, in accepting the reimposition of white rule in the South in the 1890s; this ready acceptance of an obvious retreat from the antiracist actions of the 1860s and 1870s must have been associated with a rise in white racism in the North as well.

Nevada's chief national representatives clearly accepted southern white "redemption" during the 1870s. In his *Reminiscences,* published in 1908, Senator William M. Stewart, who had served for more than twenty-seven years as one of Nevada's senators, endorsed the white supremacist view of Reconstruction and its effects. . . .

Francis G. Newlands, congressman from Nevada from 1893 through 1902 and senator from 1903 until his death in 1917, supported Chinese and Japanese exclusion on the general ground that the United States ought to have "a policy . . . which would preserve this country for the white race" and that "history teaches us that it is impossible to make a homogeneous people by the juxtaposition of races differing in color upon the same soil."

Although the process cannot yet be described fully, there must have been rising white prejudice against black professionals and businessmen, beginning in the 1890s. Dr. Stephenson [an African American] . . . had white patients in Virginia City in the 1860s and 1870s. Evidently the only black doctor in the state from the 1870s to the 1950s had more difficulty in getting white patients. . . . When the next black physician, Dr. Charles I. West, came into the state in the mid-1950s, he established his practice in the Westside of Las Vegas, which had become a sizable black ghetto by that time. Apparently before the 1970s there had never been a black physician (or other professional) in Washoe County, which had had for some time a much larger black population than the entire black population of the state at any time during the nineteenth century.

The decline among black businessmen also seems evident; there are probably fewer black businessmen in present-day Washoe County than there were in Virginia City in the 1870s, although the black population of the county is several times as large as the corresponding population of Virginia City at that time. It seems clear that most black businessmen serve mainly the black community in present-day Nevada, but this was not the case during the earlier period. The decline of black barbers is particularly striking; obviously there are far fewer black barbers in Nevada today because such barbers are chiefly serving black customers. . . .

. . . The losses forced upon the black community of Nevada at the close of the nineteenth century and the beginning of the twentieth must surely rank among the most important events in the history of black-white relations in the state.

The "Mexican Schools," 1890s–1930s

Gilbert G. Gonzalez

With an increase in the Mexican-ancestry population in the Southwest during the early twentieth century owing to large-scale immigration from Mexico, a segregated society based on a "color line" gained visibility in various southwestern communities. Attractive to employers as a source of cheap labor, Mexicans were subjected to "Mexican jobs," "Mexican wages," and "Mexican barrios," as well as to "Mexican schools." Besides having inferior teachers and resources, these schools, as Gilbert G. Gonzalez argues, were also characterized by locally legalized, or de jure, segregation. Unlike black schools in the South and Southwest, which were segregated by state law, "Mexican schools" were segregated as a result of decisions by local school boards. Thus, southwestern education, instead of being a source of sustained mobility for Mexican Americans, reinforced segregated and inferior conditions.

STUDY QUESTIONS

1. Why were "Mexican schools" established in the Southwest?

2. How did law, custom, and academic opinion create and sustain separate school systems?

3. What educational policies accounted for the higher dropout rate among Mexican-American youth?

A s early as 1892, Mexican children were being denied entrance into "American" schools in Corpus Christi (Texas). [Paul] Taylor found that "practically coincident with the entry of Mexican children to the city schools, a separate school was provided for them." By the late 1890s, enrollment in the Corpus Christi Mexican school stood at 110, and thirty years later the same school enrolled 1,320.

While Mexicans integrated into the economy and as their numbers increased, school boards established a de jure segregationist policy that was to last until midcentury. A typical scenario across the Southwest was recorded in the Ontario, California, Board of Education minutes for 11 April 1921. "Mr. Hill made the recommendation that the board select two new school sites; one in the southeastern part of the town for a Mexican school; the other near the Central School. . . ." His motion was seconded and passed unanimously. By 1920 most communities with sizable Mexican populations segregated Mexican children as a matter of course. In Texas, school districts often segregated Anglo, black, and Mexican children in a tripartite system. Although Texas law mandated the segregation of only black children, Texas custom prevailed throughout as district officials assigned each black and Mexican minority to its own school. Thus, as the pattern of Mexican residential segregation into *colonias* developed, school segregation followed. Educational theory quickly assimilated the practice, and thus academics legitimized, strengthened, and otherwise assisted in the extension of the segregation of Mexican schoolchildren.

Rather than being shaped by local or regional pressures, as some scholars have suggested, the education of Mexican children has always been an integral part of national education theory and practice. Officials practiced segregation, for example, on a national scale in addition to widespread use of progressive educational techniques such as testing, tracking, curriculum differentiation, and Americanization. Moreover, U.S. foreign policy in the decade of the 1940s played a key role in an antisegregation campaign orchestrated from Washington that affected social attitudes as well as the desegregation court decisions of the 1950s. The segregation of Mexican children attempted to extend an existing duality demarcating the colored minorities, including Mexicans from the Anglo communities. Thus, segregation reflected and recreated the social divisions within the larger society formed by residential segregation, labor and wage rate differentials, political inequality, socioeconomic disparities, and racial oppression. Public school segregation involved an extension of a prior condition to the socialization process—the psychological and socioeconomic reproduction of a social rela-

From Gilbert G. Gonzalez, *Chicano Education in the Era of Segregation*, 1990, pp. 20–27, Balch Institute Press. Reprinted by permission of Associated University Presses.

tionship dividing a dominant from a subordinate community. Education for the Mexican community therefore meant change as well as the preservation of their subordination. It brought the community into contact with new knowledge and skills, but at the same time prevented it from changing its economic and political relationship to the dominant society.

In the mid-1930s one study found that 85 percent of surveyed districts in the Southwest were segregated in one form or another, some through high school, others only through the fifth grade. In some areas, such as in the south Rio Grande Valley of Texas, strict segregation existed through most of the grades. In others, as in some of the smaller districts of California, no such uniform pattern prevailed. Nevertheless, de jure segregation of Mexican children remained common throughout the Southwest until the late forties and early fifties when various court orders declared such segregation a violation of the Constitution's equal protection clause. According to educators favoring segregation, its general purpose was to "Americanize" the child in a controlled linguistic and cultural environment, and its specific purpose was to train Mexicans for occupations considered open to, and appropriate for, them. Nevertheless, the "acculturated" Mexican child (one who had assumed the dominant society's language, dress, manners, and the like) experienced segregation as well. Although proponents justified segregation on grounds of language and culture, the essential factor involved the economic function of the Mexican community as cheap labor. Popular as well as academic opinion held that Mexicans posed an "educational problem," a consequence of an alleged intellectual, social, economical, cultural, moral, and physical inferiority. Whether U.S.-born or naturalized, many members of the dominant society commonly looked upon them as aliens or cultural outcasts whose principal function was to sell their productive human capacities, that is, their labor, in the lowest-paid occupations. Consequently, the American community perceived equal educational opportunities for Mexicans as a burden and of little value for the Mexican community. Segregation became, therefore, the ideal policy when legislators and other authorities enacted and enforced compulsory education laws. These laws created an inferior and separate education that reflected and reproduced the socioeconomic relations in the surrounding community and region.

Inadequate resources, poor equipment, and unfit building construction made Mexican schools vastly inferior to Anglo schools. In addition, school districts generally paid teachers at Mexican schools less than teachers at Anglo schools, and many times a promotion for a teacher at a Mexican school meant moving to the Anglo school. Quite often, however, teachers in Mexican schools were either beginners or had been "banished" as incompetent. One investigator, a high school teacher in Sugarland, Texas, wrote that teachers placed in a Mexican school were resentful and that "most of the teachers in the Mexican schools hope to be transferred to the school for the other whites as soon as vacancies may occur." They often realized their wishes because the frequent moving of teachers from Mexican to Anglo schools seems to have been the rule. Consequently, instruction was often left "in charge of teachers who are not specially prepared by training or experience for the particular work of teaching the Spanish-speaking pupils." Pauline R. Kibbe noted that in 1943 in one six-room Mexican school in West Texas, which enrolled 357 pupils, the head teacher "changed three times," and that in several classes a new teacher arrived "every three weeks." One wonders what degree of Americanization could take place in such a setting. Officials in urban areas elaborated better-organized programs of segregation.

For the most part, instruction periods for Mexican schools in agricultural areas coincided with farm-labor demands. Thus, school officials shortened or modified semesters depending on the dominant agricultural products of the region in which the schools were located. Moreover, children of migrant farm workers usually had little or no access to public schooling.

If, however, Mexicans attended school, whether in a segregated school, in a specific Mexican room within a nonrestricted school, or in a mixed school, the transition from Spanish to English was expected to take place in the first and second grades. Consequently, in many school districts the bulk of the children enrolled in the first two grades, with a rapid decline in enrollment by the sixth and seventh. The policy requiring Mexican children to repeat the first and second grades, combined with the practice, in many districts, of modifying the academic year to allow for child labor, tended to retard school progress. In addition, the unwritten tradition of tracking Mexican children into vocational and slow learner classes became institutionalized almost everywhere. By their sixteenth birthdays, many Mexican children had barely reached junior high, and the dropout problem, which subsequently became notorious, began to manifest itself. Since the schools advocated manual vocations, and since most Mexican families lived in poverty, many expected the majority of Mexican children to leave their segregated schools before high school in order to enter the labor force.

The legal justification for segregating Mexican children generally rested upon educational, not racial grounds. Meyer Weinberg notes that, in a 1930 unofficial opinion, California State Attorney General U. S. Webb declared segregation justifiable on the basis that Mexicans were Indians and therefore subject to the state law allowing their segregation. Webb's interpretation strained credulity as well as the law. Of course, it did not apply to *all* Mexicans in fact, but law and facts do not always converge. A 1935 revision of the California education code attempted to close Webb's loophole by legalizing the segregation of "Indians" (excepting descendants of U.S. Indians, who, after 1924, were citizens of the United States). Certainly, one could have interpreted the revised code in such a way as to justify the segregation of Mexicans given that they descended from Indians. However, it seems that the code seldom if ever applied to the segregation of the Mexican community. It made no direct mention, however, of the Mexicans even though this group comprised the most commonly segregated community in the state. Therefore, where segregation existed, it did so mainly on the basis of educational argument. In the research of Dr. George I. Sanchez—professor of education at the University of Texas, Austin—and Virgil E. Strickland on segregation in Texas, a survey of ten school districts found that the "language handicap is the official reason [to justify segregation] found in the school board minutes." However, most arguments went beyond language; a San Bernardino, California, teacher stated that segregation was the outcome of the deliberations of the Anglo community and "based largely on the theory that the Mexican is a menace to the health and morals of the rest of the community." These opinions attached "a stigma to [the Mexicans'] very being," prompting one investigator of the segregation of Mexican children to write that Americans take for granted that, among other things, "Mexicans are dirty, lawless, disease spreaders, stupid, and lazy." Not surprisingly, given the strength of such public and official opinions, the practice of an official though illegal segregation eventually anchored educational policy with regard to the Mexican community.

Not all opinions justifying segregation demonstrated such a vicious attitude toward the Mexican community. A number of prominent researchers and academics viewed segregation as the preferred method of meeting the

Children outside a segregated "Mexican school" in New Mexico, c. 1935.

educational needs of the Mexican community. They often considered this practice an educational asset for the Mexican community. Yet even here, these shallow arguments masked the same prejudices that motivated the overt racists. The Arizona State Department of Education, for example, concluded that segregation "gives opportunity for the inauguration of a special program to meet the bilingual group interests." A superintendent of a southern California district alleged that experience had demonstrated the pedagogically sound nature of segregation by showing "that Mexican children advance more rapidly when grouped by themselves," and therefore profited "most by the instruction offered in such classes."

Although 10 percent of the students in one South Texas Mexican school were tracked into the educationally mentally retarded group, one of its teachers argued that "the Mexican child is not discriminated against," and that "in the majority of cases, the [class] room is the child's best home. . . ." In describing the impact on Mexican children, another teacher wrote of "a most impressive" change in them. "Their faces radiated joy, they had thrown off the repression that held them down when they were in the schools with the other children. . . . There was no one to laugh at any peculiarity they might possess, and they were free."

These two arguments justifying segregation often intertwined. For example, the superintendent of the Garden Grove, California, elementary school district stated on the witness stand in the *Mendez* v. *Westminster* desegregation case, that integration would make Mexican children "feel inferior because of their clothing they have to wear." This same superintendent had also written on the education of Mexican children in which he justified segregation with an opposite approach.

> Because of (1) social differences between the two races; (2) much higher percentage of contagious disease (among Mexican children); (3) much higher percentage of undesirable behavior characteristics; (4) much slower progress in school, and (5) much lower moral standards, it would seem best that . . . Mexican children be segregated. . . .

Most districts that practiced segregation maintained a "Mexican" school, which admitted only Mexican children. Some districts, such as the Los Angeles City School District, segregated via districting boundaries (rather than a simple identification of nationality), because, according to one teacher, "One of the first demands from a community in which there is a large Mexican population is for a separate school." In Los Angeles, the district did not refer to these separate institutions as "Mexican schools," as in many districts, but as "neighborhood schools" and sometimes as "foreign schools." One Los Angeles school administrator wrote that neighborhood (read "Mexican") schools existed as such because "the district gerrymandered schools [so] that they can be nothing but foreign schools and remain foreign schools." The consequences of either policy were the same, although the Los Angeles system may have appeared to be a de facto system of segregation.

According to arguments raised by educators, one of the main aspects of the Mexican school was that it allowed a curriculum tailored to the needs of the student, thereby preparing him to transfer to an American elementary or junior high school. In the American school, educators expected Anglos and Americanized Mexicans to eventually compete in an integrated setting. Actually, that rarely happened. Mexicans seldom, if ever, Americanized to the extent that they no longer remained bilinguals. In fact, most retained their Mexican cultural heritage. Segregation seldom accomplished its objectives, then, and as Mexican children moved into integrated junior high, school officials tracked them into slow learner groups. This practice, wrote one teacher about a southern California school district, "appears to be a disadvantage to many of the Mexican boys and girls. With few exceptions these students are placed, as a result of the testing program, in the slower-moving classes. . . ."

However, since many, if not most, students began dropping out at this point, such integration usually affected only a minority. Thus, a different type of segregation followed Mexican children when they graduated from their Mexican school to what was, for all practical purposes, an Anglo school that opened its doors to Mexican enrollment. In the late twenties at one Los Angeles junior high, Mexican children comprised sixty out of eighty entering lower-track students; the percentage of Mexican children in lower tracks at four other schools varied from 33 to 55 percent. By the midforties the situation remained as such, prompting the superintendent of the Los Angeles County schools to comment that when the Mexican child entered the junior high, "he again finds himself segregated" into ability groups, and consequently, a "vicious cycle" of segregation was unbroken even in an "integrated" setting.

A most significant aspect of the segregated program was that it not only applied to the education of children; it also included the adults of the community, especially women. In fact, in most districts where the segregation of schoolchildren appeared, a segregated adult education program generally accompanied it. In one southern California district, educators offered language instruction for both men and women. However, for women, these courses addressed "the care of infants, cleanliness, house sanitation, and economical house management, including sewing, cooking, and thrift"; for men these programs offered "courses in thrift, in gardening, and . . . principles of the American government." Both adult and children's programs had similar objectives for substantially identical reasons, and through the same general method—the segregated school.

Segregated schools functioned not only as the center of the socialization of the Mexican child, but also as laboratories for research into the "Mexican educational problem." In the early 1920s, the California State Department of Education assigned Grace C. Stanley, formerly of the Los Angeles School District, to undertake and supervise "an experiment in the education of the foreign child." Ten schools were selected throughout southern California as centers for experimentation, with the "Mexican school" in Cucamonga as the principal station for experimentation, and it was from this project that teaching "methods were recommended throughout the State," including schools with "foreign" populations other than Mexican. Many districts established special departments entrusted with the design of the curriculum for the education of Mexican children. In the Southwest, various names identified such departments: the Department of Immigrant Education, the Department of Americanization, or simply the Department of Mexican Education. In one district in southern California, the superintendent, Merton Hill (who was soon to become the director of admissions for the University of California), ordered the Department of Mexican Education "to make a scientific study of the Mexican . . . the temperament of the race . . . those qualities and abilities that are recognized as peculiar to the Mexican people. . . ." Furthermore, the "peculiar attitudes of these good-natured and kindly people" should be "developed along the best possible lines," and their "capacities to perform different types of service should be set forth [so] that their employers may utilize them to the best interests." Such studies merely reinforced existing theories and practices subordinating the Mexican community in nearly every phase of their lives to the larger society.

Such schooling resulted in an education that recapitulated the migration of Mexicans to the United States as a supply of flexible and cheap labor. Thus, segregation grew out of policy decisions corresponding to the economic interests of the Anglo community; it became a means of domination and control, the antithesis of equality and freedom; and it was intrinsically racist both in that it was based on racial social theories, and in that it led to educational practices that reinforced a pattern of social inequality based on nationality and race.

Antimiscegenation Laws and the Filipino, 1920s–1960s

THE STAFF OF THE ASIAN AMERICAN STUDIES CENTER, THE UNIVERSITY OF CALIFORNIA, LOS ANGELES

Because the Philippines was an American territory from 1898 to 1946, Filipinos were considered American "wards" or "nationals" and could immigrate to the United States on American passports. It was therefore impossible for Congress to pass any law excluding Filipinos from immigrating, as legislators had done for other Asian immigrant groups. The number of Filipino entrants was reduced to only fifty persons a year, however, by a clause in the 1934 Tydings-McDuffie Act, which spelled out the process by which the Philippines would eventually regain its independence.

But, anti-Filipino forces found other ways to make Filipinos unwelcome. Most of the Filipinos living in the United States in the late 1920s and early 1930s were young bachelors. Some of them frequented "taxi dance halls" for recreation after long days at hard labor. These establishments employed white women who would dance with clients after the latter purchased rolls of tickets costing ten cents a dance. A number of the Filipinos became romantically involved with the women whom they met in this way, and couples began applying for licenses to get married. County clerks granted the licenses in some localities but not in others.

To put an end to interracial marriages involving Filipinos, lawmakers sought to make the existing antimiscegenation laws—originally enacted against marriages between blacks and whites and later extended to prohibit marriages between whites and "Mongolians" (meaning Chinese and Japanese)—applicable to Filipinos. In the following reading, the staff of the Asian American Studies Center at UCLA discuss how Filipinos challenged these laws in the courts. (The authors call Filipinos "Pilipinos" in this reading to honor the largely uneducated farm workers who could not pronounce the *f* sound, there being no *f* in the various languages of the Philippines.) It was not until 1967, in the *Loving* v. *Virginia* case that the U.S. Supreme Court finally declared all antimiscegenation laws unconstitutional.

STUDY QUESTIONS

1. How were the antimiscegenation laws amended to make them applicable to Filipinos?

2. What was the outcome of the efforts by Filipino Americans to challenge the antimiscegenation laws in the courts?

O ne day a Filipino came to Holtville with his American wife and their child. It was blazing noon and the child was hungry. The strangers went to a little restaurant and sat down at a table. When they were refused service, they stayed on, hoping for some consideration. But it was no use. Bewildered, they walked outside; suddenly the child began to cry with hunger. The Filipino went back to the restaurant and asked if he could buy a bottle of milk for his child.

"It is only for my baby," he said humbly.

The proprietor came out from behind the counter. "For *your* baby?" he shouted.

"Yes, sir," said the Filipino.

The proprietor pushed him violently outside. "If you say *that* again in my place, I'll bash in your head!" he shouted aloud so that he would attract attention. "You goddamn brown monkeys have your nerve, marrying our women. Now get out of this town!"

Carlos Bulosan, *America Is in the Heart*
1946

When Carlos Bulosan wrote his novel *American Is in the Heart,* a Pilipino in California and in many other states was prohibited by law from marrying a white person. That the Pilipino, a member of the brown race, could not marry whites, should hardly prove startling to those familiar with the history of American institutional racism and its various forms. Until 1948, when the California Supreme Court ruled that anti-miscegenation laws were unconstitutional, non-white races in general, including "Negroes, mulattoes, Malayans, Mongolians," could not intermarry with the white race. Nineteen years passed before the United States Supreme Court thought that a similar ruling was appropriate for the entire nation; in *Loving* v. *Virginia* (1967) it ruled that state anti-miscegenation laws . . . [violated] the due process and equal protection clauses of the Constitution. At that time, sixteen states still prohibited white interracial marriage.

Originally, white anti-miscegenation laws were an outgrowth of America's peculiar slavery institution. As early as 1661, Maryland passed the first anti-miscegenation law, aimed at prohibiting white female and black male marriages. Similar legislation soon followed such that thirty-eight states, at one time or another, prevented interracial unions between blacks and whites. California's anti-miscegenation laws, like the laws of other western states, proved to be readily adaptable. As Asian groups began to make their appear-

"Anti-Miscegenation Laws and the Pilipino" by the staff of the Asian American Studies Center, University of California, Los Angeles, from *Letters in Exile: An Introductory Reader on the History of Pilipinos in America,* ed. Jesse Quinsaat et al. (Los Angeles: University of California, Los Angeles, Asian American Studies Center, 1976), excerpt from pp. 63–70. Reprinted with permission.

ance in the [W]est in large numbers, they were simply included in the laws. Thus, in 1880, despite the few instances of Chinese-white intermarriages, Section 69 of the California Civil Code was amended to prohibit the issuance of marriage licenses to whites and "Negroes and Mongolians." The Japanese, who began arriving at the turn of the century[,] found themselves by the white ethnological definition to belong to this latter group.

Pilipinos joined the . . . list of unmixables in California in 1933. Since, anthropologically speaking, the Pilipino belonged to the Malayan race, there was some initial difficulty in concluding that the Pilipino was Mongolian. A study of how Pilipinos came to be added to the white anti-miscegenation laws is an interesting reflection on the power once held by various white racist groups as well as on the adaptability of American institutions in preventing minorities from exercising fundamental rights.

As the third group of Asian immigrants . . . recruited to fill a shortage in America's labor force, Pilipinos suffered similar racial discrimination and economic oppression which affected Chinese and Japanese. . . . What made discrimination against . . . Pilipino[s] unique, however, stemmed from [their] unique status as . . . non-alien, U.S. national[s]. In 1898, with the end of the Spanish-American [W]ar, the Philippines involuntarily became a colony of the U.S. While this [development] initially enabled Pilipinos to hurdle restrictions limiting Chinese and Japanese immigration, Pilipinos were still "wards" of the U.S. . . . [W]ith the passage and acceptance of the 1934 Tydings-McDuffie Independence Act by both U.S. and Pilipino Legislature [, providing] for an annual quota of only fifty Pilipinos to the U.S., Pilipinos became technically "aliens" and their unique status as nationals no longer existed. . . .

According to the California Department of Industrial Relations Study in 1930, less than 7 percent of the 31,092 Pilipinos admitted to California between 1920–29 were female. Of those female immigrants, about 43 percent were married. On the other hand, the majority of male Pilipino immigrants were single and between the ages of 16 and 30. The ratio of unmarried males to females was approximately 23 to 1. . . .

Although . . . Pilipino immigration to the continental United States began around 1905 and peaked during the 1920s, the status of Pilipino-white marriages in California was not clear until 1933. Until that year, no high court had ruled on the issue and the decisions of lower courts of equal jurisdiction were not in accord. The status of the intermarriage mainly rested upon the courts' arbitrary racial classification of Pilipinos. If they were ruled to be Mongolian, then previous legislation prohibited the unions, but if they were ruled to be Malayan—and not Mongolian, as some municipal courts did— then the licence was granted. Confusion on the status of the marriage was compounded by conflicting opinions of the State Attorney General and the Assistant County Counsel of Los Angeles.

The earliest opinion recorded in California is that of then Los Angeles Assistant County Counsel Edward T. Bishop. In this statement, dated May

13, 1921, Bishop advised the then Los Angeles County Clerk, L. E. Lampton:

> While there are scientists who would classify the Malayans as an off-shoot of the Mongolian race, nevertheless, ordinarily when speaking of the "Mongolians" reference is had to the yellow and not to the brown people and we believe that the legislature in Section 69 did not intend to prohibit the marriage of people of the Malay race with white persons. We are further convinced of the correctness of our conclusion when we regard the history of the situation. . . . At that time (1880) the question of the marriage of white persons with members of the brown or Malayan races was not a live one, and there was no call for a solution. We do not believe that the members of the Malayan race are "Mongolians" as that word is used in Section 69 of the Civil Code.

Although Bishop's views were not binding, the Los Angeles County Clerk issued marriage licenses to Pilipino-white couples until 1930. Bishop's opinion was written in 1921, when the number of Pilipinos in the U.S. was small, less than 6,000. But as their population increased, so did racist fears. And not surprisingly, legal interpretations later conformed to reflect and legitimize the growing alarm.

Conflicting with County Counsel Bishop's opinion was the decision of the Superior Court of Los Angeles county in *State of California* v. *Timothy S. Yatko, Jr.* In this case, the status of Pilipino-white marriages was a collateral issue. Litigated in 1925, *Yatko* involved a Pilipino, Timothy S. Yatko, Jr., who was charged with first-degree murder. Yatko, twenty-one years old at the time of his trial, allegedly stabbed to death a white man he found in bed with his wife.

In order to permit Mrs. Yatko to testify against her husband, the state questioned the legality of the marriage. The counsel for the state argued that the marriage was "null and void from the beginning and on the ground that the defendant, Yatko, was a Filipino."

Born in 1904 in Manila, Yatko came to the U.S. in 1920 after completing his second year at Manila High School. On arriving in Seattle, he worked as a mess boy on a boat from San Francisco to New York for Standard Oil Co. In 1924, he was married by a Baptist minister in San Diego to Lola Butler, a white American who was employed as a taxi-dance-hall dancer in Los Angeles. They were issued a marriage license by the San Diego County clerk. Following their marriage, she worked . . . in Los Angeles as a singer and dancer. Yatko was then working as a waiter and held no previous convictions. According to the court records, in 1925, Yatko discovered Harry L. Kidder, a white American who worked with Mrs. Yatko as a piano player, in bed with his wife, whereupon he allegedly stabbed Kidder several times. Later, Yatko surrendered himself at the police station, and signed a statement confessing to the murder which was later introduced in court.

The legal issue raised was whether Pilipinos were Mongolians and therefore prohibited from marrying white persons under existing legislation.

Arguments rested on white ethnological and anthropological opinions on the subject of race classification. But the state prosecutor also accused Malays of having a "homicidal mania" called "running amuck," which he described as a neuropathic tendency causing them without any reason or motive to kill persons of other races. He also attributed evil effects to white miscegenation generally, stating that "when the white people, or the Caucasians, came to the United States they did not intermarry with the Indians; they kept themselves pure."

Counsel for defendant Yatko argued that if this marriage would be declared void, then a great many marriages, particularly those between Indians and white persons would also be void, since, by the same ethnological standards, Indians were of the Mongolian race. The defense also mentioned that there did not exist any "Filipino problem" in California at the time the amendment to Section 60 of the Civil Code was passed by the Legislature.

A Filipino-white couple

But presiding Judge Carlos S. Hardy ruled that

> the dominant race of the country has a perfect right to exclude other
> races from equal rights with its own people and to prescribe such rights
> as they may possess . . . the Filipino is a Malay and [. . .] the Malay is a
> Mongolian. . . . Hence, it is my view that under the code of California as
> it now exists, intermarriage between a Filipino and a Caucasian would
> be void.

Lola Butler was allowed to testify[,] though her testimony was brief and
of little importance. On May 11, 1925, Timothy S. Yatko, Jr.[,] was found
guilty of first-degree murder and was sentenced to life imprisonment at San
Quentin State Prison.

Supporting the *Yatko* decision but in conflict with the opinion of County
Counsel Bishop was the legal opinion of the then [California] Attorney General U. S. Webb, who wrote on June 8, 1926[,] that "Malays belong to the
Mongoloid Race," and[,] therefore, marriages between them and white persons were prohibited by provisions of Section 60 of the Civil Code. Again, as
with Bishop's opinion, Attorney General Webb's views carried no binding
legal effect. Although his views probably influenced many Justices of the
Peace, they were not adhered to in every county in the state.

Confusing the intermarriage question still further were four conflicting
Los Angeles County Superior Court decisions following the *Yatko*, Webb
and Bishop opinions.

Stella F. Robinson v. *L. E. Lampton, County Clerk of L.A.*, litigated in
March 1930, supported the *Yatko* decision and the views of Attorney General Webb. In *Robinson*, Mrs. Stella Robinson wished to keep her daughter,
Ruby, a white, from marrying Tony V. Moreno, a Pilipino. Mrs. Robinson
petitioned the court for a writ of prohibition[,] which would have restrained
the county clerk from issuing the marriage license. Judge J. A. Smith of the
Superior Court ruled that Pilipinos were Mongolians[,] and thus prohibited
the marriage.

Opposed to the *Yatko*, *Robinson* and *Webb* opinions were the following
three court cases. In *Gavino C. Visco* v. *L.A. County* (1931), Visco petitioned for a license to marry Ruth M. Salas, a Mexican Indian. Judge Walter
Guerin, in ruling that California law did not prohibit marriages of Indians
and Pilipinos, also stated that had Ruth Salas been white, he would still have
granted the petition.

The . . . [other] cases were both civil suits seeking an annulment of
Pilipino-white marriages on the ground that these marriages violated California law. In *Estanislao P. Laddaran* v. *Emma P. Laddaran* (1931), the
Pilipino husband sought annulment; in *Ilona Murillo* v. *Tony Murillo, Jr.*
(1931), the white wife filed the petition. In both cases, the Superior Court
judges denied the petition, ruling that the marriages did not violate the California Civil Code because Pilipinos were not classified as Mongolians.

Until 1933, there was no definitive ruling on the status of Pilipino-white marriages. . . . While similar controversies probably were litigated in other California court districts, the Los Angeles decisions were of particular importance [owing] to the relatively large Pilipino population in this area.

The racial classification question was resolved in 1933, when the California Court of Appeals reviewed the case of *Salvador Roldan* v. *Los Angeles County, et al.* In 1931, Salvador Roldan and Marjorie Rogers were denied a marriage license by the county clerk. They then petitioned for a writ of mandate requiring the clerk to issue the license. Counseled by the sensationalist white woman lawyer Gladys Towles Root, and attorney George B. Bush, Roldan won his case in the county Superior Court[,] but the county appealed the decision. As in past cases, the major question in the earlier hearing as well as on appeal was whether or not the legislature in 1880 and 1905 meant to include Pilipinos in its use of the word "Mongolian." The lower court held that the Pilipino, as a Malay, was not intended to be included in the designation "Mongolian," either by legislative intent or by then-prevailing ethnological standards. On January 27, 1933, the Court of Appeals, with three judges concurring and three dissenting, affirmed that Pilipinos were not prohibited from marrying whites in California. This high court ruling superseded all lower court findings.

But the victory in the courts was short-lived. Even before the *Roldan* case was concluded on January 27, 1933, bills had already been introduced in the California Legislature to prohibit such unions. On January 18, 1933, Senator Herbert C. Jones from Santa Clara County introduced Senate Bills Nos. 175 and 176. These two bills would have amended Sections 60 and 69 of the Civil Code by adding the Malay race to the non-white groups already restricted from marrying whites. The relative ease and speed wherein these two bills passed was probably not unlike that of an emergency measure. Surely the lack of public notice and legislative opposition and debate demonstrates the relatively noncontroversial nature the measure held for both the legislators and their constituents. Both bills on March 14, 1933, passed unanimously in the State Senate Committee on the Judiciary; the very next day, both bills passed unanimously in the Senate.

Introduced in the State Assembly that same day, the bill[s] soon passed the Assembly Committee on Social Service and Welfare on March 31. Both bills passed the California Assembly on April 5, with only one opposing vote cast for Bill No. 175. On April 20, 1933, less than three months after the *Roldan* decision, and only three months after their introduction in the legislature, . . . Governor James Rolph signed the two bills into law, effective August 21, 1933. While these amendments were not to take effect until four months later, they retroactively invalidated any previous white intermarriage[s]: "*All marriages* of white persons with negroes, Mongolians, *members of the Malay race*, or mulattoes are illegal and void." [emphasis added] Furthermore, all future intermarriages were prohibited with Section 69 amended to read: ". . . no license must be issued authorizing the marriage of a white person with a negro, mulatto, Mongolian or *member of the Malay race.*" [emphasis added] Thus, *Roldan* and the previous supportive court cases had been empty victories.

Although the California Legislature believed that the 1933 amendments would halt Pilipino-white marriages, this was far from the case. Many couples travelled to other states to marry, particularly Utah, which at that time did not prohibit these unions, and later returned to California. This situation was recognized as a threat [by] California racists and on March 16, 1938, the California Assembly and Senate passed Joint Resolution No. 14, which read as a forceful appeal to states like Utah to ". . . stop the practice whereby citizens of the State of California and members of non-assimilable alien race have been defeating California marriage laws by resorting to a subterfuge of transient residence in the State of Utah."

. . . [I]n 1939, Utah passed legislation adding Malays to their anti-miscegenation laws. By that year, a Pilipino and a white person were banned from marriage in ten states by law specifically, and in three other states by implication. Some of the states were [in] the South with a long tradition of [prohibiting interracial marriage]. Georgia, South Carolina, and Virginia [had] prohibited marriage between a white and any non-white since their incorporation into the U.S. Mississippi, in prohibiting Mongolian-white marriages, also implicitly considered the inclusion of Malayans within this law. Of the western states, South Dakota (1913) was the first state to bar Malayan-white unions, followed by Nevada (1919), Arizona (1931), Wyoming (1931), California (1933) and Utah (1939).

The racial[ly] exclusive marriage laws of Oregon (1930) and Missouri (1929) already including Mongolians probably also applied to Pilipinos. Maryland made the marriages of Pilipinos and whites, and even Pilipinos and blacks, illegal in 1935. That year, Maryland['s] legislators became fearful of the interactions between Pilipinos, recruited as mess boys for the Naval Academy in Annapolis, and local white and black females.

Most of these states also made it a criminal offense to evade the law by crossing the state border, getting married in an adjoining state, and returning to residence; these out-of-state marriages were usually not legally recognized by the home state. Many of these states also provided penalties for these couples. Nevada found interracial cohabitation and fornication to be a gross misdemeanor, punishable by a fine up to $500 and up to one year['s] imprisonment. Maryland found the couple guilty of an "infamous crime" and sentenced them to prison for up to ten years. In California, in August 1930, a Salinas Superior Court judge ruled that immigrant white women who married Pilipinos would not be entitled to citizenship. In light of this ruling, the Federal District Director of Naturalization stated that women citizens marrying Pilipinos would also lose their citizenship. Most of these states even went so far as to hold that the county clerk who issued such a license, as well as the minister who solemnized such a ceremony, would be guilty of a gross misdemeanor and would be punished with the same sentences pertain[ing] to the violating couple.

While the exact number cannot be ascertained, many Pilipinos, to evade the law, crossed the border into Tijuana, Mexico. But the Mexican marriages were soon declared void by the California courts, and similar provisions were enacted by neighboring states.

California's racist marriage laws remained in effect until 1948. That year, the California Supreme Court reviewed a case in which Andrea Perez, a white woman, and Sylvester Davis, a black man, petitioned the courts to compel the county clerk of Los Angeles to issue them a marriage license. In a landmark decision, the California Supreme Court, with a close 4 to 3 vote, held that Civil Code Sections 60 and 69 were unconstitutional. While stating that marriage can be regulated as a proper function of the state, the court nonetheless held that restricting marriage solely on the basis of race violated the equal protection clause under the U.S. Constitution.

While *Perez* v. *Lippold* declared the intermarriage statutes unconstitutional, they remained on the California law books, though unenforceable, until 1959, withstanding four attempts in the California Legislature to erase the court-invalidated portions of the Civil Code.

Although California's interracial marriage laws were found unconstitutional in 1948, other states retained their statutes until 1967. During that time, court opinions continued to rule on the Pilipinos' classification as a Mongolian or Malayan, depending on the desired outcome. In one case reported by the *New York Times* in 1964, a white woman['s] and a Pilipino physician's application for a marriage license in Maryland was granted only after the circuit court discovered that the Pilipino physician had a white grandmother. In another case in 1965 involving a petition for marriage by a Pilipino male and [a] white female, the couple was denied a marriage license on the ground that the groom's part-Pilipino ancestry classified him as a Mongolian.

Housing Segregation in the Sunbelt, 1960s–1970s

ROBERT D. BULLARD AND DONALD L. TRYMAN

In the late twentieth century, Houston and other "sunbelt" cities mush-roomed as black and white migrants left the "frostbelt" of northern urban-industrial areas to seek new opportunities in the South's expanding economy. This demographic change had significant consequences for the nation. Houston and Dallas quickly became two of the United States' largest cities; in fact, Texas grew to rival California and New York in the number, size, and significance of its urban areas. But the citizens of Houston and other sunbelt cities did not share equally in the rewards produced by their city's unprecedented economic growth, despite the passage of national civil-rights legislation and the legal end of segregation.

Not only did African Americans in Houston complain more about hous-ing discrimination than did Euro-Americans, but women suffered more deeply and widely than men. Indeed, sexism combined with racism to cause minority women generally to experience what is popularly known as the double whammy. Particularly significant, African Americans were segregated from whites and Mexican Americans; they also experienced the most dis-crimination in the new areas of the city containing the preferred housing. Racism was manifest in rentals as well as in the sale of new homes. Persistent housing discrimination in turn led to increased segregation. And rather than disappearing as some have alleged, racial discrimination became more "sophisticated"— and much more difficult to prove.

STUDY QUESTIONS

1. In what ways did housing discrimination in Houston affect blacks and other minorities?

2. Why did minority women living in Houston experience the greatest dis-crimination in housing?

It has been over ten years since the Federal Fair Housing Act of 1968 pro-hibited racial discrimination in housing (with limited exceptions). How-ever, Blacks still do not receive equal treatment in the market or enjoy

From "Competition for Decent Housing: A Focus on Housing Discrimination Complaints in a Sunbelt City," by Robert D. Bullard and Donald L. Tryman, *Journal of Ethnic Studies* 7:4 (1980), pp. 51–64. Reprinted by permission of the publisher.

complete freedom. Nearly every major U.S. city has created a local fair housing department to monitor and implement fair housing policies. Since discrimination in housing continues to persist, most of these fair housing departments are still in business.

Houston's Fair Housing Ordinance . . . created the Fair Housing Division which became operational July 9, 1975. The city's Fair Housing Ordinance prohibits discrimination in the sale or rental, the financing of housing and the provision of broker services on account of race, color, sex, religion or national origins. From its inception to September 30, 1978, over 1081 complaints have been received by the Fair Housing Division.

The overall pattern of complaints seems to have come from renters. The City's Fair Housing Administrator indicates that "despite the city's public information efforts, there is a sizable portion of the population which is not yet aware of the enactment of the City's Fair Housing Ordinance. Nationwide, over 70 percent of the Black renters and over 60 percent of the Black homeowners have been discriminated against in their search for decent housing. . . .

The focus of this study centers on housing discrimination in a major growth city, Houston. Houston was selected as the focal city for several reasons: namely, (1) Houston leads the nation in housing starts, (2) it is one of the fastest growing cities in the United States, (3) it is the largest city in the South, (4) it has the largest concentration of Blacks of any city in the South (nearly 400,000 Black residents), and (5) it has been held out as a "Mecca" of the sunbelt. . . .

Black and other minority families must contend with the spiraling housing costs as other Americans along with individual and institutionalized housing discrimination. Two types of discrimination are especially relevant in housing patterns of American cities: (1) *price discrimination*, which refers to the act of charging one group a higher price than another group for identical housing, and (2) *exclusion*, which refers to any technique designed to avoid selling or renting housing in a given location to a certain group of people.

Because Blacks face a restricted housing supply, they appear to pay more than Whites of equal income for otherwise identical housing. Kain has estimated that a non-White buying a single-family home must pay 5 to 20 percent more than a White buying comparable living quarters. Other economic costs are imposed on Blacks which may include higher costs for residential services consumed and costs associated with limited availability of new housing and better quality neighborhoods.

When housing becomes tight, discrimination becomes very difficult to prove and easy to practice; often the minority prospect gets delay and red-tape and the White prospect gets the apartment. In a recent study of Houston's Section Eight Housing Program, Bullard found that some 49 percent of the relocated tenants were not satisfied with their current neighborhood.

Minority tenants, especially, expressed a feeling of being "trapped" in traditionally minority and low-income neighborhoods even though the Section 8 Housing Program has the provision for allowing tenants to select an area of their choice. White participants in the same program did not experience this discrimination by landlords. In short, landlords perceive the prejudice of their White customers and respond to it.

The National Committee Against Discrimination in Housing uncovered numerous examples of attempts by landlords to exclude Blacks. The study indicates that landlords use a variety of tactics: (1) telling Blacks that an apartment is already rented when it is not, (2) refusing to accept deposits from Blacks; (3) sending Blacks to a distant manager's office or refusing to accept their applications, and (4) carrying out more rigorous credit checks on Blacks.

Racial discrimination in housing occurs independent of income. The U.S. Department of Housing and Urban Development reports that there is a higher rate of rejection of minority applications by mortgage lending institutions than among non-minority applicants regardless of income level. The higher rejection rate occurred even when the number of years applicants were in their present position was controlled, when level of debt was controlled and when the applicant's total asset was controlled. Rejection of minority applicants who earned from $15,000 to $25,000 was 50 percent higher than for non-minority applicants earning the same amount; some 25 percent of minorities with assets of $25,000 to $30,000 were denied loans, as compared with only 12 percent of non-minorities with similar assets. The discriminatory practices of mortgage companies and other lending institutions have restricted the homeownership opportunities of middle-income minorities; such practices often subject minorities to higher housing costs and inferior housing and deny them a basic form of saving investment and accumulation of wealth through homeownership. . . .

. . . [E]very routine act, every bit of ritual in the sale or rental of a dwelling unit can be performed in a way calculated to make it either difficult or impossible to consummate a deal. Blacks are more likely to face limitations on credit, or to be unable to secure mortgages if they seek housing outside "Black" areas. The net effect of these practices is the creation of two separate housing submarkets at all rent and price levels: a highly restricted market for racial minorities, and an open, free-choice market for the White majority.

Residential segregation and housing discrimination continue to increase even in growth areas. Metropolitan centers in the South are more racially segregated than a decade ago. The opening up of opportunities to minorities in the "Sun Belt" cities has not dramatically reduced the segregation levels.

Houston is a case in point. . . . Houston is one of the fastest growing cities in the United States. . . . While the overall housing picture in Houston is booming, a sizable segment of the area['s] population continues to be ill-housed. Houston's Community Development Office has estimated that 22 percent, or 94,129 households, of all the city's households are inadequately housed; over 42 percent, or 78,247 households, of all the renter households are inadequately housed; and 8 percent, or 15,882 households, of all owner households in Houston are ill-housed.

New housing subdivisions are pushed farther from the downtown area; single-family homes in the inner-city are selling at premium prices. Previously owned homes in Houston average around $67,000 and the average price tag on new homes is $62,500. These costs have priced many lower and middle-income households out of the market.

Housing in inner-city minority areas is not reflective of the city's "booming" market. The historical patterns of segregation continue to operate in the housing search and selection process. Blacks are segregated from both Whites and Mexican-Americans. One indicator of the pattern of racial segregation is the composition of the public schools. In 1970, the Houston Independent School District had a racial and ethnic composition of 50 percent White students, 33 percent Blacks and 17 percent Hispanic students. By 1978, the Black students enrollment had climbed to 45 percent of the public school enrollment, Hispanics included 24.8 percent, and White pupil enrollment had fallen to 30.8 percent of the total enrollment. If increases continue at the current rate, Hispanics and Blacks will comprise 8 of every 10 Houston public school pupil[s].

. . . [D]ata for this paper were obtained from the Fair Housing Division of . . . Houston. The city has a population of nearly 1.6 million residents. The ethnic composition of the study city includes 26 percent Black, 14 percent Hispanic and 60 percent White; 40 percent of the city's population can be classified as an ethnic minority.

The City's Fair Housing Division became operational in July, 1975. From this date to June 30, 1978, a total of 900 housing discrimination complaints had been filed with the city agency. A proportionate stratified sample was drawn from the 900 case files yielding a total of 100 cases from this analysis. . . .

A demographic profile of the complaint sample revealed that 57 percent of the complainants were females and 43 percent were males. The ethnic composition of the sample included 57 percent who were Black, 23 percent were White, 16 percent were Hispanic and 4 percent were Asian-Americans. Over 55 percent of the complainants had attended college; and the median age for the complainants was 29. . . .

Housing discrimination complaint activity did differ among the Council Districts [the five designated areas of Houston that are represented by an elected city council member]. District C, the Southwestern Section of the city, consistently registered the largest number of complaints for each year (with the exception of 1976). District C . . . registered 29 percent of the housing discrimination complaints. However, District C had nearly two-fifths of the complaints for the years 1975, 1977 and 1978. Likewise, a substantial number of complaints were in District A (Northwest): twenty-two percent of the discrimination complaints came from the Northwestern section of the city. The Southern section of the city had the third largest number of housing discrimination complaints (19 percent of the complaints came from District D).

These data suggest that housing discrimination complaint activity occurs most frequently in the Western and Southern sections of the city (e.g., Southwest, Northwest and South). These areas have undergone a tremendous growth in housing units, particularly multi-family units. It appears that complaint activity is following the pattern of growth in the city. The Southwestern section of the city has experienced the most rapid growth of any section of the city; this section has also registered the largest number of housing discrimination complaints. Such a pattern of complaints seems to suggest that a portion of the local population may be excluded from the growth and "new prosperity" that the area is undergoing.

Two major complaint areas were indicated among the sample of complainants: First, one-third of the complaints filed were based on alleged "discrimination in terms, conditions, or privileges of sale or rental of a dwelling," and two-thirds of the complaints were based on alleged discrimination stemming from "refusal to sell, rent, or finance housing.". . .

Complaints differed somewhat between minority and White complainants. Specifically, nearly three-fourths of the minority complainants filed grievances based on "discrimination in terms and conditions," while one-half of the White complainants filed similar grievances. Overall, complaints for Whites are equally distributed between refusals and discrimination in terms and condition. On the other hand, minority complaints are heavily concentrated in the area of discrimination in terms and conditions.

Many apartment managers and landlords have altered their leasing practices which in the past may have excluded minorities. Renter complaints and dissatisfaction with the terms and conditions of housing usually come after the family is in the unit. That is, complainants expressed a feeling of being "harassed" and receiving inferior maintenance and service within the apartment complex.

The largest number of complaints filed with the local Fair Housing Division were complaints based on race/color; nearly two-thirds of the housing complaints were filed because of alleged racial discrimination.

Sex discrimination was the second most frequent type of complaint with over one-fifth of the complaints; discrimination based on national origin comprised approximately one of every ten complaints filed.

. . . [A] significant relationship exists between type of discrimination complaint and the percent [of] minority in the area of the complaint, or complaint tract. Over 45 percent of the complaints based on race or color were located in census tracts that had less than 10 percent minority residents; over two-thirds of the complaints stemming from national origin were located in census tracts that had less than 10 percent minority residents; and only one of every five sex discrimination complaints were found in tracts that had less than 10 percent minority population. However, over two fifths of the sex discrimination complaints were filed in census tracts that had from 10 to 40 percent minority residents. An additional 38 percent of the complaints based on sex discrimination were located in census tracts that had over 40 percent minority residents. In the United States, minority females are often the victim of the "double whammy": discrimination based on both sex and race. This pattern probably accounts for the relatively high percentage of sex discrimination complaints in White and minority neighborhoods.

Of the housing discrimination complaints analyzed, over 41 percent were located in census tracts that had less than 10 percent minority population; 40 percent of the complaints were located in census tracts with 10 to 40 percent minority; and 19 percent of the complaints came from census tracts with over 40 percent minority residents. While minorities make up 40 percent of the city's population, a sizable portion of the complaints occurred in predominantly white areas. The overall pattern of housing discrimination complaints appears to decrease as the percentage of minority group members increase[s] in the area.

An increasing number of families are finding themselves priced out of single-family housing. Those families who cannot afford to buy detached homes are forced into the rental market. However, apartment construction and developments are not uniformly distributed throughout the urban complex. In the case of Houston, the Southwestern sector of the city contains the largest concentration of multi-family dwelling units; nearly 58 percent of the city's multi-family units (many of which are new developments) are located in the Southwestern sector.

In locating the housing discrimination complaints according to growth of the complaint tract, . . . 50 percent of the complaints were in tracts that had undergone at least a 30 percent growth rate; 41 percent of the complaints were found in tracts that had undergone no growth to a 29 percent increase between 1970 and 1975; and 9 percent of the complaints were found in census tracts that had actually had a net loss in the number of multi-family dwelling units. These data seem to provide some support for the idea that complaint activity is more frequent in high growth areas of the city and neighborhoods which have not had a history of racially integrated housing.

As many new apartment complexes are built away from the central city, this further complicates the housing problem for minority households; few new housing developments are constructed in the central-city or minority areas. Minority households may either lease housing in the central city or venture outside their neighborhoods for housing. However, Blacks and other minority families often find insensitive and bigoted apartment managers and tenants; it does not take very long for one to "sense" when he or she is not welcome or that there is a "hidden" policy of not renting to minority families.

Segregation in housing continues to be a major problem facing the nation's cities. . . . Houston, the "Boom Town" of the sunbelt, is no exception to the rule. Blacks are segregated from both Whites and Mexican-Americans. The pattern of housing discrimination complaint activity has come largely from the renter segment of the population. . . . As few new developments are built in the inner city, many minority households search for housing in areas outside traditional minority neighborhoods. Complaints are concentrated in neighborhoods or areas that have not had a history of racially integrated housing.

Housing discrimination complaint activity is the greatest in areas of low minority concentration. This was the case for discrimination complaints based on race or color and national origin. However, a sizable proportion of the complainants who lodged grievances based on sex discrimination were also found in areas heavily populated by minorities. . . . Landlords and apartment managers continue to look with suspicion upon female-headed households and females who live alone. This appears to be the case in both White and non-White neighborhoods.

The local Fair Housing Division is responsible for implementing fair housing practices and assuring that individuals and families have equal access to the housing market. As many of the policies and practices employed by landlords, realtors, developers and lending institutions have evolved over several generations, the elimination of such practices will not be an easy one. Discrimination in housing has reached a level of sophistication that makes it easy to practice and difficult to "prove." It appears that fair housing agencies and departments will be in business for some time to come.

Jim Crow, Indian Style, 1980s

ORLAN J. SVINGEN

For many, the notion of race discrimination manifested so blatantly as to deny a group of American citizens the right to vote in the 1980s is nothing short of astonishing—unless those citizens are Native Americans living in western states. Such Indians have felt racism's effects in a variety of ways throughout their lives. They know all too well the animus that imbues discriminatory behavior, even if they do not always understand the reasons for that animosity. Part of the explanation for recent attempts to disfranchise the Crows and Northern Cheyennes has to do with population distribution and geography; the rest is a question of sociology and historical ignorance.

American Indians constitute the most numerous minority group in several western states bordering Canada. Sociologists have long recognized that overt racism is most likely to exist in areas where members of the majority culture feel threatened by the presence of a sizable minority. In the Montana counties featured in this reading by Orlan J. Svingen, Indians make up nearly half the total population, while the number of other racial minorities is quite small. I (Terry Wilson) lived for a time during the 1970s in one of these counties and was surprised at the frequency of casual racial epithets directed toward Indians—and the virtual absence of observable racism toward African Americans, Asian Americans, and Chicanos. We know little about this pattern of discrimination because it occurs mostly in remote rural communities and involves the nation's smallest minority, whose image is romantically positive elsewhere and whose existence falls outside the dichotomized history of race relations between blacks and whites.

At the root of the problem is a gross misunderstanding of Indian history. Many westerners believe that Indian tribes live on reservations *given* them by the United States, when in fact these were awarded as compensation for larger land cessions. Many Americans also falsely assume that treaty rights such as relief from certain kinds of taxation and fishing rights are a form of welfare and represent "reverse discrimination."

STUDY QUESTIONS

1. How did non-Indians who had power attempt to deny Indians their right of suffrage?

2. Why do you suppose there has been so little publicity outside Montana about the voting-rights controversy?

3. To what extent did activist Indians borrow the tactics and goals of the black civil-rights movement to battle against racism?

In June of 1986, Judge Edward Rafeedie ruled that "official acts of discrimination . . . have interfered with the rights of Indian citizens [of Big Horn County, Montana] to register and vote." Civil rights expert and ACLU [American Civil Liberties Union] attorney Laughlin McDonald later observed in the *San Francisco Examiner* that racism against Indian people in Montana was even worse than he had expected. "I thought I'd stepped into the last century," McDonald explained. "Whites were doing to Indians what people in the South stopped doing to blacks twenty years ago." Big Horn County Commissioner and area rancher Ed Miller "longs for the good old days" when Indians remained on the reservation. Angered by Rafeedie's ruling, Miller threatened to appeal the decision to the Supreme Court. "The Voting Rights Act is a bad thing," Miller complained. "I don't see no comparison with Negroes in the South." Before Janine Windy Boy and other plaintiffs filed suit against Big Horn County, "things were fine around here," Miller lamented. "Now they (Indians) want to vote," he exclaimed. "What next?"

On June 13, 1986, United States District Judge Edward Rafeedie ordered that "at-large elections in Big Horn County violate Section 2 of the Voting Rights Act. . . ." and "that a new system of election must be adopted." Judge Rafeedie's decision culminated a three-year process begun in Big Horn County by Crow and Northern Cheyenne voters who refused any longer to accept second class voting rights.

The case began its way into court in August of 1983, when Jeff Renz and Laughlin McDonald, ACLU attorneys for the plaintiffs, submitted a "Motion for Preliminary Injunction" preventing the defendants, Big Horn County, from holding a general election on November 6, 1983. The motion called for a hearing before Federal Judge James Battin in Billings, Montana. The motion and subsequent suit against Big Horn County charged that the at-large system in county commissioner and school board elections in Big Horn County diluted the Indian vote so as to disenfranchise American Indian voters.

The plaintiffs in *Windy Boy* v. *Big Horn County* argued that the at-large scheme denied the plaintiffs' rights to participate in elections and to elect representatives of their choice to county and school board offices. In Big Horn County, where non-Indians constitute fifty-two per cent of the population and American Indians form forty-six per cent, at-large elections violated the Fourteenth and Fifteenth Amendments and Section 2 of the 1965 Voting Rights Act. They asked the court to bar further at-large elections until new districts could be apportioned for the Board of Commissioners and School Districts 17H and I.

From Orlan J. Svingen, "Jim Crow, Indian Style," *American Indian Quarterly* 11 (1987), pp. 275–285. Reprinted by permission of American Indian Quarterly.

The case turned on the 1982 amendment of Section 2 of the 1965 Voting Rights Act. Amended Section 2 declares unlawful any election procedure or voting law which "results" in discrimination because of race, color, or membership in a language minority. In an earlier decision, the Supreme Court had held that Section 2 violations required proof of purposeful discrimination. Recognizing that intentional discrimination is difficult to prove, Congress amended Section 2 stating that no voting procedure can be imposed by a "State or political subdivision in a manner which results in a denial or abridgment of the right of any citizen . . . to vote."

Centuries of conflict dominate Indian-white relations and created the setting wherein late 19th and 20th century civil rights violations began. By the time Congress passed the Indian Citizenship Act in 1924, a sophisticated structure of anti-Indian policies were clearly already in place. Just as passage of the 15th Amendment precipitated countless barriers for the freedmen, the Indian Citizenship Act also failed to elevate American Indian civil rights on an equal footing with non-Indians.

Until 1924, the various states ignored Native Americans and passed numerous unchallenged laws eliminating Indian people from the political process. In 1924, however, non-Indians harboring anti-Indian attitudes now confronted Indian people armed with the protection of the 14th and 15th Amendments.

In addition to federal Indian policies of dispossession, wardship, and concentration, specific territorial and state laws affected Indian people. In 1871, Montana Territory denied voting rights to persons under "guardianship" and outlawed voting precincts at Indian agencies, trading posts in Indian Country, or "on any Indian reservation whatever. In 1884, *Elk* v. *Wilkins* held that Indians were not made citizens under the 14th Amendment because they were not persons born subject to United States jurisdiction. As such, Montana was not obliged to allow Indians to register to vote in state and county elections. The Montana Enabling Act of 1889 opened voting rights to all male citizens without regard to race or color, with the exception of Indians not taxed. At the turn of the century, two more Montana laws restricted voting rights to taxpayers only and to resident freeholders listed on city or county tax rolls. Although certain American Indians could become citizens under the Dawes and Burke Acts of 1887 and 1906, Montana systematically denied voting rights to Indian people. The State denied residency to Indian citizens living on reservations and excluded those from voting who maintained relations with a tribe. In 1911, the State Legislative Assembly declared that anyone living on an Indian or military reservation who had not previously acquired residency in a Montana county before moving to a reservation would not be regarded as a Montana resident. . . .

In 1924, Congress extended citizenship to all Indians born in the United States. Application of the 14th Amendment meant, moreover, that they were citizens of the United States "and of the State wherein they resided." Having all the basic political hardware, Congressmen could say, just as was said after Reconstruction, Indians have all the "tools" for political equality; now they are on their own. But historians recognize that Black Americans did not achieve equality with Southern whites after Reconstruction. What followed emancipation and the Reconstruction Amendments was the white response to the abolition of slavery—segregation. In addition to facing a closed society, Black Americans confronted an alien electoral system. Many lacked an understanding of political issues. Large numbers were illiterate or semi-illiterate; and . . . some even sought relief in withdrawal from associations with the white race.

Was the 1924 Indian Citizenship Act an Indian emancipation proclamation? After that legislation had formally ended the "wardship" status for Indian people, did non-Indians respond by creating a de facto form of segregation in its place? The reservation system certainly lent itself to separating Indian people from non-Indians. Instead of fearing the Africanization of Southern society, did Big Horn County and other Indian counties in the North fear an "Indianization" of the political process? . . . Although Indian people had won legal and political rights, a pattern of separation had become firmly entrenched in the minds of non-Indians—a mind-set fostered by years of acceptance of the ideology of white racial superiority.

Shortly after the passage of the Citizenship Act, the *Hardin Tribune* focused on newly-won Indian voting rights. News accounts and editorials drew front-page attention to Indian voting potential, and pondered its impact on upcoming elections. Robert Yellowtail attracted a great deal of news coverage when he ran for state office in the fall of 1924. The *Tribune* estimated 5,000, then 9,000, Montana Indians would vote in the 1924 elections, and it closely monitored the number of Indian people who registered in Big Horn County. Clearly, Big Horn County's non-Indian population dreaded the possibility of an Indian being voted into county or state office.

Three years later, state machinery hobbled Indian voting potential when the Montana Legislative assembly passed a law in 1927 dividing Montana counties into three-Commissioner districts. The law established at-large elections for county commissioners who were elected to six-year terms, on a two-year staggered basis. In order to be elected, each candidate had to win a county-wide election. On the surface, and in counties with a homogeneous population, at-large elections appeared to make county-elected officials more responsive to the wider needs of a county. It can be argued, moreover, that at-large elections were Progressive responses to the call for greater democracy in the United States. To ethnic minorities, however, Indian people included, at-large elections erased their chances for minority representation because it required a majority vote on a county-wide election. As of October, 1986, no American Indian had been elected to the Board of County Commissioners in Big Horn County. . . .

The legislative history of Senate Bill 17 establishing at-large elections reveals no overt anti-Indian bias, but its sponsorship by three senators, two of whom were from Indian counties, suggests more than coincidental ties. Senator Christian F. Gilboe from Valier, Montana, represented Pondera County, which included a portion of the Blackfeet Indian Reservation. Senator Seymour H. Porter, another sponsor of the bill, from Big Sandy, represented Choteau County, which embraced the Rocky Boy Indian Reservation. The motives behind Senate Bill 17 may remain debatable, but the results of the at-large election scheme promoted by Senators Gilboe and Porter are eminently clear to Indian people in Big Horn County.

Ten years later, more state actions crippled Indian voting in Montana. In 1937, the state mandated that all deputy voter registrars must be qualified taxpaying residents of their respective precincts. Because American Indians were exempt from certain local taxes, the state's action excluded Indian people from serving as voter registrars, thereby undermining Indian voter registration on the reservation. In the same year, Montana cancelled all voter registration and required the re-registration of all voters. Indian registration had risen steadily, but after the 1937 cancellation process, Indian voting numbers remained depressed, not returning to the pre-1937 levels until the 1980s.

Political exhortations are combined with portraits of past Indian leaders to decorate a reservation dwelling

The events of 1924 did not inaugurate an enlightened period of goodwill between Indian and non-Indian voters. Between 1924 and 1934, Indian candidates ran for state and county offices, but none won. The at-large election scheme and subsequent state actions had effectively disenfranchised American Indians in Big Horn County.

After 1937, it was clear that non-Indians had not welcomed Indian people into the political fold of state and county politics in Big Horn County. Despite the 1924 citizenship legislation, attitudes about Indians and about their political participation had changed very little. Comparing Indians elected to office before and after 1924, absolutely nothing had changed. Indian voters did not even enjoy the personal satisfaction of being sought out on a coalition basis by non-Indian candidates. Through racially polarized voting, Indian candidates were systematically defeated by non-Indian voters who elected non-Indian candidates. To Indian people in Big Horn County, voting rights conferred by citizenship were meaningless.

Comparing Indian voting rights problems with the Black historical model offers dramatic parallels with Jim Crowism and segregation. Both groups confronted the separation of races, and second-class treatment. The Black experience is useful because it dramatizes the seriousness and the pervasiveness of Indian discrimination. Throughout Southern society Black Americans had interacted with whites, but on rural reservations Indian people confronted fewer non-Indians. The relative isolation of the reservation and its inhabitants allowed racial tensions and discrimination to go unnoticed within American society.

The Black experience also draws needed attention to Indian voting issues because it invites society to conclude that Indian people have suffered indignities no longer tolerated by the courts or Black Americans. Nonetheless, the Black model has a narrow application to the American Indian experience because Blacks and American Indians represent different culture patterns. Many distinct factors affect Indian voting patterns in ways peculiar to Indian people. For example, illiteracy and semi-illiteracy rates among Indian people make it difficult to participate in elections based on the English language. Dale Old Horn, Department Head of Crow Studies at Little Big Horn College, explains that Crow is the primary language of his people. Political and social events at Crow, moreover, are conducted in Crow and English to guarantee the widest understanding. So when it comes to voting, rather than seek assistance from non-Indians in getting ballots interpreted, some Indian people simply avoid the polls.

Old Horn and Mark Small, a Northern Cheyenne rancher in Big Horn and Rosebud County, identified BIA [Bureau of Indian Affairs] paternalism as another peculiar Indian problem. State laws that all but denied the constitutionality of the 1924 Citizenship Act left Indian people traditionally dependent on the federal government and its agent, the BIA. The Bureau, Small noted, created a "false sense of security" among Indians and persuaded many to believe it would take care of their concerns. This action, in effect, promoted dependence, helplessness, and statewide voting inactivity among American Indians. By ignoring the question of Indian civil rights, Old Horn and Small agreed that the Bureau had retarded the development of full citizenship for Indian people. The question needs to be asked: "If the government is guilty of fostering federal paternalism among Indian tribes and thereby promoting state voting inactivity, is the federal government guilty of violating its trust responsibilities in the area of Indian civil rights?"

Another cultural expression affecting the voting rights question is the matter of tribal sovereignty. Some Indian people avoid confronting state and county voting rights issues because involvement with the state might be seen as inviting state jurisdiction over tribal politics. Demanding equal rights in Montana county and state elections might touch off a new round of termination discussions. Non-Indians promote these fears, Small explained, by challenging Indian people with the question: "We don't vote in your tribal elections, so why are you trying to vote in ours?"

Another far-reaching issue involving voting rights is the avoidance of bigotry and racism. Janine Windy Boy, the lead plaintiff in the Big Horn County suit and President of Little Big Horn College in Crow Agency, explains that it is a foregone conclusion: "You just don't go where you aren't wanted." Being branded a "pagan, heathen, savage, or a blanket-assed Indian" is reason enough, Old Horn observed, for some Indian people to avoid the election process. Gail Small, an attorney in Lame Deer and an enrolled member of the Northern Cheyenne, explains that Indian people have been "put down" by non-Indians so frequently that some actually internalize the criticism. "After you are told you are incompetent long enough," Small said, "some (Indian people) start believing it." These attitudes, which have historically opposed Indian political participation, have created a deep sense of alienation among Indian people towards state government.

What, then, accounts for the political wasteland for Indian people in Big Horn County extending up to the 1980s? I have argued that the historic relationship between Indians and non-Indians in the pre- and post-1924 period created a setting which was hostile to Indian participation in federal, state, and county elections. The post-1924 years inherited the wardship concept and perpetuated a system, which, whether by design or not, excluded Indian people from participation. Despite being struck down by laws, the historic barriers and stereotypes against Indian voting rights among non-Indians promote the attitude that it is inappropriate for Indian people to vote in state and county elections.

Voting rights cases involving American Indians are not new. Ample case law beginning in the mid-1970s demonstrates that Indian people meeting age and residency requirements cannot be denied voting rights. Exemptions from certain taxes no longer limit their right to vote, and election districts must be apportioned under the "one person, one vote" principle. The 1975 amendment to the Voting Rights Act requires voter registration facilities in Indian communities, and it affords special language arrangements for language minorities. Fred Ragsdale, Jr., an Indian law specialist at the University of New Mexico Law School, explains that Indian voting rights are not matters of Indian law. Ample case law precedents make this a simple citizenship question under federal law. Referring to previous voting rights cases, Ragsdale believes that "the easy ones are over with," and henceforth decisions will turn on the quality of factual questions, proof, and statistics.

If case law supporting Indian voting rights is so clearly defined by the courts, what accounts for violations of the Voting Rights Act in Big Horn County? The clearest answer is the at-large election scheme, described by Jeff Renz, co-counsel for the plaintiffs, as a form of reverse-gerrymandering in Indian counties. One might expect that Indians who comprise 46.2 percent of the Big Horn County population would have elected at least one Indian to county or state office sometime in the past sixty-two years. In response to this disturbing statistic and to the case in general, the defendants who are non-Indian officials of Big Horn County offer curious responses: (1) past problems cannot be blamed on us today, (2) nothing in Big Horn County hinders Indian voting rights, and (3) no official discrimination against Indians exists in Big Horn County.

The cumulative impact of 19th and 20th century federal Indian policies, state legislation, and racial tensions has created a cultural setting intolerant of American Indian voting rights. What else accounts for the defendant's responses to the plaintiff's charges? The skeptic, however, may argue away each separate example cited, dismissing them as the results of pre-1924 citizenship laws, pre-1965 voting procedures, or unenlightened racial attitudes. But when considered within a historic chronology—the way Indian people consider them—their impact is staggering.

Let us next turn, then, to some of the current and specific problems Crow and Northern Cheyenne people confront in Big Horn County. In terms of county employment, for example, out of 249 employees, the highest number of Indians employed by Big Horn County totaled six in 1985—or 2.4% of the County work force. Of the 100 members on twenty county citizen boards, only two Indians have ever been appointed. Membership on these boards is significant because they promote programs and provide valuable experience and county-wide name recognition for their members. Despite offers from tribal police to serve subpoenas against Indian jurors, only three Indians served on Coroner's Juries in Big Horn County between 1966 and 1983.

During the 1970s and 1980s, Indian people in Big Horn County became more vote-conscious, and a voter registration drive produced as many as 2,000 Indian registrants. At first, county officials cooperated, but as the numbers grew officials began rejecting registration cards containing minor mistakes previously overlooked. This was followed by a refusal to provide

Indian people with additional blank forms with the excuse that new ones were being printed—even through information on old and new forms was identical. Another excuse from the Clerk and Recorder's Office was that the Office had already given out large numbers of registration cards to Indians and that no more would be forthcoming until those already given out were returned.

Then in 1982, four Indian and pro-Indian candidates entered the Democratic primary election, and defeated their non-Indian opponents. The outcome shocked non-Indians in Big Horn County and prompted immediate anti-Indian sentiment. . . . [N]on-Indian Democrats charged the organizers of the voter registration drive with fraud and accused them of stealing the election. The chairman of the County Democratic party admitted that "we sort of got caught with our pants down." Disgruntled non-Indian Democrats left the party and formed the Bipartisan Campaign Committee whose sole purpose was to challenge Indian candidates from outside the Democratic party. . . .

In 1984, Gail Small, a Lame Deer attorney and a graduate of the University of Oregon Law School, ran for state representative in House District 100. . . . [W]hile campaigning east of Tongue River on Otter Creek, she knocked on the door of an area rancher and introduced herself as a candidate for state representative. . . . The rancher responded by pointing off in the distance where the ruins lay of a blockhouse fortress used in the so-called "Cheyenne Outbreak" of 1897. "It was just yesterday that we were fighting you off," he replied to Small, "and now you want me to vote for you?". . .

In both 1982 and 1984 elections, many Indian people who had registered to vote came to the polls only to learn that their names were not on the list of registered voters. Despite showing proof of registration, election judges refused to allow them to vote. Others who had voted in primary elections found their names removed from the general election registration list. . . .

Windy Boy v. *Big Horn County* offers historians a wide range of ponderables. Despite full citizenship and recent favorable decisions, Indian people still confront official discrimination against their most fundamental civil rights—social and cultural aspects aside. Clearly, the attitudes of their non-Indian counterparts have not kept pace with gains Indian people have made in the courts in recent years. Non-Indians rely on pat responses such as "Indians should look to the federal government for help," or "Indians don't pay taxes, so why should they vote in white elections?" While these attitudes persist, counties with large Indian populations will continue to oppose, challenge, and hamstring the voting rights of Indian people.

By amending Section 2 of the Voting Rights Act to consider the "results" of voting procedures rather than requiring proof of intentional discrimination, Congress has said "Let's not quibble over how intentionally or unintentionally voting rights are being denied." If election practices "result" in discrimination, a violation of federal law has occurred. This sounds simple and straightforward, but it becomes complicated when applied to the reservation setting, when compared with historic Indian policies, and when considered within the context of Indian-white counties controlled by non-Indians.

It is time for historians to survey 19th and 20th century American Indian issues with a broader perspective. Rather than applying a litmus paper test to isolated laws frozen in time and concluding that they were equally demanding to all citizens, let's ask ourselves what is the cumulative, long-term impact of these policies and laws on a culturally distinct language minority.

In the aftermath of Judge Rafeedie's decision, civil rights prospects for Crow and Northern Cheyenne people are, at best, mixed. On the positive side, abandonment of at-large districting enabled Indian people of District 2 to elect John Doyle, Jr., as Big Horn County's first Indian County Commissioner. Doyle's election reverses decades of discriminatory voting practices and illustrates the strength of Indian voting power freed from vote dilution.

On the negative side, however, anti-Indian sentiment seems as strong and defiant as ever. In the spirit of former County Commissioner Ed Miller who complained that the Voting Rights Act was "a bad thing," the defendants filed a motion of appeal in August of 1986. Subsequent to that, the *Hardin Herald* reported that an anti-Indian jurisdiction group known as Montanans Opposed to Discrimination (MOD) had become interested in the case. Composed primarily of white ranchers, MOD backed a local Secret Concerned Citizens Committee [SCCC] whose objective was to seek the basis for criminal prosecution of two of the plaintiffs in *Windy Boy*, Janine Windy Boy and James Ruegamer, and also Clarence Belue, a former "pro-Indian" County Attorney in Big Horn County. Using a $5,000 donation from MOD, SCCC sought to uncover evidence of wrong-doing for prosecuting all three. These actions, however, came to center on Windy Boy and Belue. Charges against Belue resulted in his review before the Montana State Bar Association.

Also in the wake of the decision and prior to the November 1986 election, Janine Windy Boy received a telephone call from an agent of the Federal Bureau of Investigation in Billings, Montana, asking to meet with her. The FBI explained it was investigating complaints lodged against her with the U.S. Attorney's Office. The complaint alleged that Windy Boy, President of Little Big Horn Community College at Crow Agency, had misused her office by allowing Democratic candidates and tribal officials to use community college facilities rent-free. The FBI concluded its inquiry after Windy Boy met with agents in Billings and delivered documentation disproving the allegations.

Clearly, a political setting in Big Horn County free of distrust, suspicion, and racism remains a long way off. Historic political inequality, oppression, and Indian-hating requires more than one election to usher in a period of racial harmony. One court decision such as *Windy Boy* means nothing more than non-Indians in Big Horn County can no longer "officially" ignore the

county's Indian population. Rafeedie's decision may weaken racist foundations in the county, but the old patterns of distrust, suspicion, and harassment will continue until Indian people are no longer viewed and treated as
political refugees in a white man's world.

FURTHER READING

Cletus E. Daniel, *Chicano Workers and the Politics of Fairness: The FEPC in the Southwest, 1941–1945* (Austin: University of Texas Press, 1991).

Roger Daniels, *The Politics of Prejudice: The Anti-Japanese Movement in California and the Struggle for Exclusion* (Berkeley and Los Angeles: University of California Press, 1962, 1977).

Arnoldo De Leon, *They Called Them Greasers: Anglo Attitudes Toward Mexicans in Texas, 1821–1900* (Austin: University of Texas Press, 1983).

Richard Drinnon, *Keeper of Concentration Camps: Dillon S. Myer and American Racism* (Berkeley and Los Angeles: University of California Press, 1987).

Robert F. Heizer and Alan J. Almquist, *The Other Californians: Prejudice and Discrimination Under Spain, Mexico, and the United States to 1920* (Berkeley and Los Angeles: University of California Press, 1971).

Abraham Hoffman, *Unwanted Mexican Americans in the Great Depression: Repatriation Pressures, 1929–1939* (Tucson: University of Arizona Press, 1979).

Yuji Ichioka, *The Issei: The World of the First Generation Japanese Immigrants, 1885–1924* (New York: Free Press, 1988).

Joan Jensen, *Passage from India: Asian Indian Immigrants in North America* (New Haven: Yale University Press, 1988).

Mauricio Mazón, *The Zoot-Suit Riots: The Psychology of Symbolic Annihilation* (Austin: University of Texas Press, 1984).

Jim Messerschmidt, *The Trial of Leonard Peltier* (Boston: South End Press, 1983).

Alfredo Mirande, *Gringo Justice* (Notre Dame: University of Notre Dame Press, 1987).

Gary Y. Okihiro, *Cane Fires: The Anti-Japanese Movement in Hawaii, 1865–1945* (Philadelphia: Temple University Press, 1991).

Glenn A. Phelps, "Representation Without Taxation: Citizenship and Suffrage in Indian Country," *American Indian Quarterly* 9 (1985): 135–148.

James J. Rawls, *Indians of California: The Changing Times* (Norman: University of Oklahoma Press, 1984).

Elmer R. Rusco, *"Good Time Coming?": Black Nevadans in the Nineteenth Century* (Westport, Conn.: Greenwood Press, 1975).

Elmer Clarence Sandmeyer, *The Anti-Asian Movement in California* (Urbana: University of Illinois Press, 1939, 1979).

J. M. Saniel, ed., *The Filipino Exclusion Movement, 1927–1935* (Quezon City, Philippines: Institute of Asian Studies, University of the Philippines, 1967).

Alexander Saxton, *The Indispensable Enemy: Labor and the Anti-Chinese Movement in California* (Berkeley and Los Angeles: University of California Press, 1971).

Emory J. Tolbert, *The UNIA and Black Los Angeles: Ideology and Community in the American Garvey Movement* (Los Angeles: Afro-American Studies Center, University of California, Los Angeles, 1980).

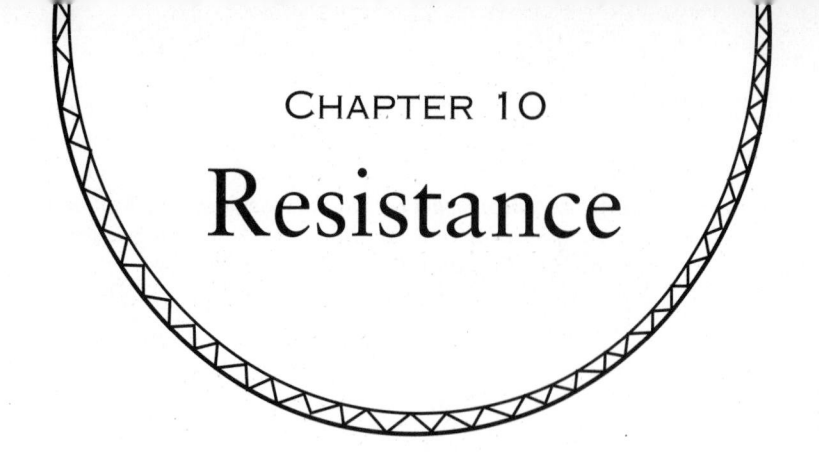

CHAPTER 10

Resistance

Subjugated and oppressed peoples of color, whether citizens or aliens, have not passively accepted the demeaning jobs, low wages, and second-class status as their lot. Rather, they have actively fought discrimination. This history of resistance is particularly significant for understanding their experiences as an integral part of western American history.

The four selections in this chapter show the wide range of forms that their resistance took. Sucheng Chan details the strikes and court battles of Asian immigrants and Asian Americans in Hawaii and California, refuting the stereotype of these people as mere sojourners ignorant of American institutions. Vicki Ruiz focuses on how Chicana cannery workers formed unions and used the boycott and strike to improve their working conditions in California, in the process highlighting the fact that women of color, as well as their male counterparts, struggled to improve their lives. Donald Fixico discusses how Native American leaders are fighting to ensure that their people benefit from the exploitation of natural energy resources on Indian reservations. Finally, Angela Davis, in the late 1960s a professor of philosophy at the University of California, Los Angeles, and now a professor of the history of consciousness at the University of California, Santa Cruz, recounts the activities and strategies of African-American leftists in Los Angeles during and following the police attack on the Black Panther party's headquarters in 1969. The four selections underline how hard peoples of color have struggled to achieve states as citizens equal under the law and offer glimpses of their resiliency and ingenuity.

FOR ANALYSIS AND DISCUSSION

1. Why was gaining the right of naturalization so important to Asian immigrants?

2. Compare and contrast the methods used by Asian- and Mexican-American workers to resist injustice.

3. How has the energy crisis affected Native American reservations?

4. Why must Native Americans ensure that the natural resources on their land not turn into a vehicle for the further exploitation of their people?

5. Do you think the Black Panther party was representative of Black activists in the 1960s? If so, why? If not, why not?

6. What conclusions can be drawn from the history of resistance by peoples of color?

Asian Americans: Resisting Oppression, 1860s–1920s

SUCHENG CHAN

One of the main complaints against Asian immigrants in years past was the idea that they were unassimilable. Opponents used Asians' alleged inability to become "real" Americans as an excuse to exclude them and to deny them participation in American political and social life. Although many Asian immigrants did retain firm ties to their homelands, it should be noted that even when these people wanted to become Americans, U.S. naturalization laws—which allowed only "free, white persons" and, after the Civil War, "persons of African ancestry" to be naturalized—prevented Asian immigrants from acquiring U.S. citizenship. A series of landmark decisions in the lower federal courts and the U.S. Supreme Court affirmed that fact. Not until the 1940s and 1950s was the right of naturalization granted to Asians.

Because they were excluded from citizenship, Asian immigrants could not vote and hence had no political power. Going on strike and filing lawsuits became their two main avenues for redressing grievances. Both are Western institutions with which few Asians were familiar before their arrival in the United States, but as strikers they nevertheless were tenacious, and as litigants persistent and sophisticated. Asian immigrants' very use of such methods challenges the stereotypical portrayal of them as a source of docile cheap labor and as unassimilable aliens.

Asian immigrants lost most of their strikes and court cases, but they did win a few notable victories. In this reading Sucheng Chan discusses some of the major strikes and law cases in which they and their descendants have been involved. The essay highlights the kinds of discrimination that concerned them the most and against which they fought the hardest.

STUDY QUESTIONS

1. Why did Asian immigrants use strikes and lawsuits as their two main forms of resistance?

2. To what extent did Asian immigrants and their descendants succeed in their fight for civil rights?

Stereotypes of Asian immigrants as plodding, degraded, and servile people—indeed, virtual slaves—notwithstanding, members of every Asian
immigrant group did stand up for their rights and fought oppression in myriad ways. Historians and sociologists of the Asian American experience have
often argued among themselves whether Asian immigrants have been discriminated against as a class, a race, or a nationality. Marxists claim that
Asian Americans have suffered because they were and are part of the proletariat; scholars and activists who consider racism as the most fundamental
issue employ race as a central category of analysis; while those with an international perspective emphasize the link between the national subjugation of
certain Asian countries and the maltreatment of their emigrants abroad.

To argue that class, or racial, or national subordination can subsume the
other two is too simplistic, for Asian immigrants have experienced all three
forms of inequality. Looking at the principal ways they have used to fight
against their lowly status—strikes, litigation, and involvement in efforts to
liberate their homelands—it is clear that the immigrants themselves realized
their suffering had multiple causes. As workers they struck for higher wages
and better working conditions; as nonwhite minorities "ineligible to citizenship" they challenged laws that denied them civil rights on account of their
race; and as proud sons and daughters of their countries of origin, they supported political movements to free those lands from foreign encroachment.

Asian immigrant workers began their struggle for equality quite early in
their history. . . . The largest strike undertaken by Chinese in the nineteenth
century occurred in June 1867 during the building of the transcontinental
railroad. At that time, Chinese workers, regardless of what tasks they performed, were paid $30 a month without board, compared to unskilled Euro-
American workers who received $30 a month with board. (Board was worth
75 cents to a dollar a day.) A few skilled ones among the latter even got as
much as $3 to $5 a day. Six days a week, the Chinese toiled from sunrise to
sundown, while subject to whipping by overseers and forbidden by the company to quit their jobs. Unhappy with their lot, 2,000 men digging tunnels in
the high Sierras went on strike, demanding $40 a month, 10 hours of work a
day for those laboring outdoors and eight hours for those inside the tunnels,
an end to corporal punishment, and the freedom to leave whenever they
desired. Their strike lasted a week—until their food ran out. The railroad
company simply stopped bringing them rations, thus starving them back to
work. The company also took the precaution of asking employment agencies
to stand ready to supply it with black workers should the Chinese strike
again. . . .

Japanese immigrant workers also have a long history of militance. . . . Seven thousand Japanese workers struck the major plantations on Oahu for four long months in 1909. . . . Despite efforts by the Japanese consul general and the well-known Protestant minister Okumura Takie to stop the strike, it quickly spread from one plantation to the next on Oahu during the latter part of May. Workers on the other islands continued working, in order to send contributions to Honolulu to support the strikers. Important associations in the Japanese community such as the Carpenters' Association, the Public Bath Operators Association, the Japanese Hotel and Inn Association, the Honolulu Retail Merchants Association, and the Barbers Association also backed the strikers. Even Chinese merchants provided food on credit. But some Japanese newspapers and other urban groups bitterly opposed the militant action.

Because the Japanese community was divided, the HSPA [Hawaiian Sugar Planters' Association] was able to use the tactic of divide and conquer to defeat the strike. . . . The plantations kept production going by hiring scabs. . . . The strike fizzled out in August when the participants ran out of all resources to keep themselves going. Three months after it was over, the planters agreed to end the practice of paying workers of different national backgrounds unequal wages, but they never fully carried out their promise. . . .

Japanese and Filipino workers . . . started organizing [again] in 1919. The Japanese formed a Federation of Japanese Labor in Hawaii to coordinate the efforts of Japanese labor organizations on the different islands. The association worked out a long list of demands, including a daily wage of $1.25, a revised bonus system that would allow men working only 15 days and women 10 days a month to qualify, 8-hour workdays, double pay for overtime, and 8 weeks of paid maternity leave for women. Filipinos, meanwhile, formed a Higher Wages Association under the leadership of Pablo Manlapit, who had founded the Filipino Federation of Labor in 1911 and the Filipino Unemployed Association in 1913.

Although the Japanese and Filipinos had agreed initially to act jointly, Manlapit unilaterally decided to begin the strike on 19 January 1920, even though the Japanese were still trying to negotiate with the HSPA in the hope of forestalling a strike. Furthermore, the Japanese thought it would be best to strike in the late spring or early summer at the height of the harvest in order to cripple the sugar industry. They also wanted to give themselves more time to build up a war chest. So they pressured Manlapit to call off the action by the Filipinos. He agreed to do so on 17 January, but discovered that he had no means of communicating with the workers, 2,600 of whom, along with 300 Spaniards and Puerto Ricans, walked off the job as planned. Left with no choice, the Japanese joined them on 1 February, pushing the total number of strikers above the 8,000 mark. . . . The planters responded by evicting 12,000 people (more than 4,000 of them children) from plantation housing in mid-February. . . .

Several days after the eviction, the Reverend Albert W. Palmer of the Central Union Church stepped in to mediate. He proposed that the unions disband themselves and that interracial labor-management committees be set up on each plantation to deal with all issues related to wages, work conditions, and living conditions. Many community leaders in Honolulu—Japanese as well as Euro-Americans—supported the Palmer plan. After heated debate, the Japanese strike leaders also decided to accept it if the HSPA would likewise do so, but the latter said it would not deal with the Federation of Japanese Labor. Thus the stalemate continued. . . .

After the failed attempt at mediation, some 3,000 Japanese and Filipino strikers and their families staged the huge 77 Cents Parade—77 cents being their average daily base wage—to counter the charges of anti-Americanism and radicalism. They marched through the streets of Honolulu carrying American flags and pictures of Abraham Lincoln. Their signs contained slogans such as "We Are Not Reds, God Forbid, But Are Brown Workers Who Produce White Sugar," "We Want to Live Like Americans," and "How Can We Live Like Americans on 77 Cents?"

The HSPA held firm, despite its estimated $12 million loss. The real issue for the planters was not wages but collective bargaining, to which they absolutely refused to accede. By the beginning of July, the weary and starving strikers decided to end the six month-long strike, but not all of them returned to work. The Japanese plantation work force in Oahu fell by over 2,000, and though the number of Filipinos increased, a large percentage of them were in fact new recruits from the Philippines. . . . By the middle of the mid-1920s, relatively few Japanese remained in the plantations of Hawaii or in the fields of California. Instead, Filipinos provided most of the agricultural labor force in the islands and all along the Pacific Coast. Not surprisingly, they became the main Asian immigrant group to engage in labor militancy. . . .

. . . [I]n the Salinas Valley of California in 1933, lettuce pickers, in cooperation with several labor contractors, formed a Filipino Labor Union (FLU) after the AFL turned down their request that it organize a union on their behalf. Seven hundred Filipino workers staged a one-day walkout in August. If failed, but the following year, when the union had some 2,000 members, it joined the Vegetable Packers Association (an AFL affiliate) in a strike in Monterey County.

The FLU wanted growers to recognize it as a legitimate union—so it could bargain with them, as the National Industrial Recovery Act required employers to do with recognized unions—and to double the wages of Filipino farm workers from 20 to 40 cents or higher per hour. During the strike, the growers shot two of the Filipinos. To avert further violence, the California Department of Industrial Relations offered to mediate through binding arbitration. The Vegetable Packers Association accepted the offer, but the Filipinos decided to continue the walkout. Meanwhile, the growers kept bringing in Mexican strike breakers to harvest the crop.

The determined strikers held on in the face of mounting hostility from every side. Newspapers in the surrounding community criticized them severely. The Vegetable Packers Association severed its ties with the FLU. The Associated Farmers of California branded the FLU a communist front group. The Salinas Grower-Shipper Association distributed pamphlets denunciating the dangers posed by Filipino militancy. Local law enforcement officers, with the help of the California Highway Patrol, arrested a number of the labor leaders for vagrancy. . . . Finally, the strike ended when local vigilantes burned to the ground a camp where hundreds of Filipino farm workers were housed.

But Filipino labor activism eventually received recognition from organized labor, however grudging it may have been. In 1936, Filipino and Mexican farm workers succeeded in persuading the AFL to grant a charter to the Field Workers Union, Local 30326, a dual-ethnic Mexican-Filipino union. Then in 1940 the AFL chartered the Federated Agricultural Laborers Association, a Filipino union, after it successfully represented thousands of asparagus cutters, Brussels sprouts pickers, celery cutters, and garlic harvesters in a series of strikes in central California.

Farm workers among Filipinos were not the only active unionists. Those working in the salmon-canning industry in Alaska likewise participated in the labor movement, usually as officers and as members of mainstream unions. In 1938 the Filipino salmon cannery workers finally got rid of the labor contractors—often individuals from their own ethnic group—who had severely exploited them. From then on, workers were hired through the union hall. But the road to success was paved with blood: the union's president and its secretary were gunned down by assassins in late 1936. . . .

In contrast to strikes where a majority of the participants (though not all of the leaders) were workers, legal action—the second method Asian immigrants used to defend their rights—was generally undertaken by more well-to-do and educated individuals. The umbrella organizations within the Chinese and Japanese immigrant communities—the Chinese Six Companies and the Japanese Association of America, respectively—usually took responsibility for retaining the Euro-American lawyers who argued their cases in court. . . .

The volume of litigation that Asian immigrants undertook is truly astonishing. . . . [T]ens of thousands of Asians sought justice through legal action. The three issues that concerned Asian immigrant litigants the most were immigration exclusion, the right of naturalization, and economic discrimination. Chinese tried hardest to fight exclusion: more than 90 percent of their reported cases arose from efforts to gain entry into the United States. Japanese, Asian Indians, and Koreans were most concerned about acquiring citizenship through naturalization, while Chinese and Japanese were determined to remove impediments to their right to earn a living. . . .

During the first few years after [Congress passed the Chinese Exclusion Act in 1882], aspiring immigrants were surprisingly successful in challenging the laws. . . . The federal officer responsible for implementing them was the collector of customs. Even though the San Francisco collector, who inspected the vast majority of the Chinese coming into the country until the turn of the century, announced that he would be as strict as possible, the Chinese he detained kept filing writs of habeas corpus, which enabled them to receive a hearing by a judge or a commissioner appointed by the court. During the first decade of exclusion, the judges allowed more than 85 percent of those whom the collector had tried to prevent from landing to enter the country— a fact that caused a public outcry. Newspapers and anti-Chinese groups castigated the judges for their decisions, but the latter, out of a firm commitment to due process, insisted that all individuals, regardless of their color or race, had the right to seek liberty through a habeas corpus proceeding.

Both the 1882 exclusion act and its 1884 amendment allowed Chinese laborers who had resided in the United States before November 1880—the date of the last treaty with China—to reenter the United States after visits to China, so long as they had the evidence required by the laws. On 1 October 1888, however, Congress unilaterally and abruptly abrogated this right, thereby denying reentry to some 20,000 laborers with the requisite certificates who were out of the country at the time.

Chae Chan Ping, a laborer who had lived in San Francisco from 1875 to 1887 and who had obtained a return certificate before departing to China for a visit, was enroute to California when the new law went into effect. He arrived on 7 October and was denied landing. The two judges in the U.S. circuit court who heard his case decided to uphold the 1888 law, even though they had earlier repeatedly defended the right of Chinese to be admitted under the 1882 and 1884 acts. Chae then took his case to the U.S. Supreme Court. . . . In an 1889 landmark decision, *Chae Chan Ping* v. *United States* (sometimes known as the *Chinese Exclusion Case*), a unanimous court decided that whereas the 1888 law and the treaties indeed seemed to be in conflict, the later document superseded the earlier ones. Moreover, whatever right Chinese laborers had to reenter the United States was "held at the will of the government, revocable at any time, at its pleasure."

When the 1882 law expired in 1892, a new and more stringent one took its place. Known as the Geary Act, it required all Chinese in the United States to register. Thereafter, any Chinese in the country caught without a registration certificate was subject to immediate deportation. Three Chinese about to be deported took their case to the U.S. Supreme Court. In *Fong Yue Ting* v. *United States* (1892), the high court held that since deportation is part of immigration and a sovereign nation has the right to decide who to let within its borders, it can rightfully compel aliens to register.

Despite these unfavorable rulings, the Chinese persevered. After an 1894 amendment gave executive officers the final say over the admission of Chinese—permitting the latter a court appearance only if they had not received a "fair hearing"—Chinese repeatedly charged that the hearings given them by the immigration officials were unfair. To put a stop to this, the U.S. Supreme Court ruled in *Lem Moon Sing* v. *United States* (1895) that district courts could no longer review Chinese habeas corpus petitions. But the exclusionists went further: they wanted to deny the courts any say over Chinese immigration altogether. In 1903 the commissioner general of immigration, acting under the secretary of commerce and labor, assumed full control over the matter. The U.S. Supreme Court affirmed this change in *United States* v. *Ju Toy* (1905), declaring that the secretary of commerce and labor had final jurisdiction over not only the entry of Chinese immigrants but that of American citizens of Chinese ancestry as well. But there was one privilege the high court refused to deny persons of Chinese ancestry: in *Wong Kim Ark* v. *United States* (1898), the court held that anyone born in the United States was a citizen and could not be stripped of the right thereof.

Recognizing the value of citizenship, Asian immigrants fought hard to gain the right of naturalization. The legal history of their struggles with regard to this issue reveals more clearly than does anything else the ambiguities, inconsistencies, and irrationality of racial exclusion. The Constitution stated that only "free white persons" could be naturalized. In 1870 the privi-

Filipino immigrant workers in Hawaii on Rizal Day Parade, 1919

lege was extended to "aliens of African nativity and to persons of African descent.". . . . [T]hough Senator Charles Sumner tried during the congressional debates over this question to strike the word "white" from the proposed statute, he failed. However, the compiler of the 1873 U.S. Revised Statutes somehow omitted the reference to "whites" in Section 2169 of Title 30, the section on naturalization. This error was corrected by an amendatory act in early 1875. Between 31 December 1873 and 18 February 1875, therefore, no racial or color restriction existed with regard to citizenship, and a number of Chinese in New York were naturalized. A court decision, *In re Ah Yup* (1878), and the 1882 Chinese exclusion law, which expressly denied the right to Chinese, closed this loophole.

As Japanese began coming, a number of them who desired naturalization challenged Section 2169. . . . When a Japanese in Massachusetts contested the statute, the U.S. circuit court, after reviewing a large body of pseudoscientific literature on ethnographic and racial classifications, declared in *In re Saito* (1894) that Japanese were not eligible because they were Mongolians. Fifteen years later, *In re Knight* (1909) held that an individual born of an English father and a mother who was half Chinese and half Japanese was insufficiently "white" to be granted citizenship. . . .

A few Japanese were naturalized, the first being Shinsei Kaneko of Riverside, California, who became a citizen in 1896 and later served as a juror and traveled abroad with an American passport. Among the others were Takuji Yamashita and Charles Hio Kono of Seattle, Washington. But these two eventually lost their citizenship when they attempted to set up a corporation—something that only citizens could do in the state of Washington. Upon reviewing their application, the secretary of state of Washington decided that the superior court that had admitted them to citizenship had erred, and he refused to grant them the incorporation papers they sought. The petitioners took their case to the U.S. Supreme Court, which held off a decision until after it had ruled on the landmark *Takao Ozawa* v. *United States* (1922) case. The justices then rescinded the citizenship granted earlier to Yamashita and Kono on the basis of the *Ozawa* decision.

The . . . *Ozawa* case [is] one of the most drawn-out suits that an Asian has ever filed in the United States. . . . Takao Ozawa was born in Japan, came to the United States as a "school boy," graduated from Berkeley High School, and attended the University of California for three years before moving to Honolulu in 1906. He spoke good English, was familiar with American institutions, married a woman brought up in the United States, sent his children to Sunday school, spoke English at home with them, reported neither his marriage nor the birth of his two children to the Japanese consulate in Honolulu, and worked for an American company. Moreover, said he, "I neither drink liquor of any kind, nor smoke, nor play cards, nor gamble, nor associate with any improper persons."

Ozawa first submitted a petition of intent in 1902 but did not follow with a petition for naturalization until 1914. When the U.S. district court in northern California denied the latter application, he tried to file in Hawaii, where he was likewise rebuffed. Undiscouraged, he appealed. Up to this point, Ozawa had acted alone, but after his case was referred to the U.S. Supreme Court in 1917, the Japanese immigrant community as well as the Japanese government became involved. The Deliberative Council of the Pacific Coast Japanese Association—the coordinating body for the Japanese Association of America and its counterpart in Canada—decided to support Ozawa's effort, but the Foreign Ministry in Tokyo opposed it. The latter did not want a negative decision to foreclose its chance for reaching a diplomatic settlement on the issue. After delays related to international power politics, the U.S. Supreme Court finally ruled on the case in 1922. It decided that Ozawa could not be naturalized because, all his qualifications notwithstanding, he was neither a free white person nor someone of African descent. In the eyes of the court, racial origins, rather than skin color, was what mattered.

The justices reversed themselves a few months later, however, in *United States* v. *Bhagat Singh Thind* (1923). . . . Thind had lived in the United States since 1913, had served in the U.S. armed forces during World War I, and had received his citizenship papers from the U.S. district court in Oregon in 1920. But Thind was known for advocating independence for India— something that the federal government found embarrassing, given the close relationship between the United States and Great Britain—and immigration officials looked for a pretext to deport him. The bureau of immigration took him to court in an attempt to "denaturalize" him. The U.S. Supreme Court upheld the federal agency, arguing that whereas Thind, as a native of India, might indeed be an Aryan ethnographically, he was nonetheless not "white." In this instance, skin color took precedence over racial classification. Following the *Thind* decision, immigration officials successfully canceled the naturalization certificates of several dozen other Asian Indians.

Though defeated in their efforts to become citizens, those Asian immigrants still in the country fought hard to defend their right to earn a living. Chinese import-export merchants and laundrymen and Japanese tenant farmers used the courts most frequently for this purpose. . . . [I]n San Francisco the board of supervisors passed 14 ordinances between 1873 and 1884 to restrict the 300 or so Chinese laundries (staffed by some 3,000 washers and ironers) in the city. One ordinance required washhouses in wooden buildings to be licensed or be subject to a fine of $1,000 or six months in jail for their owners. All the Chinese laundries were in wooden buildings. In 1885 the board rejected every Chinese license application, but granted all but one of the 80 licenses sought by non-Chinese. . . .

In defiance, about 200 Chinese laundrymen decided to keep their premises open for business. Among them was Yick Wo. (Yick Wo was actually the name of a laundry, not a man, but it was common in those days for owners of Chinese businesses to be known by their firms' names.) He arrived in San Francisco in 1861, opened a laundry two years later, and had been in business ever since. When he applied for his license in June 1885, he already had in hand permits from the city's board of fire wardens and its health officer certifying that the building housing his laundry met the city's fire and sanitation standards. The board of supervisors nevertheless denied his application. And though Yick Wo's license would not expire until October, the police filed a complaint against him and arrested him in August.

The Chinese laundry guild, the Tung Hing Tong, hired one of the most famous trial lawyers of the day to defend the entire group of laundrymen in a class action suit. Yick Wo filed a writ of habeas corpus and was released from prison, but the city appealed, the California Supreme Court upheld the ordinance, and he once again landed in jail. Then the U.S. Court of Appeals for the Ninth Circuit granted him a second habeas corpus, but would not restrain the city from enforcing the laundry ordinance. When the case went to the U.S. Supreme Court, Yick Wo argued that the ordinance was arbitrary and discriminated against persons like himself who were consequently denied due process of law.

The city responded that regulating laundries was part of its police power. Furthermore, the ordinance in question was not discriminatory since the non-Chinese laundries did not have scaffolds on their roofs for drying clothes (which the city considered to be fire hazards), whereas the Chinese ones did. The high court ruled in *Yick Wo* v. *Hopkins* (1886) that to divide laundries arbitrarily into two classes was a denial of equal protection under the law as guaranteed by the Fourteenth Amendment, which covered not only all citizens but all *persons,* including Chinese aliens. In the court's view, a law that could be applied in a discriminatory manner, even though it might be neutral on its face, was unconstitutional. . . .

Just as Chinese fought to keep their import-export stores and laundries—two of their most important means of livelihood—open, so Japanese defended time after time their right to farm. In this they were less lucky than Yick Wo had been: four landmark cases heard by the U.S. Supreme Court in 1923 cumulatively stripped away whatever rights they had enjoyed. . . . [I]n *Terrace* v. *Thompson* a unanimous court upheld the 1921 Alien Land Law of the state of Washington and denied the plaintiff the right to lease his land to a Japanese alien. The court also upheld the constitutionality of the 1920 California alien land law in *Porterfield* v. *Webb.* Sharecropping agreements were ruled illegal in *Webb* v. *O'Brien,* concerning a Californian landowner who wanted to sign a contract with a Japanese to plant, cultivate, and harvest crops, arguing that this was a contract for the performance of labor. But California's attorney general considered such an agreement a ruse that allowed Japanese aliens to possess and use land—an interpretation with which the high court concurred. Finally, *Frick* v. *Webb* forbade aliens ineligible to citizenship from owning stocks in corporations formed for the purpose of farming. According to the justices, owning such stocks would give the aliens an interest in land also.

The only positive decision Japanese tenant farmers won was *Estate of Tetsubumi Yano* (1922), in which the California Supreme Court held that the parents of two-year-old American-born Tetsubumi Yano, to whose name they had transferred 14 acres, were allowed to serve as her guardians. But their victory was short-lived. A year later, California amended Section 175(a) of its Code of Civil Procedures to prohibit aliens ineligible for citizenship from being appointed as guardians of any estate consisting in whole or in part of real property, though they could otherwise still serve as guardians to minors.

[In retrospect, what matters is not the number of strikes or lawsuits that Asian immigrants won; rather, the fact they resisted the inequities imposed on them so consistently is the best proof that they did aspire to become Americans.]

Unionization and Mexican-American Women, 1930s–1940s

Vicki L. Ruiz

Mexican workers contributed their blood, sweat, and tears to the construction of a viable new economy in the Southwest by the early twentieth century but did not reap the full fruits of their labor. Employers and others discriminated against them as a class of cheap labor, one set apart by their racial and cultural differences. Class exploitation linked with racialization produced a segmented labor market and a community in which Mexican workers and their families, along with other racial minorities, were relegated to the lowest tiers.

Yet Mexicans, far from the passive and docile people they have often been made out to be, vigorously resisted their treatment. One way involved pursuing strategies of survival, including constant occupational and residential migration throughout the region and even the country, as well as within particular communities. Another, more dramatic, course of resistance took the form of joining unions and striking. Unionization and strikes were an especially common means of resistance during the 1930s, when the Great Depression threatened even more severely than before the little that Mexicans had obtained. In the following study of the Los Angeles canneries, which employed large numbers of Mexican female workers in the 1930s, Vicki Ruiz notes these women's active role not only in joining unions such as the United Cannery, Agricultural, Packing, and Allied Workers of America (UCAPAWA) but also in leading them.

STUDY QUESTIONS

1. What methods did Mexican workers use to resist unjust discrimination?

2. What roles did kinship and neighborhood location play in cannery culture?

3. What factors accounted for the organizing success of UCAPAWA?

O n August 31, 1939, during a record-breaking heat wave, nearly all of the 430 workers at the California Sanitary Canning Company (popularly known as Cal San), one of the largest food processing plants in Los Angeles, staged a massive walkout. The following day a twenty-four-hour picket line was established in front of the plant; a long struggle seemed imminent. The primary goals of these employees, mostly Mexican women, concerned neither higher wages nor better working conditions, but recognition of their union—Local 75 of the United Cannery, Agricultural, Packing, and Allied Workers of America—and a closed shop. This strike marked the beginning of labor activism among Mexican women cannery and packing workers in southern California.

During the 1930s, Mexican women food processing operatives included young single daughters, newly married women, middle-aged wives, and widows. Occasionally, three generations worked at a particular facility—daughter, mother, and grandmother. "My father was a busboy," one former Cal San employee recalled, "and to keep the family going . . . in order to bring in a little money . . . my grandmother, my mother and brother, my sister and I all worked together at Cal San."

Kin networks formed an integral part of cannery life. Cousins, brothers, sisters, aunts, uncles, mothers, fathers, *madrinas*, *padrinos*, *niños*, and *niñas* reinforced a sense of family inside the plants. In addition, older relatives kept a protective watch over younger family members.

. . . [E]xtended family structures fostered the development of a cannery culture. A collective identity among food processing operatives within the factories emerged as a result of family ties, peer socialization, job segregation according to gender, and prevailing conditions of work. Although women composed 75 percent of the labor force in California's canneries and packing houses, they were clustered into specific departments—washing, grading, cutting, canning, and packing—and their earnings varied with production levels. In other words, they engaged in piece work. Men employees, conversely, as warehousemen and cooks, received hourly wages. Women operatives often developed friendships with their neighbors on the line, friendships that crossed family and, at times, ethnic lines. While Mexican and Mexican American women constituted the largest group of workers, many Russian women also found employment at Cal San. Their day-to-day experiences— slippery floors, peach fuzz, production speed-ups, arbitrary supervisors, and even sexual harassment—cemented feelings of solidarity among these women, as well as nurturing an "us against them" mentality in relation to management. They also shared common concerns, such as seniority status, quotas, and wages. Furthermore, women had mutual interests outside the cannery gates. While daughters might discuss problems characteristic of their age and generation, mothers talked about household responsibilities and child care.

At Cal San many Spanish-speaking and Russian Jewish workers shared another bond—neighborhood. Both Mexicans and Jews lived in Boyle Heights, an East Lost Angeles community. One writer for a Jewish publication wryly portrayed the working-class orientation of area residents:

> But there is something attractive about the atmosphere of Brooklyn Avenue. . . . It is . . . alive with radios going full blast and the clattering, clanging "B" cars pouring back the Boyle Heights workers from their daily tasks. . . . And there are "ritzy" cars from Beverly Hills . . . unloading Jews who "wouldn't think of living in Boyle Heights," but who are tied to the Ghetto by a bond that is stronger than race or religion—the mouth-watering desire for a good piece of Russian rye bread, a herring . . . and a lox sandwich. Gustatorial Jews coming back to give lip and tooth service to their own people.

Although Russian Jewish and Mexican operatives lived on different blocks, they congregated at streetcar stops during the early morning hours. Sometimes in the course of commuting or on the assembly line, interethnic friendships developed. Although most cross-cultural friendships did not extend beyond the work experience, one pair of "work buddies" attended night classes together. Of course, the degree of peer interaction varied from person to person. "I was snobbish. I just associated with my sister and a few Mexican girls," reflected one Spanish-surnamed woman. In contrast, María Rodríguez declared, "I tried to get along with everybody. It made the work go faster." The importance of neighborhood should not be underestimated because these women, if not friends, were at least passing acquaintances. Later, as UCAPAWA members, they would become allies.

Networks within the plants cut across generation, gender, and ethnicity. A detailed examination of the California Sanitary Canning Company further illuminates this unique collective identity or cannery culture. Cal San, a one-plant operation, handled a variety of crops—apricots and peaches in the summer, tomatoes and pimentos in the fall, spinach in the winter and early spring. This diversity enabled the facility, which employed approximately four hundred people, to remain open at least seven months a year.

Cal San was not highly mechanized in the women's departments. Using small kitchen knives, operatives pared fruit by hand. "And many a time you lost your knife," remembered Julia Luna Mount. "And there goes your knife down the canvas. Then you'd run looking for your knife. And you never knew who or what would get cut down the line." She further noted that the movement of the conveyor belts often made women dizzy as "half of them were anemic anyway." Indeed, on her first day at Cal San, she became so dizzy, she fainted.

Peach fuzz and vegetables stains were particularly vexing for women workers. "I could never keep myself clean, even with an apron," one recalled. Peach fuzz, in particular, caused "unbearable rashes and adhered to clothing with a vengeance. One woman took scrupulous pains in preparing for work: "I wore a big rubber apron. My mother made dish towels out of flour sacks. I'd put a bleached flour sack over my apron and then a dish towel around my waist. I was very neat . . . I didn't get dirty or wet." To avoid irritation when washing peaches, this meticulous person fashioned homemade gloves out of old stockings and carried a bottle of hand cream to use at breaks. Jealous peers referred to her as "la Reina" ("the Queen") because in addition to maintaining such a fastidious appearance, she was the fastest worker in her section. And under the piece rate system in food processing plants, speed, accuracy, and position were critical.

Women workers received very little for their labors, due to the seasonal nature of their work and the piece rate scale. In the Cal San warehouse and kitchen departments, exclusively male areas, men received an hourly wage ranging from fifty-eight to seventy cents an hour. On the other hand, in the washing, grading, cutting, and canning divisions—exclusively female areas—employees earned according to their production level. In order to make a respectable wage, a woman operative had to secure a favorable position on the line, which was always a spot near the chutes or gates where the produce first entered the department. Carmen Bernal Escobar recalled:

> There were two long tables with sinks that you find in old-fashioned houses and fruit would come down out of the chutes and we would wash them and put them out on a belt. I had the first place so I could work for as long as I wanted. Women in the middle hoarded fruit because the work wouldn't last forever and the women at the end really suffered. Sometimes they would stand there for hours before any fruit would come down for them to wash. They just got the leftovers. Those at the end of the line hardly made nothing.

Although an efficient employee standing in a favorable spot on the line could earn as much as $1.00 an hour, most women operatives averaged 30 to 35 cents. Their male counterparts, however, received from $5.25 to $6.26 per day.

Though wages were scarce, there was no "scarcity" in owner paternalism. Cal San's owners, George and Joseph Shapiro, took personal interest in the firm's operations. Both brothers made daily tours of each department, inspecting machinery, opening cans, and chatting with personnel. Sometimes a favored employee—especially if young, female, and attractive—would receive a pat on the cheek or a friendly hug; or as one informant stated, "a good pinch on the butt."

While the Shapiros kept close watch on activities within the cannery, the foreman and floor ladies exercised a great deal of autonomous authority over workers. They assigned them positions on the line, punched their time cards, and even determined where they could buy lunch. Of course, these supervisors could fire an employee at their discretion. One floor lady earned the unflattering sobriquet, "San Quentin." Some operatives, in order to make a livable wage, cultivated their friendship. "Women would bring the supervisors little *bocaditos* and little *tejiditos*—little goodies like that." At times young women dated their foremen. Some romances developed out of genuine affection; others as a means of advancement. More frequently, men used their power at work for personal ends. . . .

The supervisors, who were all Anglo, neither spoke nor understood Spanish. This language barrier contributed to increasing tensions inside the plant, especially when management had the authority to discharge an employee for speaking Spanish. Foremen also took advantage of the situation by altering production cards of operatives who spoke only Spanish. One foreman, for example, was noted for routinely cheating his Mexicana mother-in-law out of her hard-earned wages. Some women never realized that their supervisors were tampering with their cards, while others sensed something was wrong but either could not express their suspicions or were afraid to do so. Bilingual employees, cognizant of management's indiscretions, were threatened with dismissal. . . .

In 1937 a group of workers tried to establish an AFL [American Federation of Labor] union, but a stable local failed to develop. Then in July 1939, Dorothy Ray Healey, an international vice-president of UCAPAWA, began a new union campaign. Healey, a vivacious young woman of twenty-four, already had eight years of labor-organizing experience. At the age of sixteen, she had participated in a San Jose cannery strike as a representative of the Cannery and Agricultural Workers Industrial Union. She had assumed leadership positions in both the C&AWIU and the Young Communist League (YCL). Healey, in fact, chose Cal San because "there we had the good fortune . . . that about four or five UCLA students, YCLers or radicals, went to work there on summer jobs and that provided us with immediate contact." Dorothy Healey played an instrumental role in the formation and initial success of UCAPAWA Local 75.

Healey's primary task involved enrolling as many employees as possible in the union. She distributed leaflets and membership cards outside the cannery gates. Healey talked with operatives before and after work and made visits to their homes. She also sought the aid of new recruits who proselytized inside the plant during lunch time. As former Cal San employee Julia Luna Mount remembered, "Enthusiastic people like myself would take the literature and bring it into the plant. We would hand it to everybody, explain it, and encourage everybody to pay attention." Workers organizing other workers was a common trade union strategy, and within three weeks 400 out of 430 operatives had joined UCAPAWA. This phenomenal membership drive indicates not only worker receptivity and Healey's prowess as an activist but also the existence of a cannery culture. Membership cards traveled from one kin or peer network to the next. Meetings were held in workers' homes so that entire families could listen to Dorothy Healey and her recruits. The recruits themselves, by convincing family and friends, made enormous contributions to this campaign. People could not have mobilized in such numbers in so brief a time without the presence of interrelated networks within the plant. But despite the union's popularity, the Shapiros refused to recognize the union or negotiate with its representatives. As a result, members voted to strike.

On August 31, 1939, at the height of the peach season, the vast majority of Cal San employees left their stations and staged a dramatic walkout. Only thirty workers stayed behind, and sixteen of these stragglers joined the newly formed picket lines outside the plant the next day. Although the strike occurred at the peak of the company's most profitable season and elicited the support of most line personnel, management refused to bargain with the local. In fact, the owners issued press statements saying that the union did not represent a majority of the workers.

In anticipation of a long strike, Healey organized workers into several committees. A negotiating committee, a food committee, and picket details were formed hours after the walkout. The strikers' demands included union recognition, a closed shop, elimination of the piece rate system, minimal wage increases, and the dismissal of nearly every supervisor. Healey persuaded the workers to assign top priority to the closed shop demand. The striking employees realized the risk they were taking, for only one UCAPAWA local had secured a closed shop contract.

The food committee also assumed an important role. East Los Angeles grocers donated various staples, including flour, sugar, and baby food, to the Cal San strikers. Many business people obviously considered their donations as advertisements or gestures of goodwill toward their customers. But some undoubtedly acted out of a political consciousness, since earlier in the year East Los Angeles merchants had financed El Congreso De Pueblos Que Hablan Español, the first national civil rights assembly among Latinos in the United States. Whatever the cause of its success, the food committee sparked new strategies among the rank and file.

Early on, the strikers extended their activities beyond their twenty-four-hour, seven-day-a-week picket line outside the plant. They discovered a supplementary tactic—the secondary boycott. Encouraged by their success in obtaining food donations from local markets, workers took the initiative themselves and formed boycott teams. The team leaders approached the managers of various retail and wholesale groceries in the Los Angeles area, urging them to refuse Cal San products and to remove current stocks from their shelves. If a manager was unsympathetic, a small band of women picketed the establishment during business hours. In addition, the International Brotherhood of Teamsters officially vowed to honor the strike. This proved to be only a verbal commitment, for many of its members crossed the picket lines in order to pick up and deliver goods manufactured by the California Sanitary Canning Company. At one point Mexican women union members became so incensed by the sight of several Teamsters unloading their trucks that they climbed onto the loading platform and quickly "depantsed" a group of surprised and embarrassed Teamsters. The secondary boycott proved to be an effective tactic—forty retail and wholesale grocers agreed to the strikers' request.

Action by the National Labor Relations Board further raised the morale of the striking employees. U.S. Labor Commissioner Lyman Sisley affirmed Local 75's claim that it represented the majority of Cal San operatives, and the NLRB formally reprimanded the Shapiros for refusing to bargain with the UCAPAWA affiliate. The timing of the strike, the successful boycott, and favorable government decisions, however, failed to bring management to the bargaining table. After a 2 1/2-month stalemate, the workers initiated an innovative technique that became, as Healey recalled, "the straw that broke the Shapiros' back."

Both George and Joseph Shapiro lived in affluent sections of Los Angeles, and their wealthy neighbors were as surprised as the brothers to discover one morning a small group of children conducting orderly picket lines on the Shapiros' front lawns. These youngsters carried signs with such slogans as "Shapiro is starving my Mama" and "I'm underfed because my Mama is underpaid." Many of the neighbors became so moved by the sight of these children, most of whom were Mexican, that they offered their support, usually by distributing food and beverages to the young people and their adult supervisors. These youngsters, like their parents picketing the plant, maintained a twenty-four-hour vigil in front of the brothers' homes. And if this were not enough, the owners were reproached by several of the more radical members of their synagogue. After several days of community pressures, the Shapiros finally agreed to meet with Local 75's negotiating team. The strike had ended.

Once the owners met with representatives of the local, a settlement was quickly reached. Although the workers failed to eliminate the piece rate system, they did receive a five-cent wage increase, and many supervisors found themselves unemployed. More importantly, Local 75 had become the second UCAPAWA affiliate (and the first on the West Coast) to negotiate successfully a closed shop contract.

Although the strike of 1939 was the more dramatic event, the consolidation of the union became the most important task facing Cal San employees. At post-strike meetings, Dorothy Healey outlined election procedures and general operating by-laws. Male and female workers who had assumed leadership positions during the confrontation captured every major post. For example, Carmen Bernal Escobar, head of the secondary boycott committee, became "head shop steward of the women." Healey remained with the local for several months providing advice and serving as the local's first business agent. Later, the president of Local 75, Elmo Parra, also served as the business agent for Cal San.

UCAPAWA organizers Luke Hinman and Ted Rasmussen replaced Dorothy Healey at Cal San. These two men, however, directed their energies toward the union drive at the California Walnut Growers' Association plant and thus devoted little time to Cal San workers. In late 1940, Luisa Moreno, a representative of UCAPAWA, took charge of consolidating Local 75. Like Healey, Moreno had a long history of labor activism. As a professional organizer for the AFL and later for the CIO [Congress of Industrial Organizations], she had unionized workers in cigar-making plants in Florida and Pennsylvania. She helped ensure the vitality of Local 75 through various means. Moreno vigorously enforced government regulations and contract stipulations. She also encouraged workers to air any grievance immediately. On many occasions, her fluency in Spanish and English helped resolve misunderstandings between Mexican workers and Anglo supervisors.

Not all grievances were initiated by workers. Once Joseph Shapiro called the head shop stewards, the business agent, and Moreno into his office and read aloud a letter from an amused consumer: "Dear Cal San: We think your fruit is delicious, but we just can't swallow your union button." Enclosed in the envelope was an UCAPAWA pin that had been found in a Cal San can. After this incident, all union buttons had to have clasps.

Participation in civic events fostered worker solidarity and union pride. Carmen Escobar convinced Cal San operatives to enter the Los Angeles Labor Day parade. She organized construction of the plant's float—a giant cornucopia. The women who marched beside or sat atop the float dressed in white and wore flowers in their hair. At the parade ground, AFL officials made the Cal San workers wait four hours before allowing them to march. Perhaps they feared the competition, for the Cal San entry captured first place.

The employees also banded together to break certain hiring policies. With one very light-skinned exception, George and Joseph Shapiro had refused to hire blacks. With union pressure, however, in early 1942, the Shapiros relented and hired approximately thirty blacks. By mid-1941, Local 75 had developed into a strong, united democratic trade union, and its members embarked on a campaign to organize their counterparts in nearby packing plants.

In 1941, Luisa Moreno, recently elected vice-president of UCAPAWA, was placed in charge of organizing other food processing plants in southern California. She enlisted the aid of Cal San workers in consolidating Local 92 at the California Walnut Growers' Association plant. Elmo Parra, president and business agent of Local 75, headed the organizing committee. In addition, Cal San workers participated in the initial union drive at nearby Royal Packing, a plant that processed Ortega Chile products. Since 95 percent of Royal Packing employees were Mexican, the Spanish-speaking members of Local 75 played a crucial role in this UCAPAWA effort. Cal San operatives distributed leaflets and membership cards, as well as visiting workers at their homes. Leafleting and personal visits were not new to UCAPAWA professionals, but the technique of using rank-and-file union members to lay the groundwork was both innovative and effective. Cal San employees, moreover, in relating the benefits of UCAPAWA affiliation undoubtedly convinced many workers at Royal Packing of the desirability of unionization. Fueled by their successes, they organized operatives at the Glaser Nut Company and Mission Pack. The result of this spate of union activism was the formation of Local 3, which made permanent the alliance between Cal San workers and the employees of the other plants. By 1942, this local had become the second-largest UCAPAWA union.

Mexican women food processing workers took union affairs very seriously. In 1943, for example, the members of Local 3 elected Mexican women to a number of union posts. They served as major officers and executive board members. In fact, they filled eight of the fifteen elected positions of the local. These union members did not simply pay their dues and attend meetings, but also served in leadership roles.

As well as being a support group, Local 3 effectively enforced contract stipulations and protective legislation. Its members proved able negotiators during annual contract renewals. In July, 1941, for example, *UCAPAWA News* proclaimed the newly signed Cal San contract as being "the best in the state." In 1943, workers at the Walnut plant successfully negotiated an incentive plan provision in their contract. Local 3 also provided benefits to its members that few industrial locals could match—free legal advice and a hospitalization plan.

Union members also took an active part in the war effort. At Cal San, a joint labor-management production committee worked to devise more efficient processing methods. As part of the "Food for Victory" campaign, Cal San operatives increased their production of spinach to unprecedented levels. In 1942 and 1943, workers at the California Walnut plant donated one day's wages to the American Red Cross. Local 3 also sponsored a successful blood drive in late 1944. Throughout this period, worker solidarity remained strong. When Cal San closed its doors in 1945, the union arranged jobs for the former employees in the California Walnut plant.

The success of UCAPAWA at the California Sanitary Canning Company can be explained by several factors. First, prevailing work conditions heightened the attractiveness of unionization among employees. Low wages and tyrannical supervisors, as well as elements outside the plant, prompted this receptivity. These operatives, moreover, were undoubtedly influenced by the wave of CIO organizing drives under way in the Los Angeles area. One woman, for example, joined Local 75 primarily because her husband was a member of the CIO Furniture Workers Union. Along with the Wagner Act, passage of favorable legislation, such as the Fair Labor Standards Act, the Public Contracts Act, and the California minimum wage laws that set wage and hour levels for cannery personnel contributed to the rise of a strong UCAPAWA affiliate. Workers realized that the only way they could benefit from recent protective legislation was to form a union with enough clout to force management to honor these regulations. . . .

Of course, it would be unfair to downplay the dedication and organizing skills of UCAPAWA professionals Dorothy Ray Healey and Luisa Moreno in strengthening the local at Cal San. While Healey played a critical role in the local's initial successes, it was under Moreno's leadership that workers consolidated these gains and branched out to help organize employees in neighboring food processing facilities. The recruitment of minority workers by Healey and Moreno and their stress on local leadership reflect the feasibility and vitality of democratic trade unionism.

Finally, the most significant ingredient accounting for UCAPAWA's success was the phenomenal degree of worker involvement in the building and nurturing of the union. Deriving strength from their networks within the plant, Cal San operatives built an effective local. Thus, the cannery culture had, in effect, become translated into unionization. Integrated into cannery life, this UCAPAWA affiliate represented the will of the rank and file.

Tribal Leaders and Natural Energy Resources, 1970s–1980s

DONALD L. FIXICO

In this selection, American Indian historian Donald Fixico examines the dilemma faced by today's western Native American tribes living on reservations rich in natural resources. Not too long ago, some Indians made agreements with powerful corporations to allow the latter to mine the natural resources on their reservations. In many instances, however, Indians have not received due compensation for the metals and minerals taken from their lands.

Today's tribal leaders are trying to balance the grave economic condition of their people—who are generally underemployed and not sufficiently skilled to enter the mainstream labor market—against the fears of many traditionally oriented Indians that their physical and metaphysical life will be irreversibly damaged by the exploitation of these natural resources. The future of natural-resource development on Indian reservation land thus is extremely complicated, and there are no easy solutions that will satisfy both Native Americans and their non-Indian neighbors. The tribal leaders' efforts, though not an overt form of resistance, are meant to protect their people from further encroachments.

STUDY QUESTIONS

1. What have been the Indian traditionalists' arguments against tribal resource development?

2. Identify the goals of Indian leaders who favored resource development.

3. Discuss the effects of the activities of the Council of Energy Resource Tribes (CERT) on Indian mineral exploitation.

More than one hundred years ago Indian tribal leaders were forced to negotiate with white Americans and the United States government for possession of Indian lands. Today's tribal leaders face a similar situation owing to the growing energy crisis and increased demands for natural resources. Depletion of our country's mineral reserves has caused energy companies to look toward reservation lands to replenish needed oil, coal, gas, and uranium. . . .

Mining operations on Indian lands can be monetarily beneficial; tribes bestowed with large mineral deposits on their reservations receive large royalty payments. Such revenue enables the tribes to promote various programs and to improve their economies. The western tribes faced a grave dilemma, however: Should they allow mining development on their reservations? . . .

The Indians' reaction to the demand for their energy resources is twofold: one is a reluctance to allow the mining operations to continue, and the other is a progressive attitude toward increased mining to help develop tribal programs. Among the western tribes, factions for and against mining have developed among the native peoples. Some tribespeople who are conservative traditionalists oppose mining. Those who favor mining are the progressives, especially tribal leaders, but they are in the minority. Nevertheless, tribal leaders control their tribes' affairs, and they sometimes negotiate with energy companies without their people's consent. . . .

From *The Plains Indians of the Twentieth Century*, edited by Peter Iverson, pp. 220–232. Copyright © 1985 by the University of Oklahoma Press.

Mining operations are lending credence to the traditionalists' fears. Aside from harming Mother Earth and jeopardizing the relationship between nature and mankind, the companies bring more non-Indians onto the reservation. Soon the non-Indians may outnumber the native people on their own lands. In one instance, if the mining operations continue on the Northern Cheyenne Reservation, twenty non-Indians will be brought in for every Cheyenne living on the reservation. Many Indians do not want this to happen and charge that tribal leaders are allowing the abuse of their people, homelands, and culture by cooperating with energy companies. . . .

Tribal leaders have been forced to rely heavily upon non-Indian lawyers and non-Indians advisers who are experts in energy development areas and the legalities of leasing contracts. This dependency has been reduced in recent years as the number of trained Indian lawyers has grown, but lawyers still demand large fees for their services. Past relations with attorneys and non-Indian experts have caused tribal members to be distrustful of everyone. . . .

. . . Because the secretary of the interior is empowered by law to approve leases, the energy companies can control Indian lands. Supposedly the tribes would benefit from the agreement, but Indians criticize the government for failing to advise tribes correctly and not protecting them from being victimized. Lack of proper supervision by the Bureau of Indian Affairs to protect Indian interests and the bureau's urging of tribes to accept inadequate leases have angered the energy-endowed tribes.

The Northern Cheyennes have alleged that from 1969 to 1971 the United States government misadvised them. Peabody, Amax, and Chevron were given exploration and mining leases for over half of the reservation's 450,000 acres. The tribe did not realize how unfair the ill-advised agreements were until 1972, when Consolidation Coal Company offered the tribe $35 an acre, a royalty rate of 25 cents, and a $1.5 million community health center. After further investigation the Cheyenne Tribal Council charged the federal government with thirty-six violations of leasing procedures. . . .

In an effort to protect reservation resources, leaders of twenty-five western Indian tribes united in 1976 to form the Council of Energy Resource Tribes (CERT). CERT is controlled by an executive board consisting of eight tribal chairpersons and a ninth chairperson who serves as the executive director of CERT. With one-third of all coal in the West located on Indian lands, CERT takes an aggressive business approach toward energy firms to bargain in the best interests of the tribes. CERT sought advice from several OPEC [Organization of Petroleum Exporting Countries] nations over the United States government's disapproval. To halt further OPEC assistance, the federal government awarded CERT grants totaling $1,997,000 from the Department of Energy, the BIA [Bureau of Indian Affairs], and the Department of Health, Education and Welfare. Initially CERT opened offices in Denver, Colorado, and Washington, D.C., but closed the doors of the Washington Office when its 1982 budget of $6 million was cut to $3.1 million in 1983. The council educates tribes in evaluating their energy sources, in the technology of mining natural resources, and in the development of human resources and provides management studies and computer services. To prevent further exploitation of Indian lands, CERT has established a broad Indian policy "so that energy companies won't be able to pick us off one by one" according to Charles Lohah, the Acting Secretary for CERT.

It should be added that, despite its success, the organization has hardly been immune from criticism. In recent years CERT has been severely criticized by Indians who charge that it is too "pro-development" regarding reservation resources. . . .

Reservation leaders have become more successful in negotiations, and the future looks brighter for Plains and Southwest tribes. With the increased knowledge and understanding of white ways, tribal leaders are also initiating and developing new programs to help their people. It may be appropriate here to cite the advice of the Sioux leader Sitting Bull. When the mighty Sioux Nation was in decline, mostly because of white influence, Sitting Bull warned: "Take the best of the white man's road, pick it up and take it with you. That which is bad, leave it alone, cast it away. Take the best of the old Indian ways—always keep them. They have been proven for thousands of years. Do not let them die.". . .

An area of new importance opened after a court decision of 1982 in which the U.S. Supreme Court ruled that the Jicarilla Apaches could charge energy companies a severance tax for mining on their land. Two other tribes, the Shoshone and Arapahoe of Wyoming, are attempting to impose a 4 percent severance tax on oil and gas, pending approval by the secretary of the interior. With state government also taxing the mining companies, the energy firms now face double taxation. Although the state taxes are generally higher, the energy companies are challenging the right of the tribes to tax them. The 1982 ruling has opened up a new avenue for tribal income, but it is one that reservation leaders will have to fight to keep.

Many tribal leaders and reservation peoples, however, face serious problems. Some Americans assume that Indians are getting rich from royalty payments, though actually only 15 percent of the Indian population has natural resources on tribal lands. In 1982 the BIA reported that royalties on reservations totaled more than $396 million—a large sum, but if the royalties were distributed to the entire Indian population of 1.3 million (1980 census), the per capita payment would be only $290 for each person. For their oil, tribes received on the average $2 a barrel in royalties at a time when OPEC nations were demanding and receiving $40 a barrel. . . .

In negotiations with the energy companies tribal leaders are at a disadvantage. Their governments usually cannot pay for equipment to evaluate their natural resources. The requisite trained personnel and exploratory data are in short supply, forcing tribes to give up a major share of their potential wealth by leasing their lands or entering into joint ventures with energy companies.

To compound the dilemma, Indian affairs have low priority in Washington; the entire budget appropriated for Indian affairs would buy just one aircraft carrier. Worse the BIA is a frequent hindrance to tribal leaders because it also lacks the expertise that the mining firms possess in the highly competitive business of energy development. . . .

At the present time the growing demand for natural resources on Indian lands has acted as a catalyst in forcing Indians, especially tribal leaders, to choose a life-style for their peoples. They are confronted with the dilemma of a social transition from the traditional world to the white man's life-style. Within all of this turmoil, it is ironic that today's Indian leaders are negotiating with white Americans and the federal government for tribal lands as their ancestors did more than one hundred years ago.

Organizing in Black Los Angeles, 1960s

ANGELA DAVIS

In the late 1960s, Angela Davis, a doctoral candidate and political activist, obtained a position in the Philosophy Department at the University of California, Los Angeles. A communist, she sparked a controversy that embroiled the Regents of the University of California, the government, and the citizens of the state at a time when anticommunism was still a vital force in American society. At the same time, the formation and sudden growth of the Black Panther Party and the prisoners' rights movement was affecting race and community relations, as well as California politics. These social movements coalesced when the Los Angeles Police Department (LAPD) and its Special Weapons and Tactical (SWAT) Squad attacked the party's Los Angeles headquarters on Central Avenue in the heart of the city's African-American community. Shortly after, the Che-Lumumba Club supported three black convicts, the Soledad brothers, who were accused of murdering a prison guard. The following selection from Angela Davis's autobiography recounts those tense days in the late 1960s when black activists and Los Angeles residents lived amidst what seemed an armed encampment, encircled by hostile police forces.

STUDY QUESTIONS

1. Why was Angela Davis so controversial?

2. What was the Black Panthers' rationale for self-defense?

3. What tactics did the Los Angeles police employ against black leftists?

4. Why did so many people in the African-American community support the black activists after the police attack on the Black Panthers' headquarters?

The location of the LAPD Command Post had been discovered, so Franklin* told us. Someone returned to Central Avenue to get Kendra and the other comrades while we headed for the house which the chief of police had taken over as his headquarters. It was surrounded by cops, and reporters were swarming all over the place. Some of them recognized me and immediately wanted to know whether I had come to act as an "intermediary" between the police and the Panthers. I told them in so many words that I had nothing but contempt for the LAPD. My loyalties were with the sisters and brothers under attack.

The woman who lived across from the house which had been commandeered by the LAPD was indignant about the police invasion of the community. She offered us—sisters and brothers from the Panthers, the Black Student Alliance and Che-Lumumba**—the use of her house as headquarters for the resistance. A call went through to the Panther office. The sisters and brothers inside were all still alive, although most of them had been shot up and hurt in the explosion.

They said they were prepared to leave the building, but only if community people and the press could observe them coming out. They realized that if they had not defended themselves from the beginning, they might have all been shot down in cold blood. They had tried to hold out until we could gather enough people to witness the aggression, as well as to stand watch as they lay down their weapons and left the building.

A piece of white fabric was thrown out of the window. Everyone was silent. When the sisters and brothers walked out, eleven of them altogether,

* Franklin Alexander is a black activist who had joined the Communist Party, U.S.A., and worked in the party's Los Angeles branch.
** Che-Lumumba was a composite name for Che Guevara, a Latin-American revolutionary leader, and Patrice Lumumba, an African political leader.

they were all standing strong. They were bleeding, their clothes were torn, and they were dirty from the debris of the explosion. But they were still standing strong. I found out later that Peaches had been shot in both legs. Yet she had marched proudly out of the building.

When the last of the eleven had come out, a huge roar of applause and cheers surged up from the crowd. Slogans were triumphantly shouted: "Power to the People." "No more pigs in our community." This was indeed a victory. The police had crept into the community in the early hours of the morning and launched a murderous attack on the Panthers. Without a doubt, they had planned to kill as many as they could and capture the rest, thus destroying the Panther chapter in Los Angeles. But with the support of the people outside, the Panthers had emerged victorious.

With the sisters and brothers out of the building, the crowd grew bolder. One sister actually jumped out and hit one of the cops from behind. Before he realized what had hit him, she was back under the cover of the crowd.

The students Franklin had talked to earlier had made preparations for a rally. They had informed their administration that they were going to use the gym for a community meeting to protest the unwarranted police raid on the Panther headquarters. The word was passed in the crowd to move over to Jefferson for the rally.

Emotions were high. The speeches were passionate. All carried the theme of the need to protect and defend the Panthers and the need to protect and defend the community. Some of the students gave speeches, as did a brother from the Black Student Alliance, Franklin and myself. By the time the rally was over, the students had called for a walkout so that they could spread the news of the attack throughout the Los Angeles Black community. They committed themselves to help mobilize the community for the coming fight, and we all walked out of the hall singing, "I want to be a Mau Mau. Just like Malcolm X. I want to be a Mau Mau. Just like Martin Luther King."

In order to organize the resistance, a coalition was established between the Black Panther Party, the Black Student Alliance and our Che-Lumumba Club. On the basis of this coalition of the Black Left, we felt we could call for a broad united resistance emanating from all sectors of the Black community.

That night we sponsored a meeting, attended by delegates from Black organizations throughout the city. This body approved a call for a general strike two days later in the Black community. On that day, we would hold a massive protest rally on the steps of City Hall. We had about thirty-six hours to put the rally together. It was no time at all, but the quicker the community reacted in an organized way, the more effective our protest would be.

That very night, thousands of leaflets were printed. The next morning, teams saturated the community with literature about the attack and the need to resist. The local Black radio station and an underground FM station gave us free time to issue the strike call and to publicize the rally. Others announced the rally as a part of the news.

I personally recorded spot announcements and help press conferences, since my name was known in the community. Yet I also felt the need to involve myself on a grass-roots level. I needed to acquire a sense of the mood of the community—and that could not be done from behind a microphone.

A team was on its way to Jordon Down Projects in Watts to distribute leaflets. I decided to go along. In all my experience of door-to-door community work, never had I seen such unanimous acceptance of our appeal. Literally no one was abrupt, no one tried to shut us out, and all agreed that we had to resist the attack on the Panthers. Many of the people recognized me, and I was surprised that they also volunteered their support for me in the fight for my job. Virtually every person with whom I spoke made a firm promise to observe the general strike and to attend the rally the next morning.

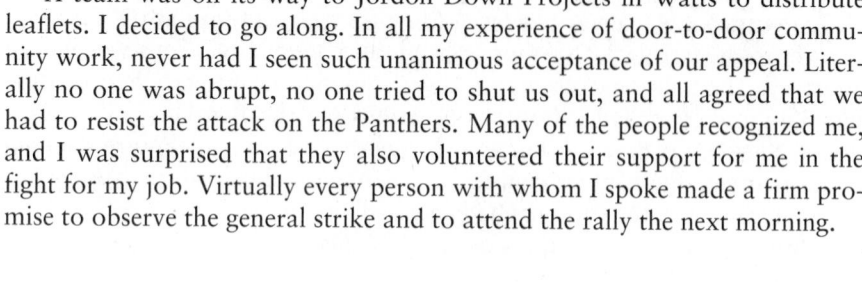

Angela Davis in jail

There were problems back at the Panther office. The woman who lived in the house behind the office had reported that early in the morning the police had returned and shot tear-gas cartridges into the office. The fumes were stronger now than shortly after the attack had halted. It was impossible to remain inside for any length of time without becoming sick.

It was decided, as a result, to hold a vigil in front of the office at all times. Participants in the vigil would form themselves into shifts in order to clean out all the debris. When the sun went down, there were still more than a hundred people taking part in the vigil. The tear-gas fumes had not abated and most of the group was clustered at the end of the block so no one would be overcome by the gas. The plans were to keep the vigil going throughout the night. Franklin led the group in freedom songs.

While the singers were warming up, I noticed some strange movements in the area: police cars creeping by—unmarked, but unmistakably police cars with agents peering out at us. I assumed that this was the normal surveillance. It seemed unlikely that they would try anything on a group which included not only the usual young movement people, but ministers, professors, politicians as well.

The singing broke into full blast. Perhaps the police felt affronted by the words of "Freedom Is a Constant Struggle" and "I Woke Up This Morning with My Mind Staid On Freedom" because they abruptly interrupted with a voice projected through a loudspeaker. "The Los Angeles Police Department had declared this an illegal assembly. If you do not move out, you will be subject to arrest. You have exactly three minutes to disperse."

Even if we had tried, we could not have dispersed in three minutes. We decided immediately not to disperse, but rather to form ourselves into a moving picket line. As long as we kept moving, we would not be an "assembly" and would theoretically have the right to remain. Senator Mervyn Dymally, a Black state senator, decided that he was going to speak to the policeman in charge, thinking he could calm them down.

The line stretched from the corner where the group had been singing, well past the office, which was near the next corner.

I moved toward the end nearest the Panther office. It was dark and difficult to determine exactly what was happening at the other corner. Suddenly there was a dash of the crowd. Thinking that this had been precipitated by nothing more serious than a show of force at the other end, I turned to calm everybody and tell them not to run. But at that moment, I saw a swarm of the black-suited cops who had executed the attack on the office the day before. They were already beating people further down, and some of them were about to converge on us.

I had been facing the crowd. I turned quickly, but before I could break into a run, I was knocked to the ground. I hit my head on the pavement and was momentarily stunned. During those seconds of semiconsciousness, I felt feet trampling on my head and body and it flashed through my mind that this was a terrible way to die.

A brother screamed, "Hey, that's Angela down there." Immediately, hands were pulling me up. I could see the billy clubs smashing into these brothers' heads. Someone told me later that as soon as the police realized who I was, they had come after me with their sticks.

Once on my feet, I ran as fast as I could.

This was insane. Clearly, the police had no intention of arresting us. They only wanted to beat us. Even Senator Dymally hadn't been immune. After his futile conversation with the chief of police, I learned later, he had been the first to be hit.

We raced through the neighborhood, across lawns, through alleys, wherever it seemed we could find temporary refuge. As I ran across a front yard with some sisters and brothers I didn't even know, I heard a voice coming from the dark porch, telling us to come in. We ran into the house, lay down on the floor and tried to catch our breath. It was a middle-aged Black woman who had opened her doors to us. When I tried to thank her, she said that after what had happened the day before, this was the very least she could do.

We were on a side street, off Central Avenue. I looked through the draperies in the front room and could see nothing except a police car cruising by. Then I noticed some of our people on a porch across the street and decided I would try to get over to that house.

In all the excitement, I hadn't noticed how badly I had been bruised by the fall. Blood was streaming down my leg and my knee was throbbing with pain. But there was no time to think about that now. I thanked the woman, said good-bye and ran toward the house across the street as fast as I could.

The family who lived there had allowed a comrade from our Party to organize a first-aid station in the house. People with blood all over their faces were already waiting to be tended, and a squad had gone out searching for others who were wounded. Apparently, people throughout the neighborhood had opened their doors. Their spontaneous show of solidarity had saved us from a real massacre.

I was worried about Kendra, Franklin, Tamu, Taboo and the rest of my Che-Lumumba comrades whom I had not yet seen. The Panther leaders not under arrest as a result of the original assault were also missing, as were key members of the Black Student Alliance. A brother from the BSA said he would accompany me around the neighborhood in order to determine what had happened to our friends. People were crowded in the storefronts along Central Avenue. By hiding in the shadows along the way, we were able to reach one of the storefronts without incident. The people we were worried about were among the crowds in the storefronts. One person had been arrested.

On Central Avenue, a squadron of cops in black jumpsuits was marching in formation. When they saw one of our people in the street, several of them would jump out of line, swing at the person with their billy clubs and then calmly fall back into the march. It appeared they were determined to hold us prisoner indefinitely in these houses and storefronts.

Later, we learned that the police in the black jumpsuits were members of the Los Angeles Police Department's counterinsurgency force—the Special Weapons and Tactical Squad. Subsequent research determined that the SWAT Squad was composed primarily of Vietnam veterans. For over a year, they had been in training, learning how to wage counterurban guerrilla warfare, learning how to "quell" riots, and obviously also how to provoke them. They had made their public debut with the attack on the Panther office. Their offensive against our vigil was their second official appearance.

The attack on us had begun around six o'clock in the evening. It wasn't until ten-thirty or eleven that it appeared we might be able to leave the houses and storefronts. Around that time, one of Senator Dymally's aides got word to us that the police were prepared to retreat if we all left the area immediately. Whether or not this guarantee was good was a matter for speculation.

Even in this moment of crisis, our most important concern was making the rally a success. Most of the organizers and speakers for the meeting were down on Central Avenue. There was only one logical explanation for this ruthless siege: the police were trying to sabotage our rally. We had to take the chance of trying to get people out of the area so that we could go on with preparations for the mass meeting.

The exit took place without incident. After almost everyone had left, Kendra and I, together with other comrades, headed for a house to hold an emergency Che-Lumumba meeting. Everyone was cautioned to shake off all police tails before arriving.

There we discussed a proposal we were going to present to other members of the coalition the next morning: a march, at the conclusion of the rally, to the county jail where the Panthers were being held. The march would culminate in a demonstration raising the demand for their immediate freedom.

In the middle of our discussions, the brother on security out front rushed into the room to tell us that the police were cruising by in unusual numbers. They had discovered our meeting place, and we had no idea what they would try to do. Our uncertainty, our firm belief based on previous experience that the Los Angeles Police would stop at nothing to crush their adversaries meant that we would have to prepare for the worst.

Weapons were checked out, loaded and distributed. In the formidable silence, in the tension-laden room, we waited in readiness. Fortunately, the attack did not materialize. Despite the excitement and the threat of an assault looming over us, we managed to get through our meeting early enough to catch a few hours' sleep before the rally. Everyone else was going home. But it was too dangerous to go to my house on Raymond Street. I had to resign myself to sleeping on Kendra and Franklin's floor.

I woke up the next morning with a terrible feeling of apprehension that only a few hundred people might show up. If the rally were poorly attended, then L.A. ruling circles, particularly the LAPD, might take it as a sign that the Black community was accepting the repression without resisting it. The police could therefore claim a mandate to escalate their aggression. They would attempt to totally obliterate the Black Panther Party and would move on to other militant Black organizations. The arbitrary police violence in the ghetto would mount.

With these fears digging at my stomach, I drove down to City Hall with Kendra, Franklin and other members of the club. It was about an hour and a half before the meeting was scheduled to begin. We arrived early to see that equipment was set up and raise the question of the march with the others.

What we saw when we arrived made us all feel euphoric. At least a thousand people were already on the steps—and four-fifths of them were Black. People were still steadily streaming into the area.

By the time the first speaker took the microphone, the crowd had swelled to eight or ten thousand strong. It was a magnificent multitude, studded with signs and banners demanding an end to police repression, demanding a halt to the offensive against the Panthers, demanding immediate release of the captured Panthers.

The speeches were powerful. As we had previously agreed, the theme of the rally—the theme of all the speeches—was genocide. The aggression against the Panthers embodied the racist policy of the U.S. government toward Black People. Carried to its logical conclusion, this policy was a policy of genocide.

The Panthers had been charged with conspiracy to assault police officers. In my speech, I turned the idea of conspiracy around and charged Ed Davis, the Chief of Police, and Sam Yorty, the mayor of L.A., with conspiring with U.S. Attorney General John Mitchell and J. Edgar Hoover to decimate and destroy the Black Panther Party.

Months later, the existence of just such a plan was revealed to the public. The government had decided to wipe out the BBP throughout the entire country. J. Edgar Hoover had called the Panthers "the greatest threat to the internal security of the country," and police forces in most of the major cities had moved on local Panther chapters.

As I emphasized in my speech, our defense of the Panthers had to be a defense of ourselves as well. If the government could carry out its racist aggression against them without fearing resistance, then it would soon be directed against other organizations and would finally engulf the entire community.

We needed more than a one-day stand. Papers circulated in the crowd to be signed by those who wanted to play an active role in organizing the mass movement we needed. By the time the speeches were over, the people were in a fighting mood. Franklin took the microphone and called for the march and demonstration. It was instantly approved with unanimous and roaring applause. We set out for the jail.

When we reached the County Courthouse where the jail was located, the collective anger was so great that the people could not be contained. Defiant throngs pressed forward through the doors of the building. So great was their rage that they began to destroy everything in sight. As they attacked the coin machines in the lobby, they were probably fantasizing about ripping down the iron bars of the jail upstairs.

There were only two ways out of the lobby—one exit on each side. If the police decided to attack, it would be a bloodbath, without a doubt. They only had to lock off the exits and we would be bottled in the building, with no place to run, no room for maneuvering.

But the crowd was ungovernable. I tried to get their attention. But my voice does not carry well without the aid of a microphone and it was drowned out in the clamor. It was Franklin who eventually assumed the role he always seems to excel in: he stood at the top of the lobby steps and with his voice blasting forth like a trumpet, he elicited complete silence from the raging demonstrators. He explained our immediate tactical disadvantages. The police had already sealed off one of the entrances. They were stationed throughout the area and could fall upon us in just a matter of minutes.

It was not enough to explain the dangers of the moment. What had to be emphasized was that the Panther prisoners would be freed by the actions of a *mass movement*. The militant protests of a movement of masses, the determined thrust of thousands of people, could force our enemy to release the sisters and brothers upstairs. Rather than waste our energies giving vent to our frustrations, we should be trying to organize ourselves into a permanent movement to defend our fighters and to defend ourselves.

The people left the courthouse and the demonstration continued outside in full force and with unabated enthusiasm. Thousands marched around the jailhouse chanting slogans of resistance.

Later, the street in front of the Panther office was overflowing with people who came down to assist in the ongoing work of this movement. In all respects, this had been an extraordinarily triumphant day. The rally had more than served its purpose. But in order to realize the potential of what we had just witnessed, much day-to-day organizing was needed. Sisters and brothers would have to commit themselves to work that might not be as visible or dramatic as what we had just done, but which, in the final analysis, would be infinitely more effective.

In the aftermath of the rally, its immediate effects could already be seen. For a while, at least, there was a noticeable let-up of police violence in the community. If you were stopped, you could see that the L.A. police were not as self-confident and certainly not as arrogant as they had been before. By the same token, the collective confidence, pride and courage of the community was definitely on the rise. I felt deeply gratified each time someone in the community expressed his satisfaction to me that something was finally being done about the brutality and insanity of the police.

FURTHER READING

Edward D. Beechert, *Working in Hawaii: A Labor History* (Honolulu: University of Hawaii Press, 1985).

Sucheng Chan, *Asian Americans: An Interpretive History* (Boston: Twayne Publishers, 1991).

Frank Chuman, *The Bamboo People: The Law and Japanese Americans* (Del Mar, Calif.: Publishers Inc., 1976).

Stephen Cornell, *The Return of the Native: American Indian Political Resurgence* (New York: Oxford University Press, 1988).

Mary Crow Dog, *Lakota Woman* (New York: Grove Weidenfeld, 1990; New York: Harper Perennial Books, 1991).

Angela Davis, *Angela Davis: An Autobiography* (New York: Random House, 1974; New York: International Publishers, 1988).

Vine Deloria, Jr., *Behind the Trail of Broken Treaties: An Indian Declaration of Independence* (New York: Delacorte Press, 1974; New York: Dell Pub. Co., 1974; Austin: University of Texas Press, 1985).

Howard A. DeWitt, "The Filipino Labor Union: The Salinas Lettuce Strike of 1934," *Amerasia Journal* 5 (1978): 1–22.

Ignacio M. García, *United We Stand: The Rise and Fall of La Raza Unida Party* (Tucson: Mexican American Studies and Research Center, University of Arizona, 1989).

Alvin M. Josephy, Jr., *Red Power: The American Indians' Fight for Freedom* (New York: American Heritage Press, 1971).

Peter Matthiessen, *In the Spirit of Crazy Horse* (New York: Viking Press, 1983; 1991; New York: Penguin Books, 1992).

Charles J. McClain, Jr., "The Chinese Struggle for Civil Rights in Nineteenth Century America: The First Phase, 1850–1870," *California Law Review* 72 (1984): 529–568.

Megumi Dick Osumi, "Asians and California's Anti-Miscegenation Laws," in *Asian and Pacific American Experiences: Women's Perspectives*, ed. Nobuya Tsuchida (Minneapolis: Asian/Pacific American Learning Resources Center, University of Minnesota, 1982).

Armando B. Rendon, *Chicano Manifesto* (New York: Collier Books, 1971).

Guadalupe San Miguel, Jr., *"Let All of Them Take Heed": Mexican Americans and the Campaign for Educational Equality in Texas, 1910–1981* (Austin: University of Texas Press, 1987).

Bobby Seale, *A Lonely Rage: The Autobiography of Bobby Seale* (New York: Times Books, 1978).

Joseph Staples Shockley, *Chicano Revolt in a Texas Town* (Notre Dame: University of Notre Dame Press, 1974).

Joyce E. Williams, *Black Community Control: A Study of Transition in a Texas Ghetto* (New York: Praeger Publishers, 1973).

John R. Wunder, "Law and Chinese in Frontier Montana," *Montana* 30 (1980): 18–31.

John R. Wunder, "The Courts and the Chinese in Frontier Idaho," *Idaho Yesterdays* 25 (1981): 23–32.

John R. Wunder, "The Chinese and the Courts in the Pacific Northwest: Justice Denied?" *Pacific Historical Review* 52 (1983): 191–211.

CHAPTER 11

Politics

It is commonly believed that racial minorities do not participate in politics. Historically, however, many have in fact done so, obstacles to such participation notwithstanding. One reason for the enduring stereotype of apolitical minorities lies in the persistence of a narrow definition of politics as encompassing only *electoral* politics. Consequently, if racial minorities do not vote or run for electoral office, some scholars have concluded that they have little interest in political affairs. Such a strict definition of politics excludes a rich variety of political activities grounded in community grassroots movements. Mutual-benefit societies, fraternal organizations, patriotic groups related to the countries of origin, and religious sodalities have all provided arenas for political action among peoples of color in the American West.

As noted by Kingsley K. Lyu in the first reading, Koreans, like most other immigrant groups in the United States, have involved themselves in the politics of their homeland by organizing several nationalist organizations to support the cause of Korean independence after Japan colonized Korea in 1910. Emory J. Tolbert then discusses African Americans' involvement in Marcus Garvey's Universal Negro Improvement Association (UNIA), a pan-Africanist organization, in the 1920s. Loretta Fowler, through extensive fieldwork among the Arapahoes, reveals the intricate dynamics of the tribal politics of one Native American group. But American electoral politics has also occupied the attention of some racial minorities in the West. Besides voting, racial minorities have struggled for effective electoral representation. In the final reading, Mario T. García describes and analyzes the successful grassroots strategy put together by Mexican Americans in 1957 to elect Raymond L. Telles as mayor of El Paso.

FOR ANALYSIS AND DISCUSSION

1. How did western peoples of color use their ethnic ties as a basis for political organizing?

2. Compare and contrast the political relationship of Koreans in America to their homeland with the connection between African-American Garveyites and Africa.

3. Compare and contrast the political tensions among the Arapahoes with the tensions among Mexican Americans in El Paso, Texas.

4. Do the various kinds of political activities described in this chapter have any goals in common? If so, what are they?

5. How do these political activities broaden the definition of "politics" in the United States?

Korean Nationalist Politics in America, 1905–1945

KINGSLEY K. LYU

Like many European immigrants, some Asians living in the United States became embroiled in the politics of their homelands. Individuals from countries trying to break the yoke of colonialism were particularly zealous in supporting efforts to liberate their countries of origin from foreign domination. Such expatriate political activities are simultaneously struggles for national independence and a form of ethnic politics on American soil. Participants often see a link between events in their homelands and difficulties that they themselves encounter in the country of settlement.

Many Chinese immigrants, for example, believed that the United States could maltreat them with impunity because China had become weak after losing several wars—first to Great Britain in 1842 and 1860, and later to Japan, in 1895. The unequal treaties imposed on China after its defeats undermined that country's sovereignty, and so its protests to the U.S. government against anti-Chinese discrimination in America fell on deaf ears. Immigrants from India, too, thought that their native land's colonial status diminished whatever civil and political rights they could claim in Canada and the United States.

Koreans in America worked harder than any other Asian immigrant group to free their homeland from colonial rule and in the process became entangled in conflicts with their fellow Koreans in the United States. Although they could barely sustain themselves on their low earnings, they still contributed about one-tenth of their income every year to support the movement for Korean independence. In this selection Kingsley Lyu describes some of the organizations set up by Koreans in America and the political rivalry among key leaders who resided at one time or another in the United States.

STUDY QUESTIONS

1. What was the main concern of Koreans in America during each of the three periods of nationalist politics that the author discusses?

2. Do you think that Koreans' intense involvement in nationalist political activities promoted or impeded their acculturation to American life?

The history of Koreans in America is in part the history of their political activities for the restoration of their national independence. The first arrival of Koreans in the United States was the Korean Diplomatic Mission, headed by Min Yong-ik, in the fall of 1883. The next was a Korean political exile named So Chae-p'il, or Philip Jaisohn, in the autumn of 1884. The principal aim of these Koreans was to strengthen Korean independence with the help of the American government. . . .

. . . On 12 January 1903, about 102 Korean men and women were imported as free laborers for the Mokuleia Sugar Plantation on Oahu. The number of Korean immigrants increased very rapidly thereafter until Korean emigration was stopped after April 1905, when Japan placed an embargo on Koreans leaving for Hawaii. A total of 7,893 Koreans, including 677 women and 465 children had immigrated to Hawaii from 20 May 1898 to 31 December 1905.

Although the emigration of Korean laborers was formally stopped after April 1905, wives and relatives of Korean immigrants were permitted to come to Hawaii. Furthermore, in order to stabilize the unmarried Koreans as a labor force for the Hawaiian sugar plantations, picture brides from Korea were permitted. The first picture bride arrived in Honolulu about 1910. The number of picture brides steadily increased until the immigration law of 1924 finally closed the door to all Oriental picture brides entering the United States. The exact number of these picture brides from Korea is not available, but based on the reports of the Board of Immigration to the Governor of Hawaii, there were about 600. . . .

Korean nationalist activities in America may be divided into three periods, namely, from 1903–1910, from 1910–1919, and from 1920–1945. The first period may be called the rise of Korean nationalism in Hawaii and the mainland United States. In this period, many Korean societies were organized among the plantation-working Koreans in the Hawaiian Islands for the mutual protection and benefit of their fellow-countrymen. . . .

Korean language schools were established as early as 1904. At first, these language schools were opened informally in Korean churches on the plantations, with pastors acting as teachers. The Methodist mission-sponsored schools alone had over 500 Korean youths enrolled in 1910. The principal objectives of these Korean language schools were not only to teach the Korean language, but to instill patriotism in the Korean youth for Korea.

. . . [I]mmigrant Koreans [maintained] . . . nationalist ties with the old country. . . . [T]hey began to organize Korean patriotic societies. The first Korean society formed in Hawaii was the Sinminhoe or New People's Soci-

From Kingsley K. Lyu, "Korean Nationalist Activities in Hawaii and the Continental United States, 1900–1945," *Amerasia Journal* 4:2 (1977), pp. 91–97. Reprinted with permission of Amerasia Journal.

ety in December 1904 at Kapaa, Kauai. The next was the Changanghoe or Self-strengthening Society at Hanapepe, Kauai. Many other Korean societies were organized thereafter. . . . [The year] 1905 [saw] the formation of the Hapsonghoe or United Party which united many Korean societies in the latter part of 1906. The Hapsonghoe was changed to the Kungminhoe or Korean National Association of Hawaii when it united with the Kongniphoe or Stand Together Society of America in February 1909.

The period from 1910 to 1919 may be called the crusading period for Korean nationalist activities in Hawaii. At that time, the Korean immigrants in the United States and Hawaii especially resented the Japanese forceful annexation of the Korean peninsula. A large majority of the Korean residents in the Hawaiian Islands were very conscious of their loss of national independence, supporting the political activities of Korean leaders morally and financially in the hope that their efforts might accelerate the restoration of their national independence.

American-educated Korean leaders arrived in Honolulu soon after Japan set up a military regime in Korea. . . . Pak Yong-man and Yi Sung-man or Syngman Rhee were two young men who had already faced bitter experiences in their youthful political activities in old Korea in the latter part of the nineteenth century. Their patriotism heightened while studying in American universities, yet they differed greatly in their political views on how to

Korean immigrants in Hawaii participating in a civic parade

restore Korean independence. Pak wanted to regain Korean sovereignty through military action while Syngman Rhee insisted that it should be done by training Korean youth as leaders and through diplomacy.

The vitally different views held by the two powerful Korean leaders in Hawaii led their followers into a whirlpool of distrust and disputes within their communities. The first controversy started in 1914. . . . The controversy went from bad to worse in 1915, resulting in the formation of the Tongnipdan or Korean Independence League in 1919 by Pak's followers. Rhee's followers meanwhile lost no time in founding the Korean Christian Church in 1917, and the Korean Women's Relief Society of Hawaii in 1919. The main objective of the latter was to assist Korean patriots who had been imprisoned as a result of the Korean independence demonstrations in 1919.

When the Korean Provisional Government was established in Shanghai in April 1919, all Korean societies in the United States and Hawaii pledged their loyalty and allegiance to the government-in-exile. Major Korean societies . . . worked harmoniously to support the Provisional Government of the Republic of Korea-in-exile, headed by Syngman Rhee himself. However, due to Rhee's autocratic methods, Koreans in Hawaii revolted against his leadership. . . . [T]his Democratization Revolt was led by his follower, Henry C. Kim, and lasted from 1929 to 1931. . . . Many thousands of dollars were spent in numerous law suits by both sides and the result was deep factionalism between Korean societies, whose members had since neglected their patriotic duties to support the Provisional Government during this period. . . .

Although Rhee was embroiled in the Democratization Revolt from 1929 to 1931, he was also busy carrying out some constructive work for the Koreans in Hawaii. One of his achievements was the building of the Korean Institute in Kalihi Valley, Honolulu, in 1923. On the side of this hilly valley he erected three buildings for classrooms and a dormitory. There he taught second-generation Korean boys and girls from the first through sixth grades. The school was closed, however, when the Japanese attack on Pearl Harbor placed the people of Hawaii under martial law. As the result of this, all foreign schools were ordered closed.

Another project Syngman Rhee carried out was the formation of the Tongjihoe or Like-minded Society and the Tongji Siksanhoe or Tongji Investment Company in 1924. He dreamed of an ideal village in which his followers might live and work together for the Korean independence movement, and this dream was partly realized when he raised the money to buy 930 acres of land near Olaa, Hawaii Island, where he built a village called the Tongji ch'on or Tongji people's village. Many of his followers subscribed to $100-shares, and devoted their time and energy to the Tongji village project. But owing to unskilled and selfish followers of his, Rhee's dream of a self-sufficient economy was shattered by 1932.

Simultaneously, Rhee was busily engaged in political and other activities on the mainland United States. He established the Korean Commission in

Washington, D.C., in April 1919 in cooperation with other Korean compatriots such as Philip Jaisohn (So Chae-p'il), Kim Kyu-sik, and Henry Chong. The Korean Commission represented the Provisional Government of the Republic of Korea-in-exile. In 1921, when the Washington Conference on the Limitation of Armaments convened in the American capital, Rhee, along with Jaisohn as chairman of the Korean Commission and Henry Chong as its secretary, presented the case of Korea before the conference. . . .

For about two years, from 1941 to December 1943, Korean nationalists in Hawaii and America were united in a single organization called the United Korean Committee in America. For the first time in the history of the Koreans in the mainland United States and Hawaii, there was a successful coordination of all political activities of Koreans living abroad in support of the Korean Provisional Government-in-exile. The chief objectives of the committee were to raise Korean independence and military funds for the Korean Commission and the Provisional Government-in-exile at Chungking, China.

The united front of the Korean nationalists in America abruptly shattered, however, when the leaders of the United Korean Committee under Kim Ho refused to support the Korean Commission after an unsuccessful attempt to take over the commission functions themselves in the fall of 1942. Kim Ho and Jacob K. M. Dunn had urged Koreans in California to oust Syngman Rhee from the chairmanship of the Korean Commission. Many patriotic Koreans protested such an unpatriotic move. . . .

The United Korean Committee in America set up its own diplomatic agency in Washington, D.C., with Jacob K. Dunn and Kim Won-yong as chief and treasurer, respectively, in the winter of 1943. The Tongjihoe then withdrew from the United Korean Committee in America. . . .

When the United Korean Committee in America stopped support of the Provisional Government [in] 1943, Korean compatriots on the island of Kauai organized the Korean National Army Service of Kauai in the winter of 1943 . . . to collect military funds in support of the Korean Provisional Government in China. . . .

The leaders of the United Korean Committee in America persisted in their antagonism to Rhee's leadership as chairman of the Korean Commission. In April 1945, the United Korean Committee in America came to San Francisco for the United Nations Conference on International Organization to hinder the Korean Provisional Government Delegation, headed by Rhee. After agreeing to form a coalition with the government delegation known as the United Korean Delegation, the United Korean Committee withdrew from the united coalition. Throughout the conference, it continued to claim that it alone was the true representative of Koreans as the Korean People's Delegation. When the assembly of world statesmen witnessed the Koreans divided into petty factions, all contending Korean delegations were denied hearings. . . .

. . . Hawaii [was] the pivot of the Korean nationalist political activities in America. There were many outstanding Korean leaders in Hawaii who lived and worked there openly, since there was freedom of speech and assembly. No foreign obstacles were in the way of the Korean nationalist movement there. Furthermore, Korean residents in Hawaii were financially better off than those living in other countries, including Korea. They raised more funds for the freedom cause than other Koreans. From this point of view, Korean immigrants in Hawaii may be called the crusaders for Korean nationalism and the architects of Korean political independence in 1948.

The UNIA in Los Angeles, 1920s

EMORY J. TOLBERT

Political activities on the part of blacks in the American West have usually reflected an abiding faith in the two-party system and in the goodwill of white Americans to accord African Americans their citizenship rights. Although African Americans have occasionally urged black migration to the Caribbean, and although many blacks did move to Canada in the late 1850s, after the Civil War they were more likely to head for the southern states, which promised opportunities formerly denied them.

By the early twentieth century, however, the rising tide of European colonialism and the subjugation of peoples of color in Africa, Asia, the Pacific Islands, and the Caribbean produced a significant new political development—pan-Africanism. A movement with nineteenth-century antecedents, pan-Africanism acquired momentum in the twentieth century as West Indians and Africans came to view themselves as sharing a common fate with African Americans. Marcus Garvey, a Jamaican-born orator and organizer, created the most significant and the largest pan-Africanist political entity, the United Negro Improvement Association (UNIA), during World War I. Although Garvey's headquarters were in New York City, small towns in California, among them Monrovia, Riverside, and Victorville, as well as larger cities such as San Diego and Los Angeles, set up branches of this new organization.

Emory Tolbert's study of the UNIA in Los Angeles, at the time the fastest-growing city in California, showcases the importance of the West Coast branch and the independence of its leaders. The infighting that Tolbert describes reveals that the Los Angeles chapter was saddled with a factionalism similar to that hampering the parent organization. The history of the Los Angeles UNIA provides a good example of the economic entrepreneurship, coordinated group efforts, and racial solidarity among black pan-Africanists in southern California and in the rest of the nation. Garvey's visits to the southern California metropolis in the early 1920s affirmed its importance to his organization.

STUDY QUESTIONS

1. Why was black nationalism, as expressed by Marcus Garvey's United Negro Improvement Association (UNIA), attractive to certain black leaders in Los Angeles?

2. What caused divisions in the UNIA in Los Angeles?

Precisely how many local black nationalist organizations were scattered throughout the black world during the years following the First World War is a topic for future study. If the Los Angeles black community is typical, however, the number would have been quite large. For the Los Angeles Forum was not the only predecessor to the local Universal Negro Improvement Association, nor were the Garveyites the first in Los Angeles to attempt to organize blacks with clear black nationalist intentions.

In 1920, the year when Garveyites organized their huge parade and convention in New York City, a Los Angeles black businessmen named John Wesley Coleman called the first and only "National Convention of Peoples of African Descent.". . . Little is known about Coleman's early effort except that it was overshadowed and absorbed by the larger and more dynamic Garvey movement. Coleman, however, was no transient zealot, but one of the older black residents of Los Angeles. After arriving in Los Angeles in 1887, he was instrumental in founding and leading the Los Angeles Forum, the People's Independent Church, the Black Masons, Shriners and Odd Fellows, and Division 156 of the Universal Negro Improvement Association. Along with Hugh Gordon, Coleman was the most persistent of black nationalists. The *California Eagle* credited Coleman's employment agency with finding jobs for 50,000 persons by 1924, and described him as a person with considerable property holdings. It was this interest in economics and devotion to Pan-Africanism that led Coleman to dissolve his organization only months after its founding and join the Garveyites.

The Los Angeles division of the UNIA was organized through the combined efforts of Coleman, Garvey's assistant president general J. D. Gordon, a community activist named W. H. "Pop" Sanders, and the editors of the *California Eagle*, Joseph Bass and Charlotta Spear Bass. Like other activists

Excerpted from Emory J. Tolbert, *The UNIA and Black Los Angeles: Ideology and Community in the American Garvey Movement* (Los Angeles, UCLA Center for Afro-American Studies Publications, 1980), pp. 49–83. Reprinted with permission.

in the Los Angeles black community, the founders of the Los Angeles UNIA were members of the Forum, an organization whose direction had become more and more nationalistic as the 1920s approached. The election of men like J. W. Coleman and Hugh Gordon to head the organization during these years strengthened that trend. But the Forum remained the one black organization that was open to blacks of all political and ideological persuasions despite its nationalist leadership, and, therefore, could not logically promote the aims of the nationalist leadership as effectively as a thorough-going black nationalist organization might. Hence the Forum remained vital while the rosters of both the Forum and the local UNIA continued to share some of the same members. To many black Angelenos the UNIA was an attractive import from the East. News of the Black Star Line* had reached the West Coast shortly after the enterprise reached national importance to blacks, and the *Negro World* had West Coast readers before the UNIA in Los Angeles was founded. . . . Indeed, few ideas caught on more rapidly and achieved a more avid following than black nationalism as interpreted by Marcus Garvey. . . .

During its most active years the Los Angeles UNIA meandered through episodes of good and bad relations with UNIA headquarters in New York. Garveyites recruited persons with multiple affiliations and widely varying interpretations of Garvey's mission. The Los Angeles UNIA became, if only for a short time, an umbrella organization that included community activists who had long seen themselves as instruments of change in the black community. Garveyism represented the hope for change through the sheer collective strength of blacks, and there were many in Los Angeles who had accepted that formula for change before the advent of Garveyism.

Formal organization for the UNIA in Los Angeles was somewhat late in coming. Before the founding convocation of the Los Angeles UNIA was held in J. D. Gordon's Tabernacle Baptist Church in January 1921, active UNIA chapters were already functioning in both San Francisco and San Diego. Garveyism in the West did not always seek out major population centers first, as might be expected. Instead, Garveyites went to relatively small black communities in southern California with the doctrine of African redemption through Garveyism, and approached larger black settlements later. In several ways the spread of Garveyism in southern California diverted from expected procedures. Although California blacks were not without centers of activity, there seemed to be less reliance on major population centers for either physical or intellectual stimuli. . . .

One of the better examples of black activism in southern California outside Los Angeles was the UNIA division in San Diego. Unlike San Francisco, whose black population was only slightly smaller than that of Los Angeles in

---

* The Black Star Line was a shipping company established and operated by the UNIA, serving ports in North America, the Caribbean, and Africa.

1920, San Diego's blacks numbered less than five thousand. Yet, Division 153 of the UNIA, which was the number given San Diego's unit, was founded a full year before the Los Angeles division. In October of 1921 the San Diego Division celebrated its second anniversary with a fifteen-car procession from the black community in southeast San Diego to Balboa Park. In the procession were a float, carloads of Black Cross nurses, and the general membership of the organization. . . . And, while it seems clear that the San Diego division never rivaled the Los Angeles division in size during the movement's peak years on the West Coast, the Garvey group in that city relied on local black talent to organize and promote African redemption without a heavy influx of activists from the Los Angeles area. In fact, although southern California blacks were sufficiently mobile during the early 1920s to sustain a lively exchange of ideas between smaller and larger communities, the distances were great enough to make autonomy necessary for each black settlement.

When Los Angeles Garveyites met to organize in 1920, they drew up a charter for submission to the parent body and elected a local newspaperman to lead the local group. Available evidence indicates that certain important black activists in Los Angeles attended. In fact, when a crisis arose in the local UNIA only nine months after it was founded, many of these activists were among the local charter members who emerged in a public dispute. The choice of the Tabernacle Baptist Church as the meeting place was logical, since its pastor was Garvey's assistant president general and it was located near the center of the black Central Avenue community.

The newspaperman chosen to lead the Los Angeles UNIA was Noah Thompson, the publisher of the short-lived *Liberator* (1912–1913) and the only black journalist in Los Angeles employed by a white-owned newspaper, the *Los Angeles Evening Express*. Thompson was listed on the editorial staff of the *Los Angeles Express* as late as 1925, and was also an occasional contributor to the *Los Angeles Times*. His assignments usually dealt with the minorities in Los Angeles, and since interest in blacks among the white press of Los Angeles seems to have been slight, Thompson's published articles were scarce. . . .

Public accomplishments by the new local UNIA leader were numerous. His role as publisher of the *Liberator* and as chairman of the (black) Soldier's and Sailors' Welfare Committee of Los Angeles during the First World War earned him sufficient popularity to become one of the five men chosen by the Los Angeles Black Workingman's Committee as possible candidates in a community struggle to place a black on the city council in 1919. Thompson also had sufficient interest in Africa and influence with California's governor, Hiram Johnson, to have been nominated for a post as United States minister to Liberia by the governor. These facts suggest that Thompson represented a prestigious choice to head the new organization, since he offered a name that was well known in both the black and white communities. They also reveal something of the nature of Garveyism and the effect of three thousand miles distance between the UNIA headquarters in New York City and the Los Angeles division.

Although black Angelenos had heard of Garvey in 1921, the specter of street-corner sermons on Garveyism and widespread selling of Black Star Line stock had not yet arrived. There is little to indicate that Garveyism was much more than the high-sounding pronouncements in the *Negro World* to many local blacks, and as such was embraced more in theory than in substance. . . .

Because of their distance from the parent organization, Los Angeles Garveyites were spared the details of UNIA headquarters infighting and, consequently, built an organization that, initially at least, leaned heavily upon the ideals of Garveyism and its African dream, drawing interested blacks from many strata. *California Eagle* editor Joseph Bass, who was a charter member of the local UNIA, wrote: "The Universal Negro Improvement Association applies and appeals to all classes regardless of nationality, religion or social standing so long as you are of African descent or a part of what is called the colored group." . . .

UNIA Division 156 of Los Angeles was part of a general spread of Garveyism between 1920 and 1921. According to UNIA parent body records recently uncovered in New York City, by 1926 there were sixteen divisions and chapters of the UNIA in California. . . .

This spread of Garveyism in California occurred rapidly, but relatively late in the movement's history. By July 1921 Hugh Gordon, invoking his brother's name and drawing upon his own notoriety as a Forum president in Los Angeles and a well-known former resident of Riverside, established UNIA divisions in both Riverside and San Bernardino. Recruitment was the order of the day; mass meetings were held to outline UNIA programs with hopes of generating a larger membership. A year later UNIA branches had been organized in Watts, Duarte, Monrovia, and in the black colony at Victorville. . . . The small divisions and chapters of the UNIA were sometimes products of UNIA divisions in larger cities, some of them stemming from urban Garveyites' activities among their rural cousins. . . . The structure of the UNIA allowed unlimited growth since only seven people were required to form a division. Besides, the growth-conscious parent body dispatched charters to even the smallest groups of blacks who expressed an interest in organizing. . . .

Gordon's brief career as Garvey's right-hand man brought him an opportunity to enact lifelong dreams of high-level influence in the black struggle. The 1921 UNIA parent body letterhead listed Marcus Garvey as president general and only J. D. Gordon as his assistant president general. While the other assistant presidents general were titularly of equal rank with Gordon, his position as Garvey's personal assistant allowed him to remain in the New York City headquarters and, consequently, rendered him much more power-

A partial front page from the California Eagle of October 1, 1921, reporting a failed attempt by the Los Angeles branch of the UNIA to force division president Noah Thompson to resign

ful than the others. While Garvey was out of the country, Gordon played a major role in the running of UNIA headquarters, hence much of the blame for the financial problems that Garvey's supporters alleged had cropped up while Garvey was away fell on Gordon's shoulders.

In January of 1921, while he was still assistant president general and while Marcus Garvey was away from UNIA headquarters, J. D. Gordon corresponded with a white Los Angeles minister and entrepreneur named John Scott. Since it is the only correspondence that has been preserved from Gordon's stint in office, it deserves close scrutiny. Also, something of the importance of the land speculation fever in the West and its influence on black nationalists, as well as J. D. Gordon's personal interpretation of the goals of the UNIA, are revealed in these letters. Indeed, if John Scott's proposal was typical of the financial involvements Reverend Gordon entertained, some of the suspicion he drew from his UNIA colleagues can be more easily understood. For it is clear that Gordon had personal investments that required considerable sums of money for their support.

Reverend Gordon and white Universalist minister John Scott cooperated in an Arizona land project in 1921 which evidently was intended to purchase property for a Negro university there. . . . UNIA policy on white philanthropy was one of consistent opposition, since the themes of racial autonomy and independence did not allow for preening moneyed whites. . . .

Scott persisted in his effort to persuade Gordon to involve the UNIA in his Arizona land scheme. From Scott's later correspondence to the Tuskegee Institute, it appears he planned a Tuskegee-style school in Arizona which would be initially supported by white benefactors. Land would also be made available for black farming communities with the goal of eventually producing an autonomous black community. In a second letter to Scott, Gordon refused his proposal outright, citing the UNIA's Liberian Construction Project of 1921 as his reason for denying any further financial commitments for the UNIA. Yet, his private business arrangements with Mr. Scott continued, since he noted in the same letter that he had made a payment on land in Arizona.

Gordon's confrontation with Garvey at the 1921 convention, therefore, saw two ambitious and strong-willed men at odds over the direction of the organization's finances. American-born, educated, older than Garvey and a veteran of years of black nationalist activism and church leadership, Gordon was not at all willing to absorb all of the blame for the organization's financial irregularities. After being discredited in the pages of the *Negro World*, Gordon returned to Los Angeles until Garvey's visit in 1922. . . .

When the *California Eagle* referred to the Los Angeles division of the UNIA as "the largest body of enthusiastic Garvey followers of any unit west of Chicago," the estimated membership of the local branch was one thousand. Interest in Garvey, however, extended beyond the official membership. When both the *California Eagle* and the *Negro World* reported a crowd of ten thousand spectators at the UNIA parade during Garvey's Los Angeles visit in June 1922, that number represented almost half of the total black population of southern California. . . .

By the first week of November 1921 the split among local Garveyites was completed. The parent body revoked the local division's charter and made it clear that members of the Thompson faction were not welcome in the UNIA. One of the essential elements in the dispute had been the matter of local control over UNIA activities, since Thompson's supporters had argued that the movement could be best served by strengthening local branches. The emphasis on black nationalism and the future establishment of a strong African government did not satisfy the local need for direct knowledge about the use of funds and the status of the Black Star Line. . . . Thompson's group was attracted more to the economic aspect of the UNIA than to the spiritual thrust toward black unity and a romance with Africa. Therefore, the meeting of the second week in November 1921 saw the Thompson faction, which was clearly the majority, forming the Pacific Coast Negro Improvement Association (PCNIA).

Tabernacle Baptist Church, the birthplace of the original Los Angeles UNIA, was filled to capacity for the initial gathering of the neo-Garveyites. The founders of this new organization contended that their quarrel was not with Garvey, but with the behavior of his lieutenants (particularly Captain Gaines), who they felt were leading the organization in improper directions. Attorney Hugh MacBeth, a member of the Thompson faction, asserted: "The Garvey spirit will be the guiding one with reservations that ignorance shall not be installed over and above intelligence. Truth will be the watchword and sane business methods instead of haphazard and irregular effusions which would bring disrepute and disgrace."

While the insurgents occupied Tabernacle Baptist, the regular UNIA was meeting on a vacant lot on Los Angeles's Hooper Avenue, stripped of most of its membership and awaiting further aid from the parent body. The PCNIA, whom a *California Eagle* columnist called "Pretty Cute Negroes in Accounting," went to the heart of UNIA financial problems with their complaints. . . .

The *California Eagle* declared in its November 19, 1921, issue that the "UNIA is no more." As might be expected, Noah Thompson was elected president of the PCNIA, with Joseph Bass, of the *California Eagle*, as secretary. The intention was to restrict the new organization to the West Coast initially, although the possibility for expansion was not ruled out. These men and women considered themselves Garveyites and apparently saw their initiative as a means of bringing the rest of the organization to what they regarded to be financial responsibility. They were the "intelligent" Garveyites of the West Coast, a judgment that they felt Garvey was not able to make because he did not know them personally. To these neo-Garveyites, their explosion had been the result of a misunderstanding, since Garvey had been influenced by press accounts of the West Coast schism and had received an unfavorable report on the insurgents from Captain Gaines. Thompson's supporters had apparently sent telegrams to Garvey to defend their position, but were angered when they received no answers and Captain Gaines arrived to reorganize Division 156.

Unencumbered by East Coast interference and a parent body into which funds seemed to vanish, Thompson's association planned to purchase a "big business block" on Central Avenue at the cost of $35,000, and raised $3,000 in a single meeting to launch the project. . . .

When the stout black Jamaican came to Los Angeles a police escort led his parade down Central Avenue. The UNIA brass band and a float representing the hoped-for Republic of Africa comprised the parade as it brought Garvey to Trinity Auditorium. There a representative of Los Angeles Mayor Cryer delivered a welcoming speech and Garvey's recruiting and peacemaking campaign in Los Angeles began. The *California Eagle* estimated the crowd witnessing the parade at 10,000 and the Trinity Auditorium audiences at 1,000 on one occasion and 800 to 900 on another. Among his several speeches was one Garvey gave before the Los Angeles Forum, where he complimented Noah Thompson as the strongest figure at the 1921 convention and a worthy representative of the local division. Once Thompson's bruised feelings were soothed the local UNIA appeared on its way to unity; but the question of parent body finances remained. Some former members of the Los Angeles UNIA were never satisfied with official explanations of the association's finances and never became active again in the organization. Noah Thompson was one of them.

Chandler Owen's visit to Los Angeles had done more than establish a chapter of the Friends of Negro Freedom. Owen had seen in Noah Thompson's Pacific Coast Negro Improvement Association a group of local blacks who were intensely interested in financial speculation, especially the kind that was locally controlled and prudently executed. The Garvey visit in June 1922 seemed to signal the end of the PCNIA, but not of local black financial investment. By the time of Garvey's visit, a Noah Thompson–Chandler Owen alliance was well under way, and Thompson had already given up any idea of reuniting with Garvey's movement.

The months that followed Garvey's grand entrance into Los Angeles found Noah Thompson more active than ever, for Los Angeles blacks were engaging in a renaissance of cooperative economics without the official help of the Garvey movement. The PCNIA became the California Development Company in September 1923. Writing in the *Messenger*, Thompson noted that the new company was headed by Chandler Owen and managed by Morgan Stokes, a black newcomer from Colorado. By 1924 the California Development Company had purchased an apartment house in the midst of what Thompson called "the Harlem of Los Angeles" and was using it to house out-of-state blacks who had come to examine business opportunities in the city. Owen had visited Los Angeles in May 1923 as part of a speaking tour and had spoken before the local Friends of Negro Freedom, the group he had organized on an earlier visit. At a luncheon in his honor, Owen met the black business community of Los Angeles and discussed his new company. Noah Thompson joined with other blacks in business to form the "Commercial Council of Los Angeles" in April 1924. This group's purpose was to encourage California blacks to study the conditions of Negroes in California and then engage in cooperative economics to improve those conditions throughout the state. As chairman of the council's Department of Statistics and Records, Thompson compiled lists of black businesses and businessmen in Los Angeles. By that time Thompson was also an assistant instructor in journalism in the extension division of the University of California's southern branch.

The economic renaissance of black Los Angeles also included other projects. In 1924 Dr. Wilbur Gordon, businessman E. S. Blodgett, and a group of well-to-do Los Angeles blacks formed the Liberty Savings and Loan Association. That same year the Golden State Mutual Insurance Company was formed, with backing from many of the same blacks who had financed the savings and loan. In addition, the Unity Finance Company was formed and capitalized at $200,000, once again in the boom year of 1924. . . .

[A] second trip to the West Coast [was] made by Garvey and his entourage. At this November 1923 visit Garvey had an opportunity to measure the impact of his earlier efforts in Los Angeles and to determine whether his fading prestige in the East was holding up in California. The months between Garvey's Los Angeles visits had been trying ones. During that time James Eason, one of Garvey's assistant presidents general, had argued with Garvey in a heated exchange during the August 1922 UNIA convention. Not long afterward Eason was assassinated and the blame for the act ascribed to Garvey by his critics. J. D. Gordon, who had returned to New York City with Garvey after his last visit to Los Angeles, had once again left UNIA headquarters for his California home, this time permanently. And most important, Garvey had been tried and convicted of using the mails to defraud, sentenced to a $1000 fine and five years in prison, and incarcerated for three months in New York City's Tombs prison until his supporters were able to gain his release on bail in September 1923.

Suffering from asthma, Garvey left Tombs prison for the warmer climates of the western United States, taking his wife with him to enjoy the vacation. The Garveys stayed in California for two weeks in November 1923, touring the state from San Francisco to San Diego and making stops at Oakland and Los Angeles. There was time to visit Hollywood and see how motion pictures were made, and sufficient leisure to tour the black settlements in southern California.

Garvey spoke in Los Angeles in the auditorium of Reverend L. B. Brown's New Tabernacle Baptist Church. J. D. Gordon, who was in Los

Angeles and pastoring the original Tabernacle Baptist Church, had apparently lost many of the Garveyites in his congregation to Brown's new church. For when Gordon made his final official break with the UNIA, the New Tabernacle Baptist Church became the logical refuge for local Garveyism and the best place for Garvey to make his speech. Unlike the previous visit, there was no parade, the *California Eagle* did not give his arrival advance publicity, and the mayor sent no representative to greet the president general. Nevertheless, a crowd of more than 1,500 packed the church to hear Garvey speak for an hour and a half. There was agreement between the *Negro World* and the avidly anti-Garvey *California Eagle* on the size and spirit of the meeting. To the *California Eagle* reporter, Garvey was "more fiery than ever," spell-binding his audience throughout the lengthy speech. Mrs. Garvey's report to the *Negro World* described caravans of automobiles and trucks from surrounding areas coming to hear Garvey.

The second Garvey visit attracted great interest, but not exclusively UNIA members and sympathizers. This time Garvey was coming to the West fresh from a type of notoriety he could have done without. Garvey was now the most controversial figure in black America, and likely to draw huge crowds wherever he went on the strength of that reputation. If the crowds of black Los Angeles in June 1922 were filled with the curious as well as the faithful, the crowd of November 1923 attracted even more of the curious. Garvey and the UNIA were engaged in a battle for survival and black Los Angeles knew it. This time Garvey left Los Angeles without reenlisting J. D. Gordon, but he left a nucleus of local support that remained intact until the early 1930s.

Garvey's second departure was not a last gasp for Los Angeles Garveyism, but the UNIA faithfuls held the local group together for another full decade. Between 1923 and 1933 more than fifty reports were sent to the *Negro World* by Los Angeles Garveyites, reviewing the progress of the UNIA in southern California. The Garvey loyalists, who had withstood the onslaught of the PCNIA and the Friends of Negro Freedom, were joined by later black immigrants to Los Angeles to preserve the local division. These Garveyites comprised the bulk of the rank and file interviewed in this study, for they were contributors to UNIA projects long after most of black America had turned away from Garveyism. With the coming of the Great Depression, however, Garveyism began a rapid decline in Los Angeles. The growing pressure of poverty created disputes among local Garveyites over the proper use of what little money the organization managed to raise. Finally, the local division collapsed when it was unable to meet payments on a hall that had been purchased over the objections of some of its members. By 1934, UNIA meetings in Los Angeles had ended and local Garveyites no longer stalked Central Avenue with their cries for a free Africa.

Arapahoe Politics in Wyoming, 1960s–1970s

LORETTA FOWLER

The internal workings of tribal politics everywhere in the United States are complex and often impenetrable to outsiders. In most instances, popularly elected council representatives serve the communities that are under a particular tribe's authority. Many tribes operate according to written constitutions mandated under the Indian Reorganization Act (1934), but these Anglo-American forms should not mislead the casual observer, for real decision-making generally occurs within an unofficial milieu of traditional practices of governance, familial and clan association, and a host of cultural influences. Some of these are survivals of an ancient past, whereas others are of more recent origins. Loretta Fowler's long years of fieldwork among the Arapahoes living on the Wind River Reservation in west-central Wyoming afforded her a rich opportunity in which to observe tribal politics. Her analysis tellingly illuminates one Indian group's way of managing its affairs.

STUDY QUESTIONS

1. How does Arapahoe politics revise the notion that people of color in the United States have an aversion to politics?

2. In Arapahoe politics, how is people's behavior affected by the generation to which they belong?

The organization of Arapahoe society in four broad age groups still affects all social interaction. One Arapahoe explained "Indian politics" this way: "When I want something to get done, I talk first to the elders, then the younger generation, and then maybe the young people." Associated with each age group is a specific kind of leadership potential. (Children have no political role.)

People who have lived over sixty years usually are considered to have the greatest amount of wisdom. They must be wise to have lived so long; and having lived so long, they may have acquired knowledge of spiritual matters. Their judgments, when given, are most respected. Their opinion is still

Reprinted from *Arapahoe Politics, 1851–1978: Symbols in Crisis of Authority* by Loretta Fowler, pp. 267–270 and 273–276, by permission of the University of Nebraska Press. Copyright © 1982 by the University of Nebraska Press.

required on most tribal matters of any importance. They are called upon to recall and interpret past events—to monitor tradition. The Arapahoes also expect elders to exert a tempering influence on the "younger generation," although elders generally do not try to control behavior directly.

The ceremonial elders—the "old people," who have ultimate authority in all tribal religious rituals—are considered to have completed the requisite "degrees" to communicate most directly and effectively with the supernatural. . . .

The Arapahoes are wary of persons other than ceremonial elders (or their apprentices) who seek through fasting and prayer to have visions. The vision experience is closed particularly to "young people." During 1974–75 a few young Arapahoe men formed a chapter of the American Indian Movement (AIM) at Wind River and some went into the hills to fast. The elders expressed grave apprehensions that they would err or misuse supernatural power, and thereby bring disaster on the tribe. . . . It is their responsibility to counsel younger people and "grandsons" against socially disruptive or violent acts. Ceremonial elders, guardians of tradition, are also considered to be legitimately endowed with the right to change tradition. Today, as in the past, old men may innovate in the ceremonial realm, and because of the supernatural sanction given to their acts (as long as disaster does not follow), these changes are not considered to be in conflict with the "Arapahoe way" of doing things. . . .

At the funeral of an old woman whose husband was important in tribal ceremonials, an Arapahoe leader acting as announcer said, "The old people are what holds this reservation together. We must listen to them and respect them." He was reaffirming before a tribal gathering the belief that wisdom, supernatural beneficence, social harmony, and perpetuation of Arapahoe tradition—all are linked with advanced age. Thus elders play a key part in monitoring the reputations of their juniors, and the "younger generation" and "youths" defer to them and are constantly attuned to their interpretations and reactions.

The "younger generation"—persons in their mid-forties to late fifties—are thought to be not so capable of a life of "good thoughts" but more skilled in dealing with whites (and in speaking English). Success in dealing with the white world is indicated by completion of military service, educational attainment, or achievement in some other sphere of activity involving interaction with the institutions of the wider society. Education is of value only when it is applied on behalf of the tribe, and when it does not interfere with "common sense." Common sense is indicated by one's deference to the elders and by demonstrated loyalty to the Arapahoe community. As the wife of one councilman remarked proudly, "He came home from college to be an Indian." Thus individuals are "educated" if they are successful in dealings with whites and use this success to help other Arapahoes; education is not necessarily related to progress in school, nor does lack of formal education keep one from acquiring a reputation as an "educated" person. People of the "younger generation" are considered to be mature enough to become apprentices to the ceremonial elders.

"Young people" under forty are not considered to be fully mature. They occasionally apprentice themselves to sodalities and help with club projects, but they are still presumed to be too unstable to take on responsibilities of any significance. As one elder explained when talk turned to a man in his early thirties who was known to want a leadership position, "He is kind of liquid, unsettled, and this affects his frame of mind." The position of young Arapahoes today (as in the past) is often frustrating. As one individual commented, "You find all over this reservation if a young guy tries to say something they snicker and say he is too young. It makes a guy want to quit." Young people, however, may motivate older Arapahoes to accept innovations. . . .

Individuals interested in positions of leadership are advised to "watch on" and thus to earn the respect of others by accumulating experience. A Business Council position is acquired through years of service in the clubs, which are viewed as stages on the avenue leading to a council position. One elderly Arapahoe made this observation: "If you start out from the bottom, like on the Powwow Committee, and really work, you have a chance." And another Arapahoe remarked, "If you want to be a leader, throw your hat in the ring. You can join a club and get your name used." Persons who become impatient fail to earn the respect of others. Individuals who run for the council and lose are frequently characterized as "too fast": they behaved inappropriately for their age or "experience."

Elders aid an individual at birth, at death, and whenever they are exposed to dangerous or threatening experiences. At a tribal gathering an older man, a veteran of World War II, gave his Indian name to a youth who was leaving for military duty in Vietnam. The naming ceremony was performed to help ensure the young man's safe return. As the name was associated with the veteran's successful battle experiences, so it would aid the youth in similar circumstances.

Younger club members defer to older members and new councilmen defer to those with more years of service. A newly elected councilman is a kind of apprentice to his colleagues. There have been occasions when two classificatory siblings have served at the same time on the Business Council, and the younger of the two felt an obligation to defer to his senior and to refrain from participating extensively in his presence. In 1969–70, when I attended all council meetings, the youngest and most recently elected council member had the least responsibility and status. He was almost always the one who ran errands for the other members. He sat closest to the door and frequently left meetings to check on something for the other councilmen or to summon someone into the council room. By the late 1970s he was one of the senior councilmen; he had worked his way up. . . .

The Arapahoe Business Council is made up of members of the younger generation who are thought to have accumulated experience and shown marked level-headedness. Most of them are veterans, and have the reputation of being sociable and even-tempered in their relations with other Arapahoes. Council members exhibit deference to elders and may consult them on important tribal business, particularly on proposed innovations, even though this kind of business is supposedly for the Business Council alone to decide. . . .

Arapahoes place great stress on the obligation to be generous. In the Arapahoe view, sharing is an expression of tribal loyalty—one's well-being depends on the well-being of all. As one elder explained it, "A person tries to survive, to get food for his family. It's the same with the tribe. It has to survive. The individual is just one unit of the tribe." Requests from relatives or friends are very rarely refused, and ideally aid is given to others whenever possible. Those who earn a good living are expected to give conspicuous and liberal financial aid to others. Arapahoes often express this imperative thus: "Whenever anybody tries to get ahead, everybody tries to pull him down."

The recent increase in income, due to the per capita payments*, has not been used primarily to improve family economic status, but has been channeled into the tribal network of reciprocity. Elderly people frequently comment that the food and gifts that were distributed at the Sun Dance before the days of per capita payments were much less plentiful than they are today. Families spend several hundred dollars on the food and gifts that are exchanged among participants in the Sun Dance. . . .

People who at any time appear laggard in participating in the networks of reciprocity are labeled "stingy" or "out of themselves." The strength of their commitment to the tribe is questioned. One man who for a time was the butt of considerable criticism was described this way: "He lives like a white man. His children said they didn't need the per capita. Their father's salary is enough for them to spend on what they want. People said they should get off the reservation if they are that good off." The man lived no more "like a white man" than many others, but members of his family had become too boastful about their economic situation, and community pressure was exerted to censure this immodesty and to encourage a generous donation to the next tribal celebration.

Similarly, people who are enrolled but not full participants in reciprocal exchange may be called "breeds" or "just like a breed" (that is, *kho'nih'óóOoo*, "half white man"). People remark, "The breeds, they don't know you when you're in distress." When the child of one such family wanted to compete in the regional Frontier Days Rodeo, the Entertainment

---

* The Department of the Interior issues quarterly checks to individual Arapahoes for their shares of agricultural and mineral leasing of reservation land and resources.

Committee refused to sponsor him. "It would be like that money just went right out of the tribe. We wouldn't get anything back."

Arapahoes who wish to earn respect must demonstrate generosity above the norm. And people in positions of leadership are expected to aid any Arapahoe or "foreign Indian" on request. As one elder put it, "If you want to be an important man, you give away. . . . This is to keep your name known to the people, to let them know what you are going to do for the tribe. You give away if you want to be recognized. . . . Not to say thanks for electing me, but for your judgment, your recognition of me." Failure to reassure other Arapahoes of one's generosity is, for business councilmen, a sure way to damage one's reputation. One councilman who failed to win reelection was criticized before the election for repeatedly refusing to give aid when he was asked for it. One woman who was refused use of the man's telephone remarked, "He only thinks of himself.". . .

One of the striking features of Arapahoe political life, compared to that on many other Plains reservations, is the absence of public accusations of graft on the part of the council leadership. During the 1965–78 era, no council member failed to be reelected or resigned because of misuse of tribal funds; departures from the council are usually due to personal problems or to difficulty in bearing up under the pressure of council duties. One councilman, sent to an eastern city to attend a conference, failed to attend the meeting and instead used his expense money for personal entertainment. The other councilmen and the elders took him so severely to task that he soon repaid the sum to the tribe's account. By repaying the money the man atoned for his "mistake."

These moral imperatives—getting along with people, keeping a low profile, respecting the elders, being fair-minded, and helping others by sharing—influence behavioral choices. The degree to which an individual conforms to these ideals, or convinces others that he conforms to them, affects his reputation in the community and thus his perceived readiness for leadership. Political opposition is expressed in accusations of unsociability or dissension, immodesty or an overbearing manner, inattentiveness to the teachings of elders, favoritism, or stinginess.

Political success depends on the degree to which people are reassured of an individual's commitment to tribal life and values. During one recent election, one candidate generated considerable negative comment. The following remarks were typical: "He doesn't want to be Arapahoe. He talks like he could go to Washington and he will be a businessman someday. He won't stay Arapahoe. Probably will go to Denver. He probably won't even take his per capita payments or anything that's Arapahoe." In fact, the man was no more skilled in the English language, no more successful occupationally, and no less dependent on the per capita payment than many men who were far more respected. But he was at that time unskilled in reassuring others, through appropriate behavior, that he could be relied on to conform to Arapahoe ideals of political behavior. The observation that "he won't stay Arapahoe" is telling in another respect. It is quite possible that cultural identity can change and that an individual can alter Arapahoe perceptions and evaluations of his character.

The Politics of Status, 1950s

MARIO T. GARCÍA

Mexican Americans have been involved in politics in the United States since the American acquisition in 1848 of what today is the Southwest. Following the U.S. takeover, some Mexican Americans pursued what can be called a politics of accommodation by attempting to integrate themselves politically into the new American system. Others embraced a politics of resistance and rebelled against new forms of subordination that they experienced.

During the Mexican Revolution of 1910, some Mexicans on the north side of the border backed the various revolutionary factions that had emerged. Others supported the Euro-American political machines operating in south Texas, El Paso and its environs, New Mexico, and elsewhere. After World War II, a new generation of Mexican Americans—the so-called Mexican-American Generation—provided a more representative leadership, one that would obtain greater gains for Mexican Americans in general and would secure for itself a more respectable political status. Perhaps the best example of this new movement was the campaign to elect Raymond L. Telles as mayor of El Paso in 1957, the subject of this study by Mario T. García.

STUDY QUESTIONS

1. Why did Mexican-American community leaders perceive Raymond Telles to be a viable candidate for mayor of El Paso?

2. What electoral strategy did Telles pursue that ultimately proved successful in his campaign to be mayor? Do you think that such a strategy would still be viable today? Why or why not?

3. What does Telles's campaign reveal about race and ethnic relations in American politics?

The election of Raymond L. Telles as mayor of El Paso in 1957 was a major breakthrough in the Mexican-American Generation's quest for political representation and status in the United States. A personal triumph for Telles, his election also symbolized a political victory for the entire Mexican-American community of this key southwestern border city. After over one hundred years of limited and inadequate political participation in local affairs, Mexican Americans concluded in 1957 that the time had come for electing one of their own as mayor of a city numbering almost 250,000 with one half the population being of Mexican descent. Telles became the first Mexican American to be elected mayor of a major southwestern city in this century. His election and subsequent administration (1957–1961) stimulated additional Mexican-American electoral initiatives and, more important, gave Mexican Americans a growing confidence in themselves as American citizens and as political actors. Hence, the Telles story is part of the larger and ongoing struggle by Mexican Americans to eliminate a legacy of second-class citizenship. This [selection] is a case study of the 1957 election. . . .

Who was Raymond Telles and why did the Mexican-American leadership of El Paso consider him to be the most "electable" Mexican? Born in 1915 in the barrio of south El Paso, Telles, unlike most other Mexican Americans, received a good elementary and high school education in Catholic schools. Graduating from high school in the midst of the Great Depression, Telles attended business school and worked for the Works Progress Administration until moving to a better clerical job at the federal correctional institution at La Tuna, Texas, just north of El Paso. Being drafted into the army two years later in 1941 only accelerated Telles's personal mobility besides providing helpful background experience for his future political career. Telles entered as a private and returned home a decorated major in the Army Air Force. Back in El Paso, Telles's father, Ramón, who had always been involved in south-side politics along with Telles's politically ambitious younger brother, Richard, and a number of returning Mexican-American veterans—the *veteranos*—saw in Raymond Telles their hopes for political influence if not power. In 1948 they convinced a reluctant Telles to run for the position of county clerk. In a heated race in which his incumbent opponent stooped to racial baiting, Telles achieved a stunning victory with a slim margin of 563 votes. He swept the south-side and Lower Valley barrios as Mexican Americans turned out in large numbers, but he likewise received good support from the Anglo north side. For nine years, Telles proved to be a model administrator and was repeatedly reelected without opposition. In the meantime his Mexican-American admirers continued to promote his image as a civic leader. While county clerk, Telles held high

From Mario T. García, *Mexican Americans: Leadership, Ideology, and Identity, 1930–1960*, pp. 113–133, 1990. Reprinted by permission of Yale University Press.

offices in organizations such as the Boy Scouts, Girl Scouts, the El Paso Tuberculosis Association, the El Paso Boys Club, and the Southwestern Sun Carnival Association. He also joined the chamber of commerce. Tall, not particularly dark-skinned, elegant in appearance, an impeccable dresser, thoroughly bilingual, a modest man by nature but with a warm and generous personality, a happily married man and the father of two daughters, Telles stood out as *the* candidate for an aspiring Mexican-American community. . . .

In 1955 Mexican-American leaders (excluding Ramón Telles, who had died in 1950) encouraged Raymond Telles to run for mayor. Telles, however, expressed ambivalence about the prospects of a Mexican-American candidate and concluded that the political climate was not right. "In other words," he recalls, "for me to win, there had to be a very special issue, an issue whereby people would vote against the other group and not necessarily in favor of me. So at that time I decided that the issue wasn't there." One year later Mexican Americans again assessed their chances of winning the 1957 mayoral election. "We were hungry to get one of our men to be a mayor of the city," "Kiko" Hernández of LULAC [League of United Latin American Citizens] explains. "We had that burning desire. You know when people have that burning desire that's when they get hot." The veteranos, LULAC officials such as Alfonso Kennard, Richard Telles, and others, again approached Telles. "I wanted to see Raymond become mayor," LULACer Lelo Jacques notes, "because I knew that if Raymond would be mayor that some day Raymond would be a congressman."

Telles agreed this time. He now believed conditions to be propitious for two reasons. First, the city's annexation of the Lower Valley, downriver from El Paso, initiated by the Hervey administration and concluded by the incumbent one, had produced anger and discontent among Lower Valley residents. This protest might effectively be organized into a solid bloc of voters. Second, Mayor Tom Rogers had not been elected by the voters and probably was vulnerable. Rogers, a businessman, had been appointed mayor by the city council in consultation with the city's Anglo business and financial elites—the so-called kingmakers—after Mayor W. T. Misenhimer resigned following his election, citing health reasons. "I decided at that time that it was possible [to win]," Telles remembers his decision. "I knew it wasn't going to be easy. I knew it was going to take a lot of money, which I didn't have and it was going to be very difficult getting people to run with me." Telles had lingering trepidations but by late 1956 was in the race.

Albert Armendáriz, one of the few Mexican-American lawyers and a past national president of LULAC, recalls being present at a strategy meeting with Telles in November 1956. One crucial discussion concerned getting Mexican Americans to pay their poll taxes. Telles, however, was the perfect candidate to excite Mexican-American voters. If Mexican Americans would not vote for Telles, they would not vote for anyone else. Yet the Mexican-

American vote would not be enough. Telles would, as in 1948, need some Anglo support. Mexican Americans, such as Armendáriz, believed Telles could appeal to Anglos and not threaten them. "We chose him [Telles] because he's diplomatic-looking; he's light-skinned; he's impeccable; he speaks perfect English," Armendáriz notes. "I mean here was a qualified Mexican American to be mayor. And that was the thing we were looking for. We didn't want to postulate a person for mayor that was going to be rejected on the basis: 'Hey, he's not qualified.'". . .

In organizing his campaign, Telles began with a strong family foundation including his wife, Delfina, and his two brothers: Joe, who ran the family business, Ramón's Transfer, and, of course, Richard. The youngest Telles brother, a key to Raymond's election in 1948, would be invaluable again through his political and business contacts among Mexican Americans. Richard had inherited from his father an astute political instinct along with a combative personality. In the 1948 campaign, he had masterminded a strategy for getting Mexican Americans to the polls. A nonveteran, Richard, unlike Raymond, had gone into business for himself and operated both a cantina [bar] and a vending company (juke boxes, pinball machines, and cigarettes) serving other bars in the south and southeast barrios of El Paso. Through his business contacts and as Democratic precinct chairman in the south side, Richard organized an informal political network that in later years would come to be referred to by his political enemies as the "organization." The 1948 campaign had allowed him the opportunity to apply his political talents at the service of his older brother. "You had to be tough in those days to exist," Richard recalls of this first political battle.

Outside the family, the veteranos stood ready to literally march once more for Telles. Indeed, the 1948 election had inaugurated a new force in Mexican-American politics in El Paso that influenced Raymond Telles's political future. Returning from a war to save democracy, Mexican-American veterans resolved to have democracy at home. Victims of discrimination before being drafted and encountering it again on their return, especially on job applications, the veteranos organized to achieve equality of opportunity for Mexican Americans in El Paso. "We came back with new ideas," veterano leader David Villa remembers. As part of their reform program the veteranos hoped to build effective Mexican-American political representation in local government. They wanted to break with the older tradition referred to by historian John Higham as "received leadership," in which Anglo politicians handpicked accommodating Mexican Americans to act as "leaders" for the Mexican-American community. Instead, they sought a more authentic or "internal leadership" that emanated from within the people. To achieve this the veteranos led by Gabriel Navarrete, David Villa, and others formed the Segura–McDonald branch of the VFW [Veterans of Foreign Wars] (named after two Mexican Americans from El Paso killed in the war). Although prohibited from directly engaging in politics as a VFW group, they engaged in political action on an individual basis. When Telles announced for county clerk, the veteranos mobilized to support their fellow veteran not only because he was Mexican American but because they believed he could do the job. "We had to make . . . a start someplace," recalls Navarrete, a school friend of Telles's. "We thought Telles was the best man for that position. . . . We wanted a qualified man." In addition, a more active LULAC through both the men's and women's councils could assist in registering voters.

Finally, Telles could count on the support of the *El Paso Herald-Post* and its editor, Ed Pooley. Without the support of one of El Paso's two newspapers, Telles believed that his campaign would get nowhere and simply be dismissed as a nonviable ethnic effort. Representing a loose coalition of liberal small businessmen, professionals, and union leaders, Pooley and the *Herald-Post* desired to democratize El Paso politics. Liberalism in El Paso generally meant supporting a more open political process in local government and greater attention by local government to the needs of the masses in the city. The conservative liberal dichotomy also contained an ethnic dimension. Most Mexican Americans supported liberal rather than conservative political candidates. "Now the man that I owe a lot, and I'll never forget, is Mr. Ed M. Pooley," Telles recalls.

As in 1948, Telles started with a Mexican-American base. He could not possibly win without a large Mexican-American vote not only south of the tracks, but in the central districts now housing many Mexican Americans who made it out of the barrio. Mexican Americans would have to be mobilized and registered to pay their poll taxes. Moreover, with the Lower Valley annexation, Telles could expand his base to include this area, containing at least 50 percent Mexican Americans, which he carried in the 1948 county election. If he could win big in Mexican-American precincts and in the Lower Valley, Telles knew he had a chance to be mayor. However, he likewise recognized as in 1948 that he could not run an open ethnic campaign. Such a strategy would undoubtedly cause a backlash among Anglo voters. Telles did not deceive himself. He understood that most Anglos would perceive him as a Mexican-American candidate regardless of what he did. But if he accented the ethnic appeal, even more Anglos would register to vote just to keep a Mexican out of the mayor's office. He would also risk the chance of scaring away those Anglo liberals and moderates he hoped to attract. "I realized," he recalls, "that the odds were very much against me because my name was Telles." He believed that the odds would be even greater against him if he ran an ethnic campaign. Hence, Telles decided on a "People's Ticket campaign." He would stress that he stood for El Paso's common man against the elite "kingmakers." Telles the populist could appeal to both Mexican Americans and Anglos. Finally, Telles would conduct an issues-oriented campaign while relying on Pooley's *Herald-Post* to aggressively and polemically attack the Rogers ticket. "See, the name of the ticket was the

People's Ticket," Telles explains, "and we wanted to give the impression that we were dealing with all the people not just one sector, cause if we had ever given the impression that we were there representing only the Mexican Americans we would've been killed. I mean, we would've never gotten anywhere."

Telles and his supporters concluded that three objectives had to be achieved in the carrying out of their strategy. First they had to select a ticket that would complement the populist theme and help Telles with Anglo voters. Second, as in 1948, Telles would run a nonethnic "public" campaign stressing his administrative background and proposals for reforming city government. Finally, as he had done nine years before, Richard Telles would operate an ethnic "non-public" campaign. Richard would mobilize the Mexican-American vote and turn it out on election day. The Telles campaign would consequently possess different personalities in different areas of El Paso. Telles would appeal as an American populist throughout the city, while in the southern precincts Richard would ensure that ethnic loyalty tied Mexican Americans to his brother. As in 1948, this strategy did not translate into a split personality or opportunism on Telles's part. He personally found no comfort in running as an ethnic candidate and believed it more appropriate to present himself as an American citizen who believed in a democratic form of city government. At the same time, he astutely realized that to win he or his supporters had to specifically organize Mexican Americans.

The selection of a ticket proved to be no easy task. Few Anglos desired to run on a ticket headed by a Mexican American. Telles hoped to entice businessmen candidates to counter Rogers's emphasis on a business approach to city government. Telles: "So I tried gaining these men, but I found it was not possible. 'Cause I approached several of them and several of them said yes and then a couple of days later they came back and said sorry." Consequently, he turned to citizens with less prominent business backgrounds. Ernest Craigo, an insurance man, agreed to be on the ticket. Telles had known Craigo in the Air Force Reserve. Jack White, a service manager for a local auto dealer, also joined the campaign. More important, Telles acquired the services of Ted Bender, a local television and radio personality, and Ralph Seitsinger, a Lower Valley businessman. El Pasoans knew Bender as the "friendly weatherman" and could identify with him. His daily radio and television appearances would indirectly publicize the campaign. Seitsinger turned down being on the ticket at first but agreed to locate a suitable candidate from the Lower Valley. He could not. "Don't get on that Mexican ticket," he heard Lower Valley bankers tell potential candidates. Unable to find a running mate for Telles, Seitsinger joined the ticket himself. Telles had wanted Seitsinger all along. Seitsinger likewise proved an asset by contributing $3,000 to the campaign and by getting a Lower Valley contractor, Joe Yarborough, to substantially fund Telles's efforts. Telles complemented the Seitsinger selection by naming Ray Marantz as campaign manager. Marantz possessed no political experience but had Lower Valley contacts through his insurance business.

Having chosen a ticket and organized a campaign structure and strategy, Telles formally announced his candidacy on January 22, one day before the filing deadline. "Ours is the People's Ticket," his announcement emphasized, "and if elected, it will be a City Government by the people and for the people of El Paso. We shall bow to no bosses." Telles pledged that his administration would more effectively represent all the people of the city. "Ours will be an administration that serves no special interest or particular area; rather we propose to offer conscientious service to the entire community." Telles reminded voters that as county clerk he had fulfilled all his campaign promises.

Formally in the race, Telles swiftly mobilized to register Mexican-American voters before the poll tax deadline on the last day of January. Voter registration had been done earlier, but Telles's announcement triggered off a frenzy of activity. From campaign headquarters in downtown El Paso, the Telles organization plotted their voter registration drive. Campaign manager Marantz remembers that they stressed registering those Mexican Americans who had never voted, including the elderly. Telles estimated that he would need at least 90 percent of the Mexican-American vote. Voter registration consisted of various methods. The LULAC people, although barred by their constitution from endorsing political candidates, assisted Telles by feverishly selling poll taxes to Mexican Americans. LULAC Council 132, for example, hosted a dance and charged the price of a poll tax for admission. It also sponsored films at the Colón Theatre in south El Paso, where admission was purchase of a poll tax. LULACers likewise set up poll tax booths in southeast El Paso as well as going door to door. They got Mexican-American merchants and grocers to become deputy registrars and to sell poll taxes in their stores. Francisco "Kiko" Hernández, who sold poll taxes at his drugstore in southeast El Paso, remembers that he and other LULACers helped those who could not pay their poll taxes by finding work for them. LULACers further went to barrio churches and sold poll taxes after Sunday masses. Conrad Ramírez, LULAC official at the time, notes receiving much support on poll tax sales in southeast El Paso from Los Compadres, a community group of Mexican Americans working out of Our Lady of Light Church and led by people such as Mrs. Frank Maldonado. Mexican-American women, especially members of LULAC Ladies Councils 9 and 335, were particularly active in voter registration. Lucy Acosta, for example, recalls selling poll taxes along with other women in front of the local Sears and J. C. Penney's as well as the Popular and the White House department stores. In all, LULAC sold 4,378 poll taxes and won the Junior Chamber of Commerce Poll Tax Contest. At Smeltertown, where hundreds of Mexican Americans worked at the ASARCO plant, Mexican-American officers of the International Union of Mine, Mill and Smelter Workers registered voters for Telles.

El Continental, the city's Spanish-language newspaper, aided Telles's voter registration drive by alerting voters to where they could pay their poll taxes. Finally, Richard Telles and his veterano allies, as in 1948, gathered poor Mexican Americans and assembled a formidable bloc of pro-Telles voters. . . .

If Raymond Telles conducted his public campaign in organized political forums and in the newspapers and television, he approved of his unofficial campaign being carried out in the streets, alleys, cantinas, community centers, and homes of the barrio. There, Richard Telles put his organizing talents to work and proved indispensable to his brother's campaign. "Richard was *the man,*" Ted Bender recalls. And Lelo Jacques of LULAC notes that Richard was the "Mexican Lyndon Johnson—master politician." Intensely loyal to Raymond and harboring his own political ambitions, Richard understood that ethnicity was the name of the game in the election. Raymond might officially present himself as a public servant above ethnicity, but Richard mobilized the Mexican-American hunger for the election of one of their own as mayor. Mexican Americans were tired of being treated as second-class citizens and hoped that through the electoral process they could achieve political respectability and eliminate barriers to equal opportunities. "We started feeling the pressure of social justice," Richard explains. "We wanted a little cut of the pie."

Richard concentrated solely on the Mexican-American neighborhoods in south and southeast El Paso in establishing his own campaign organization separate from official Telles headquarters in downtown El Paso. "We stayed away from it completely," he recalls. "We knew what we had to do, and we did it from our office in South El Paso." He ran the Mexican-American campaign out of his own business quarters at 8th and St. Vrain, in the same house his father had built for the family. Here, veterano Navarrete explains, the nuts and bolts of the campaign took place. "He knew precincts," Ralph Seitsinger says of Richard, "he knew who was there, he knew who were the workers." Only a massive Mexican-American turnout would elect his brother, and Richard believed only he could organize the vote. Marantz might be the official campaign manager, but Ritchie Telles was the unofficial one and as he puts it: "When it came down to strategy and all that very few people knew how to handle South and East El Paso." He might have added that he was one of the few.

As in the 1948 campaign, Richard Telles's first task consisted in registering Mexican Americans to vote. With the veteranos of the Segura–McDonald VFW club along with additional veterans from the southside Marcos Armijo VFW unit, Telles again assembled a sophisticated political organization in the best tradition of American ethnic politics. He and the veteranos overcame the discriminating poll tax by appealing everywhere for money. "The money was the number one thing," Richard emphasizes. "We hocked our souls." To legitimize these and other campaign operations, Richard organized out of his office the Southside Democratic Club, composed primarily of veteranos who could not officially engage in politics as a VFW group. A diversity of sources contributed funds. Kiko Hernández recalls that many Mexican-American merchants, like himself, gave out of their own pockets. Even the mayor of Juárez, René Mascarenas, who had attended Cathedral High School in El Paso with Raymond, provided financial assistance. With these funds, Richard and over 700 Mexican-American members of the two VFW clubs along with other volunteers fanned throughout the barrios to register voters and assist those who could not afford the poll tax. As in 1948 the Telles forces made use of Richard's business contacts in the cantinas and used these establishments as organizing center. "It was the easiest way to organize," Richard says of the cantina strategy. At the cantinas, Mexican Americans could purchase their poll taxes, or if they did not have the $1.75 Telles supporters gave it to them. In addition, Richard selected district coordinators and precinct captains who supervised door-to-door contacts encouraging registration. The veteranos likewise held dances where Mexican Americans purchased admission by buying a poll tax. The Women's Auxiliaries of the VFW aided these efforts as well as by selling poll taxes at community halls.

To publicize the campaign, Richard took advantage of border culture by purchasing time on Juárez radio stations across the border that provided cheaper rates than in El Paso. The Spanish-language political advertisements easily reached across the narrow Rio Grande and into Mexican-American homes. These ads, along with the campaign in general, also made Raymond Telles something of a political hero in Juárez. Moreover, in his headquarters Richard stored posters and bumper stickers which volunteers distributed widely two weeks before the election. Richard, along with coordinator David Villa, also personally visited local community organizations such as PTAs in south-side schools, where he called on Mexican-American parents to vote for his brother and to "stand up and be counted." Besides organized efforts, word-of-mouth spread news of the Telles campaign. Druggist Hernández remembers talking to his customers about the election as well as displaying Telles posters in his windows.

Registering voters and publicizing the campaign, Richard likewise educated Mexican Americans on the process of voting. Voter education became doubly important because city officials for the first time employed voting machines in the city election. Richard believed that the use of the machines in an election with a Mexican-American candidate was no coincidence. He saw it as an attempt to intimidate potential Mexican-American voters. To overcome these obstacles, Richard ingeniously devised mock voting machines out of empty refrigerator boxes. He placed these samples at every precinct before and during election day to demonstrate to the people how to operate the machines. The mock-ups resembled a regular machine and volunteers instructed voters how to pull the correct lever alongside each of the People's Ticket candidates. "Don't be scared," Ray Marantz recalls instructors telling voters, "go ahead and vote. You have the privilege and the right to vote." In addition, Ted Bender remembers that some Mexican Americans received a string with knots like a rosary. Telles supporters instructed voters to take this string into the regular voting machine, hang the string alongside the names of candidates, and pull the lever where the knots corresponded to one of the People's Ticket candidates. Other voters memorized a nonexistent telephone number provided by the Telles people each of whose figures matched the correct placement on the ballot of each candidate of the People's Ticket. Although these tactics undoubtedly disturbed the Rogers campaign, it put up no serious challenge to them. "I don't see how they let us," Kiko Hernández still wonders about the mock-machine outside Jefferson High School, "but we did it."

On election day, Richard finely orchestrated his organization to deliver the vote. From his command headquarters in his office, he observed on a big board the total number of registered voters in each Mexican-American precinct and the actual number voting as the day progressed. Telles broke down a list of all registered voters and delegated his volunteers to be responsible not only for particular areas but specific individuals. Every registered Mexican American received individual attention from a volunteer. "We had no computer or anything," Telles recalls. "We'd take those lists, take the names down, break this into streets, break them into numbers, and go from there. It was a hell of a job!" In a separate room at headquarters, David Villa operated three telephones connecting him with district coordinators and precinct captains, who would request information on which precinct a particular voter was eligible to vote in. In the field, volunteers including veteranos and LULACers contacted people in their homes to see if they had voted. Others drove voters to the polls. Mary Lou Armendáriz recalls taking her children along with her as she drove voters to the polls throughout the entire day. Each volunteer reported to a precinct captain who, along with district coordinators, reported regularly to central headquarter. Still others, including young Mexican women sent over to help by Juárez Mayor Mascarenas, passed out sample ballots at each precinct. "We made sure that every man who had a poll tax went out to vote," Richard explains. "We physically picked the people up from their homes and brought them to vote." As he supervised the election turnout both from his office and in the streets, Richard grew confident that his brother had won.

With the help of the veteranos, the LULACers, and countless others plus the excitement of his brother's candidacy, Richard Telles masterminded the most impressive Mexican-American vote in El Paso's history. Whether Raymond won or lost, Richard had displayed the political strength of Mexican Americans when organized. "I don't think that there has ever been," lawyer Armendáriz stresses, "as high a participation in any political campaign of a Mexican-American community as we experienced on this day when we elected Raymond Telles."

With the flurry of activity on election day, the campaign came to an end. Only the results awaited. Campaign manager Marantz believed that Telles and Rogers were even although no scientific polls existed. In its afternoon edition, the *Herald-Post* headlined a Telles lead determined from polling voters in certain precincts. The paper estimated that the rest of the People's Ticket held substantial margins over their opponents. El Pasoans voted in record numbers. The *Herald-Post* predicted a final vote of at least 30,000, almost double that in the 1955 city election. The polls closed at 7 P.M. and Telles, exhausted from the campaign, waited for the returns at home. He believed he had failed to get the vote out and had lost. Early returns from pro-Rogers precincts only darkened his mood. Telles reconciled himself to possible defeat. However, precinct returns from the south side soon lifted Telles's hopes. "Then I decided well, gee whiz maybe I better go down to the Court House and see what's going on." At the court house, both Telles and Rogers supporters clustered around to hear the returns from the last precinct boxes. "I knew how far behind we were, of course," Telles recalls, "'cause they were being counted-tabulated all the time and I knew that we had certain precincts of ours which would come in pretty heavy for us, you know, and it started coming in and sure enough before too long after that we pulled up side by side and then we starting pulling away." By 10 P.M. officials finished the count and announced the results. With a record city election vote of 34,883, Telles upset Rogers by 2,754 votes: 18,688 to 15,934 (53.97 percent of the vote for Telles). Moreover, the entire People's Ticket won with even larger margins. Telles supporters celebrated well into the next day. Veterano Navarrete remembers that he and other elated volunteers paraded around the court house and staged a brief victory march into south El Paso.

Telles won because his strategy worked. His sterling military and political record, his dignified personal appearance, and his avoidance of an ethnic public campaign disarmed all but the most racist Anglo voters. The opposition could not isolate him as a threat to the city's interests or portray him as a radical Mexican American. Consequently, Telles gained a certain percentage of Anglo voters while conceding to Rogers only a minute fraction of Mexican-American ones. With Pooley's help, Telles instead placed Rogers on the defensive by exploiting issues such as the Lower Valley annexation. At the same time, Telles remained calm when his opponents counterattacked. Moreover, through the work of Richard Telles, the veteranos, and the LULACers, Telles effectively mobilized Mexican-American voters. "That was a revolution, not an election," one Mexican American exclaimed.

FURTHER READING

Bong-Youn Choy, *Koreans in America* (Chicago: Nelson-Hall, 1979).

Fay G. Cohen, *Treaties on Trial: The Continuing Controversy over Northwest Indian Fishing Rights* (Seattle: University of Washington Press, 1986).

Yen Le Espiritu, *Asian American Panethnicity: Bridging Institutions and Identities* (Philadelphia: Temple University Press, 1992).

Ignacio M. García, *United We Win: The Rise and Fall of La Raza Unida Party* (Tucson: Mexican American Studies and Research Center, University of Arizona, 1989).

Mario T. García, *Mexican Americans: Leadership, Ideology, and Identity, 1930–1960* (New Haven: Yale University Press, 1989).

Richard A. García, "Class, Consciousness, and Ideology: The Mexican Community of San Antonio, Texas, 1930–1940," *Aztlan* 9 (1978): 23–70.

Daniel K. Inouye with Lawrence Elliott, *Journey to Washington* (Englewood Cliffs, N.J.: Prentice-Hall, 1967).

Mark Juergensmeyer, "The Ghadar Syndrome: Immigrant Sikhs and Nationalist Pride," in *Sikh Studies: Comparative Perspectives on a Changing Tradition*, ed. Mark Juergensmeyer and N. Gerald Barrier (Berkeley, Calif.: Berkeley Religious Studies Series, 1979).

Him Mark Lai, "The Kuomintang in Chinese American Communities Before World War II," in *Entry Denied: Exclusion and the Chinese Community in America, 1882–1943*, ed. Sucheng Chan (Philadelphia: Temple University Press, 1991).

Michael Lawson, *Damned Indians: The Pick-Sloan Plan and the Missouri River Sioux, 1944–1980* (Norman: University of Oklahoma Press, 1982).

L. Eve Armentrout Ma, *Revolutionaries, Monarchists, and Chinatowns: Chinese Politics in the Americas and the 1911 Revolution* (Honolulu: University of Hawaii Press, 1990).

D'Arcy McNickle, *Wind from an Enemy Sky* (San Francisco: Harper & Row, 1978; Albuquerque: University of New Mexico Press, 1988).

Guadalupe San Miguel, Jr., *"Let Them All Take Heed": Mexican Americans and the Campaign for Educational Equality in Texas, 1910–1981* (Austin: University of Texas Press, 1987).

Bobby Seale, *Seize the Time: The Story of the Black Panther Party and Huey P. Newton* (New York: Random House, 1970; Baltimore: Black Classic Press, 1991).

John Staples Shockley, *Chicano Revolt in a Texas Town* (Notre Dame: University of Notre Dame Press, 1974).

Graham D. Taylor, *The New Deal and American Indian Tribalism: The Administration of the Indian Reorganization Act, 1934–1945* (Lincoln: University of Nebraska Press, 1980).

Emory J. Tolbert, *The UNIA and Black Los Angeles: Ideology and Community in the American Garvey Movement* (Los Angeles: Afro-American Studies Center, University of California, Los Angeles, 1980).

William Wei, *The Asian American Movement* (Philadelphia: Temple University Press, 1993).

Charles Wilkinson, *American Indians, Time, and the Law: Native Societies in a Modern Constitutional Democracy* (New Haven: Yale University Press, 1987).

CHAPTER 12

Survival

For Chicanos and Native Americans, it has taken a major, if not always conscious, effort of endurance and will to ensure continued existence as discrete ethnic groups within the majority culture. Each community, whatever its size and location, has necessarily sought strategies for survival as a cultural entity. Ultimately, for members of these two minority groups, survival depends on the group's—not the individual's—endurance as recognizable and different "others."

In this chapter, Richard A. García uses San Antonio, Texas, as a case study in the creation of a Mexican-American culture distinct from earlier Mexican immigrant cultures. Veronica Tiller concentrates on the internal dynamics of the Jicarilla Apaches as that tribe adapted the Indian New Deal for its own purposes. And Duane Champagne examines the Alaskan Tlingits' struggle to maintain a viable culture in the face of extreme pressures from Euro-Americans to acculturate. In all three instances, members of these ethnic enclaves preserved elements of their cultural heritage while selectively borrowing from outsiders to survive the journey into the present and future.

FOR ANALYSIS AND DISCUSSION

1. Discuss the notion of cultural and political duality as it was developed by Mexican Americans before World War II.

2. Describe how the Jicarilla Apaches effectively adapted the Indian Reorganization Act to their own ends in their struggle for cultural survival.

3. How has the Tlingit institution of the potlatch acted as a conveyor of tribal traditions?

4. What is the role of landownership in Native American and Mexican-American survival?

5. Discuss the social, cultural, political, and economic pressures exerted by the majority society on minority groups.

6. Which term, *persistence* or *survival*, do you think better explains the efforts of Mexican Americans and Native Americans to maintain separate group identities today?

The Mexican-American Mind, 1930s

RICHARD A. GARCÍA

By the 1930s, Mexican communities in the United States—composed of both descendants of the earlier, nineteenth-century communities and more recent immigrants—were changing very perceptibly. A new biological and political generation was coming of age, reflecting as well as creating new ideas, inspirations, goals, and views. This is what has come to be called the Mexican-American Generation. While by no means identical in their outlook and goals, members of this generation recognized that they were no longer a vanquished, isolated, nineteenth-century people nor an inward-looking immigrant community. Instead they were Americans of Mexican descent—that is, *Mexican Americans,* a term introduced during this period and widely adopted during World War II and the postwar era.

Besides attempting to deal with dual identities—as Mexicans and as Americans—and trying to reconcile their double heritage to create or invent a new Mexican-American ethnic identity, the leadership that emerged launched a significant civil-rights movement, one that is not well known in this country. In the following essay, Richard A. García examines San Antonio as a case study of this nascent Mexican-American Generation. He compares the group's distinctive philosophy with the views of the immigrant generation of Mexicans, and specifically those of "Los Ricos," the upper-middle-class political exiles from the Mexican Revolution of 1910 who had settled in San Antonio and attempted to keep the Mexican mind looking southward, maintaining "lo mexicano" as its reference point.

STUDY QUESTIONS

1. Why did members of the Mexican-American Generation feel the need to assert a separate identity?

2. What are some of the distinctive elements in their philosophy?

The intellectual history of Mexicans between 1929 and 1941 is best understood as the expression of a sociocultural crisis. It was a decade of an intellectual search for community by the rising middle class. The Mexican American mind emerged in the 1930s as a product of social differentiation, the crisis of the Depression, the Americanization role of such institutions as the family, the Catholic Church, and the educational system, the Mexican and American ethos of the city, the ideas and ideology of the exiled Mexican "Ricos" and the rise of the League of United Latin American Citizens (LULAC), as well as the relative absence of constant immigration.

The consciousness of a community is a difficult process to ascertain, but by examining the hegemonic position of the dominant social classes, there is some certainty, nevertheless, of determining when a new set of ideals, values, and opinions begin to become predominant in a community. During the 1930s there began to emerge in San Antonio, Texas, a minute, but viable Mexican middle class. The ideas and ideology of this social stratum were articulated by LULAC. This organization exhibited a new set of ideological tools from which to view the self and society. As a result of LULAC's activities the San Antonio Mexican community began to acquire a new set of ideas and values, in fact, a new sense of ethnicity which defined its forms of social, political, and intellectual life. This new zeitgeist of Mexican-Americanism, which differed from the idea of just being "Mexicano," although it varied from social stratum to social stratum, was by the 1930s and the 1940s a cohesive collective cluster of ideas that permeated the extensive Mexican communities throughout the Southwest.

The development of the Mexican American mind, however, was in crisis during the 1930s in the Southwest, specifically in San Antonio, Texas, which is the focus of this paper. The emerging reality of this new mentality threatened the dominant cultural-intellectual hegemony of "Los Ricos," the exiled Mexican upper class of the community. This paper does not want to suggest that prior to the 1930s there were not any individuals who identified themselves as Mexican Americans, Latin Americans, or Mexicano Texanos. What is being suggested in this paper is that the 1930s was the period in which a whole community, in this case San Antonio, began to become aware of a new mentality—a Mexican American one—that was being advocated, programmed, and institutionalized by the voice of the developing middle class organization: the League of United Latin American Citizens. In order to fully understand the process of this intellectual development we must first focus on the development of the ethos of the city, the social differentiation within

Excerpted from Richard A. García, "The Mexican American Mind: A Product of the 1930's" in *History, Culture, and Society: Chicano Studies in the 1980s*, ed. Mario T. García and Francisco Lomeli (Ypsilanti, Mich.: National Association for Chicano Studies and Bilingual Press, 1983), pp. 67–91. Reprinted by permission of the Bilingual Review Press.

the Mexican community, the impact of the institutions on the Mexicans, and finally the ideas and ideology of "Los Ricos" and of LULAC. . . .

The very economic structure of San Antonio helped to divide the Mexicans economically into the working class and the lower middle class. The American workplace values were being fused with the Mexican cultural ones. The extent, of course, depended on the occupation. These different American occupations affected the Mexicans' lives by influencing the family's cultural and intellectual matrix. Moreover, because of the extensive Mexican population there had developed since the late nineteenth century an upper middle class of Mexican entrepreneurs and professionals that serviced the Mexican community with grocery stores, barber shops, furniture stores, drug stores, etc. This nascent class was strengthened by the middle class emigrés during the great migration. Each of these classes had their own ideas and ideology, although they still were within the intellectual parameters of "el espíritu de la raza." Both American and Mexican intellectual and cultural traditions affected their daily lives. . . . In addition to the laboring class and the sectors of the middle class, there was also a very small number of approximately 100 families of exiled Mexican "Ricos" at the top of this socioeconomic pyramid by the 1930s. The upper middle class Mexicans, socially and culturally, were intertwined with "Los Ricos," and residentially "segregated" themselves in the Prospect Hill area of the West Side or in the San Pedro district, another enclave on the West Side. Others, like some of the "Ricos," moved outside of the "Mexican Quarter." But regardless of birthplace or residence, the employment situation was difficult during the thirties, although there were some Mexicans, such as the small shop owners, who managed to maintain their shops. . . .

Although the culture and society of San Antonio's "Latin Quarter" was divided into three worlds—the laboring class, the middle class, and "Los Ricos"—they intersected on the issues of health, education, immigration and deportation, as well as politics. In these areas, many times, the two upper classes worked together to help the working class. However, the cultural hegemony was still held by "Los Ricos," although the "counter culture" of the Mexican American middle class was slowly rearing its head. But, regardless of the differences in culture, society, or class, the Mexicans in San Antonio faced the common problems of racism and discrimination. These were unwanted unifying factors that insidiously weaved their way into the core of the community. Like cancer, racism did not respect any class or status group. If nationalism was the positive unifying thread in the West Side, racism was the negative. Both kept Mexicans separated and segregated. If acculturation promised relief, racism did not. Mexicans became Americanized, but discrimination kept them, for the most part, Mexicans. The intellectual dilemma was clear; they were not quite Americans, but neither were they quite Mexicans. The synthesis was Mexican Americanism, although the "Ricos" tried to keep them on the Mexican side of the hyphen by asserting their intellectual role.

"Los Ricos" of San Antonio were a *comprador* class. For the most part, they had no economic or political base in San Antonio or throughout the Southwest. These exiled Mexicans always "faced South" toward Mexico and were more interested in the politics of Mexico and the rest of the world rather than in San Antonio. Yet, they still supported any improvement of the economic, the social or the political conditions for the Mexican in the United States, whether they were working class or middle class. In spite of these activities in San Antonio, these "Ricos," who included many of the political refugees who settled in San Antonio between 1908 and 1914 as well as many of the religious refugees who came in the 1920s, were "persons, largely from Mexico's upper classes, [who] looked upon San Antonio more as a refuge than as a permanent home. Some of them left San Antonio as soon as conditions in Mexico permitted, but others remained."

This Mexican comprador class was exemplified by Ignacio E. Lozano and his newspaper, *La Prensa*. The newspaper was referred to as *"un faro del pensamiento"* (an intellectual light). Lozano was referred to at a banquet in 1937 as "the highest representative of Mexico" and a person who "ought to be an example for all Mexicans." These eulogies were from both the middle class Mexicans and "Los Ricos" who were trying to have Lozano elected as the president of the national organization *Alianza Hispano Americana*, which was headquartered in Arizona. This organization rivaled the LULACs and was more representative of Mexicans like "Los Ricos" who identified themselves more as Spanish (Hispanos) than as Mexicans. There were some middle class persons who aligned themselves closer to this sector of the population than to the growing Mexican American one in order not to be identified with the poor Mexicans. For the "Spanish" "Ricos" and the aspiring Mexicano, Lozano was the "Champion of the Mexican People" and the "new Moses," as many referred to him. . . .

"Los Ricos" felt that they were the "class people" (*gente decente*) that could return Mexico to normalcy, and that they were also the ones who could conserve the "spirit of La Raza" within the hearts of the Mexicans in the United States. Both "Los Ricos" and LULAC agreed on the preservation of this spirit, but LULAC and the middle class were adapting to the Americanization in their lives. The exiled businessmen and writers of *La Prensa*, however, always wanted to return to Mexico; they wanted La Patria. These "Ricos" were only building a feeling and a spirit in San Antonio. They were promoting a Mexican past and a tradition in which they hoped to envelop all the sectors of the West Side community. In juxtaposition, and not necessarily in constant conflict, was the middle class's everyday activities which were building a "new" sense of community. But, this "new order" was one of American traditions; it was a community based on the present not on the past. Change and time favored the Mexican American middle class since their dreams coincided with reality; the dreams of the "Ricos" did not. Nevertheless, the "Ricos" helped to maintain the Mexican cultural ethos that provided the continuity from the past to the present which the middle class used to support its ideological activities in the present while moving to the future.

This "spirit of La Raza" could best be maintained, the "Ricos" believed, through everyday cultural activities. Therefore, through the cultural activities which emanated from the Casino Social, through the sale of Mexican books, through the sale of Mexican music, and through the speaking and writing of its intellectuals, the "Ricos" of San Antonio continued to maintain the Mexican "spirit" and "soul"—*La Cultura*—despite the sea of acculturation. The "Ricos" were attempting to foster a "high culture" on the Mexicans of San Antonio and the Southwest. They were attempting to develop a sophisticated leadership and a *clase de gente decente*. Mexican leaders and the Mexican *élan vital*, the "Ricos" believed, could be built on the anvil of culture. For the "Ricos," artists were an integral part, if not the cornerstone, of Mexican culture. For the "Ricos" culture and politics were intertwined. . . .

Unfortunately, "Los Ricos" always saw San Antonio through a nationalist ideology, rather than a class analysis. Mexicans, whether they were rich or poor, were Mexicans, according to "Los Ricos." LULAC, for "Los Ricos," was not the expression of an emerging class. It was just a different gestalt. Classes for "Los Ricos" did not exist. Consequently, their wish for a social and cultural homogeneity was idealistic, both for San Antonio and Mexico. They could not have just one culture and one society. Their ideology had no reality; in contrast, LULAC's ideology was based on the emerging reality of the 1930s.

The ideas and ideology of the League of United Latin American Citizens were the intellectual waves of the future for the Mexicans in San Antonio's West Side. It was the expression of a new consciousness; in fact, a new order. As the *LULAC News* stated: ". . . in 1929, with the great social upheaval of the Depression just ahead, the Texas wind carried a whisper of hope to the most native of all Texas' sons, the Mexican Americans." Within the extensive Mexican community of "Los Ricos" there was forming a Mexican American mind. It was partially a product of the Mexican middle class' search for community during the 1920s and especially the 1930s. In 1939, J. Montiel Olvera, the compiler of the *Latin American Yearbook of San Antonio*, described this new mentality as one isolated from the intellectual roots that nourished it: the Anglo-American and the Hispano-American minds. This Mexican American mind flourished within the middle class of entrepreneurs: restaurateurs, bakers, barbers, shoestore owners, butchers, furniture store owners, gasoline station owners, jewelers, tailors, druggists, cleaner and laundry owners, and among the over 350 grocery store owners of the Mexican community as well as the small but significant number of professionals, doctors, and lawyers. It was from these Mexican citizens that a culturally cohesive and intellectually conscious Mexican American middle class developed. Their way of thinking and feeling—their lifestyle—was different from "Los Ricos" and "Los Pobres.". . . . The consciousness of this small, but growing middle class was formulated and articulated by the LULAC members who sought, in general, "the promotion of the effective exercise of American citizenship, the cultural advancement of persons of Mexican ancestry, and the effacement of public school racial distinctions. . . ."

The general basis for the "new consciousness" began in the nineteenth and twentieth centuries, but specifically it began in 1921 when the Order of the Sons of America was founded in San Antonio by a cadre of World War I veterans and other politically conscious individuals. . . . All were middle-class Mexicans. [John] Solís explained their effort in the following manner: "we didn't have anything [as Mexicans] in 1921[;] we decided to organize our people to try and better the condition of Mexican Americans here in San Antonio and Bexar County." The first year, according to Solís, thirty-seven people joined the organization whose general goal was "to develop better American citizens and urge education," and in October of 1921 the Order of the Sons of America, the first consciously Mexican American group, was chartered by the State of Texas. The other goals of the organization were also general, but straightforward: the achievement of economic, social, and racial equality with other Americans, the attainment of social and economic opportunity, and political power. The vehicles for achieving these goals were the Order of the Sons of America Councils that were established throughout Texas. The main membership requirement, because of their goals, was American citizenship. Also a major emphasis was placed on the members learning and speaking the English language. . . .

With the closing of the "Roaring Twenties" two things became clear to these Mexicans who aspired to be Mexican Americans. They needed a very clear social and political program and they needed organizational unification. Therefore, in 1927, a call for a unification meeting of the major organizations—Order of the Sons of America, the Knights of America, the League of Latin American Citizens, and Los Caballeros de América—was issued. This call was made by Corpus Christi leader Ben Garza, the Head of Council IV of the Order of the Sons of America, the largest of the Mexican American organizations. The meeting, which was held at Harlingen, Texas, was the first of a series of meetings toward eventual unification. Such prominent San Antonio leaders as Alonzo S. Perales, Juan Solís, M. C. Gonzales, Maricio Machado, and James Tafolla attended. Three other major leaders attending were from South Texas, Ben Garza, J. T. Canales, and Luis Sáenz. These series of meetings finally culminated on February 17, 1929, at Obreros Hall. At this last major meeting, on May 18 and 19 of 1929, after much discussion, compromise, and argument, Ben Garza, the president of the sessions, and M. C. Gonzales, the secretary, announced that the League of United Latin American Citizens (LULAC) was now the single representative body of the Mexican American middle class. The acronym LULAC contained the central principles of the organization:

L—For *Love* of country and fellowman

U—For *Unity* of purpose

L—For *Loyalty* to country and principles

A—For *Advancement* of a people

C—For *Citizenship*, true and unadulterated

With unification and a common philosophical goal—to make Mexicans into Mexican Americans—LULAC began immediately to spread and attempt to "uplift" cultural pride, increase the rate of American citizenship, and educationally advance the Mexican population to a new Mexican American consciousness throughout Texas, but especially in the San Antonio area. By 1933, LULAC chapters had spread from Texas to Arizona, New Mexico, Colorado, California and even the District of Columbus and other Eastern States. Wherever there was a Mexican middle class community, LULAC was embraced. Because the organization's growth by 1937 was in part due to the work of the women, the Texas LULAC leadership decided to give them equal leadership privileges and councils. However, their councils were to be composed solely of women. A dual organizational structure, therefore, was established. Mrs. F. I. Montemayor was elected the first woman to the LULAC general office. In addition to this women's section, LULAC established the Junior LULACs between 1938 and 1939 under the sponsorship of the adult councils. The LULAC leadership throughout the thirties sought to incorporate the whole Mexican family within the organizational structure. . . .

Throughout the 1930s the LULACs were conscious that they had a historical-philosophical mission to accomplish. If the family, the church, the educational system, and the political arena were the institutional transmitters of change for the Mexican American generation, the LULAC members were the active bearers of change via ideas and ideology. In 1932 LULAC President M. C. Gonzales placed LULAC into historical perspective: "We are here on a mission. To make living conditions better for the coming and succeeding generations; not to accomplish that work is to fail in our duties." Then M. C. Gonzales underlined the LULAC's major task as the vehicle of the Mexican American generation of the 1930s. This task was the hegemonic confrontation with "Los Ricos" of San Antonio, who were only building a Mexican consciousness. " 'Los Ricos' were never part of our [everyday] life," remembered Gonzales; "their newspaper, *La Prensa*, kept the image of Mexico alive, but never the welfare of Mexican American citizens of the United States or Texas." This role of "Los Ricos," however, was seen as useful by LULAC because it helped to preserve the "Spanish-Mexican culture." . . .

LULAC's "uplifting" mission was helped by the fact that by the thirties there were numerous towns and cities in the Southwest, including San Antonio, that already contained a population of Mexicans who were second- and third-generation American citizens. This generational situation was a drawback to "Los Ricos'" philosophy. These Mexicans were being changed by the institutions and their own decisions to change. Many times these native Mexican Americans welcomed their Mexican "relatives," but by the Depression decade they began to establish some social distance between themselves and the poor Mexicans. LULAC, as well as the community institutions, helped them form this distinctiveness. . . .

In addition to pursuing this goal of material progress for all and bringing a new sense of dual consciousness, the San Antonio Mexican middle class led by LULAC sought specifically to eliminate racial prejudice, gain equality before the law, gain equal educational facilities, and gain equal political representation in local, state, and national politics. However, LULAC, as the conscious vehicle of the middle class mind, acknowledged that, as Weeks had noted, "the greatest stumbling block in the way of accomplishing this end is the Mexican American himself, who possesses no clear conception of the significance of the privileges and duties of his American citizenship." In other words, LULAC had to first direct its activities to its own middle class before it could help the rest of the Mexican community. LULAC, therefore, sought to arouse the middle class "to a consciousness of that citizenship," Weeks wrote. LULAC also sought to educate the upper and middle class sectors in their political and civil rights and their obligations. Weeks observed that the LULAC members were the "intelligent class of Mexican Americans" and that they were not necessarily interested in the Mexican national nor the Mexican agricultural transient. . . .

Thus, the "Mexican mind" during the 1930s was pitted against the Mexican American one. During this decade the "Ricos" sought to address themselves to *la época de la concordia*—the time of unification in Mexico. They sought to have "*los mejicanos de afuera* remember that they were Mexican and that they should return to work for Mexico." The LULACs, on the other hand, sought to address their "search for community," also reminding the West Siders to remain Mexican, but to remember they were *mejicanos de adentro*, and thus their loyalties were to their present home, the United States. A LULAC leader forcefully responded to "Los Ricos'" cry of betrayal: "The Mexicans [Los Ricos] say we're trying to Americanize, and get away from Mexican patriotism. We have to be American citizens [since we live in the United States] whether we want to or not." LULAC "faced North" and pursued the reality of their everyday existence in the United States; they looked toward the present and the future. "Los Ricos," however, always "faced South"; they remembered the past and wished to continue it. Regardless of their present exile in the United States, they continued to be Mexicans, from Mexico. Paul Taylor observing this hegemonic confrontation wrote "that if [community] dissensions were avoided, its [LULAC] program followed, and if its appeal to the working class succeeded, the

Mexican-American mind would prevail." Taylor observed this, LULAC believed it, and most of the Mexican community, after a decade, accepted it. A continuing sense of cultural ethnicity rather than just a political and philosophical Americanization persisted with "astonishing tenacity" from 1929 through 1941 in the Mexican community. . . .

. . . Mexican Americans did not seek to become assimilated. They sought a duality: Mexican in culture and social activity, but American in philosophy and politics. Within the latter role they sought to adhere to democratic ideals such as civic virtue, equality, right of education, and the right of citizenship. They sought to acquire the use of the English language, but maintain the right to Spanish. LULAC's ideals, intentions, and activities were beyond suspicion: they were for the community.

The New Deal and the Jicarilla Apaches, 1930s

VERONICA E. VELARDE TILLER

The number of Indian historians is quite small, and those who have written about their own tribes smaller still. In this reading, Veronica E. Velarde Tiller analyzes how the Indian Reorganization Act (IRA) of 1934 affected her own people, the Jicarilla Apaches.

The Jicarillas occupy a reservation in northern New Mexico. That they are there at all is a tribute to their tenacity in holding firmly to their autonomy in the face of Spanish, Mexican, and Anglo-American policymakers. (The United States unsuccessfully attempted to amalgamate them with the Mescalero Apaches in the 1870s and 1880s.) Tiller's tribal history, from which the following excerpts are taken, emphasizes that the Jicarillas have continually been spirited participants in forging their own destinies. The period of the IRA was no exception: the tribe initially opposed the legislation and embraced its programs only after being convinced that doing so would positively affect their economic and cultural future.

The IRA marked a significant departure from past acculturationist Indian policy. It was designed to improve economic conditions among the tribes, to ensure their political autonomy, and to bolster native cultural and spiritual values. It is not surprising that such ambitious plans carried out in the crucible of the Great Depression would rouse strong suspicions as well as great hope from tribal peoples long subjected to the assimilationist caprices of Washington, D.C. The Jicarillas' experience provides an example of how the IRA worked on one reservation inhabited by a single tribe. Other tribes either never participated or had less happy interactions with the administration of Commissioner of Indian Affairs John Collier. Like much of the rest of the legislation offered by President Franklin D. Roosevelt's New Deal, the IRA eludes easy analysis as wholly effective or ineffective, positive or negative.

STUDY QUESTIONS

1. What changes in Indian life did the Indian Reorganization Act attempt to bring about?

2. What part did the Jicarillas play in implementing the New Deal?

3. Do you think the Indian Reorganization Act, as it was applied to the Jicarillas, had a positive or negative impact on the tribe? Explain your answer.

The Wheeler-Howard Act of June 15, 1934, also known as the Indian Reorganization Act, began a new era for many tribes throughout the United States, among them the Jicarilla Apaches, who accepted the provisions of this act on August 3, 1937. The impact of this new legislation on the reservation economy and political organization was practically immediate. The tribe adopted a constitution, bylaws, and a corporate charter that made it possible to implement other IRA programs: the relinquishing of allotments, the purchase of the Wirt Trading Post, the acquisition of livestock, and the adoption of conservation programs. All of this amounted to a visible increase in individual and tribal income, which, in turn, improved social conditions on the reservation. As a result, the Jicarillas changed from a dying, poverty-stricken race to a prosperous people with a thriving livestock economy. . . .

The Indian Reorganization Act was passed in the hope of reversing the trend started by the Dawes Act of 1887. It was given additional support by the findings of congressional investigations and surveys conducted before 1934. Specifically, it was passed in response to the recommendations of the Meriam Report of 1928, which condemned the Dawes Act and other federal Indian policies that had contributed to the dire economic and social conditions prevalent on Indian reservations.

The Indian Reorganization Act was primarily directed toward Indians who desired land or who had some land holdings that could be consolidated.

From *The Jicarilla Apache Tribe: A History, 1846–1970* by Veronica E. Velarde Tiller, pp. 159, 161, 164–167, and 169–178, by permission of the University of Nebraska Press. Copyright © 1983, 1992 by the University of Nebraska Press.

Its emphasis was undoubtedly economic improvement, social enhancement being only a secondary consideration. Economic advancement hinged to a large degree on the land base, without which the IRA really could not be implemented. On the Jicarilla Apache Reservation, all the necessary prerequisite conditions were present.

At the turn of the century, legislation had provided for the sale of timber on the Jicarilla Reservation. The money realized from the sale had been used to purchase livestock for eventual distribution to individual Jicarillas on a per capita basis. By the 1920s, when more funds became available from the proceeds of timber, several more distributions of sheep were made. To provide for the increasing herds, the southern portion of the reservation was added by Executive Order in 1908. By the 1930s, the Jicarillas already had livestock and thousands of acres of grazing lands at their disposal. . . .

[John] Collier [Commissioner of the Bureau of Indian Affairs] had great faith in the advice and opinions of anthropologists, and used many of these scholars to implement his programs. Among these was Morris E. Opler, whose opinions and observations about the untenable situation on the Jicarilla Reservation received considerable attention in Washington.

Opler's report stemmed from his visit to the reservation during 1934 for a study on Apache culture. The duration of his visit made it possible for him to get fairly well acquainted with the people and their situation. The main point of his report was that the Jicarilla reservation was under the absolute control of Emmitt Wirt, the post trader, and his son-in-law's father, J. Denton Simms. Both of these men had a profound influence on the Jicarillas; and they had become well-entrenched over the past decades. Wirt's control amounted to an economic stranglehold; he had a virtual monopoly on trading with the Indians due to their physical isolation. By extending credit, he bound them to his store through indebtedness. They were penalized severely for any deviation in their trading patterns. . . . Wirt, according to Opler, was dictatorial and ruthless. He not only had complete economic control over the Indians, but he controlled agency affairs as well. His control was made possible partly because of his political connections with the Republican party of southern Colorado and northern New Mexico, and partly because of his long acquaintance with and residence on the reservation. . . .

The reports of Opler . . . perhaps had some truth in them, although, interestingly, [his] opinions are in direct contrast to those popularly held about Wirt. Occasionally, similar views are found in some of the pre-1934 inspection reports. . . . "The story of the Jicarillas cannot be divorced from Emmitt Wirt. He came to the reservation in 1889. He was gruff and determined on the outside, but there is an interchange of sympathy and understanding with the Indians.". . .

Wirt was of particular interest to the Collier administration. In part, the success and adoption of the act hinged on this man's support; at least, his power had to be circumvented. Wirt's noncommittal and vague attitude toward the IRA kept the administration guessing. Collier wanted to size up his attitude without alienating him in case this elderly man still had the power attributed to him in the reports. Another and more important reason for this keen interest in Wirt was that once the Jicarilla organized a formal government and took out a charter, the purchase of the old trader's store was on their agenda. Without Wirt's cooperation, this might not be possible.

The more immediate concern of Collier was, of course, getting the Jicarillas to accept the IRA so that a program of economic development could begin. In spite of initial opposition, the Jicarillas gradually yielded to the tactful pressure applied by the administration, and by 1936 there was a willingness to accept the IRA. In February 1937, the first draft of the proposed "Jicarilla Apache Constitution and By-Laws," similar to other tribal constitutions, was circulating among concerned personnel for review and comments. After it was approved by officialdom, an election was held on July 3, 1937, in which the constitution was overwhelmingly accepted and ratified by the voters, 247 to 2. It was approved by the secretary of the interior a month later, on August 4, 1937.

The new constitution provided for a tribal government to consist of a representative tribal council of eighteen members from the six districts on the reservation: La Jara area was district one; Boulder and Stinking Lake area was district two; Horse Lake and Burns Canyon were districts three and four, respectively; district five covered the La Juita and Carracus area; and the largest areas, Dulce and Dulce Lake, made up district six. All of these districts were located in the northern part of the reservation because that was where the Jicarillas had their permanent homes. A councilman had to live within the district he represented and he had to be at least twenty-eight years old. . . .

Members of the Jicarilla Apache Tribe who were twenty-one or older could cast ballots in their respective districts. Membership in the tribe was defined as follows: it included all persons of Indian blood whose names appeared on the official census roll of 1937 of the Jicarilla Apache Tribe, and all children of one-fourth or more Indian blood not affiliated with another tribe, born after the completion of the 1937 census roll, as well as any member of the tribe resident on the Jicarilla Reservation. Membership by adoption could be acquired by a three-fourths majority vote of the tribal council and the approval of the secretary of the interior. All members were granted equal rights to life, liberty, industrial pursuits, and the economic resources and activities of the tribe. No person could be denied the right to worship as he pleased, to speak or write his opinions, assemble with others, or to petition for the redress of grievances. . . .

One of the main ideas of the IRA was to preserve the Indian tribes as cultural entities, and this was reflected in the Jicarilla constitution. The council had the power to expend funds for the good of the entire tribe, for its own expenses, and to extend aid to the needy. In deference to tradition, the coun-

Jicarilla Apaches at a summer encampment in 1935

cil was accorded the duty of preserving peace and order. Still reflecting the spirit of the IRA, it was clearly stated in the constitution that all resolutions and regulations passed by the council were subject to review by the secretary of the interior (after the superintendent had approved or disapproved them within ten days). . . .

This new government was truly representative of Jicarilla society. The election districts were set up to correlate with the settlements or local groups defined by the peoples themselves. The Jicarillas had a tendency to live with or near their own bandsmen, and they named their people according to the geographic area they inhabited. For example, those who lived in district one were referred to as La Jara people; the Canyon people lived at Burns Canyon; and the Sagebrush people were from district five. Those who lived near the agency were called "Around the House" people, the house being the agency headquarters. They were considered a group apart because they were Ollero and Llanero intermixed and had no special leader. It was well known which districts were Ollero, which were Llanero, and which were mixed.

The Jicarillas were still a conservative people in 1936, the majority of them adhering to traditional customs and religion. The first elected council was quite representative of the majority. About five of the members were traditional leaders whose fathers were chiefs or headmen. For example, Anastacio Julián was the son of a former chief of one Llanero clan, Juan Julián. Albert Velarde was the son of the Ollero chief Huerito Mundo, and the Vicentis and Vigils also represented the descendants of Augustine Vigil and Vicentito. Ramón Tafoya and Dotayo Veneno also came from a family closely related to the family of San Pablo and Santiago Largo, former Llanero chiefs.

The majority of the leaders also represented the religious beliefs of the people. They were men who practiced and appreciated their Apache religion. Out of the eighteen members, ten were either medicine men of one kind or another, or spiritual leaders. . . . Not all of them were active at the time of their election, but their later service as medicine men or participation as spiritual leaders indicated their strong belief in, and commitment to, the religion of their ancestors. The remaining seven were not necessarily nonbelievers; however, they were neither as active nor as visible as the rest. They, too, represented a good number of Jicarillas with similar persuasions on religious matters. This large number of Jicarilla men who believed in their religion was an indication that the tribe was not only well represented traditionally, but also that in spite of their exposure to missionary activity, the majority had not completely given up their own beliefs. . . .

The five wealthiest men on the reservation in 1936, John Mills Baltazar, DeJesús Campos Serafín, Grover Vigil, Lindo Vigil, and Laell Vicenti, were on the council. These men were not always the wealthiest on the reservation, but they were never considered poor by Jicarilla standards. Only the Vigils represented inherited wealth. When the Jicarillas returned from the

Mescalero Apache Reservation in 1886–87, Augustine Vigil, the patriarch, was the only one who could have been considered well-off. He had a large herd of sheep and horses. He was able to hold on to his wealth and increase his holdings as time went on. Only two men on the council could be considered poor; they had fewer than seventy head of sheep each. The remaining had moderate to medium-high incomes.

One conclusion that may be drawn is that the ability to accumulate wealth was an indication of motivation, incentive, and perhaps leadership, and, as in other societies, it was rewarded. Or one can conclude that this council, like many other governing bodies, was made up of the rich, who had vested interests in the government. The composition of this Jicarilla body might upset the popular belief that among Indians, the poorer ones were usually the traditionalists and the rich ones were the progressives, and that it was the traditional Indians who practiced ancestral religion and customs, whereas progressives did not. This certainly was not the case with the Jicarillas. It was their belief that one's ability to obtain economic wealth was enhanced by retaining one's religion. This conviction, however, became the exception rather than the rule as time went on.

In terms of educational background, five of the older, traditional leaders who were members of the council had had no formal schooling. Their practical experience, however, compensated for their lack of educational training. The remaining thirteen had been to school at least through the sixth grade. The best educated councilor was Norman TeCube, who had finished high school and attended Sherman Institute in California. He was also the youngest member of the council and served as its interpreter. The average age was about fifty years, ranging from TeCube, who was about thirty, to Garfield Velarde, the dean of the council at eight-two. . . .

The council was a good one. It was responsive to the needs of all the people, cautious in its spending, and deliberate in its decisions. Its main problem was the lack of adequate education that was badly needed to run the affairs of an increasingly complex corporation. This made the councilmen rely heavily on the superintendents, who at times were all-knowing benevolent father figures. Toward the end of the 1940s, these councilmen were unjustly being labeled as too traditional and too conservative. They were pushed aside by the superintendents, who wanted more "progressive" and younger men. To them these younger "progressives," regardless of intellect or experience, were synonymous with progress. These "progressives" seemed more willing to go along with the superintendent in all that he wanted or ordered. The older leaders did not go along as easily and this presented a problem for the agency. . . .

Although at first the Jicarillas rejected the IRA, once they accepted its terms, they were ensured a vital economic pattern of growth. The Jicarillas became a model for which Collier often congratulated both himself and Stover. The accomplishments did not go unpublicized and with good reason, for the Jicarillas entered into an unmatched era of economic development. The establishment of the tribal government was only the necessary beginning.

One of the first items of business was taking out a corporate charter. On September 4, 1937, the Jicarillas voted to become a chartered federal corporation under the name of Jicarilla Apache Tribe, composed of all members of the tribe. The tribal council was to act as the governing board with the powers to own, hold, manage, operate, and dispose of real and personal property, subject to certain limitations, such as the prohibition of the sale or mortgage of any lands within the Jicarilla Reservation. All natural resources were to be used cautiously and they were to be protected through the employment of conservation practices. The corporation was not to sign any leases involving a period longer than ten years except mineral leases, or those requiring substantial improvements to land. All contracts were to be approved by the secretary of the interior. This charter surely reflected the spirit of the IRA. . . .

One of the first actions of the council was to secure a loan from the revolving credit fund in the amount of $85,000 to purchase the Wirt trading post. It was to be called the Jicarilla Apache Cooperative Store, and it was to be managed by a person hired by the corporation. The manager was not only to run the enterprise, but he was to determine the amount of credit to be extended to the members of the tribe. Credit was a necessary feature of this operation since the tribal members received their monetary incomes twice a year if they were sheepmen and once a year if they were cattlemen. The manager of the store was to be supervised by the superintendent and the Tribal Executive Committee. The supervisors were to review the credit records every three months. In case of a difference of opinion between the council and the manager, the decision of the superintendent prevailed. From the net profits of the store, 50 percent was to be repaid to the government each year; 20 percent was to be placed in a reserve account for operating expenses; and 30 percent was to be distributed in dividends to the members. If per-capita payments were to exceed $10,000, the approval of 75 percent of the voters and that of the secretary of the interior was necessary for distribution. When the 20 percent share of the profits set up in the reserve account equaled $100,000, no further deposits were necessary and this 20 percent was then available for distribution on a per-capita basis.

In the supporting materials that were included with the application for this loan, it was made clear that the manner in which Wirt operated his trading post would continue. For half a century, Wirt had been the manager-operator. In this capacity he had advanced credit to the Indians to buy food and to carry on their livestock business. Expenses incidental to the operation of the business, such as shearing, lambing, and herding, had been funded through the store. Payments were made twice a year and credit was kept under strict control by Wirt. "This has been due to Mr. Wirt's intimacy with the Indians, which gave him a knowledge whereby credit was not extended beyond the borrower's ability to repay and secondly, a gentlemen's agreement existed between Mr. Wirt and every Indian borrowing from the store regarding repayments of the indebtedness and delivery of Indian products. When wool and lamb sales were made, which were marketed through the store, the proceeds were applied to indebtedness to the store. Debit balances of the accounts were carried on the books to be paid from anticipated returns from future operations, and credit balances are paid in cash at the time the transaction is completed."

The operation of the store under new management was to continue along the established traditional lines, though a few variations were made. Several branch stores were proposed throughout the reservation, but only one, at Otero, was approved. With the purchase of the store, the Jicarillas also bought Wirt's residence and all his landholdings. The majority of the funds were for the store, its inventory and all unliquidated debts of Jicarillas, which amounted to about $20,000. The application was submitted on September 28, 1937, and shortly thereafter, it was approved.

The Jicarilla Apache Cooperative Store became the hub around which the wheel of Jicarilla economy revolved. There was no part of the life of the Jicarilla people that was not influenced by this enterprise directly or indirectly. The entire economy was handled through the store.

By 1940, two years after it came into existence, it was doing very well financially. All obligations to the revolving credit fund had been met and dividends were paid to the tribal members both on a consumers' cooperative basis and on a per capita basis. The volume of business was increasing yearly, going from approximately $125,000 in 1939 to $270,000 in 1949. This cooperative was not only a retail service for the tribe, but a wholesale enterprise for all their collective products, individually produced. It also provided a means of setting up deserving individuals in the livestock business. . . .

This enterprise was so successful that the tribe decided in 1942 to invest the amount that would have gone for per-capita payments in United States defense bonds. In addition, the Cooperative Store decided to purchase a $100 bond for each month of 1942. The Indian Office approved this investment since the Jicarilla corporation had more than sufficient capital to carry on its operations. This required a slight change in the loan agreement. Since this seemed too cumbersome, it was decided that rather than using per-capita dividends, a certain amount from the cash reserve would be used instead. What plan the administration finally decided on was not determined, but nonetheless, the tribe did buy almost $1,000,000 worth of bonds by the time the war had ended. Since some of the livestock men used these dividends to pay off part of their debts at the store, how the purchase of the bonds affected their credit payments was also not determined. The important thing seemed to be the Jicarilla participation in America's victory.

By 1945, three years ahead of schedule, the tribe had paid off their loan from the government. Part of the success of this enterprise was the general prosperity made possible by the IRA program, the demand for agricultural products during the war, and the good leadership and agency administration. Even more important was the pride engendered among the people in owning their own business and the development of a sense of responsibility toward the use of credit, on which their livelihood depended. . . .

A lingering concern was taken care of in 1943. In that year the council adopted an ordinance by which all allotments were to be surrendered to the tribe by transferring their titles to the United States government; the titles were to be held in trust for the tribe. The increase in the value of the individual's share in the tribal asset was considered sufficient compensation for the surrender of the allotted lands or interests in the lands.

To make an equitable distribution of the tribal lands, now held in tribal ownership, every head of family was given the opportunity to apply for an assignment of sufficient land for a home site and, if available, irrigable land for farming. The assignments were exclusive so long as the assignee made continuous and beneficial use of the land. Improvements on the property were considered the private possessions of each individual. Every adult member of the tribe was also entitled to a proportionate share of the grazing lands until the range was in use to full capacity. There was to be an agreement among all the land users as to how the grazing lands in the summer and winter ranges were to be used. The maximum acreage permitted was a range unit sufficient to run one thousand head of sheep or its equivalent in cattle, provided everyone had been given the opportunity to make an application. Surplus land was granted temporarily to livestock owners who needed it; but if someone who had not received any other land assignment needed it, the surplus land had to be given up. The range capacity was not to be exceeded. All the animals were registered with the council so that land use could be monitored. A land code, which contained all these provisions, was adopted by the council and approved by the secretary. This system of land assignments remained in effect until the late 1950s when all Jicarilla livestock operators were essentially taxed for the use of the range. They had to pay grazing fees according to the number of head of livestock owned.

At the time, the Jicarillas were fairly well satisfied with these arrangements. Most of the people registered their home sites, which in most cases were where they had lived over the years and where they or their parents had been assigned allotments. The system had simply verified the existing pattern of land use. There was little or no problem with the use of the southern portion of the reservation since those ranges had been used on a communal basis since the 1920s.

Besides the land assignments, other matters were also given effective consideration. An Old People's Herd, a flock of sheep belonging to senior citizens and incapacitated members of the tribe, was established. The authority for this was written into the constitution, but it grew out of an existing arrangement, initiated as a result of a sheep issue made on December 4, 1930. The money for this issue was appropriated out of tribal funds derived from the sale of timber. Each member received an equivalent of 14 2/7 sheep, representing a $100 investment. A problem arose for seventy Jicarillas who were too old or too incapacitated to care for their sheep and who, in a short time, would not have any visible means of support. So the plan was devised whereby all these Indians brought their sheep together to form a flock of about 1,000; this was designated the Old People's Herd. The expense for running this herd was the responsibility of the Tribal Council. . . .

By and large, the Indian Reorganization Act was beneficial to the Jicarilla way of life. It had dramatic effects on the economy, especially the livestock sector. This in turn increased tribal and individual incomes and, therefore, improved the standard of living. In the 1940s there was a rapid increase in the number of animals owned by the Jicarillas. For example, sheep alone totaled 32,319 in 1940; a high of 37,312 was reached in 1944, but beginning in 1946 there was a noticeable decrease. In this same decade, the income from livestock and livestock products rose from about $120,000 in 1940 to approximately $320,000 in 1948. The number of families having agricultural income over $1,000 also increased during the 1940s.

The rise in income had obvious implications for the Jicarillas. Clearly it meant previously unknown prosperity. It also meant better living conditions. The new prosperity had beneficial effects socially. The attitude of the people toward education gradually improved. Health care became more readily available. Perhaps the best indication of the new spirit created by these changing circumstances was the increase in the population.

Politically, the IRA had a tremendous impact on the Jicarilla Apaches. The constitution and the corporate charter proved to be important stepping stones toward the establishment of a modern legally recognized tribe. Before 1937, the Jicarillas had held uncertain legal status. The Dawes Act required the allotment of lands, but on the Jicarilla Reservation only the northern portion had been allotted, while the southern addition was communally owned. The Dawes policy was also to sever the trustee relationship: yet administratively, from the 1920s on, the Bureau actually increased its involvement in Jicarilla affairs. The Jicarillas were not being hurt by the Dawes policies because they were benefiting from the continuing guardianship of the federal government. This situation had caused confusion in the minds of the Jicarillas when confronted with the IRA, but once they formally accepted it, their legal status was made clear.

The Tlingits' Struggle for Ethnic Survival in Alaska, 1860s–1980s

DUANE CHAMPAGNE

American Indian sociologist Duane Champagne is interested in how native cultures worldwide have developed "strategies and conditions of political and cultural survival." In this reading, he uses the Tlingit peoples of the Pacific Northwest as a historical example of one Native American group's struggle to maintain a culturally and politically integrated society. His work serves as a classic example of modern ethnohistorical approaches to the subject of America's indigenous peoples—studies that include the research of ethnographers, anthropologists, historians, political scientists, environmentalists, and sociologists.

Alaska's native peoples (comprising Aleuts; Inuits, or Eskimos, and American Indians) are among the least-known indigenous societies within the United States. This northernmost state's relative isolation, geographically and climatically, from the rest of the nation is certainly a factor, as is scholars' preoccupation with early English, French, and Spanish colonization, at the expense of the Russian frontier experience. In the 1790s the Tlingits first encountered Russian fur traders under the command of Alexander Baranov. He had established a brutal regime of fur gathering among the Aleuts but found the Tlingits not only fearless but resistant to his plans to subjugate them. Having acquired firearms from British and American traders, the Tlingits continuously threatened Russian hegemony in southeastern Alaska until the United States purchased the territory in 1867.

Beginning in the 1870s, the Tlingits' population declined, and their traditional culture was significantly altered. Their land base reduced, they faced worsening economic conditions in the early twentieth century. Not content to accept the new order, the tribespeople joined with other groups in 1912 to form the Alaska Native Brotherhood. Champagne traces the attempts of the Tlingits (usually in conjunction with others) to revive their traditions and cope with the exigencies of modern life through political organization.

STUDY QUESTIONS

1. Describe Tlingit tribal life before the native people's contact with Euro-Americans.

2. How effective was the Alaska Native Brotherhood in asserting Indian values, beliefs, and aspirations?

3. What role has the potlatch played in the Tlingits' social and political survival?

The Pacific Northwest, an ecological zone abundant with fish and wildlife, provided an economic base for a variety of complex cultures. The cultures located in this region, which extends from the Alaska panhandle down to northern California, share a variety of cultural orientations and institutional complexes. The most readily apparent feature is the potlatch, or "giveaway," in which wealth is accumulated and distributed in public displays. Giveaways are prominent in many other North American societies—among the Northern Cheyenne and other plains nations, for example. This emphasis on accumulation of wealth has gained the attention of many scholars, who proffer something of an analogy to the acquisitive emphasis in Western societies. These orientations toward accumulating wealth early on attracted many of the northwesterners into trade and market relations with Westerners. Oftentimes, however, the primary purpose of the potlatch was not economic reinvestment, as is the case with market-oriented, rational capitalist entrepreneurship, but to enhance social status, honor ancestors, or seal marriage agreements. The potlatch should be understood from within its own cultural and institutional framework, and not be too easily compared with self-interested materialism.

The institutional relations within which the potlatch is embedded vary from case to case. The potlatch among the Tlingit, for example, is primarily associated with events initiated by funerals; among the Kwakiutl the potlatch is used to validate the marriage arrangements of the firstborn. Similarly, the northwest coast nations share a common mythological tradition in which the trickster figure Raven is a central character; in the southwest, a similar trickster figure is known as Coyote. The belief in rebirth is predominant in the northwest, but the visions of cosmological order vary from society to society. . . . The Tlingit believe that the dead travel to an other-worldly house, although some spirits might perish on the way; from this house, some spirits may be recalled to rebirth within the same clan as their earlier existences.

Just as views of the cosmos and the potlatch vary in the northwest, so does social organization. The Tlingit were organized by two moieties with about 25 clans in each division. They lived in the Alaska panhandle, the northernmost region of the northwest culture area, and as one proceeds south the forms of kinship and social organization range toward more decentralized and segmentary forms. Finally, to add yet another dimension of complexity to the diversity of the Pacific Northwest, the region is currently divided into three geopolitical zones. Most groups in the lower 48 states ("the lower 48"), in present-day Washington, Oregon, and northern California, were subdued and placed on reservations prior to the end of the

From *American Indian Societies: Strategies and Conditions of Political and Cultural Survival* by Duane Champagne (Cultural Survival, Inc., 1989), pp. 110–123. Reprinted by permission of Cultural Survival, Inc.

nineteenth century, and therefore suffered early administrative and economic restrictions. The groups in present-day British Columbia came under the administration of the Canadian government, which in some ways was more direct and restrictive than the American system. The third group of cases are the Tlingit, and parts of the Tsimshian and Haida, who are located in southeast Alaska. The Alaskans were not forced onto reservations and their administration has been indirect compared to the rest of the American- and Canadian-administered northwestern groups. Alaska was a territory from 1867 to 1960, and only a few small reservations were established there. The remainder of the Alaska natives were held in an ambiguous and relatively undefined relation to the US government up until the early 1970s. The Tlingit in Alaska, then, found themselves under less direct colonial administration than the other northwestern culture societies.

The example to be proffered here of social change in the northwest region will be the Tlingit, with reference to the associated Tsimshian and Haida segments located in Alaska. These groups have formed a remarkable institutional response to American contact during the twentieth century. They have enhanced their social unity by revising the potlatch ceremonies to make them reciprocal between the two major moieties. They have centralized and differentiated their political relations by forming the Alaska Native Brotherhood and have accepted further changes in political and economic differentiation by adopting the Tlingit-Haida Central Council in the 1960s and forming the Sealaska Corporation in the 1970s.

Tlingit social organization was decentralized and segmentary. It had no society-wide political center, and political and social loyalties went to kinship groups and villages. These organizational features would not indicate the likelihood of the subsequent centralization and differentiation in social and political organization. Nevertheless, Tlingit society was integrated by the potlatch ceremony, which was carried on by reciprocal arrangements between clan segments from two opposite moieties. In addition, Tlingit culture supported a hierarchical social order, encouraged competition for social status, and emphasized the accumulation of wealth. All of these features have some congruence with Western societies, and therefore may have eased Tlingit adaptations to American society. But, as will be argued, Tlingit social and political centralization and differentiation cannot be understood as a result deriving from the characteristics of internal institutional and cultural order. The political and economic conditions of contact and the interpenetration of Western values played a central role in explaining the increased social and political solidarity and increased economic and political differentiation of Tlingit society during the twentieth century.

Tlingit society was divided into two moieties, usually named Eagle and Raven. . . . Each moiety has about 25 matrilineal clans. Members of the Raven moiety must marry members of the Eagle moiety, although during the present century the strictness of this rule has lapsed. Nevertheless, it is still possible to find young men who will only marry women from the opposite moiety in order not to shame or embarrass their parents.

Each clan is further subdivided into clan segments, which were located in 14 different villages in the Tlingit country. A clan may have segments in one or several villages, but no clan had segments in all villages. The primary political and social loyalties were given to the clan segment, or house. The clan segment occupied a separate communal house, which was further divided into lineages with rank order within the house. The villages were not corporately organized, although the highest-ranked man within the highest-ranked house was the headman of the village. However, his authority was nominal, because the headmen of the houses in the village managed their own affairs. The village government was composed of the headmen of the houses. There was no regular political authority above the houses or villages, and each house was sovereign and derived its rank order from its past prestige in giving goods away in the potlatch.

The Tlingit houses had rights to territory, and to fishing on certain rivers, and each owned ceremonial equipment, a house, a store of songs, dances, music, and mythological tales. The leader of the house managed the house estate, a job that included augmenting the wealth of the house and sponsoring potlatches that enhanced its prestige. The house headman was usually the immediate nephew of the previous headman, although the position was not necessarily hereditary. The leading positions were generally determined by the aristocratic lineages within the house, those who could trace their ancestry most directly to the mythical founders of the house or clan. The farther one's lineage was from the central mythical lineage, the less prestige and rank was conferred. At least during the more intensely competitive contact period, the ability of a leader to produce wealth and enhance the social prestige of the house was a more important criterion for leadership than was birth in a high lineage.

Since house social rank depended on the leadership and acquisitive abilities of the house leader, the failure to appoint their most capable men to leadership positions could easily result in the decline of prestige and rank of the house. Rank order was maintained through community evaluation of the worth of one's potlatches, which required extensive accumulation and give-away of material goods. Houses were openly competitive in acquiring and displaying wealth, dances, and songs, since the potlatch was the primary means of status mobility in Tlingit society. House members were bound to contribute to the wealth of the house in order to advance its status. Houses were assigned rank according to their performance at potlatches. . . .

Although potlatches determined the rank order of the houses, individuals received unique potlatch names or titles that designated their in-house rank—aristocrat, commoner or slave. Slaves, usually captured enemies and bastard children, received little status and were sometimes ceremonially executed and placed under the corners of a house during ceremonies. When slaves died they were often left to rot on the beaches, without any ceremony or recognition of interment. The titles of aristocrats and commoners graded into one another, and, as was already mentioned, there were advancement opportunities for ambitious individuals. . . .

The potlatch was the central institution of Tlingit social integration. The round of potlatch reciprocities was initiated by the death of a member of one of the houses. The members of the house and moiety of the deceased did not handle the body or funeral arrangements; these duties were carried out by the house and relatives of the spouse of the deceased, who were members of the opposite moiety. The spouse's house and relatives prepared the body for cremation and provided material and social comforts for the bereaved. The potlatch, then, was a way to pay back the members of the spouse's house, who had comforted the bereaved during their time of sorrow. If the deceased was of no special rank, then a return potlatch at some future date would settle the matter and end the period of mourning. If the deceased was the headman of the house, however, an elaborate sequence of ceremonies was initiated in order to establish the next head of the house with appropriate rank. Such activities might include building a new house, raising new totem poles, and granting new titles for those to be honored with higher ranks. . . .

The potlatch, however, was more than an exchange of goods and services. The cultural justification for the potlatch was that it was a ceremony intended to honor the clan ancestors. By giving away a large amount of accumulated wealth the bereaved house was not only repaying for services rendered, but it was believed that the spirit of the donated goods went to benefit or honor clan ancestors. The more wealth given away, the more the house rose in community prestige for loving and honoring its clan ancestors. During the potlatch ceremonies, the deceased members of the house and clan are remembered, and their formal names are called out. . . .

At the time of early contact with Westerners, the Tlingit were politically decentralized and their polity and kinship organization were not differentiated. Tlingit mythology gave legitimacy to particularistic identities among the clans and houses, since each clan had its own origin myth. Even in the potlatch, at this early time, the reciprocal obligations were carried out between houses related by marriage; the clan and moiety were only symbolically entered into these obligations, meaning that the integrative effects of the potlatch tended to be particularistic, and based on kin ties. Thus, the structure of Tlingit society does not indicate that it would become more centralized, solidary, and differentiated under conditions of contact with American or Western societies. Of all the societies encountered thus far, only the Tlingit have norms and values that favor internal competition, extensive social inequality, and material acquisitiveness, all of which have affinities with the cultures of Western societies. Nevertheless, Tlingit institutions must be considered within their own social context; they do not form one-to-one correspondences with Western inequality, materialism, or competitive self-interest.

The earliest sustained contact that Tlingit had with Westerners came through the fur trade in the eighteenth century. The Russians had colonized Alaska in the late eighteenth century, but had not succeeded in politically subduing the Tlingit. The fur trade, representing a new source of wealth, opened up new opportunities for the Tlingit. By the 1820s, the Tlingit had overexploited their supplies of tradeable furs, and thereafter monopolized trade routes to the interior tribes. Those houses closest to the trade routes had an economic advantage, and consequently rose in wealth and rank.

In 1867 the United States purchased Alaska from Russia, but it did not establish an administrating government until 1877. The Tlingit in Alaska came under less administrative domination than the Indians who were put on reservations in the lower 48. The territorial and civil rights of the Alaska natives had not been defined in the Alaska sale. In 1878 the first fish canneries opened at Klawock and Sitka, and soon several canning companies had appropriated the traditional salmon runs of the Tlingit. In 1897 the native fisherman were prohibited from using fish traps, which had been used for

Yakutat natives dressed in dancing costumes for a potlatch ceremony in 1904

generations for subsistence. The Tlingit had no legal recourse against the intrusions of the fishing companies, and most lost control over their subsistence livelihood. Many Tlingit turned to commercial fishing, and others, mainly women, turned to wage labor in the canning plants.

Many Tlingit actively participated in the new labor markets and took advantage of commercial fishing opportunities. House headmen encouraged their kinfolk to accept the new economic opportunities. Tlingit were not necessarily seeking wealth for economic reinvestment, but to pursue traditional goals of raising personal and house prestige through the potlatch system. House leaders did not oppose the exploitation of market opportunities, even though young people began to reject the discipline of the economically communal house. Many moved to towns, started to invest in American-style homes, and became more interested in personal accumulation. By the 1890s the younger generations were less willing to live under the constraints of the house and less willing to share economic wealth. Strong identification with house and clan remained, but house control over individual economic action weakened. . . .

Several critical conditions and events arose near the turn of the twentieth century. The Tlingit population was noticeably declining and by 1900 had reached a low point of about 5,000, having declined from an earlier estimated population of 10,000. The potlatch ceremonies were coming under increasing censure from American missionaries, who regarded them as a waste of material resources and a pagan rite that emphasized ancestor worship. Perhaps the last great, traditional potlatch occurred in 1904; by 1912 the potlatches were banned, and some ceremonial goods and artifacts were confiscated by the US government. . . .

As American citizens began to outnumber natives in southeast Alaska, the Tlingit were reduced to minority status. In 1902 the US government established the Tongass National Forest, appropriating nearly 16 million acres of land that had been claimed by the southeastern natives. Territorial dispossession and changing economic conditions and relations were major problems among the Tlingit, but the issue of civil rights was also considered important.

In 1912 the Alaska Native Brotherhood (ANB) held its first organizational meeting at Juneau in the office of the superintendent of the Bureau of Indian Affairs. In 1915 an auxiliary organization, the Alaska Native Sisterhood (ANS), was formed. Native leaders had observed the organization of the Alaska territorial government and thought that only through a territory-wide native organization could native Alaskans defend and further their interests in civil rights and economic incorporation and protect the subsistence economy. ANB was originally created to facilitate the Alaska native transition to American economic life and citizenship. Its roots—it was organized primarily by Tlingits and one Tsimshian—did not derive primarily from traditional culture and organization, but was organized along the model of a Presbyterian religious society. . . . The founders of the Alaska Native Brotherhood had all participated in religious societies. The experience they gained proved fundamental to the establishment of the ANB.

By the late 1920s ANB had received support and participation from nearly all the villages in the Alaska panhandle. ANB promoted political integration on the basis of Christian principles of individual social responsibility and commitment. It was not organized by traditional social structural principles, but the members embraced Christian principles of voluntary participation and attitudes of progress and change. In fact, the early founders—and some contemporary leaders—refused to recognize traditional culture and kinship organization. ANB's written constitution scrupulously adhered to parliamentary procedures.

Thus, ANB represented a centralization and differentiation of political organization among the Tlingit. The values, organization, and mode of political integration of the new organization were based largely on Christian principles rather than on Tlingit values. The new political center was differentiated from kinship and Tlingit mythology. ANB leaders supported increased social solidarity through participation in potlatches and also promoted a more secular political solidarity through commitments to the organization.

Until the early 1950s ANB formally disassociated itself from traditional culture and social order. In the 1950s potlatches were again openly celebrated, and many Tlingit wished to have dances and ceremonies during recreational periods of ANB grand camp meetings. This led to bitter debate, but ended with the approval of dances and traditional entertainment. Despite the formal differentiation of ANB organization from Tlingit culture and social organization, ANB is informally supported by Tlingit social order. The clan-moiety system and potlatch ceremonies provided an underlying social consensus in support of the organization and its goals. Clan leaders urged participation in ANB, and the traditional generosity of giving wealth away at potlatches was in part transferred to giving material and service contributions to support ANB. Families and individuals gained community recognition for their regular and sizable contributions in support of ANB, just as they had gained recognition in their support of potlatches. . . .

As a political organization ANB has a long record of distinguished service. It successfully challenged discriminatory laws. . . . Between 1929 and 1959 ANB successfully engineered a land claim suit against the United States for its appropriation of the Tongass and Glacier Bay national parks. In 1929 its lawyers secured the right for native children to attend public schools. In 1945 the Alaska territorial government passed an antidiscrimination law as the result of intense lobbying by ANB leaders. In 1946 several ANB leaders were elected to the Alaska territorial House and Senate. During the 1920s and 1930s the organization represented cannery workers in labor disputes and attempted to gain better wages and better working conditions; its union activities were later turned over to the Congress of Industrial Organizations. ANB continues to be active in protecting the subsistence economy for Alaska natives against state, federal, and international laws restricting hunting and fishing rights. In 1968 the southeast natives were awarded $7.5 million for lands lost in the early part of the century, a decision that brought to a close a land claim movement initiated in 1929. ANB is highly mobilized within Alaska state politics; its members are expected to vote and help get voters to the polls. Its strategy has always been one of working within the American political order, never one of challenging that order.

Over the past three decades Tlingit economic and political organizations have become more specialized, and the kinship-ceremonial complex continues to provide a consensual ground for further institutional differentiation and change. In 1959, the Tlingit-Haida Central Council (THCC) won the long-standing land claim case. THCC was created by ANB in 1939 to pursue the land claim against the United States; the ANB, which was open to universal membership, could not represent the specific land claims of the Tlingit and Haida tribes. THCC was delegated administration of the $7.5 million settlement claim. After some controversy, the Tlingit and Haida decided to keep the settlement money as a capital fund and spend only the interest to provide services to the Tlingit and Haida people. In the lower 48 land claims are usually distributed per capita and therefore do not provide a financial base for government or economic enterprise.

In recent years THCC has come to operate much in the same way as the reservation governments in the lower 48, except that THCC is not subject to direct administrative controls and veto powers from BIA. THCC manages social welfare programs and acts for the legal interests of the Tlingit and Haida of Alaska. . . .

Since 1971, the formation of the Sealaska Corporation has introduced a powerful economic institution into southeast Alaska. The Alaska Native Claims Settlement Act of 1971 (ANCSA) authorized the creation of 12 regional economic corporations and numerous village corporations. ANCSA was the result of intense lobbying and grew out of the energy conditions of the late 1960s. ANCSA authorized that the regional corporations would control most of the money and land granted by the act—$962.5 million and 44 million acres of land—which was intended to ensure that BIA did not gain direct control over Alaska native land, money, and organizations. The Alaska native leadership, familiar with the administrative controls that BIA exercised over the reservation governments and communities in the lower 48, considered such control a major obstacle to self-government and economic self-sufficiency. Most Alaska natives, however, knew little about corporate economic enterprises. The relative absence of BIA administrative regulation over Alaska native corporations and community associations allowed the Alaska natives considerable political and economic freedoms, freedoms not generally available to the native communities of the lower 48.

Nevertheless, freedom from regulation also entails the risk of business losses, and therefore losses of land, money, and other assets. The corporations are profit-oriented organizations, and as such must compete in the domestic and international markets. Possible bankruptcy will mean the loss of native control over land and assets.

About 16,000 native people in southeast Alaska were initially granted 100 shares of stock in Sealaska, which had total assets of $400 million. Shareholders have the right to elect members to the board of directors, which is responsible for Sealaska's economic performance. Since Sealaska controls most Tlingit and Haida natural and economic resources, membership on the board and corporate management jobs have become the most prestigious posts in contemporary Tlingit-Haida society. Sealaska wields considerably more economic power and material and political resources than either THCC or ANB, and hence has attracted much of the experienced and able leadership. Election to the board of directors is a highly competitive and expensive undertaking. Mobilizing kinship ties helps to some extent, but one must also have administrative experience, some business acumen, and proven ability to compete within the American economy.

Overall Sealaska has not shown strong returns on its initial investment. Some corporations have invested their initial settlement money in interest-bearing instruments and have collected higher returns. The Sealaska board of directors, however, has taken an active approach in investing and managing a variety of businesses, and it has argued that this active approach will prove more beneficial in terms of experience, economic autonomy, and generation of jobs than a passive investment approach. During the early 1980s Sealaska's annual revenues were around $250 million, which placed it on the Fortune 1000 list. However, a combination of poor market conditions and a few unfortunate business decisions have contributed to Sealaska's marginal profitability.

Sealaska aggressively invests in and manages a portfolio of companies engaged in construction, sea transportation, lumbering, and fishing. It has also made special efforts to employ qualified shareholders, and about 17 percent of the work force are shareholders. Although it has a firm commitment to profitability and viability within the American corporate world, one of Sealaska's major goals is to preserve the heritage of land and culture. Many members of the community believe that Sealaska must ultimately serve this latter purpose.

Whether Sealaska will achieve its long-range goals of profitability and cultural preservation remains to be seen. In 1991 Sealaska shareholders will have the right to vote for public sale of shares or for keeping the shareholders exclusively among the southeastern natives and their descendants. Up until 1988, the original ANCSA law required that all shares of the regional corporations become available for public sale in 1991. This stipulation greatly agitated the Alaska native community, because it implied that the corporations might well be bought by larger American corporations, thereby leaving the land and natural resources in the hands of American corporate managers. AFN was able to secure a change in the ANCSA law, which now gives the shareholders the right to vote on selling shares publicly. The general opinion appears to be that the shareholders of ANCSA corporations will vote not to make shares available to the general public.

Over the past century the Tlingit and Haida of Alaska have demonstrated a capacity for political and economic institution building. At present, Sealaska, THCC, ANB, and the traditional kinship-ceremonial complex act in concert in their pursuit of Tlingit and Haida political, economic, and cultural interests. The relations of key participants in the four major institutions resemble interlocking corporate directorships. Members of Sealaska's board are often people who have served as past presidents or members on the executive committee of THCC, have put in long service as members of ANB, and often are members of ANB's executive committee. Most people who are active in ANB, THCC, and the Sealaska Corporation also bear the obligations of leadership of their clan in contemporary potlatch ceremonies. Some are heads of their clans, members of the board of directors of Sealaska, and leaders in both THCC and ANB all at the same time, although this is not common. ANB is considered the most respected of the newly differentiated institutions, although in more recent years Sealaska's economic power and, to a much lesser extent, THCC's control over governmental resources, have eclipsed the role of ANB.

A combination of conditions are necessary for explaining Tlingit and Haida political and economic institution building. First, the Alaska geopolitical environment, which did not entail BIA administrative regulation over native institutions, contributed to the possibilities for Tlingit-Haida institution building. Similar levels of economic and political differentiation and institutional stability are not generally found among the reservation communities of the lower 48. Second, the competitive, acquisitive, and hierarchical orientations of Tlingit society facilitated active participation in markets and acceptance of American competitive and stratified economic and political institutions. Third, the Tlingit-Haida moiety and potlatch system provided a consensual social solidarity that supported more differentiated political institutions designed to protect native interests within the context of American political institutions and market economy. For example, a combined Eagle and Raven, which symbolizes the societal unity for the Tlingit and Haida as well as Tsimshian, composes the logo for both ANB and the Sealaska Corporation. Fourth, the interpenetration of American and Christian values and organizational models among the leaders of ANB is critical to understanding the formation of the more differentiated and politically integrated ANB, since traditionally particularistic house loyalties were not the basis of ANB's political unity or organization.

The most critical component appears to be the underlying social solidarity of the potlatch system, since without consensus we would expect that the introduction of more differentiated forms of political organization and new norms of political solidarity would fail to become institutionalized and would break the community into conservative and "progressive" factional cleavages, as we have seen among the Sioux on the plains. Prior to 1960, the relative freedom from administrative regulation within the Alaska political environment did not lead to similar developments in political centralization and differentiation and economic incorporation among the Athapascans, Aleuts and Eskimos, who were also resident native groups in Alaska over the same period as the Tlingit and Haida. . . . [T]he situation changed drastically after 1960, but the southeastern natives with their moiety structure, potlatch complex, and competitive, hierarchical, and acquisitive cultural orientations were actively engaged in economic entrepreneurship, wage labor, and political institution building well before the political movements of the 1960s in Alaska. Consequently, Tlingit social solidarity and cultural orientations help explain their relative propensity for adopting political and economic change.

FURTHER READING

Gloria Anzaldua, *Borderlands/La Frontera: The New Mestiza* (San Francisco: Spinsters/Aunt Lute Press, 1987).

Arthur L. Campa, *Hispanic Culture in the Southwest* (Norman: University of Oklahoma Press, 1979).

Sandra Cisneros, *Woman Hollering Creek and Other Stories* (New York: Random House, 1991).

James A. Clifton, *The Prairie People: Continuity and Change in Potawatomi Indian Culture, 1665–1965* (Lawrence: Regents Press of Kansas, 1977).

John W. Connor, *Tradition and Change in Three Generations of Japanese Americans* (Chicago: Nelson-Hall, 1977).

Lucha Corpi, *Delia's Song* (Houston: Arte Publico Press, 1989).

Stephen S. Fugita and David J. O'Brien, *Japanese American Ethnicity: The Persistence of Community* (Seattle: University of Washington Press, 1991).

Richard A. García, *Rise of the Mexican American Middle Class: San Antonio, 1929–1941* (College Station: Texas A&M University Press, 1991).

Margaret A. Gibson, *Accommodation Without Assimilation: Sikh Immigrants in an American High School* (Ithaca, N.Y.: Cornell University Press, 1988).

Won Moo Hurh and Kwang Chung Kim, *Korean Immigrants in America: A Structural Analysis of Ethnic Confinement and Adhesive Adaptation* (Cranbury, N.J.: Associated University Presses, 1984).

George Jackson, *Blood in My Eye* (Baltimore: Black Classic Press, 1991).

Joseph G. Jorgensen, *The Sun Dance Religion: Power for the Powerless* (Chicago: University of Chicago Press, 1972).

William M. King, *Going to Meet a Man: Denver's Last Legal Public Execution, 17 July, 1886* (Miwot, Colo.: University Press of Colorado, 1990).

Chalsa M. Loo, *Chinatown: Most Time, Hard Time* (New York: Praeger Publishers, 1991).

Huey Newton with J. Herman Blake, *Revolutionary Suicide* (New York: Harcourt Brace Jovanovich, 1973; New York: Ballantine Books, 1974).

Kenneth R. Philp, ed., *Indian Self-Rule: First-Hand Accounts of Indian-White Relations from Roosevelt to Reagan* (Salt Lake City: Howe Brothers, 1986).

Deward E. Walker, Jr., *Conflict and Schism in Nez Perce Acculturation: A Study of Religion and Politics* (Pullman: Washington State University Press, 1968).

Terry P. Wilson, *The Underground Reservation: Osage Oil* (Lincoln: University of Nebraska Press, 1985).

CHAPTER 13

Wartime

Both world wars profoundly shaped U.S. history, but it was the Second World War, which saw fighting in the Pacific as well as in Europe, that affected the American West to such a degree that race relations have never been the same again in the region. Westerners of European ancestry viewed the Japanese as alien and hostile and in 1942 interned more than 112,000 people of Japanese ancestry, two-thirds of them Americans citizens, in ten relocation centers scattered in the American West. In this chapter's first reading, Roger Daniels discusses the divisions among the internees and considers the effects of conflict, discord, and political debate concerning their situation on their lives.

In the Pacific theater, Navajo soldiers, employing their own language, assisted the American military by radioing secret messages from one command post to another to confound the Japanese army and navy. In the second selection, Cozy Stanley Brown, one of the "code talkers," relates his life on the reservation as well as his recruitment, training, and experiences in the Pacific and helps to clarify why a disproportionate number of Native Americans joined the U.S. armed forces.

Along the United States' Pacific coast, meanwhile, thousands of black migrants from the South settled in the San Francisco Bay Area, Los Angeles, and San Diego to work in war industries. In the third reading, Albert Broussard analyzes the impact of their presence on civil rights and race relations in San Francisco. Erasmo Gamboa in the final essay examines the bracero program, under which tens of thousands of Mexican workers were imported to cultivate and harvest crops in the 1940s throughout the American West, including the Pacific Northwest region.

FOR ANALYSIS AND DISCUSSION

1. What important changes—social, economic, cultural, and other—did World War II bring to the American West?

2. What justifications were given for incarcerating more than 112,000 Japanese immigrants and Japanese Americans during World War II? Do these justifications stand up under scrutiny? Explain your answer.

3. What was noteworthy about Navajo participation in the U.S. armed forces?

4. How were the exceptional war records of Native Americans and Japanese Americans used to shape public policy after the war?

5. Compare and contrast the African Americans who migrated to the San Francisco Bay Area with the Mexican braceros who went to the Pacific Northwest, in terms of their working conditions and quality of life.

6. Did race relations change in the American West during the war? If so, how?

The Incarceration of Japanese Americans During World War II

ROGER DANIELS

After Japan bombed the American naval station at Pearl Harbor, Hawaii, on December 7, 1941, the United States entered World War II, a war that would deeply affect Americans. Men and women of all ethnic backgrounds served in the military during the global conflict; large numbers of women took up "men's work" in factories and shipyards; some African Americans and other racial minorities finally gained access to jobs that had previously been closed to them; and thousands of Chinese and Filipino aliens were naturalized in mass ceremonies so that they could serve in the armed forces.

When the war had broken out, aliens of Japanese, German, and Italian nationality living in the United States were branded as "enemy aliens." The leaders among them were taken into custody and interned at camps operated by the U.S. Justice Department. After this initial roundup, federal policy toward the three groups of enemy aliens diverged: Germans and Italians were kept under surveillance, but Japanese immigrants and their American-born children living along the Pacific coast—almost 113,000 persons—were rounded up and incarcerated in so-called relocation centers administered by the War Relocation Authority.

Some writers have called these centers concentration camps, but many Americans, particularly those of Jewish ancestry, have argued that the term is misused because, in their minds, that nomenclature should be reserved for the camps run by the German Nazis. Whatever they are called, the temporary assembly centers and the more permanent relocation centers were grim places of confinement ringed by barbed wire and guarded by armed sentries. Families were crowded into tiny, bare compartments in barracks; meals were served in mess halls; toilets initially had no partitions. In contrast to the "official" view of the War Relocation Authority that depicted the camps as relatively tension-free and happy places, this study by Roger Daniels probes the conflicts that spread through these camps, both among the internees and between them and their keepers.

STUDY QUESTIONS

1. Do you think that the relocation centers should be called concentration camps? Defend your answer.

2. What were the sources of tension in the camps?

3. Why did officials ask the internees to fill out a loyalty questionnaire even though the government had earlier declared that it was impossible to separate the loyal from the disloyal?

4. Why did the Tule Lake Relocation Center have more problems than the other camps?

Eight months after Pearl Harbor, on August 7, 1942, all the West Coast Japanese Americans had been rounded up, one way or another, and were either in Wartime Civil Control Administration (WCAA) Assembly Centers or War Relocation Authority (WRA) camps. By November 3 the transfer to WRA was complete; altogether 119,803 men, women, and children were confined behind barbed wire. Almost six thousand new American citizens would be born in the concentration camps and some eleven hundred were sent in from the Hawaiian Islands. The rest—112,704 people—were West Coast Japanese. Of these, almost two-thirds—64.9 percent—were American-born, most of them under 21 and 77.4 percent under 25. Their foreign-born parents presented a quite different demographic profile. More than half of them—57.2 percent—were over 50. The camps, then, were primarily places of confinement for the young and the old, and since young adults of the second generation were, in the main, the first to be released, the unnatural age distribution within these artificial communities became more and more disparate as time went by.

Life in these places was not generally brutal; there were no torture chambers, firing squads, or gas ovens waiting for the evacuated people. The American concentration camps should not be compared, in that sense, to Auschwitz or Vorkuta. They were, in fact, much more like a century-old American institution, the Indian reservation, than like the institutions that flourished in totalitarian Europe. They were, however, places of confinement ringed with barbed wire and armed sentries. Despite WRA propaganda about community control, there was an unbridgeable gap between the Caucasian custodians and their Oriental charges; even the mess halls were segregated by race. Although some of the staff, particularly those in the upper echelons of the WRA, disapproved of the racist policy that brought the camps into being, the majority of the camp personnel, recruited from the local labor force, shared the contempt of the general population for "Japs.". . .

Most of the existing literature about the camps stresses the cooperation and compliance of the inmates, thus perpetuating the basic line of both the WRA and the JACL. [Japanese American Citizens League]. Like most successful myths, this one contains elements of truth. There was little spectacular, violent resistance; no desperate attempts to escape; even sustained mass

From *Concentration Camps, North America: Japanese in the United States and Canada during World War II* by Roger Daniels (Robert E. Krieger Pub. Co., Inc., 1981), pp. 104–117 and 122–129. Reprinted by permission of the author.

civil disobedience rarely occurred. But from the very beginning of their confinement, the evacuated people were in conflict, both with their keepers and
with each other. These conflicts started even before the evacuation began,
grew in the Assembly Centers, and were intensified in the concentration
camps; their effects are still felt in the contemporary Japanese American
community as the questioning and often angry members of the third, or San-
sei, generation—many of whom began their lives behind barbed wire or in
exile—question the relative compliance of most of their parents a quarter
century ago.

Although resignation rather than resistance was the more common
response of the internees, resistance, both active and passive, did occur and
was more frequent and significant than is generally realized. . . . The most
effective early opposition to the JACL and its deliberate policy of collaboration came not from the older generation but from the Kibei, American-born
Japanese who had been sent back to Japan for education or employment.
The older Issei generation seemed to feel powerless: they were, after all,
enemy aliens, and treatment of them was generally in accord with the
Geneva Convention. The partly Americanized Kibei, who were, whatever
their loyalties, American citizens, led what might be called the "right-wing"
opposition among the evacuee population. Some of them, and many Issei as
well, were undoubtedly rooting for Imperial Japan. The bulk of the early
active conflict within the internee population was between the Nisei and the
Kibei, with the former blaming the latter for everything that went wrong. . . .

Sometimes these "Kibei" attacks received great support from the camp
populations; one of them led to the most serious outbreak of violence in the
entire evacuation, the Manzanar riot of December 6, 1942. The previous
evening Fred Tayama, a restaurant owner who had been a leading JACL
official, was attacked by an unknown group and beaten seriously enough to
require hospitalization. Although he could not positively identify his attack-
ers, the WRA authorities arrested several Kibei [whose] . . . arrest sparked a
mass demonstration led not by a Kibei but by Joe Kurihara, a Hawaiian
Nisei who was the most effective anti WRA-JACL agitator in the camp. A
veteran of the United States Army who had been wounded in World War I,
Kurihara was understandably embittered by his imprisonment. . . .

After some fruitless discussions with the Manzanar management, another
and more heated mass meeting was held about 6 P.M. . . . The WRA authorities . . . called in the military police, who pushed the crowd back from the
jail but failed to disperse it. The troops then tear-gassed the crowd of several
hundred, mostly teen-agers and young men, which scattered in great confusion, but re-formed later. At this juncture the troops, apparently without
orders, fired submachine guns, shotguns, and rifles into the unarmed crowd.
Two young men were killed and ten other evacuees were treated for gunshot
wounds, as was one soldier, apparently hit by a ricocheting army bullet. . . .
Sixteen malcontents were sent to isolation camps in Moab, Utah, and Leupp,

Arizona, and 65 of the most prominent JACL leaders were taken into protective custody at an abandoned Civilian Conservation Corps camp in the Mohave Desert. . . .

Four months later a trigger-happy military policeman at Topaz was responsible for another death. Camp regulations forbade any alien to approach an outer fence, and when an elderly and obviously harmless Issei man did so and allegedly failed to respond to a command of "Halt!" the sentry shot and killed him in broad daylight. A mass funeral was held and much indignation was expressed, but there was no significant prisoner violence at Topaz. At all the camps there were, at one time or another, protest demonstrations and "strikes" over this or that inequity, but other serious internal violence was avoided except for the crisis at Tule Lake in late 1943 and early 1944. . . .

These outbreaks of violence were obviously not characteristic of camp life, whose salient feature was probably boredom and mild discomfort. Normal family life was obviously impossible. . . . Not only semiprivate housing, but public feeding created problems for parents. . . . The children, particularly the teen-agers, had a degree of freedom within the confines of the camp far greater than they would have known on the outside. Among the parents, the authority of the father was greatly reduced; not only did he have less control over his children, but he also often lost his traditional role as provider. If he was an alien, his citizen children were in a superior legal position to him. If his wife worked, she brought in the same meager wage as he did. . . .

. . . [T]he camps . . . were not static places. . . . [E]ven as the evacuation and relocation began, two significant groups of Japanese Americans were allowed to leave reception centers and relocation camps: the college students who left permanently and the farm workers who left temporarily. On October 1, 1942, new WRA "leave clearance procedures" went into effect which eventually enabled many of the Nisei to reenter civilian life. . . . During 1943 some 17,000 evacuees were allowed to leave and reenter civilian life. The great majority of these were Nisei between 18 and 30. The increasing shortage of skilled and semiskilled civilian labor undoubtedly facilitated their absorption into the economy with, all things considered, a minimum of friction. Chicago, in particular, became the favorite city for relocatees, with many others being attracted to Denver and Salt Lake City. The WRA helped by setting up local resettlement committees of volunteers from civic and religious groups in the receiving communities which cooperated with field offices set up by the WRA. . . .

The decision to allow "leaves" still left the question of loyalty unsettled in the minds of many within the WRA, and, when it became known outside the centers that some "Japs" were being turned loose, all kinds of protests were made. . . .

In the meantime, the United States Army had decided that it needed Japanese American manpower. . . . [T]he Army had decided to recruit an all-

Nisei combat team of about 5000 men drawn from both the Hawaiian Islands and the Relocation Centers. Obviously, only "loyal" Japanese Americans would volunteer or be acceptable for such a unit, and the Army directed that the loyalty of the Nisei males of military age be determined by a questionnaire. . . .

The WRA quickly adapted the Army's proposal to its own purposes. Instead of administering the loyalty questionnaire to male Nisei over seventeen years of age, the agency decided to determine administratively the loyalty of all internees over seventeen, regardless of sex or nationality. National publicity was given to the decision. On January 28, 1943, War Secretary Stimson announced the decision to form an all-Nisei combat team. Three days later, President Roosevelt issued a public statement praising the decision. . . .

The resulting questionnaire was singularly inappropriate. First distributed on February 10, 1943, it was headed "Application for Leave Clearance." Many of the Issei, particularly the more elderly, had no desire to leave the camps, so the very title created confusion. The public announcement of the Japanese American combat team had already created all kinds of rumors in the camps, and, it must be remembered, the inmates had little reason to trust the United States government. But the most serious problems were created by questions 27 and 28 on the questionnaire, which had originally been intended for Nisei of military age.

> No. 27. Are you willing to serve in the armed forces of the United States on combat duty, wherever ordered?
>
> No. 28. Will you swear unqualified allegiance to the United States of America and faithfully defend the United States from any or all attack by foreign or domestic forces, and forswear any form of allegiance or obedience to the Japanese emperor, to any other foreign government, power or organization?

What aged Issei or women of any age were to make of question 27 is hard to say. But even worse was question 28. For the Issei, who were by law ineligible because of race to become United States citizens, it was asking them voluntarily to assume stateless status, and, in addition, a violation of the Geneva Convention governing the treatment of enemy aliens. Eventually, the question was rewritten for Issei to read:

> No. 28. Will you swear to abide by the laws of the United States and to take no action which would in any way interfere with the war effort of the United States?

This, of course, was a more proper question which many Issei were able to answer affirmatively, but great confusion had already been caused. For the Nisei, both questions created problems. Some contended that question 28 was a trap and that to forswear allegiance to Japan was to confess that such allegiance had once existed. Many answered question 27 conditionally, saying things like: "Yes, if my rights as citizen are restored," or "No, not unless the government recognizes my right to live anywhere in the United States." Some simply answered "No-No" out of understandable resentment over their treatment and others refused to fill out the forms at all. On the other hand, the JACLers viewed the questionnaire and the opportunity to volunteer as a way to redeem their questioned loyalty. As a former University of California student who volunteered wrote to Monroe Deutsch, it was "a hard decision. . . . I know that this will be the only way that my family can resettle in Berkeley without prejudice and persecution."

Out of the nearly 78,000 inmates who were eligible to register almost 75,000 eventually filled out the questionnaires. Approximately 6700 of the registrants answered "No" to question 28; nearly 2000 qualified their answers in one way or another, and thus were set down in the government's books as "disloyal"; and a few hundred simply left the question blank. The overwhelming majority—more than 65,000—answered "Yes" to question 28. More than 1200 Nisei volunteered for combat and about two-thirds of them were eventually accepted for military service. . . .

Although originally designed as a method of getting volunteers for an Army program, the loyalty questionnaires were eventually used by the WRA as a basis for separating the "loyal" from the "disloyal" and shipping the latter to Tule Lake, which became a segregation center for "disloyals," with "loyal" inmates shipped out to other camps and segregants moved in. Apart from the spurious nature of the loyalty determination, other factors entered into the decision of individuals to go to Tule Lake or remain there. Family loyalties, the desire to remain where they were, and often sheer resentment and disillusionment were as significant as "loyalty" or "disloyalty.". . . Eventually, more than 18,000 Japanese Americans were segregated at Tule Lake; almost a third of these were family members of segregants rather than segregants themselves. Another third were "Old Tuleans," many of whom just simply did not want to move. . . .

Predictably, Tule Lake became a trouble spot and was turned over to the Army for a time and placed under martial law. Even there some inmates were accused by others of being "*inu*," and several serious beatings and one murder occurred. During the period of Army control one evacuee was shot and killed by a sentry, who, although exonerated by both civilian and military courts, seems to have overreacted. Within Tule Lake, a strong minority movement for what was called "resegregation" grew up. Its proponents, strongly pro-Japanese and desirous of returning to Japan, objected to the presence of a majority, who, despite their presumably "disloyal" status, had no such orientation or desire. Eventually more than a third of those at Tule Lake formally applied for repatriation to Japan after the war; of the 7222 persons who did so, almost 65 percent were American-born. . . .

. . . [L]ike the "No" answer on question 28, statements made about repatriation and citizenship renunciation were motivated by many factors. Chief, of course, was the fact that the incarcerated people were subject to all kinds of pressures, real and imaginary. . . . [T]he fear of being thrust back, virtually penniless, into a hostile, wartime atmosphere was frightening. Many, as we have seen, went to or stayed at Tule Lake because it seemed to offer a kind of refuge in an otherwise stormy world. . . .

But trouble and reluctance to leave were not confined to Tule Lake. Protests and resistance to resettlement characterized the history of the other nine camps even after the "disloyals" had been segregated. Heart Mountain, Wyoming, often classified as a "happy camp," is a good case in point. From the very beginning there had been conflict and organized resistance there. In October and November 1942, protests and demonstrations occurred over the erection of the standard barbed wire fence surrounding the camp, which had not yet been erected when the evacuees began to arrive in August. The fence and other guard facilities were denounced in a petition signed by half the adults in the camp as "devoid of all humanitarian principles . . . an insult to any free human being." The fence, of course, stayed, but other, more pragmatic protests continued. . . . One of the major inarticulated premises behind the segregation of "disloyals" at Tule Lake, an assumption shared by WRA administrators and "loyal" JACLers alike, was that with "troublemakers" removed, the camps would become more placid and that resistance and protest would all but cease. At Heart Mountain such was not the case; there was more tangible protest, and protest of greater consequence, after segregation than before. As it turned out, almost all the key leaders . . . remained at Heart Mountain after segregation because they had either answered "Yes-Yes" to the crucial questions or had so qualified their answers that they were not "eligible" for segregation.

One such leader was Kiyoshi Okamoto. . . . In November 1943 he formed what he called a "Fair Play Committee of One" and began to agitate and speak to his fellow prisoners about doing something to clarify the legal status of the incarcerated Nisei. . . . Soon he was running "open forums" in the camp, and he attracted a number of followers who eventually formed what they called the Fair Play Committee. . . .

Although it had considerable support, the Fair Play Committee would not have had much impact had not the Army changed the rules again. On January 20, 1944, War Secretary Stimson announced that because of the fine record of Nisei volunteers normal selective service procedures would again be applied to Japanese Americans, both inside and outside the camps. (Actually, the fact that there were not enough volunteers from the camps was equally a factor.) The WRA and the JACL had long urged such a step, and of course it had been an issue raised during the loyalty-registration crisis. The *Sentinel* [a newspaper published by the Japanese American internees in the Heart Mountain Relocation Camp], now under the editorship of Haruo Omura but still following the JACL line, hailed Stimson's announcement as "the most significant development in returning Japanese Americans to full civic status," but it soon had to admit that "to say that the War Department's announcement . . . brought joy to the hearts of all draft-age men would be misleading and inaccurate." Nevertheless the *Sentinel* urged Heart Mountaineers to avoid another "senseless" round of "endless questions" and "picayune issues."

By mid-February the Fair Play Committee members had allies outside the camp: Samuel Menin, a Denver attorney, was advising them about their legal rights, and James Omura, who had been one of the few Japanese Americans to take an anti-JACL line at the Tolan Committee hearings before the evacuation and was now resettled in Denver, opened the columns of the Denver *Rocky Shimpo*, of which he was English language editor, to the Fair Play Committee. In addition, with funds raised from a $2 membership fee, the Committee purchased a mimeograph machine and began to distribute its own bulletin within Heart Mountain. The Committee members were warned both by camp authorities and local selective service officials against counseling draft resistance. The evacuee dissidents contended that they were merely advising Nisei to get a clarification of their rights, and an FBI investigation in February could find no indictable behavior. . . .

As a counterweight to the Fair Play Committee, the evacuee community council, perhaps at the instigation of the WRA circulated a petition to President Roosevelt accepting the draft but mildly protesting other aspects of government policy. Opposed by the Fair Play Committee, the petition was viewed as a test of strength. Only slightly over a third of the adult inmates signed, much to the disappointment of the Heart Mountain administration. Shortly after the test of strength, the first tangible results of the Fair Play Committee's agitation appeared: in the first weeks of March twelve Nisei refused to board the bus to take their selective service physicals, and an increasing number of potential draftees were promising to do likewise.

At this juncture the *Heart Mountain Sentinel* launched a full-scale attack on the Committee, and the *Rocky Shimpo* retaliated with a blast at the camp paper. . . . Naturally the question of loyalty came up. The *Sentinel* suggested that the leading spirits, at least, of the Fair Play Committee had answered questions 27 and 28 untruthfully, thus implying that they should be sent to Tule Lake, while the Committee leadership insisted that the real disloyalty to American democracy and its traditions was the "patriotism equals submission" formula of the *Sentinel* and the JACL.

The *Sentinel* couched some of its arguments in pragmatic terms insisting that "fighting against issues that are beyond our control . . . is a waste of time and space." The real fallacy of the resisters' case was, according to the *Sentinel*:

> The contention that a restriction of our rights means a loss of those rights. We don't lose any rights unless the constitution itself is changed. . . . If the Supreme Court rules evacuation was constitutional, then we will not have been deprived of any rights.

Whatever the merits of the debate, many Heart Mountain draft eligibles were won to the militants' position. By the end of March 1944, 54 of the 315 evacuees ordered to report for physicals had failed to do so. Late that month the Fair Play Committee, broadening its attack, began to agitate for a general strike at Heart Mountain. Predictably, the WRA reacted. The project director was informed from Washington that a reexamination of the papers of Fair Play Committee leader Kiyoshi Okamoto had discovered evidence of disloyalty; he was quickly taken into custody and shipped off to Tule Lake. Okamoto's "transfer" angered his fellow protestants; Isamu Horino, also a Fair Play Committee leader, in order to dramatize the lack of freedom, publicly announced his intention of leaving Heart Mountain and tried in broad daylight to walk out the main gate. Naturally, the military police stopped him, and, with this overt evidence of "disloyalty," the administration soon shipped him off to Tule Lake. . . .

On April 1, 1944, Project Director Robertson wrote to WRA Director Dillon Myer, arguing that Omura's editorials in the *Rocky Shimpo* bordered on "sedition" and asked for an investigation of the newspaper, whose assets were administered by the Alien Property Custodian, its original owners having been Issei and thus enemy aliens. The following week, in what can hardly have been a coincidence, the *Sentinel* attacked Omura as "the number one menace to the post-war assimilation of the Nisei," insisted that he was "responsible for wrecking the lives" of the draft evaders, and charged that he was "prostituting the privileges of freedom of the press to advocate an un-American stand." By the end of April federal officials had seized Omura's records and correspondence, and the Alien Property Custodian fired him and his staff. The Heart Mountain resistance was all but dead; only if its exponents could be vindicated in the courts would it stay alive.

Before his transfer to Tule Lake, Okamoto had written to the American Civil Liberties Union asking for help in testing the constitutionality of drafting citizens who were behind barbed wire. In mid-April, American Civil Liberties Union Director Roger Baldwin, in a public letter, disassociated himself and his organization from the Fair Play Committee fight. The dissidents had, Baldwin admitted, "a strong moral case," but, he insisted, "no legal case at all.". . .

On May 10, 1944, a federal grand jury in Cheyenne indicted the draft resisters, whose number had grown to 63. They were tried the next month in the largest mass trial for draft resistance in our history. The defense, by attorney Menin, argued that the defendants violated the draft orders only to clarify their ambiguous draft status and that no felonious intent was involved. The court was not impressed. Federal District Judge T. Blake Kennedy found all 63 guilty and sentenced them to three years' imprisonment and, in a memorandum, questioned their loyalty: "If they are truly loyal American citizens they should . . . embrace the opportunity to discharge the duties [of citizenship] by offering themselves in the cause of our National Defense."

An appeal filed by their attorney, which also argued that the defendants had been deprived of liberty without due process of law, was rejected in March 1945 by the Tenth Circuit Court of Appeals in Denver, and the Supreme Court refused *certiorari.*

In the meantime, however, other charges were brought against the Heart Mountain resisters and one of their allies. The same federal grand jury that had indicted the draft resisters had also brought in an indictment against seven members of the Fair Play Committee's executive council . . . and editor James Omura for unlawful conspiracy to counsel, aid, and abet violations of the draft. The indictments were kept secret by federal authorities until after the initial conviction of the draft violators themselves. A few days after the first convictions, the *Sentinel*, perhaps in on the secret, argued that those who encouraged the draft resisters not to report "deserve penitentiary sentences even more than those convicted. On July 21, 1944, the indictments were made public and the eight defendants arrested.

The seven evacuee defendants were represented by Abraham Lincoln Wirin, a Southern California ACLU [American Civil Liberties Union] attorney whose views about the evacuation and other matters were often more libertarian than those of the national body; Omura was represented by a Denver attorney, Sidney Jacobs. Jacobs unsuccessfully tried to get a separate trial for Omura on the grounds that he had never seen the other defendants (he had corresponded with some of them) before they appeared in court together. Wirin, using an argument that probably would have been successful two decades later, tried to get the case dismissed on the grounds that evacuees were systematically excluded from jury duty. The government contended that the Fair Play Committee was a conspiracy against the selective service system in particular and the war effort in general. Editor Omura was found innocent, but all seven of the evacuees were found guilty and sentenced to terms of four and two years' imprisonment.

After the verdict, Nisei war hero Ben Kuroki, who had been a government witness, told the press:

> These men are fascists in my estimation and no good to any country. They have torn down [what] all the rest of us have tried to do. I hope that these members of the Fair Play Committee won't form the opinion of America concerning all Japanese-Americans.

Attorney Wirin filed an appeal contending that there was insufficient evidence and that the judge's instructions to the jury were improper. More than a year later the Tenth Circuit Court of Appeals, in a 2–1 decision, upheld Wirin's second contention while rejecting the first, and the defendants were free. But even while this was going on, resistance to the draft was continuing at Heart Mountain, although on a reduced scale. Between the summer of 1944 and the closing of the camp in November 1945, 22 more men were indicted and convicted for draft resistance, bringing the total of such convictions at Heart Mountain to 85. To put draft resistance into numerical perspective, more than 700 Heart Mountain men did board the bus for their draft physicals, and 385 were inducted; of these 11 were killed and 52 wounded. Nor was the Heart Mountain case an isolated one; similar figures for both draft resistance and compliance can be tabulated for the other regular camps.

This account of the "loyal" Japanese American resistance—what I have called the "left opposition"—is highly significant. It calls into question the stereotype of the Japanese American victim of oppression during World War II who met his fate with stoic resignation and responded only with superpatriotism. This stereotype, like most, has some basis in reality. Many Japanese Americans, conforming to the JACL line, honestly felt that the only way they could ever win a place for themselves in America was by being better Americans than most. Whether or not this kind of passive submission is the proper way for free men to respond to injustice and racism, is, of course, a matter of opinion. But it is important to note that not all "loyal" Japanese Americans submitted; the resistance of the Heart Mountain Fair Play Committee and of other individuals and groups in the other camps, has been almost totally ignored and in some instances deliberately suppressed by chroniclers of the Japanese Americans. The JACL–WRA view has dominated the writing of the evacuation's postwar history, thereby nicely illustrating E. H. Carr's dictum that history is written by the winners. The authors of these works have in some cases been ignorant of the nature and scope of the "left opposition"; others, more knowledgeable, have either consciously underplayed it or suppressed it completely, hoping thereby, in their view at least, to manage and improve the image of an oppressed people. There are those, however, who will find more heroism in resistance than in patient resignation.

Navajo Code Talker, 1940s

COZY STANLEY BROWN

One of the puzzling anomalies of American Indian history is the extraordinary record of voluntary service among Native Americans in the U.S. military during wartime. During the first and second world wars, the Korean War, and the Vietnam War, Indians responded to the call to arms in proportionately vastly greater numbers than any other racial segment of the nation's population. Subject to the draft for the first time when World War II began, many Indians opted not to wait to be drafted and volunteered for duty. Before peace came in 1945, more than 25,000 Native Americans were in uniform, while another 40,000 had left their homes to work in war industries.

During and after the fighting, an explanation was advanced to account for the high rate of Indian volunteerism in defense of a nation that had conquered Native American homelands. Government spokesmen cited patriotism and a lingering "warrior tradition," and they later used Native Americans' fine war record to support the move toward a policy that would end the federal government's guardianship of Indians and their reservation homes. Navajo serviceman Cozy Stanley Brown in this reading suggests another motivation: "to protect my land and my people because the elderly people said that the earth was our mother."

Cozy Brown became a "code talker," one of a group of Navajos who significantly aided the U.S. war effort. Brown and his companions thwarted Japanese attempts to break the U.S. communications codes in the Pacific by using not only the Navajo language, but also the intricate Navajo cosmology, to communicate in code. Navajo spiritual beliefs include a number of creators, heroes, monsters, and tribe members that the code talkers used to refer to white military persons and operations. Even if the Japanese could have cracked the Navajo language, they lacked the cultural understanding to penetrate the religious symbolism and make sense of the translation. Brown's personal story, told in his own words and reflecting tribal rhythms, dramatically illustrates not only Indians' participation in World War II but also that conflict's enormous impact on Navajo life.

STUDY QUESTIONS

1. How did the U.S. entry into World War II affect the Navajos?

2. What were the most notable changes that Cozy Stanley Brown experienced after he left the reservation?

3. Do you think that the code talkers' success was due to cultural as well as linguistic aspects of tribal culture? Explain.

Jones Van Winkle: A man named Cozy S. Brown from Chinle, Arizona, will relate to you some of his story about the war he went through. He was one of the Code Talkers in the Second World War. He will talk mainly about his life history. . . .

Cozy Stanley Brown: Thanks for giving me the time to relate my story. My name is Cozy S. Brown, 50 years of age. I was born on December 5, at

Excerpted from Broderick H. Johnson, ed., *Navajo and World War II*. Navajo Community College Press, 1977, pp. 52–61. Reprinted by permission.

dawn, in about 1925 or 1926. It was where Del Muerto Canyon and Canyon de Chelly connect. That was what I was told. My mother is Mary Steward Brown. My father was Jack Brown, who died four years ago. His Navajo name was Tall Boss (Naat'áanii Nééz), and he was a well known medicine man. . . .

My clan is the Deer Spring (Biih bitoodnii) which is the same as the Bitter Water clan (Tódích'íí'nii). I was born for the Red Running Into Water People (Táchíí'nii), which is the same as the Tobacco People (Nát'oh dine'é). I was raised with sheep and goats, and I grew up with my late grandmother's assistance. As soon as I was old enough to realize what was happening, I began to herd sheep and goats. . . .

My grandmother was born at Fort Sumner (Hwééldi or Bosque Redondo) over at the eastern edge of New Mexico. She was four years old when the Navajos were allowed to walk back to the Navajo Reservation. . . . After I got bigger I noticed my father was working at the trading post called Upper House of Thunderbird Trading Post, which is now Thunderbird Lodge. I grew up near that trading post. . . . In the fall, when school was about to begin, I cried because I wanted to go to school with my sisters and brothers. I told my parents that I would like to go, but they kept telling me that I was too young. Later, my parents got together and discussed it and agreed to let me enroll.

Jones: How old were you then?

Cozy: I was six years old. One afternoon, a saddled horse was brought in front of our hogan. They told me to wash up and get ready to go some place. I ate my lunch and I was forced to go right away. So we started to travel on horseback. At that time there weren't many vehicles.

Jones: What year was that?

Cozy: I think it was around 1931 or 1932. My father and I rode double on the horse. Before we left, the trader, who was my father's employer, came out of the post and asked us where we were going. My father replied, "We are going to school." Then the trader said, "What will you name him?" At that time Navajo children had no English names. My father looked at the trader and said, "His name will be Cozy." That was how I got my English name. My father registered me with that name at the school.

Jones: The trader had that name, too?

Cozy: Yes, the trader's name was Cozy. His last name was McSparron. That was how I got my name.

I was taken to Chinle Boarding School, where I attended for six years. I liked school, and they took good care of me. It was like a military setup. They used to be wakened early in the mornings, and we ran long distances very early.

We used to form a single line and do calisthenics. . . . I attended and did very well for six years at the Chinle school. I was involved in all of the activities. . . . The way I thought about it was that the Anglos and various other

Indian tribes helped me in those activities and in many other teachings. They helped me learn many things and I forced myself to get the best out of whatever classes they offered me. It didn't take me too long to learn the white man's language.

I was one of the boy scouts and dorm leaders. They told us to work for our own clothes at school; so I worked for those clothes. I did all of those things until I finished the 6th grade.

Then they told me to choose what high school I would like to go to—Fort Wingate or Shiprock, but I already had chosen to attend Shiprock. I guess some of my teachers from Chinle had been transferred to that high school, and they wanted me to attend it. Four of us were chosen to go to that school. . . .

I came home when school was out and spent my summer vacation there. When school started again in the fall, I returned. I attended until it was time for school to be out. Then they asked me if I wanted to stay that summer and work in the fields. That was fine with me; so I spent the summer planting and working crops. I did that for four summers. In early fall, when school was about to begin again, I went home for only three weeks or so before going back to school.

When I reached the 12th grade and it was close to my graduation, I heard that the Japanese and the United States had gotten into war. It was December 7, 1941. At that time I was old enough to qualify for the military service; so I thought about it. As our parents used to say, "You have to think about things before you get into them."

Later, it was announced that some Navajos would be needed to go into training. They told us we would learn some things pertaining to the war. They gave us two weeks to think about it. I did my own thinking, and I didn't inquire of my parents; and I decided to go ahead and enter the Service.

Six of us signed up for the training. . . . They told us to go home for a week which we did; and we were told to return to Window Rock, Arizona, for a physical examination. Navy doctors examined us, and we were physically all right. . . . We left there for Fort Wingate, New Mexico, where we met many others. There we took the oath that marked us as American soldiers. Then we took the Greyhound bus to San Diego. The next morning military clothing was issued to us.

Jones: What year was that?

Cozy: It was May 4, 1942. That was when we took our oath. We had eight weeks training at the Marine Corps Boot Training Camp. We were trained for only eight weeks because the war was going on and they were lacking soldiers. That was why we were forced to get the training quickly. There were 20 of us who completed the eight weeks of training and were highly honored. . . . Twenty-eight of us left the training camp, and one guy named Mr. Johnson was already at the camp we were headed for. So with him, it made 29 of us. There we learned infantry tactics.

Jones: What was the name of that place?

Cozy: That was in Camp Elliott, close to San Diego, California. Afterward, it was the Navy Training Center. . . . We were at that camp to learn basic things. The main reason for us Navajos was our language. They liked to use our language in war to carry messages. So we were taught how to use the radio. We had to do that in a hurry at that time. . . . Then, we got together and discussed how we would do it. We decided to change the name of the airplanes, ships and the English ABC's into the Navajo language. We did the changing. For instance, we named the airplanes "dive bombers" for ginitsoh (sparrow hawk), because the sparrow hawk is like an airplane—it charges downward at a very fast pace. We called the enemy ana'i, just like the old saying of the Navajos. The name ana'i also is used in the Navajo Enemy Way ceremony. We changed the English alphabet to the Navajo language, like for the letter T we used tashii (turkey), tsin (stick), and tliish (snake) in Navajo. We usually used the harmful animals' names that were living in our country for the alphabet. . . .

Navajo code talkers during World War II

. . . We did that for eight weeks, when eight men were selected. I was one of them. They told us to get ready, but we had no idea where we were going, because they were not allowed to tell us. . . .

Jones: Were the eight men Navajos?

Cozy: Yes, they were Navajos. . . .

Jones: What was the name of the place?

Cozy: New Caledonia. The eight of us got off at that island and spent the night there. The next morning we were divided and assigned to different ships. Three of us were assigned to one ship and the other code talkers were divided among the other ships. . . . The men were divided into groups, and placed in different areas in the jungle. We had discussed again how we would use the Navajo language, and we informed the officers. . . .

Long ago our elderly people had many bad hardships. Accordingly, I guess we decided to go to war and protect our people from having other hardships. . . .

We were code Talkers for four months at Guadalcanal. That was the time we took advantage of our enemy. It was like the old saying of our elderly Navajo people, "Only the Navajos had the whole world in their hands," or "the Navajos created the earth." According to that, the Navajo people helped the American soldiers, and the enemy never did overcome them. That was why I had faith and believed what our elderly people said. . . .

We left Guadalcanal . . . for a place named Melvin in Australia. It was located in the south part of the country. The place was similar to our Reservation. The Anglos were also similar to the white men on our Reservation, because they had come from the same countries—like England. . . . They treated us like their own relatives, and they chose each of us to be with one family. . . .

When we were still in Melvin, a group of American Navajo soldiers arrived there. There were 29 of us that first went into war. We were divided among the 2nd, 3rd, 4th, 5th and 6th Marine Divisions. I guess they had noticed that Code Talkers were important and very helpful in the war; so they sent us more Navajo soldiers to learn. . . . We taught them the skills we had learned in our training as Code Talkers. . . . After we had completed [training] we moved to a place called New Guinea. . . . The main place for us was called the Aru Islands. We helped the Army fight the enemies there. . . . Afterward, the war cooled down in New Guinea; so we moved from that place on Christmas Eve to the New Britain Islands. We arrived on December 25. There were Japanese soldiers on that island. . . . We spent three or four months there.

. . . Then we moved to another place from there, but it was still among the Russell Islands (Solomon Islands). The Army raided the enemies in Bougainville the same time we did. They won the island from the enemy that day. Then we moved to another place in the Solomons. . . . At that time I had spent a year and 10 months overseas.

Jones: What year was that?

Cozy: It was in 1944. We moved to a place called Palau Island. The Island was long in length and narrow in width. When we got there we started combat with the air enemy. There was an airport and a high mountain peak. There were holes in the mountain where many enemies were hidden, and they used them for protection. That was where we had bad hardships, but we killed all of the enemies that were near the beach, also those in other areas besides the mountain peak. We had a hard time exploding the mountain because it was made of quartz rock. We tried to kill the enemies that were on the mountain. We would kill two or three at a time during the night when we snuck up on them.

Jones: What did you use to kill them?

Cozy: We used guns. . . . Flamethrowers and napalm bombs helped a lot, though. . . .

We spent two months there. One day when I was operating the radio, a call came in from the Hawaiian Islands. At that time we called the Hawaiian Islands "Abalone Shell Water" in Navajo—like the abalone shell water they use in the Squaw Dance ceremony today. The call was for Major General Vandegrift at the 7th Regiment's Division headquarters. I wrote down the codes in Navajo. After the call, I gave my notes to one of the Anglos who was a de-coder. He changed the codes into English. Our names appeared, and we were ordered to return home because we had completed our war duty in action.

Jones: What year was that?

Cozy: It still was in 1944, during the fall season. . . .

Jones: While you were over there, did you kill any enemies?

Cozy: Yes, I killed some enemies.

Jones: How close did you kill one?

Cozy: I was holding one enemy in my hands when I killed him.

Jones: You were holding him with your hands?

Cozy: Yes, I held him with my hands. That was when I brought back the scalp of an enemy.

Jones: While you held him, what weapon did you use to kill him?

Cozy: I used a knife to cut his head off and I pulled out a bunch of sideburns, which I was taught to do by a medicine man called Stewart Greyeyes. He is still living today. He also performed the ceremony on me before I left for war. I brought one of the enemy's scalps home. The Squaw Dance was performed on me for the enemy scalp that I brought home with me.

Jones: A Squaw Dance was performed for you?

Cozy: Yes, I took a furlough for 35 days to have a Squaw Dance for me. After my leave was over, I went back to the east coast and from there they transferred me to the west to a place called Quantico. I took high speed radio training there. Then I returned to San Diego. I was told to instruct the new American soldiers that had just arrived for training. I worked as an instructor for almost a year. . . .

Jones: Before you left for overseas, did they perform a Blessing Way chant on you, or the Enemy Way chant?

Cozy: My uncle, Stewart Greyeyes, performed a Blessing Way and an Enemy Way chant on me. . . .

Jones: When you returned did they perform a Squaw Dance on you?

Cozy: When I returned, they again performed an all-night vigil of the Blessing Way chant. When I got home things were all ready for a Squaw Dance. So, that evening, plans were made for me to have the ceremony performed. We took the Squaw Dance prayer stick to Chinle Valley, to a man named Mr. Red Canyon. The dance was performed very well for me. From there, my mind began to function well again.

Jones: You really believe in Navajo ceremonies?

Cozy: Yes, because I was mainly raised with them. I guess my grandfathers, grandmothers, my father and mother used the Navajo ceremonies. I also believe in Anglo religion, like the Catholic religion. The prayers and the stories are similar to Navajo legends and prayers. That is how I think about the two religions. Some parts of the legends are slightly different. . . .

Jones: After going through the Military Service overseas what was your main reason for coming back to live on the Reservation?

Cozy: My main reason for going to war was to protect my land and my people because the elderly people said that the earth was our mother. That was why our elderly Navajos blessed the earth with corn pollen. There are Anglos and different Indian tribes living on the earth who have pride in it. That was my main reason for fighting in the war; also, I wanted to live on the earth in the future. Some of our men are in the Military Services today for the same reasons. One of my nephews is in the Marine Corps today. He probably thinks the same way I thought when I was in the Service. The Anglos say "Democracy," which means they have pride in the American flag. We Navajos respect things the same way they do.

Jones: So the main things you went into war for were the land, its people, the living things and things that are sacred. Also, the water and the sacred mountains which surround our Reservation.

Cozy: Yes, that was the way it was. Like the Navajo people get their blessings from the four sacred mountains, our mother the earth, father the sun and the air we breathe.

That idea was told to me by my late father. Our grandchildren and our young relatives will carry on those beliefs in the future, if we tell them and if they have knowledge of sacred things. Those are some of the reasons I went to war—and because I had pride in all of those things.

The younger generations need to know the stories and lives of the older people and of the past. I hope that what I have said will be useful in telling the important things done by the Navajos in the Second World War.

Civil-Rights Leaders in San Francisco, 1940s

ALBERT S. BROUSSARD

Albert Broussard's essay focuses on disagreements among historians concerning World War II's effects on African-American leaders and their tradition of activism. Ironically, while the booming shipbuilding industries on the West Coast sparked a mass black migration to the region from the South, segregated unions, as well as competition for jobs and for housing, limited opportunities for African Americans and intensified racism in the American West during the war. San Francisco attracted the largest number of westward-bound migrants, its black population swelling 600 percent during the war, providing new leaders and new followers for civil-rights struggles and protests.

Broussard also discusses continuities in the black activist tradition in San Francisco. Significantly, while newcomers provided important leadership for civil-rights efforts, interracial alliances presented a new dimension for race relations in the San Francisco Bay Area. Local chapters of the National Urban League and the National Council for Negro Women were organized, and integrated alliances, among them the Bay Area Council against Discrimination and the Council for Civic Unity, opened a new chapter in race relations in the mid-twentieth century. Their activities spread to the East Bay communities of Richmond, Berkeley, and Oakland. Broussard encourages more in-depth studies of the war's effects on western black communities and their traditions of social activism.

STUDY QUESTIONS

1. What social factors impeded the growth of the black community in San Francisco before World War II?

2. Which industries drew blacks to the West Coast during World War II?

3. How did race relations in the San Francisco Bay area change during World War II?

The Second World War brought significant social, political, economic and demographic changes to black communities throughout the nation. The West was no exception. Blacks migrated to western cities in unprecedented numbers to work in the wartime defense industries, and West Coast cities like San Francisco, Oakland, Portland, and Seattle attempted to integrate thousands of black migrants into their communities between 1941 and 1945. The war also brought changes in race relations in western cities as blacks challenged longstanding racial barriers and pushed for full equality. Black activism in Western cities, however, predate the Second World War, and the struggle against the increased discrimination that accompanied wartime opportunities was led by men and women already experienced in protest. Historians examining this period have described it as a critical turning point with little acknowledgment of either important continuities with the past or the ambiguities of wartime progress. Richard M. Dalfiume, for example, has asserted that "anyone studying American race relations from the years 1939–1945 will find it difficult not to conclude that this period marks a watershed in recent Negro history." Dalfiume believed that these years were critical in the development of black militancy and assertiveness throughout the nation and he called the World War II era "the forgotten years of the Negro Revolution."

However, few studies have explored the impact of World War II on blacks in the West, and the Dalfiume thesis remains substantially untested. Gerald D. Nash, in a recent study on the impact of World War II on the West wrote: "Wartime mobilization brought rapid changes in the relations between minorities and their fellow citizens in the West." On the eve of war, Nash continued, black westerners were "passive and subdued, excluded from many spheres of the region's activities." He concluded that World War II had a "crucial impact" in the West in "stimulating the movement for equal rights." This essay will evaluate the impact of World War II on San Francisco's black community, and illustrate the continuity of prewar ideology and programs with the transition in black leadership that occurred during the Second World War era.

More than one million blacks left the South during the war; most of them migrated to northern and western cities in search of better paying jobs. California, in particular, was a focal point for western black migrants. The statewide increase of 258,900 in black population between 1940 and 1950 was greater than the volume of black migration to any other state. Eighty-five percent of all western migrants came to California, and most crowded into large urban centers like San Francisco, Oakland, Los Angeles, and San Diego, San Francisco's black population increased by more than six hundred

From "Strange Territory, Familiar Leadership: The Impact of World War II on San Francisco's Black Community" by Albert S. Broussard, *California History* 65:1 (1986), pp. 18–25. Reprinted by permission of the California Historical Society.

percent between 1940 and 1945. By 1950, 43,460 blacks resided in a city that had contained fewer than 5,000 Afro-Americans a decade earlier. More blacks migrated to San Francisco between 1940 and 1950 than the combined totals of every decennial census of San Francisco's black population in the previous nine decades.

Many factors had curtailed the growth of San Francisco's black community prior to 1941. Blacks found it extremely difficult to advance in other than unskilled, menial jobs. Most labor unions also excluded blacks or segregated them into "Jim Crow" auxiliaries, making it difficult for blacks to advance in the skilled and semiskilled sectors. The Great Depression also curbed black migration into San Francisco, as the menial jobs that blacks occupied were the first to be eliminated in periods of economic distress. By 1940, more than fifteen percent of black San Franciscans were unemployed, and the black press did not encourage Afro-Americans to migrate to San Francisco to better their economic prospects.

World War II, however, transformed the nation's economy, and the San Francisco Bay Area suddenly became a haven for black migrants. The immediate availability of jobs in defense industries provided the major impetus for the large black in-migration into the Bay Area. By 1943, according to the local Chamber of Commerce, the Bay Area was the "largest shipbuilding center in the world." Blacks migrated to San Francisco by the thousands each month between 1941 and 1945, crowding into established black settlements, such as the Fillmore District in the Western Addition, and creating new ones, such as Hunter's Point. Sue Bailey Thurman recalled that blacks were "scattered all over the city in 1942," when she first arrived. By 1944, when she returned to San Francisco, there were almost "40,000 blacks living in the city," she estimated. "It had changed in just that time." Similarly, the local Urban League's executive director, Seaton W. Manning, wrote that the "migration of Negroes into San Francisco and the Bay Area is still continuing and I find it hard to believe that there are any Negroes left in Texas and Louisiana.

This dramatic increase in population had several significant consequences. By 1945, blacks became a majority of the city's non-white population, forging ahead of both the Chinese and the Japanese. Between 1940 and 1945, their proportion of the non-white population increased from fifteen percent to fifty-eight percent. The large number of black migrants from southern states such as Louisiana, Texas, and Oklahoma also gave the city's black community a decidedly southern flavor, much to the dismay of many long-time black San Franciscans. During the post-war era, blacks would celebrate "Juneteenth," the day that Texas slaves learned of their emancipation. This day had little meaning to black San Franciscans before the war. Finally, white San Franciscans were much more likely to have contact with blacks than ever before in jobs, schools, and public accommodations. Prior to 1940, according to Charles S. Johnson, who conducted an extensive study of black war workers in San Francisco, "the small number of Negro inhabitants were to some degree lost in the city's population complex." By 1945, however, blacks were the most visible non-white group in San Francisco and, for the first time, competing with whites for housing, employment, and public facilities.

The large black migration prompted particularly intense competition for housing. Although San Francisco's wartime housing was in short supply, the city avoided the chaos and violence of a northern city like Chicago, where three-fourths of the racial incidents reported by the Chicago Commission on Human Relations involved housing. Nonetheless, the competition for housing heightened racial tensions and prompted a more rigid pattern of residential segregation than was evident before the war. "[Housing] segregation is practiced almost rigidly with the use [of] occupancy clauses in deed and leases restricting colored races to certain well defined areas of the city," reported the *Christian Science Monitor*. Housing discrimination was so widespread in San Francisco that Davis McEntire, professor of Social Welfare at the University of California, estimated that "not less than eighty to ninety percent of the residence areas in the San Francisco Bay Area communities are closed to non-Caucasian entry." Charles S. Johnson noted that "underlying the entire question of Negro housing in San Francisco—both public and private—is the issue of residential segregation." Similarly, Seaton W. Manning wrote that "it is not necessarily by choice that Negro families live in the Western Addition." By 1960, Tarea Hall Pittman, acting director of the NAACP's West Coast Regional Office, testified before the United States Commission on Civil Rights that "residential segregation based on race is the general rule in the towns and cities in the West." Thus, rather than serving as a catalyst to gain improved housing opportunities, World War II stimulated increased white hostility to black residential integration in San Francisco and intensified residential concentration in the black community.

Black San Franciscans made their greatest gains in the employment sector. By 1943, black workers comprised almost thirteen percent of the labor force in the Bay Area's four leading shipbuilding companies. In other areas, racial barriers toppled at a much slower pace, although blacks gained positions in jobs from which they had heretofore been excluded. In 1942 after a bitter struggle, the San Francisco Municipal Railway System hired Audley Cole, its first black conductor. By 1944, Harry Kingman, the Fair Employment Practices Committee's West Coast regional director, reported that "700 Negro platform operators" were employed. The San Francisco Unified School District also broke the color barrier in 1944 when it hired Josephine Cole, the city's first black teacher. . . . While black workers continued to lag behind white workers, they were also aware that San Francisco's labor force had fewer racial barriers than before the war and that limited mobility was possible.

World War II also raised the expectations of black San Franciscans that full equality might be achievable. Robert Flippin, a prominent black leader and social worker, believed that San Francisco was "in the embryonic stage of developing a truly democratic[,] mutually agreeable and successful pattern of biracial living." Thus, a recent black migrant, such as Joseph James, used this occasion to challenge successfully the system of segregated auxiliary unions through the courts. Several blacks wrote Franklin D. Roosevelt to protest racial discrimination in the workplace. . . . These letters revealed that some black workers believed that they possessed an ally in the White House, but they also illustrated a sense of urgency among black San Franciscans to eliminate the remaining vestiges of racial discrimination.

Despite their small numbers, black San Franciscans had not been "passive and subdued" before World War II—as Gerald D. Nash concluded about black westerners in general. Quite the contrary, they had fought racial discrimination wherever it reared its head from the turn of the twentieth century. The San Francisco branch of the NAACP [National Association for the Advancement of Colored People], organized in 1915, had challenged the showing of the movie, "The Birth of A Nation," protested discrimination in Civil Service employment, New Deal Programs, and public accommodations. The branch also supported the NAACP's national anti-lynching campaign and its efforts to free the Scottsboro boys and sent contributions to assist blacks after the 1917 race riot in East St. Louis.

Given the activism of San Francisco's black community prior to the war, it would be inaccurate to conclude that World War II produced a "watershed" in black consciousness. Nor did the war radically change the programs, ideologies, or strategies of San Francisco's black leadership, in spite of a significant in-migration of educated and professional blacks. The wartime black leadership, much of it composed of new personnel, differed not in the nature of their demands for racial equality, but rather, in the urgency of their message. These men and women played an active role in the Bay Area civil rights struggle during the 1940s and the 1950s, and they were prominent figures in organizing local chapters of the National Urban League and the National Council for Negro Women.

One of the most significant changes in black leadership during the wartime era was the willingness to form interracial alliances to fight for racial progress. The NAACP had been the only effective interracial organization in San Francisco prior to 1940, and whites had never played a major role in the local branch's affairs. After 1940, however, blacks and whites were almost zealous in courting one another, and whites played a much greater role in several local civil rights organizations, including the Bay Area Council Against Discrimination and the Council for Civic Unity. No longer were whites merely token executive board members and welcomed into these organizations principally for their status in the community and their financial contributions. By the end of the war, whites were as likely as blacks to be heading a Bay Area civil rights organization. Of the seven leading civil rights organizations in San Francisco between 1940 and 1946, only the local chapters of the NAACP, National Urban League, and National Council of Negro Women retained consistent policies of electing black chief executives. The Bay Area Council Against Discrimination, Council for Civic Unity, American Council on Race Relations, and California Federation for Civic Unity, though interracial, were dominated by white officers and board members. Blacks did not protest the presence of whites as presidents and executive directors of civil rights organizations as they would during the 1960s. Instead, San Francisco's interracial leadership appeared to reach a consensus that achieving racial equality required a joint effort.

Howard Thurman and Seaton Manning epitomized the new black leader who operated with a broad interracial constituency. By the outbreak of World War II, Howard Thurman was among the most respected black theologians in the nation. A prolific scholar, Thurman wrote almost two dozen books during his lifetime. He also occupied academic posts at Morehouse College, Howard University, and Boston University. The editors of *Life Magazine* felt that Thurman demonstrated such promise that they named him one of the ten most influential ministers in America.

Thurman resigned from his comfortable position . . . at Howard University because he welcomed the challenge of establishing an interracial alliance between black and white San Franciscans. In 1943, Thurman was invited to pastor an interracial church in the city's black community. Alfred G. Fisk, a Presbyterian clergyman and professor of philosophy at San Francisco State College, would ultimately take to hyperbole in his effort to sway Thurman to move to the West Coast. "San Francisco, so it seems to me now, is doomed if you do not come. There is no one in the nation who could do what you could do here," Fisk unabashedly exclaimed. Indeed, racial tensions had magnified as a result of the large scale black influx within a relatively few years. But there was no indication that quick tempers produced Fisk's dismal portrayal of "tensions rising to the breaking point, the outbreak of violence and more general rioting only averted by a hair's breadth." San Franciscans had not gone that far.

Howard Thurman was deeply moved by the challenge that this opportunity provided and began making preparations almost immediately to relocate to San Francisco. However, Thurman's open pronouncements that God and destiny were both playing some part in his decision, did not prevent him from encouraging his contacts to use their influence to support this endeavor. He assured Fisk that Channing Tobias and Mary McLeod Bethune "have offered to write their friends around the Bay urging them to give every encouragement by attendance and in other ways to the project."

Within six months, the experiment was officially launched. The church, officially named the Church for the Fellowship of All Peoples, was the first "fully integrated" church in America, according to Thurman. Fellowship

Church catered primarily to the city's black elite and white liberals. Within a decade after its organization, Thurman moved the church out of the black community altogether, fearing that it would become a predominantly black church and lose its original purpose. Nonetheless, Howard Thurman illustrated the type of new black leader who served San Francisco's multiracial communities, rather than the black community exclusively. . . .

. . . Blacks throughout the entire Bay Area suffered a disproportionally high unemployment rate relative to white workers between 1945 and 1950. In 1946, non-whites, primarily blacks, comprised twenty percent of all persons receiving unemployment insurance, though they accounted for only five percent of the Bay Area's population. A year later, the California State Employment Services reported that the black unemployment rate was thirty percent, and that unemployment among Bay Area black women was six times as high as the statewide rate. The sociologist Wilson Record noted disparagingly by the end of the decade: "Conservative estimates indicate that at least one-third of all Negroes in the Bay Area labor force are unable to find jobs."

Black woman workers in one of the shipyards in the San Francisco Bay Area

The World War II black migration also brought a greater number of professional black women into the Bay Area than ever before. Some of these females vied for leadership positions within black organizations. Others, worked in interracial societies, churches, community centers, and women's clubs. Sue Bailey Thurman and Frances Glover were typical of this emerging group of black professional women.

Sue Bailey Thurman had never allowed being a woman or her marriage to the renowned black minister, Howard Thurman, to compromise her potential. After receiving undergraduate degrees from both Spelman and Oberlin colleges, Thurman taught briefly at Hampton Institute before joining the national staff of the YWCA to work with southern and eastern colleges. She also found time while raising a family to chair the archival and museum departments of the National Council of Negro Women. Additionally, Thurman founded and edited the *Aframerican Woman's Journal*, the official publication of the National Council of Negro Women. . . . [A]t the urging of Mary McLeod Bethune she organized a local chapter of the National Council of Negro Women in 1945. Supporting her husband in the day-to-day affairs of the Fellowship Church, Thurman directed the church's Intercultural Workshop and traveled extensively. Her travels included serving as a delegate to the first Inter-American Congress of Women in Guatemala in 1947, and visits to India, Burma, Ceylon, and Cuba. In 1949, she led a delegation to the UNESCO conference in Paris. In 1948, Sue Bailey Thurman received recognition in a nationwide poll as an "outstanding woman of the year."

Frances B. Glover's life paralleled Sue Bailey Thurman's in several respects, although the two women followed different career paths. Like Thurman, Glover also followed her husband to San Francisco when he was selected as the San Francisco Urban League's Industrial Secretary. Glover had also worked with Mary McLeod Bethune as an assistant in the National Youth Administration's Division of Negro Affairs in northern Ohio. . . . Glover served as managing editor of the San Francisco *Sun-Reporter,* the city's largest black newspaper. She also served as secretary to the board of directors at the Central YWCA and a member of the Board of Trustees of Fellowship Church. The achievements of both women illustrated that opportunities were beginning to open for black women both during and after the Second World War.

Indeed, World War II had a profound effect upon San Francisco's black community. The war triggered a black demographic revolution between 1940 and 1950, it stimulated an upsurge in multiracial activism and black protest, and it opened many new opportunities for black workers. The large black influx also broadened the black leadership class, as a sizable number of black professionals migrated to San Francisco for the first time. Gerald D. Nash argues correctly that, "Wartime mobilization brought rapid changes in the relations between minorities and their fellow citizens in the West." Nash, however, overestimates the extent of change.

Although significant, these changes were not so far-reaching that they marked a "watershed" in San Francisco's race relations. Black San Franciscans had been protesting injustices for decades before the war, albeit with mixed success. The new racial climate during the war was more favorable for the implementation of their demands for equal opportunity. Instead of conceptualizing this era as a "watershed," William H. Chafe's analysis of the Second World War is more accurate for San Francisco. "The war itself proved more decisive to the longterm history of change in race relations," wrote Chafe. "Although little was accomplished in the way of permanent progress toward equality, the changes which did occur laid the foundations for the development of mass protest activity in subsequent years."

Braceros in the Pacific Northwest, 1942–1947

Erasmo Gamboa

During World War II, thousands of young Mexican Americans volunteered for military service. They fought with great valor in both the European and Pacific theaters of war and were one of the most highly decorated ethnic groups in the war effort. Mexican-American women served too, joining the armed forces as WACS and WAVES.

Mexican-American wartime contributions extended to the home front. As before, Mexican Americans performed much of the needed labor in western agriculture, mining, smelting, manufacturing, and various services. Their efforts were complemented by the importation of tens of thousands of Mexican nationals, brought to the United States to work under the bracero program. (The word *bracero* comes from the Spanish *brazos*—"arms.") The program resulted from an agreement between the U.S. and Mexican governments. As its name indicates, the imported workers were valued for their arms—arms that would pick and pack crops all over the West.

For farm operators and shippers, the program represented a huge subsidy from the federal government that guaranteed a cheap and organized labor supply during wartime. The program was so valued by farm operators that it was continued until 1964, long after the war ended.

From the perspective of the braceros, the program provided jobs. But as Erasmo Gamboa documents, the workers experienced much misery and discrimination wherever they worked. Despite their migratory existence, braceros built a strong sense of community in the labor camps and organized work stoppages and strikes to defend themselves against exploitation.

Although little celebrated, the Mexican braceros made a significant contribution to the Allied victory against fascism during World War II.

STUDY QUESTIONS

1. Why was the bracero program established?

2. Why did Mexicans participate in this program?

3. What were the most important factors that shaped the bracero experience in the Pacific Northwest?

Between 1943 and 1947, the United States government contracted with approximately 47,000 bracero agricultural laborers in Mexico to work in the northwestern states of Idaho, Oregon, and Washington. Despite the large number, little is known about the experiences of these men. In contrast, the history and administrative details of the agricultural bracero program in California and other southwestern states have been well documented. . . .

During the Second World War, the U.S. War Manpower Commission's call for record-shattering farm production exerted tremendous pressure on an already labor-starved western agricultural economy. One result was a demand for Mexican workers to which Congress responded in August 1942 with Public Law-45 (PL-45), a binational agreement authorizing the importation of agricultural workers from Mexico. . . . Within a year, Mexican nationals had become a vital mainstay in northwestern farm production; only California recruited more workers. Of the 220,640 laborers who entered the country under PL-45, approximately twenty-one percent were contracted by northwestern farmers.

The braceros' experiences in the Pacific Northwest were shaped by their background, the attitude of growers and northwestern communities, and the federal bureaucracy. Government officials expected the workers to live in tent camps under spartan conditions with few organized social activities. Overall, the men endured much racial discrimination from employers and local communities alike. On the job, they suffered many accidents not only because of their unfamiliarity with farm machinery, but also because farmers had little regard for their safety. As a rule, braceros received low wages, and when they organized strikes to win increases, they encountered quick and sometimes violent resistance from growers and local officials. Although these experiences differ little from those of braceros in the Southwest, the record of the workers in the two regions significantly diverged.

"Braceros in the Pacific Northwest: Laborers on the Domestic Front, 1942–1947" by Erasmo Gamboa, from *Pacific Historical Review* 56 (1987), pp. 378–398. Reprinted by permission of University of California Press.

Life was difficult for the braceros because they were young and came from rural areas steeped in traditional Mexican culture. . . . [T]he greater number were between twenty and thirty years of age. . . . For most, their sojourn to the United States would be the first separation from their immediate and extended families which were (and are) so important in Mexican culture. Thus they arrived ill-prepared to cope with the strain of hostile and unfamiliar circumstances and the tensions and emotion surrounding the war effort. Not surprisingly, many men became distraught and feigned illness or wrote to their families asking to be recalled for reasons of supposed sickness or death before the end of their seasonal contracts. . . .

Poor living conditions also heightened the desire of many workers to return to Mexico. In the Northwest, the braceros generally lived in mobile tent camps designed to go where needed among the widely dispersed agricultural areas. As a rule, six workers lived together in a 16′ by 16′ tent furnished with folding cots, one blanket per person, and stove heaters when available. Although each individual was entitled to bring seventy-seven pounds of personal effects from Mexico, in reality most arrived with little more than a change of clothes. Within time, the workers scavenged for discarded crates or boxes and placed them inside the tents for storage and seating. These makeshift creations, along with personal pictures of loved ones, tokens of remembrance, or knickknacks purchased locally, completed the interior.

During the summer, the men were often driven from the tents by 100 degree temperatures, and in fall and winter, the fabric structures offered little protection from the inclement Northwest weather. Stoves, if provided, were virtually ineffective because the loose sides of the tent allowed heat to escape quite easily. Moreover, the frequent lack of adequate supplies of kerosene, coal, or dry wood meant that the stove heaters were often useless. . . . Although the specter of hypothermia was present, the braceros faced a more serious threat from fires as they struggled to keep warm with the combination of kerosene, old stoves, and highly flammable tents. Besides frequent tent fires, there were also destructive explosions. . . .

When fires occurred, the design of the mobile camps' water systems added to the danger. Water tanks, pipes, and pumps were entirely above ground and readily froze increasing the peril of fire. Water barrels with handpumped fire extinguishers were also useless during freezing temperatures. . . .

Although the braceros complained strongly about their living accommodations, they grumbled most about the poor quality of food served in the camps. The meals lacked variety and appeal because the kitchen facilities in the tent camps were often makeshift and deficient by most standards. Moreover, northwestern federal officials, unlike those in the Southwest, gave local grower committees the responsibility for feeding the braceros in the labor centers. . . .

In the Northwest, as in California, meals were the source of more discontent and work stoppages than any other single aspect of camp life. In July 1943, Mexicans at the Skagit County camp north of Seattle went on strike in order to call attention to the terrible kitchen services. Workers there started their daily routine with breakfast at 4:30 A.M. Seven and a half hours later, they stopped work to eat a noon lunch consisting of three sandwiches: one contained meat, one egg spread, and another jelly. A sweet roll and half pint of milk were also provided. The camp, improvised at the county fairgrounds, had no refrigeration; therefore by lunch time, the sandwiches, prepared the day before, were unappetizing and the milk was "sour or blinky.". . . Workers were not provided containers to carry coffee or milk, so they used anything they could find without much thought to sanitation. This doubtlessly contributed to bracero camps in the Northwest having an unusually high incidence of food poisoning. . . .

Leisure time activities, a key to the physical and social well being of most persons, were just as precious to the braceros—yet the men had little to do during their off hours. In most camps, Mexican movies projected outdoors on tent walls were a bright spot in an otherwise dull routine. . . . When films were not available, the braceros found other ways to pass time during non-working hours. On Sundays, they sometimes requested Catholic priests to offer mass in camp. They also frequently pooled their resources to purchase radios or jukeboxes, which they stocked with Spanish records. Others passed idle hours with handicraft work, such as fashioning rings out of scrap pipe or suitcases from discarded wood.

Beyond the limited leisure activities, the social highlight of the year at most camps was the celebration of Mexican Independence. The Office of Labor, in the War Food Administration, sanctioned the festival because officials recognized it as an excellent way to sustain morale and a dedication to task among the imported work force. State farm labor officials also encouraged local communities to cooperate with the celebrations at the labor camps. . . . Another much-celebrated occasion in the camps was Cinco de Mayo, the anniversary of the defeat of the French in Mexico. At Medford, Oregon, in 1944, more than a thousand attended the celebration. . . .

These two celebrations, which brought the braceros and public together, stood in stark contrast to widespread anti-Mexican sentiment usually faced by the workers. In the Northwest, Idaho developed the most notorious reputation for discrimination. Prejudice became so common and deep-seated that in 1946 the Mexican government threatened to forbid its workers to go into the state and two years later made good on its threat. Consequently, Idaho, like Texas, was blacklisted by the Mexican government for its mistreatment of braceros. . . .

Antipathy against Mexicans developed outside of Idaho as well. In Seattle, the Reverend U. G. Murphey, chairman of the Evacuees Service Counsel which worked on behalf of Japanese Americans relocated in internment camps, was unsympathetic toward the Mexican men, and although PL-45 did not provide for permanent residency, he opposed any settlement of braceros. Meanwhile, the school superintendent at Boardman, Oregon, asked Senator Rufus C. Holman why the braceros in the state could not be conscripted into the military. At Stanwood, Washington, braceros had an altercation with some high school students and a local marshal outside a restaurant resulting in a near "race riot." Not long thereafter, the camp manager at Medford, Oregon, reported that a Mexican national was attacked in public "without provocation" and severely injured by five young men. After the assault, the battered man was arrested on a charge of being intoxicated. During his arraignment the judge acknowledged that "those who made the attack should have been arrested instead." As it turned out, the bracero had been staggering and presumed drunk "due to the beating received and not due to alcoholism as claimed.". . .

Braceros faced another severe form of discrimination from health authorities. Some hospitals refused to treat them, and this prejudice prompted the chief of operations at the U.S. Office of Labor in Portland to suggest that the federal government establish infirmaries in areas where Mexicans could not obtain needed medical care. Sometimes, the workers were denied treatment on racial grounds, while on other occasions health practitioners doubted the

Braceros from Mexico doing their laundry in a labor camp

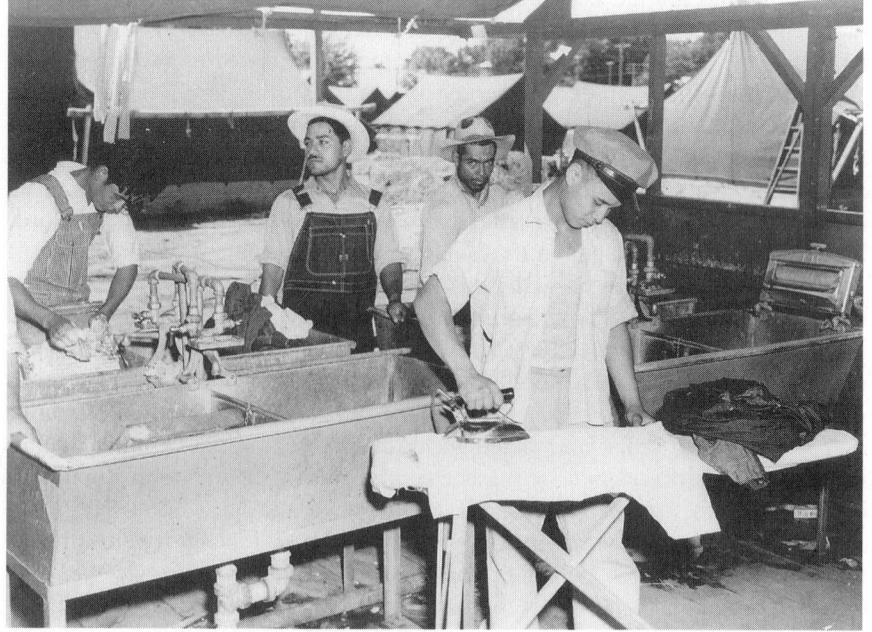

men's ability to pay their medical expenses and feared they would be left with outstanding bills. . . . When medical authorities and community hospitals treated the braceros, the workers usually received minimal attention. . . .

In addition to poor living conditions, discrimination and minimal health care, braceros faced unpleasant and dangerous work conditions because some farmers had little concern for the welfare of the men. At times, growers required that the braceros work during extremely cold weather, although the men were not acclimatized and lacked proper clothing. . . .

The growers' lack of concern for the men's welfare was reflected in numerous work-related accidents which resulted from poor safety and the braceros' inexperience with the hazards of working near powerful farm machinery. At Weiser, Idaho, Apolinar Calderón accidentally severed a finger while working on a seed harvester. In Oregon, Primitivo Mosqueda suffered serious injuries to the temporal region, lacerations, and a fractured skull when his head was pinned between two pieces of farm equipment causing "a portion of an end of a bolt to pierce down in the skull to an unbelievable distance." In another instance, as workers were having lunch, a tractor ran over a milk bottle sending glass flying into the braceros' food. One worker accidently swallowed a fragment and spent three days in the hospital after doctors removed the glass from his throat. At Kennewick, Washington, Pedro Correa Armenta lost his sight in a work-related accident. Following an unsuccessful operation to restore his vision, he was repatriated to Mexico. Often the braceros were killed or critically injured in accidents while being transported to and from work in open flatbed trucks. The return trip was the most dangerous because the workers had to ride atop loose loads of potatoes, sugar beets, or lightly secured vegetable and fruit boxes. . . . [T]he number of accidents involving trucks was particularly grave in the Northwest. . . .

The braceros could legally do little more than complain to Mexican government officials to improve working conditions because their contracts prohibited work stoppages or strikes. In the Southwest these prohibitions kept labor disturbances to a minimum. As Ernesto Galarza noted, dissatisfied workers had but two alternatives: "either shut-up or go back." Doubtlessly, southwestern braceros staged labor protests—there was a serious disturbance near Fullerton, California, in 1943—but no general pattern of strikes emerged. In the Northwest, on the other hand, braceros were constantly on strike, and this made the region unique among other parts of the country.

Just months after the braceros arrived in the Northwest, they initiated the first strike and established a pattern that continued until PL-45 expired in 1947. At Burlington, Washington, a local Mexican American convinced the braceros to halt work because farmers were paying higher wages to Anglos doing similar work. The growers ended the work stoppage by reminding the Mexicans that strikes were prohibited under the terms of their contract and by giving the Mexican American a "friendly warning against inciting a riot in a government camp." The "instigator" at once left and the workers returned to their jobs.

Most bracero strikes were not so easy to put down. Idaho, which had the lowest wage scales and the most recalcitrant farmers, experienced many serious labor disturbances despite the state legislature's approval, in February 1943, of a strong measure to curb labor unrest. The law prohibited union organizers from entering, without the owner's consent, "any ranch, farm, feeding and shearing plant or other agricultural premise" to solicit members, collect dues, or promote a strike. Picket lines and consumer boycotts were also illegal. . . .

The longest and best coordinated work stoppage involved more than 600 braceros from four camps near Nampa, Idaho, in June 1946. The timing of the walkout was critical to the growers primarily because their crops were ready for harvest and because prisoners of war, who had earlier been used as agricultural workers, were no longer available. The strike was in protest to a higher wage scale in the western part of Canyon County where growers had to compete with Oregon farmers. . . . In an attempt to control the strike, a Spanish-speaking farm labor supervisor negotiated with the braceros until they finally agreed to call off the strike on the promise that the Mexican consul would push for a hearing before the county wage stabilization board.

Twelve days later, the workers and growers got an opportunity to testify before the wage board. The braceros presented their case for a uniform wage of $.70 an hour. The growers responded that some workers were paid as much as $.75 because they were skilled "American laborers" employed year around, but as for the braceros, they were paid adequately at a $.60 rate. In the end, the growers convinced the hearing examiners to rule that "there was no evidence presented that warranted a change, either increase or decrease, in the existing scale."

The Mexican consul, in a move to force an increase in wages, threatened the growers: "Considering that ample opportunity has been given Farmers Associations [of the] Nampa District to revise discriminatory attitudes toward contracted Mexican Nationals, please proceed to remove workers at your earliest convenience unless seventy cents per hour prevailing wage in nearby areas is recognized before Monday, July 22nd." This threat was reinforced by Carl G. Izett of the Federal Production and Marketing Administration offices in Portland who argued that a solution to the workers' protest was "critical" to the continuation of the bracero program. The labor dispute ended, however, without either an increase in wages or repatriation. Although made uneasy by the consul's threat and the braceros' "extremely rebellious attitude," the growers persuaded local law enforcement officials to break the strike by arresting the strikers on spurious felony charges.

Braceros organized similar protests over working conditions in other areas of the Northwest. . . . The pattern of labor unrest among braceros in the Pacific Northwest must be seen in light of circumstances peculiar to the region and the men's motive for coming to the United States. They came to earn sufficient money to take back to Mexico but this was not always possible because of working conditions or low wages. Most braceros left terrible living conditions in Mexico, yet the tent camps left much to be desired and the food was deplorable. When the workers protested, northwestern farmers searched for another source of cheap labor.

The expiration of PL-45 in April 1947 gave growers added reason to stop bringing braceros in the Pacific Northwest. The new legislative authorization for the bracero program, PL-40, contained major administrative changes, including payment by employers of all transportation costs from Mexico. As a result, braceros were replaced by Mexican American workers on northwestern farms, although southwestern states continued to recruit Mexican nationals in record numbers until 1964.

FURTHER READING

John Adair and Evon Z. Vogt, "Navajo and Zuni Veterans," *American Anthropologist* 51 (1949): 547–568.

Carl Allsup, *The American G.I. Forum: Origins and Evolution* (Austin: Center for Mexican American Studies, University of Texas, distributed by the University of Texas Press, 1982).

Alison R. Bernstein, *American Indians and World War II: Toward a New Era in Indian Affairs* (Norman: University of Oklahoma Press, 1991).

Roger Daniels, *Concentration Camps, North America: Japanese in the United States and Canada During World War II* (Malabar, Fla.: Robert E. Krieger Pub. Co., 1986).

Ernesto Galarza, *Merchants of Labor: The Mexican Bracero Story* (Charlotte, N.C.: McNally & Loftin, 1964; Santa Barbara: McNally & Loftin, West, 1978).

Erasmo Gamboa, *Mexican Labor and World War II: Braceros in the Pacific Northwest, 1942–1947* (Austin: University of Texas Press, 1990).

Mario T. García, "Americans All: The Mexican-American Generation and the Politics of Wartime Los Angeles, 1941–1945," *Social Science Quarterly* 65 (June 1984): 278–289.

James D. Harrington, *Yankee Samurai: The Secret Role of Nisei in America's Pacific Victory* (Detroit: Pettigrew Enterprises, 1979).

Chester B. Himes, *If He Hollers, Let Him Go* (Garden City, N.Y.: Doubleday Doran, 1945; New York: Berkley Pub. Corp., 1964; New York: Signet Books, 1971; New York: New American Library, 1971; Chatham, N.J.: Chatham Bookseller, 1972; New York: Thunder Mouth Press, 1986; London: Pluto, 1986).

Tom Holm, "Fighting a White Man's War: The Extent and Legacy of American Indian Participation in World War II," *Journal of Ethnic Studies* 9 (1981): 69–81.

Thomas James, *Exile Within: The Schooling of Japanese Americans, 1942–1945* (Cambridge, Mass.: Harvard University Press, 1987).

Christina M. Lim and Sheldon H. Lim, "In the Shadow of the Tiger: The 407th Air Service Squadron, Fourteenth Air Force, CBI, World War II," in *Chinese America: History and Perspectives, 1993* (San Francisco: Chinese Historical Society of America, 1993).

Raul Morin, *Among the Valiant: Mexican Americans in World War II and Korea* (Alhambra, Calif.: Borden Pub. Co., 1963, 1966).

Douglas W. Nelson, *Heart Mountain: The History of an American Concentration Camp* (Madison: State Historical Society of Wisconsin, 1976).

Peter Phan, "Familiar Strangers: The Fourteenth Air Service Group Case Study of Chinese American Identity During World War II," in *Chinese America: History and Perspectives, 1993* (San Francisco: Chinese Historical Society of America, 1993).

Tamotsu Shibutani, *The Derelicts of Company K: A Sociological Study of Demoralization* (Berkeley and Los Angeles: University of California Press, 1978).

Chester Tanaka, *Go for Broke: A Pictorial History of the Japanese American 100th Battalion and the 442nd Regimental Combat Team* (Richmond, Calif.: Go for Broke, 1982).

They Talked Navajo: The United States Marine Corps Navajo Code Talkers of World War II (Window Rock, Ariz.: Navajo Tribal Museum, 1972).

Dorothy S. Thomas and Richard Nishimoto, *The Spoilage: Japanese American Evacuation and Resettlement During World War II* (Berkeley and Los Angeles: University of California Press, 1946).

Evon Z. Vogt, *Navajo Veterans: A Study in Changing Values* (Cambridge, Mass.: Harvard University Press, 1951).

CHAPTER 14

Protest

The 1960s witnessed some of the most tumultuous political developments in American history. Social movements to overcome racial, ethnic, and gender inequality swept the country. Westerners were very much involved in these significant social movements. Drawing on their own particular community experiences, and seeking to understand the racial discrimination against their people, as well as the history of struggles to combat such discrimination, a militant generation of peoples of color came of age during the 1960s and early 1970s.

The new and dynamic oppositional movements launched by this 1960s generation combined older goals for civil rights with more innovative objectives based on identity and culture. Activists fervently challenged earlier generations and their alleged failures to fight against racism and an accompanying erosion of ethnic cultures. Youth centered, and operating largely out of universities, colleges, and high schools, the 1960s generation employed militant direct-action strategies such as sit-ins, boycotts, mass rallies, and marches to secure their demands.

The following selections explore aspects of this militant generation. Carlos Muñoz, Jr., examines the ethnic roots of the Chicano student movement, which saw itself as the vanguard of "El Movimiento." Alma M. García shows how a women's movement arose out of Chicanas' dissatisfaction with the Chicano movement. Sucheng Chan provides an overview of the changes affecting young Asian Americans as they rediscovered their ethnic roots and invented a pan-Asian identity. Karen Miller illustrates how the struggle to establish black studies and other ethnic studies programs or departments was a part of this social revolution. Finally, Judith Antell, through oral history, recaptures the hopes and frustrations of Native Americans in the San Francisco Bay Area as they dramatically reoccupied Alcatraz Island.

FOR ANALYSIS AND DISCUSSION

1. How were the political movements that emerged in the 1960s similar to or different from the political activism in which earlier generations (as described in Chapters 10 and 11) had engaged?

2. How did each of the movements discussed in this chapter define "opposition"?

3. How did ethnicity intertwine with politics in each of these movements?

4. Why was it mainly young people in educational institutions who participated in these movements?

5. What did each of these movements hope to achieve?

6. In what ways did they redefine the American dream?

 # Chicano Protest Politics, 1960s

CARLOS MUÑOZ, JR.

The 1960s witnessed an acceleration of political activity among a new generation of Mexican Americans: the Chicano Generation. Feeling the burden of a long history of discrimination and exploitation in the United States, members of the Chicano Generation were also influenced by the drive for black civil rights and by the black power movement, as well as by the general youth rebellion of the 1960s. Coming of age in a radical political climate, the Chicano Generation represented the most challenging political movement in Chicano history.

Skeptical of the American dream and rejecting earlier Mexican-American strategies to achieve pluralism and integration, the Chicano movement opted for an oppositional position based on the resurgence or invention of Chicano ethnic nationalism centered around a new identity—*Chicanismo*—that called on Chicanos to rediscover their Mexican roots and culture and to use them as political weapons against acculturation. This new political movement would recapture not only a lost homeland—*Aztlán*—but also a soul. In his study of the role of youth and students who served as the vanguard of the movement, Carlos Muñoz, Jr., records the early influences on, and the development of "El Movimiento."

STUDY QUESTIONS

1. What non-Chicano influences inspired Chicano youth to embrace political activism?

2. What new political directions did the Los Angeles school "blow-outs" signal for the Chicano Generation?

T
he dramatic emergence of the civil rights movement generated reform in education and politics. Although chiefly aimed at benefiting African Americans, the movement created a political atmosphere beneficial to Mexican American working-class youth, for it gave them more access to institutions of higher education. Their access to college was no longer limited to patronage by the YMCA and the Protestant and Catholic churches, as had

From *Youth, Identity, Power: The Chicano Movement* by Carlos Muñoz, Jr. (Verso Publishers, 1989), pp. 50–53, 58–59, and 64–72. Reprinted by permission of Verso.

been the case in the 1930s, nor was it limited to veterans with G.I. Bill benefits, as it had largely been in the 1940s. There were now hundreds of youth of Mexican descent attending college as a direct result of federal educational programs made possible by the civil rights movement and implemented especially during the Johnson administration.

The growing numbers of Mexican American students on college campuses did not come close to representing a significant proportion of the Mexican American population: Mexican American youth remained severely underrepresented. Neither did they produce a visible Mexican American student activism. But from those numbers came a few student activists who, between 1963 and 1967, participated in some activities and organizations of the civil rights movement. Some of them became active indirectly or directly as members of the Student Nonviolent Coordinating Committee [SNCC]. For example, Maria Varela became a key SNCC organizer in Alabama, where she established an adult literacy project. She was from New Mexico and before joining SNCC had been a cofounder of Students for a Democratic Society at the University of Michigan. Elizabeth ("Betita") Sutherland Martinez, a civil rights activist of Mexican descent, became the director of the New York City SNCC office in 1964 and also worked in Mississippi. Others participated in the 1963 March on Washington organized by Dr. Martin Luther King, Jr., and the Southern Christian Leadership Conference. At San Jose State College in Northern California, a few Mexican American students joined a campus protest when a Black student was denied admission.

In the mid-1960s, some of those who had participated in SNCC and other organizations or who had been influenced by the civil rights movement came to the realization that Mexican Americans were not a concern of the Black civil rights leadership and its allies. The War on Poverty programs created by the Johnson administration did not initially address poverty in the *barrios* of the South and Midwest. The first organized student effort in the nation to bring specific attention to the needs of Mexican Americans and youth in particular took place on the San Jose State College campus in 1964 when Armando Valdez organized the Student Initiative (SI). Valdez was a member of Students for a Democratic Society [SDS] and a supporter of SNCC. He recruited some students from the handful of Mexican Americans on campus at that time and others from the ranks of white liberal student activists. The objectives of Student Initiative focused on pressuring the campus administration to create programs to recruit Mexican American students and tutorial programs to help them survive once they entered college.

Mexican American student activists were also exposed to a more radical politics during the early 1960s as left political organizations resurfaced from the underground where they had been driven during the McCarthy era. Communist and socialist youth groups became visible on college campuses as did nonsocialist New Left groups like SDS. Campus protest against the Vietnam War was also becoming visible, as manifested in the "teach-ins" organized by white liberal and leftist faculty and students.

In 1964 Luis Valdez and Roberto Rubalcava, student activists at San Jose State, became associated with the Progressive Labor Party (PL); as an undergraduate student Valdez had been active in the Viva Kennedy Clubs and in MAPA [Mexican American Political Association]. Valdez and Rubalcava travelled to Cuba as part of a PL delegation, and their first-hand observation of the Cuban revolution inspired them to produce the first radical manifesto written by Mexican American student activists. The manifesto read in part:

> The Mexican in the United States has been . . . no less a victim of American imperialism than his impoverished brothers in Latin America. In the words of the Second Declaration of Havana, tell him of "misery, feudal exploitation, illiteracy, starvation wages," and he will tell you that you speak of Texas; tell him of "unemployment, the policy of repression against the workers, discrimination . . . oppression by the oligarchies," and he will tell you that you speak of California; tell him of US domination in Latin America, and he will tell you that he knows that Shark and what he devours, because he has lived in its very entrails. The history of the American Southwest provides a brutal panorama of nascent imperialism.

The manifesto represented a radical departure from the political thought of the Mexican-American Generation and a harsh critique of its political leadership. . . .

Valdez returned from Cuba and after graduating from college joined the radical San Francisco Mime Troupe, where he continued to refine his critique of the assimilationist and accommodationist perspective of the Mexican-American Generation and worked to develop a new cultural identity and politics for Mexican Americans. Some of that thinking came to fruition when he joined the farmworkers' struggle in Delano, California in 1965 and founded the Teatro Campesino. Many of the ideas behind the conceptualization of the Chicano identity and the development of the Chicano Generation of the late 1960s emanated from the ideas of Luis Valdez and the cultural work of his Teatro Campesino. Key members of the Teatro were student activists he recruited from college campuses in Northern California. One of the most prominent of them was Ysidro Ramon Macias, an undergraduate activist at the University of California, Berkeley. Macias became one of the Teatro's original playwrights; his influential play *The Ultimate Pendejada* dramatized the rejection of the assimilationism of Mexican-American identity and the emergence of Chicano identity. . . .

By 1966, student activists, though still relatively few in number, were seriously discussing the formation of distinct Mexican American student organizations on their campuses throughout the Southwest. By the fall of 1967 organizations had emerged on several college campuses in Los Angeles and on two campuses in Texas. At St. Mary's College in San Antonio, Texas it was named the Mexican American Youth Organization (MAYO). At the University of Texas at Austin it was called the Mexican American Student

Organization (MASO), later changing its name to MAYO. In the Los Angeles area, chapters of the United Mexican American Students (UMAS) were
formed at UCLA; California State College, Los Angeles; Loyola University;
University of Southern California; California State College, Long Beach; and
San Fernando State College. At East Los Angeles Community College,
another group organized as the Mexican American Student Association
(MASA).

At about the same time, the Student Initiative organization at San Jose
State College in Northern California changed its name to the Mexican Amer-
ican Student Confederation (MASC). Chapters followed at Fresno State,
Hayward State, and Sacramento State colleges. The following year, 1968,
students formed a chapter of UMAS at the University of Colorado at Boul-
der, and a MASC chapter at the University of California, Berkeley. By 1969
UMAS chapters were emerging in other parts of the Southwest. The first
UMAS chapter in the Midwest was organized at the University of Notre
Dame by Gilbert Cárdenas, a first-year graduate student in sociology and
former undergraduate member of UMAS in California.

Ideologically, most of these new student organizations had objectives
similar to those of the Mexican Youth Conferences of the 1930s and the
Mexican-American Movement of the 1940s. They emphasized the theme of
"progress through education," and concentrated on activities related to

Chicano youth marching in a demonstration as the Brown Berets

recruitment of Mexican American students and helping them stay in college. The new student organizations worked with Mexican American professionals to raise scholarship funds for needy students, and sought their advice on matters relating to the education of Mexican Americans. Some of the student activists themselves attended college with help from scholarships made available by middle-class organizations like LULAC [League of United Latin American Citizens]. With few exceptions, the new student groups mirrored the political consciousness of the Mexican-American Generation of the 1930s and were committed to the development of a new generation of professionals who could play a leading role in the betterment of the Mexican American community within the context of middle-class politics.

These student organizations did not yet represent a student movement in political terms. But as they came into direct contact with community politics and learned more about the Chávez and Tijerina movements they came to represent a student movement in the making. By the end of 1967, the antiwar and Black Power movements had become other sources of growing militancy among some of the student leaders. The politics of the times were now characterized by mass protest, and the fact that the main protagonists in the unfolding drama were white and Black radical youth did not go unnoticed by the leadership of the Mexican American student organizations. Some of them joined with SDS and the Black student unions in planning campus protests. . . .

On the morning of 3 March 1968, shouts of "Blow Out!" rang through the halls of Abraham Lincoln High School, a predominantly Mexican American school in East Los Angeles. Over a thousand students walked out of their classes, teacher Sal Castro among them. Waiting for them outside the school grounds were members of UMAS and various community activists. They distributed picket signs listing some of the thirty-six demands that had been developed by a community and student strike committee. The signs of protested racist school policies and teachers and called for freedom of speech, the hiring of Mexican American teachers and administrators, and classes on Mexican American history and culture. As might be expected, the signs that caught the attention of the mass media and the police were those reading "Chicano Power!"; "Viva La Raza!"; and "Viva La Revolución!" By the afternoon of that day, several thousand more students had walked out of five other *barrio* high schools to join the strike. The strike brought the Los Angeles city school system, the largest in the nation, to a standstill and made news across the country; a *Los Angeles Times* reporter interpreted the strike as "The Birth of Brown Power." Over ten thousand students had participated by the time the Los Angeles "blow-outs" ended a week and a half later.

But the strike accomplished something much more important than shaking up school administrators or calling public attention to the educational problems of Mexican American youth. Although not one of its original objectives, the strike was the first major mass protest explicitly against racism undertaken by Mexican Americans in the history of the United States. As such, it had a profound impact on the Mexican American community in Los Angeles and in other parts of the country, and it generated an increased political awareness along with visible efforts to mobilize the community. This was manifested in the revitalization of existing community political organizations and the emergence of new ones, with youth playing significant leadership roles.

Overnight, student activism reached levels of intensity never before witnessed. A few Mexican American student activists had participated in civil rights marches, anti-Vietnam War protests, and had walked the picket lines for the farmworker movement. But the high school strike of 1968 was the first time students of Mexican descent had marched en masse in their own demonstration against racism and for educational change. It was also the first time that they had played direct leadership roles in organizing a mass protest. The slogans of "Chicano Power!"; "Viva La Raza!"; and "Viva La Revolución!" that rang throughout the strike reflected an increasing militancy and radicalism in the ranks of UMAS and other student organizations. The nature of these concerns and the momentum built up among Mexican American students—both in high school and on college campuses—broke the ideological bonds that characteristically keep student organizations, and students in general, from questioning authority and the status quo. Membership grew as those organizations and their leaders became protagonists in struggles for change in Mexican American communities. The strike moved student activism beyond the politics of accommodation and integration which had been shaped by the Mexican-American Generation and the community's middle-class leadership.

However, it was not student activists who conceived of the strike; the idea originated with Sal Castro, the teacher at Lincoln High School who had walked out with his students. . . . [H]e had become disillusioned with the Democratic Party and with Mexican American middle-class leadership. . . . [H]e had played a prominent role in the "Viva Kennedy" campaign in 1960, serving as the student coordinator of the Southern California campaign. He was a Korean War–era veteran attending college on the G.I. Bill at the time. Like other veterans, he played a role in MAPA and was a founder of the Association of Mexican American Educators. . . .

But by 1964 Castro had come to the realization that the Democrats did not have the interests of Mexican Americans at heart and that corruption was inherent in the political system. A product of the *barrio* schools in East Los Angeles, Castro returned to the neighborhood as a teacher only to find that racism toward Mexican American youth remained virulent. Through the AMAE [Association of Mexican American Educators] organization he worked hard to make reforms within the school bureaucracy but was not able to accomplish much. Like other middle-class leaders, he saw that the civil rights movement ignored Mexican Americans and that they were low on the agenda of the War on Poverty and in education reform plans. But unlike most other middle-class leaders, Castro came to the conclusion that his people needed their own civil rights movement and that the only alternative in the face of a racist educational system was nonviolent protest against the schools. He therefore prepared to sacrifice his teaching career, if necessary, in the interest of educational change for Mexican American children. The strike made Castro one of the movement's leaders.

The strike of 1968 went beyond the objectives of Castro and others concerned only with improving education. It was the first loud cry for Chicano Power and self-determination, serving as the catalyst for the formation of the Chicano student movement as well as the larger Chicano Power Movement of which it became the most important sector. . . .

After the strike the UMAS leadership urged the members to assume a more political role in both the community and on campus and to think in terms of being part of a student movement. In the first Mexican American student organization newsletter to be published and distributed throughout the Southwest, the UMAS chapter at California State College, Los Angeles, described its role:

> UMAS is cognizant of the social, economic, and political ills of our Mexican people. The desire of UMAS is to play a vital role in the liberation of the Mexican American people from second class citizenship. To do this we see our role to stand united in the effort to affect social change for the betterment of our people. We believe the ills that beset our people are not products of our culture, but that said ills have been inflicted by the institutions which today comprise the establishment in the American society.

This first newsletter urged students to participate in the Poor People's March on Washington scheduled for later in the spring of 1968 and to join the Mexican American delegation to it being led by Reies López Tijerina. It also called on students to support Sal Castro, who had been suspended by the Los Angeles Board of Education for his role in the strike and for his continued support for change in the schools. Finally, UMAS advocated an "internal and external" plan of action for the student movement:

> [Recognizing] that the system cannot be changed overnight, we feel it is necessary that we work within the existing framework to the degree that it not impede our effectiveness. It is historically evident that working within the existing framework is not sufficient; therefore, our external approach will consist of exerting outside pressure on those institutions that directly affect the Mexican American community.

The term *Chicano* appeared often—mostly interchangeably with *Mexican American*—but UMAS advanced no particular ideology for the student movement at this point. . . . UMAS continued to stress educational issues, involvement in the community to assist high school students and defend them from harassment by racist teachers, the need to establish tutorial programs, and efforts to increase enrollments of Mexican American college students. . . .

In the weeks following the strike, the leadership of each UMAS chapter in the Los Angeles area formed a coordinating body called UMAS Central. The first newsletter of this group called on Chicanos to take pride in their Mexican identity and on students to see themselves as a political vanguard.

> We have begun to recognize our role as an organizational agent through which Chicano students are able to recognize themselves as Mexicans and to take pride in it. We are the avant-garde of the young Mexican American liberation movement. We formulate a philosophy for our people and we provide the hope for the future of Mexicans of all generations. We recognize ourselves as a generation of doers as well as thinkers. . . . We are resolved to perpetuate an atmosphere of respect and dignity for our people. . . . We are the agents of progress and unity. We demanded social justice for a people too long oppressed.

Militancy in the ranks of the developing student movement accelerated as a consequence of the response to the strike on the part of the power structure of the city of Los Angeles and the implementation of directives from the Federal Bureau of Investigation. On 4 March 1968, FBI Director J. Edgar Hoover issued a memo to local law enforcement officials across the country urging them to place top priority on political intelligence work to prevent the development of nationalist movements in minority communities. Hoover's chief goal was to undermine the Black Power Movement, but his directive was considered applicable to other similar movements. . . .

On 2 June 1968, three months after the strike and two days before California's primary elections, thirteen young Mexican American political activists who had been identified as leaders of the emerging "Brown Power" movement were indicted by the Los Angeles County Grand Jury on conspiracy charges for their roles in organizing the strike. The indictments charged that the thirteen activists had conspired to "willfully disturb the peace and quiet" of the city of Los Angeles and disrupt the educational process in its schools. They were characterized as members of communist "subversive organizations" or outside agitators intent on radicalizing Mexican American students. Each of the thirteen activists faced a total of sixty-six years in prison if found guilty.

None of the "LA Thirteen" were in fact communists or members of "subversive organizations." They included Sal Castro; Eliezer Risco, editor of a new community newspaper named *La Raza*; and Patricio Sanchez, a member of MAPA. The remaining ten were all student activists and key leaders of their respective organizations. . . . Instead of preventing the rise of another "nationalist movement," the indictments of the LA Thirteen simply fueled the fire of an emerging radicalism among Mexican American students.

Several weeks later, Mexican American graduating seniors at San Jose State College and members of the audience walked out during commencement exercises. Approximately two hundred people were involved in the demonstration. They denounced the college for its lack of commitment to the surrounding Mexican American community, as shown by the low enrollment of Mexican American students on campus. The walkout was also a protest against the inadequate training of professionals such as teachers, social workers, and policemen, who, after graduating, would work in the Mexican American community with no understanding of the culture and needs of that community, or—most important—of how their own racism affected their dealings with Mexican Americans. . . .

That walkout was the first protest activity undertaken by Mexican American students on a college campus. Five months later, in November 1968, Mexican American students became part of the strike at San Francisco State College, organized by the Third World Liberation Front (TWLF). It was marked by violent confrontations between students and the police, and many students were injured. The strike began over issues initially raised by Black students and lasted until March 1969. Although the students' demands mostly focused on the needs of Black students, one demand called for the creation of a Department of Raza Studies under the umbrella of a proposed School of Ethnic Studies. The TWLF also demanded open admission for all third world students. The San Francisco State strike was significant because it marked the first time that Mexican American and other third world student activists united to create a politically explosive "rainbow" coalition.

In October 1968, the Mexican American Student Confederation took over the office of Charles Hitch, president of the University of California system, to protest his refusal to discontinue the purchase of grapes while Chávez's farmworkers were on strike—part of a national campaign to boycott grapes in support of the UFW. The takeover of Hitch's office resulted in the arrest of eleven MASC members for trespassing and unlawful assembly. This was the first in a series of third world student confrontations with university authorities on the Berkeley campus, which eventually culminated in the formation of another Third World Liberation Front and student strike.

Patterning itself after the Third World Liberation Front at San Francisco State across the Bay, the TWLF at Berkeley organized its own student strike, which lasted from January through April 1969. It was the first major third world student confrontation within the University of California system, and one of the most violent to occur at any of the university's campuses: many students were arrested or became victims of police violence.

In contrast to the strike at San Francisco State, Mexican American students played a leading role in the organization of the Third World Liberation Front and the strike on the UC Berkeley campus. The strike was aimed at exposing the university's lack of commitment to meeting the educational needs of third world people. Although there were many differences within the TWLF, the strike demands incorporated previous issues raised by both African American and Mexican American student activists. The TWLF demanded the creation of a Third World College with departments of Mexican American, Black [Native American,] and Asian-American studies. It also demanded sufficient resources for the proposed college to involve itself in minority communities and contribute effectively to their development. TWLF demanded that the new college be under the full control of its students, faculty, and representatives of the community; "self-determination" was to be its principle of governance. Other demands called for open admission for all third world people and poor working-class whites and the recruitment of third world faculty and staff.

There were other high school student strikes throughout the Southwest during 1969, patterned after the 1968 strike in Los Angeles. In Denver, Colorado and Crystal City, Texas, high school strikes also resulted in significant political developments beyond the immediate issues of educational change. In Denver, the strike contributed to the further development of the Crusade for Justice and made Corky Gonzáles a national leader of the emerging Chicano movement. In contrast to the relatively violence-free student strike in Los Angeles, the Denver demonstrations resulted in violent confrontations between police, students, and members of the Crusade for Justice, and Corky Gonzáles was himself arrested. After his release he praised the striking students for risking "revolutionary" actions to make history: "You kids don't realize you have made history. We just talk about revolution. But you act it by facing the shotguns, billies, gas, and mace. You are the real revolutionaries."

In Crystal City, a high school strike contributed directly to the founding of La Raza Unida Party, a second electoral revolt in that city that resulted in the party's takeover of city government and the school system, and the making of José Angel Gutiérrez into another national leader of the Chicano Movement.

The movement was given further impetus by other events that took place in 1968, the year that was the turning point of the decade. The antiwar movement became a potent political force in national politics as mass protest against the war in Vietnam dramatically increased. . . . It was also the year that Dr. Martin Luther King, Jr., led the Poor People's March on Washington, which included a contingent of Mexican Americans. Later in the year Dr. King and Senator Robert F. Kennedy were assassinated. Even more important, 1968 was also the year of international student uprisings from Paris and Berlin to Tokyo to Mexico City. . . . Between 1968 and 1969, Mexican American student militancy intensified as more and more of them became convinced that they were part of an international revolution in the making.

From the ranks of these militant students came artists, poets and actors who collectively generated a cultural renaissance and whose work played a key role in creating the ideology of the Chicano movement. In Oakland, California, the first group of radical artists organized themselves as the Mexican American Liberation Art Front (MALAF). Elsewhere in the Bay Area, José and Malaquias Montoya, Esteban Villa, René Yañez, Ralph Maradiaga and Rupert García produced posters whose striking art reflected the movement's quest for identity and power. Other artists emerged in other parts of the nation, and by 1970 a distinct Chicano art movement was in full bloom, which, in addition to radical poster art included a Chicano mural art in the tradition of the Mexican revolutionary artists David Alfaro Sequieros, José Clemente Orozco, and Diego Rivera.

Poets and writers produced campus and community underground newspapers, which replaced student organizational newsletters as the main form of movement communication. These newspapers led to the formation of an independent Chicano Press Association. In addition to Berkeley's *El Grito,* radical poets and writers created other magazines such as *Con Safos* in Los Angeles and *El Pocho Che* in San Francisco.

Student activists also created numerous campus and community-based "guerilla" theater groups patterned after the Teatro Campesino. By 1970 these groups had become part of a national Chicano theater movement called Teatros Nacionales de Aztlán.

The student strikes in the community and on the college campus, in conjunction with the political upheavals of the late sixties, thus generated the framework for the eventual transformation of student activist organizations into a full-blown student movement with clear social and political goals and an ethnic nationalist ideology that came to be known as cultural nationalism.

Chicana Feminist Discourse, 1970s

ALMA M. GARCÍA

The Chicano movement of the late 1960s and early 1970s represented one of the most significant political efforts by Mexican Americans to confront the historic exploitation that generations of Chicanos had endured since the U.S. acquisition of the Southwest in 1848. The movement called for a resurgence of Chicano nationalism as a way of forging a new and radical political movement based on a new identity. While the Chicano movement was an oppositional force in the context of American politics, it also possessed various internal contradictions, not the least of which centered on the issue of gender and on the dubious relationship of women to the movement.

In this essay, Alma M. García rediscovers the voices of Chicanas within the movement. She analyzes their evolution as both nationalists and feminists and examines the tensions between the two positions. As nationalists, some Chicanas challenged such nationalist concepts as *la familia*—the family—that conveyed pride in Chicano culture but also perpetuated patriarchical relationships that were oppressive to women. Their feminist critiques of Chicano nationalism elicited hostile reactions and charges that Chicana women were betraying their culture. Yet despite this backlash, Chicana feminists, for the sake of preserving ethnic bonds, remained within the Chicano movement even while criticizing its continuing sexism.

STUDY QUESTIONS

1. Why did some Chicana feminists feel compelled to remain in the Chicano movement even as they criticized its sexist dimensions?

2. What do Chicana feminists hope to accomplish?

3. How are their goals similar to or different from those of white feminists?

Between 1970 and 1980, a Chicana feminist movement developed in the United States that addressed the specific issues that affected Chicanas as women of color. The growth of the Chicana feminist movement can be traced in the speeches, essays, letters, and articles published in Chicano and Chicana newspapers, journals, newsletters, and other printed materials.

During the sixties, American society witnessed the development of the Chicano movement, a social movement characterized by a politics of protest. The Chicano movement focused on a wide range of issues: social justice, equality, educational reforms, and political and economic self-determination for Chicano communities in the United States. Various struggles evolved within this movement: the United Farmworkers unionization efforts; the New Mexico Land Grant movement; the Colorado-based Crusade for Justice; the Chicano student movement; and the Raza Unida Party.

Chicanas participated actively in each of these struggles. By the end of the sixties, Chicanas began to assess the rewards and limits of their participation. The 1970s witnessed the development of Chicana feminists whose activities, organizations, and writings can be analyzed in terms of a feminist movement by women of color in American society. Chicana feminists outlined a cluster of ideas that crystallized into an emergent Chicana feminist

From "The Development of Chicana Feminist Discourse, 1970–1980" by Alma M. García, *Gender and Society* 3 (1989), 217–218 and 221–228. Reprinted by permission of Sage Publications, Inc.

debate. In the same way that Chicano males were reinterpreting the historical and contemporary experience of Chicanos in the United States, Chicanas began to investigate the forces shaping their own experiences as women of color. . . .

Throughout the seventies and . . . eighties, Chicana feminists have been forced to respond to the criticism that cultural nationalism and feminism are irreconcilable. In the first issue of the newspaper, *Hijas de Cuauhtemoc* [*Daughters of Cuauhtemoc*], Anna Nieto Gomez stated that a major issue facing Chicanas active in the Chicano movement was the need to organize to improve their status as women within the larger social movement. Francisca Flores, another leading Chicana feminist, stated:

> [Chicanas] can no longer remain in a subservient role or as auxiliary forces in the [Chicano] movement. They must be included in the front line of communication, leadership and organizational responsibility. . . . The issue of equality, freedom and self-determination of the Chicana— like the right of self-determination, equality, and liberation of the Mexican [Chicano] community—is not negotiable. Anyone opposing the right of women to organize into their own form of organization has no place in the leadership of the movement.

Supporting this position, Bernice Rincon argued that a Chicana feminist movement that sought equality and justice for Chicanas would strengthen the Chicano movement. Yet in the process, Chicana feminists challenged traditional gender roles because they limited their participation and acceptance within the Chicano movement.

Throughout the seventies, Chicana feminists viewed the struggle against sexism within the Chicano movement and the struggle against racism in the large society as integral parts of Chicana feminism. As Nieto Gomez said:

> Chicana feminism is in various stages of development. However, in general, Chicana feminism is the recognition that women are oppressed as a group and are exploited as part of *la Raza* people. It is a direction to be responsible to identify and act upon the issues and needs of Chicana women. Chicana feminists are involved in understanding the nature of women's oppression.

Cultural nationalism represented a major ideological component of the Chicano movement. Its emphasis on Chicano cultural pride and cultural survival within an Anglo-dominated society gave significant political direction to the Chicano movement. One source of ideological disagreement between Chicana feminism and this cultural nationalist ideology was cultural survival. Many Chicana feminists believed that a focus on cultural survival did not acknowledge the need to alter male-female relations within Chicano communities. For example, Chicana feminists criticized the notion of the "ideal Chicana" that glorified Chicanas as strong, long-suffering women who had endured and kept Chicano culture and the family intact. To Chicana feminists, this concept represented an obstacle to the redefinition of gender roles. Nieto stated:

> Some Chicanas are praised as they emulate the sanctified example set by [the Virgin] Mary. The woman *par excellence* is mother and wife. She is to love and support her husband and to nurture and teach her children. Thus, may she gain fulfillment as a woman. For a Chicana bent upon fulfillment of her personhood, this restricted perspective of her role as a woman is not only inadequate but crippling.

Chicana feminists were also skeptical about the cultural nationalist interpretation of machismo. Such an interpretation viewed machismo as an ideological tool used by the dominant Anglo society to justify the inequalities experienced by Chicanos. According to this interpretation, the relationship between Chicanos and the larger society was that of an internal colony dominated and exploited by the capitalist economy. Machismo, like other cultural traits, was blamed by Anglos for blocking Chicanos from succeeding in American society. In reality, the economic structure and colony-like exploitation were to blame.

Some Chicana feminists agreed with this analysis of machismo, claiming that a mutually reinforcing relationship existed between internal colonialism and the development of the myth of machismo. According to Sosa Riddell, machismo was a myth "propagated by subjugators and colonizers, which created damaging stereotypes of Mexican/Chicano males." As a type of social control imposed by the dominant society on Chicanos, the myth of machismo distorted gender relations within Chicano communities, creating stereotypes of Chicanas as passive and docile women. At this level in the feminist discourse, machismo was seen as an Anglo myth that kept both Chicanos and Chicanas in a subordinate status. As Nieto concluded:

> Although the term "machismo" is correctly denounced by all because it stereotypes the Latin man . . . it does a great disservice to both men and women. Chicano and Chicana alike must be free to seek their own individual fulfillment.

While some Chicana feminists criticized the myth of machismo used by the dominant society to legitimate racial inequality, others moved beyond this level of analysis to distinguish between the machismo that oppressed both men and women and the sexism in Chicano communities in general, and the Chicano movement in particular, that oppressed Chicana women. According to Vidal, the origins of a Chicana feminist consciousness were prompted by the sexist attitudes and behavior of Chicano males, which constituted a "serious obstacle to women anxious to play a role in the struggle for Chicana liberation."

Furthermore, many Chicana feminists disagreed with the cultural nationalist view that machismo could be a positive value within a Chicano cultural value system. They challenged the view that machismo was a source of masculine pride for Chicanos and therefore a defense mechanism against the dominant society's racism. Although Chicana feminists recognized that Chicanos faced discrimination from the dominant society, they adamantly disagreed with those who believed that machismo was a form of cultural resistance to such discrimination. Chicana feminists called for changes in the ideologies responsible for distorting relations between women and men. One such change was to modify the cultural nationalist position that viewed machismo as a source of cultural pride.

Chicana feminists called for a focus on the universal aspects of sexism that shape gender relations in both Anglo and Chicano culture. While they acknowledged the economic exploitation of all Chicanos, Chicana feminists outlined the double exploitation experienced by Chicanas. Sosa Riddell concluded: "It was when Chicanas began to seek work outside of the family groups that sexism became a key factor of oppression along with racism." Francisca Flores summarized some of the consequences of sexism:

> It is not surprising that more and more Chicanas are forced to go to work in order to supplement the family income. The children are farmed out to a relative to baby-sit with them, and since these women are employed in the lower income jobs, the extra pressure placed on them can become unbearable.

Thus, while the Chicano movement was addressing the issue of racial oppression facing all Chicanos, Chicana feminists argued that it lacked an analysis of sexism. Similarly, Black and Asian American women stressed the interconnectedness of race and gender oppression. Hooks analyzes racism and sexism in terms of their "intersecting, complementary nature." She also emphasizes that one struggle should not take priority over the other. White criticizes Black men whose nationalism limited discussions of Black women's experiences with sexist oppression. The writings of other Black feminists criticized a Black cultural nationalist ideology that overlooked the consequences of sexist oppression. Many Asian American women were also critical of the Asian American movement whose focus on racism ignored the impact of sexism on the daily lives of women. The participation of Asian American women in various community struggles increased their encounters with sexism. As a result, some Asian American women developed a feminist consciousness and organized as women around feminist issues.

The systematic analysis by Chicana feminists of the impact of racism and sexism on Chicanas in American society and, above all, within the Chicano movement was often misunderstood as a threat to the political unity of the Chicano movement. As Marta Cotera, a leading voice of Chicana feminism, pointed out:

> The aggregate cultural values we [Chicanas] share can also work to our benefit if we choose to scrutinize our cultural traditions, isolate the positive attributes and interpret them for the benefit of women. It's unreal

that *Hispanas* have been browbeaten for so long about our so-called conservative (meaning reactionary) culture. It's also unreal that we have let
men interpret culture only as those practices and attitudes that determine
who does the dishes around the house. We as women also have the right
to interpret and define the philosophical and religious traditions beneficial to us within our culture, and which we have inherited as our tradition. To do this, we must become both conversant with our history and
philosophical evolution, and analytical about the institutional and
behavioral manifestations of the same.

Such Chicana feminists were attacked for developing a "divisive ideology"—
a feminist ideology that was frequently viewed as a threat to the Chicano
movement as a whole. As Chicana feminists examined their roles as women
activists within the Chicano movement, an ideological split developed. One
group active in the Chicano movement saw themselves as "loyalists" who
believed that the Chicano movement did not have to deal with sexual
inequities since Chicano men as well as Chicano women experienced racial
oppression. According to Nieto Gomez, who was not a loyalist, their view
was that if men oppress women, it is not the men's fault but rather that of
the system.

Even if such a problem existed, and they did not believe that it did, the
loyalists maintained that such a matter would best be resolved internally
within the Chicano movement. They denounced the formation of a separate
Chicana feminist movement on the grounds that it was a politically dangerous strategy, perhaps Anglo inspired. Such a movement would undermine
the unity of the Chicano movement by raising an issue that was not seen as a
central one. Loyalists viewed racism as the most important issue within the
Chicano movement. Nieto Gomez quotes one such loyalist:

> I am concerned with the direction that the Chicanas are taking in the
> movement. The words such as liberation, sexism, male chauvinism, etc.,
> were prevalent. The terms mentioned above plus the theme of individual-
> ism is a concept of the Anglo society; terms prevalent in the Anglo
> women's movement. The *familia* has always been our strength in our cul-
> ture. But it seems evident . . . that you [Chicana feminists] are not con-
> cerned with the *familia*, but are influenced by the Anglo woman's
> movement.

Chicana feminists were also accused of undermining the values associated
with Chicano culture. Loyalists saw the Chicana feminist movement as an
"anti-family, anti-cultural, anti-man and therefore an anti-Chicano movement." Feminism was, above all, believed to be an individualistic search for
identity that detracted from the Chicano movement's "real" issues, such as
racism. Nieto Gomez quotes a loyalist as stating:

> And since when does a Chicana need identity? If you are a real Chicana
> then no one regardless of the degrees needs to tell you about it. The only
> ones who need identity are the *vendidas*, the *falsas*, and the opportunists.

The ideological conflicts between Chicana feminists and loyalists persisted throughout the seventies. Disagreements between these two groups became exacerbated during various Chicana conferences. At times, such confrontations served to increase Chicana feminist activity that challenged the loyalists' attacks, yet these attacks also served to suppress feminist activities.

Chicana feminist lesbians experienced even stronger attacks from those who viewed feminism as a divisive ideology. In a political climate that already viewed feminist ideology with suspicion, lesbianism as a sexual lifestyle and political ideology came under even more attack. Clearly, a cultural nationalist ideology that perpetuated such stereotypical images of Chicanas as "good wives and good mothers" found it difficult to accept a Chicana feminist lesbian movement.

Cherrie Moraga's writings during the 1970s reflect the struggles of Chicana feminist lesbians who, together with other Chicana feminists, were finding the sexism evident within the Chicano movement intolerable. Just as Chicana feminists analyzed their life circumstances as members of an ethnic minority and as women, Chicana feminist lesbians addressed themselves to the oppression they experienced as lesbians. As Moraga stated:

> My lesbianism is the avenue through which I have learned the most about silence and oppression. . . . In this country, lesbianism is a poverty—as is being brown, as is being a woman, as is being just plain poor. The danger lies in ranking the oppressions. The danger lies in failing to acknowledge the specificity of the oppression.

Chicana, Black, and Asian American feminists experienced similar cross-pressures of feminist-baiting and lesbian-baiting attacks. As they organized around feminist struggles, these women of color encountered criticism from both male and female cultural nationalists who often viewed feminism as little more than an "anti-male" ideology. Lesbianism was identified as an extreme derivation of feminism. A direct connection was frequently made that viewed feminism and lesbianism as synonymous. Feminists were labeled lesbians, and lesbians as feminists. Attacks against feminists—Chicanas, Blacks, and Asian Americans—derived from the existence of homophobia within each of these communities. As lesbian women of color published their writings, attacks against them increased.

Responses to such attacks varied within and between the feminist movements of women of color. Some groups tried one strategy and later adopted another. Some lesbians pursued a separatist strategy within their own racial and ethnic communities. Others attempted to form lesbian coalitions across racial and ethnic lines. Both strategies represented a response to the marginalization of lesbians produced by recurrent waves of homophobic sentiments in Chicano, Black, and Asian American communities. A third response consisted of working within the broader nationalist movements in these communities and the feminist movements within them in order to challenge their heterosexual biases and resultant homophobia. As early as 1974, the "Black

Feminist Statement" written by a Boston-based feminist group—the Combahee River Collective—stated: "We struggle together with Black men against racism, while we also struggle with Black men against sexism." Similarly, Moraga challenged the white feminist movement to examine its racist tendencies; the Chicano movement, its sexist tendencies; and both, their homophobic tendencies. In this way, Moraga argued that such movements to end oppression would begin to respect diversity within their own ranks.

Chicana feminists as well as Chicana feminist lesbians continued to be labeled *vendidas* or "sellouts." Chicana loyalists continued to view Chicana feminism as associated, not only with melting into white society, but more seriously, with dividing the Chicano movement. Similarly, many Chicano males were convinced that Chicana feminism was a divisive ideology incompatible with Chicano cultural nationalism. Nieto Gomez said that "[with] respect to [the] Chicana feminist, their credibility is reduced when they are associated with [feminism] and white women." She added that, as a result, Chicana feminists often faced harassment and ostracism within the Chicano movement. Similarly, Cotera stated that Chicanas "are suspected of assimilating into the feminist ideology of an alien [white] culture that actively seeks our cultural domination."

Chicana feminists responded quickly and often vehemently to such charges. Flores answered these antifeminist attacks in an editorial in which she argued that birth control, abortion, and sex education were not merely "white issues." In response to the accusation that feminists were responsible for the "betrayal of [Chicano] culture and heritage," Flores said, "Our culture hell"—a phrase that became a dramatic slogan of the Chicana feminist movement.

Chicana feminists' defense throughout the 1970s against those claiming that a feminist movement was divisive for the Chicano movement was to reassess their roles within the Chicano movement and to call for an end to male domination. Their challenges of traditional gender roles represented a means to achieve equality. In order to increase the participation of and opportunities for women in the Chicano movement, feminists agreed that both Chicanos and Chicanas had to address the issue of gender inequality. Furthermore, Chicana feminists argued that the resistance that they encountered reflected the existence of sexism on the part of Chicano males and the antifeminist attitudes of the Chicana loyalists. Nieto Gomez, reviewing the experiences of Chicana feminists in the Chicano movement, concluded that Chicanas "involved in discussing and applying the women's question have been ostracized, isolated and ignored." She argued that "in organizations where cultural nationalism is extremely strong, Chicana feminists experience intense harassment and ostracism."

 # The Asian-American Movement, 1960s–1980s

SUCHENG CHAN

The civil-rights movement was launched in the late 1950s and early 1960s as African Americans increasingly refused to sit in the backs of buses in the Deep South and as black and white students took direct action to integrate lunch counters and other public facilities in various parts of the country. Few Asian Americans participated in this first phase of the movement. Indeed, it was not until the mid-1960s that Asian-American high school and college students, mostly on East and West Coast campuses, became actively involved in the social-protest movements sweeping the country.

The Asian-American movement that began in the late 1960s can be seen as an offshoot of the civil-rights movement, but by the time it got under way, the concept of black power had overtaken the integrationist approach of earlier years. In a climate that valued racial and ethnic separatism and community power, Asian-American activists demanded the establishment of Asian-American studies programs on university campuses, exposed the ineffectiveness of the conservative leaders who had ruled over America's Chinatowns, Japantowns, and Manilatowns, and set up social-service agencies to serve better the needs of aging, poor, needy, and disfranchised workers.

Much of the radicalism in the Asian-American movement has been spent, but many of the community agencies it spawned are still functioning, and many of its activists remain dedicated to their cause, now serving an ever more heterogeneous immigrant clientele. Just as important, the ethnic pride and cultural awakening that accompanied this political activism have found expression in an outpouring of poems, short stories, novels, plays, posters, paintings, films, and dances that explore the Asian-American experience. Some of these creative works have received critical acclaim and have become part of a new multiethnic American culture.

STUDY QUESTIONS

1. What led to the emergence of an Asian-American movement?

2. In what sense can the creative writing and artwork that have appeared since the late 1960s be considered products of the Asian-American movement?

The great social movements sweeping the U.S. since the 1960s have . . . transformed the lives of many Asian Americans. Though the number of Asian American activists during these years was small in comparison to the Asian American population as a whole, they have nonetheless earned a secure place in U.S. history by creating a new world for themselves and their communities. . . .

As renewed immigration revitalized Asian American communities, a small number of the American-born second, third, and fourth generations grappled with their identity, questioned their position in American society, and took part in a social movement that shook to the core their communities. . . . By the time that the civil rights movement started by Afro- and Euro-American youths began to attract Latinos and Asian Americans, it had taken a separatist turn as black power advocates split from Euro-American liberals and radicals. Thus, as Asian Americans became involved in the fight for civil rights, they did so largely in a nonintegrated setting, but they were greatly influenced by the political style of the black activists. . . .

The antiwar movement attracted considerably more attention among Asian Americans than did the civil rights struggles. Youthful Asian Americans, who had been trying so hard to assimilate—indeed, to forget, or even deny, their cultural heritage—suddenly with the unwitting aid of the television evening news realized that the people being killed by American forces in that war were Asians. The more radical among them perceived a direct link between imperialism abroad and racism at home. Asian American draftees found themselves caught in the bind of fighting against people who looked like themselves. . . .

Still another development that influenced the style of the nascent Asian American movement was China's Great Proletarian Cultural Revolution which began in 1966 and ended ten years later. Like the Red Guards, Asian American activists, though far smaller in number, challenged all authority, recited slogans from the "Little Red Book" of Chairman Mao Tse-tung, denounced individuals and institutions, spent countless hours in meetings, practiced collective leadership and a democratic workstyle, and engaged in sectarian struggles among themselves. Instead of going to the countryside to learn from the masses as Red Guards in China were doing, the Asian American activists rediscovered—or rather, discovered for the first time—their own ethnic communities and sought to organize workers and establish social service agencies there. The activists—who may be broadly divided into the young professionals with a reformist orientation, and college students and others who considered themselves revolutionaries—tackled serious problems that had never before been properly addressed, but their success was uneven.

Excerpted from Sucheng Chan, *Asian Californians*, 1991, pp. 139–141, 160–167. Reprinted by permission from Material for Today's Learning, Inc.

Their youthful inexperience, their preoccupation with style, the strenuous resistance of the establishment within Asian American communities . . . , and the lack of responsiveness by the white power structure, which was more concerned about the more numerous and more militant blacks than about Asian Americans, proved stumbling blocks. The greatest resistance came from within their own ethnic groups. When they called attention to the hidden problems in their communities—such as the overcrowded and unsanitary conditions in Chinatown's tenements or the exploitation of immigrant workers in restaurants and sewing factories—in order to make claims on government resources, many traditional community leaders reacted in anger. They wanted, instead, to take care of these problems themselves and condemned any attempt to wash dirty linen in public.

Still, the activists accomplished a great deal. They showed other Asian Americans (including members of the middle class and even the conservative establishment) the efficacy of political action. Though they themselves usually disapproved of electoral politics, their efforts to bring about social change encouraged moderate Asian Americans to exercise their political power. Many of the community social service agencies they established, such as local health clinics staffed with bilingual professionals and organizations of law students and young lawyers providing free or low-cost legal services, have endured even in the face of severe cutbacks in federal funding. In education, bilingual programs, though their quality is uneven, exist in many school districts, while ethnic studies programs struggle for survival and legitimacy on university campuses. In the world of culture, writers, artists, actors, musicians, and dancers have produced creative works that portray realistically the Asian historical and contemporary experience in America....

. . . The novels, short stories, plays, paintings, sculptures, dances, and movies of Asian Americans, especially since the 1970s, contain many complex themes, but the search for identity runs as a common thread through most of them. Some writers, like Frank Chin, assert the unique identity of Asian Americans by rejecting both Asian immigrant and Euro-American culture. "As far as I'm concerned," states Chin, who first attracted wide public attention in 1972 with his play *The Chickencoop Chinaman*, "Americanized Chinese who came over in their teens and later to settle here and American born Chinamen have nothing in common, culturally, intellectually, emotionally. . . . We're not interchangeable. Our sensibilities are not the same." Chin depicts Chinatown as a decrepit, decayed, and dying community, from which his protagonists, such as the ones in his short stories "Food for All His Dead" (1972) and "Yes, Young Daddy" (1975), try desperately to escape while lashing out at the racist society that has emasculated them. Not only does Chin not seem to like immigrants, but he is also sarcastic toward some of his fellow Asian American writers who have won approval from Euro-American critics. When Maxine Hong Kingston, author of *The Woman Warrior: Memoirs of a Girlhood among Ghosts* (1976) received favorable reviews, Chin attacked her for attempting to "cash in on the feminist fad." He was equally critical of David Henry Hwang, author of *FOB*, which won the Obie award for the best new off-Broadway play in 1980–1981, and several other well-received plays, including *The Dance and the Railroad* (1981), *Family Devotions* (1981), and *M. Butterfly*, winner of the Tony Award for the best play of 1988. According to Chin, Hwang "works very hard to kiss-up to the white racist stereotypes of the Chinese and Chinese Americans."

In contrast to Chin's negative portrayal of immigrant communities are the short stories of the late Toshio Mori, who saw Japanese ethnic neighborhoods as a source of emotional sustenance for their inhabitants. Mori had a special ability to render pictures of everyday life and the quiet heroism of ordinary people. His anthologies, *Yokohama, California* (1949) and *The Chauvinist and Other Stories* (1979), provide glimpses of individuals who find ways to live in dignity in spite of discrimination and boredom. The aged gardener in "Operator, Operator," for example, is too old to work but nonetheless sits by his telephone waiting for calls that may bring employment, while the protagonist of "The Chauvinist" pretends to be a deaf-mute who has "become deaf to survive the living" and who "in spirit grab[s] the grits of life, scraping for crumbs while cooking up the great feast of life." Amidst gray surroundings, his characters create more interesting worlds in their minds.

The especially painful aspects of the Asian American past have captivated playwrights. The effects of discrimination on a Japanese American family in rural California is the subject of Momoko Iko's *The Gold Watch* (1974). Wakako Yamauchi's *And the Soul Shall Dance* (1977) portrays the hardships of two Japanese American farm families in the Imperial Valley during the Great Depression and the longing of some members to return to Japan, while her *12-I-A* (1982) dramatizes the responses of Japanese Americans to life in the internment camps, ranging from rebellion to superpatriotism. Genny Lim depicts Chinese immigrants in the detention barracks of Angel Island in *Paper Angels* (1982), in which the characters express nostalgia for China and regret its political weakness while voicing anger over their maltreatment at the hands of U.S. immigration officials.

The moral dilemmas faced by many Asian Americans have also been the subject of theatrical creation. In *Honey Bucket* (1976), Mel Escueta portrays the life of a Filipino-American who fought in the Vietnam war and had to live with the guilt of having killed fellow-Asian men, women, and children. Writing the play became a form of therapy for Escueta, himself a Filipino American Vietnam veteran, who had to deal with "the whole wrenching sadness" of that experience. *Point of Order* (1983) by Rick Shiomi confronts the decision that Gordon Hirabayashi made when he disobeyed orders to leave for an internment camp.

Some of the historical themes that have fascinated playwrights have also been made the subject of films. Loni Ding has produced *Nisei Soldier: Stan-*

dard Bearer for an Exiled People (1984) and *The Color of Honor* (1987) about the World War II experiences of Japanese Americans who volunteered for service in the army while their families were incarcerated in camps. *The Color of Honor*, with its compelling vignettes of many individuals who served, as well as some who refused to do so, was aired on the Public Broadcasting System network in January 1989 in eleven major metropolitan areas across the U.S. It introduced many American viewers, perhaps for the first time, to the human dimensions of the gross injustice that was perpetrated upon an entire ethnic group. Another fine film, *Unfinished Business* (1984), by Steven Okazaki, depicts the moral courage of Korematsu, Yasui, and Hirabayashi as these men reflected on the circumstances that led them to resist an order that so many others obeyed. *Unfinished Business* is especially effective in bringing out the intergenerational continuity in the Asian American experience. By capturing something of the Asian American activist spirit, as it is expressed by the young lawyers who took up the three men's cause, it offers hope that the wrongs done the fathers and mothers can sometimes be righted by the sons and daughters.

The experiences of other Asian Americans have also been graphically rendered on film and videotape. *Mississippi Triangle* (1983), by Christine Choy, deals with an unusual group of Chinese Americans—the descendants of Chinese men who settled in the Mississippi Delta and who, in many cases, married black women. The story of this group, when compared to that of Chinese Californians, reminds us that the Asian American experience is by no means a homogeneous one. *Carved in Silence* (1988), by Felicia Lowe, explores the legacy of Angel Island, an immigration station in San Francisco Bay in which thousands of aspiring Chinese immigrants were held—sometimes for years—as their right to land was minutely investigated.

Dollar a Day, Ten Cents a Dance (1984), by Mark Schwartz and Geoffrey Dunn, brings to life old Filipino farmworkers who toiled for decades to bring in California's harvests. *In No One's Shadow* (1988), by Naomi and Antonio De Castro, portrays the history of Filipinos in many regions of the country, including Louisiana, where dozens (probably men originally brought to Mexico during the voyages of the Manila galleons) had settled in the 1780s, long before any Filipinos came to Hawaii and California. New immigrants from India are shown in *The New Puritans: The Sikhs of Yuba City* (1987), by Ritu Sarin and Tenzing Sonam. Scenes of a traditional wedding ceremony taking place in the 1980s in a California town are juxtaposed against conversations with Asian Indian teenagers speaking accentless American English—highlighting the coexistence of Asian and Euro-American cultures in their families. The struggle of Vietnamese refugee fishermen for survival can be seen in *Monterey's Boat People* (1982), by Spencer Nakasako, a film that explores in a balanced way the conflicting concerns of local Euro-American residents and their new neighbors. *Becoming American* (1982), by Ken Levine, follows a Hmong family as it found its way from a refugee camp in Thailand to Seattle, recording for posterity the sense of bewilderment that these newcomers experienced as they learned to cope with modern Western life.

Aside from making documentaries, a few Asian Americans have also produced commercial films. Wayne Wang's *Chan Is Missing* (1981), which became the talk of the art film circuit, offers an insider's view of a contemporary American Chinatown. As the audience is drawn into the efforts of a middle-aged man and his nephew to solve a mystery (the disappearance of a friend who made off with a large sum of money), we meet a range of characters who indirectly convey the message that Chinese Americans, like other people, are not all cut from the same cloth. A subsequent film of Wang's, *Dim Sum* (1987), sensitively portrays the relationship between an aging Chinese American mother and one of her daughters, exploring, in the process, not only intergenerational relationships, but also changing Chinese American attitudes towards marriage, the family, and the community. Another commercial film, *The Wash* (1988), by Philip Kan Gotanda, author of half a dozen plays, also probes new roles that older Asian Americans now feel free to assume. In the film, a sixty-year-old Japanese American woman leaves her husband for a younger man, but feels obligated, nevertheless, to return weekly to her former home to do her husband's laundry. The dumbfounded reaction of her daughter upon encountering the mother's lover on a Sunday morning visit, the woman's own poignant justification of her right to happi-

Asian-American youth demonstrating against U.S. involvement in the war in Vietnam

ness, her husband's stoic attempt to cope with his loss, all pull at the heart-strings in ways that no scholarly studies of the Asian American experience can possibly do. Because the film speaks eloquently about universal human concerns, it, like *Dim Sum*, entices a non-Asian audience as well as an Asian American one.

Asian American writers, playwrights, and filmmakers have tackled important aspects of their people's history in the U.S., but as their works proliferate, critics have noticed that there are significant gender differences in how the men and women artists deal with their subjects. Asian American male writers have generally not depicted women sympathetically (Toshio Mori is an exception), but Asian American women writers have transformed the difficult and complex lives of their mothers, sisters, and daughters into works of art. The childhood of girls born of Chinese immigrant parents is compellingly portrayed by Maxine Hong Kingston, who weaves together myth and reality to convey a sense of the rich yet troubling cultural legacy under which Chinese Americans live. The narrator in her *The Woman Warrior* (1976) is confused not only by her multiple role models, ranging from Fa Mu Lan, the legendary sword-wielding woman warrior of Chinese history, to Moon Orchid, the abandoned and abused aunt of the narrator, but also by at least three different cultures which surround her: Chinese tradition as it was practiced in China, the culture created by the emigrant villagers in California, and the culture of white America. "How do you separate what is peculiar to childhood, to poverty, insanities, one family, your mother who marked your growing with stories, from what is Chinese? What is Chinese tradition and what is the movies?"

Writing the book became for Kingston a way to unravel the various forces that shaped her childhood. Because children were not allowed to question what they did not understand, "Those of us in the first American generation have had to figure out how the invisible world the emigrants built around our childhoods fit in solid America. . . . The emigrants confused the gods. They must try to confuse their offspring as well, who, I suppose, threaten them in similar ways—always trying to get things straight, always trying to name the unspeakable." To escape the psychological grip of the legends they were told and the superstitious beliefs they were taught, the narrator's siblings "made up their minds to major in science and mathematics" in order to develop rational views of life. The narrator herself, however, became a writer, and to her, "The reporting is the vengeance—not the beheading, not the gutting, but the words. And I have so many words—'chink' words and 'gook' words too. . . ." And, it might be added, the misogynous words of male relatives and fellow villagers.

Playwrights Bernadette Cha, Barbara Noda, and Velina Hasu Houston explore the relationships among women and between women and men. Bernadette Cha's *Salted Linen* (1981) is set against the backdrop of the Korean War and probes the disagreement between a mother and daughter searching for their lost husband/father. In her *Aw Shucks!* (1981), Barbara Noda describes the lives of three Asian American lesbians, a minority within a minority, as they grapple with the dilemma of making public their sexual orientation. Velina Hasu Houston, the daughter of a black American father and a Japanese mother, has written a trilogy (1985) about Japanese war brides. In the first play, *Asa Ga Kimashita*, a Japanese woman leaves her family for the city where she discards traditional ways and falls in love with an American soldier who is half black and half Native American. The second play, *American Dreams*, depicts the war bride and her husband trying to adjust to life in New York, while in the third, *Tea*, four of five Japanese war brides living in Kansas—where they were "the first yellow faces in a land of yellow hair and yellow wheat"—gather at the funeral of the fifth who had gone crazy, shot her husband (because "he laughed at my soy sauce once too often"), and apparently committed suicide. The five women's different adaptations to American society are poignantly depicted.

Another popular theme of women writers has been the seemingly crazy women for whom madness is not only a form of rebellion but also a way to retain their creative impulse. These mad women become mirrors reflecting the contradictions in the lives of sane people. In "The Legend of Miss Sasagawara" (1950), Hisaye Yamamoto contrasts the hopeful daydreams of two young Nisei girls in an internment camp with the bizarre behavior of an unloved spinster who had gone insane. In her poem "Crazy Alice" (1978), Janice Mirikitani creates another memorable female character who shocks a wedding party by showing up with disheveled hair and torn clothes and asking who the bride is, only to be told she is Alice's own daughter.

Perhaps to get away from the painful and serious subject matter of so many Asian American works, some playwrights have used the detective story as a light-hearted device for looking at—perhaps spoofing—Asian American community life. Rick Shiomi's *Yellow Fever* (1982) uses the doings of the private eye Sam Shizake—styled after gumshoe Sam Spade—to take his audience on a tour of the Japanese American community in Vancouver, introducing them to a variety of archetypical characters.

A number of writers have been especially concerned with capturing the language of Asian Americans. Milton Murayama, author of *All I Asking for Is My Body* (1975), a novel about Japanese Americans on a Hawaiian plantation, initially published the work himself because he wanted to make sure that the pidgin he so carefully preserved would not be "corrected" into standard English. Jeffrey Paul Chan, whose *Auntie Tsia Lays Dying* (1972) relates the tale of a Chinese immigrant woman, was afraid that editors would force him to change the ungrammatical title. Japanese American poets Ron Tanaka, Garrett Hongo, and Janice Mirikitani interweave Japanese words and expressions into their English poems, while Chinese American novelist Louis Chu inserts literal translations of Cantonese colloquial expressions and swear words into the dialogues in his novel, *Eat a Bowl of Tea* (1961).

Asian American audio, visual, and performing artists have also gained national visibility during the last two decades. From the small but significant beginning made by Chris Iijima, Joanne Miyamoto, and Charlie Chin who recorded *A Grain of Sand* (1973), the first Asian American album, many musical groups have sprung up, composing songs drawing on a variety of cultural traditions. The emphasis in the 1970s on creating art for the people produced hundreds, perhaps thousands, of beautiful and striking posters and mural paintings on the walls and bulletin boards of Asian American community centers. Dance companies performing works choreographed by Asian Americans have also appeared and remain in existence largely because of the dedication of their members.

Regardless of the medium or the genre or the artistic quality of individual pieces, Asian American works of art play a vital role in capturing, reconstructing, and preserving the past. They give voice to the perceptions, feelings, thoughts, and aspirations of a heterogeneous group whose members have until recently been seen as quiet, unassertive, and foreign. By breaking silence, Asian American writers and artists are shattering the negative stereotypes that have dominated the wider public's view of their people. In the process, they are forging a pan-Asian American consciousness that cuts across national origins and class backgrounds.

Black Studies and Higher Education, 1960s–1980s

KAREN KARLETTE MILLER

Black studies departments in American colleges and universities grew out of the civil-rights movement. Most of them were started not in the South, the region that is usually the focal point in studies of the African-American struggle for equality, but in California and the Northeast. Although we typically associate civil-rights protest, violence, and troop intervention with places like Little Rock, Arkansas, and Selma, Alabama, violence and force occurred also at state institutions of higher learning in San Francisco, Berkeley, and Los Angeles in 1968 and 1969 as the movement to establish ethnic studies programs gained momentum and as black students became increasingly militant.

California's black students, empowered by calls for black power and racial pride, demanded a revamping of the curriculum and the hiring of African-American faculty at San Francisco State College and several campuses of the University of California. The controversy provoked considerable debate and led to some bloodshed at these schools, yet the establishment of African-American studies departments or programs facilitated the introduction of La Raza (or Chicano), Native American, Asian-American, and women's studies at about the same time. The following selection examines this controversial change in higher education.

STUDY QUESTIONS

1. What role did students play in getting black studies and other ethnic studies programs established?

2. How did the Black Studies Department at the University of California, Santa Barbara, attempt to differentiate itself from the more traditional departments?

There was nothing conventional about black studies' entry into the academy. Even on campuses that did not experience strikes, demonstrations, vandalism, and other student demands, the eruption of turmoil at other universities prompted administrative committees to work toward increasing the black presence in the curriculum and in the academic community in general. Disruptions on the scale of those at the University of California, Berkeley, or at San Francisco State College profoundly influenced general perceptions of black studies and black students in the late 1960s. To understand the evolution of black studies, it is necessary to understand the civil-rights and black power movements of which it was a part. This history is what sets black studies apart from many of its humanities and social-science counterparts. . . .

The black power movement and riots in predominantly black communities during the "long, hot summers" of 1965 and 1966 contributed to interracial hostility, suspicion, and an erosion of white support for black activism. Angry and frustrated blacks, weary of the gradualist approach of the civil-rights movement, rioted in Watts, Detroit, Newark, and elsewhere. Instead of "We Shall Overcome," Afro-Americans now sang "We Shall Overrun." Moderate blacks and sympathetic whites advised the frustrated to be patient, but to little avail. . . . Though it had seemed acceptable to charge

Karen K. Miller, "Black Studies in California Higher Education, 1965–1980" (Ph.D. diss., University of California, Santa Barbara, 1986), edited excerpt from pp. 18–20, 25–26, and 135–142. This selction was excerpted by Douglas Henry Daniels and edited by Sucheng Chan.

The author gratefully acknowledges the generous assistance and support of Carl V. Harris, Patricia Cline Cohen, and the Center for Black Studies at the University of California, Santa Barbara.

the South with racism, segregation, and discrimination, white "backlash" hardened when these same charges were leveled against American society and its institutions in general. In the public mind and in the mass media, the civil-rights movement associated with Martin Luther King, Jr., his methods of nonviolence and passive resistance, and the goal of racial integration had been supplanted by "black militancy"—a phrase used to describe blacks who were "against nonviolence as a tactic and integration as a goal." In short, the concept of black power heightened racial tensions. . . .

The specific sequence of events that led to the development of formal black studies programs and departments varied, depending on the individual campus. Each campus, however, reflected and was affected by the racial tensions of the period. Students complained about institutional racism and educational irrelevance. They talked about black nationalism. Private citizens and unsympathetic members of the university perceived these criticisms as ungracious responses to institutional efforts to give a break to poverty-stricken, academically deficient minorities. To many Californians, black students asked for more than universities could or should provide. Given the apparent proliferation of opportunities for minority students, their rocking the boat with complaints seemed incomprehensible. Student unrest constituted a particularly volatile issue for California's citizens because of the impending 1968 elections and the important role played by state bond issues for financing public higher education in the state's university and state-college systems. In addition, there was the issue of charging resident California students an educational fee to attend one of the state's public institutions of higher learning. Parents and alumni, private citizens and public servants, political groups and organizations all wrote their representatives and university administrators asking about black student unrest, particularly on public university campuses.

One incident that generated letters from California citizens occurred on October 14, 1968, at the University of California, Santa Barbara (UCSB). Twenty members of the Black Student Union (BSU) took over North Hall, the building that housed the campus computer center. They made eight demands, including "development of a College of Black Studies with black instructors, and a graduate program in Afro-American Studies." They also demanded hiring more black career staff and administrative personnel and the formation of a commission to "investigate problems resulting from personal and individual racism." Though students threatened to destroy the computer center during the nine-and-a-half-hour occupation, the situation ended peacefully after administrators promised to investigate and take action to redress BSU grievances. . . .

Administrators who consented to student demands for a black studies unit had a stake in the program's survival, if there were people in whom they believed the program could be safely entrusted. Antagonists, however, opposed black studies programs partially because the decision to establish them often was made without extensive consultation with the faculty. If it were possible to revamp rather than raze a program, not only would doing so preserve administrative credibility, but it could also salvage the initial investment in the program. . . .

Another factor that kept some programs alive may have been a fear of resurgent turmoil. In addition to the protests at the Santa Barbara and Berkeley campuses over administrative changes, students and some faculty at San Francisco State College discussed, but did not undertake, another strike action when college president S. I. Hayakawa fired all of the black studies faculty at the end of the 1969–1970 academic year. In 1975 black students at UCSB occupied the North Hall computer center once again amidst rumors that the Center for Black Studies might be disestablished.

Patricia Thornton, former acting dean of the School of Ethnic Studies at San Francisco State, was one of those fired "without reason" in 1970. Attempts to organize a strike failed principally because, as Thornton recalled,

> When we had demonstrations, they now had helicopters, they had cameras on the roofs, they had police . . . on horseback. They were just overtly intimidating us from demonstrating peacefully. They would beat people brutally without any provocation whatsoever. . . . [But] the department was reopened the next year. There were people in the Arts area that argued that the community needed the Black Studies Department even if it wasn't autonomous; and, we [who were fired] were not going to concede the autonomy of the Black Studies Department.

As approval of Afro-American studies programs lessened the intensity of racial conflict on campuses, protests against American involvement in the Vietnam War surfaced. . . . Unrest at UCSB, for instance, diverted attention away from the Black Studies Department and toward incidents that culminated in the burning of the Bank of America in the nearby community of Isla Vista in early 1970.

A lack of substantial progress in increasing the proportion of black academic and administrative personnel outside of black studies might also be a factor in the survival of some programs. Jonas Richmond and David Blackwell, faculty members at Berkeley for more than twenty-five years, recalled a noticeable increase in black faculty during and shortly after the black student movement began and the Afro-American Studies Program there was established. James Hirabayashi, an anthropologist at San Francisco State, maintains that "minority hiring among the ethnic studies faculty increased, but not in campuswide faculty appointments." At UCSB, the number of black scholars increased from one at the end of the 1968–1969 school year to twelve at the end of the 1984–1985 academic year. Of those twelve, ten are or were affiliated with the Black Studies Department. Although the motives were not always the most altruistic, institutions that otherwise might have dismantled their black studies program or department did not do so. The people affiliated with black studies probably played a significant role in the survival of each program or department. Where there was a willingness and ability to move toward program development consistent with traditional academic standards and structure, black studies survived. The shifts away from direct activism were, in many cases, voluntary. . . . At the same time, there was an element of coercion—a recognition that continued insistence on the "right" to be different from other segments of the academy would likely result in dissolution.

Compromise and conformity on the part of blacks studies faculty did not necessarily mean a wholesale abandonment of the "education for liberation" premise. Rather, strategies for racial uplift and educational relevance were recast in a more "traditionally academic" mold. At the University of California, Berkeley, for instance, there remained a commitment to serve the interests of the surrounding black community, but not by direct action. Attention shifted toward the "theoretical and pedagogical issues presented in classroom instruction." This shift in emphasis is justified, according to William Banks, who chaired the Afro-American Studies Department at Berkeley for some years, because

> . . . Afro-American Studies, in structuring community-involved educational activities, recognized that the primary focus of the activity must be the intellectual growth of the student, not service to the community. It is hard not to imagine that a corps of solidly trained and motivated college graduates would not be of invaluable service to communities and societies at large.

In other words, as Barbara Christian, another Berkeley Afro-American studies faculty member, reiterated, black scholars increasingly realized that "ideas were weapons as much as community activity." Part of the process of developing in that direction, according to Christian, was hiring scholars with a commitment to "solid methodology and sensitivity to the important issues related to Afro-American life and culture and the knowledge and information that is derived from such systematic and imaginative intellectual inquiry." Though the strategies diverged from earlier rhetoric, the goals remained the same—that is, in Christian's words, "teaching, research, and public service can contribute to [the] building of a more humane and just society."

The movement toward hiring academically trained faculty with advanced degrees who potentially could receive tenure reflected the need for stability as well as credibility in black studies. Lecturers and temporary appointees were used to augment, not supersede, the permanent faculty. During the initial phase, the emphasis on hiring black people in Afro-American studies and the number of programs slated to begin during the 1969–1970 academic year far exceeded the supply of scholars available to move into newly created tenure-track positions. At the same time, however, students deemphasized degrees and stressed blackness, commitment, experience, teaching ability, and political perspective. "A good many 'courses,'" Donald Henderson wrote, "were to be designed and taught by students." *The temporary nature of students and lecturers hired on year-to-year contracts contributed to a "revolving door" situation in black studies, not necessarily because of a lack of ability but because it was hard to plan systematically, given the turnover in personnel.

Lack of career security was implicit in this situation. At San Francisco State, Berkeley, Santa Barbara, and elsewhere, many of the temporary faculty divided their time between teaching and working for advanced degrees in the hope of moving into tenure-track positions. But their teaching loads and their graduate studies often precluded sustained research that would lead to the publications necessary for tenure. Furthermore, as Gerard Pigeon, former chair of UCSB's Black Studies Department, has argued, pressures affected tenure-track and temporary faculty alike. Even after ten years in operation, the faculty

> were all given demanding administrative assignments. Their duties as administrators, coupled with the necessity of collecting, organizing, and teaching a newly formed discipline, forced them to somewhat neglect their publications. Moreover, having to answer the ever increasing needs of students for counseling and tutoring, they channeled their energy into areas not recognized by the university for advancement and promotion. As a result, when the tension eased and no threat was to be feared, they were either terminated, denied tenure, or advised to look for [jobs at] other institutions. . . . Many times instructors had to go out of their specialties so we could offer more diversity to interested students. This action in turn put more pressure on the already overburdened teachers [who] . . . had to devote more time to research not necessarily related to their specialties in order to prepare adequate material for their classes. As a result, . . . their publication records suffered and they were faced with the eventuality of dismissal.

Given the small number of faculty members in the department and the comparatively high student-to-faculty ratio, releasing faculty from their teaching duties so they might improve their research and publication records posed another set of problems. Rather than adopt that strategy, Pigeon recalls, "we have always been stopped by the fact that this action would reduce our enrollment and therefore open our flank to criticism and possible dismemberment of the department." Pressures of the sort described by Pigeon did not disappear, despite the department's seeking out qualified tenure-track and tenured faculty.

It would be overstating the case to argue that still existing black studies programs and departments are now entrenched in the academy. In earlier

---

* Donald Henderson, "What Direction Black Studies?" in Henry Richards, ed., *Topics in Afro-American Studies* (Buffalo: Black Academy Press, 1978).

years, bitterly divisive confrontations within and outside of black studies weakened it, but by the 1980s retrenchment in the field winnowed out the weakest programs and left the survivors in varying stages of development. Black studies practitioners, with some exceptions, now seem less concerned with survival. It is no longer a burning question. . . . Rather, debate presently centers on resolving differences in teaching styles, determining what theories to use to explain certain phenomena, and defining research methods within black studies. A secondary debate entails which structural arrangement holds the most promise for black studies' future. Many issues still under consideration are holdovers from the initial period because the rush to get programs under way left little time to forge a consensus about what legitimately constitutes black studies.

 The Occupation of Alcatraz Island, 1969–1970

JUDITH ANTELL

American Indians' occupation of Alcatraz Island in 1969 marked a major event in the civil-rights struggle waged by Native Americans in the 1960s and 1970s. In this reading, Judith Antell, a mixed-blood Chippewa and one of the first two persons to earn a doctorate in ethnic studies, interviews Rosalie McKay, a Pomo Indian who is head librarian of the Native American Studies Library at the University of California, Berkeley, about her experience as a participant in the Alcatraz takeover. The interview offers insights into the dynamics of male-female interactions within the urban Indian community and Native American women's roles as leaders.

Seventy-eight Indians landed on Alcatraz before dawn on November 20, 1969. They claimed the land "in the name of all American Indians by right of discovery." They had chosen Alcatraz because the grounds of the former prison were not in use and under federal law could revert back to the original owners; Indians had once lived on the island. Attracting support from Native Americans nationwide, a shifting group of "Indians of All Tribes" held their ground for nineteen months before being removed by federal marshals. The protesters' hope was to focus media attention on Indians' struggle for self-determination and for the redress of past grievances perpetrated by a nation whose government had failed to fulfill treaty obligations and whose public had largely forgotten or ignored its native survivors. The American public responded to this and other political confrontations staged by Indian activists to promote justice during the following decade. Alcatraz acted as a catalyst to activism, provided a continuing sense of pride for individual Native Americans, and proved the efficacy of pan-Indian organization.

STUDY QUESTIONS

1. What did the Native Americans who occupied Alcatraz Island want?

2. Do you think that the occupation was a success? If so, in what ways? If not, why not?

3. Compare the struggles of the Indians to those of other U.S. minority groups fighting for their civil rights.

Rosalie McKay found her own life affected and changed by the occupation of Alcatraz Island in November 1969. While living there with her children, Rosalie traveled almost every day to Merritt College and the University of California, Berkeley, in order to complete fall-semester classes at both institutions. As one of the first permanent residents of Alcatraz, Rosalie found that her fellow students at Merritt College were very interested in her. As the result of an encounter with a classmate at this time, she also discovered that outward appearances can be deceiving.

> I was still finishing up at Merritt. It was the winter quarter at Merritt and I was taking one class at UC and two at Merritt. I would talk about Alcatraz in my public speaking class at Merritt. The teacher said the only reason she gave me a high grade was because of the subject since my voice wouldn't carry to the back of the room. But everybody would get real quiet and listen and she said the only reason was because I was telling about Alcatraz.
>
> There was a policeman who was taking our class. He was very rigid and things were either black or white. He wore short, cropped hair and that's when the hippies were letting it all hang out. I can't remember what he would talk about in class but everybody would disagree with him right off because he was a policeman. And I didn't really have anything to say to him during the whole class. And then we were taking a break one day and he came over to me and gave me a check for $25 for Alcatraz and he said, "I have a boat and I can take supplies out to the island. Get in touch with me." And I couldn't believe it because he seemed so rigid and anti-everything. And here he was with all these feelings way underneath.

"American Indian Women Activists" (Ph.D. diss., University of California, Berkeley, 1989) by Judith Antell, edited excerpt from pp. 99–106 and 108–115. Reprinted by permission of the author.

In spite of the inconveniences of daily travel back and forth from the island to the mainland in order to continue her classes and in spite of her obviously altered personal life, Rosalie managed to finish both fall and spring semesters of the school year 1969–1970.

> At first at our meetings on Alcatraz we decided that the college students would have first dibs on the first boat out in the morning, and that worked out all right for a while. I would go to classes and I was still keeping my apartment because I was in low-income housing and I didn't want to lose my place, so I just kept on paying rent. And I was getting food stamps so we would donate our food stamps to Alcatraz whenever we needed food. But for a while we really didn't need to because people were donating food and we had food galore.
>
> Then some people started getting into trouble on the mainland. I think some of them were stealing copper from the island and selling it. And then there were other things. People were getting DUI's [driving under the influence] or speeding tickets or things where they had to show up in court early in the mornings. So those people started taking the first boat and a lot of us who were taking classes started missing them.
>
> I started doing really bad in my foreign language class because you have to be there every day. I ended up getting an F and that dragged my grade point way down. I went from being on the Dean's List to being on probation.

While Rosalie was coming to the mainland for classes, her children were being educated on the island.

> We started a school on Alcatraz. It was a good school, and the teachers who worked there really cared and were doing it their way. I think the children who went there really benefitted. All my kids went to school there and Elvin, my oldest, ended up tutoring the younger kids.

I was interested to know if the children's schooling on Alcatraz Island was considered by the public school system to be adequate for their promotion to the next grade the following year. Schooled on the island from November until May, they missed most of the regular school year on the mainland. Rosalie explained to me that the children went back into public school the following year and advanced without problem into the next grades. This was due largely to the fact that Indian sympathizers working in the Oakland public schools completed the necessary paperwork, attesting to the fact that the children had indeed been in school while on the island. As I offered congratulations for the political savvy of having sympathizers strategically positioned in government bureaucracy, Rosalie pointed out that the level of sophistication was, in fact, quite limited.

> I don't think we were sophisticated. We missed a lot of things that we could have done. I don't think any of us, maybe one or two, had done anything in offices or organization development, and it was like experi-

menting to see if this or that was going to work. Finally we would get it down to the way that it would be if we had studied it and got there in maybe a month's time. Instead it took us maybe a year, just by trial and error.

I asked about the people who came to Alcatraz during the seven months Rosalie and her family lived on the island. What were their tribal affiliations, their jobs, their family lives like back on the mainland? Were they students, members of tribal governments, BIA [Bureau of Indian Affairs] bureaucrats, urban politicos, working-class families, or the professional elite? Had all these people come to stay on Alcatraz for the same reasons? Was there a shared ideology among the occupants, or was every person pursuing his or her individual path? Rosalie shared with me her perspective as one person on Alcatraz with hundreds of others.

There were some professional people. Some people had quit their jobs and come out there. People came from all over the country. We had offices off the island and on the island both, and the professional people kind of took over and ran everything, and that was okay because nobody else knew how to do anything. The majority of us did not know. I was around the office a lot where I saw what was happening. And even though these people were more sophisticated than I was, I could see that they were learning too. They might have been working in offices but the majority weren't directors. There might have been one or two directors in the group, but they couldn't do everything. We had to have a PR place because we just had letters, letters, letters. And, of course, the TV was out there all the time. And we had a lot of money coming in and we just didn't know how to handle everything and some of it got lost. I think that was our downfall—the fact that we didn't have it together politically and in an organizational sense. We lacked management.

The organization and management of the Alcatraz occupation, as described by Rosalie, did have the markings of a spontaneous, largely grass-roots effort. How had it happened, I wanted to know.

The way I see it, it was the students at Berkeley and San Francisco State. We used to meet together all the time for picnics and everything. We would invite one another to our student meetings and they would have something going on, and we'd all go and stay over there, or they would all come over to Berkeley. California Indian Education was starting up at this time and we started meeting. We were also becoming more and more aware politically because of our Indian Studies Program. The first person I remember saying that we should do something about what we were studying and what was happening was Richard Oakes. At the time *The New Indian* was the popular book and we all had to read it. And I think it was Mel Thom who said "Action Now!" instead of just talking about it.

Set in the late 1960s, the takeover of Alcatraz was, of course, part of a much larger movement for social change promoted by people of color in America. I wondered if Rosalie had been able to place the occupation of Alcatraz in its larger context, if she understood at the time, in 1969, that it was part of a bigger picture. I also wondered how being part of the Alcatraz takeover affected Rosalie's sense of Indianness, her racial identity. How did she see herself as an Indian woman in relation to other people, other women of color? How did she see herself in contrast to whites?

> I knew that things were wrong, but I think Alcatraz made me more aware that we could speak out against them, whereas before I would never dream of saying, "Hey, that's not right." Because you just didn't do that. The white people were supreme.

I found this somewhat contradictory considering that Rosalie has told me she never thought whites were superior and that, in fact, she had ridiculed them for their lack of intelligence. Why had she found it so difficult to speak out against whites in the past? Why had she handled tense racial situations with passive aggression? . . .

> It was fear of repercussions. And being around my mother and watching her behavior when the social worker would come around. She would make us hide, for one thing. So right there there's a fear instilled in us. I experience it even now when I have to talk to an administrator or a white book dealer. When I first see a white man in a suit and tie, something stops me for a second. So I stop and think, "Hey, this guy has all the fears and everything that we do." And I make it work. But I think about it even now.
>
> Before Alcatraz I used to think they had ways of putting you down if you said something back. I don't know what I thought they could do to me. Maybe I thought they could take my welfare money away from me because I was acting smart. I thought they had a lot of control, which they did. But I didn't know the extent of it. They've always had so much control in our lives.
>
> But it was Alcatraz and being around other people who felt the same way that changed me. It's not that I thought whites were smart. I didn't. But they had control. The difference is that they had control, and they showed that. I saw it at Stewart [Indian School], I saw it in the towns around the reservation, I saw it in Hawthorne [town near Stewart] where we were discriminated against. They were in total control. I knew they weren't any smarter than I was, and yet they had all this power over me. I hated it.

Just as I searched for information about Rosalie's attitude toward and experiences with the issue of race, I also pursued with her the topic of gender, specifically differences in her perceptions of and relationships with men and women. I wanted to know if white men and women acted out their privileged positions in different manners, if there were distinctions in the ways they imposed power on others.

> White men are usually in high places, and it seems that they have more control. But white women, the ones I've been around, always seem so patronizing. It's like somebody fawning over a little kid and talking baby talk or treating them like they're not human beings. They act like you can't think or hear. They talk louder, like maybe you don't know something and if the they increase the volume they can get through. . . .

The attention paid by the media to the Alcatraz takeover brought newspeople from all over the world. These reporters, journalists, and photographers stayed for varying lengths of time on or near the island, and it became clear to the residents of Alcatraz that it would be in the best interest of the occupation to establish a public relations center on the island, operated and

Sioux tribal members staking claim to Alcatraz Island

controlled by Indians. Rosalie volunteered to help in this center. It was especially through this work that she realized the significance of the takeover.

> I was typing, answering letters and stuff. That's when the impact of it got
> to me, the enormity of what we were doing. We were getting letters from
> all over the world, and it was just great.

Support for the Indians on Alcatraz came in many ways. Letters to be
sure, but also gifts of money, food, and clothes. Some of the donations were
more funny than useful. "We were getting some really goofy things. High
heels and formals and it was freezing out there, it was the middle of winter.
We would go to the gym and play around in the high heels and big, fancy
hats." Support and interest from around the world created the necessity not
only for a public relations center on the island but also for regular meetings,
to keep residents, as well as guests, informed of political strategies, current
events, and other issues of concern.

> We had general meetings every day, and we would talk about negotia-
> tions and other things. At one time we talked about negotiations with
> then Governor Reagan, and some people said, "We don't need to deal
> with the honkies; we don't even need to do that." Very few people had
> the political sophistication to know that you have to negotiate for any-
> thing. That's a sign of maturity when you realize you always have to
> compromise. But a lot of us were naive and said, "Let's just do it!" The
> meetings were really a good thing because you got to meet a lot of differ-
> ent people. You didn't always sit by the same people, so you got to
> exchange information on your tribe. The kids really benefited by realiz-
> ing that there are so many tribes.
>
> The whole community was made aware of who was on the island and
> when and where the meetings would take place. At first we were going to
> put out an information sheet because rumors were being started all over
> the place. But it was hard because we didn't have any money to print.
> And then somebody on the mainland agreed to print for free, and we
> decided to do a newsletter. We had spokesmen, and there was a good
> reason for that because when they stole our land, they just went up to
> anybody and made them a chief and said, "Here, let's make a deal." And
> this way, by having spokespersons, the government officials had to go to
> certain people to talk. At meetings we always decided what was going to
> happen, whether we were going to set up a deadline or whatever. And
> then whoever went to represent us followed our directions.

Rosalie used the terms "us" and "we" so often I came to the conclusion
that the women on the island certainly weren't excluded from the political
process and that most probably the men and women worked cooperatively
together. Was I right? Were women, as well as men, among the leaders of
this occupation movement?

Yes, they were. And there didn't seem to be any conflict. There was a good mix always. Women were involved in Alcatraz from the very beginning. Some of them swam from the boat going over for the first time. Women and men. Some of the Indian women had already been involved on community boards, like the San Francisco Indian Center Board. A friend of mine, in particular. Her mother and a bunch of other women had started the Indian Center, and it was just like sitting around over coffee one day and saying, "We ought to get together and get a place." At Alcatraz, two people rose to the top as leaders. LaNada Means and Richard Oakes, one woman and one man. He stayed on the island, and she stayed on the mainland. When I think of Alcatraz, I always think of those two. They had leadership qualities and were able to hold a crowd's attention. Richard would always open the meetings, and LaNada always did a lot of PR. It seems like she was more involved in dealing with the government.

What kind of qualities does an Indian woman possess in order to become a leader in Indian politics?

I think first of all you have to care about your community. I think you also have to have some charisma. I think LaNada had that quality. I've known women with every imaginable personality who have become leaders. There was a lady on Alcatraz who had a lot of bed partners, and she used to tease and joke about it. She was crazy and she didn't dress "nicely," and yet she was on the council and she could speak in front of the cameras. If you saw her, you would never think this lady was a leader. But she commanded respect in a different way. I thought she was great. I thought she could handle any sort of situation. And she was physically strong. If we went off the island and got into it with anybody and she was along, we always knew we had our slack!

After laughing about this, Rosalie continued, "But she was smart, too, and her ideas carried some weight."

Rosalie's comments about this woman's tendency to have many bed partners reminded me of a conversation I had with another Indian woman about how women might be politically compromised as a result of their promiscuity. I asked Rosalie if she knew of ways in which Indian women had been discredited as leaders or perhaps prevented from becoming leaders. She suggested incompetence was a primary factor, and, in her opinion, sexual habits had little to do with an Indian woman's ability to achieve or maintain a public position.

She might get more votes, in fact. I think she might draw people to her side. Maybe men think they will get something if they say, "I voted for you."

As Rosalie and I continued to talk about Indian women in politics, our conversation focused mainly on work at the grassroots level. Rosalie has been part of the Oakland Indian community for nearly twenty years, and I was interested to learn her point of view concerning Indian community work in an urban setting. The questions I asked her related especially to the roles of women.

> It's usually all women who are on the boards and come to meetings. Men are busy with their jobs, or they're on their union boards or whatever. We have a hard time convincing them that the Indian community is just as important. Any man who ran for a board seat probably got it just because we wanted the male perspective. But I could probably count on my fingers how many of the men took the job seriously. And there's a lot of tension between the men. I never noticed anything between the women. We had the greatest group!

At this point I asked Rosalie if she felt the men she worked with had a greater need than women for personal attention and recognition. Her response was a strong, "Yes!"

> Men want to be the star. They want everybody to laugh at their jokes. It is competition all the way. I think they learn it from Little League on up.

I was curious to know if Indian men were really able to respect and acknowledge the contributions of Indian women, given the fact that the men seemed to need so much attention themselves. Do men outwardly give respect to the efforts of Indian women?

> No. They give respect to other men and to themselves. I don't think they give respect to women. On Alcatraz I didn't notice this, though. LaNada really commanded respect. I think the reason for that is that she came out and said what she thought. She had a following around her all the time, male and female, and she just stood out. Whether they resented it or not, I don't remember. I don't remember anybody resenting her. But one time at a community meeting here in Oakland I remember I made a suggestion, and everybody stopped and listened to me, and then they just picked up where they had left off and went on. And I thought maybe they didn't hear me. But now I know they did. And a little while later, one of the men said the same thing I did, and then they considered it. And I thought, "Well, what am I doing here?" It was a real putdown. This has also been done to me by non-Indian men at Ethnic Studies Department meetings on the Berkeley campus. I think men in general have a tendency to do this—not only Indian men.

Rosalie talked about the competitiveness of Indian men and how she felt that tendency was encouraged from an early age. That led me to wonder about leadership qualities in women. In what ways did Indian women learn to become community leaders? In what arenas did they practice decision making and other organizational skills? In the black community, for example, women have historically been instrumental in politics through a number of channels, including women's associations often connected to churches. Have Indian women had similar avenues for social training?

I think about that a lot because we don't have anything. I started thinking about this because of these young, black girls from Mills College who use the library here. I have been really impressed with their leadership qualities. They belong to Urban League and black women's associations that get them when they are in high school. I talked to one girl a real long time and she was telling me all the things they go through. And it is to get more power in this society. I was thinking if we could only have something like that to grab our youngsters while they are coming up. We don't have anything for these young kids, especially. I know a lot of women who are interested in community work, but nobody is interested in working with the teenagers. So if our young women get involved with community work, it might be because they just stumble into it. But some young Indian women and men do get experience, sometimes from their parents or other relatives or friends who are active. Some of our young people are quite knowledgeable, but we do need to do more.

FURTHER READING

Paula Gunn Allen, *Recovering the Feminine in American Indian Tradition* (Boston: Beacon Press, 1986).

Russel Lawrence Barsh and James Y. Henderson, *The Road: Indian Tribes and Political Liberty* (Berkeley and Los Angeles: University of California Press, 1980).

Sucheng Chan and L. Ling-chi Wang, "Racism and the Model Minority: Asian-Americans in Higher Education," in *The Racial Crisis in American Higher Education*, ed. Philip G. Altbach and Kofy Lomotey (Albany: State University of New York Press, 1991).

Stephen Cornell, *The Return of the Native: American Indian Political Resurgence* (New York: Oxford University Press, 1988).

Vine Deloria, Jr., *We Talk, You Listen: New Tribes, New Turf* (New York: Macmillan, 1970).

Adam Fortunate Eagle, *Alcatraz! Alcatraz! The Indian Occupation of 1969–1971* (Berkeley: Heyday Books, 1992).

Yen Le Espiritu, *Asian American Panethnicity: Bridging Institutions and Identities* (Philadelphia: Temple University Press, 1992).

F. Chris García, ed., *La Causa Politica: A Chicano Politics Reader* (Notre Dame: University of Notre Dame Press, 1974).

Juan Gomez-Quinones, *Chicano Politics: Reality and Promise, 1940–1990* (Albuquerque: University of New Mexico Press, 1990).

G. Louis Heath, ed., *The Black Panther Leaders Speak: Huey P. Newton, Bobby Seale, Eldridge Cleaver and Company Speak Out Through the Black Panther Party's Official Newspaper* (Metuchen, N.J.: Scarecrow Press, 1976).

Karen Karlette Miller, "Black Studies in California Higher Education, 1965–1980" (Ph.D. dissertation, University of California Santa Barbara, 1986).

Carlos Muñoz, Jr., *Youth, Identity, Power: The Chicano Movement* (London: Verso, 1989).

Stan Steiner, *La Raza: The Mexican Americans* (New York: Harper & Row, 1969).

Stan Steiner, *The New Indians* (New York: Harper & Row, 1967; New York: Dell Pub. Co., 1968).

William Wei, *The Asian American Movement* (Philadelphia: Temple University Press, 1993).

CHAPTER 15

Diversity

R ace, ethnic, and gender relations in the American West have become extremely complex over the past few decades. Although Asian immigration was curtailed by the 1930s, people from Mexico have continued to cross the border in large numbers. And, as we have seen, during World War II, masses of African Americans migrated to the Pacific coast to work in the region's shipyards and war industries. After Congress revamped U.S. immigration laws in 1965, large-scale immigration to America from Asia began anew. Since 1975, a million refugees have come to the United States from Vietnam, Cambodia, and Laos. Meanwhile, people from El Salvador, Nicaragua, Guatemala, Cuba, and other Latin American countries have been entering the country in sizable numbers as immigrants, refugees, and asylum seekers.

Although virtually all regions of the United States have felt the impact of this influx, a disproportionately large percentage of the Asian and Spanish-speaking immigrants have settled in California and Texas. The result, as the 1990 U.S. census of population shows so clearly, is the emergence of a truly multiethnic, multicultural, multilingual society in the American West.

The readings in this chapter document this growing diversity. David M. Reimers briefly discusses the history of what became the Immigration Reform and Control Act of 1986—a law that deeply affected undocumented immigrants, particularly from Mexico. Kwang Chung Kim and Won Moo Hurh correct some misperceptions about Asian Americans' socioeconomic status. Qui-Phiet Tran studies the fiction produced by Vietnamese refugee writers to get an idea of how these expatriates feel and think about their losses and the challenges they face as new Americans. The short excerpts by Mee Her and Ge Lor, two Hmong from Laos, and by Sirathra Som and Salouth Soman, two Cambodians, poignantly profile some refugees who have managed to survive and thrive in the American West.

FOR ANALYSIS AND DISCUSSION

1. Although we have been using the umbrella term *peoples of color,* it is important to recognize that many differences exist among and within the groups considered in this book. What are some of the differences between men and women of color in the West? between the more successful immigrants and refugees and those who are still destitute?

2. What do immigrants and refugees who come to the United States gain, and what do they lose?

3. In what ways are the subjective experiences of some of these refugees different from their observable characteristics?

4. How is the presence of these diverse groups changing the nature of American society?

5. What are the pros and cons of continuing to admit so many immigrants and refugees to the United States?

Controlling the "New" Latino Immigration, 1980s–Present

DAVID M. REIMERS

Mexican immigration to the United States is not a recent phenomenon; as earlier chapters have revealed, it has roots in the nineteenth and early twentieth centuries. Because Mexican immigrants have been flowing across the border into the United States for decades, the Mexican-ancestry population is made up of old and new immigrants as well as of Mexican Americans whose families have been living here for generations. During the 1970s and 1980s, a dramatic spurt in Mexican immigration occurred, particularly of persons who entered without documents—the so-called undocumented aliens or illegals. At the same time, the number of Latino immigrants and refugees from Central America and the Caribbeans rose.

While these recent Mexican and Latino immigrants are more widely scattered throughout the country than were their earlier counterparts, the majority of them enter the southwestern and western labor markets. Consequently, during the 1990s and into the next century, immigration, particularly that of Latinos and Asians, will continue to be a central issue in these regions.

To gain greater control over this Latino influx, the U.S. Congress debated for years over what eventually became the Immigration Reform and Control Act of 1986. As David M. Reimers observes, this act was a "delicate compromise providing for a limited amnesty, employer sanctions, and modifications for the . . . temporary workers program."

STUDY QUESTIONS

1. What "problems" did the 1986 Immigration Reform and Control Act try to address?

2. What is the difference between "undocumented" aliens and people allowed into the country under a temporary-worker program such as the Special Agricultural Worker program?

3. Why did Congress think that employer sanctions were necessary?

In 1982, a coalition developed, led by Democratic Representative Romano Mazzoli and Senator Alan Simpson, to enact a comprehensive immigration reform bill. The Reagan administration . . . set up a task force composed of representatives from many agencies to . . . make recommendations. . . . Reagan wanted an expansion of a temporary worker program. . . . When this proved unpopular, the [Reagan] administration supported the Mazzoli-Simpson bill, but did not consider it a priority item. Proponents of immigration reform could point to growing unemployment and said their bill was not only immigration reform, but also a "jobs bill" as well. They also pointed to public opinion polls taken in the 1970s and one in the fall of 1983, all of which overwhelmingly supported employer sanctions and expressed the public belief that undocumented immigrants caused unemployment. . . .

Basically, the Simpson-Mazzoli bill measure was a delicate compromise providing for a limited amnesty, employer sanctions, and modifications in the H-2 temporary workers program* to possibly admit more temporary agriculture workers. In the Senate the bill as finally passed in August 1982 included a limit of 425,000 on legal immigration, not counting refugees and modified the brothers and sisters fifth preference.** The House committees responsible for the bill eliminated the cap on legal immigration and restored the brothers and sisters of U.S. citizens preference and instead concentrated on the illegal issue.

The Senate passed their bill by an 81 to 18 vote, but in the House it was a different matter. When the representatives finally debated the bill in December, during a special session of Congress, not enough time was left to resolve the issues. Hispanic groups, especially, opposed the employer sanctions proviso, and they had allies who disliked other provisions. Supporters either lacked enthusiasm from representatives in areas where immigration was not an issue or they lacked time to overcome objections to particular parts of the bill. No doubt the confusion of the administration about immigration and its lack of interest also hurt.

In 1983 the Senate again considered and passed the Simpson-Mazzoli measure by a lopsided margin. In the House, however, several committees controlled by the Democrats altered the Senate version. Even these changes were inadequate to ward off defeat. Sensitive to Hispanic organizational

---

From *Still the Golden Door: The Third World Comes to America*, by David M. Reimers, 1985, 2nd rev. ed., pp. 242–252. © Columbia University Press, New York. Reprinted with the permission of the publisher.

* The H-2 program, part of earlier immigration legislation, permits the entry of temporary immigrant workers when it can be certified that a temporary labor shortage exists.
** The brothers and sisters fifth preference refers to family reunification procedures allowing direct kin of legal immigrants to move to the United States and receive permanent resident status.

pressures, Speaker Tip O'Neill told reporters in October that the House would not consider the bill in 1983. The Speaker said that the bill would not be voted upon because the President would veto it. While some administration leaders denied that the President would veto the act, others noted concerns about the cost of an amnesty to illegal aliens and the problems in formulating a worker identification policy. Several weeks later, after much political and editorial outcry, O'Neill indicated a shift and said the bill would be considered by the House in the next session of Congress.

Finally, in June 1984 the House of Representatives held a lengthy debate on the bill and passed it. The debates were heated at times, and the representatives voted on a series of amendments before considering the final bill. The Senate had passed the bill easily, by a four to one margin; but in the House the final vote was extremely close, 216 to 211. . . .

As in the past, the controversial issues dealt with undocumented aliens and temporary workers. Most of the arguments were familiar. Those who favored a compromise wanted an amnesty for undocumented aliens already here in exchange for employer sanctions. This compromise did not satisfy Hispanics and their supporters who wanted stricter enforcement of the labor laws, a generous amnesty, and no sanctions. Nor did it satisfy those, like William McCollum of Florida, who said an amnesty rewarded people for entering illegally and punished those who waited in line for visas. In the end, Romano Mazzoli and his allies won, and employer sanctions and an amnesty carried.

Issues related to the enforcement of the compromise prompted considerable debate. The representatives worried about discriminations against Hispanics and by a 404 to 9 vote included provisions prohibiting discrimination against job applicants because of national origin or alienage. This provision was not in the Senate bill and later caused trouble in conference. The House also rejected use of a national identification card and instead suggested that other documents could be used and left to the future other means of identification.

Congressman Mazzoli had not favored a temporary worker program, but after fierce lobbying, representatives from states wanting laborers to pick their crops managed to win House support for an expanded temporary worker program. This angered organized labor and many others, but its supporters insisted these workers were needed to replace the undocumented ones.

The close votes for individual parts of the bill and the narrow victory of five votes for the final bill indicated the deep divisions about immigration. Because the vote was so close and the House bill differed from the Senate one in several key areas, passage of the Simpson-Mazzoli bill appeared in doubt. Moreover, the Democratic candidates for President and Vice-President said that they opposed the bill. Vice-President George Bush told a group of Hispanics that the administration did not favor any bill that might lead to discrimination against them. But the President indicated another reason for trouble. The administration said it did not wish the federal government to bear the full cost of legalization of undocumented aliens, who would become eligible for governmental assistance programs.

In spite of the gloomy outlook for a conference bill that both houses could accept and the President would sign, House and Senate conferees attempted to find a solution. Although these members of Congress managed to compromise on the dates for legalization for those who had entered illegally and discrimination provisions, they could not agree on funding. But Congress was eager to adjourn so that its members would have time to campaign for the fall elections. Thus Simpson-Mazzoli failed again in 1984.

When the newly elected Congress met in 1985, prospects for passage in the Senate appeared strong again, especially after Senator Simpson became assistant majority leader. Moreover, amnesty was made more acceptable because of promises for increased enforcement of the immigration laws. In September the Senate approved the bill 69 to 30, but the House was a different matter in 1985. However, Peter Rodino, chairman of the House Judiciary Committee, assumed leadership for immigration when he introduced a bill of his own. Rodino had been opposed to a Simpson-Rodino earlier draft that had included cutting the fifth preference for brothers and sisters of U.S. citizens. But the brothers and sisters change was now dropped as were earlier suggestions for a cap on legal immigration. Neither was Rodino especially enthusiastic about temporary worker programs for growers, but compromise on that issue proved to be possible.

As the Simpson-Rodino Act worked its way through Congress in 1986 the usual arguments were heard and critical compromises were required for final passage and acceptance by the White House. Of course, central to the final bill were amnesty and employer sanctions. The cutoff for an amnesty was finally fixed at January 1, 1982; those undocumented aliens who had entered the United States before that date and had remained there since were eligible. Employer sanctions made it unlawful to knowingly employ undocumented aliens. Congress rejected the controversial concept of a national identity card; instead employers could verify an alien's standing by examining a combination of documents and papers. For violators of the law, fines were assessed, but for a "pattern or practice" of hiring undocumented immigrants, criminal penalties could be imposed, including a jail sentence.

While employer sanctions and an amnesty were the heart of the IRCA [Immigration Reform and Control Act], crucial for its passage were provisions for temporary foreign workers to harvest perishable crops and a Special Agricultural Workers (SAW) amnesty. The Senate draft included a temporary agriculture worker program which many representatives opposed. Proponents of help for growers were reportedly losing strength in Congress by 1986, but they nonetheless were able to insist upon some provisions for agricultural workers, which Representative Charles Schumer provided.

Schumer proposed that undocumented aliens who had worked for at least 20 (later increased to 90) days in agriculture between May 1985 and May 1986 be allowed to become temporary aliens and then permanent resident aliens. The final bill also permitted growers to bring foreign farm workers into the country if they convinced the government they were needed. Rodino called Schumer's proposal "a compromise very, very delicately arrived at," and said that "it is the only political reality that will bring together all the forces" working for the bill. Moreover, the final bill included another victory for growers: a section prohibiting INS [Immigration and Naturalization Service] officials from questioning a grower's farm workers unless they had a search warrant or the farm owner's permission.

In some ways the SAW program was the most remarkable part of IRCA. It was adopted without hearings and without a thorough examination of how it would work. Indeed, it had not been discussed much in the past. The House committee, using estimates from the Congressional Budget Office (CBO) said, "Workers covered under the special agriculture workers provision are estimated to total about 250,000." Republican dissenters claimed that this provision was drafted in haste and that no one knew exactly how many workers SAW would produce, and said that "Guesses range from 200,000 to over 1,000,000." Furthermore, they noted, "There is nothing in the legislation to require SAW's continued employment in agriculture." The result was, as Representative Dan Lungren of California pointed out, that SAW was a "second legalization" program, one not carefully crafted like the main amnesty provision. One Republican, James Sensenbrenner, Jr., noted another problem:

> With document fraud at an all time high in the United States, fears have been raised about the possibility of fraudulent documents being used in the amnesty program. People must prove they have lived and worked in the U.S. since 1982. The Schumer workers only have to account for 60 [sic] days, with documents which would be difficult, if not impossible, to verify, and easy to draw up.

Of course some representatives did not like any amnesty. But they lacked the votes to block SAW, and their attempts to kill the regular amnesty provision failed by a narrow margin in the House. On the other side were those who worried about employer sanctions leading to racial and ethnic discrimination. Addressing the concerns of Hispanics and civil libertarians, the representatives also insisted upon antidiscrimination provisions, which the Senate accepted. If the General Accounting Office (GAO) found discrimination against foreign-looking individuals or resident aliens, then Congress was to reconsider employer sanctions. . . .

In the end the various compromises won enough support from those not necessarily satisfied with individual sections of IRCA and it passed easily in the Senate (63–24) and by a 238 to 173 margin in the House. Many members insisted that is was the best bill obtainable, and even 5 of the 11-member Hispanic caucus favored it. Hispanics and their allies wanted a later cut-off day for amnesty than January 1, 1982; it was the best they could get, and the amnesty coupled with the antidiscrimination provisions won their votes. Some feared a less generous bill would be enacted if IRCA went down to defeat. Conservatives, on the other hand, favored the Simpson-Rodino Act because of employer sanctions and the prospect of increased border supervision.

Estimates had varied as to the number of persons eligible for amnesty. After a slow start 1.7 million applied for the regular legalization. A majority were Mexican. SAW proved to be the surprise. CBO estimates were way short of the final number, and even INS's high guess of 600,000 turned out to be off by a half; when the deadline ended in 1988, 1.3 million persons had claimed amnesty under the SAW divisions. There were also mostly Mexicans who made up 2.2 million of the 3 million total amnesty applications. INS officials had one explanation for the large number of SAW; fraud on a massive scale. After reviewing the applications, INS in 1989 identified about 400,000 cases of possible fraud. At the same time it confessed that it lacked the funds and manpower to prosecute individual applicants. In some spots, said Jack Bass, assistant commissioner for investigations, fraud was "rampant if not totally out of control." Charles Schumer, author of the compromise SAW program, admitted it was "too open," and that INS lacked the resources to track down fraud. Critics noted that it "was a weak program and it was poorly articulated in law."

Growers had insisted upon provisions for temporary farm workers because they could no longer hire illegal aliens. Some growers did claim a shortage existed, but the federal government was not convinced. Farmers were able to find laborers, either by hiring SAW workers, Americans, regular immigrants or by continuing to use undocumented workers.

Problems also emerged in the regular legalization program. . . . INS officials quickly discovered that families could be disrupted because of the cutoff date. If the husband arrived before January 1982, but the wife and children at a later date, the family members would have to apply for admission from their country under the second preference; but in countries like Mexico, that preference was backed up for years. INS indicated that it would not deport such individuals, but Congress wanted to be certain of avoiding hardship for families. After holding hearings on this issue the legislators included in the Immigration Act of 1990 a provision that provided for a stay of deportation for spouses and children of undocumented aliens who were eligible for amnesty. They then could wait (and work) in the United States while their applications for admission were pending.

The concern by Hispanics and civil libertarians that the employer sanctions might lead to discrimination appeared to be well founded. Several investigations by state agencies and the GAO revealed that discrimination occurred. Civil rights and Hispanic organizations called for a repeal of employer sanctions, and they had supporters in Congress. But Congress did not include this provision in the sweeping 1990 Immigration Act. The discrimination issue remained troubling, however, and indicated how shaky that IRCA was.

The main issue for many who believed that American borders were out of control was employer sanctions. For them IRCA was critical. The task of prosecuting employers who violated the law, even with increased funding and personnel for INS, was huge. Nevertheless, in August 1987, INS issued the first citation; and in 1988 a Maryland firm, the operator of Wendy's Restaurants, received the first criminal fine under IRCA. Others followed.

In 1986 INS had reported a record 1.6 million undocumented aliens apprehended, and the first year after passage of IRCA, the number dropped; by 1989 it was approximately half of that amount. As employers reported shortages of workers, it appeared that the new law might deter undocumented immigration. But then apprehensions began to climb again, and in 1990 they topped one million. Several scholarly studies concluded that it was not possible to measure the precise impact of IRCA in such a short time; and they noted that in addition to IRCA, economic conditions also affected the illegal flow and that increased personnel along the border could account for changes in apprehensions.

Moreover, effective enforcement of IRCA depended upon documentary evidence given by employees. INS officials and scholars said smugglers were still active and that the traffic in fake documents was as brisk as ever, only the price was higher. For employers, there was little incentive to be sure that these documents were authentic, for they were not required to do so. Most employers had opposed IRCA, and some were convicted for employing undocumented aliens, but it was not easy to prove that employers knowingly hired illegals. IN 1989, INS reported that of 900 aliens it arrested at workplaces, 233 admitted having counterfeit Social Security cards and 142 a fake green card. Wayne Cornelius, director of the Center for United States–Mexican Studies at the University of California at San Diego, put it in 1990, "Employer sanctions may have seemed a real barrier at first, but now they are just one more hurdle to overcome."

Certainly IRCA did not end horror stories of desperate illegal aliens trying to enter the United States. In 1987 the Border Patrol found 19 undocumented aliens locked in a railroad trailer in West Texas in 120-degree heat. About the same time, the Patrol also found 18 such aliens who suffocated to death in a Texas box car. Two years later four dead undocumented aliens were discovered confined in a trailer. And in early 1991 New York City police rescued undocumented Chinese aliens who had been smuggled from China. After paying thousands of dollars to get to America, they had been kidnapped and held as virtual slaves until rescued.

That persons faced with poverty at home in Mexico or the Caribbean or civil war and violence in Central America would seek a better life in America was understandable, even after the passage of IRCA. If caught, they did as so many did before the 1986 Immigration Reform and Control Act became law—they simply tried again. And for thousands of others who overstayed their visas, there were jobs in American cities.

In response, INS and its allies called for more personnel for IRCA and border enforcement. They also suggested proposals with an old history: counterfeit-proof green cards, improved Social Security cards, and a national ID system. Another familiar proposal was to create a large ditch along the United States border with Mexico. The Federation of Americans for Immigration Reform (FAIR) went further. It called for a beefed-up INS and the construction of a 12-foot-high fence along the area most used by border crossers.

Proposals for elaborate fences and national ID cards ran into the usual opposition and had little chance for passage. Whatever impact IRCA had was clearly limited. Although long discussed, it contained too many compromises and hasty provisions (like SAW) to be fully effective. Moreover, the United States continued to be attractive to many people. Evidence exists that those crossing the border consisted of proportionately more Central Americans and Mexicans eager to stay in the United States rather than working seasonally. Some authorities also believed that the latest undocumented immigrants heading north included more women and children and even some professionals. Among the visa abusers, those who entered with visitors' permits and then stayed, were a number of well-educated people, such as the Irish and Israelis. What they shared in common was a search for a better life. Barring a major economic collapse in the United States, which would dry up employment, they would still try to find a place in the American economy and society.

Korean Americans and the Model Minority Myth, 1970s–Present

KWANG CHUNG KIM AND WON MOO HURH

Since 1966, when sociologist William Petersen published an influential article dubbing Asian Americans the "successful minority," many scholars and journalists have depicted Americans of Asian origin as the "model minority." They have based their argument on three indexes: Asian Americans' high level of educational attainment, their high family income, and their low rate of social deviance.

Some Asian-American scholars have criticized the political implications of this myth of a model minority. At the height of the civil-rights and black power movements, such portrayals of Asian-American success contained the message that the United States is indeed a land of opportunity; if African Americans and Latino Americans do not seem to be "making it" in America, this failure must be due to their own "deficiencies." After all, it was implied, despite the discrimination that Asian immigrants also have suffered, they are pulling themselves up by their bootstraps by dint of their reverence for education, their hard work, and the strength of their families.

Critics of the model-minority thesis point out that if Asian Americans have a high level of education attainment, it is partly owing to a U.S. immigration policy that favors the entry of well-educated professionals. If Asian-American family income is high, part of the explanation is that the average Asian-American family has several income earners who pool their income. If Asian Americans' rate of social deviance is low, the reason is that, in the mid-1960s, the number of Asian-American youths was still small, so that those who got into trouble formed only a tiny fraction of the young people arrested for crime and juvenile delinquency. Kwang Chung Kim and Won Moo Hurh analyze the success image as it applies to Korean Americans, the vast majority of whom have come to the United States only since the late 1960s.

STUDY QUESTIONS

1. How did the image of Asian Americans as particularly successful—a "model minority"—arise?

2. What purpose did such an image serve?

3. To what extent do you think Asian Americans do indeed constitute a "model minority"?

4. How do the authors validate or refute this stereotype?

Asian Americans have been recently depicted as "successful" or "model" ethnic groups despite their past sufferings from prejudice and discrimination. This image of Asian Americans and their reputed position in the American racial and ethnic hierarchy raises several questions. First, to what degree is this image valid? Second, how has the success of Asian Americans been empirically measured and interpreted? Third, what are the implications of such an image for race/ethnic relations in the United States? In establish-

---

From Kwang Chung Kim and Won Moo Hurh, "Korean Americans and the 'Success' Image: A Critique," *Amerasia Journal* 10:2 (1983), pp. 3–4 and 6–16. Reprinted with permission of Amerasia Journal.

ing answers to these questions, we will examine recent Korean immigrants in Los Angeles.

A review of the literature reveals a number of interesting trends. During the mid-1960s, both the major mass media and scholarly works promoted the image of Asian Americans as successful minorities. The media first cited Japanese and Chinese Americans as minorities that had attained success in American society. In the 1970s, Koreans were included in this success story as were recent refugees from Indochina. Currently the success theme is applied to most Asian ethnic groups.

Scholarly support and promotion of the success theme has continued to the present, although the bulk of this literature was written prior to the mid-1970s. During the late 1970s, however, a number of scholarly and government publications disputed or rejected the alleged socioeconomic success of Asian Americans in American society.

In this study those who support the success image of Asian Americans will be referred to as "proponents" while those who dispute or reject the idea, as "critics." Proponents and critics can be distinguished from one another by their ethnicity and by the types of organizations with which they are affiliated. In general, the proponents are either non-Asian scholars or reporters with ties to major American mass media while the critics are scholars of Asian ancestry or representatives of government agencies such as the U.S. Commission on Civil Rights and its state advisory committees. There are of course exceptions. For example, Harry Kitano's *Japanese Americans: The Evolution of a Subculture* is one of the most quoted books in support of the success image of Asian Americans. In contrast, non-Asian scholars such as Edna Bonacich and John Modell in their analysis of Japanese American small business have directly challenged the success story theme. Although Asian Americans are by no means united in their effort to repudiate the success story image, they are clearly the principal critics. . . .

Proponents utilize three socioeconomic variables to measure the level of social status and privileges of Asian Americans: 1) education (mean years of schooling, the proportion of those with college education), 2) occupation (the proportion of those in professional-technical occupations or in white collar occupations), and 3) earnings (individual or family).

By these criteria, Japanese Americans have achieved a level of education similar to that of whites since the early 1940s. As of 1960, both native and foreign-born Chinese Americans have also approximately achieved equal or even higher levels of education to that of whites. Today Korean immigrants as well as native and foreign-born Pilipino Americans exhibit similarly high levels of educational achievement.

In terms of economic achievement, prior to World War II a high proportion of Japanese and Chinese Americans were in small business. Japanese, for example, engaged in truck farming while the Chinese operated laundries and restaurants. This small business tradition has changed little, although wartime relocation greatly reduced the number of Japanese small businesses. In the postwar period a high proportion of young Japanese and Chinese Americans gained access to professional and technical occupations because of their high education. Increased access to professional-technical positions and continued participation in small businesses has resulted in a higher proportion of Japanese and Chinese Americans in white-collar occupations than whites. Among Korean immigrants the occupational distribution is similar. The high proportion of Asian Americans in white collar occupations and their high rate of labor force participation have resulted in a median family income which nearly equals or surpasses that of whites. The 1980 Census shows that the annual median family income of Asian and Pacific Americans was $22,075 while that of white families was $20,840.

These data have led proponents to conclude that Asian American are successful. Implicit in the success theme are three crucial political messages. First, if Asian Americans are successful, then they no longer need public policies designed to benefit deprived minorities—the benefit denying function. Second, Asian American success validates the widely-held assumption that the United States is a land of opportunity—the system preserving function. Third, in this land of opportunity, if a minority group fails to achieve a high socioeconomic status, then the minority is responsible for its own failure—the minority blaming function. In this context, Asian American achievement was explicitly contrasted to black Americans in the 1960s when black urban unrest was at its height and the civil rights movement was gaining momentum.

Critics of the proponents' approach are primarily concerned with the exclusion of minority groups from full participation in American society. Exclusion would make it relatively more difficult for minority groups to attain a level of social status and privileges similar to that of the dominant group. Under this condition, minority groups may have to pay a higher price than the dominant group. Utilizing an approach similar to equity theory or distributive justice theory, critics compare minority groups and the dominant group in terms of both their respective costs or investments, and rewards or achievements.

The critics maintain that Asian Americans can be considered successful only if they have paid a price equal to that of whites for the same social status and privileges. In this comparison, "whites" refer mainly to white males. Asian Americans can be considered disadvantaged and discriminated against if: 1) they are equal to whites in rewards or achievements, but have made greater costs or investments, or 2) they attain less than whites in rewards or achievements, but have made equal costs or investments. In both cases, the reward (achievement) rate per unit of cost (investment) is smaller for Asian Americans than whites. Critics argue that the existence of a differential rate of reward would demonstrate that Asian Americans experience disadvantage, discrimination, injustice and/or inequity. Using the above conceptual framework, critics analyze Asian Americans' socioeconomic achievement in terms of education, labor market position, and earnings.

Since Asian Americans have attained a high level of education, a central question from the perspective of the critics is the relative costs they may have paid for this achievement. According to Chun: "If members of a minority group view education as the only means of social mobility and invest heavily in their children's college education at a disproportionate sacrifice to family finances, should that college education be regarded necessarily as a sign of success of this group?"

While the proponents are primarily concerned with analyzing the occupational profiles of Asian Americans, critics examine also the types of industries and specific firms employing Asian American labor. This combined approach measures the labor market position of Asian Americans. Critics raise the basic question: When the qualifications of Asian Americans and white workers are equal, is the quality of jobs comparable for both groups?

The earnings of Asian Americans, analyzed in terms of investments (e. g., education, job experience) and labor market position, are compared by critics to those of white workers. This analysis is, however, complicated because family income is often used as the basis of comparison. This frequently conceals a number of investment factors since:

> high income may be the result of longer work hours or sacrificed weekends. It follows that for the household income to be a usable index for purposes of group comparison, one has to make adjustments for the number of wage earners and the number of hours worked. In addition, since education is known to be a substantial contributor to occupational mobility as well as higher income, the level of wage income should be adjusted at least for wage earner's education.

Utilizing the contrasting approaches of proponents and critics of the Asian American success story, we will analyze the socioeconomic status of Korean immigrants. . . .

The majority of Koreans working in the United States immigrated after the revision of the U.S. Immigration and Naturalization Act of 1965. . . . Presently Los Angeles has the largest Korean American population in the United States. We interviewed six hundred fifteen Korean immigrant adults (281 males and 334 females), who resided in Los Angeles. . . .

The interviewees have lived in the United States for slightly more than six years on the average . . . with most (79 percent of the males and 82 percent of the females) in the economically active ages (21–50 years old). . . . The overwhelming majority of the respondents (87 percent of the males and 72 percent of the females) are married.

In terms of education, the respondents fall into three categories: 1) non-college graduates, i.e., those who have not completed a college education either in Korea or the United States and who are not currently enrolled as students, 2) Korean-college graduates, and 3) American-college graduates.

More than 40 percent of both males . . . and females . . . are Korean-college graduates which indicates that Korean migration has been a highly selective process favoring college graduates. An additional 19 percent of the male . . . and 8 percent of the female . . . respondents are American-college graduates. . . . Another ten percent of the respondents are currently enrolled as college students.

A great majority of both male (. . . 86 percent) and female (. . . 64 percent) respondents are currently employed. The rate of employment is especially high among married women (68 percent) which, according to the 1980 Census, is higher than that of white married women (49 percent) and black married women (60 percent).

In terms of occupation, the interviewees are divided into five categories: 1) professionals and semi-professionals, 2) proprietors and managers, 3) other white-collar workers, 4) skilled workers, and 5) semi-skilled or unskilled workers. The majority of the male respondents are either professionals and semi-professionals (26 percent) or proprietors and managers (34 percent). A similar finding is observed for female respondents with about half employed either as professionals and semi-professionals (21 percent) or as proprietors and managers (29 percent). Regardless of sex, virtually all the proprietors and managers own and/or manage small businesses. A small proportion of the respondents are employed in other types of white-collar occupations. . . . In total, a little more than two-thirds of the sample are employed in white-collar occupations.

The relationship between education and current occupation is evident among the men. Half of the American-college graduates . . . are currently employed as professionals and semi-professionals while about 40 percent of the Korean-college graduates . . . are engaged in small businesses. At the same time, nearly two-thirds of the non-college graduates . . . are currently employed either in blue-collar or service occupations with a remaining one-third engaged mainly in self-employed small businesses. This distribution indicates that a majority of the small businessmen are Korean-college graduates . . . while non-college graduates constitute the majority of blue-collar or service workers (. . . 61 percent). . . .

In terms of the employment status of family members, two types of Korean immigrant families are identified. The majority of the married respondents (. . . 54 percent) indicate that only the husband and wife are employed in their families. Another third of the married respondents (. . . 32 percent) report that only the husband is employed. Thus in our sample the husband and wife are the major wage earners with other family members seldom contributing to the family income. . . .

. . . [A]bout two-thirds of the families . . . report that their annual income exceeds the [1970] national median of $17,000. In families with both husbands and wives employed, more than half . . . of the families have annual incomes above the [1970] national family income median of $23,000. . . .

The following aspects of the Korean experience, however, lend support to critics: 1) a high proportion of Korean immigrants are currently engaged in small business as owner-operators; 2) employed Korean immigrants tend to work longer hours; and 3) [the majority of work colleagues or customers tend also to be minority members.]

A clear majority of the employed respondents (86 percent) are full-time workers. A large proportion of them work more than eight hours a day. The proportion of overtime workers is especially high among small business operators with 72 percent of the males . . . and 65 percent of the females . . . who work more than an eight-hour day. One-third of the male respondents in other occupations also work for more than eight hours a day. Moreover, the majority of employed respondents, irrespective of sex, report that they work every Saturday or on certain Sundays. . . .

. . . [A] high proportion of those employed in other occupations appear to work in segregated settings as indicated by the ethnicity of their major work colleagues. . . . In his discussion of minority labor market experiences, Becker makes a distinction between two types of segregation; one is characterized by a disproportionate concentration of minority workers in certain occupational categories, the other, by the separation of white and minority workers in the same occupation across different places of employment. The former is referred to as occupational segregation, the latter as workplace segregation. In our study we observe both types of segregation. The heavy concentration of Korean immigrants in small businesses illustrates occupational segregation while the segregation of Korean workers with minority workers is indicative of workplace segregation. What these two types of segregation signify is that Korean immigrants either hold an inferior occupation or work under unfavorable conditions.

Several comments can be made on the inferior quality of Korean small business. First, Korean enterprises are heavily concentrated in two labor-intensive and highly competitive industries, retail trade and selected services. Because of competitive pressures, small businessmen are often required to invest additional hours of labor in the enterprise and to utilize family labor. Korean small business is thus characterized by the use of cheap labor.

Second, other studies of Korean enterprises in the Los Angeles area suggest that their scale of business is small both in terms of number of employees and in volume of annual sales. . . . [T]wo-thirds of Korean small businesses in the Los Angeles area hire five persons or less. . . . [N]ine-tenths of the small businesses have no more than ten employees. Virtually all of the businesses indicate that their annual sales volume does not exceed one million dollars. In this sense, Korean small business may be generally classified as "small" or "family" small businesses.

Third, since retail and service industries generally deal with local markets, the fortunes of such small businesses depend upon a good location. Like other minority small businesses, Korean small businesses are generally excluded from the "mainstream" markets. They are usually concentrated in the "protected" markets of their own ethnic community or in the markets of other minority groups such as Blacks and Mexicans. . . . In these . . . markets, the profit-margin is small, and an overriding concern is with "business security" which refers both to earnings and physical safety. . . .

Fourth, small business is highly vulnerable to the business cycle and other economic trends and often suffer from a high rate of business failure. This is also true of Korean small business. But for most Korean small businessmen, as for Chinese small businessmen, small business is "a matter of economic necessity, not profit-mongering" in their struggle to establish a solid economic base in the United States. Therefore, Korean small businessmen remain in the field of small business in spite of a high risk rate and endure the problem of occupational immobility in the absence of other attractive occupational opportunities.

Fifth, . . . the majority of current Korean small businessmen are Korean-college graduates. Managing small businesses thus involves a considerable underutilization of their educational resources. In sum, Korean small business possesses the typical features of minority-owned small business in the United States: 1) a heavy concentration in the retail and service sectors, 2) small scale of business establishments, 3) predominance in the underprivileged market, and 4) a high rate of business failure. However, Korean small business differs in two significant ways: 1) a higher proportion of Korean immigrants are engaged in small business, and 2) their business expansion comes from their active penetration in[to] the market of other minority groups. Through such penetration, Korean small businessmen emerge as a middleman minority.

A basic contention of labor market segmentation theory is that white male workers dominate the relatively favorable labor markets making entry difficult for minority workers. This condition forces members of minority groups to gravitate into the more easily accessible but relatively unfavorable labor markets or remain unemployed.

This position has been empirically supported by a number of past studies. It is also supported in our study by the fact that the male non-small business respondents who work mostly with minority workers or in a mixed setting of white and minority workers earn considerably less than those whose major work colleagues are whites. Among the female respondents, the ethnicity of work colleagues seems to affect their individual earnings less than their male counterparts, after adjusting for occupation. This may derive from the fact that white female workers in general are also to some extent segregated in their employment. Therefore, we contend that Korean immigrants are segregated in the American labor market and mainly restricted to inferior occupations or unfavorable work conditions. . . .

Our analysis of the experiences of Korean immigrants in Los Angeles leads us to mixed conclusions. Using the socioeconomic criteria favored by proponents, Korean immigrants can be considered a successful ethnic group in the United States. . . . [O]ur findings also demonstrate that certain segregated conditions exist which generally keep Korean immigrants a disadvantaged minority within the American labor market. Therefore, we conclude that basing the success image of Korean immigrants solely on the proponents' approach is inadequate to understand the complex experiences of Korean immigrants in the United States.

 Vietnamese Artists and Writers in America, 1975–Present

QUI-PHIET TRAN

Compared to other Asian immigrant groups, Vietnamese have resided in America for a relatively short time. Few Vietnamese had settled in the United States before 1975, when a communist government assumed power in South Vietnam. As Saigon fell, some 130,000 individuals—Vietnamese who either had held high positions in the government and armed forces or had worked for Americans and their dependents—were evacuated under chaotic conditions. They were flown to U.S. bases in the Philippines, Guam, and Hawaii for temporary processing and then housed in four camps on the U.S. mainland for several months before being released into American society, usually under the care of sponsors.

This first wave of refugees had hardly been resettled when a new exodus from Vietnam began in 1978. Called the "boat people," these thousands of Vietnamese, many of Chinese ancestry, left their country in small, overcrowded, unseaworthy boats to escape harsh economic conditions and political repression. It has been estimated that half of those who fled perished at sea. The United States, France, Australia, and other countries have taken in the refugees and continue to admit them, but tens of thousands remain in refugee camps in Hong Kong, Thailand, and the Philippines.

In 1980 the governments of the Socialist Republic of Vietnam and the United States established the Orderly Departure Program, which has regularized the exodus and allowed Vietnamese to enter the United States not as refugees but as immigrants. American-born children of Vietnamese ancestry are also becoming visible. Today almost a million persons of Vietnamese ancestry live in the United States, some 40 percent of them in California.

Scholars have completed many studies of the refugees, but with the exception of some short oral histories, the refugees themselves have published very little in English about their experiences. By analyzing the themes in the short stories penned by Vietnamese now living in the United States, Qui-Phiet Tran offers insight into how these newest Asian Americans perceive themselves and their situation.

STUDY QUESTIONS

1. What are the similarities and the differences between immigrants and refugees?

2. What feelings do the Vietnamese refugee writers now living in America express?

The Vietnamese exodus to America and other countries following the fall of Saigon since 1975 has had no parallel in Vietnam's history. Although emigration becomes a repetitive pattern in a country such as Vietnam that has undergone so many social, political, and military upheavals in the past, this most recent experience has been unknown to the Vietnamese. In just thirteen years over two million citizens have left their country and become refugees scattered in most parts of the world. Their escape to a new haven, however, is one of the greatest tragedies that has ever befallen modern man. Many of them did not reach the shores of the free world safely and happily. During their long ordeal they perished on the high seas or were subject to all kinds of humiliation and torture caused by piracy, rape, and starvation. But even their safe arrival in an asylum country does not guarantee that their nightmare will soon be over. The interminable waiting in squalid refugee camps before a third country deigns to pick them up adds to the devastating ordeal they have already undergone so long. In addition, the refugees' euphoria of being resettled quickly gives way to feelings of uncertainty, fear, and alienation caused by the culture shock, linguistic and cultural differences, role-reversal in the family, and the like that they experience in the new land. These problems coupled with their unwillingness to leave their native country make these émigrés regard their coming to the West as an uprooting, a dismemberment they cannot quickly get over.

A striking characteristic of this exodus is the presence of numerous intellectuals, artists, and writers, many of whom were key figures in the pre-1975 South Vietnamese literary scene. These people and the "new" artists and writers (those who never practiced art and literature at home before) have lent a remarkable "ideological" nature to their flight from Vietnam. It is this large group of artists and writers and their interpretations of their ordeal at

---

From Qui-Phiet Tran, "Exiles in the Land of the Free: Vietnamese Artists and Writers in America, 1975 to the Present," *Journal of the American Studies Association of Texas* 20 (1989), pp. 101–109.

home and in the new world that are the focus of this short essay. Spokesmen for the refugees, these men and women provide through their art insights into their fellow people's problems, attitudes, aspirations, and perspectives in the new land.

Stunned at first by the 1975 political events and their anguish at being suddenly transplanted from their native land, Vietnamese artists and writers soon plunged themselves into numerous cultural and literary activities. For these authors—old and new—the urge of creativity was so compelling that despite their lack of time (many of them labored in sweatshops for their living), they managed to write and publish a great deal. This 1975 group—so called to distinguish from the second group, the "boat people," who began to come in 1977—was most active during the years 1975 to 1977. Their writings center on the following themes: nostalgia, guilt, and exile.

Nostalgia. For most artists and writers their paradise was the Vietnam of the pre-1975 era. Laden with innumerable memories because of their country's long history, the Vietnamese tend to identify with the past rather than with the present and the future. The 1975 political events and their sudden exile cut off what is considered to be their lifeblood—the past. Most Vietnamese exiles, Le Tat Dieu explains, seem to be in a state of somnambulism when in America: "The real world, the American world that they are living in, is as elusive as a dream. The lost world, the one that exists only in their dream, appears immensely real." For the first time, Vietnamese literature, which used to have no room for masochistic themes, seems to give free rein to the treatment of the joy of suffering. This "maddening remembrance of things past" and the resulting motif of "digging rivers and mountains for human images" can be found not only in literature but also in art. Although modern Vietnamese art is essentially European, Vietnamese artists turn away from American themes and solely preoccupy themselves with the Vietnamese past. More successful because of their emotional appeal are the performing arts, particularly music. In addition to the booming of pre-1975 music, which treats the themes of war, suffering, despair, and alienation, there came into vogue numerous new sentimental songs carrying significant titles such as "Songs of Humiliation," "Songs of Exile," "Regrets for Saigon," etc. If Western music was popular in most Vietnamese shows before 1975, it no longer interests Vietnamese audiences and performers overseas. "Those unfortunate refugees," remarks Le Tat Dieu, "will continue to be obsessed with their past until death."

Guilt. Nostalgia for the past, though poignant, cannot be equated with the guilt most Vietnamese feel for those who stayed. Despite their difficulty in adjusting to life in the new land and their harsh view of America, the refugees who arrived in 1975 consider themselves very lucky compared to their many other relatives, friends, colleagues, and comrades-at-arms whom they envision to be languishing at home. Since 1975 self-recrimination caused by their anguish at having "betrayed" those who stayed has been a favorite theme in the writings of many exile authors. For some, like the novelist Vo Phien, being exiled means depriving one's life of its meaning because individual destiny is inseparable from national identity. Enjoying for the first time in America "a peaceful springtime," which he never had in his war-torn Vietnam, Vo Phien suddenly perceives "the horrible vacuum of an existence that has no worries and no future" because he has been "struck out from the path of suffering my people are traveling." While writers like Vo Phien see exile as a complete detachment from national destiny and a cause for unassuageable self-accusation, others still perceive the link between those who left and those who stayed. From their vantage point these authors view their coming to the West as an opportunity for them to speak out on behalf of those who are stranded at home. Apparently to exorcise their guilt, a great part of these authors' works are devoted to the popularization of their heroes who are able to maintain their human values even in the most adverse circumstances. In one of her well-known exile stories Tran Dieu Hang writes about the friendship between three women, two of whom remain in Vietnam and every day fight against the death instinct but never for a moment forget their exiled friend in the States. In her turn, the latter is no less loyal to them. In addition to appointing her two friends the other mothers of her infant, she tries to immortalize their memories by vowing to pass on their legacy to her child's generation. By apotheosizing love thus, the young mother's guilt is absolved. Self-recrimination is also deftly spared in the writings of the others who romanticized about their protagonists' exploits in resisting the new regime, elevating them, as it were, to a semi-divine status. By trying to return to "the path of suffering" being traveled by those who did not leave, these authors have identified with their nation's destiny and therefore have sublimated their exile experience.

Exile. Not only are the Vietnamese haunted by the ghosts of the past, they are also confronted with the realities of their new condition. Unlike other immigrants who had come to America before them, the new exiles from Vietnam generally see this haven as a penal colony. The picture of a Vietnamese refugee in exile [as depicted in] Vietnamese literature, though complex, is a most depressing one. It is, first of all, that of "a clown" who plays a ridiculous role in "the racial assimilation drama"—"a yellow American with a wan smile and a bleeding heart." It is also that of "a tattered puppet," and even worse, "a new slave." But the pathetic, Kafkaesque portrait of a Vietnamese exile since 1975 is that of a stranger totally lost and alienated, driven insane by "mountains of grief and agony," and doomed to eternal penance for making America his home. Thus, ironically, the 1975 evacuation from Saigon is seen as "a brutal uprootedness," "the calculated driving of the Vietnamese to the wasteland." Thus, the refugees' "new life" is interpreted as a banishment, "the wearing away of both body and soul," in brief, "a slow death."

Important factors such as cultural differences, language barriers, and changes in socio-economic status can account for refugee behavior patterns similar to those described above. As soon as the immigrants become settled in, their frustration about the new country will gradually disappear as has happened to many Vietnamese who used to be very bitter about America. However, this theory does not seem to work for this group of Vietnamese artists and writers, particularly those who had fought in the war, who have lived here since 1975. Their bitterness to the point of hostility to America originates from their feeling of being "betrayed" by their former ally, from their anger of being forced to lay down their arms so soon, from their guilt of leaving their comrades-at-arms behind, and from their impression of being reduced to an insignificant role in their new country.

Vietnamese writers' feeling of isolation is intensified not only by their excessive obsession with their past, their frustration about their "unfinished mission," but also by their dissatisfaction with America's culture which they find incompatible with their own. Exile Vietnamese literature not only reflects this Vietnamese attitude toward America's cultural values, but also provides insightful comparisons between oriental and American minds. Essentially, the following American values are most strongly criticized by Vietnamese writers:

Material civilization. Vietnamese are appalled by American life, which they find too hectic, mechanical, competitive, and insecure as opposed to "the quiet and leisure of the Orient." Because of their addiction to work, Americans, observe Vietnamese writers, do not realize that the Tao of living consists in toiling and enjoying oneself at the same time. "Both the bird that flies in the sky and the fish that swims in the water are hunting for prey and enjoying themselves at the same time. The small fish that flickers about in Chuang-tseu's *Nam-hua chen-ching* looks as if he was having fun, but in fact he is at work. The butterfly that is gathering pollen is in fact having a good time." Similarly, in Vietnamese and other oriental societies, work is imbued with poetic beauty because "recreation becomes mingled with labor." Americans, they conclude, are progressive but unfortunate because they are so hard pressed by their materialistic civilization.

Social and moral values. Americans' feverish existence not only prevents them from enjoying leisure, but also deprives them of the opportunity to appreciate the value and benefits of human feelings. Although Americans feel the need for this sort of moral and emotional sustenance to cope with the depression of modern life, they do not often have access to these luxuries in their highly technological society. Because of their reliance on professional institutions to resolve problems of the human heart, Americans, the Vietnamese observe, do not highly value loyal friendship and matrimony, filial piety, and the like, which are primary ideals in oriental societies. Rather, they develop a cult of individualism and privacy, sometimes to the point of isolation. "Americans," declares Vo Phien, "are easy to be acquainted, but hard to become intimately associated with. . . . They are incapable of loving

Vietnamese "boat people" seeking refuge

long because of their shortness of emotions." Despite their warm hospitality shown for the refugees, Americans are found to be cold. "America is cold because it is a great power," comments sarcastically a prominent, pre-1975 woman novelist on the United States and its people.

The Vietnamese do not see the calm appearance of an American's secluded life as a token of an unperturbed solitude beneficial to intellectual pursuits, but as a manifestation of extreme loneliness because of the lack of friends and beloved ones. Americans are lonely, Vo Phien explains, because they care little for the past and do not want to get entangled in "the web of favors and gratitude, memories and remembrances," which is so important in Vietnamese life. Interestingly, some writers interpret America's treatment of old age as an attempt to deny the past and its emotional intricacies and provide a nice comparison between the two cultures: "Unlike Orientals who believe that the Golden Age is behind them, Americans are convinced that it hovers in front of them. Why should Americans care for old age when they are concerned only with the future?" But the cult of the future is a paradox because children are practically discriminated against. In his novel about America, *Dong Cua Tran Gian (Shutting the Doors to the Human World)*, Le Tat Dieu writes about a young widow who has three children and whose boyfriend runs away when she gets pregnant. Because she cannot afford to let the baby arrive, she resorts to abortion. Still, the family cannot find a place to live because all landlords refuse to accept children. In revenge, her oldest child burns down the houses of those who have turned his family away. The central theme of the novel is obvious: when separating the old from the young, modern American society destroys the link between the past and the future.

As suggested by the novel and other observations by Vietnamese writers, violence is a key aspect of American life. "Looking dignified and composed is the appearance of many Americans. Behind it is all insanity." Shocked by what they see on the television and in real life, the Vietnamese deplore the decline of American ethics and attribute it to the excessive freedom enjoyed by Americans, particularly young people. Stories have been told about many families who had at first refused to leave refugee camps for fear of violence. They and many writers express the wish "to return to our civilized life" where—except for the war, which was seen as "a natural calamity," part of the "Will of Heaven"—everything was so peaceful and safe.

Vietnamese writers' gloomy views of America are not entirely caused by their bitterness about their forced exile but by their frustration about irreconcilable dissimilarities between American and Vietnamese cultures as well. These feelings become acute when they realize they have to adopt America as their other country, accept its institutions, and live up to its norms. The greatest threat that faces most Vietnamese Americans is loneliness, which they are not accustomed to. Native Americans, Vo Phien writes, are better off than Vietnamese Americans because they are used to being independent and they have their church and their community. Vietnamese Americans are unfortunate because eventually they will be scattered over many parts of the country and "will not be able to find a warm shelter from this cold, windswept society."

This maudlin trend of regretting the past and lamenting the present suddenly gives way to an outburst of wrath and agony manifested in the writings of the boat people who began to arrive in 1977. Unlike those who came in 1975, this group claims to leave Vietnam with a clear ideological purpose—to seek freedom and to tell the world about the "Vietnam in blood and tears." With this vociferous group now predominating the literary scene, there is a sudden shift from the literature of exile to the literature of protest. Not only literature but also music and art are seethed with the boat people's misery and anger. The hellish human drama portrayed below by an ex-convict explains this explosion and the reasons for the new literature: "I am one of the many people who were burned by the most terrible fire in the world—Communism. Its heat made me look to death as the only solution. Many nights awakened and finding myself quiver among those human worms, I wished I had found a nail or a razor blade. But, that inner voice suddenly spoke to me again and again: 'Write! Do not die!'" In just two years—1977 and 1978—when the exodus of the boat people reached its climax, exile Vietnamese literature witnessed a second spectacular phenomenon. Hundreds of magazines, newspapers, books of prose and poetry have been published in Vietnamese and several languages to alarm the world about the inferno of Vietnam and the ordeal of the boat people. In contrast to the attractive but unreal image of Vietnam's past that haunts the minds of the first group, the picture of Vietnam's present portrayed by the second group is one of the darkest and most heartbreaking realism. It is, first of all, a wasteland where death reaches not only the human, but also the animal and vegetal life. "Trees stand barren on the fields covered with bones / Birds have broken wings, finding no place to land." In the writings of this group the country appears as a netherworld, "a phantom city where countless bandaged souls parade silently and grimly to an immense cemetery." But the most horrible picture of Vietnam is of a hell seething with human misery and agony, one which is darker and naturally more realistic than Dante's inferno. Unlike Dante's characters, who are shadows and therefore experience only illusory suffering, Vietnamese writers' protagonists writhe under tortures because they are corporeal. The common picture of Vietnamese modern man is a war prisoner shut up in a cage where he wallows in filth, vermin, and excrement, and is ravaged by maddening hunger and different kinds of torments: "Handfuls of rice mixed with feces / Drops of turbid water rank with urine smell / Torrid during the day, biting cold at night / Lashes cutting through the flesh of a swollen body / Resounding interrogations blasting the brains like a revolving grinder." The dehumanization is so extreme—and absurd—that the poet (and the reader) wonders if he, a human, is really going through the process.

To explain this absurdity of the human condition the Vietnamese mention a mysterious inexorable fate that they believe they are trapped in. In exile Vietnamese literature man's attempts to escape are doomed to failure. The voyage to freedom immediately becomes the voyage to death in the sea or to an eternal exile and isolation in the haven. Nature, man's best friend in traditional Vietnamese literature, also turns against him as if it was concurrent with fate to destroy him: "No more blue sky / No more sea-gulls on the reefs / The sea is blind and revengeful / Roaring while it sinks human lives." But the cruelest thing fate does to the Vietnamese refugee is its deception. In the writings of the boat people just when the escapees beam with joy on seeing the shores of freedom within their reach, death usually intervenes and takes away their lives or those of their beloved ones. Unlike Dante's characters who can aspire for their *purgatorio* or even *paradisio*, man in modern Vietnamese literature is condemned to an eternal inferno.

But the Vietnamese damned refuse to perish in their inferno. To do so, they create a dialectical paradox—accept the destruction of their physical bodies but deny the death of their souls. During his crucifixion, the poet "learn[s] to smile / To remember my idyllic love / To dream my most beautiful dream / In order to prolong my last breath." Similarly, during their dark moments of exile in America Vietnamese artists and writers still cherish the hope of returning to Vietnam eventually, or at least dream about metamorphosing into the Chuang-tseu butterfly to transcend their crude realities. This mode of salvation is an echo of the romantic Taoist tradition that has been an essential element of Vietnamese literature over ten centuries and has contributed to the nation's survival during its most turbulent historical periods.

Writing in *War's Other Voices: Women Writers on the Lebanese Civil War*, Miriam Cooke explains why these women (and men) write: "When wars are over, many write to construct the war, or just understand it, or idealistically, by writing war to end all wars." This observation can apply to Vietnamese exile literature in America. Because for most Vietnamese authors exile is a traumatic experience that resulted from their native country's longest war, they have to write about it to understand it and, hopefully, transcend it. But writing has a far more important purpose for these émigrés now regarding themselves as Americans: explaining the meaning of their unique ordeal to their fellow Americans who have granted them asylum. Speaking for his fellow artists and writers in one of his most critical stories about America, Le Tat Dieu comments on the Vietnamese contribution to the American pluralistic culture as follows:

> God does not cease to enrich America. This immense garden of the American soul which has seen the blooming of myriad flowers of myriad colors is now witnessing the burgeoning of newer flowers with even newer colors. In this garden which contains a treasure of human experience one can find not only flowers of greatest happiness, but also those of greatest sorrows ever grown by the human kind.

Hmong and Cambodian Voices, 1970s–Present

MEE HER, GE LOR, SIRATHRA SOM, AND
SALOUTH SOMAN

When escapees from Vietnam, Laos, and Cambodia began entering the United States in the 1970s, officials lumped them together as "Indochinese refugees." Euro-Americans soon learned, however, that *Indochinese* is not a favored term, because it harks back to the name *Indochina,* by which the French referred collectively to their five colonies in mainland Southeast Asia. (Though the French cultural legacy remains in their countries, the Vietnamese, Cambodians, and Laotians do not have fond memories of the political subjugation and economic exploitation they experienced under French colonial rule.) Most people today consequently call these immigrants Southeast Asian refugees. Yet this designation is still inaccurate, for it erases the many differences—in history, culture, language, religion, and social organization—that exist among the various groups.

In mainland Southeast Asia historically and even today, perhaps the most significant division is between hill tribespeople and lowlanders. The ethnic groups living in the mountains practice slash-and-burn agriculture—the practice of clearing plots in the jungle for cultivation by chopping down and then burning all the trees and other foliage—and move continually from one locality to another. Of the hill tribespeople from Laos who have immigrated to America, the Hmong are most numerous and the best known. Thousands of them had been recruited by the U.S. Central Intelligence Agency to fight against communist forces in the 1960s. When a communist government came to power in Laos in 1975, the lives of these people were endangered, and tens of thousands of them trekked through jungles and crossed the Mekong River into Thailand, where they lived for years in refugee camps before being resettled.

The lowland people, on the other hand, cultivate rice in flooded paddies and lead a sedentary existence. Most of the Cambodian immigrants to the United States are lowlanders, the survivors of what has been called an Asian holocaust. Between April 1975 and December 1978, Cambodia was ruled by the Khmer Rouge, Cambodian communists led by the ideologue Pol Pot. As soon as the Khmer Rouge took over Phnom Penh, Cambodia's capital, they ordered its residents, as well as people in other towns, to evacuate to the countryside. The evacuees, however, were given few means of subsistence. Starvation, exposure to the elements, forced labor, and executions resulted in the death of more than a million Cambodians—in a country with a total population of only 7 million—in the three and a half years during which the regime held power. Mee Her, Ge Lor, Sirathra Som, and Salouth Soman are among the lucky few who have overcome their traumatic experiences and become self-reliant Americans.

STUDY QUESTIONS

1. What difficulties do refugees from Southeast Asia encounter?

2. How have some of them overcome their hardships?

3. How has coming to the United States affected the relationship between parents and children in refugee households?

BOWLING TO FIND A LOST FATHER
MEE HER

We all held our breath as the ball slowly rolled down the alley. Then, just as it was about to hit the pins, it dropped into the gutter. Ahh . . . We sighed in disappointment. My father slowly turned toward us. His eyes sparkled like those of a little boy, and a big smile was printed on his face. Then he joyfully chuckled as he walked to his seat. I never thought my father would enjoy playing with us. . . . But on that evening when I taught him how to bowl, I did more than teach him how to hit pins. I had taken the first step toward bridging a gap which had been created between him and his children.

My father had never played with us. I guess that came with his Hmong orientation in valuing hard work. He told us that play was a waste of meaningful time which could be better used for productivity.

If we were still living in Laos where children don't have to go to school, and all they do is work in the field with parents, my father's orientation would be the ideal. There, children would work hard on the farms, then, during break times, they would listen to parents tell stories of their own childhood. Parents also either would teach "music" lessons to their children with instruments that they created out of bamboo sticks or they would teach them how to blow and make music out of leaves. This kept the relationship between children and their parents close. But in this country, where every-

"Bowling to Find a Lost Father" by Mee Her excerpted from *Passages: An Anthology of the Southeast Asian Refugee Experience*, comp., Katsuyo K. Howard (California State University, Fresno, 1990), pp. 195–197. Reprinted with permission.

"Learning American Farming" by Ge Lor; "The Donut Queen" by Sirathra Som; and "Beyond the Killing Fields" by Salouth Soman excerpted from *Voices from Southeast Asia: The Refugee Experience in the United States*, by John Tenhula (New York: Holmes & Meier, 1991), pp. 153–154, 178–181, and 184–185. Copyright © 1991 by Homes & Meier Publishers, Inc. Reprinted by permission of the publisher.

thing is so sophisticated, parents don't know how to be close to their children.

I remembered my relationship with my father as a child. We went everywhere together. He took me to the hospital where he worked, to the fields, or to feed the stock on the farm. I remember the times my father took me to the hospital with him. . . . I felt so close to him. However, since we came to this country, my relationship with my father has changed. He no longer knows how to be the father he used to be for us. He began to build walls around us by becoming so overly protective. He did not let us play outside or go out with our friends, using concepts of hard work to keep us at home like dutiful Hmong children. I felt emotionally distant from him. Somehow the gap seemed so great that neither he nor his children knew how to bridge it. As it turned out, I ignored our relationship altogether.

It wasn't until my third year in college that I decided to make my first move to recreate the relationship between my father and me. I had moved away from home when I started college. The time and distance made me miss the closeness that I used to have with him. . . . It must have been frightening to live with children who did not live in the same world that he did. He couldn't play video games with them or couldn't understand ear-busting rock 'n' roll. He didn't even know how to play soccer or volleyball! And those were the things that his children did for enjoyment in this country.

Poor Dad. It was not his fault that he did not know how to be included in our lives. It was just that he didn't know how to get involved with his children. That was why my brothers and sisters and I decided to introduce my father to bowling.

I remember that day well when my brothers, sisters, dad and I went bowling. Dad was a little hesitant to come with us, but we all persuaded him. When we got to the bowling alley, we showed him how to hold the ball. Then we taught him how to throw the ball. It was a little bit foreign for me to be the one teaching my father, and I sensed that Father felt odd, too. But once he got the hang of it, he did well. He even made a couple of strikes!

I think it was much more than bowling that father enjoyed. It was the emotional closeness that he felt with us which made him come back to bowl again. The next time we went bowling, he was teaching the younger children to bowl. As I watched him beam so happily with the kids, it occurred to me that this was the beginning of building a bridge across a long-created gap between Dad and his children.

LEARNING AMERICAN FARMING
GE LOR

We were highland people in Laos. I had worked for an American company and left Laos for Thailand in 1979. After one year of living in Kansas, my family—a wife and two sons—moved to Fresno, California. We moved mostly because there were no other Laotian [Hmong] people in Kansas. When we arrived, we met other Laotian people from Providence and Minnesota. They came to California for the same reasons. There are now about 23,000 Laotians in Fresno County.

The one thing that we could do that everyone else was doing in Fresno was farming. But this was a different kind of farming. We are talking about hi-tech farming, not the hand-tool farming we were used to in Laos. It's not so simple as turning the soil and planting seeds. Farming here is very modern, and to compete, we had to learn about these new techniques.

I was part of a program that helped train thirty-five new farmers in hi-tech farming skills in 1981. . . . The program was from the federal government, and we were supposed to eventually teach other refugees about farming. Our idea was to get involved in planting cash crops that we could work on as a community. It would be crops that the large farmers didn't want to grow. For many Laotians, farming is a good job because it doesn't require English and all of the family can work on it at the same time. Laotians have large families so this could be a good thing for business. . . .

. . . I learned . . . farming as a big business. How to rent and lease land, to hope for some venture capital to buy land. How to guess when and what crops might bring a profit. I never thought of farming as such a serious business. What I learned was more business than agriculture.

We had the idea of forming Laotian cooperative gardening that would be able to use the Laotian people in cash-crop ventures that would be long-term profitable for the people—not just to supplement incomes, but that would be their main source of income. We made many mistakes. What we learned was that there is a lot of competition in the United States, especially from Mexico, for bringing in these crops. You must really understand marketing and distribution . . . getting your fruits and vegetables out when they are ready.

. . . [I]n 1982, . . . because we had no venture capital available through any of the banks, about twenty of us started a cooperative farm that would, we hoped, bring in about a hundred families total. . . . [O]ur first crop was cherry tomatoes. They had brought in a good price the year before. . . . The market price for tomatoes is usually top price, but what we did not know was that all other farmers would plant cherry tomatoes. What happened was that the market was flooded and by then Mexico was sending tomatoes at even a lower price. Most important, these tomatoes all came ripe at once and we had not planned for the transportation of them. . . . We had no way to move them and they were rotting in the fields. It was a disaster. . . .

I hope Laotian people make it as farmers. I am part of a cooperative now that is hoping for a government contract for vegetables and fruits for Merced Air Force Base and possibly a base in Texas. . . . We have the workers but what we need is the ability to buy and improve the transport system. We need a Laotian trucking association with coolers. Then we need heavy farm equipment. I think it will come in time but it takes so long.

THE DONUT QUEEN
SIRATHRA SOM

I was born in the capital, Phnom Penh, and led a very comfortable life. I can still see the school I went to as a child. I see the trees on the street and I think of the familiar things that made my life happy. I grew up a happy child with friends and school to keep me busy. My parents were educated but we were not what you would call rich. . . .

The role of women in Cambodia is very defined. . . . Women are wives and mothers—those are the roles. We never questioned any of it. Not me, not my mother—we accepted it. If you grew up in a society where the rules are established and the community obeys them, then you just go along with it. You ask no questions—just go with it. . . . My marriage, of course, was arranged. I was young, and before we left the country I had two babies. I fit the traditional role of a good wife and mother and listener.

No one can forget the final days in Cambodia. It was only yesterday in my mind. Cambodia fell before Vietnam, and by early April we had to leave. My husband worked for the U.S. Agency for International Development, so we would be in a dangerous position if we stayed. No question about it, we would have been killed. I was twenty-two then. We left on April 7, 1975, and went to Camp Pendleton and were released to a sponsor in Texas three weeks later.

All of my family and my husband's family were killed, all of my friends. No one was left. It was like a plague of death and everyone is gone. The Khmer Rouge killed everyone. All of my family were educated people—those were the ones that Pol Pot wanted most to destroy.

We arrived in California with nothing, nothing. Only the clothes we were wearing. I could not speak English and everybody looked threatening to me. Simple things seemed complicated. Colors were different, sounds were different. Each day was filled with more questions than answers.

My first job was at the Sheraton Hotel in San Francisco as a domestic, and I earned $2.50 an hour. I was lucky to get the job—there were a lot of people who wanted it. . . . For me there was no question of whether I should work or stay at home. One of the first things you learn in America is that you need money. . . . [W]e needed two incomes and I went to work. I know my husband did not like it, but it could not be helped. The journey here created problems for us and this work situation was one of them. I could work easier than he could and I began to do well and I supported the family. I became the breadwinner.

He had bad feelings about this, I understood this, but the feelings got worse. It's hard for me to talk about it. I understood his pain but there was nothing I could do about it to help him. Eventually, we were divorced. Divorced! This would be unheard-of in Cambodia where you are married once and that is it for life. But he could not make the changes here. . . .

. . . In 1976, I persuaded Winchell's Donuts to give me a manager franchise and to work off the $5,000 fee. Then I started a small Winchell's shop in Berkeley and was able to pay off the franchise fee in four months. I built up one business and sold it in five months. I doubled the money I had paid for it. In 1982, when I was visiting some friends in Stockton, I noticed a run-down Oriental food store being mismanaged, and the owners were glad to sell it. The Asia food store is doing very well today. The store is ideally located in a busy shopping center within a few blocks of a new housing sub-division full of Asian refugee farm workers.

I began with nothing and now I have something. For me, that's what is great about America. I know the Cambodian men say I am tough—so what? By American standards you need to be good at business to survive. So maybe I am tough. But it is very hard work. I am working every morning at four-thirty in one of my six donut stores. I want to buy that McDonald's hamburger store next door, that is my next investment.

BEYOND THE KILLING FIELDS
SALOUTH SOMAN

. . . I had the courage last month to see the film about the life of Dith Pran [*The Killing Fields*] on videocassette at a house of a friend of mine. For me this took a great deal of courage. I always said that I would never do it, never see it because there are too many painful memories for me. . . . The memories of the escape and the terrible things that happened to all of us have permanently made scars on our souls for our entire lives. We are wounded and there is little we can do to respond to the pain except get through our days the best we can. For those with children it is easier. I lost my wife and two babies trying to escape. There is never a day I can forget this, never. But this is not to say that we do not try to forget about some of it. . . .

. . . Every day, every day again and again and again we try to get along here with our lives. So much of it is not pleasurable, even after many years here, we fight it. But that, for me, is what *The Killing Fields* is about: it is a story of survival at many levels.

I visit friends in Philadelphia and they tell me about the problems they have with their children and how they are disappointed with them. I am silent and inside of me I cry. I cry for my lost babies and my wife. I cry for the other family that I have lost and for my village that is gone. But I say nothing. I do not tell what is really in my heart, that they should be so happy that they have children and all of those things. You cannot say too much. But this is from *The Killing Fields*, too. We must learn to see the past as it was—the past—and move on with our lives as Americans. That is why we are here—to be Americans.

FURTHER READING

Harley L. Browning and Rodolfo O. De La Garza, eds., *Mexican Immigrants and Mexican Americans: An Evolving Relation* (Austin: Center for Mexican American Studies, University of Texas, 1986).

Nathan Caplan, John K. Whitmore, and Marcella H. Choy, *The Boat People and Achievement in America: A Study of Family Life, Hard Work, and Cultural Values* (Ann Arbor: University of Michigan Press, 1989).

Sucheng Chan, ed., *Hmong Means Free: Life in Laos and America* (Philadelphia: Temple University Press, 1994).

Roger Daniels, *Coming to America: A History of Immigration and Ethnicity in American Life* (New York: HarperCollins, 1990).

James T. Fawcett and Benjamin V. Carino, eds., *Pacific Bridges: The New Immigration from Asia and the Pacific Islands* (Staten Island, N.Y.: Center for Migration Studies, 1987).

Timothy P. Fong, *America's First Suburban Chinatown: The Remaking of Monterey Park, California* (Philadelphia: Temple University Press, 1993).

James A. Freeman, *Hearts of Sorrow: Vietnamese American Lives* (Stanford: Stanford University Press, 1989).

Lawrence H. Fuchs, *The American Kaleidoscope: Race, Ethnicity, and the Civic Culture* (Middletown, Conn.: Wesleyan University Press, 1990).

David W. Haines, ed., *Refugees as Immigrants: Cambodians, Laotians, and Vietnamese in America* (Totowa, N.J.: Rowan & Littlefield Pub., 1989).

Katsuyo K. Howard, comp., *Passages: An Anthology of the Southeast Asian Refugee Experience* (Fresno: Southeast Asian Student Services, California State University, Fresno, 1990).

Susan E. Keefe and Amado M. Padilla, *Chicano Ethnicity* (Albuquerque: University of New Mexico Press, 1987).

Ivan Light and Edna Bonacich, *Immigrant Entrepreneurs: Koreans in Los Angeles, 1965–1982* (Berkeley and Los Angeles: University of California Press, 1988).

Gil Loescher and John A. Scanlan, *Calculated Kindness: Refugees and America's Half-Open Door, 1945–Present* (New York: Free Press, 1986).

Lucy Nguyen-Hong-Nhiem and Joel Martin Halpern, eds., *The Far East Comes Near: Autobiographical Accounts of Southeast Asian Students in America* (Amherst: University of Massachusetts Press, 1989).

Alejandro Portes and Robert L. Bach, *Latin Journey: Cuban and Mexican Immigrants in the United States* (Berkeley and Los Angeles: University of California Press, 1984).

Alejandro Portes and Ruben G. Rumbaut, *Immigrant America: A Portrait* (Berkeley and Los Angeles: University of California Press, 1990).

David M. Reimers, *Still the Golden Door: The Third World Comes to America* (New York: Columbia University Press, 1985, 1992).

David Rieff, *Los Angeles: Capital of the Third World* (New York: Touchstone, 1991).

Joanna C. Scott, *Indochina's Refugees: Oral Histories from Laos, Cambodia and Vietnam* (Jefferson, N.C.: McFarland & Co., 1989).

Earl Shorris, *Latinos: A Biography of the People* (New York: W. W. Norton, 1992).

Paul J. Strand and Woodrow Jones, Jr., *Indochinese Refugees in America: Problems of Adaptation and Assimilation* (Durham, N.C.: Duke University Press, 1985).

John Tenhula, *Voices from Southeast Asia: The Refugee Experience in the United States* (New York: Holmes & Meier, 1991).

Usha Welaratna, *Beyond the Killing Fields: Voices of Nine Cambodian Survivors in America* (Stanford: Stanford University Press, 1993).

Thomas Weyr, *Hispanic U.S.A.: Breaking the Melting Pot* (New York: Harper & Row, 1988).

PHOTO CREDITS